LITERATURE AND SCIENCE IN THE NINETEENTH CENTURY

THE material in this anthology comes from novels, plays, poetry, essays, scientific articles, lectures, treatises, and textbooks written throughout the course of the nineteenth century. It demonstrates the fertile exchange of ideas that took place between writers in very different disciplines, and reveals fascinating dialogues and confluences, as well as instructive distinctions.

It was not until the 1830s that the word 'science' began to take on its modern meaning, and by the end of the century it had already divided into the branches we recognize today: medicine and psychology, zoology, geology, astronomy, mathematics and technology, sociology, and genetics. At the same time creative writers were exploring these emerging fields in their fiction and verse and using images, metaphors, and narrative techniques that fed both kinds of writing. Both scientists and literary authors wrote for a common audience, and their work was published side by side in periodicals and journals such as *Household Words* and the *Westminster Review*. *Literature and Science in the Nineteenth Century* shows how such juxtapositions fed a hunger for knowledge, and with what excitement writers sought to communicate their discoveries.

LAURA OTIS is Associate Professor of English at Hofstra University, and the author of *Organic Memory* (1994), *Membranes* (1999), and *Networking: Communicating with Bodies and Machines in the Nineteenth Century* (2001). Awarded a MacArthur Fellowship for her interdisciplinary studies of the nervous system, she is currently working at the Max Planck Institute for the History of Science in Berlin.

T0060998

OXFORD WORLD'S CLASSICS

*For over 100 years Oxford World's Classics have brought
readers closer to the world's great literature. Now with over 700
titles—from the 4,000-year-old myths of Mesopotamia to the
twentieth century's greatest novels—the series makes available
lesser-known as well as celebrated writing.*

*The pocket-sized hardbacks of the early years contained
introductions by Virginia Woolf, T. S. Eliot, Graham Greene,
and other literary figures which enriched the experience of reading.
Today the series is recognized for its fine scholarship and
reliability in texts that span world literature, drama and poetry,
religion, philosophy and politics. Each edition includes perceptive
commentary and essential background information to meet the
changing needs of readers.*

OXFORD WORLD'S CLASSICS

Literature and Science in the Nineteenth Century
An Anthology

Edited with an Introduction and Notes by
LAURA OTIS

OXFORD
UNIVERSITY PRESS

OXFORD

UNIVERSITY PRESS

Great Clarendon Street, Oxford OX2 6DP

Oxford University Press is a department of the University of Oxford.
It furthers the University's objective of excellence in research, scholarship,
and education by publishing worldwide in

Oxford New York

Auckland Bangkok Buenos Aires Cape Town Chennai
Dar es Salaam Delhi Hong Kong Istanbul Karachi Kolkata
Kuala Lumpur Madrid Melbourne Mexico City Mumbai Nairobi
São Paulo Shanghai Singapore Taipei Tokyo Toronto

with an associated company in Berlin

Oxford is a registered trade mark of Oxford University Press
in the UK and in certain other countries

Published in the United States
by Oxford University Press Inc., New York

First published as an Oxford World's Classics paperback 2002
Reissued 2009

British Library Cataloguing in Publication Data

Data available

Library of Congress Cataloging in Publication Data

Data available

ISBN 978–0–19–955465–2

13

Typeset in Ehrhardt
by RefineCatch Limited, Bungay, Suffolk
Printed in Great Britain by
Clays Ltd, Elcograf S.p.A.

ACKNOWLEDGEMENTS

THIS anthology could never have emerged without all of the people who have suggested new ways to see the relationship between nineteenth-century literature and science. First, I would like to thank Robert Mighall, who recommended me as a potential editor, and my own editor Judith Luna, whose forthright advice and persistent enthusiasm for the project have kept me working these past four years. I am also deeply grateful to Hofstra University, which has granted me a full four years of research leave to work on this and other projects.

Research for this anthology was conducted almost entirely at the University of Chicago Libraries, and I would like to thank all of the librarians there who helped me locate texts. I am especially indebted to Jay Satterfield, Krista Ovist, Barbara Gilbert, Jessica Westphal, and Debra Levine in the Department of Special Collections. I am grateful to the University of Chicago Libraries for allowing me to reproduce these texts, and I thank Françoise Meltzer for inviting me to work at the University of Chicago as a fellow of the Comparative Literature Department. Some work was done at the New York Public Library, the Great Neck Public Library, and the New York Academy of Medicine, and there I would like to thank Caroline Duroselle-Melish, Reference Librarian of Historical Collections. I am also grateful to the Cambridge University Library for allowing me to browse its collection of nineteenth-century journals, and to Ellen Garske at the Max Planck Institute Library in Berlin for her assistance in obtaining additional sources.

I would like to thank Thomas D. Brock for permission to reproduce his translation of Louis Pasteur's 'On the Organized Bodies Which Exist in the Atmosphere' (1861), originally published in his anthology, *Milestones in Microbiology*, Madison, University of Wisconsin Press, 1989.

I am deeply indebted to all of the scholars who have offered feedback and introduced me to new texts. I am most grateful to my reader Helen Small, whose comments have made this a much more representative, thought-provoking anthology than it might have been. As an honest and helpful critic, Helen has greatly enhanced my knowledge of nineteenth-century British culture. I am also indebted to her as a writer, for all of my introductions have benefited from her insightful rephrasing. Her assistance with the selection and analysis of texts cannot be underestimated. I would like to thank Helen's student, Julia Reid, for suggesting Richard A. Proctor's essay 'The Photographic Eyes of Science,' and Alison Winter for her suggestions of texts illustrating Victorian thoughts about mesmerism. I am grateful to Pamela K. Gilbert for introducing me to sensation novels, particularly to the work of Braddon. I owe a great deal to Gillian Beer, whose lectures at the University of Chicago in May 1998 opened my eyes to many issues in nineteenth-century mathematics and physics. I am grateful for her suggestions about Carroll's, Maxwell's, and Kipling's works and for her own inspiring studies of nineteenth-century literature and science. I thank her student Jeff Mackowiak for his friendly support and his interesting study of Maxwell's poetry. I am indebted to the many scholars at the University of Chicago whose feedback has shaped this anthology, particularly Larry Rothfield. I thank my colleague George Greaney at Hofstra for his assistance with the classical references, and John Bryant, Scott Harshbarger, JoAnn Krieg, and Julia Markus for their suggestions about Melville, Wordsworth, Whitman, and Browning respectively. I am grateful to my friends in the Society for Literature and Science whose thoughts have inspired my work during the past four years, among them Carol Colatrella, N. Katherine Hayles, Steve Kern, Tim Lenoir, George Levine, Richard Menke, Sid Perkowitz, David Porush, and Susan Squier. Finally, I would like to thank Sander Gilman, whose undying friendship and support have kept up my spirits as I have followed the connections between literature and science.

CONTENTS

Telecommunications

Bodies and Machines

SCIENCES OF THE BODY

Animal Electricity

Experimental Medicine and Vivisection

EVOLUTION   235

The Present and the Past

The Individual and the Species

Sexual Selection

Mesmerism and Magnetism

Dreams and the Unconscious

Nervous Exhaustion

INTRODUCTION

In the 1830s the English word 'science' began to take on its modern meaning. Robert Southey commented in 1834 that 'the medical profession . . . was an art . . . before it became a science', implying that it had advanced from a practical skill to a systematic, theoretically informed body of knowledge. At the 1833 meeting of the British Association, William Whewell proposed the term 'scientist' for investigators who until then had been known as natural philosophers.[1] In the nineteenth century 'science' came to signify the study of the natural and physical world. Until that time it had denoted any sort of knowledge or skill, including the 'science' of boxing.

In contrast, the notion of a 'split' between literature and science, of a 'gap' to be 'bridged' between the two, was never a nineteenth-century phenomenon. Certainly educational reformers and scientists creating new fields debated what science and literature *were*, and how much time students should devote to each. In the popular press, however, the two commingled and were accessible to all readers. Scientists quoted well-known poets both in their textbooks and in their articles for lay readers, and writers we now identify as primarily 'creative' explored the implications of scientific theories. Science was not perceived as being written in a 'foreign language'—a common complaint of twenty-first-century readers. As a growing system of knowledge expressed in familiar words, science was in effect a variety of literature.

'Literature', declared Matthew Arnold, 'is a large word.' Its breadth is immediately observable in the nineteenth-century popular press, the most important print medium for exchanges between writers from all fields. In nineteenth-century periodicals, magazines, and newspapers, articles on scientific issues were set side by side with fiction, poetry, and literary criticism. In the early 1850s the

---

[1] Southey, *Doctor*, 120 (1862), 294 (cited in *OED*). At the 1833 meeting of the British Association, William Whewell stated that 'some ingenious gentleman' had proposed the term 'scientist' to describe investigators of natural phenomena. This gentleman may have been either a member of the audience or Whewell himself (Richard Yeo, *Defining Science: William Whewell, Natural Knowledge and Public Debate in Early Victorian Britain* (Cambridge: Cambridge University Press, 1993), 110–11).

liberal journal the *Westminster Review* began offering an overview of 'contemporary literature'. This section included reviews of works in theology, philosophy, politics, sociology, travel, science, history, and biography, as well as belles lettres. In its first year (1850) Dickens's popular family magazine *Household Words* carried articles on respiration, chemistry, and the hippopotamus, interspersed with serialized novels. At the intellectual *Westminster Review*, George Eliot similarly helped to prepare essays on astronomy, biology, mesmerism, and vivisection. Matthew Arnold, who had famously defined culture as 'the best which has been thought and uttered in the world', protested that 'literature' meant much more than fiction; it could include 'everything written with letters or printed in a book'.

In the nineteenth century, as Western economies became more industrial than agricultural, educational reformers protested that the traditional curriculum of Greek and Latin literature—which had given aristocrats and gentry the 'stamp of the educated man'—failed to prepare the new professional classes for modern life. Technological advances and transformative new theories had made science as essential to culture as Horace's poetry had once seemed to be. In 1880, at the opening of a science college for middle- and working-class students, Thomas Henry Huxley claimed provocatively that 'for the purpose of attaining real culture, an exclusively scientific education is at least as effectual as an exclusively literary education'. Huxley later qualified this remark, adding that an education focusing purely on science was as skewed as one focusing solely on literature. His insistence on the cultural centrality of science disturbed Matthew Arnold, who protested that Huxley was defining 'literature' much too narrowly. Arguing that Euclid's *Elements* and Newton's *Principia* could be read as cultural documents, Arnold submitted that 'all knowledge that reaches us through books is literature'.

But what does this statement finally tell us? Scientific writing is not literature, and, as Sally Shuttleworth puts it, 'to reduce science to literature by insisting that science is a kind of writing' misrepresents the work of authors in both fields.[2] Literary and scientific writing have different goals and, usually, different reading contexts. To do justice to both it is as important to study their differences as

---

[2] 'Introduction', in John Christie and Sally Shuttleworth (eds.), *Nature Transfigured: Science and Literature, 1700–1900* (New York: St Martin's, 1989), 3.

their similarities.[3] In juxtaposing texts by literary and scientific writers, this anthology aims to illustrate both common and divergent patterns in the techniques of nineteenth-century authors. There is no doubt that at the time, scientists and novelists actively reflected upon the affinities and differences between their tasks. The idea that science 'divorces itself from literature' arose from sheer ignorance, protested the physicist John Tyndall in 1874. Anyone who read the works of successful scientists could see immediately that most good scientists were also imaginative writers. The ability to express oneself articulately was essential for the communication and progress of science.

Breadth of reading also played a central role in science, because to establish their authority as writers many scientists needed to show a familiarity with the canonical texts of the Western literary tradition. By the nineteenth century scientific knowledge was spread most effectively not through face-to-face encounters but through the printed word. A close acquaintance with the literary heritage could be crucial to a scientist's ability to obtain an audience and make a favourable impression in society. To win the confidence of educated readers, nineteenth-century scientists made frequent references to the fiction and poetry of the day and to that of earlier generations. By doing so, they declared an affinity, sometimes of thought but more often of culture, with respected authors and, indirectly, with their readers. When nineteenth-century scientists quoted Greek and Roman authors, they defined their knowledge as 'cultured' and therefore non-threatening. Charles Lyell's *Principles of Geology* (1830–3) won a wide readership not just because he provided convincing evidence for gradual geological change but because he used literary references to Milton, Scott, and Wordsworth to present geology as a respectable, gentlemanly pursuit.[4]

Many nineteenth-century scientists were effectively gentlemen scholars and received the same classical education as literary writers from élite backgrounds. Those scientists who did not come from the socially privileged classes had even more to gain by establishing reputations as men of humane learning. With no government

---

[3] See N. Katherine Hayles, *Chaos Bound: Orderly Disorder in Contemporary Literature and Science* (Ithaca, NY: Cornell University Press, 1990), 3.

[4] James A. Secord, 'Introduction' to Lyell's *Principles of Geology* (Harmondsworth: Penguin, 1997), pp. xvii–xxix.

support for research, the social niche of the professional scientist did not exist for much of the nineteenth century. It began to emerge only at mid-century, first in Germany, then in other European nations and the United States, when universities began to establish themselves as research centres. Investigators who were independently wealthy, like Sir Francis Galton or George John Romanes, could fund their own research; others, like Claude Bernard, kept themselves in the laboratory through lucrative marriages. But other experimental scientists had to support themselves through teaching, journalism, medical practice, engineering, or military service, so that many would-be physicists got their start in other fields. Hermann von Helmholtz, who performed pioneering work in physics and physiology, studied medicine for economic reasons. John Tyndall and Thomas Henry Huxley, two of England's greatest popularizers of science, began writing and lecturing for the general public in order to survive financially. For aspiring scientists, it paid to be well read.

In addition to facing economic problems, nineteenth-century scientists encountered resistance when they challenged the expertise and authority of non-scientists. For centuries, discussions of human origins and behaviour had been dominated by theologians and philosophers, so that when scientists wrote they had to defend their right to address these questions. Like literary writers, they often did so by incorporating the voices of accepted authorities, particularly those of religious texts. The concessions to religion in Darwin's *The Origin of Species* are unmistakable with its references to 'powers, having been originally breathed into a few forms'. While Darwin sometimes used religious phrases unconsciously, his keen awareness of language suggests that he crafted his final paragraph to appease readers. Knowing how deeply his arguments threatened the traditional understanding of humanity's place in the universe, he presented his theory as complementary to religious teachings, not as a replacement for them.

Literary writers, who for centuries had told their stories in the cultural language of biblical tales, were able to challenge accepted views of human nature by interweaving traditional stories with new narratives made available by science. The devastating flood at the conclusion of George Eliot's *The Mill on the Floss* undercuts her long narrative of gradual change, defying the notion that 'time heals all wounds'. The innovative use of well-known tales was as essential to literature as it was to science.

At the most fundamental level, scientific explanation of the world is akin to the processes of reading and writing. Whether studying skull structures, geological layers, or bird populations, scientists were deciphering sign systems and interpreting texts. Both the geologist Charles Lyell and the neurobiologist Santiago Ramón y Cajal compared themselves with the linguist Jean François Champollion, who decoded the Egyptian hieroglyphics on the Rosetta stone. Highly conscious of their roles as communicators, scientists did not need critics like Arnold to point out their affinity to ordinary writers. They illustrated it themselves in their own texts.

Scientists knew that like literary writers, they relied heavily on imagination. Only a comparison of the unknown with the known can create new forms of understanding, so that metaphor plays a key role in original thought. As Gillian Beer has observed, scientific writing is most like fiction when it is struggling to say something new, at which time it relies heavily upon comparisons. Metaphor, in Beer's words, 'can allow insight without consequences'.[5] Whether studying physical or biological events, scientists depicted the world imaginatively so that they could draw inferences about invisible phenomena based on observable effects. Picturing the unknown, they acted like novelists or poets, inviting readers to imagine hidden worlds.

In 1852 the physicist Michael Faraday apologized to readers of his *Experimental Researches in Electricity* (1839–55) because he had incorporated passages 'of a speculative and hypothetical nature'. Such writing, he confessed, would be more at home in the Philosophical Magazine than in the Philosophical Transactions of the Royal Society, but he included it because it was indispensable to his theories. Studying the interrelation of electricity and magnetism, Faraday struggled to explain how forces could act at a distance. With little formal training in mathematics, he solved the problem by reasoning visually, proposing that electricity and magnetism exerted their power through 'lines of force'. Such lines could never themselves be observed, but the characteristic pattern of metal shavings around a magnet suggested their structure. Faraday called such imagined structures 'wonderful aids in the hands of the experimentalist and mathematician', reflecting that 'not only are they useful in rendering the vague idea more clear for the time, giving it

[5] Gillian Beer, *Darwin's Plots: Evolutionary Narrative in Darwin, George Eliot, and Nineteenth-Century Fiction* (London: Routledge and Kegan Paul, 1983), 3, 14.

something like a definite shape . . . but they lead on, by deduction and correction, to the discovery of new phenomena'.

To complement his factual evidence for evolution in *The Origin of Species*, Charles Darwin offered readers a series of 'Imaginary Illustrations', scenes which encouraged them to picture natural selection at work. While Darwin's factual evidence was extensive, he knew that he could never be persuasive unless he could make readers see what he saw. His goal was not just to help them imagine the unknown, but to make them interpret familiar events in new ways. In 1859 his readers would have been very accustomed to such appeals to their imaginations. Nineteenth-century periodicals offered numerous travel narratives, responding to a cultural desire to 'see' the world. In 1854 *Household Words* published 'An Imaginary Voyage' to South America, inviting readers to see through the eyes of an 'imaginary traveller'. When Darwin presented his theory of natural selection, he knew that readers were used to such voyages, and he drew on their capabilities to recreate the evolutionary process. Like novelists who 'took' readers into imaginary worlds, Darwin appealed to his readers to imagine the development of life as he described it.

At times, Darwin worried that his writing sounded too literary and feared that his metaphors would lead readers astray. The phrase 'natural selection', for instance, might suggest an active agent doing the selecting. Occasionally, Darwin's 'Nature' comes across as a literary character, a conscious being who is making decisions. Considering Darwin's desire to stimulate readers' imaginations, the anthropomorphism may well have been intentional. Like literary writers, nineteenth-century scientists sometimes created characters to embody or personify challenging ideas.

Explaining a key exception to the second law of thermodynamics, the physicist John Clerk Maxwell asked readers to 'conceive a being' who opened a door between compartments, allowing fast-moving particles to enter a chamber of higher temperature. Though Maxwell's being—who quickly became a 'demon'—is no developed literary character, it was created for a similar purpose. In communicating the limitations of the second law, Maxwell was telling a story, and his story needed a protagonist. Here again scientific writers followed the example of the popular press, which conveyed unfamiliar theories and situations by creating characters. *Household*

Words offered readers the 'Life of a Salmon' and 'The Collier at Home' and presented 'The Laboratory in the Chest' as a dialogue between a middle-aged man and his bright young nephew. Readers found new theories accessible when they were voiced by sympathetic characters, and scientific writers responded to their audience's needs.

A scientific narrative, of course, aims primarily to communicate, not to entertain, and the necessary differences between literary and scientific writing led many nineteenth-century scientists to use fiction as a freer mode in which to explore provocative scientific ideas. The physicians Oliver Wendell Holmes and S. Weir Mitchell turned to literature because in stories there is not the same need for 'proof'. While readers of nineteenth-century fiction demanded consistency and plausibility, they expected different kinds of 'evidence' than those required by scientific journals. The neurologist Mitchell published textbooks about his patients' phantom limb pains, but when trying to develop his theory that people's bodies shaped their notions of identity, he turned to the short story form. Ironically, readers found Mitchell's story so realistic that they mistook it for an actual case. Mitchell's tale, 'The Case of George Dedlow,' may not have been recognized as fiction because the neurologist published it anonymously. Holmes, his mentor, had warned him not to use his own name, hinting that a scientist known as a fiction writer would never be taken seriously. Even though scientists and literary writers engaged readers with the same strategies, the scientists usually tried to maintain some distance between themselves and those whose imaginations were supposedly unrestricted by reason.

It would be inaccurate, though, to depict nineteenth-century literature as a realm in which the imagination had comparatively free reign. Novelists of the period were greatly concerned with facts. Many, like George Eliot, performed careful research in order to make their works not just credible but historically accurate. In the nineteenth century romantic writing, in which the imagination was praised as the prime source of literary inspiration, increasingly gave way to realistic and naturalistic narratives, in which the story-teller shared many goals with medical and scientific writers. Lawrence Rothfield has shown that the shift in emphasis from observation to experimentation in medicine from the 1860s onward corresponded to more detailed, penetrating depictions of characters and their environments in realistic fiction.[6]

It is thus no surprise that nineteenth-century scientists found they could be more persuasive by using the story-telling techniques of fiction writers. Darwin, who took a volume of Milton's poems on his five-year voyage on the *HMS Beagle*, described the struggle for life through references to Milton's poetic images. Whether or not he consciously drew upon the poet, Milton offered him a way to communicate his observations. Milton's rewriting of Genesis allowed Darwin to imagine the Creation as a long, continuous process, nurturing his developing concept of evolution.[7]

In their quest to redraw the boundaries between 'truth' and 'untruth', nineteenth-century scientists cited novelists and philosophers who had already questioned these limits. Introducing a case study of mesmeric anaesthesia, John Elliotson acknowledged his readers' scepticism by quoting the French philosopher Bernard Fontanelle and the popular gothic novelist 'Monk' Lewis. Elliotson's choice of epigraphs reveals a great deal about his own hopes and his readers' expectations. The quotation from Lewis reads: 'I never said it was possible. I only said it was true.' Next to this Elliotson has placed a line from Fontanelle, who spread Copernicus's view of the solar system: 'the truth does not always look like truth.' Together, these voices from 'low' and 'high' culture challenge readers who doubt that mesmerism can anaesthetize a patient, defining their scepticism as closed-mindedness.

As science gained prestige, literary writers in turn gained credibility by incorporating the voices of scientists. This strategy worked particularly well in the American 'tall tale' genre. Writers like Edgar Allan Poe and Mark Twain consciously imitated scientists' styles and use of evidence, exploiting their own writing techniques to play with scientists' ideas and encourage readers to rethink them. If readers mistook the fiction for science, it was merely part of the game. If they discovered the 'truth', they might subsequently read science and fiction in a new light, resisting writers' strategies to exploit their credibility.

For most of the nineteenth century scientists and novelists shared

---

[6] Lawrence Rothfield, *Vital Signs: Medical Realism in Nineteenth-Century Fiction* (Princeton: Princeton University Press, 1992).

[7] Beer, *Darwin's Plots*, 34–6.

a common vocabulary and common literary techniques. Thus far I
have emphasized this form of kinship because it is the least obvious
and most challenging to demonstrate. But it is also crucial to recognize that the same *subjects* occupied both scientific and literary
writers. The quest for 'origins' developed simultaneously in studies
of language, geology, zoology, and numerous other fields, although
many scholars would have agreed that philosophically, 'origin' was a
shaky concept. From the mid-eighteenth century onwards, European philologists explored the family trees of modern languages,
hoping to define nations and peoples more accurately by identifying
their linguistic ancestors. In English novels, the search for origins
had long been accepted as a plot-driving device. The identification
of one's 'true' family and assumption of one's rightful social position
provided closure to many complex stories, narratives as different as
Tom Jones and *Oliver Twist*. By offering readers a 'great tree' sup-
plemented by a complex, branched diagram, Darwin made his
claims more believable, conveying them through a familiar narrative.
Like the philology and literature of his day, Darwin's writing reflects
the assumption that origins establish identity, yet conveys a strong
conviction that 'origins' are fictions.

Herbert Spencer's question, 'What is an individual?' also links a
great number of fields. In the natural sciences, writers debated the
'independence' of cells, which since the 1830s had been presented as
the fundamental units of life. As evolutionary theory became more
widely accepted, natural scientists speculated that the cells of complex organisms might be the descendants of unicellular ancestors,
retaining considerable autonomy. When the philosopher George
Henry Lewes protested that the cell had 'usurped' the role of the
unified organism, his resistance to cellular autonomy reflected his
vision of society. Like his partner, George Eliot, Lewes believed that
consciousness and selfhood could never be associated with a single
unit, only with the complex interactions in a neural or social 'web'.
The physicist James Clerk Maxwell also faced the question of individual *v.* group behaviour when he studied the movements of gas
particles.[8] Using statistical laws to describe the behaviour of matter,
Maxwell found that one could not predict the movements of large
groups of molecules by studying those of individual ones. In physics,

---

[8] Selma B. Brody, 'Physics in *Middlemarch*: Gas Molecules and Ethereal Atoms',
Modern Philology, 85 (1987), 46–8.

physiology, sociology, and literature, the relationship between personal and collective identity remained unclear. As writers confronted the problem, they imitated each other's ways of describing it, experimenting with one another's metaphors while defending their own moral interpretations of the world around them.

Perhaps the most disturbing question nineteenth-century writers faced was what it meant to be human. The rapid development of industrialization, physiology, evolutionary theory, and the mental and social sciences challenged the traditional view of people as uniquely privileged beings created in the divine image. While religion remained a powerful social and ideological force, it became increasingly difficult for educated writers to refer to a 'soul'. Too many other fields offered alternative explanations of human behaviour, from muscle reflexes to inherited memories. If nineteenth-century physiological psychologists were right, and human thoughts and actions could be explained by the laws of chemistry and physics, it was unclear how people could be distinguished from the machines on which they increasingly depended. As Samuel Butler pointed out, many human lives, such as those of stokers and colliers, were already being used to serve machinery.

A Note on the Anthology

Because the divisions between scientific fields have changed so greatly since the nineteenth century, organizing an anthology of nineteenth-century literature and science has been a tremendous challenge. Throughout the nineteenth century new discoveries created needs for new disciplines, so that the 'great tree' of science produced ever more branches and sub-branches. In the late 1830s, for example, the theory that all living organisms were composed of cells led to the growth of histology. By the 1860s it was inspiring the development of cellular pathology and bacteriology. Nineteenth-century writers experienced an overwhelmingly rapid succession of observations, theories, and technological developments: in physics, the articulation of thermodynamic laws and the rise of statistical mechanics; in engineering, the development of mechanized industry, the railways, the telegraph, the telephone, and gas and electric lighting; in the natural sciences, cell theory, evolutionary theory, and experimental physiology; and in medicine, anaesthesia, anaesepsis, and germ theory. Viewing these achievements in retrospect, one runs the risk of imposing twenty-first-century boundaries on newly emerging fields. Nineteenth-century readers and writers would not have classified the texts in this anthology as readers would today. To make the selections more accessible to today's readers, however, I have introduced some twenty-first-century categories, classifying the texts under the headings of Mathematics, Physical Science, and Technology; Sciences of the Body; Evolution; Sciences of the Mind; and Social Sciences. By creating these divisions, I have to some degree overridden nineteenth-century writers' perceptions that they were contributing to a fluid, less differentiated body of knowledge. I have also included texts about mathematical and technological achievements which would then have been regarded as 'arts' rather than 'sciences', indicating the use of practical skill rather than systematic inquiry.

In ordering these categories, however, I have tried to represent the nineteenth-century understanding of knowledge more faithfully. In the late 1820s the French philosopher Auguste Comte began arguing that human knowledge had developed progressively and that its fields could be organized hierarchically, according to how recently they had emerged and how 'scientific' they were. The numerous advocates of Comte's positivistic philosophy understood mathematics and physics as the source of rigorous laws and consequently the foundation on which other disciplines might be based. For this reason, I have placed 'Mathematics, Physical Science, and Technology' first. I have placed 'Sciences of the Body' and 'Evolution' next because over the course of the century writers studying human thought and behaviour turned increasingly to physiological and evolutionary theories. Again reflecting a prominent nineteenth-century hierarchy, I have placed 'Sciences of the Mind' before 'Social Sciences', since the social sciences, as the 'youngest' field of inquiry, were seen as relying on studies of individual minds. I have avoided the terms 'biology', 'psychology', and 'sociology', which belong more to the twentieth than to the nineteenth century.

This anthology invites readers to explore the fertile exchange of images, metaphors, and narrative techniques among writers who today—though not in their own day—are regarded as members of very different disciplines. Within each category, I have placed literary and scientific texts side by side in chronological order. In selecting these texts, I have not attempted to offer a comprehensive history of any of the fields considered or even to include their most influential writers. Each discipline has its canonical texts, but my goal has been to illustrate the relationships between scientific and literary writing. While this anthology excludes some well-known figures, it offers readers an opportunity to discover some lesser-known writers whose work reveals the passage of ideas between science and fiction.

Because of the great diversity of nineteenth-century scientific issues, I have focused on British and American fiction writers and the scientists with whom they exchanged ideas. Since many nineteenth-century writers read French, German, and Italian, some of the scientific texts in those languages included here were not translated until the twentieth century. Wherever possible, I have used nineteenth-century translations so that today's readers can confront the same texts that nineteenth-century readers would have encountered.

This anthology aims to reveal dialogues and confluences, leaving it to readers to characterize and define them. None of these short selections can do justice to the writers' complex bodies of work, but I hope that they will invite readers to explore nineteenth-century literature and science in greater depth, leading to new discoveries about the affinities and distinctions of science and fiction.

SELECT BIBLIOGRAPHY

Mathematics, Physical Science, and Technology

Beer, Gillian, *George Eliot* (Brighton: Harvester, 1986).
—— *Open Fields: Science in Cultural Encounter* (New York: Oxford University Press, 1996).
Brock, W. H., McMillan, N. D., and Mollan, R. C. (eds.), *John Tyndall: Essays on a Natural Philosopher*, Historical Studies in Irish Science and Technology (Dublin: Royal Dublin Society, 1981).
Cahan, David (ed.), *Hermann von Helmholtz and the Foundations of Nineteenth-Century Science* (Berkeley: University of California Press, 1994).
Gillispie, Charles Coulston, *The Edge of Objectivity: An Essay in the History of Scientific Ideas* (Princeton: Princeton University Press, 1960).
Hacking, Ian, *The Taming of Chance* (Cambridge: Cambridge University Press, 1990).
Haight, Gordon, *George Eliot: A Biography* (Oxford: Oxford University Press, 1968).
Hayles, N. Katherine, *Chaos Bound: Orderly Disorder in Contemporary Literature and Culture* (Ithaca, NY: Cornell University Press, 1990).
—— *The Cosmic Web: Scientific Field Models and Literary Strategies in the Twentieth Century* (Ithaca, NY: Cornell University Press, 1984).
Haynes, Roslynn D., *From Faust to Strangelove: Representations of the Scientist in Western Literature* (Baltimore: Johns Hopkins University Press, 1994).
Hyman, Anthony, *Charles Babbage: Pioneer of the Computer* (Princeton: Princeton University Press, 1982).
Kittler, Friedrich A., *Discourse Networks 1800/1900*, tr. Michael Metteer (Stanford, Calif.: Stanford University Press, 1990).
Krasner, James, *The Entangled Eye: Visual Perception and the Representation of Nature in Post-Darwinian Narrative* (New York: Oxford University Press, 1992).
Kuhn, Thomas S., *The Structure of Scientific Revolutions*, 2nd edn. (Chicago: University of Chicago Press, 1970).
Lenoir, Timothy (ed.), *Inscribing Science: Scientific Texts and the Materiality of Communication* (Stanford, Calif.: Stanford University Press, 1998).
Mackowiak, Jeff, 'Maxwell's "Quaint Verses" as Commonplace Book', unpublished essay, 4 June 1999.

Marvin, Carolyn, *When Old Technologies Were New: Thinking about Electric Communication in the Late Nineteenth Century* (New York: Oxford University Press, 1988).

Paulos, John Allen, *Once Upon a Number: The Hidden Mathematical Logic of Stories* (New York: Basic Books, 1998).

Schivelbusch, Wolfgang, *The Railway Journey: The Industrialization of Time and Space in the Nineteenth Century* (Berkeley: University of California Press, 1986).

Seltzer, Mark, *Bodies and Machines* (New York: Routledge, 1992).

Simmons, Jack, *The Victorian Railway* (New York: Thames and Hudson, 1991).

Standage, Tom, *The Victorian Internet: The Remarkable Story of the Telegraph and the Nineteenth Century's On-line Engineers* (New York: Walker, 1998).

Twain, Mark, *The Science Fiction of Mark Twain*, ed. David Ketterer (Hamden, Conn.: Shoestring Press–Archon Books, 1984).

Winter, Alison, 'A Calculus of Suffering: Ada Lovelace and the Bodily Constraints on Women's Knowledge in Early Victorian England', in Christopher Lawrence and Steven Shapin (eds.), *Science Incarnate: Historical Embodiments of Natural Knowledge* (Chicago: University of Chicago Press, 1998).

Sciences of the Body

Ackerknecht, Erwin H., 'Anticontagionism between 1821 and 1867', *Bulletin of the History of Medicine*, 22 (1948), 562–93.

Brock, Thomas, *Milestones in Microbiology* (Madison: University of Wisconsin Press, 1989).

—— *Robert Koch: A Life in Medicine and Bacteriology* (Madison: Science Tech Publishers; Berlin: Springer, 1988).

Corbin, Alain, *The Foul and the Fragrant: Odor and the French Social Imagination*, tr. Miriam L. Kochan and Roy Porter (Cambridge, Mass.: Harvard University Press, 1986).

de Kruif, Paul, *Microbe Hunters* (New York: Harcourt, Brace, and World, 1953).

Dubos, René, *Louis Pasteur: Free Lance of Science* (New York: Scribner, 1976).

Epstein, Julia, *Altered Conditions: Disease, Medicine, and Storytelling* (New York: Routledge, 1995).

Finer, S. E., *The Life and Times of Sir Edwin Chadwick* (London: Methuen, 1952).

Ford, Brian J., *Single Lens: The Story of the Simple Microscope* (New York: Harper and Row, 1985).

Forrester, John, 'Lydgate's Research Project in *Middlemarch*', *George Eliot–George Henry Lewes Newsletter*, 16–17 (1990), 2–6.

Foucault, Michel, *The Birth of the Clinic: An Archaeology of Medical Perception*, tr. A. M. Sheridan Smith (New York: Vintage-Random House, 1975).

French, Richard D., *Antivivisection and Medical Science in Victorian Society* (Princeton: Princeton University Press, 1975).

Furst, Lillian, 'Struggling for Medical Reform in *Middlemarch*', *Nineteenth-Century Literature*, 48 (1993–4), 341–61.

Gilman, Sander L., *Disease and Representation: Images of Illness from Madness to AIDS* (Ithaca, NY: Cornell University Press, 1988).

Greenberg, Robert A., 'Plexuses and Ganglia: Scientific Allusion in *Middlemarch*', *Nineteenth-Century Fiction*, 30 (1975–6), 33–52.

Hamlin, Christopher, 'Edwin Chadwick and the Engineers, 1842–1854: Systems and Antisystems in the Pipe-and-Brick Sewers War', *Technology and Culture*, 33 (1992), 680–709.

Haraway, Donna, *Simians, Cyborgs, and Women: The Reinvention of Nature* (London: Free Association, 1991).

Jacyna, L. S., 'The Romantic Programme and the Reception of Cell Theory in Britain', *Journal of the History of Biology*, 17 (1984), 13–48.

Koch, Robert, *Essays of Robert Koch*, tr. K. Codell Carter, Contributions in Medical Studies, no. 20 (New York, Westport, Conn., and London: Greenwood Press, 1987).

Laqueur, Thomas, *Making Sex: Body and Gender from the Greeks to Freud* (Cambridge, Mass.: Harvard University Press, 1990).

Latour, Bruno, *The Pasteurization of France*, tr. Alan Sheridan and John Law (Cambridge, Mass. and London: Harvard University Press, 1988).

Lawrence, Christopher, and Shapin, Steven (eds.), *Science Incarnate: Historical Embodiments of Natural Knowledge* (Chicago: University of Chicago Press, 1998).

Levine, George, *The Realistic Imagination: English Fiction from Frankenstein to Lady Chatterley* (Chicago: University of Chicago Press, 1981).

Lewis, Richard Albert, *Edwin Chadwick and the Public Health Movement, 1832–1854* (London: Longman's, Green 1952).

McCarthy, Patrick J., 'Lydgate, "The New Young Surgeon" of *Middlemarch*', *Studies in English Literature*, 10 (1970), 805–16.

Mason, Michael York, '*Middlemarch* and Science: Problems of Life and Mind', *Review of English Studies*, 22 (1971), 151–69.

Mellor, Anne K., *Mary Shelley: Her Life, Her Fiction, Her Monsters* (New York: Methuen, 1988).

Menke, Richard, 'Fiction as Vivisection: G. H. Lewes and George Eliot', *English Literary History*, 67 (2000), 617–53.

Metz, Nancy Aycock, 'Discovering a World of Suffering: Fiction and the Rhetoric of Sanitary Reform—1840–1860', *Nineteenth-Century Contexts*, 15 (1991), 65–81.

Otis, Laura, *Membranes: Metaphors of Invasion in Nineteenth-Century Literature, Science, and Politics* (Baltimore: Johns Hopkins University Press, 1999).

Pera, Marcello, *The Ambiguous Frog: The Galvani–Volta Controversy on Animal Electricity*, tr. Jonathan Mandelbaum (Princeton: Princeton University Press, 1992).

Poovey, Mary, 'Domesticity and Class Formation: Chadwick's 1842 Sanitary Report' in David Simpson (ed.), *Subject to History: Ideology, Class, Gender* (Ithaca, NY: Cornell University Press, 1991).

—— *Making a Social Body: British Cultural Formation, 1830–1864* (Chicago: University of Chicago Press, 1995).

Rothfield, Lawrence, *Vital Signs: Medical Realism in Nineteenth-Century Fiction* (Princeton: Princeton University Press, 1992).

Scarry, Elaine, *The Body in Pain: The Making and Unmaking of the World* (Oxford: Oxford University Press, 1985).

Serres, Michel, *The Parasite*, tr. Lawrence R. Schehr (Baltimore: Johns Hopkins University Press, 1982).

Shaw, George Bernard, *Address Delivered at the Annual Meeting of the British Union for the Abolition of Vivisection* (London: n.p., 1909).

Shuttleworth, Sally, *George Eliot and Nineteenth-Century Science: The Make-Believe of a Beginning* (Cambridge: Cambridge University Press, 1984).

Sontag, Susan, *Illness as Metaphor and AIDS and Its Metaphors* (New York: Anchor-Doubleday, 1989).

Virchow, Rudolf, *Collected Essays on Public Health and Epidemiology* [1879], ed. L. J. Rather, 2 vols. (Canton, Mass.: Science History Publications, 1985).

Wormald, Mark, 'Microscopy and Semiotic in *Middlemarch*', *Nineteenth-Century Literature*, 50 (1995–6), 501–24.

Evolution

Bailey, J. O., 'Evolutionary Meliorism in the Poetry of Thomas Hardy', *Studies in Philology*, 60 (1963), 569–87.

Beer, Gillian, *Darwin's Plots: Evolutionary Narrative in Darwin, George Eliot, and Nineteenth-Century Fiction* (London: Routledge and Kegan Paul, 1983).

Bowler, Peter J., *Evolution: The History of an Idea* (Berkeley: University of California Press, 1984).

Christie, John, and Shuttleworth, Sally (eds.), *Nature Transfigured: Science and Literature, 1700–1900* (New York: St Martin's, 1989).

Cosslett, Tess, *The 'Scientific Movement' and Victorian Literature* (Brighton: Harvester; New York: St Martins, 1982).

Desmond, Adrian, *The Politics of Evolution: Morphology, Medicine, and Reform in Radical London* (Chicago: University of Chicago Press, 1989).

Glicksberg, Charles I., 'Hardy's Scientific Pessimism', *Western Humanities Review*, 6 (1952), 273–83.

Gould, Stephen Jay, *Ontogeny and Phylogeny* (Cambridge, Mass.: Belknap-Harvard University Press, 1977).

—— *Time's Arrow, Time's Cycle: Myth and Metaphor in the Discovery of Geological Time* (Cambridge, Mass.: Harvard University Press, 1987).

Greenacre, Phyllis, *The Quest for the Father: A Study of the Darwin–Butler Controversy, as a Contribution to the Understanding of the Creative Individual*, Freud Anniversary Lecture Series (New York: International Universities Press, 1963).

Hardy, Florence Emily, *The Life of Thomas Hardy 1840–1928* (London: Macmillan, 1962).

Henkins, Leo, *Darwinism in the English Novel, 1860–1910: The Impact of Evolution on Victorian Fiction* [1940] (New York: Russell and Russell, 1963).

Jann, Rosemary, 'Darwin and the Anthropologists: Sexual Selection and Its Discontents', *Victorian Studies*, 37 (1994), 287–306.

Jordanova, Ludmilla J. (ed.), *Languages of Nature: Critical Essays on Science and Literature* (London: Free Association Press, 1986).

Knoepflmacher, U. C., and Tennyson, G. B. (eds.), *Nature and the Victorian Imagination* (Berkeley: University of California Press, 1977).

Koestler, Arthur, *The Case of the Midwife Toad* (New York: Random House, 1972).

Levine, George, *Darwin and the Novelists: Patterns of Science in Victorian Fiction* (Chicago: University of Chicago Press, 1988).

—— (ed.), *One Culture: Essays in Science and Literature* (Madison: University of Wisconsin Press, 1987).

Mayr, Ernst, and Provine, William B. (eds.), *The Evolutionary Synthesis: Perspectives on the Unification of Biology* (Cambridge, Mass.: Harvard University Press, 1980).

Millgate, Michael, *Thomas Hardy: A Biography* (New York: Random House, 1982).

Morton, Peter R., *The Vital Science: Biology and the Literary Imagination 1860–1900* (London: Allen and Unwin, 1984).

Newton, William, 'Chance as Employed by Hardy and the Naturalists', *Philological Quarterly*, 30 (1951), 154–75.

Otis, Laura, *Organic Memory: History and the Body in the Late Nineteenth and Early Twentieth Centuries* (Lincoln, Nebr.: University of Nebraska Press, 1994).

Raby, Peter, *Samuel Butler: A Biography* (London: Hogarth Press, 1991).

Robinson, Roger, 'Hardy and Darwin', in Norman Page (ed.), *Thomas Hardy: The Writer and His Background* (London: Bell and Hyman; New York: St Martin's, 1980).

Secord, James A., *Controversy in Victorian Geology: The Cambrian-Silurian Dispute* (Princeton: Princeton University Press, 1986).

—— 'Introduction' to Charles Lyell, *Principles of Geology* (Harmondsworth: Penguin, 1997).

—— *Victorian Sensation: The Extraordinary Publication, Reception, and Secret Authorship of Vestiges of the Natural History of Creation* (Chicago: University of Chicago Press, 2000).

Stevenson, Lionel, *Darwin among the Poets* (Chicago: University of Chicago Press, 1932).

Turner, Frank M., *Between Science and Religion: The Reaction to Scientific Naturalism in Victorian England* (New Haven: Yale University Press, 1974).

Yeo, Richard, *Defining Science: William Whewell, Natural Knowledge and Public Debate in Early Victorian Britain* (Cambridge: Cambridge University Press, 1993).

Zaniello, Tom, *Hopkins in the Age of Darwin* (Iowa City: University of Iowa Press, 1988).

Sciences of the Mind

Boring, Edwin G., *A History of Experimental Psychology*, 2nd edn. (New York: Appleton, 1950).

Bynum, W. F., Porter, Roy, and Shepherd, Michael (eds.), *The Anatomy of Madness: Essays in the History of Psychiatry*, 3 vols. (London: Tavistock, 1985).

Clarke, Edwin, and Jacyna, L. S., *Nineteenth-Century Origins of Neuroscientific Concepts* (Berkeley: University of California Press, 1987).

Donnelly, Michael, *Managing the Mind: A Study of Medical Psychology in Early Nineteenth-Century Britain* (London: Tavistock, 1983).

Earnest, Ernest Penney, *S. Weir Mitchell: Novelist and Physician* (Philadelphia: University of Pennsylvania Press, 1950).

Ellenberger, Henri F., *The Discovery of the Unconscious: The History and Evolution of Dynamic Psychiatry* (New York: Basic Books, 1970).

Foucault, Michel, *Madness and Civilization: A History of Insanity in the Age of Reason*, tr. Richard Howard (New York: Vintage-Random House, 1965).

Gilbert, Pamela K., *Disease, Desire, and the Body in Victorian Women's Popular Novels* (Cambridge: Cambridge University Press, 1997).

Gilman, Sander L., *Seeing the Insane* (New York: Wiley, 1982).

Hunter, Kathryn Montgomery, *Doctors' Stories: The Narrative Structure of Medical Knowledge* (Princeton: Princeton University Press, 1991).

Jacobus, Mary, Keller, Evelyn Fox, and Shuttleworth, Sally (eds.), *Body Politics: Women and the Discourses of Science* (New York: Routledge, 1990).

Jordanova, Ludmilla J., *Sexual Visions: Images of Gender in Science and Medicine between the Eighteenth and Twentieth Centuries* (Madison: University of Wisconsin Press, 1989).

Logan, Peter Melville, *Nerves and Narratives: A Cultural History of Hysteria in Nineteenth-Century British Prose* (Berkeley: University of California Press, 1997).

Micale, Mark S., and Porter, Roy (eds.), *Discovering the History of Psychiatry* (New York: Oxford University Press, 1994).

Oppenheim, Janet, *'Shattered Nerves': Doctors, Patients, and Depression in Victorian England* (New York: Oxford University Press, 1991).

Poirier, Suzanne, 'The Weir Mitchell Rest Cure: Doctor and Patients', *Women's Studies*, 10 (1983), 15–40.

Porter, Roy, *A Social History of Madness: The World through the Eyes of the Insane* (New York: Weidenfeld and Nicolson, 1988).

—— and Bynum, W. F. (eds.), *Medical Fringe and Medical Orthodoxy 1750–1850* (London: Croom Helm, 1987).

—— and Porter, Dorothy, *In Sickness and in Health: The British Experience, 1650–1850* (New York: Blackwell, 1989).

Rein, David, *S. Weir Mitchell as a Psychiatric Novelist* (New York: International Universities Press, 1952).

Scull, Andrew (ed.), *Madhouses, Mad-Doctors and Madmen: The Social History of Psychiatry in the Victorian Era* (London: Athlone, 1981).

Showalter, Elaine, *The Female Malady: Women, Madness, and English Culture 1830–1980* (New York: Viking-Penguin, 1987).

Shuttleworth, Sally, and Bourne Taylor, Jenny (eds.), *Embodied Selves: An Anthology of Psychological Texts, 1830–1890* (Oxford: Clarendon Press, 1998).

Small, Helen, *Love's Madness: Medicine, the Novel, and Female Insanity 1800–1865* (Oxford: Clarendon Press, 1996).

Winter, Alison, *Mesmerized: Powers of Mind in Victorian Britain* (Chicago: University of Chicago Press, 1998).

Social Sciences

Arata, Stephen, *Fictions of Loss in the Victorian Fin de Siècle* (Cambridge: Cambridge University Press, 1996).

Brantlinger, Patrick, 'Bluebooks, the Social Organism, and the Victorian Novel', *Criticism*, 14 (1972), 328–44.

—— *Rule of Darkness: British Literature and Imperialism 1830–1914* (Ithaca, NY: Cornell University Press, 1988).

Chamberlin, J. Edward, and Gilman, Sander L., *Degeneration: The Dark Side of Progress* (New York: Columbia University Press, 1985).

Cullen, Michael J., *The Statistical Movement in Early Victorian Britain: The Foundations of Empirical Social Research* (New York: Barnes and Noble, 1975).

Dyos, H. J., 'The Slums of Victorian London', *Victorian Studies*, 11 (1967), 5–40.

Fontana, Ernest, 'Lombroso's Criminal Man and Stoker's *Dracula*', *Victorian Newsletter*, 66 (1984), 25–7.

Foucault, Michel, *Discipline and Punish: The Birth of the Prison*, tr. Alan Sheridan (New York: Vintage-Random House, 1977).

Gallagher, Catherine, 'The Body versus the Social Body in the Works of Thomas Malthus and Henry Mayhew', *Representations*, 14 (1986), 83–106.

—— *The Industrial Reformation of English Fiction: Social Discourse and Narrative Form, 1832–1867* (Chicago: University of Chicago Press, 1985).

Gould, Stephen Jay, *The Mismeasure of Man* (New York: Norton, 1981).

Greenway, John L., 'Seward's Folly: *Dracula* as a Critique of "Normal Science."', *Stanford Literature Review*, 3 (1986), 213–30.

Jann, Rosemary, 'Saved by Science?: The Mixed Messages of Stoker's *Dracula*', *Texas Studies in Literature and Language*, 31 (1989), 273–87.

Lightman, Bernard (ed.), *Victorian Science in Context* (Chicago: University of Chicago Press, 1997).

Mighall, Robert, *A Geography of Victorian Gothic Fiction: Mapping History's Nightmares* (Oxford: Oxford University Press, 1999).

Nordon, Pierre, *Conan Doyle*, tr. Frances Partridge (London: Murray, 1966).

Paradis, James, and Postlewait, Thomas (eds.), *Victorian Science and Victorian Values: Literary Perspectives* (New York: New York Academy of Sciences, 1981).

Scarry, Elaine (ed.), *Literature and the Body: Essays on Populations and Persons* (Baltimore: Johns Hopkins University Press, 1988).

Smith, Roger, *The Fontana History of the Human Sciences* (London: Fontana-HarperCollins, 1997).

Smith, Sheila M., *The Other Nation: The Poor in English Novels of the 1840s and 1850s* (Oxford: Clarendon Press, 1980).

Stepan, Nancy, *The Idea of Race in Science: Great Britain, 1800–1960* (Hamden, Conn.: Archon, 1982).

Stoler, Ann Laura, *Race and the Education of Desire: Foucault's History of Sexuality and the Colonial Order of Things* (Durham, NC: Duke University Press, 1995).

Further Reading in Oxford World's Classics

Austen, Jane, *Pride and Prejudice*, ed. James Kinsley.

Braddon, Mary Elizabeth, *Lady Audley's Secret*, ed. David Skilton.

Brontë, Charlotte, *Jane Eyre*, ed. Margaret Smith and Sally Shuttleworth.

Carroll, Lewis, *Alice's Adventures in Wonderland/Through the Looking-Glass*, ed. Roger Lancelyn Green.

Collins, Wilkie, *The Moonstone*, ed. John Sutherland.

Darwin, Charles, *The Origin of Species*, ed. Gillian Beer.

De Quincey, Thomas, *The Confessions of an English Opium-Eater*, ed. Grevel Lindop.

Dickens, Charles, *Bleak House*, ed. Stephen Gill.

—— *Dombey and Son*, ed. Alan Horsman, introd. Dennis Walder.

—— *Hard Times*, ed. Paul Schlicke.

Eliot, George, *Daniel Deronda*, ed. Graham Handley.

—— *The Lifted Veil and Brother Jacob*, ed. Helen Small.

—— *Middlemarch*, ed. David Carroll and Felicia Bonaparte.

—— *The Mill on the Floss*, ed. Gordon S. Haight.

Engels, Friedrich, *The Condition of the Working Class in England*, ed. David McLellan.

Gaskell, Elizabeth, *North and South*, ed. Angus Easson and Sally Shuttleworth.

Gissing, George, *The Nether World*, ed. Stephen Gill.

Haggard, H. Rider, *She*, ed. Daniel Karlin.

Hardy, Thomas, *Jude the Obscure*, ed. Patricia Ingham.

—— *A Pair of Blue Eyes*, ed. Alan Manford.

—— *Tess of the D'Urbervilles*, ed. Juliet Grindle and Simon Gatrell.

—— *Two on a Tower*, ed. Suleiman M. Ahmad.

Poe, Edgar Allan, *Selected Tales*, ed. David Van Leer.

Schreiner, Olive, *The Story of an African Farm*, ed. Joseph Bristow.

Shelley, Mary, *Frankenstein* (the 1818 text), ed. Marilyn Butler.

—— *The Last Man*, ed. Morton D. Paley.

Stevenson, Robert Louis, *The Strange Case of Dr Jekyll and Mr Hyde/ Weir of Hermiston*, ed. Emma Letley.
Stoker, Bram, *Dracula*, ed. Maud Ellmann.
Whitman, Walt, *Leaves of Grass*, ed. Jerome Loving.
Wilde, Oscar, *The Picture of Dorian Gray*, ed. Isobel Murray.

CHRONOLOGY

	Events	Publications
1800	Alessandro Volta develops the battery as a source of electricity.	William Herschel, *On the Power of Penetrating into Space by Telescopes*
1801		Xavier Bichat, *General Anatomy*
1809		Jean Baptiste de Lamarck, *Zoological Philosophy*
1813		Jane Austen, *Pride and Prejudice*
1815	Final defeat of Napoleon.	
1818		Mary Shelley, *Frankenstein*
1820	Johann Christian Oersted discovers electro-magnetic induction.	
1822		Thomas De Quincey, *Confessions of an English Opium-Eater*
1824		George Combe, *Elements of Phrenology*
1825	Opening of the first public railway line.	
1826		Mary Shelley, *The Last Man* Johann Gaspar Spurzheim, *Phrenology in Connection with the Study of Physiognomy*
1830	Revolution in France and crowning of a 'Citizen King'.	Sir Charles Lyell, *Principles of Geology* (1830–3)
1832	First Reform Bill in England.	Charles Babbage, *On the Economy of Machinery and Manufactures* J. R. M'Culloch, *A Dictionary, Practical, Theoretical, and Historical of Commerce and Commercial Navigation*
1833		Marshall Hall, 'On the Reflex Function'
1835		James Cowles Prichard, *A Treatise on Insanity*
1837	Victoria becomes Queen of England.	
1839	Theodor Schwann proposes that all living organisms are composed of individual cells.	Michael Faraday, *Experimental Researches in Electricity* (1839–55)

	Events	Publications
1840	Fox Talbot invents the calotype photograph.	Chauncey Hare Townsend, *Facts in Mesmerism* William Whewell, *Philosophy of the Inductive Sciences*
1842		Sir Edwin Chadwick, 'An Inquiry into the Sanitary Condition of the Labouring Population of Great Britain'
1843		Thomas Carlyle, *Past and Present* John Elliotson, *Surgical Operations without Pain in the Mesmeric State* Oliver Wendell Holmes, 'The Contagiousness of Puerperal Fever'
1844	Opening of the first public telegraph line.	
1845		Friedrich Engels, *The Condition of the Working Class in England* Harriet Martineau, *Letters on Mesmerism* Edgar Allan Poe, *Tales*
1846	Ether is first used as a general anaesthetic.	Nathaniel Hawthorne, 'The Birthmark'
1847	Chloroform is first used as a general anaesthetic.	Charles Dickens, *Dombey and Son* (1847–8) Charlotte Brontë, *Jane Eyre* James Esdaile, *Mesmerism in India* Hermann von Helmholtz, 'On the Conservation of Force' Augustus de Morgan, *Formal Logic* Alfred, Lord Tennyson, *The Princess*
1848	Political uprisings in France, Prussia, and Austria.	
1850	Hermann von Helmholtz measures the velocity of a nerve impulse.	Robert Knox, *The Races of Men* Alfred, Lord Tennyson, *In Memoriam*
1851	Great Exhibition in London.	Henry Mayhew, *London Labour and the London Poor*
1852		Charles Dickens, *Bleak House* (1852–3)
1853	Crimean War (1853–6).	
1854		Charles Dickens, *Hard Times*
1855		Elizabeth Gaskell, *North and South* Walt Whitman, *Leaves of Grass* (1st edn.)
1856		Herman Melville, 'Bartleby the Scrivener'
1857	Armed uprisings against British colonial forces in India.	

	Events	Publications
1858		Rudolf Virchow, *Cellular Pathology*
1859		Charles Darwin, *The Origin of Species* George Eliot, 'The Lifted Veil'
1860		George Eliot, *The Mill on the Floss* Thomas Laycock, *Mind and Brain*
1861	US Civil War (1861–5).	Louis Pasteur, 'On the Organized Bodies Which Exist in the Atmosphere' Oliver Wendell Holmes, *Elsie Venner*
1862		Mary Elizabeth Braddon, *Lady Audley's Secret*
1864		Herbert Spencer, *Principles of Biology* (1864–7)
1865		Claude Bernard, *An Introduction to the Study of Experimental Medicine*
1867		Joseph Lister, 'Illustrations of the Antiseptic System'
1868		Wilkie Collins, *The Moonstone*
1870	Franco-Prussian War (1870–1).	Henry Maudsley, *Body and Mind*
1871	Paris Commune.	Lewis Carroll, *Through the Looking-Glass* Charles Darwin, *The Descent of Man* George Eliot, *Middlemarch* (1871–2) James Clerk Maxwell, *Theory of Heat*
1872		Samuel Butler, *Erewhon* S. Weir Mitchell, *Wear and Tear*
1873		Thomas Hardy, *A Pair of Blue Eyes*
1874		William B. Carpenter, *Principles of Mental Physiology* Ernst Haeckel, *The Evolution of Man*
1876	Alexander Graham Bell invents the telephone.	George Eliot, *Daniel Deronda* Cesare Lombroso, *The Criminal Man*
1877	Thomas Edison develops the phonograph.	George Henry Lewes, *The Physical Basis of Mind*
1879	Thomas Edison produces the electric light bulb.	
1880		Samuel Butler, *Unconscious Memory* Thomas Henry Huxley, *Science and Culture*
1881	Louis Pasteur vaccinates sheep against anthrax at Pouilly-le-Fort.	August Weismann, *Essays on Heredity* (1881–5)
1882	Robert Koch identifies the tuberculosis bacillus; the British Society for Psychical Research is founded.	Matthew Arnold, 'Literature and Science' Thomas Hardy, *Two on a Tower*

Events	Publications
1883 Robert Koch discovers the cholera bacillus.	Wilkie Collins, *Heart and Science* Sir Francis Galton, *Inquiries into Human Faculty and Its Development* O. Schreiner, *The Story of an African Farm*
1884 A Prime Meridian conference is held to discuss universal adoption of standard time.	
1885 Louis Pasteur produces the rabies vaccine.	
1886	Robert Louis Stevenson, *The Strange Case of Dr Jekyll and Mr Hyde*
1887 Physicists Michelson and Morley find no experimental evidence for the 'ether' through which light waves supposedly move.	Henry Rider Haggard, *She*
1888	George John Romanes, *Mental Evolution in Man*
1889 Eiffel Tower constructed.	George Gissing, *The Nether World*
1890	William James, *Principles of Psychology* Oscar Wilde, *The Picture of Dorian Gray*
1891	Thomas Hardy, *Tess of the D'Urbervilles*
1892	Charlotte Perkins Gilman, 'The Yellow Wall-Paper' Max Nordau, *Degeneration*
1893	Sarah Grand, *The Heavenly Twins*
1895 The Lumière brothers develop moving pictures for public entertainment.	Wilhelm Conrad Roentgen, 'On a New Kind of Rays' H. G. Wells, *The Time Machine* Thomas Hardy, *Jude the Obscure*
1896 Guglielmo Marconi produces the wireless telegraph.	H. G. Wells, *The Island of Dr Moreau*
1897	Bram Stoker, *Dracula*
1898 Spanish-American War.	Henry James, 'In the Cage' George Bernard Shaw, *Mrs Warren's Profession*
1899 Boer War (1899–1902).	Walter Besant, *East London*
1900 Gregor Mendel's genetic experiments, supporting a two-allele model, are rediscovered and made public; the A, B, and O blood groups are discovered, making transfusions possible.	

LITERATURE AND SCIENCE
IN THE
NINETEENTH CENTURY

PROLOGUE: LITERATURE AND SCIENCE

EDGAR ALLAN POE

Sonnet—To Science (1829)

Science true daughter of Old Time thou art
    Who alterest all things with thy peering eyes.
Why preyest thou thus upon the poet's heart,
    Vulture, whose wings are dull realities?
How should he love thee? or how deem thee wise,
    Who wouldst not leave him in his wandering
To seek for treasure in the jewelled skies.
    Albeit he soared with an undaunted wing?
Hast thou not dragged Diana from her car?
    And driven the Hamadryad* from the wood
To seek a shelter in some happier star?
    Hast thou not torn the Naiad* from her flood,
The Elfin from the green grass, and from me
The summer dream beneath the tamarind tree?

JOHN TYNDALL

The Belfast Address (1874)

The impregnable position of science may be described in a few
words. We claim, and we shall wrest from theology, the entire
domain of cosmological theory. All schemes and systems which thus
infringe upon the domain of science must, in so far as they do this,
submit to its control, and relinquish all thought of controlling it.
Acting otherwise proved always disastrous in the past, and it is simply fatuous to-day. Every system which would escape the fate of an
organism too rigid to adjust itself to its environment, must be plastic
to the extent that the growth of knowledge demands. When this

truth has been thoroughly taken in, rigidity will be relaxed, exclusiveness diminished, things now deemed essential will be dropped, and elements now rejected will be assimilated. The lifting of the life is the essential point; and as long as dogmatism, fanaticism, and intolerance are kept out, various modes of leverage may be employed to raise life to a higher level.

Science itself not unfrequently derives motive power from an ultra-scientific source. Some of its greatest discoveries have been made under the stimulus of a non-scientific ideal. This was the case among the ancients, and it has been so amongst ourselves. . . .

It has been said by its opponents that science divorces itself from literature; but the statement, like so many others, arises from lack of knowledge. A glance at the less technical writings of its leaders—of its Helmholtz, its Huxley, and its Du Bois-Reymond*—would show what breadth of literary culture they command. Where among modern writers can you find their superiors in clearness and vigour of literary style? Science desires not isolation, but freely combines with every effort towards the bettering of man's estate. Single-handed, and supported, not by outward sympathy, but by inward force, it has built at least one great wing of the many-mansioned home which man in his totality demands. And if rough walls and protruding rafter-ends indicate that on one side the edifice is still incomplete, it is only by wise combination of the parts required, with those already irrevocably built, that we can hope for completeness. There is no necessary incongruity between what has been accomplished and what remains to be done. The moral glow of Socrates, which we all feel by ignition, has in it nothing incompatible with the physics of Anaxagoras* which he so much scorned, but which he would hardly scorn to-day.

THOMAS HENRY HUXLEY

From *Science and Culture* (1880)

I hold very strongly by two convictions—The first is, that neither the discipline nor the subject-matter of classical education is of such direct value to the student of physical science as to justify the expenditure of valuable time upon either; and the second is, that for the purpose of attaining real culture, an exclusively scientific education is at least as effectual as an exclusively literary education.

I need hardly point out to you that these opinions, especially the latter, are diametrically opposed to those of the great majority of educated Englishmen, influenced as they are by school and university traditions. In their belief, culture is obtainable only by a liberal education; and a liberal education is synonymous, not merely with education and instruction in literature, but in one particular form of literature, namely, that of Greek and Roman antiquity. They hold that the man who has learned Latin and Greek, however little, is educated; while he who is versed in other branches of knowledge, however deeply, is a more or less respectable specialist, not admissible into the cultured caste. The stamp of the educated man, the University degree, is not for him.

I am too well acquainted with the generous catholicity of spirit, the true sympathy with scientific thought, which pervades the writings of our chief apostle of culture to identify him with these opinions; and yet one may cull from one and another of those epistles to the Philistines, which so much delight all who do not answer to that name, sentences which lend them some support.

Mr Arnold tells us that the meaning of culture is 'to know the best that has been thought and said in the world.' It is the criticism of life contained in literature. That criticism regards 'Europe as being, for intellectual and spiritual purposes, one great confederation, bound to a joint action and working to a common result; and whose members have, for their common outfit, a knowledge of Greek, Roman, and Eastern antiquity, and of one another. Special, local, and temporary advantages being put out of account, that modern nation will in the intellectual and spiritual sphere make most progress, which most thoroughly carries out this programme. And what is that but saying that we too, all of us, as individuals, the more thoroughly we carry it out, shall make the more progress?'

We have here to deal with two distinct propositions. The first, that a criticism of life is the essence of culture; the second, that literature contains the materials which suffice for the construction of such a criticism.

I think that we must all assent to the first proposition. For culture certainly means something quite different from learning or technical skill. It implies the possession of an ideal, and the habit of critically estimating the value of things by comparison with a theoretic standard. Perfect culture should supply a complete theory of life, based upon a clear knowledge alike of its possibilities and of its limitations.

But we may agree to all this, and yet strongly dissent from the assumption that literature alone is competent to supply this knowledge. After having learnt all that Greek, Roman, and Eastern antiquity have thought and said, and all that modern literatures have to tell us, it is not self-evident that we have laid a sufficiently broad and deep foundation for that criticism of life which constitutes culture.

Indeed, to any one acquainted with the scope of physical science, it is not at all evident. Considering progress only in the 'intellectual and spiritual sphere,' I find myself wholly unable to admit that either nations or individuals will really advance, if their common outfit draws nothing from the stores of physical science. I should say that an army, without weapons of precision and with no particular base of operations, might more hopefully enter upon a campaign on the Rhine, than a man, devoid of a knowledge of what physical science has done in the last century, upon a criticism of life.

MATTHEW ARNOLD

Literature and Science (1882)

What Professor Huxley says, implies just the reproach which is so often brought against the study of *belles lettres*, as they are called: that the study is an elegant one, but slight and ineffectual; a smattering of Greek and Latin and other ornamental things, of little use for any one whose object is to get at truth. So, too, M. Renan* talks of the 'superficial humanism' of a school-course which treats us as if we were all going to be poets, writers, orators, and he opposes this humanism to positive science, or the critical search after truth. And there is always a tendency in those who are remonstrating against the predominance of letters in education, to understand by letters *belles lettres*, and by *belles lettres* a superficial humanism, the opposite of science or true knowledge.

But when we talk of knowing Greek and Roman antiquity, for instance, which is what people have called humanism, we mean a knowledge which is something more than a superficial humanism, mainly decorative. 'I call teaching *scientific*,' says Wolf, the critic of Homer, 'which is systematically laid out and followed up to its original sources. For example: a knowledge of classical antiquity is scientific when the remains of classical antiquity are correctly studied in the original languages.' There can be no doubt that Wolf* is perfectly right, that all learning is scientific which is systematically laid out and followed up to its original sources, and that a genuine humanism is scientific.

When I speak of knowing Greek and Roman antiquity, therefore, as a help to knowing ourselves and the world, I mean more than a knowledge of so much vocabulary, so much grammar, so many portions of authors, in the Greek and Latin languages. I mean knowing the Greeks and Romans, and their life and genius, and what they were and did in the world; what we get from them, and what is its value. That, at least, is the ideal; and when we talk of endeavouring to know Greek and Roman antiquity as a help to knowing ourselves and the world, we mean endeavouring so to know them as to satisfy this ideal, however much we may still fall short of it.

The same as to knowing our own and other modern nations, with the aim of getting to understand ourselves and the world. To know the best that has been thought and said by the modern nations, is to know, says Professor Huxley, 'only what modern *literatures* have to tell us; it is the criticism of life contained in modern literature.' And yet 'the distinctive character of our times,' he urges, 'lies in the vast and constantly increasing part which is played by natural knowledge.' And how, therefore, can a man, devoid of knowledge of what physical science has done in the last century, enter hopefully upon a criticism of modern life?

Let us, I say, be agreed about the meaning of the terms we are using. I talk of knowing the best which has been thought and uttered in the world; Professor Huxley says this means knowing *literature*. Literature is a large word; it may mean everything written with letters or printed in a book. Euclid's *Elements* and Newton's *Principia* are thus literature. All knowledge that reaches us through books is literature. But by literature Professor Huxley means *belles lettres*. He means to make me say, that knowing the best which has been thought and said by the modern nations is knowing their *belles lettres* and no more. And this is no sufficient equipment, he argues, for a criticism of modern life. But as I do not mean, by knowing ancient Rome, knowing merely more or less of Latin *belles lettres*, and taking no account of Rome's military and political and legal and administrative work in the world; and as, by knowing ancient Greece, I understand knowing her as the giver of Greek art, and the guide to a free and right use of reason and to scientific method, and the founder of our mathematics and physics and astronomy and biology—I understand knowing her as all this, and not merely knowing certain Greek poems, histories, and speeches—so as to the knowledge of modern nations also. By knowing modern nations, I mean not merely knowing their *belles lettres*, but knowing also what has been done by such men as Copernicus, Galileo, Newton, Darwin.

MATHEMATICS, PHYSICAL SCIENCE, AND TECHNOLOGY

John Tyndall called imagination 'the mightiest instrument of the physical discoverer'. In physics, he believed—the scientific field that is sometimes considered 'farthest' from literature—the imagination was indispensable for modelling forces accessible to the senses only through secondary effects. As nineteenth-century scientists studied the relationships between heat, motion, magnetism, and electricity, they relied extensively on metaphors in order to compare one force to another. Their analogies allowed them not just to publicize their findings but to theorize about how one force might be 'translated' into another. When conveying their ideas, physicists called upon readers to use their imagination just as they themselves had used it.

Both mathematicians and literary writers used gambling as a way to represent the action of random chance, as a social and evolutionary force. Even if nature and society were governed by random occurrences rather than unknown laws, people might still gain control of their circumstances by making probability a science and learning to make predictions.

Gambling, hypothesized the mathematician John Venn, was the opposite of insurance, representing a misguided effort to control what could only be tamed through systematic study. When George Eliot introduced her novel *Daniel Deronda* with a scene of gambling, she suggested how powerfully random chance affects people's lives. Despite nineteenth-century scientists' emphasis on the human will, Eliot's opening conveys how little control people had over most aspects of their existence. With her formidable scientific knowledge, Eliot understood the importance of probabilities not just for mathematics and physics but for the emerging social sciences, which often used statistics to present themselves as legitimate fields of knowledge. As a novelist, Eliot knew the creative value of randomness for plot construction and for suggesting the complex affinities between words. By the time *Daniel Deronda* appeared, games of chance had become as powerful a metaphor for scientists as for literary writers.

In the early nineteenth century interest in probabilities developed rapidly as international commerce demanded more accurate calculations of risks. The science of probabilities, proposed the mathematician George Boole, was to the traditional 'gut instinct' what a thermometer was to the physical sensation of heat. Justifying his field through analogy, he proposed that it substituted numerical values for vague impressions. But numbers, observed Boole, were not the only medium in which the laws of probability held. The fact that words and characters recur with predictable frequencies had allowed the archaeologist Sir Austen Henry Layard to decipher cuneiform tablets. Like creative writers, nineteenth-century scientists and mathematicians were well aware of what language could do, and they thought actively about the connections words suggested. Michael Faraday, for instance, wrote that he used the words 'static' and 'dynamic' 'merely as names, without pretending to have a clear notion of the physical condition which they seem meaningly to imply'.

In formulating their theories, scientists introduced all of the random associations borne by ordinary language, and like literary writers, they struggled to express themselves in words whose meanings were interwoven with history. When the mathematician Ada Lovelace outlined the principles of Charles Babbage's calculating engine, she lamented the ambiguities that ordinary language introduced into mathematical discussions. In designing the analytical engine, Babbage tried not just to build a sophisticated calculating machine but to redesign language, devising a system of mechanical notation more appropriate for representing moving machine parts. As Augustus de Morgan argued, the relationship between a word and its referent was as essential to mathematics as it was to literature.

Lewis Carroll, a gifted story-teller and mathematician, implied that since logic was written in this flawed medium, the 'game of logic' was one of identification. Traditional logical syllogisms consist of two or more premises and a conclusion that follows from them, but the nature of language makes it easy to mimic true syllogisms with words like 'if', 'then', and 'therefore'. In a system in which words have multiple, context-dependent meanings and readers have been trained to seek meanings in terms of pre-set patterns, distinguishing the true syllogisms from the false ones that so closely resemble them becomes a formidable challenge.

In *Through the Looking-Glass*, Carroll celebrates language's confluences as a delightful game. Alice's frustrating dialogues suggest that words acquire their meanings more from their relations with other words than from the referents pre-assigned to them. Carroll's emphasis on puns and literal readings reveals language's many coincidences. When Alice passes through the looking-glass, the characters she encounters mimic traditional logic but make erratic leaps based on the 'sound' rather than the 'sense' of words. This phenomenon, Carroll suggests, is equally common on Alice's own side of the glass.

In the nineteenth century discoveries about language, matter, and energy inspired writers from diverse fields to use their creativity to convey unfamiliar concepts. Trained as a biologist, H. G. Wells used fiction to explore a new understanding of time. By mid-century the rapid advancement of science and technology had encouraged some writers to view time linearly, in terms of progress. Positivists argued that if scientific knowledge continued its rapid growth, people might someday achieve moral enlightenment and world peace. Wells's time traveller, however, argues that time is much more complex and accessible than his listeners imagine.

Both physicists and literary writers challenged the notion that humankind could anticipate a more civilized, prosperous future. Mimicking the style of the biblical Revelation, Thomas Carlyle 'prophesied' that nineteenth-century technology and the 'sooty desperation' it had created were leading to an apocalypse in which the unstable social order would be overthrown. In 1852 William Thomson's formulation of the second law of thermodynamics challenged the positivistic view of time. According to Thomson, whenever energy changed forms, some was irrecoverably lost and could never again be used to do work. Thomson presented his findings to lay readers by showing that the sun's capacity was finite. In the distant future, the sun would cease emitting energy, so that the world as people knew it could no longer exist. Wells played on popular awareness of thermodynamics when he presented time as fluid, resisting notions of intellectual and moral progress.

By 1871 Thomson's theory of gradual energy loss had become a scientific 'law', and like Wells, the physicist James Clerk Maxwell used a fictional 'character' to challenge it. Maxwell described matter in terms of the movements of individual particles, enhancing scientists' understanding of gases by presenting them in terms of statistical laws. To indicate an important exception to the second law, a case in which fast-moving particles might unexpectedly move from a cooler to a warmer compartment, Maxwell asked readers to 'conceive a being' who selectively opened a portal between the two compartments. Since the movements of particles were random and could be described only in terms of probabilities, such a migration was possible, but highly unlikely. In a popular lecture eight years later, the physicist William Thomson called Maxwell's 'being' 'a creature of imagination' invented for a specific purpose. The 'demon' persisted in the public imagination, however. Like literary characters, scientific ones tended to take on their own lives.

Because imagination played a central role in both scientific and literary texts, vision became a key metaphorical vehicle in nineteenth-century writing. The eye functioned figuratively as the mind's eye, so that vision represented the imaginative power in general. Both scientific and literary works made numerous references to the eye and the instruments that enhanced its powers. Introducing readers to the power of telescopes, the astronomer William Herschel began by reviewing what the human eye itself could see of the stars. He then presented the telescope as an extension of the natural eye, one which possessed a greater resolving power but functioned according to the same principles. In Herschel's writing, the 'power of penetrating into space' is the ability to imagine what one cannot see.

Half a century later, in his *Outlines of Astronomy*, the mathematician John Herschel asked the reader 'to station himself . . . in some open situation whence a good general view of the heavens can be obtained'. While this request at first seems literal, it soon becomes clear that he is taking readers on an imaginative journey, asking them to picture stars that seem spread out on a dome over their heads. His astronomy textbook relies on this initial entreaty to readers to imagine themselves imagining.

Writing primarily for scientists, Faraday appealed directly to his readers' imaginative power when he theorized about lines of force. What is the best response for scientists, he asked, when faced with a phenomenon whose effects they can observe but which they can never see directly? Because he was not a skilled mathematician, Faraday relied on his visual imagination to explain the interaction of electrical and magnetic forces. So impressed was Faraday by the lines he could see in his mind's eye that he contended they had a real 'physical existence'.

More than half a century later, the German physicist Wilhelm Roentgen also found himself facing an invisible, entirely unknown phenomenon. Like Faraday's descriptions, Roentgen's modest, lucid characterization of X-rays addresses a question essential to nineteenth-century physics: how does one characterize what one cannot see? Roentgen took a practical course, comparing the unknown rays to other energy forms and documenting their effects on various substances, including film. Many physicists responded like Faraday, however, reasoning visually about processes they could never observe.

Unlike Faraday, many nineteenth-century investigators came from privileged backgrounds. Because it was nearly impossible to earn one's living as a scientist—outside of medicine or engineering, which left little time for research—the field was largely restricted to investigators who were independently wealthy. Consequently, most of them received a classical as well as scientific training, particularly the study of Greek and Roman literature. When scientists formulated their ideas, they incorporated their knowledge of the classics, not just to communicate their thoughts to lay readers but to 'brainstorm' with one another. In both literary and scientific writing, emerging theories blended with classical myths to form a common cultural language.

In Thomas Hardy's *Two on a Tower*, modern astronomy challenges the traditional association of the stars with fate. Hardy's stated purpose in the novel was to compare the feelings generated by an 'ill-starred' romance with the immense reality of an indifferent universe. While Hardy's characters develop original theories about the heavens, the stars' Greek names suggest the persistence of older ways of thinking. This contrast is equally apparent in William Herschel's writings when he uses mathematical formulae to characterize stars named after mythological characters. Herschel, who wrote about the stars more than eighty years before Hardy, makes no attempt to alert readers to any potential conflict. For him, as for most early nineteenth-century astronomers, there was no conflict involved.

James Clerk Maxwell's ironic poems interweave mathematical references with literary allusions. Like Carroll's stories, they offer the scientist creative plays on words that stimulate scientific thinking. In its form, Maxwell's 'Tyndallic Ode' suggests Horace, but it relies on a special kind of pun: a confluence created by a visual image. In this poem, an inverted isosceles triangle symbolizes two very different concepts: an Assyrian harp and a quaternion operator used in calculations essential to electrical and magnetic studies. Maxwell's comic ode honours the mathematician Peter Guthrie Tait, who worked with quaternion operators. Like a dream image, Maxwell's triangle bears condensed meanings.

In the 1830s electromagnetic studies like Faraday's allowed European and American engineers to construct electrical telegraphs. Developed rapidly in the 1850s, telegraph networks replaced the older, unreliable semaphore system so that messages could be sent instantaneously. When asking the US Congress to finance his electromagnetic telegraph in 1837, Samuel Morse presented it as a national nervous system. In 1877, when public telephones became available, a writer explaining their development revealed that Alexander Graham Bell, like Morse, had thought in terms of the human body. Before constructing his receiver, Bell consulted an ear specialist so that his device might function as efficiently as the human organ. For nineteenth-century inventors the resemblance between sensory organs and technical devices was more than an informative metaphor; it inspired the design of communications devices.

In their effort to achieve credibility, fiction writers describing communications technologies used the same strategies as scientists. In 1891, five years before the wireless telegraph was invented, Mark Twain published the tall tale 'Mental Telegraphy' in which a narrator argues that thoughts can be transmitted from mind to mind. At first, Twain's anecdotes about coincidental discoveries seem to offer convincing evidence for thought-transmission because they are interspersed with scientific references. One begins to doubt the narrator only when he innocently invokes 'mental telegraphy' to explain scientific and literary disputes about authorship. The real subject of Twain's tale is plagiarism, an issue as essential to science as it is to literature.

As Henry James suggests in his telegraphic story 'In the Cage', technology feeds the imagination. Trapped in a dull office, his protagonist attempts to enter her wealthy customers' lives, picturing her mind and body as the centre of a vast network. In James's story, the telegraph fails to deliver the knowledge or relationships it promises, and the feeling of connectedness offered by technological communications proves illusory. As James implies, however, technology inspires its users to think, particularly about their own bodies and identities.

As mechanized industry developed, writers from all fields compared bodies to machines. Hermann von Helmholtz helped his listeners understand the principle of conservation of energy by 'translating' mechanical work into labour performed by the body. Trained as a physician, Helmholtz began his career by studying the relationship between heat and work in living bodies and discovered thermodynamics through these studies of 'animal heat.' For him, the body–machine analogy was much more than a device to communicate his idea.

While a great variety of technical developments altered Western societies in the nineteenth century, it is worthwhile to focus on the railways, since debates about the new mode of transportation raised issues central to discussions of technology in general. In the 1830s and 1840s England's growing railway networks changed people's conception of distance. Their advocates, mainly middle-class industrialists, argued that the new system of communication would create near-organic unity and promote social harmony, as Morse claimed about the telegraph.

Charles Dickens—who often travelled in trains and himself survived a railway accident in 1865—took a very different view. In *Dombey and Son*, he offers two troubling depictions of trains, both of which associate the railways with death. The first is metaphorical: Mr Dombey, who has just lost his only son, experiences the train as the relentless force that took the young boy's life. The second is literal: Carker, who is fleeing Dombey after having cheated him for years, experiences the train as an avenging monster that grinds him up.

While Dickens uses trains to symbolize forces crushing people's humanity, Walt Whitman's elegy 'To a Locomotive in Winter' presents a locomotive as heroic because of its resemblance to a human body. To Whitman, the machine seems alive because of its ability to resist the frigid elements. Here nature becomes the threatening force, and the reader is invited to identify with the machine that resists it.

Butler's *Erewhon* uses humour to approach the most disturbing aspects of nineteenth-century technology, 'quoting' a rambling prophet who questions oft-cited 'differences' between people and machines. Butler, who was deeply interested in evolutionary theory, depicts machines as developing and growing, with the potential to acquire consciousness. The prophet's warnings about machines ring true because both structurally and stylistically his argument sounds a great deal like Darwin's. When he mentions the number of people (miners, engineers, etc.) who live to serve machines, his evolutionary argument becomes highly convincing. Both Butler and Babbage, who had proposed that some mental labour could be performed more efficiently by steam, anticipate the central concerns of twentieth-century science fiction.

In nineteenth-century Europe, the rapid development of technology encouraged all those who used it to rethink their notions of mind, body, and identity. Through their comparisons of bodies and machines, scientists and literary writers contributed to a new cultural understanding of selfhood. Both, in turn, revised their understanding of the body as an entity increasingly dependent on tools and open to outside forces.

Mathematics

ADA LOVELACE

Sketch of the Analytical Engine (1843)

In the early 1820s the mathematician Charles Babbage designed a steam-powered calculating machine, the 'difference engine', to generate tables of data without the errors introduced by human 'calculators'. In the mid–1830s he abandoned the difference engine and began building a much more versatile, powerful machine, the analytical engine. While few British scientists appreciated Babbage's new creation, Italian mathematician Luigi Federico Menabrea (1809–96) admired Babbage's work and wrote a lucid, informative article explaining its importance to lay readers. The mathematician Ada Lovelace, a close friend of Babbage's, translated Menabrea's article for British readers and added several insightful explanatory notes, offering original contributions to mathematical theory. The following passage is taken from Lovelace's first note to her translation of Menabrea.

In studying the action of the Analytical Engine, we find that the peculiar and independent nature of the considerations which in all mathematical analysis belong to *operations*, as distinguished from *the objects operated upon* and from the *results* of the operations performed upon those objects, is very strikingly defined and separated.

It is well to draw attention to this point, not only because its full appreciation is essential to the attainment of any very just and adequate general comprehension of the powers and mode of action of the Analytical Engine, but also because it is one which is perhaps too little kept in view in the study of mathematical science in general. It is, however, impossible to confound it with other considerations, either when we trace the manner in which that engine attains its results, or when we prepare the data for its attainment of those results. It were much to be desired, that when mathematical processes pass through the human brain instead of through the medium of inanimate mechanism, it were equally a necessity of things that the reasonings connected with *operations* should hold the same just place as a clear and well-defined branch of the subject of analysis, a fundamental but yet independent ingredient in the science, which they must do in studying the engine. The confusion, the difficulties, the contradictions which, in consequence of a want of accurate distinctions in this particular, have up to even a recent period encumbered mathematics in all those branches involving the consideration of negative and impossible quantities, will at once occur to the reader who is at all versed in this science, and would alone suffice to justify dwelling somewhat on the point, in connexion with any subject so peculiarly fitted to give forcible illustration of it, as the Analytical Engine. It may be desirable to explain, that by the word *operation*, we mean *any process which alters the mutual relation of two or more things*, be this relation of what kind it may. This is the most general definition, and would include all subjects in the universe. In abstract mathematics, of course operations alter those particular relations which are involved in the considerations of number and space, and the *results* of operations are those peculiar results which correspond to the nature of the subjects of operation. But the science of operations, as derived from mathematics more especially, is a science of itself, and has its own abstract truth and value; just as logic has its own peculiar truth and value, independently of the subjects to which we may apply its reasonings and processes. Those who are accustomed to some of the more modern views of the above subject, will know that a few fundamental relations being true, certain other combinations of relations must of necessity follow; combinations unlimited in variety and extent if the deductions from the primary relations be carried on far enough. They will also be aware that one main reason why the separate nature of the science of operations has been little felt, and in general little dwelt on, is the *shifting* meaning of many of the symbols used in mathematical notation. First, the symbols of *operation* are frequently *also* the symbols of the *results* of operations. We may say that these symbols are apt to have both a *retrospective* and a *prospective* signification. They may signify either relations that are the consequence of a series of processes already performed, or relations that are yet to be effected through certain processes. Secondly, figures, the symbols of *numerical magnitude*, are frequently *also* the symbols of *operations*, as when they are the indices of powers. Wherever terms have a shifting meaning, independent sets of considerations are liable to become complicated together, and reasonings and results are frequently falsified. Now in the Analytical Engine the operations which come under the first of the above heads, are ordered and combined by means of a notation and of a train of mechanism which belong exclusively to themselves; and with respect to the second head, whenever numbers meaning *operations* and not *quantities* (such as the indices of powers), are inscribed on any column or set of columns, those columns immediately act in a wholly separate and independent manner, becoming connected with the *operating mechanism* exclusively, and re-acting upon this. They never come into combination with numbers upon any other columns meaning *quantities*; though, of course, if there are numbers meaning *operations* upon *n* columns, these may *combine amongst each other*, and will often be required to do so, just as numbers meaning *quantities* combine with each other in any variety. It might have been arranged that all numbers meaning *operations* should have appeared on some separate portion of the engine from that which presents numerical *quantities*; but the present mode is in some cases more simple, and offers in reality quite as much distinctness when understood.

The operating mechanism can even be thrown into action independently of any object to operate upon (although of course no *result* could then be developed). Again, it might act upon other things besides *number*, were objects found whose mutual fundamental relations could be expressed by those of the abstract science of operations, and which should be also susceptible of adaptations to the action of the operating notation and mechanism of the engine. Supposing, for instance, that the fundamental relations of pitched sounds in the science of harmony and of musical composition were susceptible of such expression and adaptations, the engine might compose elaborate and scientific pieces of music of any degree of complexity or extent.

The Analytical Engine is an *embodying of the science of operations*, constructed with peculiar reference to abstract number as the subject of those operations. . . .

Those who view mathematical science not merely as a vast body of abstract and immutable truths, whose intrinsic beauty, symmetry and logical completeness, when regarded in their connexion together as a whole, entitle them to a prominent place in the interest of all profound and logical minds, but as possessing a yet deeper interest for the human race, when it is remembered that this science constitutes the language through which alone we can adequately express the great facts of the natural world, and those unceasing changes of mutual relationship which, visibly or invisibly, consciously or unconsciously to our immediate physical perceptions, are interminably going on in the agencies of the creation we live amidst: those who thus think on mathematical truth as the instrument through which the weak mind of man can most effectually read his Creator's works, will regard with especial interest all that can tend to facilitate the translation of its principles into explicit practical forms.

The distinctive characteristic of the Analytical Engine, and that which has rendered it possible to endow mechanism with such extensive faculties as bid fair to make this engine the executive right-hand of abstract algebra, is the introduction into it of the principle which Jacquard* devised for regulating, by means of punched cards, the most complicated patterns in the fabrication of brocaded stuffs. It is in this that the distinction between the two engines lies. Nothing of the sort exists in the Difference Engine. We may say most aptly that the Analytical Engine *weaves algebraical patterns* just as the Jacquard-loom weaves flowers and leaves. Here, it seems to us, resides much more of originality than the Difference Engine can be fairly entitled to claim. We do not wish to deny to this latter all such claims. We believe that it is the only proposal or attempt ever made to construct a calculating machine *founded on the principle of successive orders of differences*, and capable of *printing off its own results*; and that this engine surpasses its predecessors, both in the extent of the calculations which it can perform, in the facility, certainty and accuracy with which it can effect them, and in the absence of all necessity for the intervention of human intelligence *during the performance of its calculations*. Its nature is, however, limited to the strictly arithmetical, and it is far from being the first or only scheme for constructing *arithmetical* calculating machines with more or less of success.

The bounds of *arithmetic* were however outstepped the moment the idea of applying the cards had occurred; and the Analytical Engine does not occupy common ground with mere 'calculating machines.' It holds a position wholly its own; and the considerations it suggests are most interesting in their nature. In enabling mechanism to combine together *general* symbols, in successions of unlimited variety and extent, a uniting link is established between the operations of matter and the abstract mental processes of the *most abstract* branch of mathematical science. A new, a vast, and a powerful language is developed for the future use of analysis, in which to wield its truths so that these may become of more speedy and accurate practical application for the purposes of mankind than the means hitherto in our possession have rendered possible. Thus not only the mental and the material, but the theoretical and the practical in the mathematical world, are brought into more intimate and effective connexion with each other. We are not aware of its being on record that anything partaking in the nature of what is so well designated the *Analytical* Engine has been hitherto proposed, or even thought of, as a practical possibility, any more than the idea of a thinking or of a reasoning machine.

AUGUSTUS DE MORGAN

From *Formal Logic* (1847)

Connected with ideas are the *names* we give them; the spoken or written sounds by which we think of them, and communicate with others about them. To have an idea, and to make it the subject of thought as an idea, are two perfectly distinct things: the *idea of an idea* is not the idea itself. I doubt whether we could have made thought itself the subject of thought without language. As it is, we give names to our ideas, meaning by a name not merely a single word, but any collection of words which conveys to one mind the idea in another. Thus a-man-in-a-black-coat-riding-along-the-high-road-on-a-bay-horse is as much the name of an idea as man, black, or horse. We can coin words at pleasure; and, were it worth while, might invent a single word to stand for the preceding phrase.

Names are used indifferently, both for the objects which produce ideas, and for the ideas produced by them. This is a disadvantage, and it will frequently be necessary to specify whether we speak ideally or objectively. In common conversation we speak ideally and think we speak objectively: we take for granted that our own ideas are fit to pass to others, and will convey to them the same ideas as the objects themselves would have done. That this may be the case, it is necessary first, that the object should really give us the same ideas as to others; secondly, that our words should carry from us to our correspondents the same ideas as those which we intended to express by them. How, and in what cases, the first or the second condition is not fulfilled, it is impossible to know or to enumerate. But we have nothing to do here except to observe that we are only incidentally concerned with this question in a work of logic. We presume fixed and, if objective, objectively true ideas, with certain names attached: so that it is never in doubt whether a name be or be not properly attached to any idea. This method must be followed in all works of science: a conceivably attainable end is first presumed to be attained, and the consequences of its attainment are studied. Then, after-wards, comes the question whether this end is always attained, and if not, why. The way to mend bad roads must come at the end, not at the beginning, of a treatise on the art of making good ones.

Every name has a reference to every idea, either affirmative or negative. The term *horse* applies to every thing, either positively or negatively. This (no matter what I am speaking of) either *is* or *is not* a horse. If there be any doubt about it, either the idea is not precise, or the term *horse* is ill understood. A name ought to be like a boundary, which clearly and undeniably either shuts in, or shuts out, every idea that can be suggested. It is the imperfection of our minds, our lan-guage, and our knowledge of external things, that this clear and undeniable inclusion or exclusion is seldom attainable, except as to ideas which are *well within the boundary*: at and near the boundary itself all is vague. There are decided greens and decided blues: but between the two colours there are shades of which it must be unsettled by universal agreement to which of the two colours they belong. To the eye, green passes into blue by imperceptible gradations: our senses will suggest no place on which all agree, at which one is to end and the other to begin.

But the advance of knowledge has a tendency to supply means of precise definition. Thus, in the instance above cited, Wollaston and Fraunhofer* have discovered the black lines which always exist in the spectrum of solar colours given by a glass prism, in the same relative places. There are definite places in the spectrum, by the help of which the place of any shade of colour therein existing may be ascertained, and means of definition given.

When a name is complex, it frequently admits of definition, nominal or real. A name may be said to be *defined nominally* when we can of right substitute for it other terms. In such a case, a person may be made to know the meaning of the word without access to the object of which it is to give the idea. Thus, an *island* is completely defined in 'land surrounded by water.' In definition, we do not mean that we are necessarily to have very precise terms in which to explain the name defined: but, as the terms of the definition so is the name which is defined; according as the first are precise or vague, clear or obscure, so is the second. Thus there may be a question as to the meaning of *land*: is a marsh sticking up out of the water an island? Some will say that, as opposed to water, a marsh is land, others may consider marsh as intermediate between what is commonly called [dry] land and water. If there be any vagueness, the term island must partake of it: for island is but short for 'land surrounded by water,' whether this phrase be vague or precise. This sort of definition is *nominal*, being the substitution of names for names. It is complete, for it gives all that the name is to mean. An island, as such, can have nothing necessarily belonging to it except what necessarily belongs to 'land surrounded by water.' By *real* definition, I mean such an explanation of the word, be it the whole of the meaning or only part, as will be sufficient to separate the things contained under that word from all others. Thus the following, I believe, is a complete definition of an *elephant*; 'an animal which naturally drinks by drawing the water into its nose, and then spirting it into its mouth.' As it happens, the animal which does this is the elephant only, of all which are known upon the earth: so long as this is the case, so long the above definition answers every purpose; but it is far from involving all the ideas which arise from the word. Neither sagacity, nor utility, nor the production of ivory, are necessarily connected with drinking by help of the nose. And this definition is purely objective; we do not mean that every idea we could form of an animal so drinking is to be called an elephant. If a new animal were to be discovered, having the same mode of drinking, it would be a matter of pure choice whether it should be called elephant or not. It must then be settled whether it shall be called an elephant, and that race of animals shall be divided into two species, with distinctive definitions; or whether it shall have another name, and the definition above given shall be incomplete, as not serving to draw an entire distinction between the elephant and all other things.

It will be observed that the nominal definition includes the real, as soon as the terms of substitution are really defined: while the real definition may fall short of the nominal.

When a name is clearly understood, by which we mean when of every object of thought we can distinctly say, this name does or does not, contain that object—we have said that the name applies to everything, in one way or the other. The word man has an application both to Alexander and Bucephalus:* the first *was* a man, the second *was not*. In the formation of language, a great many names are, as to their original signification, of a purely negative character: thus, parallels are only lines which do *not* meet, aliens are men who are *not* Britons (that is, in our country). If language were as perfect and as copious as we could imagine it to be, we should have, for every name which has a positive signification, another which merely implies all other things: thus, as we have a name for a tree, we should have another to signify every thing that is not a tree. As it is, we have sometimes a name for the positive, and none for the negative, as in *tree*: sometimes for the negative and none for the positive, as in *parallels*: sometimes for both, as in a frequent use of *person* and *thing*. In logic, it is desirable to consider names of inclusion with the corresponding names of exclusion: and this I intend to do to a much greater extent than is usual: inventing names of exclusion by the prefix not, as in tree and not-tree, man and not-man. Let these be called *contrary*, or *contradictory*, names.

Let us take a pair of contrary names, as man and not-man. It is plain that between them they represent everything imaginable or real, in the universe. But the contraries of common language usually embrace, not the whole universe, but some one general idea. Thus, of men, Briton and alien are contraries: every man must be one of the two, no man can be both. Not-Briton and alien are identical names, and so are not-alien and Briton. The same may be said of integer and fraction among numbers, peer and commoner among subjects of the realm, male and female among animals, and so on. In order to express this, let us say that the whole idea under consider-ation is *the universe* (meaning merely the whole of which we are considering parts) and let names which have nothing in common, but which between them contain the whole idea under consider-ation, be called contraries *in, or with respect to, that universe*. Thus, the universe being mankind, Briton and alien are contraries, as are soldier and civilian, male and female, &c.: the universe being animal, man and brute are contraries, &c.

Names may be represented by the letters of the alphabet: thus A, B, &c., may stand for any names we are considering, simple or com-plex. The contraries may be represented by not-A, not-B, &c., but I shall usually prefer to denote them by the small letters a, b, &c. Thus, everything in the universe (whatever that universe may embrace) is either A or not-A, either A or a, either B or b, &c. Nothing can be both B and b; every not-B is b, and every not-b is B: and so on.

No language, as may well be supposed, has been constructed beforehand with any intention of providing for the wants of any metaphysical system. In most, it is seen that the necessity of provid-ing for the formation of contrary terms has been obeyed. Our own language has borrowed from the Latin as well as from its parent: thus we have *imperfect, disagreeable*, as well as *unformed* and *witless*. There is a choice of contraries without very well settled modes of appropriation: standing for different degrees of contrariety. Thus we have *not perfect* which is not so strong a term as *imperfect*; and *not imperfect*, the contrary of a contrary, which is not so strong as *perfect*. The wants of common conversation have sometimes retained a term and allowed the contrary to sink into disuse; sometimes retained the contrary and neglected the original term; sometimes have even introduced the contrary without introducing any term for the ori-ginal notion, and allowed no means of expressing the original notion except as the contrary of a contrary. If we could imagine a perfect language, we should suppose it would contain a mode of signifying the contrary of every name: this indeed our own language may be said to have, though sometimes in an awkward and unidiomatic manner. One inflexion, or one additional word, may serve to signify a contrary of any kind: thus *not man* is effective to denote all that is other than man. But there is a wider want, which can only be partially supplied, for its complete satisfaction would require words almost beyond the power of arithmetic to count: and all that has been done to make it less consists, in our language and in every other, mostly in the formation of compound terms, be they substantive and adjective, double substantives, or any others.

GEORGE BOOLE

From *An Investigation of the Laws of Thought* (1854)

A distinguished writer* has thus stated the fundamental definitions of the science [of probability]:

'The probability of an event is the reason we have to believe that it has taken place, or that it will take place.'

'The measure of the probability of an event is the ratio of the number of cases favourable to that event, to the total number of cases favourable or contrary, and all equally possible' (equally likely to happen).

From these definitions it follows that the word *probability*, in its mathematical acceptation, has reference to the state of our knowledge of the circumstances under which an event may happen or fail. With the degree of information which we possess concerning the circumstances of an event, the reason we have to think that it will occur, or, to use a single term, our *expectation* of it, will vary. Probability is expectation founded upon partial knowledge. A perfect acquaintance with *all* the circumstances affecting the occurrence of an event would change expectation into certainty, and leave neither room nor demand for a theory of probabilities.

Though our expectation of an event grows stronger with the increase of the ratio of the number of the known cases favourable to its occurrence to the whole number of equally possible cases, favourable or unfavourable, it would be unphilosophical to affirm that the strength of that expectation, viewed as an emotion of the mind, is capable of being referred to any numerical standard. The man of sanguine temperament builds high hopes where the timid despair, and the irresolute are lost in doubt. As subjects of scientific inquiry, there is some analogy between *opinion* and *sensation*. The thermometer and the carefully prepared photographic plate indicate, not the intensity of the sensations of heat and light, but certain physical circumstances which accompany the production of those sensations. So also the theory of probabilities contemplates the numerical measure of the circumstances upon which expectation is founded; and this object embraces the whole range of its legitimate applications. The rules which we employ in life-assurance, and in the other statistical applications of the theory of probabilities, are altogether independent of the *mental* phaenomena of expectation. They are founded upon the assumption that the future will bear a resemblance to the past; that under the same circumstances the same event will tend to recur with a definite numerical frequency; not upon any attempt to submit to calculation the strength of human hopes and fears.

Now experience actually testifies that events of a given species do, under given circumstances, tend to recur with definite frequency, whether their true causes be known to us or unknown. Of course this tendency is, in general, only manifested when the area of observation is sufficiently large. The judicial records of a great nation, its registries of births and deaths, in relation to age and sex, &c., present a remarkable uniformity from year to year. In a given language, or family of languages, the same sounds, and successions of sounds, and, if it be a written language, the same characters and successions of characters recur with determinate frequency. The key to the rude Ogham inscriptions,* found in various parts of Ireland, and in which no distinction of words could at first be traced, was, by a strict application of this principle, recovered. The same method, it is understood, has been applied to the deciphering of the cuneiform records recently disentombed from the ruins of Nineveh by the enterprise of Mr Layard.*

Let us endeavour from the above statements and definitions to form a conception of the legitimate object of the theory of Probabilities.

Probability, it has been said, consists in the expectation founded upon a particular kind of knowledge, viz., the knowledge of the relative frequency of occurrence of events. Hence the probabilities of events, or of combinations of events, whether deduced from a knowledge of the particular constitution of things under which they happen, or derived from the long-continued observation of a past series of their occurrences and failures, constitute, in all cases, our data. The probability of some connected event, or combination of events, constitutes the corresponding *quaesitum*, or object sought. Now in the most general, yet strict meaning of the term 'event,' every combination of events constitutes also an event. The simultaneous occurrence of two or more events, or the occurrence of an event under given conditions, or in any conceivable connexion with other events, is still an event. Using the term in this liberty of application, the object of the theory of probabilities might be thus defined. Given the probabilities of any events, of whatever kind, to find the probability of some other event connected with them.

Events may be distinguished as simple or compound, the latter term being applied to such events as consist in a combination of simple events. In this manner we might define it as the practical end of the theory under consideration to determine the probability of some event, simple or compound, from the given probabilities of other events, simple or compound, with which, by the terms of its definition, it stands connected.

Thus if it is known from the constitution of a die that there is a probability, measured by the fraction ⅙, that the result of any particular throw will be an ace, and if it is required to determine the probability that there shall occur one ace, and only one, in two successive throws, we may state the problem in the order of its *data* and its *quaesitum*, as follows:

FIRST DATUM.—Probability of the event that the first throw will give an ace = ⅙.

SECOND DATUM.—Probability of the event that the second throw will give an ace = ⅙.

QUAESITUM.—Probability of the event that either the first throw will give an ace, and the second not an ace; the first will not give an ace, and the second will give one.

Here the two data are the probabilities of simple events defined as the first throw giving an ace, and the second throw giving an ace. The quaesitum is the probability of a compound event,—a certain disjunctive combination of the simple events involved or implied in the data. Probably it will generally happen, when the numerical conditions of a problem are capable of being deduced, as above, from the constitution of things under which they exist, that the data will be the probabilities of *simple* events, and the quaesitum the probability of a *compound* event dependent upon the said simple events. Such is the case with a class of problems which has occupied perhaps an undue share of the attention of those who have studied the theory of probabilities, viz., games of chance and skill, in the former of which some physical circumstance, as the constitution of a die, determines the probability of each possible step of the game, its issue being some definite combination of those steps; while in the latter, the relative dexterity of the players, supposed to be known *à priori*, equally determines the same element. But where, as in statistical problems, the elements of our knowledge are drawn, not from the study of the constitution of things, but from the registered observations of Nature or of human society, there is no reason why the data which such observations afford should be the probabilities of simple events. On the contrary, the occurrence of events or conditions in marked combinations (indicative of some secret connexion of a causal character) suggests to us the propriety of making such concurrences, profitable for future instruction by a numerical record of their frequency. Now the data which observations of this kind afford are the probabilities of compound events. The solution, by some general method, of problems in which such data are involved, is thus not only essential to the perfect development of the theory of probabilities, but also a perhaps necessary condition of its application to a large and practically important class of inquiries.

JOHN VENN

From *The Logic of Chance* (1866)

Closely connected with Insurance, as an application of Probability, though of course by contrast, stands Gambling. Though we cannot, in strictness, term either of these practices the converse of the other, it seems nevertheless correct to say that they spring from opposite mental tendencies. Some persons, as has been said, find life too monotonous for their taste, or rather the region of what can be predicted with certainty is too large and predominant in their estimation. They can easily adopt two courses for securing the changes they desire. They may, for one thing, aggravate and intensify the results of events which are comparatively incapable of prevision, these events not being in themselves of sufficient importance to excite any strong emotions. The most obvious way of doing this is by betting upon them. Or again, they may invent games or other pursuits, the individual contingencies of which are entirely removed from all possible human prevision, and then make heavy money consequences depend upon these contingencies. This is gambling proper, carried on mostly by means of cards and dice and the roulette.

The gambling spirit, as we have said, seeks for the excitement of uncertainty and variety. When therefore people make a long continued practice of playing, especially if the stakes for which they play are moderate in comparison with their fortune, this uncertainty from the nature of the case begins to diminish. The thoroughly practised gambler, if he possesses more than usual skill (in games where skill counts for something), must be regarded as a man following a profession, though a profession for the most part of a risky and exciting kind, to say nothing of its ignoble and often dishonest character. If, on the other hand, his skill is below the average, or the game is one in which skill does not tell and the odds are slightly in favour of his antagonist, as in the gaming tables, one light in which he can be regarded is that of a man who is following a favourite amusement; if this amusement involves a constant annual outlay on his part, that is nothing more than what has to be said of most other amusements.

We cannot, of course, give such a rational explanation as the above in every case. There are plenty of novices, and plenty of fanatics, who go on steadily losing in the full conviction that they will eventually come out winners. But it is hard to believe that such ignorance, or such intellectual twist, can really be so widely prevalent as would be requisite to constitute them the rule rather than the exception. There must surely be some very general impulse which is gratified by such resources, and it is not easy to see what else this can be than a love of that variety and consequent excitement which can only be found in perfection where exact prevision is impossible.

It is of course very difficult to make any generalization here as to the comparative prevalence of various motives amongst mankind; but when one considers what is the difference which most quite ordinary whist players feel between a game for 'love' and one in which there is a small stake, one cannot but assign a high value to the influence of a wish to emphasize the excitement of loss and gain.

I would not for a moment underrate the practical dangers which are found to attend the practice of gambling. It is remarked that the gambler, if he continues to play for a long time, is under an almost irresistible impulse to increase his stakes, and so re-introduce the element of uncertainty. It is in fact this tendency to be thus led on, which makes the principal danger and mischief of the practice. Risk and uncertainty are still such normal characteristics of even civilized life, that the mere extension of such tendencies into new fields does not in itself offer any very alarming prospect. It is only to be deprecated in so far as there is a danger, which experience shows to be no trifling one, that the fascination found in the pursuit should lead men into following it up into excessive lengths.

LEWIS CARROLL

From *Through the Looking-Glass* (1871)

Everything was happening so oddly that she didn't feel a bit surprised at finding the Red Queen and the White Queen sitting close to her, one on each side: she would have liked very much to ask them how they came there, but she feared it would not be quite civil. However, there would be no harm, she thought, in asking if the game was over. 'Please, would you tell me—' she began, looking timidly at the Red Queen.

'Speak when you're spoken to!' the Queen sharply interrupted her.

'But if everybody obeyed that rule,' said Alice, who was always ready for a little argument, 'and if you only spoke when you were spoken to, and the other person always waited for *you* to begin, you see nobody would ever say anything, so that—'

'Ridiculous!' cried the Queen. 'Why, don't you see, child—' here she broke off with a frown, and, after thinking for a minute, suddenly changed the subject of the conversation. 'What do you mean by "If you really are a Queen"? What right have you to call yourself so? You can't be a Queen, you know, till you've passed the proper examination. And the sooner we begin it, the better.'

'I only said "if"!' poor Alice pleaded in a piteous tone.

The two Queens looked at each other, and the Red Queen remarked, with a little shudder, 'She *says* she only said "if"—'

'But she said a great deal more than that!' the White Queen moaned, wringing her hands. 'Oh, ever so much more than that!'

'So you did, you know,' the Red Queen said to Alice. 'Always speak the truth—think before you speak—and write it down afterwards.'

'I'm sure I didn't mean—' Alice was beginning, but the Red Queen interrupted her impatiently.

'That's just what I complain of! You *should* have meant! What do you suppose is the use of a child without any meaning? Even a joke should have some meaning—and a child's more important than a joke, I hope. You couldn't deny that, even if you tried with both hands.'

'I don't deny things with my *hands*,' Alice objected.

'Nobody said you did,' said the Red Queen. 'I said you couldn't if you tried.'

'She's in that state of mind,' said the White Queen, 'that she wants to deny *something*—only she doesn't know what to deny!'

'A nasty, vicious temper,' the Red Queen remarked; and then there was an uncomfortable silence for a minute or two.

The Red Queen broke the silence by saying to the White Queen, 'I invite you to Alice's dinner-party this afternoon.'

The White Queen smiled feebly, and said 'And I invite *you*.'

'I didn't know I was to have a party at all,' said Alice; 'but if there is to be one, I think *I* ought to invite the guests.'

'We gave you the opportunity of doing it,' the Red Queen remarked: 'but I daresay you've not had many lessons in manners yet?'

'Manners are not taught in lessons,' said Alice. 'Lessons teach you to do sums, and things of that sort.'

'Can you do Addition?' the White Queen asked. 'What's one and one and one and one and one and one and one and one and one and one?'

'I don't know,' said Alice. 'I lost count.'

'She can't do Addition,' the Red Queen interrupted. 'Can you do Subtraction? Take nine from eight.'

'Nine from eight I can't, you know,' Alice replied very readily: 'but—'

'She can't do Substraction,' said the White Queen. 'Can you do Division? Divide a loaf by a knife—what's the answer to that?'

'I suppose—' Alice was beginning, but the Red Queen answered for her. 'Bread-and-butter, of course. Try another Subtraction sum. Take a bone from a dog: what remains?'

Alice considered. 'The bone wouldn't remain, of course, if I took it—and the dog wouldn't remain; it would come to bite me—and I'm sure *I* shouldn't remain!'

'Then you think nothing would remain?' said the Red Queen.

'I think that's the answer.'

'Wrong, as usual,' said the Red Queen: 'the dog's temper would remain.'

'But I don't see how—'

'Why, look here!' the Red Queen cried. 'The dog would lose its temper, wouldn't it?'

'Perhaps it would,' Alice replied cautiously.

'Then if the dog went away, its temper would remain!' the Queen exclaimed triumphantly.

Alice said, as gravely as she could, 'They might go different ways.' But she couldn't help thinking to herself, 'What dreadful nonsense we *are* talking!'

'She can't do sums a *bit*!' the Queens said together, with great emphasis.

'Can *you* do sums?' Alice said, turning suddenly on the White Queen, for she didn't like being found fault with so much.

The Queen gasped and shut her eyes. 'I can do Addition,' she said, 'if you give me time—but I can't do Substraction, under *any* circumstances!'

'Of course you know your A B C?' said the Red Queen.

'To be sure I do,' said Alice.

'So do I,' the White Queen whispered: 'we'll often say it over together, dear. And I'll tell you a secret—I can read words of one letter! Isn't *that* grand? However, don't be discouraged. You'll come to it in time.'

Here the Red Queen began again. 'Can you answer useful questions?' she said. 'How is bread made?'

'I know *that*!' Alice cried eagerly. 'You take some flour—'

'Where do you pick the flower?' the White Queen asked. 'In a garden, or in the hedges?'

'Well, it isn't *picked* at all,' Alice explained: 'it's *ground*—'

'How many acres of ground?' said the White Queen. 'You mustn't leave out so many things.'

'Fan her head!' the Red Queen anxiously interrupted. 'She'll be feverish after so much thinking.' So they set to work and fanned her with bunches of leaves, till she had to beg them to leave off, it blew her hair about so.

'She's all right again now,' said the Red Queen. 'Do you know Languages? What's the French for fiddle-de-dee?'

'Fiddle-de-dee's not English,' Alice replied gravely.

'Who ever said it was?' said the Red Queen.

Alice thought she saw a way out of the difficulty this time. 'If you'll tell me what language "fiddle-de-dee" is, I'll tell you the French for it!' she exclaimed triumphantly.

But the Red Queen drew herself up rather stiffly, and said 'Queens never make bargains.'

'I wish Queens never asked questions,' Alice thought to herself.

'Don't let us quarrel,' the White Queen said in an anxious tone. 'What is the cause of lightning?'

'The cause of lightning,' Alice said very decidedly, for she felt quite certain about this, 'is the thunder—no, no!' she hastily corrected herself. 'I meant the other way.'

'It's too late to correct it,' said the Red Queen: 'when you've once said a thing, that fixes it, and you must take the consequences.'

From *The Game of Logic* (1886)

FALLACIES

And so you think, do you, that the chief use of Logic, in real life, is to deduce Conclusions from workable Premisses, and to satisfy yourself that the Conclusions, deduced by other people, are correct? I only wish it were! Society would be much less liable to panics and other delusions, and *political* life, especially, would be a totally different thing, if even a majority of the arguments, that are scattered broadcast over the world, were correct! But it is all the other way, I fear. For *one* workable Pair of Premisses (I mean a Pair that lead to a logical Conclusion) that you meet with in reading your newspaper or magazine, you will probably find *five* that lead to no Conclusion at all: and, even when the Premisses *are* workable, for *one* instance, where the writer draws a correct Conclusion, there are probably *ten* where he draws an incorrect one.

In the first case, you may say 'the *Premisses* are fallacious': in the second, 'the *Conclusion* is fallacious.'

The chief use you will find, in such Logical skill as this Game may teach you, will be in detecting '*Fallacies*' of these two kinds.

The first kind of Fallacy—'Fallacious Premisses'—you will detect when, after marking them on the larger Diagram,* you try to transfer the marks to the smaller. You will take its four compartments, one by one, and ask, for each in turn, 'What mark can I place *here*?'; and in *every* one the answer will be 'No information!', showing that there is *no Conclusion at all*. For instance,

> 'All soldiers are brave; }
> Some Englishmen are brave. }
> ∴ Some Englishmen are soldiers.'

looks uncommonly *like* a Syllogism, and might easily take in a less experienced Logician. But *you* are not to be caught by such a trick! You would simply set out the Premisses, and would then calmly remark 'Fallacious *Premisses*!': you wouldn't condescend to ask what *Conclusion* the writer professed to draw—knowing that, *whatever* it is, it *must* be wrong. You would be just as safe as that wise mother was, who said 'Mary, just go up to the nursery, and see what Baby's doing, *and tell him not to do it!*'

The other kind of Fallacy—'Fallacious Conclusion'—you will not detect till you have marked *both* Diagrams, and have read off the correct Conclusion, and have compared it with the Conclusion which the writer has drawn.

But mind, you mustn't say '*Fallacious* Conclusion,' simply because it is not *identical* with the correct one: it may be a *part* of the correct Conclusion, and so be quite correct, *as far as it goes*. In this case you would merely remark, with a pitying smile, '*Defective*

Conclusion!' Suppose, for example, you were to meet with this Syllogism:—

> 'All unselfish people are generous; ⎫
> No misers are generous.   ⎭
> ∴ No misers are unselfish,'

the Premisses of which might be thus expressed in letters:—

> 'All x' are m; ⎫
> No y are m.'   ⎭

Here the correct Conclusion would be 'All x' are y'' (that is, 'All unselfish people are not misers'), while the Conclusion, drawn by the writer, is 'No y are x',' (which is the same as 'No x' are y,' and so is *part* of 'All x' are y'.') Here you would simply say '*Defective* Conclusion!' The same thing would happen, if you were in a confectioner's shop, and if a little boy were to come in, put down twopence, and march off triumphantly with a single penny-bun. You would shake your head mournfully, and would remark 'Defective Conclusion! Poor little chap!' And perhaps you would ask the young lady behind the counter whether she would let *you* eat the bun, which the little boy had paid for and left behind him: and perhaps *she* would reply 'Sha'n't!'

But if, in the above example, the writer had drawn the Conclusion 'All misers are selfish' (that is, 'All y are x'), this would be going *beyond* his legitimate rights (since it would assert the *existence* of y, which is not contained in the Premisses), and you would very properly say 'Fallacious Conclusion!'

Now, when you read other treatises on Logic, you will meet with various kinds of (so-called) 'Fallacies', which are by no means *always* so. For example, if you were to put before one of these Logicians the Pair of Premisses

> 'No honest men cheat;   ⎫
> No dishonest men are trustworthy.' ⎭

and were to ask him what Conclusion followed, he would probably say 'None at all! Your Premisses offend against *two* distinct Rules, and are as fallacious as they can well be!' Then suppose you were bold enough to say 'The Conclusion is "No men who cheat are trustworthy",' I fear your Logical friend would turn away hastily—

perhaps angry, perhaps only scornful: in any case, the result would be unpleasant. *I advise you not to try the experiment!*

'But why is this?' you will say. 'Do you mean to tell us that all these Logicians are wrong?' Far from it, dear Reader! From *their* point of view, they are perfectly right. But they do not include, in their system, anything like *all* the possible forms of Syllogism.

They have a sort of nervous dread of Attributes beginning with a negative particle. For example, such Propositions as 'All not-*x* are *y*,' 'No *x* are not-*y*,' are quite outside their system. And thus, having (from sheer nervousness) excluded a quantity of very useful forms, they have made rules which, though quite applicable to the few forms which they allow of, are no use at all when you consider all possible forms.

Let us not quarrel with them, dear Reader! There is room enough in the world for both of us. Let us quietly take our broader system: and, if they choose to shut their eyes to all these useful forms, and to say 'They are not Syllogisms at all!' we can but stand aside, and let them Rush upon their Fate! There is scarcely anything of yours, upon which it is so dangerous to Rush, as your Fate. You may Rush upon your Potato-beds, or your Strawberry-beds, without doing much harm: you may even Rush upon your Balcony (unless it is a new house, built by contract, and with no clerk of the works) and may survive the foolhardy enterprise: but if you once Rush upon your *Fate*—why, you must take the consequences!

GEORGE ELIOT

From *Daniel Deronda* (1876)

Was she beautiful or not beautiful? and what was the secret of form or expression which gave the dynamic quality to her glance? Was the good or the evil genius dominant in those beams? Probably the evil; else why was the effect that of unrest rather than of undisturbed charm? Why was the wish to look again felt as coercion and not as a longing in which the whole being consents?

She who raised these questions in Daniel Deronda's mind was occupied in gambling: not in the open air under a southern sky, tossing coppers on a ruined wall, with rags about her limbs; but in one of those splendid resorts which the enlightenment of ages has prepared for the same species of pleasure at a heavy cost of gilt mouldings, dark-toned colour and chubby nudities, all correspondingly heavy—forming a suitable condenser for human breath belonging, in great part, to the highest fashion, and not easily procurable to be breathed in elsewhere in the like proportion, at least by persons of little fashion.

It was near four o'clock on a September day, so that the atmosphere was well-brewed to a visible haze. There was deep stillness, broken only by a light rattle, a light chink, a small sweeping sound, and an occasional monotone in French, such as might be expected to issue from an ingeniously constructed automaton. Round two long tables were gathered two serried crowds of human beings, all save one having their faces and attention bent on the tables. The one exception was a melancholy little boy, with his knees and calves simply in their natural clothing of epidermis, but for the rest of his person in a fancy dress. He alone had his face turned towards the doorway, and fixing on it the blank gaze of a bedizened child stationed as a masquerading advertisement on the platform of an itinerant show, stood close behind a lady deeply engaged at the roulette-table.

About this table fifty or sixty persons were assembled, many in the outer rows, where there was occasionally a deposit of new comers, being mere spectators, only that one of them, usually a woman, might now and then be observed putting down a five-franc piece with a simpering air, just to see what the passion of gambling really was. Those who were taking their pleasure at a higher strength, and were absorbed in play, showed very distant varieties of European type: Livonian* and Spanish, Graeco-Italian and miscellaneous German, English aristocratic and English plebeian. Here certainly was a striking admission of human equality. The white bejewelled fingers of an English countess were very near touching a bony, yellow, crab-like hand stretching a bared wrist to clutch a heap of coin—a hand easy to sort with the square, gaunt face, deep-set eyes, grizzled eyebrows, and ill-combed scanty hair which seemed a slight metamorphosis of the vulture. And where else would her ladyship have graciously consented to sit by that dry-lipped feminine figure prematurely old, withered after short bloom like her artificial flowers, holding a shabby velvet reticule before her, and occasionally putting in her mouth the point with which she pricked her card? There too, very near the fair countess, was a respectable London tradesman, blond and soft-handed, his sleek hair scrupulously parted behind and before, conscious of circulars addressed to the nobility and gentry, whose distinguished patronage enabled him to take his holidays fashionably, and to a certain extent in their distinguished company. Not his the gambler's passion that nullifies appetite, but a well-fed leisure, which in the intervals of winning money in business and spending it showily, sees no better resource than winning money in play and spending it yet more showily—reflecting always that Providence had never manifested any disapprobation of his amusement, and dispassionate enough to leave off if the sweetness of winning much and seeing others lose had turned to the sourness of losing much and seeing others win. For the vice of gambling lay in losing money at it. In his bearing there might be something of the tradesman, but in his pleasures he was fit to rank with the owners of the oldest titles. Standing close to his chair was a handsome Italian, calm, statuesque, reaching across him to place the first pile of napoleons* from a new bagful just brought him by an envoy with a scrolled mustache. The pile was in half a minute pushed over to an old bewigged woman with eyeglasses pinching her nose. There was a slight gleam, a faint mumbling smile about the lips of the old woman; but the statuesque Italian remained impassive, and—probably secure in an infallible system which placed his foot on the neck of chance— immediately prepared a new pile. So did a man with the air of an emaciated beau or worn-out libertine, who looked at life through one eyeglass, and held out his hand tremulously when he asked for change. It could surely be no severity of system, but rather some dream of white crows, or the induction that the eighth of the month was lucky, which inspired the fierce yet tottering impulsiveness of his play.

But while every single player differed markedly from every other, there was a certain uniform negativeness of expression which had the effect of a mask—as if they had all eaten of some root that for the time compelled the brains of each to the same narrow monotony of action.

Deronda's first thought when his eyes fell on this scene of dull, gas-poisoned absorption was that the gambling of Spanish shepherd-boys had seemed to him more enviable:—so far Rousseau* might be justified in maintaining that art and science had done a poor service to mankind. But suddenly he felt the moment become dramatic. His attention was arrested by a young lady who, standing at an angle not far from him, was the last to whom his eyes travelled. She was bending and speaking English to a middle-aged lady seated at play beside her; but the next instant she returned to her play, and showed the full height of a graceful figure, with a face which might possibly be looked at without admiration, but could hardly be passed with indifference.

The inward debate which she raised in Deronda gave to his eyes a growing expression of scrutiny, tending farther and farther away from the glow of mingled undefined sensibilities forming admiration. At one moment they followed the movements of the figure, of the arms and hands, as this problematic sylph bent forward to deposit her stake with an air of firm choice; and the next they returned to the face which, at present unaffected by beholders, was directed steadily towards the game. The sylph was a winner; and as her taper fingers, delicately gloved in pale-grey, were adjusting the coins which had been pushed towards her in order to pass them back again to the winning point, she looked round her with a survey too markedly cold and neutral not to have in it a little of that nature which we call art concealing an inward exultation.

But in the course of that survey her eyes met Deronda's, and instead of averting them as she would have desired to do, she was unpleasantly conscious that they were arrested—how long? The darting sense that he was measuring her and looking down on her as an inferior, that he was of different quality from the human dross around her, that he felt himself in a region outside and above her, and was examining her as a specimen of a lower order, roused a tingling resentment which stretched the moment with conflict. It did not bring the blood to her cheeks, but sent it away from her lips. She controlled herself by the help of an inward defiance, and without other sign of emotion than this lip-paleness turned to her play. But Deronda's gaze seemed to have acted as an evil eye. Her stake was gone. No matter; she had been winning ever since she took to roulette with a few napoleons at command, and had a considerable reserve. She had begun to believe in her luck, others had begun to believe in it: she had visions of being followed by a *cortège* who would worship her as a goddess of luck and watch her play as a directing augury. Such things had been known of male gamblers; why should not a woman have a like supremacy? Her friend and chaperon who had not wished her to play at first was beginning to approve, only administering the prudent advice to stop at the right moment and carry money back to England—advice to which Gwendolen had replied that she cared for the excitement of play, not the winnings. On that supposition the present moment ought to have made the flood-tide in her eager experience of gambling. Yet when her next stake was swept away, she felt the orbits of her eyes getting hot, and the certainty she had (without looking) of that man still watching her was something like a pressure which begins to be torturing. The more reason to her why she should not flinch, but go on playing as if she were indifferent to loss or gain. Her friend touched her elbow and proposed that they should quit the table. For reply Gwendolen put ten louis* on the same spot: she was in that mood of defiance in which the mind loses sight of any end beyond the satisfaction of enraged resistance; and with the puerile stupidity of a dominant impulse includes luck among its objects of defiance. Since she was not winning strikingly, the next best thing was to lose strikingly. She controlled her muscles, and showed no tremor of mouth or hands. Each time her stake was swept off she doubled it. Many were now watching her, but the sole observation she was conscious of was Deronda's, who, though she never looked towards him, she was sure had not moved away. Such a drama takes no long while to play out: development and catastrophe can often be measured by nothing clumsier than the moment-hand. 'Faites votre jeu, mesdames et messieurs,'* said the automatic voice of destiny from between the mustache and imperial of the croupier; and Gwendolen's arm was stretched to deposit her last poor heap of napoleons. 'Le jeu ne va plus,'* said destiny. And in five seconds Gwendolen turned from the table, but turned resolutely with her face towards Deronda and looked at him. There was a smile of irony in his eyes as their glances met; but it was at least better that he should have kept his attention fixed on her than that he should have disregarded her as one of an insect swarm who had no individual physiognomy.

H. G. WELLS

From *The Time Machine* (1895)

The Time Traveller (for so it will be convenient to speak of him) was
expounding a recondite matter to us. His grey eyes shone and twin-
kled, and his usually pale face was flushed and animated. The fire
burnt brightly, and the soft radiance of the incandescent lights in the
lilies of silver caught the bubbles that flashed and passed in our
glasses. Our chairs, being his patents, embraced and caressed us
rather than submitted to be sat upon, and there was that luxurious
after-dinner atmosphere, when thought runs gracefully free of the
trammels of precision. And he put it to us in this way—marking
the points with a lean forefinger—as we sat and lazily admired his
earnestness over this new paradox (as we thought it) and his
fecundity.

'You must follow me carefully. I shall have to controvert one or
two ideas that are almost universally accepted. The geometry, for
instance, they taught you at school is founded on a misconception.'

'Is not that rather a large thing to expect us to begin upon?' said
Filby, an argumentative person with red hair.

'I do not mean to ask you to accept anything without reasonable
ground for it. You will soon admit as much as I need from you. You
know of course that a mathematical line, a line of thickness *nil*, has
no real existence. They taught you that? Neither has a mathematical
plane. These things are mere abstractions.'

'That is all right,' said the Psychologist.

'Nor, having only length, breadth, and thickness, can a cube have a
real existence.'

'There I object,' said Filby. 'Of course a solid body may exist. All
real things—'

'So most people think. But wait a moment. Can an *instantaneous*
cube exist?'

'Don't follow you,' said Filby.

'Can a cube that does not last for any time at all, have a real
existence?'

Filby became pensive. 'Clearly,' the Time Traveller proceeded,
'any real body must have extension in *four* directions: it must have
Length, Breadth, Thickness, and—Duration. But through a natural

infirmity of the flesh, which I will explain to you in a moment, we incline to overlook this fact. There are really four dimensions, three which we call the three planes of Space, and a fourth, Time. There is, however, a tendency to draw an unreal distinction between the former three dimensions and the latter, because it happens that our consciousness moves intermittently in one direction along the latter from the beginning to the end of our lives.'

'That,' said a very young man, making spasmodic efforts to relight his cigar over the lamp; 'that . . . very clear indeed.'

'Now, it is very remarkable that this is so extensively overlooked,' continued the Time Traveller, with a slight accession of cheerfulness. 'Really this is what is meant by the Fourth Dimension, though some people who talk about the Fourth Dimension do not know they mean it. It is only another way of looking at Time. *There is no difference between Time and any of the three dimensions of Space except that our consciousness moves along it.* But some foolish people have got hold of the wrong side of that idea. You have all heard what they have to say about this Fourth Dimension?'

'*I* have not,' said the Provincial Mayor.

'It is simply this. That Space, as our mathematicians have it, is spoken of as having three dimensions, which one may call Length, Breadth, and Thickness, and is always definable by reference to three planes, each at right angles to the others. But some philosophical people have been asking why *three* dimensions particularly—why not another direction at right angles to the other three?—and have even tried to construct a Four-Dimensional geometry. Professor Simon Newcomb* was expounding this to the New York Mathematical Society only a month or so ago. You know how on a flat surface, which has only two dimensions, we can represent a figure of a three-dimensional solid, and similarly they think that by models of three dimensions they could represent one of four—if they could master the perspective of the thing. See?'

'I think so,' murmured the Provincial Mayor; and, knitting his brows, he lapsed into an introspective state, his lips moving as one who repeats mystic words. 'Yes, I think I see it now,' he said after some time, brightening in a quite transitory manner.

'Well, I do not mind telling you I have been at work upon this geometry of Four Dimensions for some time. Some of my results are curious. For instance, here is a portrait of a man at eight years old, another at fifteen, another at seventeen, another at twenty-three, and so on. All these are evidently sections, as it were, Three-Dimensional representations of his Four-Dimensioned being, which is a fixed and unalterable thing.'

'Scientific people,' proceeded the Time Traveller, after the pause required for the proper assimilation of this, 'know very well that Time is only a kind of Space. Here is a popular scientific diagram, a weather record. This line I trace with my finger shows the movement of the barometer. Yesterday it was so high, yesterday night it fell, then this morning it rose again, and so gently upward to here. Surely the mercury did not trace this line in any of the dimensions of Space generally recognized? But certainly it traced such a line, and that line, therefore, we must conclude was along the Time-Dimension.'

'But,' said the Medical Man, staring hard at a coal in the fire, 'if Time is really only a fourth dimension of Space, why is it, and why has it always been, regarded as something different? And why cannot we move about in Time as we move about in the other dimensions of Space?'

The Time Traveller smiled. 'Are you so sure we can move freely in Space? Right and left we can go, backward and forward freely enough, and men always have done so. I admit we move freely in two dimensions. But how about up and down? Gravitation limits us there.'

'Not exactly,' said the Medical Man. 'There are balloons.'

'But before the balloons, save for spasmodic jumping and the inequalities of the surface, man had no freedom of vertical movement.'

'Still they could move a little up and down,' said the Medical Man.

'Easier, far easier down than up.'

'And you cannot move at all in Time, you cannot get away from the present moment.'

'My dear sir, that is just where you are wrong. That is just where the whole world has gone wrong. We are always getting away from the present moment. Our mental existences, which are immaterial and have no dimensions, are passing along the Time-Dimension with a uniform velocity from the cradle to the grave. Just as we should travel *down* if we began our existence fifty miles above the earth's surface.'

'But the great difficulty is this,' interrupted the Psychologist. 'You *can* move about in all directions of Space, but you cannot move about in Time.'

'That is the germ of my great discovery. But you are wrong to say that we cannot move about in Time. For instance, if I am recalling an incident very vividly I go back to the instant of its occurrence: I become absent-minded, as you say. I jump back for a moment. Of course we have no means of staying back for any length of Time, any more than a savage or an animal has of staying six feet above the ground. But a civilized man is better off than the savage in this respect. He can go up against gravitation in a balloon, and why should he not hope that ultimately he may be able to stop or accelerate his drift along the Time-Dimension, or even turn about and travel the other way?'

'Oh, *this*,' began Filby, 'is all—'

'Why not?' said the Time Traveller.

'It's against reason,' said Filby.

'What reason?' said the Time Traveller.

'You can show black is white by argument,' said Filby, 'but you will never convince me.'

Physical Science

SIR WILLIAM HERSCHEL

From *On the Power of Penetrating into Space by Telescopes* (1800)

If now it be admitted that the expressions we have laid down are such as agree with well known facts, we may proceed to vision at a distance; and first with respect to the naked eye.

Here the power of penetrating into space, is not only confined by nature, but is moreover occasionally limited by the failure in brightness of luminous objects. Let us see whether astronomical observations, assisted by mathematical reasoning, can give us some idea of the general extent of natural vision. Among the reflecting luminous objects, our penetrating powers are sufficiently ascertained. From the moon we may step to Venus, to Mercury, to Mars, to Jupiter, to Saturn, and last of all to the Georgian planet.* An object seen by reflected light at a greater distance than this, it has never been allowed us to perceive; and it is indeed much to be admired, that we should see borrowed illumination to the amazing distance of more than 18 hundred millions of miles; especially when that light, in coming from the sun to the planet, has to pass through an equal space, before it can be reflected, whereby it must be so enfeebled as to be above 368 times less intense on that planet than it is with us, and when probably not more than one-third part of that light can be thrown back from its disk.

The range of natural vision with self-luminous objects, is incomparably more extended, but less accurately to be ascertained. From our brightest luminary, the sun, we pass immediately to very distant objects; for, Sirius, Arcturus,* and the rest of the stars of the first magnitude, are probably those that come next; and what their distance may be, it is well known, can only be calculated imperfectly from the doctrine of parallaxes,* which places the nearest of them at least 412530 times farther from us than the sun.

In order to take a second step forwards, we must enter into some preliminary considerations, which cannot but be attended with considerable uncertainty. The general supposition, that stars, at least those which seem to be promiscuously scattered, are probably one with another of a certain magnitude, being admitted, that after a certain number of stars of the first magnitude have been arranged about the sun, a farther distant set will come in for the second place. The situation of these may be taken to be, one with another, at about double the distance of the former from us.

By directing our view to them, and thus penetrating one step farther into space, these stars of the second magnitude* furnish us with an experiment that shews what phaenomena will take place, when we receive the illumination of two very remote objects, equally bright in themselves, whereof one is at double the distance of the other. The expression for the brightness of such objects, at all distances, and with any aperture of the iris, according to our foregoing notation, will be a^2l/D^2;* and a method of reducing this to an experimental investigation will be as follows.

Let us admit that a Cygni, β Tauri,* and others, are stars of the second magnitude, such as are here to be considered. We know, that in looking at them and the former, the aperture of the iris will probably undergo no change; since the difference in brightness, between Sirius, Arcturus, a Cygni, and β Tauri, does not seem to affect the eye so as to require any alteration in the dimensions of the iris; a, therefore becomes a given quantity, and may be left out. Admitting also, that the latter of these stars are probably at double the distance of the former, we have D^2 in one case four times that of the other; and the two expressions for the brightness of the stars, will be l for those of the first magnitude, and $\frac{1}{4}l$ for those of the second.

The quantities being thus prepared, what I mean to suggest by an experiment is, that since sensations, by their nature, will not admit of being halved or quartered, we come thus to know by inspection what phaenomenon will be produced by the fourth part of the light of a star of the first magnitude. In this sense, I think we must take it for granted, that a certain idea of brightness, attached to the stars which are generally denominated to be of the second magnitude, may be added to our experimental knowledge; for, by this means, we are informed what we are to understand by the expressions

$$\frac{a^2\,l}{\odot^2},\ \frac{a^2\,l}{|\text{Sirius}|^2},\ \frac{a^2\,l}{|\beta\,\text{Tauri}|^2}. \quad [\odot = \text{the sun}]$$

We cannot wonder at the immense difference between the brightness of the sun and that of Sirius; since the two first expressions, when properly resolved, give us a ratio of brightness of more than 170 thousand millions to one; whereas the two latter, as has been shewn, give only a ratio of four to one.

What has been said will carry us, with very little addition, to the end of our unassisted power of vision to penetrate into space. We can have no other guide to lead us a third step than the same beforementioned hypothesis; in consequence of which, however, it must be acknowledged to be sufficiently probable, that the stars of the third magnitude may be placed about three times as far from us as those of the first. It has been seen, by my remarks on the comparative brightness of the stars, that I place no reliance on the classification of them into magnitudes; but, in the present instance, where the question is not to ascertain the precise brightness of any one star, it is quite sufficient to know that the number of the stars of the first three different magnitudes, or different brightnesses, answers, in a general way, sufficiently well to a supposed equally distant arrangement of a

Physical Science

first, second, and third set of stars about the sun. Our third step forwards into space, may therefore very properly be said to fall on the pole-star, on γ Cygni, ε Bootis,* and all those of the same order.

As the difference, between these and the stars of the preceding order, is much less striking than that between the stars of the first and second magnitude, we also find that the expressions

$$\frac{a^2\,l}{\overline{\beta\,\text{Tauri}}|^2}, \text{ and } \frac{a^2\,l}{\overline{\text{Polaris}}|^2},$$

are not in the high ratio of 4 to 1, but only as 9 to 4, or 2¼ to 1.

Without tracing the brightness of the stars through any farther steps, I shall only remark, that the diminution of the ratios of brightness of the stars of the 4th, 5th, 6th, and 7th magnitude, seems to answer to their mathematical expressions, as well as, from the first steps we have taken, can possibly be imagined. The calculated ratio, for instance, of the brightness of a star of the 6th magnitude, to that of one of the 7th, is but little more than 1⅓ to 1; but still we find by experience, that the eye can very conveniently perceive it. At the same time, the faintness of the stars of the 7th magnitude, which require the finest nights, and the best common eyes to be perceived, gives us little room to believe that we can penetrate much farther into space, with objects of no greater brightness than stars.

But, since it may be justly observed, that in the foregoing estimation of the proportional distance of the stars, a considerable uncertainty must remain, we ought to make a proper allowance for it; and, in order to see to what extent this should go, we must make use of the experimental sensations of the ratios of brightness we have now acquired, in going step by step forward: for, numerical ratios of brightness, and sensations of them, as has been noticed before, are very different things. And since, from the foregoing considerations, it may be concluded, that as far as the 6th, 7th, or 8th magnitude, there ought to be a visible general difference between stars of one order and that of the next following, I think, from the faintness of the stars of the 7th magnitude, we are authorized to conclude, that no star, eight, nine, or at most ten times as far from us as Sirius, can possibly be perceived by the natural eye.

The boundaries of vision, however, are not confined to single stars. Where the light of these falls short, the united lustre of sidereal systems will still be perceived. In clear nights, for instance, we may see a whitish patch in the sword-handle of Perseus,* which contains small stars of various sizes, as may be ascertained by a telescope of a moderate power of penetrating into space. We easily see the united lustre of them, though the light of no one of the single stars could have affected the unassisted eye.

Considerably beyond the distance of the former must be the cluster discovered by Mr MESSIER,* in 1764; north following H Geminorum.* It contains stars much smaller than those of the former cluster; and a telescope should have a considerable penetrating power, to ascertain their brightness properly, such as my common 10-feet reflector. The night should be clear, in order to see it well with the naked eye, and it will then appear in the shape of a small nebula.

Still farther from us must be the nebula between η and ζ Herculis, discovered by Dr HALLEY,* in 1714. The stars of it are so small that it has been called a Nebula; and has been regarded as such, till my instruments of high penetrating powers were applied to it. It requires a very clear night, and the absence of the moon, to see it with the natural eye.

Perhaps, among the farthest objects that can make an impression on the eye, when not assisted by telescopes, may be reckoned the nebula in the girdle of Andromeda, discovered by SIMON MARIUS, in 1612.* It is however not difficult to perceive it, in a clear night, on account of its great extent.

From the powers of penetrating into space by natural vision, we proceed now to that of telescopes.

THOMAS CARLYLE

From *Past and Present* (1843)

Certainly it were a fond imagination to expect that any preaching of mine could abate Mammonism; that Bobus of Houndsditch will love his guineas less, or his poor soul more, for any preaching of mine! But there is one Preacher who does preach with effect, and gradually persuade all persons: his name is Destiny, is Divine Providence, and his Sermon the inflexible Course of Things. Experience does take dreadfully high school-wages; but he teaches like no other!

I revert to Friend Prudence the good Quaker's refusal of 'seven thousand pounds to boot.' Friend Prudence's practical conclusion will, by degrees, become that of all rational practical men whatsoever. On the present scheme and principle, Work cannot continue. Trades' Strikes, Trades' Unions, Chartisms;* mutiny, squalor, rage and desperate revolt, growing ever more desperate, will go on their way. As dark misery settles down on us, and our refuges of lies fall in pieces one after one, the hearts of men, now at last serious, will turn to refuges of truth. The eternal stars shine out again, so soon as it is dark *enough*.

Begirt with desperate Trades' Unionism and Anarchic Mutiny, many an Industrial *Law-ward*, by and by, who has neglected to make laws and keep them, will be heard saying to himself: 'Why have I realised five hundred thousand pounds? I rose early and sat late, I toiled and moiled, and in the sweat of my brow and of my soul I strove to gain this money, that I might become conspicuous, and have some honour among my fellow-creatures. I wanted them to honour me, to love me. The money is here, earned with my best lifeblood: but the honour? I am encircled with squalor, with hunger, rage, and sooty desperation. Not honoured, hardly even envied; only fools and the flunky species so much as envy me. I am conspicuous,—as a mark for curses and brickbats. What good is it? My five hundred scalps hang here in my wigwam: would to Heaven I had sought something else than the scalps; would to Heaven I had been a Christian Fighter, not a Chactaw* one! To have ruled and fought not in a Mammonish but in a Godlike spirit; to have had the hearts of the people bless me, as a true ruler and captain of my people; to have felt my own heart bless me, and that God above instead of Mammon below was blessing me,—this had been something. Out of my sight, ye beggarly five hundred scalps of banker's-thousands: I will try for something other, or account my life a tragical futility!'

Friend Prudence's 'rock-ledge,' as we called it, will gradually disclose itself to many a man; to all men. Gradually, assaulted from beneath and from above, the Stygian* mud-deluge of Laissez-faire, Supply-and-demand, Cash-payment the one Duty, will abate on all hands; and the everlasting mountain-tops, and secure rock-foundations that reach to the centre of the world, and rest on Nature's self, will again emerge, to found on, and to build on. When Mammon-worshippers here and there begin to be God-worshippers, and bipeds-of-prey become men, and there is a Soul felt once more in the huge-pulsing elephantine mechanic Animalism of this Earth, it will be again a blessed Earth.

'Men cease to regard money?' cries Bobus of Houndsditch: 'What else do all men strive for? The very Bishop informs me that Christianity cannot get on without a minimum of Four thousand five hundred in its pocket. Cease to regard money? That will be at Doomsday in the afternoon!'—O Bobus, my opinion is somewhat different. My opinion is, that the Upper Powers have not yet determined on destroying this Lower World. A respectable, ever-increasing minority, who do strive for something higher than money, I with confidence anticipate; ever-increasing, till there be a sprinkling of them found in all quarters, as salt of the Earth once more. The Christianity that cannot get on without a minimum of Four thousand five hundred, will give place to something better that can. Thou wilt not join our small minority, thou? Not till Doomsday in the afternoon? Well; *then*, at least, thou wilt join it, thou and the majority in mass!

But truly it is beautiful to see the brutish empire of Mammon cracking everywhere; giving sure promise of dying, or of being changed. A strange, chill, almost ghastly dayspring strikes up in Yankeeland itself: my Transcendental* friends announce there, in a distinct, though somewhat lankhaired, ungainly manner, that the Demiurgus Dollar is dethroned; that new unheard-of Demiurgusships, Priesthoods, Aristocracies, Growths and Destructions, are already visible in the gray of coming Time. Chronos is dethroned by Jove; Odin by St Olaf: the Dollar cannot rule in Heaven forever. No; I reckon, not. Socinian* Preachers quit their pulpits in Yankeeland, saying, 'Friends, this is all gone to coloured cobweb, we regret to say!'—and retire into the fields to cultivate onion-beds, and live frugally on vegetables. It is very notable. Old godlike Calvinism declares that its old body is now fallen to tatters, and done; and its mournful ghost, disembodied, seeking new embodiment, pipes again in the winds;—a ghost and spirit as yet, but heralding new Spiritworlds, and better Dynasties than the Dollar one.

Yes, here as there, light is coming into the world; men love not darkness, they do love light. A deep feeling of the eternal nature of Justice looks out among us everywhere,—even even through the dull eyes of Exeter Hall; an unspeakable religiousness struggles, in the most helpless manner, to speak itself, in Puseyisms* and the like. Of our Cant, all condemnable, how much is not condemnable without pity; we had almost said, without respect! The *in*articulate worth and truth that is in England goes down yet to the Foundations.

Some 'Chivalry of Labour,' some noble Humanity and practical Divineness of Labour, will yet be realised on this Earth. Or why *will*; why do we pray to Heaven, without setting our own shoulder to the wheel? The Present, if it will have the Future accomplish, shall itself commence. Thou who prophesiest, who believest, begin thou to fulfil. Here or nowhere, now equally as at any time! That outcast help-needing thing or person, trampled down under vulgar feet or hoofs, no help 'possible' for it, no prize offered for the saving of it,— canst not thou save it, then, without prize? Put forth thy hand, in God's name; know that 'impossible,' where Truth and Mercy and the everlasting Voice of Nature order, has no place in the brave man's dictionary. That when all men have said 'Impossible,' and tumbled noisily elsewhither, and thou alone art left, then first thy time and possibility have come. It is for thee now; do thou that, and ask no man's counsel, but thy own only, and God's. Brother, thou hast possibility in thee for much: the possibility of writing on the eternal skies the record of a heroic life. That noble downfallen or yet unborn 'Impossibility,' thou canst lift it up, thou canst, by thy soul's travail, bring it into clear being. That loud inane Actuality, with millions in its pocket, too 'possible' that, which rolls along there, with quilted trumpeters blaring round it, and all the world escorting it as mute or vocal flunky,—escort it not thou; say to it, either nothing, or else deeply in thy heart: 'Loud-blaring Nonentity, no force of trumpets, cash, Long-acre art, or universal flunkyhood of men, makes thee an Entity; thou art a *Non*entity, and deceptive Simulacrum, more accursed than thou seemest. Pass on in the Devil's name, unworshipped by at least one man, and leave the thoroughfare clear!'

Not on Ilion's or Latium's plains;* on far other plains and places henceforth can noble deeds be now done. Not on Ilion's plains; how much less in Mayfair's drawingrooms! Not in victory over poor brother French or Phrygians;* but in victory over Frost-jötuns, Marsh-giants,* over demons of Discord, Idleness, Injustice, Unreason, and Chaos come again. None of the old Epics is longer possible. The Epic of French and Phrygians was comparatively a small Epic: but that of Flirts and Fribbles, what is that? A thing that vanishes at cock-crowing,—that already begins to scent the morning air! Game-preserving Aristocracies, let them 'bush' never so effectually, cannot escape the Subtle Fowler. Game seasons will be excellent, and again will be indifferent, and by and by they will not be at all. The Last Partridge of England, of an England where millions of men can get no corn to eat, will be shot and ended. Aristocracies with beards on their chins will find other work to do than amuse themselves with trundling-hoops.

SIR JOHN HERSCHEL

From *Outlines of Astronomy* (1849)

Suppose the reader to station himself, on a clear evening, just after sunset, when the first stars begin to appear, in some open situation whence a good general view of the heavens can be obtained. He will then perceive, above and around him, as it were, a vast concave hemispherical vault, beset with stars of various magnitudes, of which the brightest only will first catch his attention in the twilight; and more and more will appear as the darkness increases, till the whole sky is over-spangled with them. When he has awhile admired the calm magnificence of this glorious spectacle, the theme of so much song, and of so much thought,—a spectacle which no one can view without emotion, and without a longing desire to know something of its nature and purport,—let him fix his attention more particularly on a few of the most brilliant stars, such as he cannot fail to recognize again without mistake after looking away from them for some time, and let him refer their apparent situations to some surrounding objects, as buildings, trees, &c., selecting purposely such as are in different quarters of his horizon. On comparing them again with their respective points of reference, after a moderate interval, as the night advances, he will not fail to perceive that they have changed their places, and advanced, as by a general movement, in a westward direction; those towards the eastern quarter appearing to rise or recede from the horizon, while those which lie towards the west will be seen to approach it; and, if watched long enough, will, for the most part, finally sink beneath it, and disappear; while others, in the eastern quarter, will be seen to rise as if out of the earth, and, joining in the general procession, will take their course with the rest towards the opposite quarter.

If he persist for a considerable time in watching their motions, on the same or on several successive nights, he will perceive that each star appears to describe, as far as its course lies above the horizon, a circle in the sky; that the circles so described are not of the same magnitude for all the stars; and that those described by different stars differ greatly in respect of the parts of them which lie above the horizon. Some, which lie towards the quarter of the horizon which is denominated the SOUTH, only remain for a short time above it, and disappear, after describing in sight only the small upper segment of their diurnal circle; others, which rise between the south and east, describe larger segments of their circles above the horizon, remain proportionally longer in sight, and set precisely as far to the west-ward of south as they rose to the eastward; while such as rise exactly in the east remain just twelve hours visible, describe a semicircle, and set exactly in the west. With those, again, which rise between the east and north, the same law obtains; at least, as far as regards the time of their remaining above the horizon, and the proportion of the visible segment of their diurnal circles to their whole circumferences. Both go on increasing; they remain in view more than twelve hours, and their visible diurnal arcs are more than semicircles. But the magni-tudes of the circles themselves diminish, as we go from the east, northward; the greatest of all the circles being described by those which rise exactly in the east point. Carrying his eye farther north-wards, he will notice, at length, stars which, in their diurnal motion, just graze the horizon at its north point, or only dip below it for a moment; while others never reach it at all, but continue always above it, revolving in entire circles round ONE POINT called the POLE, which appears to be the common centre of all their motions, and which alone, in the whole heavens, may be considered immoveable. Not that this point is marked by any star. It is a purely imaginary centre; but there is near it one considerably bright star, called the Pole Star, which is easily recognized by the very small circle it describes; so small, indeed, that, without paying particular attention, and referring its position very nicely to some fixed mark, it may easily be supposed at rest, and be, itself, mistaken for the common centre about which all the others in that region describe their circles; or it may be known by its configuration with a very splendid and remarkable *constellation* or group of stars, called by astronomers the GREAT BEAR.

He will further observe, that the apparent relative situations of all the stars among one another, is not changed by their diurnal motion. In whatever parts of their circles they are observed, or at whatever hour of the night, they form with each other the same identical groups or configurations, to which the name of CONSTELLATIONS has been given. It is true, that, in different parts of their course, these groups stand differently with respect to the horizon; and those towards the north, when in the course of their diurnal movement they pass alternately above and below that common centre of motion described in the last paragraph, become actually inverted with respect to the horizon, while, on the other hand, they always turn the same points towards the pole. In short, he will perceive that the whole assemblage of stars visible at once, or in succession, in the heavens, may be regarded as one great constellation, which seems to revolve with a uniform motion, as if it formed one coherent mass; or as if it were attached to the internal surface of a vast hollow sphere, having the earth, or rather the spectator, in its centre, and turning round an axis inclined to his horizon, so as to pass through that fixed point or *pole* already mentioned.

Lastly, he will notice, if he have patience to outwatch a long winter's night, commencing at the earliest moment when the stars appear, and continuing till morning twilight, that those stars which he observed setting in the west have again risen in the east, while those which were rising when he first began to notice them have completed their course, and are now set; and that thus the hemisphere, or a great part of it, which was then above, is now beneath him, and its place supplied by that which was at first under his feet, which he will thus discover to be no less copiously furnished with stars than the other, and bespangled with groups no less permanent and distinctly recognizable. Thus he will learn that the great constellation we have above spoken of as revolving round the pole is co-extensive with the whole surface of the sphere, being in reality nothing less than a universe of luminaries surrounding the earth on all sides, and brought in succession before his view, and referred (each luminary according to its own visual ray or direction from his eye) to the imaginary spherical surface, of which he himself occupies the centre. There is always, therefore (he would justly argue), a star-bespangled canopy over his head, by day as well as by night, only that the glare of daylight (which he perceives gradually to efface the stars as the morning twilight comes on) prevents them from being seen. And such is really the case. The stars actually continue visible through telescopes in the daytime; and, in proportion to the power of the instrument, not only the largest and brightest of them, but even those of inferior lustre, such as scarcely strike the eye at night as at all conspicuous, are readily found and followed even at noonday,—unless in that part of the sky which is very near the sun,—by those who possess the means of pointing a telescope accurately to the proper places. Indeed, from the bottoms of deep narrow pits, such as a well, or the shaft of a mine, such bright stars as pass the zenith may even be discerned by the naked eye; and we have ourselves heard it stated by a celebrated optician, that the earliest circumstance which drew his attention to astronomy was the regular appearance, at a certain hour, for several successive days, of a considerable star, through the shaft of a chimney. Venus in our climate, and even Jupiter in the clearer skies of tropical countries, are often visible, without any artificial aid, to the naked eye of one who knows nearly where to look for them. During total eclipses of the sun, the larger stars also appear in their proper situations.

But to return to our incipient astronomer, whom we left contemplating the sphere of the heavens, as completed in imagination beneath his feet, and as rising up from thence in its diurnal course. There is one portion or segment of this sphere of which he will not thus obtain a view. As there is a segment towards the north, adjacent to the pole above his horizon, in which the stars *never set*, so there is a corresponding segment, about which the smaller circles of the more southern stars are described, in which they *never rise*. The stars which border upon the extreme circumference of this segment just graze the southern point of his horizon, and show themselves for a few moments above it, precisely as those near the circumference of the northern segment graze his northern horizon, and dip for a moment below it, to re-appear immediately. Every point in a spherical surface has, of course, another diametrically opposite to it; and as the spectator's horizon divides his sphere into two hemispheres—a superior and inferior—there must of necessity exist a depressed pole to the south, corresponding to the elevated one to the north, and a portion surrounding it, perpetually beneath, as there is another surrounding the north pole, perpetually above it.

'Hic vertex nobis semper sublimis; at illum
Sub pedibus nox atra videt, manesque profundi.'—VIRGIL

One pole rides high, one, plunged beneath the main,
Seeks the deep night, and Pluto's dusky reign.

To get sight of this segment, he must travel southwards. In so doing, a new set of phenomena come forward. In proportion as he advances to the south, some of those constellations which, at his original station, barely grazed the northern horizon, will be observed to sink below it and set; at first remaining hid only for a very short time, but gradually for a longer part of the twenty-four hours. They will continue, however, to circulate about the same point—that is, holding the same invariable position *with respect to them* in the concave of the heavens among the stars; but this point itself will become gradually depressed with respect to the spectator's horizon. The axis, in short, about which the diurnal motion is performed, will appear to have become continually less and less inclined to the horizon; and by the same degrees as the northern pole is depressed the southern will rise, and constellations surrounding it will come into view; at first momentarily, but by degrees for longer and longer times in each diurnal revolution—realizing, in short, what we have already stated.

MICHAEL FARADAY

From *Experimental Researches in Electricity* (1839–55) (1852)

I have recently been engaged in describing and defining the lines of magnetic force, *i.e.* those lines which are indicated in a general manner by the disposition of iron filings or small magnetic needles, around or between magnets; and I have shown, I hope satisfactorily, how these lines may be taken as exact representants of the magnetic power, both as to disposition and amount; also how they may be recognized by a moving wire in a manner altogether different in principle from the indications given by a magnetic needle, and in numerous cases with great and peculiar advantages. The definition then given had no reference to the physical nature of the force at the place of action, and will apply with equal accuracy whatever that may be; and this being very thoroughly understood, I am now about to leave the strict line of reasoning for a time, and enter upon a few speculations respecting the physical character of the lines of force, and the manner in which they may be supposed to be continued through space. We are obliged to enter into such speculations with regard to numerous natural powers, and, indeed, that of gravity is the only instance where they are apparently shut out.

It is not to be supposed for a moment that speculations of this kind are useless, or necessarily hurtful, in natural philosophy. They should ever be held as doubtful, and liable to error and to change; but they are wonderful aids in the hands of the experimentalist and mathematician. For not only are they useful in rendering the vague idea more clear for the time, giving it something like a definite shape, that it may be submitted to experiment and calculation; but they lead on, by deduction and correction, to the discovery of new phaenomena, and so cause an increase and advance of real physical truth, which, unlike the hypothesis that led to it, becomes fundamental knowledge not subject to change. Who is not aware of the remarkable progress in the development of the nature of light and radiation in modern times, and the extent to which that progress has been aided by the hypotheses both of emission and undulation? Such considerations form my excuse for entering now and then upon speculations; but though I value them highly when cautiously advanced, I consider it as an essential character of a sound mind to hold them in doubt; scarcely giving them the character of opinions, but esteeming them merely as probabilities and possibilities, and making a very broad distinction between them and the facts and laws of nature.

In the numerous cases of force acting at a distance, the philosopher has gradually learned that it is by no means sufficient to rest satisfied with the mere fact, and has therefore directed his attention to the manner in which the force is transmitted across the intervening space; and even when he can learn nothing sure of the manner, he is still able to make clear distinctions in different cases, by what may be called the affections of the lines of power; and thus, by these and other means, to make distinctions in the nature of the lines of force of different kinds of power as compared with each other, and therefore between the powers to which they belong. In the action of gravity, for instance, the line of force is a straight line as far as we can test it by the resultant phaenomena. It cannot be deflected, or even affected, in its course. Neither is the action in one line at all influenced, either in direction or amount, by a like action in another line; *i.e.* one particle gravitating toward another particle has exactly the same amount of force in the same direction, whether it gravitates to that one alone or towards myriads of other like particles, exerting in the latter case upon each one of them a force equal to that which it can exert upon the single one when alone: the results of course can combine, but the direction and amount of force between any two given particles remain unchanged. So gravity presents us with the simplest case of attraction; and appearing to have no relation to any physical process by which the power of the particles is carried on between them, seems to be a pure case of attraction or action at a distance, and offers therefore the simplest type of the cases which may be like it in that respect. My object is to consider how far magnetism is such an action at a distance; or how far it may partake of the nature of other powers, the lines of which depend, for the communication of force, upon intermediate physical agencies.

There is one question in relation to gravity, which, if we could ascertain or touch it, would greatly enlighten us. It is, whether gravitation requires *time*. If it did, it would show undeniably that a physical agency existed in the course of the line of force. It seems equally impossible to prove or disprove this point; since there is no capability of suspending, changing, or annihilating the power (gravity), or annihilating the matter in which the power resides.

When we turn to radiation phaenomena, then we obtain the highest proof, that though nothing ponderable passes, yet the lines of force have a physical existence independent, in a manner, of the body radiating, or of the body receiving the rays. They may be turned aside in their course, and then deviate from a straight into a bent or a curved line. They may be affected in their nature so as to be turned on their axis, or else to have different properties impressed on different sides. Their sum of power is limited; so that if the force, as it issues from its source, is directed on to or determined upon a given set of particles, or in a given direction, it cannot be in any degree directed upon other particles, or into another direction, without being proportionately removed from the first. The lines have no dependence upon a second or reacting body, as in gravitation; and they require time for their propagation. In all these things they are in marked contrast with the lines of gravitating force.

When we turn to the electric force, we are presented with a very remarkable general condition intermediate between the conditions of the two former cases. The power (and its lines) here requires the *presence* of two or more acting particles or masses, as in the case of gravity; and cannot exist with one only, as in the case of light. But though two particles are requisite, they must be in an *antithetical* condition in respect of each other, and not, as in the case of gravity, alike in relation to the force. The power is now dual; there it was simple. Requiring two or more particles like gravity, it is unlike gravity in that the power is limited. One electro-particle cannot affect a second, third and fourth, as much as it does the first, to act upon the latter its power must be proportionately removed from the former, and this limitation appears to exist as a necessity in the dual character of the force; for the two states, or places, or directions of force must be equal to each other.

With the electric force we have both the static and dynamic state. I use these words merely as names, without pretending to have a clear notion of the physical condition which they seem meaningly to imply. Whether there are two fluids or one, or any fluid of electricity, or such a thing as may be rightly called a current, I do not know; still there are well-established electric conditions and effects which the words *static*, *dynamic*, and *current* are generally employed to express; and with this reservation they express them as well as any other. The lines of force of the *static* condition of electricity are present in all cases of induction. They terminate at the surfaces of the conductors under induction, or at the particles of non-conductors, which, being electrified, are in that condition. They are subject to inflection in their course, and may be compressed or rarefied by bodies of different inductive capacities; but they are in those cases affected by the intervening matter; and it is not certain how the line of electric force would exist in relation to a perfect vacuum, *i.e.* whether it would be a straight line, as that of gravity is assumed to be, or curved in such a manner as to show something like physical existence separate from the mere distant actions of the surfaces or particles bounding or terminating the induction. No condition of *quality* or *polarity* has as yet been discovered in the line of static electric force; nor has any relation of *time* been established in respect of it.

The lines of force of dynamic electricity are either limited in their extent, as in the lowering by discharge, or otherwise of the inductive condition of static electricity; or endless and continuous, as closed curves in the case of a voltaic circuit. Being definite in their amount for a given source, they can still be expanded, contracted, and deflected almost to any extent, according to the nature and size of the media through which they pass, and to which they have a direct relation. It is probable that matter is always essentially present; but the hypothetical aether may perhaps be admitted here as well as elsewhere. No condition of quality or polarity has as yet been recognized in them. In respect of *time*, it has been found, in the case of a Leyden discharge, that time is necessary even with the best conductors; indeed there is reason to think it is as necessary there as in the cases dependent on bad conducting media, as, for instance, in the lightning flash.

Three great distinctions at least may be taken among these cases of the exertion of force at a distance; that of gravitation, where propagation of the force by physical lines through the intermediate space is not supposed to exist; that of radiation, where the propagation does exist, and where the propagating line or ray, once produced, has existence independent either of its source, or termination; and that of electricity, where the propagating process has intermediate existence, like a ray, but at the same time depends upon both extremities of the line of force, or upon conditions (as in the connected voltaic pile) equivalent to such extremities. Magnetic action at a distance has to be compared with these. It may be unlike any of them; for who shall say we are aware of all the physical methods or forms under which force is communicated? It has been assumed, however, by some, to be a pure case of force at a distance, and so like that of gravity; whilst others have considered it as better represented by the idea of streams of power. The question at present appears to be, whether the lines of magnetic force have or have not a physical existence; and if they have, whether such physical existence has a static or dynamic form.

WILLIAM THOMSON, LORD KELVIN

On the Age of the Sun's Heat (1862)

The second great law of Thermodynamics involves a certain principle of *irreversible action in nature*. It is thus shown that, although mechanical energy is *indestructible*, there is a universal tendency to its dissipation, which produces gradual augmentation and diffusion of heat, cessation of motion and exhaustion of potential energy through the material universe. The result would inevitably be a state of universal rest and death, if the universe were finite and left to obey existing laws. But it is impossible to conceive a limit to the extent of matter in the universe; and therefore science points rather to an endless progress, through an endless space, of action involving the transformation of potential energy into palpable motion and thence into heat, than to a single finite mechanism, running down like a clock, and stopping for ever. It is also impossible to conceive either the beginning or the continuance of life, without an overruling creative power; and, therefore, no conclusions of dynamical science regarding the future condition of the earth, can be held to give dispiriting views as to the destiny of the race of intelligent beings by which it is at present inhabited.

The object proposed in the present article is an application of these general principles to the discovery of probable limits to the periods of time, past and future, during which the sun can be reckoned on as a source of heat and light. . . .

At his surface the sun's temperature cannot, as we have many reasons for believing, be incomparably higher than temperatures attainable artificially in our terrestrial laboratories.

Among other reasons it may be mentioned that the sun radiates heat, from every square foot of his surface, at only about 7,000 horse power. Coal, burning at a rate of a little less than a pound per two seconds, would generate the same amount; and it is estimated that, in the furnaces of locomotive engines, coal burns at from one pound in thirty seconds to one pound in ninety seconds, per square foot of grate-bars. Hence heat is radiated from the sun at a rate not more than from fifteen to forty-five times as high as that at which heat is generated on the grate-bars of a locomotive furnace, per equal areas.

The interior temperature of the sun is probably far higher than that at his surface, because direct conduction can play no sensible part in the transference of heat between the inner and outer portions of his mass, and there must be an approximate *convective* equilibrium of heat throughout the whole, if the whole is fluid. That is to say, the temperatures, at different distances from the centre, must be approximately those which any portion of the substance, if carried from the centre to the surface, would acquire by expansion without loss or gain of heat.

The sun being, for reasons referred to above, assumed to be an incandescent liquid now losing heat, the question naturally occurs, How did this heat originate? It is certain that it cannot have existed in the sun through an infinity of past time, since, as long as it has so existed, it must have been suffering dissipation, and the finiteness of the sun precludes the supposition of an infinite primitive store of heat in his body.

The sun must, therefore, either have been created an active source of heat at some time of not immeasurable antiquity, by an overruling decree; or the heat which he has already radiated away, and that which he still possesses, must have been acquired by a natural process, following permanently established laws. Without pronouncing the former supposition to be essentially incredible, we may safely say that it is in the highest degree improbable, if we can show the latter to be not contradictory to known physical laws. And we do show this and more, by merely pointing to certain actions, going on before us at present, which, if sufficiently abundant at some past time, must have given the sun heat enough to account for all we know of his past radiation and present temperature.

It is not necessary at present to enter at length on details regarding the meteoric theory, which appears to have been first proposed in a definite form by Mayer, and afterwards independently by Waterston:* or regarding the modified hypothesis of meteoric vortices, which the writer of the present article showed to be necessary, in order that the length of the year, as known for the last 2,000 years, may not have been sensibly disturbed by the accessions which the sun's mass must have had during that period, if the heat radiated away has been always compensated by heat generated by meteoric influx.

. . . We may now believe that all theories of complete, or nearly complete, contemporaneous meteoric compensation, must be rejected; but we may still hold that—

Meteoric action . . . is . . . not only proved to exist as a cause of solar heat, but it is the only one of all conceivable causes which we know to exist from independent evidence.*

The form of meteoric theory which now seems most probable, and which was first discussed on true thermodynamic principles by Helmholtz,* consists in supposing the sun and his heat to have originated in a coalition of smaller bodies, falling together by mutual gravitation, and generating as they must do according to the great law demonstrated by Joule,* an exact equivalent of heat for the motion lost in collision.

That some form of the meteoric theory is certainly the true and complete explanation of solar heat can scarcely be doubted, when the following reasons are considered:

(1) No other natural explanation, except by chemical action, can be conceived.

(2) The chemical theory is quite insufficient, because the most energetic chemical action we know, taking place between substances amounting to the whole sun's mass, would only generate about 3,000 years' heat.

(3) There is no difficulty in accounting for 20,000,000 years' heat by the meteoric theory.

It would extend this article to too great a length, and would require something of mathematical calculation, to explain fully the principles on which this last estimate is founded. It is enough to say that bodies, all much smaller than the sun, falling together from a state of relative rest, at mutual distances all large in comparison with their diameters, and forming a globe of uniform density equal in mass and diameter to the sun, would generate an amount of heat which, accurately calculated according to Joule's principles and experimental results, is found to be just 20,000,000 times Pouillet's estimate of the annual amount of solar radiation. The sun's density must, in all probability, increase very much towards his centre, and therefore a considerably greater amount of heat than that must be supposed to have been generated if his whole mass was formed by the coalition of comparatively small bodies. On the other hand, we do not know how much heat may have been dissipated by resistance and minor impacts before the final conglomeration; but there is reason to believe that even the most rapid conglomeration that we can conceive to have probably taken place could only leave the finished globe with about half the entire heat due to the amount of potential energy of mutual gravitation exhausted. We may, therefore, accept, as a lowest estimate for the sun's initial heat, 10,000,000 times a year's supply at present rate, but 50,000,000 or 100,000,000 as possible, in consequence of the sun's greater density in his central parts.

The considerations adduced above, in this paper, regarding the sun's possible specific heat, rate of cooling, and superficial temperature, render it probable that he must have been very sensibly warmer one million years ago than now; and, consequently, that if he has existed as a luminary for ten or twenty million years, he must have radiated away considerably more than the corresponding number of times the present yearly amount of loss.

It seems, therefore, on the whole most probable that the sun has not illuminated the earth for 100,000,000 years, and almost certain that he has not done so for 500,000,000 years.* As for the future, we may say, with equal certainty, that inhabitants of the earth cannot continue to enjoy the light and heat essential to their life, for many million years longer, unless sources now unknown to us are prepared in the great storehouse of creation.

JOHN TYNDALL

On Chemical Rays, and the Light of the Sky (1869)

Whether we see rightly or wrongly—whether our intellection be real or imaginary—it is of the utmost importance in science to aim at perfect clearness in the description of all that comes, or seems to come, within the range of the intellect. For if we are right, clearness of utterance forwards the cause of right; while if we are wrong, it ensures the speedy correction of error. In this spirit, and with the determination at all events to speak plainly, let us deal with our conceptions of aether waves and molecules. Supposing a wave, or a train of waves, to impinge upon a molecule so as to urge all its parts with the same motion, the molecule would move bodily as a whole, but because they are animated by a *common motion* there would be no tendency of its constituent atoms to separate from each other. *Differential motions* among the atoms themselves would be necessary to effect a separation, and if such motions be not introduced by the shock of the waves, there is no mechanical ground for the decomposition of the molecule.

It is, however, difficult to conceive the shock of a wave, or a train of waves, so distributed among the atoms as to cause no strain amongst them. For atoms are of different weights, probably of different sizes; at all events it is almost certain that the ratio of the mass of the atom to the surface it presents to the action of the waves is different in different cases. If this be so, and I think the probabilities are immensely in favour of its being so, then every wave which passes over a molecule tends to decompose it—tends to carry away from their weightier and more sluggish companions those atoms which, in relation to their mass, present the largest resisting surfaces to the motion of the waves. The case may be illustrated by reference to a man standing on the deck of a ship. As long as both of them share equally the motions of the wind or of the sea, there is no tendency to separation. In chemical language, they are in a state of combination. But a wave passing over it finds the ship less rapid in yielding to its motion than the man; the man is consequently carried away, and we have what may be regarded as decomposition.

Thus the conception of the decomposition of compound molecules by the waves of aether comes to us recommended by *à priori* probability. But a closer examination of the question compels us to supplement, if not materially to qualify, this conception. It is a most remarkable fact, that the waves which have thus far been found most effectual in shaking asunder the atoms of compound molecules are those of least mechanical power. *Billows*, to use a strong comparison, are incompetent to produce effects which are readily produced by *ripples*. It is, for example, the violet and ultra-violet rays of the sun that are most effectual in producing these chemical decompositions; and, compared with the red and ultra-red solar rays, the energy of these 'chemical rays' is infinitesimal. This energy would probably in some cases have to be multiplied by millions to bring it up to that of the ultra-red rays; and still the latter are powerless where the smaller waves are potent. We here observe a remarkable similarity between the behaviour of chemical molecules and that of the human retina. The energy transmitted to the eye from a candle-flame half a mile distant is more than sufficient to inform consciousness; while waves of a different period, possessing twenty thousand million times this energy, have been suffered to impinge upon my own retina, with an absolute unconsciousness of any effect whatever—mechanical, physiological, chemical, or thermal.

Whence, then, the power of these smaller waves to unlock the bonds of chemical union? If it be not a result of their strength, it must be, as in the case of vision, a result of their periods of recurrence. But how are we to figure this action? I should say thus; the shock of a single wave produces no more than an infinitesimal effect upon an atom or a molecule. To produce a larger effect, the motion must *accumulate*, and for wave-impulses to accumulate, they must arrive in periods identical with the periods of vibration of the atoms on which they impinge. In this case each successive wave finds the atom in a position which enables that wave to add its shock to the sum of the shocks of its predecessors. The effect is mechanically the same as that due to the timed impulses of a boy upon a swing. The single tick of a clock has no appreciable effect upon the unvibrating and equally long pendulum of a distant clock; but a succession of ticks, each of which adds, at the proper moment, its infinitesimal push to the sum of the pushes preceding it, will, as a matter of fact, set the second clock going. So likewise a single puff of air against the prong of a heavy tuning-fork produces no sensible motion, and, consequently, no audible sound; but a succession of puffs, which follow each other in periods identical with the tuning-fork's period of vibration, will render the fork sonorous. I think the chemical action of light is to be regarded in this way. Fact and reason point to the conclusion that it is the heaping up of motion on the atoms, in consequence of their synchronism with the shorter waves, that causes them to part company. This I take to be the mechanical cause of these decompositions which are effected by the waves of aether. . . .

With regard to the colour of the sky; how is it produced, and can we not reproduce it? This colour has not the same origin as that of ordinary colouring matter, in which certain portions of the white solar light are extinguished, the colour of the substances being that of the portion which remains. A violet is blue because its molecular texture enables it to quench the green, yellow, and red constituents of white light, and to allow the blue free transmission. A geranium is red because its molecular texture is such as quenches all rays except the red. Such colours are called colours of absorption; but the hue of the sky is not of this character. The blue light of the sky is all *reflected* light, and were there nothing in our atmosphere competent to reflect the solar rays we should see no blue firmament, but should look into the darkness of infinite space. The reflection of the blue is effected by perfectly colourless particles. Smallness of size alone is requisite to ensure the selection and reflection of this colour. Of all the visual waves emitted by the sun, the shortest and smallest are those which correspond to the colour blue. On such waves small particles have more power than upon large ones, hence the predominance of blue colour in all light reflected from exceedingly small particles. The crimson glow of the Alps in the evening and in the morning is due, on the other hand, to *transmitted* light; that is to say, to light which in its passage through great atmospheric distances has its blue constituents sifted out of it by repeated reflection.

It is possible, as stated, by duly regulating the quantity of vapour, to make our precipitated particles grow from an infinitesimal and altogether ultra-microscopic size to masses of sensible magnitude; and by means of these particles, in a certain stage of their growth, we can produce a blue which shall rival, if it does not transcend, that of the deepest and purest Italian sky. Let this point be in the first place established. Associated with our experimental tube is a barometer, the mercurial column of which now indicates that the tube is exhausted. Into the tube I introduce a quantity of the mixed air and nitrite of butyl vapour sufficient to depress the mercurial column one-twentieth of an inch; that is to say, the air and vapour together exert a pressure of one six-hundredth of an atmosphere. I now add a quantity of air and hydrochloric acid sufficient to depress the mercury half an inch further, and into this compound and highly attenuated atmosphere I discharge the beam of the electric light. The effect is slow; but gradually within the tube arises this splendid azure, which strengthens for a time, reaches a maximum of depth and purity, and then, as the particles grow larger, passes into whitish blue. This experiment is representative, and it illustrates a general principle. Various other colourless substances of the most diverse properties, optical and chemical, might be employed for this experiment. The *incipient cloud* in every case would exhibit this superb blue; thus proving to demonstration that particles of infinitesimal size, without any colour of their own, and irrespective of those optical properties exhibited by the substance in a massive state, are competent to produce the colour of the sky. . . .

We have thus far illuminated our incipient cloud with ordinary light, and found the portion of this light reflected laterally from the cloud in all directions round it to be perfectly polarised. We will now examine the effects produced when the light which illuminates the cloud is itself polarised. In front of the electric lamp, and between it and the experimental tube, is placed this fine Nicol's prism* which is sufficiently large to embrace and to polarise the entire beam. The prism is now placed so that the plane of vibration of the light emergent from it, and falling upon the cloud, is vertical. How does the cloud behave towards this light? This formless aggregate of infinitesimal particles, without definite structure, shows the two-sidedness of the light in the most striking manner. It is absolutely incompetent to reflect upwards or downwards, while it freely discharges the light horizontally, right and left. I turn the polarising Nicol so as to render the plane of vibration horizontal; the cloud now freely reflects the light vertically upwards and downwards, but it is absolutely incompetent to shed a ray horizontally to the right or left.

Fix your attention upon one of those reflecting particles. Figure it as a little sphere with the beam of the electric light impinging upon it. Let us call that diameter which coincides with the direction of the beam, the *axis* of the sphere; one of its *poles* would then be turned towards the light, and the other in the opposite direction. The equator of the little sphere would of course be midway between its poles. Now, conceive a parallel of latitude drawn upon the sphere at an angular distance of 45 degrees from the pole; that is to say, midway between the pole and the equator. Then what occurs with ordinary light is this: all the vibrations tangent to the little circle, which I have called a parallel of latitude, are reflected perfectly polarised; but all vibrations executed at right angles to the circle go unreflected through the little sphere. If, instead of ordinary light, we use polarised light, it is clear that at two opposite points of the little circle the vibrations are executed along the tangents, while at two other opposite points they are executed at right angles to the tangents. In the former case the particle *reflects* the light, in the latter it *transmits* the light unreflected. What is true of a single particle is true of all, and hence the inability of the incipient cloud formed of such particles to reflect light in two directions, while it freely reflects it in two others. The entire facts are now placed before you. The reflecting particle and the waves of aether are of course both beyond the range of the senses, but to the intellect the conceptions here introduced are just as easy as if, in illustration, I had pointed to the poles, equator, and parallel of latitude of an ordinary terrestrial globe.

Suppose the atmosphere of our planet to be surrounded by an envelope impervious to light, with an aperture on the sunward side, through which a solar beam could enter and cross our atmosphere. Surrounded on all sides by air not directly illuminated, the track of the sunlight would resemble that of the electric beam in a dark space filled with our incipient cloud. The course of the sunbeam would be *blue*, and it would discharge laterally in all directions round it, light in precisely the same polarised condition as that discharged from the incipient cloud. In fact, the azure revealed by the sunbeam would be the azure of such a cloud. And if, instead of permitting the ordinary light of the sun to enter the aperture, a Nicol's prism were placed there, which should polarise the sunlight on its entrance into our atmosphere, the particles producing the colour of the sky would act precisely like those of our incipient cloud. In two directions we should have the solar light reflected; in two others unreflected. In fact, out of such a solitary beam, traversing the unilluminated air, we should be able to extract every effect shown by our incipient cloud. In the production of such clouds we virtually carry bits of the sky into our laboratories, and obtain with them all the effects obtainable in the open firmament of heaven.

On the Scientific Use of the Imagination (1870)

This essay was originally a lecture delivered to the British Association at Liverpool, 16 September 1870.

[Previously] I had been thinking much of light and heat, of magnetism and electricity, of organic germs, atoms, molecules, spontaneous generation, comets, and skies. With one or another of these I now sought to reform an alliance, and finally succeeded in establishing a kind of cohesion between thought and Light. The wish grew within me to trace, and to enable you to trace, some of the more occult operations of this agent. I wished, if possible, to take you behind the drop-scene of the senses, and to show you the hidden mechanism of optical action. For I take it to be well worth the while of the scientific teacher to take some pains, and even great pains, to make those whom he addresses copartners of his thoughts. To clear his own mind in the first place of all haze and vagueness, and then to project into language which shall leave no mistake as to his meaning—which shall leave even his errors naked—the definite ideas he has shaped. A great deal is, I think, possible to scientific exposition conducted in this way. It is possible, I believe, even before an audience like the present, to uncover to some extent the unseen things of nature; and thus to give not only to professed students, but to others with the necessary bias, industry, and capacity, an intelligent interest in the operations of science. Time and labour are necessary to this result, but science is the gainer from the public sympathy thus created.

How then are those hidden things to be revealed? How, for example, are we to lay hold of the physical basis of light, since, like that of life itself, it lies entirely without the domain of the senses? Philosophers may be right in affirming that we cannot transcend experience; but we can, at all events, carry it a long way from its origin. We can also magnify, diminish, qualify, and combine experiences, so as to render them fit for purposes entirely new. We are gifted with the power of Imagination—combining what the Germans call Anschauungsgabe and Einbildungskraft*—and by this power we can lighten the darkness which surrounds the world of the senses. There are tories even in science who regard imagination as a faculty to be feared and avoided rather than employed. They had observed its action in weak vessels, and were unduly impressed by its disasters. But they might with equal justice point to exploded boilers as an argument against the use of steam. Bounded and conditioned by cooperant Reason, imagination becomes the mightiest instrument of the physical discoverer. Newton's passage from a falling apple to a falling moon was, at the outset, a leap of the imagination. When William Thomson tries to place the ultimate particles of matter between his compass points, and to apply to them a scale of millimetres, he is powerfully aided by this faculty. And in much that has been recently said about protoplasm and life, we have the outgoings of the imagination guided and controlled by the known analogies of science. In fact, without this power, our knowledge of nature would be a mere tabulation of co-existences and sequences. We should still believe in the succession of day and night, of summer and winter; but the soul of Force would be dislodged from our universe; causal relations would disappear, and with them that science which is now binding the parts of nature to an organic whole.

JAMES CLERK MAXWELL

From *Theory of Heat* (1871)

ON THE KINETIC THEORY OF GASES

A gaseous body is supposed to consist of a great number of molecules moving with great velocity. During the greater part of their course these molecules are not acted on by any sensible force, and therefore move in straight lines with uniform velocity. When two molecules come within a certain distance of each other, a mutual action takes place between them, which may be compared to the collision of two billiard balls. Each molecule has its course changed, and starts on a new path. I have concluded from some experiments of my own that the collision between two hard spherical balls is not an accurate representation of what takes place during the encounter of two molecules. A better representation of such an encounter will be obtained by supposing the molecules to act on one another in a more gradual manner, so that the action between them goes on for a finite time, during which the centres of the molecules first approach each other and then separate.

We shall refer to this mutual action as an Encounter between two molecules, and we shall call the course of a molecule between one encounter and another the Free Path of the molecule. In ordinary gases the free motion of a molecule takes up much more time than that occupied by an encounter. As the density of the gas increases, the free path diminishes, and in liquids no part of the course of a molecule can be spoken of as its free path.

In an encounter between two molecules we know that, since the force of the impact acts between the two bodies, the motion of the centre of gravity of the two molecules remains the same after the encounter as it was before. We also know by the principle of the conservation of energy that the velocity of each molecule relatively to the centre of gravity remains the same in magnitude, and is only changed in direction.

Let us next suppose a number of molecules in motion contained in a vessel whose sides are such that if any energy is communicated to the vessel by the encounters of molecules against its sides, the vessel communicates as much energy to other molecules during their encounters with it, so as to preserve the total energy of the enclosed system. The first thing we must notice about this moving system is that even if all the molecules have the same velocity originally, their encounters will produce an inequality of velocity, and that this distribution of velocity will go on continually. Every molecule will then change both its direction and its velocity at every encounter; and, as we are not supposed to keep a record of the exact particulars of every encounter, these changes of motion must appear to us very irregular if we follow the course of a single molecule. If, however, we adopt a statistical view of the system, and distribute the molecules into groups, according to the velocity with which at a given instant they happen to be moving, we shall observe a regularity of a new kind in the proportions of the whole number of molecules which fall into each of these groups.

And here I wish to point out that, in adopting this statistical method of considering the average number of groups of molecules selected according to their velocities, we have abandoned the strict kinetic method of tracing the exact circumstances of each individual molecule in all its encounters. It is therefore possible that we may arrive at results which, though they fairly represent the facts as long as we are supposed to deal with a gas in mass, would cease to be applicable if our faculties and instruments were so sharpened that we could detect and lay hold of each molecule and trace it through all its course.

For the same reason, a theory of the effects of education deduced from a study of the returns of registrars, in which no names of individuals are given, might be found not to be applicable to the experience of a schoolmaster who is able to trace the progress of each individual pupil.

The distribution of the molecules according to their velocities is found to be of exactly the same mathematical form as the distribution of observations according to the magnitude of their errors, as described in the theory of errors of observation. The distribution of bullet-holes in a target according to their distances from the point aimed at is found to be of the same form, provided a great many shots are fired by persons of the same degree of skill.

We have already met with the same form in the case of heat diffused from a hot stratum by conduction. Whenever in physical phenomena some cause exists over which we have no control, and which produces a scattering of the particles of matter, a deviation of observations from the truth, or a diffusion of velocity or of heat, mathematical expressions of this exponential form are sure to make their appearance.

It appears then that of the molecules composing the system some are moving very slowly, a very few are moving with enormous velocities, and the greater number with intermediate velocities. To compare one such system with another, the best method is to take the mean of the squares of all the velocities. This quantity is called the Mean Square of the velocity. The square root of this quantity is called the Velocity of Mean Square. . . .

LIMITATION OF THE SECOND LAW OF THERMODYNAMICS

Before I conclude, I wish to direct attention to an aspect of the molecular theory which deserves consideration.

One of the best established facts in thermodynamics is that it is impossible in a system enclosed in an envelope which permits neither change of volume nor passage of heat, and in which both the temperature and the pressure are everywhere the same, to produce any inequality of temperature or of pressure without the expenditure of work. This is the second law of thermodynamics, and it is undoubtedly true as long as we can deal with bodies only in mass, and have no power of perceiving or handling the separate molecules of which they are made up. But if we conceive a being whose faculties are so sharpened that he can follow every molecule in its course, such a being, whose attributes are still as essentially finite as our own, would be able to do what is at present impossible to us. For we have seen that the molecules in a vessel full of air at uniform temperature are moving with velocities by no means uniform, though the mean velocity of any great number of them, arbitrarily selected, is almost exactly uniform. Now let us suppose that such a vessel is divided into two portions, A and B, by a division in which there is a small hole, and that a being, who can see the individual molecules, opens and closes this hole, so as to allow only the swifter molecules to pass from A to B, and only the slower ones to pass from B to A. He will thus, without expenditure of work, raise the temperature of B and lower that of A, in contradiction to the second law of thermodynamics.

This is only one of the instances in which conclusions which we have drawn from our experience of bodies consisting of an immense number of molecules may be found not to be applicable to the more delicate observations and experiments which we may suppose made by one who can perceive and handle the individual molecules which we deal with only in large masses.

In dealing with masses of matter, while we do not perceive the individual molecules, we are compelled to adopt what I have described as the statistical method of calculation, and to abandon the strict dynamical method, in which we follow every motion by the calculus.

It would be interesting to enquire how far those ideas about the nature and methods of science which have been derived from examples of scientific investigation in which the dynamical method is followed are applicable to our actual knowledge of concrete things, which, as we have seen, is of an essentially statistical nature, because no one has yet discovered any practical method of tracing the path of a molecule, or of identifying it at different times.

I do not think, however, that the perfect identity which we observe between different portions of the same kind of matter can be explained on the statistical principle of the stability of the averages of large numbers of quantities each of which may differ from the mean. For if of the molecules of some substance such as hydrogen, some were of sensibly greater mass than others, we have the means of producing a separation between molecules of different masses, and in this way we should be able to produce two kinds of hydrogen, one of which would be somewhat denser than the other. As this cannot be done, we must admit that the equality which we assert to exist between the molecules of hydrogen applies to each individual molecule, and not merely to the average of groups of millions of molecules.

To the Chief Musician upon Nabla
A TYNDALLIC* ODE (1874)

A nabla is a triangle-shaped harp. In mathematics, the quaternion operator has the same shape. Maxwell supported the use of quaternions—
which could be used to represent complex numbers—in physics because
of their usefulness in electrodynamics, while other physicists dismissed
them as 'empty language'. Because the mathematician Peter Guthrie Tait
advocated the use of quaternions, Maxwell called him the 'chief musician
upon Nabla'.

I

I come from fields of fractured ice,
    Whose wounds are cured by squeezing,
Melting they cool, but in a trice,
    Get warm again by freezing.
Here, in the frosty air, the sprays
    With fern-like hoar-frost bristle,
There, liquid stars their watery rays
    Shoot through the solid crystal.

II

I come from empyrean* fires—
    From microscopic spaces,
Where molecules with fierce desires,
    Shiver in hot embraces.
The atoms clash, the spectra flash,
    Projected on the screen,
The double D, magnesian *b*,
    And Thallium's living green.*

III

We place our eye where these dark rays
    Unite in this dark focus,
Right on the source of power we gaze,
    Without a screen to cloak us.

Then where the eye was placed at first,
　　We place a disc of platinum,
It glows, it puckers! will it burst?
　　How ever shall we flatten him!

IV

This crystal tube the electric ray
　　Shows optically clean,
No dust or haze within, but stay!
　　All has not yet been seen.
What gleams are these of heavenly blue?
　　What air-drawn form appearing,
What mystic fish, that, ghostlike, through
　　The empty space is steering?

V

I light this sympathetic flame,
　　My faintest wish that answers,
I sing, it sweetly sings the same,
　　It dances with the dancers.
I shout, I whistle, clap my hands,
　　And stamp upon the platform,
The flame responds to my commands,
　　In this form and in that form.

VI

What means that thrilling, drilling scream,
　　Protect me! 'tis the siren:
Her heart is fire, her breath is steam,
　　Her larynx is of iron.
Sun! dart thy beams! in tepid streams,
　　Rise, viewless exhalations!
And lap me round, that no rude sound
　　May mar my meditations.

VII

Here let me pause.—These transient facts,
　　These fugitive impressions,
Must be transformed by mental acts,
　　To permanent possessions.

Then summon up your grasp of mind,
    Your fancy scientific,
Till sights and sounds with thought combined,
    Become of truth prolific.

VIII

Go to! prepare your mental bricks,
    Fetch them from every quarter,
Firm on the sand your basement fix
    With best sensation mortar.
The top shall rise to heaven on high—
    Or such an elevation,
That the swift whirl with which we fly
    Shall conquer gravitation.

Professor Tait, Loquitur (1877)

Will mounted ebonite* disk
    On smooth unyielding bearing,
When turned about with motion brisk
    (Nor excitation sparing),
Affect the primitive repose,
    Of + and − in a wire,
So that while either downward flows,
    The other upwards shall aspire?
Describe the form and size of coil,
    And other things that we may need,
Think not about increase of toil
    Involved in work at double speed.
I can no more, my pen is bad,
    It catches in the roughened page—
But answer us and make us glad,
    THOU ANTI-DISTANCE-ACTION SAGE!
Yet have I still a thousand things to say,
    But work of other kinds is pressing—
So your petitioner will ever pray
    That your defence be triple *messing*.*

Answer to Tait

The mounted disk of ebonite
  Has whirled before, nor whirled in vain;
Rowland of Troy,* that doughty knight,
  Convection currents did obtain
In such a disk, of power to wheedle,
From its loved North the subtle needle.

'Twas when Sir Rowland, as a stage
  From Troy to Baltimore, took rest
In Berlin, there old Archimage*
  Armed him to follow up this quest;
Right glad to find himself possessor
Of the irrepressible Professor.

But wouldst thou twirl that disk once more.
  Then follow in Childe Rowland's train,
To where in busy Baltimore
  He brews the bantlings of his brain;
As he may do who still prefers
One Rowland to two Olivers.*

But Rowland,—no, nor Oliver,—
  Could get electromotive force,
Which fact and reason both aver,
  Has change of some kind as its source,
Out of a disk in swift rotation
Without the least acceleration.

But with your splendid roundabout
  Of mighty power, new-hung and greasy,
With galvanometer so stout,
  A new research would be as easy;
A test which might perchance disclose,
Which way the electric current flows.

Take then a coil of copper pure,
  And fix it on your whirling table;
Place the electrodes firm and sure
  As near the axis as you're able,

And soon you'll learn the way to work it,
With galvanometer in circuit.

Not while the coil in spinning sleeps,
   On her smooth axle swift and steady;
But when against the stops she sweeps,
   To watch the light-spot then be ready,
That you may learn from its deflexion
The electric current's true direction.

It may be that it does not move,
   Or moves but for some other reason;
Then let it be your boast to prove
   (Though some may think it out of season,
And worthy of a fossil Druid),
That there is no Electric Fluid.

To Hermann Stoffkraft, Ph.D.,
the Hero of a recent work called 'Paradoxical Philosophy'

A PARADOXICAL ODE (1878)
[After Shelley]

I

My soul is an entangled knot,
Upon a liquid vortex wrought
By Intellect, in the Unseen residing,
   And thine doth like a convict sit,
   With marlinspike* untwisting it,
Only to find its knottiness abiding;
    Since all the tools for its untying
    In four-dimensioned space are lying,
    Wherein thy fancy intersperses
    Long avenues of universes,
    While Klein and Clifford fill the void
    With one finite, unbounded homaloid,*
And think the Infinite is now at last destroyed.

II

But when thy Science lifts her pinions
In Speculation's wild dominions,
We treasure every dictum thou emittest,
While down the stream of Evolution
We drift, expecting no solution
But that of the survival of the fittest.
Till, in the twilight of the gods,
When earth and sun are frozen clods,
When, all its energy degraded,
Matter to aether shall have faded;
We, that is, all the work we've done,
As waves in aether, shall for ever run
In ever-widening spheres through heavens beyond the sun.

III

Great Principle of all we see,
Unending Continuity!
By thee are all our angles sweetly rounded,
By thee are our misfits adjusted,
And as I still in thee have trusted,
So trusting, let me never be confounded!
Oh never may direct Creation
Break in upon my contemplation;
Still may thy causal chain, ascending,
Appear unbroken and unending,
While Residents in the Unseen—
Aeons and Emanations—intervene,
And from my shrinking soul the Unconditioned screen.

WILLIAM THOMSON, LORD KELVIN

The Sorting Demon of Maxwell (1879)

The word 'demon,' which originally in Greek meant a supernatural
being, has never been properly used as signifying a real or ideal
personification of malignity.

Clerk Maxwell's 'demon' is a creature of imagination having

certain perfectly well-defined powers of action, purely mechanical in their character, invented to help us to understand the 'Dissipation of Energy' in nature.

He is a being with no preternatural qualities, and differs from real living animals only in extreme smallness and agility. He can at pleasure stop, or strike, or push, or pull any single atom of matter, and so moderate its natural course of motion. Endowed ideally with arms and hands and fingers—two hands and ten fingers suffice—he can do as much for atoms as a pianoforte player can do for the keys of the piano—just a little more, he can push or pull each atom *in any direction.*

He cannot create or annul energy; but just as a living animal does, he can store up limited quantities of energy, and reproduce them at will. By operating selectively on individual atoms he can reverse the natural dissipation of energy, can cause one half of a closed jar of air, or of a bar of iron, to become glowing hot and the other ice-cold; can direct the energy of the moving molecules of a basin of water to throw the water up to a height and leave it there proportionately cooled (1 deg. Fahrenheit for 772 ft. of ascent); can 'sort' the molecules in a solution of salt or in a mixture of two gases, so as to reverse the natural process of diffusion, and produce concentration of the solution in one portion of the water, leaving pure water in the remainder of the space occupied; or, in the other case, separate the gases into different parts of the containing vessel.

'Dissipation of Energy' follows in nature from the fortuitous concourse of atoms. The lost motivity is essentially not restorable otherwise than by an agency dealing with individual atoms; and the mode of dealing with the atoms to restore motivity is essentially a process of assortment, sending this way all of one kind or class, that way all of another kind or class.

The classification, according to which the ideal demon is to sort them, may be according to the essential character of the atom; for instance, all atoms of hydrogen to be let go to the left, or stopped from crossing to the right, across an ideal boundary; or it may be according to the velocity each atom chances to have when it approaches the boundary: if greater than a certain stated amount, it is to go to the right; if less, to the left. This latter rule of assortment, carried into execution by the demon, disequalises temperature and undoes the natural diffusion of heat; the former undoes the natural diffusion of matter.

By a combination of the two processes, the demon can decompose water or carbonic acid, first raising a portion of the compound to dissociational temperature (that is, temperature so high that collisions shatter the compound molecules to atoms), and then sending the oxygen atoms this way, and the hydrogen or carbon atoms that way; or he may effect decomposition against chemical affinity otherwise, thus:—Let him take in a small store of energy by resisting the mutual approach of two compound molecules, letting them press as it were on his two hands, and store up energy as in a bent spring; then let him apply the two hands between the oxygen and the double hydrogen constituents of a compound molecule of vapour of water, and tear them asunder. He may repeat this process until a considerable proportion of the whole number of compound molecules in a given quantity of vapour of water, given in a fixed closed vessel, are separated into oxygen and hydrogen at the expense of energy taken from translational motions. The motivity (or energy for motive power) in the explosive mixture of oxygen and hydrogen of the one case, and the separated mutual combustibles, carbon and oxygen, of the other case, thus obtained, is a transformation of the energy found in the substance in the form of kinetic energy of the thermal motions of the compound molecules. Essentially different is the decomposition of carbonic acid and water, in the natural growth of plants, the resulting motivity of which is taken from the undulations of light or radiant heat, emanating from the intensely hot matter of the sun.

The conception of the 'sorting demon' is merely mechanical, and is of great value in purely physical science. It was not invented to help us to deal with questions regarding the influence of life and of mind on the motions of matter, questions essentially beyond the range of mere dynamics.

THOMAS HARDY

From *Two on a Tower* (1882)

He brought a little lantern from the cabin, and lighted her up the winding staircase to the temple of that sublime mystery on whose threshold he stood as priest.

The top of the column was quite changed. The tub-shaped space within the parapet, formerly open to the air and sun, was now arched over by a light dome of lath-work covered with felt. But this dome was not fixed. At the line where its base descended to the parapet there were half a dozen iron balls, precisely like cannon-shot, standing loosely in a groove, and on these the dome rested its whole weight. In the side of the dome was a slit, through which the wind blew and the North Star beamed, and towards it the end of the great telescope was directed. This latter magnificent object, with its circles, axes, and handles complete, was securely fixed in the middle of the floor.

'But you can only see one part of the sky through that slit,' said she.

The astronomer stretched out his arm, and the whole dome turned horizontally round, running on the balls with a rumble like that of nearing thunder. Instead of the star Polaris, which had first been peeping in upon them through the slit, there now appeared the countenances of Castor and Pollux.* Swithin then manipulated the equatorial, and put it through its capabilities in like manner. . . .

Then they proceeded to scan the sky, roving from planet to star, from single stars to double stars, from double to coloured stars, in the cursory manner of the merely curious. They plunged down to that at other times invisible stellar multitude in the back rows of the celestial theatre: remote layers of constellations whose shapes were new and singular; pretty twinklers which for infinite ages had spent their beams without calling forth from a single earthly poet a single line, or being able to bestow a ray of comfort on a single benighted traveller.

'And to think,' said Lady Constantine, 'that the whole race of shepherds, since the beginning of the world,—even those immortal shepherds who watched near Bethlehem,—should have gone into their graves without knowing that for one star that lighted them in their labours, there were a hundred as good behind trying to do so! . . . I have a feeling for this instrument not unlike the awe I should feel in the presence of a great magician in whom I really believed. Its powers are so enormous, and weird, and fantastical, that I should have a personal fear in being with it alone. Music drew an angel down, said the poet; but what is that to drawing down worlds!'

'I often experience a kind of fear of the sky after sitting in the observing-chair a long time,' he answered. 'And when I walk home afterwards I also fear it, for what I know is there, but cannot see, as one naturally fears the presence of a vast formless something that only reveals a very little of itself. That's partly what I meant by saying that magnitude, which up to a certain point has grandeur, has beyond it ghastliness.'

Thus the interest of their sidereal observations led them on, till the knowledge that scarce any other human vision was travelling within a hundred million miles of their own gave them such a sense of the isolation of that faculty as almost to be a sense of isolation in respect of their whole personality, causing a shudder at its absoluteness. At night, when human discords and harmonies are hushed, in a general sense, for the greater part of twelve hours, there is nothing to moderate the blow with which the infinitely great, the stellar universe, strikes down upon the infinitely little, the mind of the beholder; and this was the case now. Having got closer to immensity than their fellow-creatures, they saw at once its beauty and its frightfulness. They more and more felt the contrast between their own tiny magnitudes and those among which they had recklessly plunged, till they were oppressed with the presence of a vastness they could not cope with even as an idea, and which hung about them like a nightmare.

He stood by her while she observed; she by him when they changed places. Once that Swithin's emancipation from a trammelling body had been effected by the telescope, and he was well away in space, she felt her influence over him diminishing to nothing. He was quite unconscious of his terrestrial neighbourings, and of herself as one of them. It still further reduced her towards unvarnished simplicity in her manner to him.

The silence was broken only by the ticking of the clock-work which gave diurnal motion to the instrument. The stars moved on, the end of the telescope followed, but their tongues stood still. To expect that he was ever voluntarily going to end the pause by speech was apparently futile. She laid her hand upon his arm.

He started, withdrew his eye from the telescope, and brought himself back to the earth by a visible—almost painful—effort.

'Do come out of it,' she coaxed, with a softness in her voice which any man but unpractised Swithin would have felt to be exquisite. 'I feel that I have been so foolish as to put in your hands an instrument to effect my own annihilation. Not a word have you spoken for the last ten minutes.'

'I have been mentally getting on with my great theory. I hope soon to be able to publish it to the world. What, are you going? I will walk with you, Lady Constantine. When will you come again?'

'When your great theory is published to the world.'

RICHARD A. PROCTOR

The Photographic Eyes of Science (1883)

To the poet of old, who could judge only by what his eyes showed him, the starlit heavens, the moon walking in brightness, the sun rejoicing as a giant to run his course, the planets, which

> Seemed to move,
> Carrying through ether in perpetual round
> Decrees and resolutions of the gods,*

stood first among the wonders and the mysteries of nature. 'The heavens declare the glory of God, the firmament sheweth his handy-work,' was no vain saying, even among men who could know but a small part of the real significance of the scene displayed to their view. For to them the stars were but bright points of light, not suns as they are to us; the sun and moon were but two lamps moving athwart the sky for the benefit of earth, the greater light to rule the day, the lesser light to rule the night; and the strange movements of the planets as they pursue

> Their wandering course—now high, now low, then hid—
> Progressive, retrograde, and standing still,*

had no meaning save in relation to this small earth.

With the invention of the telescope came discoveries which at once gave an entirely new meaning to the celestial scenery. The waves which come from each orb in space, to fall in ordinary course upon that small surface through which light passes to tell its message from without, were now gathered on a larger surface, yet brought, after being so gathered, into the same visual knowledge-field, there to tell of greater wonders than the eye of man had yet seen, or even than it had been given to the mind of man to conceive. For note that before such inventions as have revealed the feebleness of our own unaided senses, men naturally regarded what they saw and heard and felt as all that is; whereas now that stars and suns outside our range of vision have been brought into our ken, there is no limit to the range of our conceptions. We feel that what we now know of the wonders of the star depths may be as utterly insignificant compared with what *is*, as is the starscape seen and estimated by the eye compared with the galaxy revealed by the great Herschelian gauging telescopes.

Nor was it less in what it interpreted than in what it showed that the telescope widened men's conceptions of the universe. It showed the planets as worlds—some greater, some less, than our earth—but all much vaster than the earth as she had been regarded in ancient times. If it did not actually reveal the stars as suns, it taught men very plainly that they are so. The scale of the visible universe was widened enormously at the very time when the visible universe was shown to be but the minutest corner of the real universe.

Yet what the telescope has taught men has been really taught through the eye; only what has been actually seen by telescopic observers can be regarded as so much added to our knowledge. And even that far wider expansion of our knowledge arising from legitimate inference has been attained only by a process of sampling carried on by the eye,—though with its powers increased and in a sense multiplied.

Now the eye is an organ which does certain work in a certain way, which possesses certain powers and certain weaknesses. The telescope may increase its powers in some ways, but in others it cannot help the organ to which it is but an adjunct. For instance, whether with or without telescopic aid the eye requires a certain time to receive and dispose of an impression. It may receive an impression in less than the hundred thousandth part of a second. That it does so is shown when we see a lightning flash; which certainly does not last so long. But it does not dispose of the impression, so as to be ready independently to receive new impressions, in less than the tenth of a second. When we look at a moving body, especially at a body in swift motion, we recognise the difficulties arising from this peculiarity of eyesight; for we find that the mind is quite unable to separate the different impressions received during each tenth of a second, or rather existing simultaneously all the time that we are looking at a swiftly-moving body. If the eye were an absolutely perfect organ, receiving and disposing of each impression in an indefinitely minute portion of time, and if the mind could deal with all the successive images thus conveyed to it, we could see a cannon ball distinctly at every point of its flight, we could watch separately each spoke of a wheel of a swiftly-advancing railway train—nay, the details of a swiftly revolving top or gyroscope could all be as distinctly seen as if the body were at rest.

Thus is the eye defective in that it cannot always with sufficient rapidity deal with the impressions it receives. We shall presently see that in an important class of scientific observations this is not only a defect, but renders the eye absolutely useless for special forms of work. There are cases in science like the case of the ball as it leaves the mouth of the cannon, where the eye does not see *ill*, but *not at all*. There are other cases where it sees the thing that is not,—where scientific observation conducted by the eye alone indicates results as remote from the truth as the apparent stillness of a sleeping top.

The eye has another defect, which, regarding sight as an organ of scientific research, is still more serious. The eye receives an impression, though it does not dispose of it, in a very minute fraction of a second. After that short space of time (too short to be appreciable) has past, the impression received does not increase in strength, though the object observed may be kept in the field of view, unchanged in position, for a much longer time. The brain may, indeed, in the course of time, become conscious of more in the field of view than had been noticed at first; and if the conditions of light, &c., are varying, more may actually become visible; but in the one case all that is finally recognised had been seen (though not noticed) from the beginning; in the latter case all that becomes visible under particular conditions of light and shade is visible at once, not through any gradual strengthening of an impression at first imperfectly received. If the eye could, by continually gazing on an object, gain a continually strengthening impression of the object, more being seen as minute after minute passed, it is obvious that many objects in the heavens which now escape ordinary, or even telescopic vision, might be seen if looked at long enough. A nebula, for instance, so faint as to be quite imperceptible at a momentary view, might be seen after a minute's looking, or (failing that) after ten minutes or an hour of steady gazing. But we know that, so far from this being the case, the eye cannot bear to be directed at the same object for any great length of time. It wearies, the object becomes less and less distinct, and at last the eye is obliged to seek rest. The experiment of looking for awhile at a dark object on a bright ground or *vice versâ*, or at a coloured object, and then turning the eye to a uniform white or light grey surface, shows clearly that the longer the eye is used in steady looking at an object the less clearly it sees the object. For instance, when we turn the eye to the uniform light-tinted surface, we see as a dark object there the bright object we had been looking at; in other words, the part of the retina on which the rays of light from the bright object had fallen has become in a certain degree insensible to the action of light, so that before it was turned from the bright object it received a less brilliant impression than it had at the beginning of the observation.

It is obvious, also, that if by any means one of the defects here considered could be removed or corrected, the other would be increased.

There are, however, other, and for scientific research more serious defects in ordinary vision than those just considered. In observation more than mere seeing is required. It is essential that either a trustworthy record should be taken of what has been seen, or that the memory should be perfect to recall it—to give a faithful picture of what has been seen, or a clear and correct description. Otherwise the observer alone knows what has been seen, and the cause of science—that is, the knowledge of facts by many persons—is not advanced.

In all these three points in which the eye of man is defective, an eye provided by science is practically free from fault, or if it is not yet quite free from fault, promises soon to become so. . . .

We must speak, however, rather of the photographic eyes than of the photographic eye of science. For the eye which takes views in the minutest fraction of a second cannot, clearly, be regarded as the same eye which requires hundreds of thousands of times as long to take a single view; nor can either be regarded as the same eye which, neither with exceeding haste nor with exceeding deliberation, takes just and truthful portraits of celestial objects, seen less truly by the human eye, and either misjudged or misunderstood. With its three eyes—the eye of keenness, the eye of patient watchfulness, and the eye of artistic truth, photography promises to be a Cerberus* to the science of the future, whose watchfulness will prevent the admission of error and detect truths which otherwise would escape us. But, indeed, with photography, spectroscopy, polariscopy,* and other aids, science promises soon to be Argus-eyed.*

WILHELM CONRAD ROENTGEN

On a New Kind of Rays (1895)

If the discharge of a fairly large induction-coil be made to pass
through a Hittorf vacuum-tube, or through a Lenard tube, a Crookes
tube,* or other similar apparatus, which has been sufficiently
exhausted, the tube being covered with thin, black card-board which
fits it with tolerable closeness, and if the whole apparatus be placed
in a completely darkened room, there is observed at each discharge a
bright illumination of a paper screen covered with barium platino-
cyanide, placed in the vicinity of the induction-coil, the fluorescence
thus produced being entirely independent of the fact whether the
coated or the plain surface is turned towards the discharge-tube.
This fluorescence is visible even when the paper screen is at a distance of two metres from the apparatus.

It is easy to prove that the cause of the fluorescence proceeds from
the discharge-apparatus, and not from any other point in the conducting circuit.

The most striking feature of this phenomenon is the fact that an
active agent here passes through a black card-board envelope, which
is opaque to the visible and the ultra-violet rays of the sun or of the
electric arc; an agent, too, which has the power of producing active
fluorescence. Hence we may first investigate the question whether
other bodies also possess this property.

We soon discover that all bodies are transparent to this agent,
though in very different degrees. I proceed to give a few examples:
Paper is very transparent; behind a bound book of about one thousand pages I saw the fluorescent screen light up brightly, the
printers' ink offering scarcely a noticeable hindrance. In the same
way the fluorescence appeared behind a double pack of cards; a
single card held between the apparatus and the screen being almost
unnoticeable to the eye. A single sheet of tin-foil is also scarcely
perceptible; it is only after several layers have been placed over one
another that their shadow is distinctly seen on the screen. Thick
blocks of wood are also transparent, pine boards two or three centimetres thick absorbing only slightly. A plate of aluminium about
fifteen millimetres thick, though it enfeebled the action seriously,
did not cause the fluorescence to disappear entirely. Sheets of hard

rubber several centimetres thick still permit the rays to pass through them. Glass plates of equal thickness behave quite differently, according as they contain lead (flint-glass) or not; the former are much less transparent than the latter. If the hand be held between the discharge-tube and the screen, the darker shadow of the bones is seen within the slightly dark shadow-image of the hand itself. Water, carbon disulphide, and various other liquids, when they are examined in mica vessels, seem also to be transparent. That hydrogen is to any considerable degree more transparent than air I have not been able to discover. Behind plates of copper, silver, lead, gold, and platinum the fluorescence may still be recognized, though only if the thickness of the plates is not too great. Platinum of a thickness of 0.2 millimetre is still transparent; the silver and copper plates may even be thicker. Lead of a thickness of 1.5 millimetres is practically opaque; and on account of this property this metal is frequently most useful. A rod of wood with a square cross-section (20 × 20 millimetres), one of whose sides is painted white with lead paint, behaves differently according as to how it is held between the apparatus and the screen. It is almost entirely without action when the X-rays pass through it parallel to the painted side; whereas the stick throws a dark shadow when the rays are made to traverse it perpendicular to the painted side. In a series similar to that of the metals themselves their salts can be arranged with reference to their transparency, either in the solid form or in solution.

The experimental results which have now been given, as well as others, lead to the conclusion that the transparency of different substances, assumed to be of equal thickness, is essentially conditioned upon their density: no other property makes itself felt like this, certainly to so high a degree.

The following experiments show, however, that the density is not the only cause acting. I have examined, with reference to their transparency, plates of glass, aluminium, calcite, and quartz, of nearly the same thickness; and while these substances are almost equal in density, yet it was quite evident that the calcite was sensibly less transparent than the other substances, which appeared almost exactly alike. No particularly strong fluorescence of calcite, especially by comparison with glass, has been noticed.

All substances with increase in thickness become less transparent. In order to find a possible relation between transparency and thickness, I have made photographs in which portions of the photographic plate were covered with layers of tin-foil, varying in the number of sheets superposed. Photometric measurements of these will be made when I am in possession of a suitable photometer.* . . .

The justification for calling by the name 'rays' the agent which proceeds from the wall of the discharge-apparatus I derive in part from the entirely regular formation of shadows, which are seen when more or less transparent bodies are brought between the apparatus and the fluorescent screen (or the photographic plate).

I have observed, and in part photographed, many shadow-pictures of this kind, the production of which has a particular charm. I possess, for instance, photographs of the shadow of the profile of a door which separates the rooms in which, on one side, the discharge-apparatus was placed, on the other the photographic plate; the shadow of the bones of the hand; the shadow of a covered wire wrapped on a wooden spool; of a set of weights enclosed in a box; of a galvanometer in which the magnetic needle is entirely enclosed by metal; of a piece of metal whose lack of homogeneity becomes noticeable by means of the X-rays, etc.

Another conclusive proof of the rectilinear propagation of the X-rays is a pin-hole photograph which I was able to make of the discharge-apparatus while it was enveloped in black paper; the picture is weak but unmistakably correct.

I have tried in many ways to detect interference phenomena* of the X-rays; but, unfortunately, without success, perhaps only because of their feeble intensity.

Experiments have been begun, but are not yet finished, to ascertain whether electrostatic forces affect the X-rays in any way.

In considering the question what are the X-rays—which, as we have seen, cannot be cathode rays—we may perhaps at first be led to think of them as ultra-violet light, owing to their active fluorescence and their chemical actions. But in so doing we find ourselves opposed by the most weighty considerations. If the X-rays are ultra-violet light, this light must have the following properties:

(*a*) On passing from air into water, carbon disulphide, aluminium, rock-salt, glass, zinc, etc., it suffers no noticeable refraction.

(*b*) By none of the bodies named can it be regularly reflected to any appreciable extent.

(*c*) It cannot be polarized by any of the ordinary methods.

(*d*) Its absorption is influenced by no other property of substances so much as by their density.

That is to say, we must assume that these ultra-violet rays behave entirely differently from the ultra-red, visible, and ultra-violet rays which have been known up to this time.

I have been unable to come to this conclusion, and so have sought for another explanation.

There seems to exist some kind of relationship between the new rays and light rays; at least this is indicated by the formation of shadows, the fluorescence and the chemical action produced by them both. Now, we have known for a long time that there can be in the ether* longitudinal vibrations besides the transverse light-vibrations; and, according to the views of different physicists, these vibrations must exist. Their existence, it is true, has not been proved up to the present, and consequently their properties have not been investigated by experiment.

Ought not, therefore, the new rays to be ascribed to longitudinal vibrations in the ether?

I must confess that in the course of the investigation I have become more and more confident of the correctness of this idea, and so, therefore, permit myself to announce this conjecture, although I am perfectly aware that the explanation given still needs further confirmation.

Telecommunications

SAMUEL F. B. MORSE

Letter to the Hon. Levi Woodbury, Secretary of the US Treasury

New York City University,
September 27, 1837.

Dear Sir: In reply to the inquiries which you have done me the honor to make, in asking my opinion 'of the propriety of establishing a system of telegraphs for the United States,' I would say, in regard to the general question, that I believe there can be scarcely two opinions, in such a community as ours, in regard to the advantage which would result, both to the Government and the public generally, from the establishment of a system of communication by which the most speedy intercourse may be had between the most distant parts of the country. The mail system, it seems to me, is founded on the universally admitted principle that the greater the speed with which intelligence can be transmitted from point to point, the greater is the benefit derived to the whole community. The only question that remains, therefore, is, what system is best calculated, from its completeness and cheapness, to effect this desirable end?

With regard to telegraphs constructed on the ordinary principles,* however perfected within the limits in which they are necessarily confined, the most perfect of them are liable to one insurmountable objection—They are useless the greater part of the time. In foggy weather, and ordinarily during the night, no intelligence can be transmitted. Even when they can transmit, much time is consumed in communicating but little, and that little not always precise.

Having invented an entirely new mode of telegraphic communication, which so far as experiments have yet been made with it, promises results of almost marvelous character, I beg leave to present to the Department a brief account of its characteristics.

About five years ago, on my voyage home from Europe, the electrical experiment of Franklin,* upon a wire some four miles in length, was casually recalled to my mind in a conversation with one of the passengers, in which experiment it was ascertained that the electricity travelled through the whole circuit in a time not appreciable, but apparently instantaneous. It immediately occurred to me that if the presence of electricity could be made visible in any desired part of this circuit, it would not be difficult to construct a system of signs by which intelligence could be instantaneously transmitted. The thought, thus conceived, took strong hold of my mind in the leisure which the voyage afforded, and I planned a system of signs, and an apparatus to carry it into effect. I cast a species of type, which I had devised for this purpose, the first week after my arrival home; and although the rest of the machinery was planned, yet, from the pressure of unavoidable duties, I was compelled to postpone my experiments, and was not able to test the whole plan until within a few weeks. The result has realized my most sanguine expectations.

As I have contracted to have a complete apparatus made to demonstrate at Washington by the 1st of January, 1838, the practicability and superiority of my mode of telegraphic communication by means of electro-magnetism, (an apparatus which I hope to have the pleasure of exhibiting to you,) I will confine myself in this communication to a statement of its peculiar advantages.

First. The fullest and most precise information can be almost instantaneously transmitted between any two or more points, between which a wire conductor is laid: that is to say, no other time is consumed than is necessary to write the intelligence to be conveyed, and to convert the words into the telegraphic numbers. The numbers are then transmitted nearly instantaneously, (or, if I have been rightly informed in regard to some recent experiments in the velocity of electricity, two hundred thousand times more rapidly than light!*) to any distance, where the numbers are immediately recognised, and reconverted into the words of the intelligence.

Second. The same full intelligence can be communicated at any moment, irrespective of the time of day or night, or state of the weather.

This single point establishes its superiority to all other modes of telegraphic communication now known.

Third. The whole apparatus will occupy but little space, (scarcely six cubic feet, probably not more than four;) and it may, therefore, be placed, without inconvenience, in any house.

Fourth. The record of intelligence is made in a permanent manner, and in such a form that it can be at once bound up in volumes convenient for reference if desired.

Fifth. Communications are secret to all but the persons for whom they are intended.

These are the chief advantages of the electro-magnetic telegraph over other kinds of telegraphs, and which must give it the preference, provided the expense and other circumstances are reasonably favorable. . . .

If the circuit is laid through the air the first cost* would doubtless be much lessened. This plan of making the circuit has some advantages, but there are also some disadvantages, the chief of which latter is, that, being always in sight, the temptation to injure the circuit to mischievously disposed persons is greater than [if] the first [wires] were buried out of sight beneath their feet. As an offset, however, to this, an injury to the circuit is more easily detected. With regard to danger from wantonness, it may be sufficient to say that the same objection was originally made in the several cases, successfully of water pipes and railroads and yet we do not hear of wantonness impairing any of these. Stout spars, of some thirty feet in height, well planted in the ground and placed about 350 feet apart, would in this case be required, along the tops of which the circuit might be stretched. Fifteen such spars would be wanted to a mile. This mode would be as cheap probably as any other, unless the laying of the circuit in water should be found most eligible. . . .

The cost of printing in the first instance of a telegraph dictionary should perhaps also be taken into account, as each officer of the government as well as many others would require a copy should this mode of telegraphic communication go into effect. This dictionary would contain a full vocabulary of all the words in common use in the English language, with the numbers regularly affixed to each word.

The stations in the case of this telegraph may be as numerous as are desired, the only additional expenses for that purpose being the adding of the transmitting and receiving apparatus for each station.

The cost of supporting a system of telegraph on this plan (when a circuit is once established) would, in my opinion, be much less than on the common plans, yet, for want of experience in this mode, I would not affirm it positively.

As to the propriety of connecting the system of telegraphs with any existing department of Government, it would seem most natural to connect a telegraphic system with the Post Office Department, for, although it does not carry a mail, it is another mode of accomplishing the principal object for which the mail is established, to wit, the rapid and regular transmission of intelligence. If my system of telegraphs should be established, it is evident that it would have little rest day or night.

The advantages of communicating intelligence instantaneously in hundreds of instances of daily occurrence would warrant such a rate of postage (if it may be so called) as would amply defray all expenses of the first cost of establishing a system and of guarding it and keeping it in repair.

As every word is numbered, an obvious mode of writing might be, a charge of a certain amount for so many numbers. I presume that five words can certainly be transmitted in a minute; for, with the imperfect machinery I now use, I have recorded that rate, at the distance of a half a mile.

In conclusion I would say, that if the perfecting of this new system of telegraphs (which may justly be called the American telegraph, since I can establish my claims to priority in the invention) should be thought of as public utility, and worthy of the attention of the Government, I shall be ready to make any sacrifice of personal service and of time in its accomplishment.

In the meantime I remain, sir, with sincere respect and high personal esteem,

Your most obedient, humble servant,
Sam'l F. B. Morse

Hon. Levi Woodbury
   Secretary of the Treasury
    D.C.

ANONYMOUS

The Telephone (1878)

Of all modern inventions connected with the transmission of tele-graphic signals, the telephone, devised by Mr Alexander Graham Bell, has excited the most wide-spread interest and wonder. Wher-ever Mr Bell has appeared before the public to give an account of his invention and the researches which have led up to it, crowds have assembled to hear him. Nor is this astonishing; for the telephone professes not only to convey intelligible signals to great distances without the use of a battery, but to transmit in facsimile the tones of the human voice, so that a voice shall be as certainly recognised when heard over a distance of a few hundreds of miles as if its owner were speaking in the room by our side. And the telephone does not fall short of its profession. Scientific men have had their wonder and curiosity aroused even more than the unscientific public, since a sci-entific man appreciates the enormous difficulties to be overcome before such an instrument can be realised. Had any hardy speculator a few years ago proposed a telephone which should act on the principle, and be constructed in the form, of Mr Bell's instrument, he would probably have been considered a lunatic. The effects are so marvellous; the exciting causes at first sight so entirely inadequate to produce them. For a telephonic message differs as widely from an ordinary telegraphic message as a highly finished oil-painting differs from a page of print. In the one you have only white and black, black symbols on a white ground, the symbols being limited in number, and recurring again and again with mere differences of order. The painting, on the other hand, discloses every variety of colour and arrangement. No sharp lines of discontinuity offend the eye; on the contrary, the tints shade off gradually and softly into each other, presenting tone and depth in endless variety. The page of print is unintelligible without the aid of a key; the painting tells its story plainly enough to any one who has eyes to see. . . .

No skill or training is required for the effective use of the telephone. The operator has merely to press the instrument to his ear to hear distinctly every sound transmitted from the distant end. For this, it is true, an effort of attention is required, and some persons use the instrument at the first trial with more success than others. Individuals differ in the facility with which they are able to concentrate their attention on one ear, so as to be practically insensible to what goes on around them. But this habit of attention is readily acquired, and when it is once acquired, the telephone may be used by any one who has ears to hear and a tongue to speak. In sending a message, the instrument is held about an inch in front of the mouth, and the sender merely talks into the mouthpiece in his ordinary natural manner. The words are repeated by the instrument at the other end of the circuit with the same pitch, the same cadences, and the same relative loudness. But what strikes one the most is that the *character* of the speaker's voice is faithfully preserved and reproduced. Thus one voice is readily distinguished from another. No peculiarity of inflection is lost. . . .

Now the great interest which attaches to Mr Bell's telephone, and the intense wonder and curiosity it has aroused, are due to its power of conveying absolutely unaltered every peculiarity of voice or musical instrument. A violin note reappears as a violin note; it cannot be mistaken for anything else. And in the case of a human voice, it is not less easy to distinguish one speaker from another than it would be if the speakers were in the room close by instead of being miles or even hundreds of miles away. This is the charm of the new telephone; this it is which renders it immeasurably superior to anything of the kind which preceded it.

Mr Bell's researches in electric telephony began with the artificial production of musical sounds, suggested by the work in which he was then engaged in Boston, viz., teaching the deaf and dumb to speak. Deaf mutes are dumb merely because they are deaf. There is no local defect to prevent utterance, and Mr Bell has practically demonstrated by two thousand of his own pupils that when the deaf and dumb know how to control the action of their vocal organs, they can articulate with comparative facility. Striving to perfect his system of teaching, it occurred to Mr Bell that if, instead of presenting to the eye of the deaf mute a system of symbols, he could make visible the vibrations of the air, the apparatus might be used as a means of teaching articulation. In this part of his investigations Mr Bell derived great assistance from the phonautograph.* He succeeded in vibrating by the voice a style of wood, about a foot in length, attached to the membrane of the phonautograph; and with this he obtained enlarged tracings of the vibrations of the air, produced by the vowel sounds, upon a plane surface of smoked glass. Mr Bell traced a similarity between the manner in which this piece of wood was vibrated by the membrane of the phonautograph and the manner in which the ossiculae of the human ear were moved by the tympanic membrane. Wishing to construct an apparatus closely resembling the human ear, it was suggested to him by Dr Clarence J. Blake, a distinguished aurist of Boston, that the human ear itself would be still better, and a specimen was prepared. Our readers are aware that the tympanic membrane of the ear is connected with the internal ear by a series of little bones called respectively the malleus, the incus, and the stapes, from their peculiar shapes, and that by their means the vibrations of the tympanic membrane are communicated to the internal ear and the auditory nerves. Mr Bell removed the stapes, and attached to the end of the incus a style of hay about an inch in length. Upon singing into the external artificial ear, the style of hay was thrown into vibration, and tracings were obtained upon a plane surface of smoked glass passed rapidly underneath. The curves so obtained are of great interest, each showing peculiarities of its own dependent upon the vowel sound that is sung. Whilst engaged in these experiments, Mr Bell's attention was arrested by observing the wonderful disproportion which exists between the size and weight of the membrane—no thicker than tissue paper—and the weight of the bones vibrated by it, and he was led to inquire whether a thicker membrane might not be able to vibrate a piece of iron in front of an electro-magnet. The experiment was at once tried. A piece of steel spring was attached to a stretched membrane of gold-beater's skin and placed in front of the pole of the magnet. This answered very well, but it was found that the action of the instrument was improved by increasing the area of metal, and thus the membrane was done away with and an iron plate substituted for it. It was important, at the same time, to determine the effect produced by altering the strength of the magnet; that is, of the current which passed round the coils. The battery was gradually reduced from fifty cells to none at all, and still the effects were observed, but in a less marked degree. The action was in this latter case doubtless due to residual magnetism; hence, in the present form of apparatus a permanent magnet is employed. Lastly, the effect of varying the dimensions of the coil was studied, when it was found that the sounds became louder as its length was diminished; a certain length was, however, ultimately reached, beyond which no improvement was effected, and it was found to be only necessary to enclose one end of the magnet in the coil of wire.

Such was the instrument that Mr Bell sent to the Centennial Exhibition at Philadelphia. The following is the official report of it, signed by Sir William Thomson and others:—

'Mr Alexander Graham Bell exhibits an apparatus by which he has achieved a result of transcendent scientific interest,—a transmission of spoken words by electric currents through a telegraph wire. To obtain this result Mr Bell perceived that he must produce a variation of strength of current as nearly as may be in exact proportion to the velocity of a particle of air moved by the sound, and he invented a method of doing so,—a piece of iron attached to a membrane, and thus moved to and fro in the neighbourhood of an electro-magnet,—which has proved perfectly successful. The battery and wire of this electro-magnet are in circuit with the telegraph wire and the wire of another electro-magnet at the receiving station. This second electro-magnet has a solid bar of iron for core, which is connected at one end by a thick disc of iron to an iron tube surrounding the coil and bar. The free circular end of the tube constitutes one pole of the electro-magnet, and the adjacent free end of the bar core the other. A thin circular iron disc, held pressed against the end of the tube by the electro-magnetic attraction and free to vibrate through a very small space without touching the central pole, constitutes the sounder by which the electric effect is reconverted into sound. With my ear pressed against this disc, I heard it speak distinctly several sentences. . . . I need scarcely say I was astonished and delighted. So were others, including some judges of our group, who witnessed the experiments and verified with their own ears the electric transmission of speech. This, perhaps the greatest marvel hitherto achieved by the electric telegraph, has been obtained by appliances of quite a homespun and rudimentary character. With somewhat more advanced plans and more powerful apparatus, we may confidently expect that Mr Bell will give us the means of making voice and spoken words audible through the electric wire to an ear hundreds of miles distant.'

MARK TWAIN

Mental Telegraphy (1891)

A Manuscript with a History

NOTE TO THE EDITOR.—By glancing over the enclosed bundle of rusty old manuscript, you will perceive that I once made a great discovery: the discovery that certain sorts of things which, from the beginning of the world, had always been regarded as merely 'curious coincidences'—that is to say, accidents—were no more accidental than is the sending and receiving of a telegram an accident. I made this discovery sixteen or seventeen years ago, and gave it a name—'Mental Telegraphy.' It is the same thing around the outer edges of which the Psychical Society of England* began to grope (and play with) four or five years ago, and which they named 'Telepathy.' Within the last two or three years they have penetrated toward the heart of the matter, however, and have found out that mind can act upon mind in a quite detailed and elaborate way over vast stretches of land and water. And they have succeeded in doing, by their great credit and influence, what I could never have done—they have convinced the world that mental telegraphy is not a jest, but a fact, and that it is a thing not rare, but exceedingly common. They have done our age a service— and a very great service, I think.

In this old manuscript you will find mention of an extraordinary experience of mine in the mental telegraphic line, of date about the year 1874 or 1875—the one concerning the Great Bonanza book. It was this experience that called my attention to the matter under consideration. I began to keep a record, after that, of such experiences of mine as seemed explicable by the theory that minds telegraph thoughts to each other. In 1878 I went to Germany and began to write the book called *A Tramp Abroad*.* The bulk of this old batch of manuscript was written at that time and for that book. But I removed it when I came to revise the volume for the press; for I feared that the public would treat the thing as a joke and throw it aside, whereas I was in earnest.

At home, eight or ten years ago, I tried to creep in under shelter of an authority grave enough to protect the article from ridicule—the *North American Review*. But Mr Metcalf was too wary for me.* He said that to treat these mere 'coincidences' seriously was a thing which the *Review* couldn't dare to do; that I must put either my name or my *nom de plume* to the article, and thus save the *Review* from harm. But I couldn't consent to that; it would be the surest possible way to defeat my desire that the public should receive the thing seriously, and be willing to stop and give it some fair degree of attention. So I pigeon-holed the MS, because I could not get it published anonymously.

Now see how the world has moved since then. These small experiences of mine, which were too formidable at that time for admission to a grave magazine—if the magazine must allow them to appear as something above and beyond 'accidents' and 'coincidences'—are trifling and commonplace now, since the flood of light recently cast upon mental telegraphy by the intelligent labors of the Psychical Society. But I think they are worth publishing, just to show what harmless and ordinary matters were considered dangerous and incredible eight or ten years ago. . . .

We are always mentioning people, and in that very instant they appear before us. We laugh, and say, 'Speak of the devil,' and so forth, and there we drop it, considering it an 'accident.' It is a cheap and convenient way of disposing of a grave and very puzzling mystery. The fact is it does seem to happen too often to be an accident.

Now I come to the oddest thing that ever happened to me. Two or three years ago I was lying in bed, idly musing, one morning—it was the 2d of March—when suddenly a red-hot new idea came whistling down into my camp, and exploded with such comprehensive effectiveness as to sweep the vicinity clean of rubbishy reflections, and fill the air with their dust and flying fragments. This idea, stated in simple phrase, was that the time was ripe and the market ready for a certain book; a book which ought to be written at once; a book which must command attention and be of peculiar interest—to wit, a book about the Nevada silver mines. The 'Great Bonanza' was a new wonder then, and everybody was talking about it. It seemed to me that the person best qualified to write this book was Mr William H. Wright,* a journalist of Virginia, Nevada, by whose side I had scribbled many months when I was a reporter there ten or twelve years before. He might be alive still; he might be dead; I could not tell; but I would write him, anyway. I began by merely and modestly suggesting that he make such a book; but my interest grew as I went on, and I ventured to map out what I thought ought to be the plan of the work, he being an old friend, and not given to taking good intentions for ill. I even dealt with details, and suggested the order and sequence which they should follow. I was about to put the manuscript in an envelope, when the thought occurred to me that if this book should be written at my suggestion, and then no publisher happened to want it, I should feel uncomfortable; so I concluded to keep my letter back until I should have secured a publisher. I pigeon-holed my document, and dropped a note to my own publisher, asking him to name a day for a business consultation. He was out of town on a far journey. My note remained unanswered, and at the end of three or four days the whole matter had passed out of my mind. On the 9th of March the postman brought three or four letters, and among them a thick one whose superscription was in a hand which seemed dimly familiar to me. I could not 'place' it at first, but presently I succeeded. Then I said to a visiting relative who was present:

'Now I will do a miracle. I will tell you everything this letter contains—date, signature, and all—without breaking the seal. It is from a Mr Wright of Virginia, Nevada, and is dated the 2d of March—seven days ago. Mr Wright proposes to make a book about the silver mines and the Great Bonanza, and asks what I, as a friend, think of the idea. He says his subjects are to be so and so, their order and sequence so and so, and he will close with a history of the chief feature of the book, the Great Bonanza.'

I opened the letter, and showed that I had stated the date and the contents correctly. Mr Wright's letter simply contained what my own letter, written on the same date, contained, and mine still lay in its pigeon-hole, where it had been lying during the seven days since it was written.

There was no clairvoyance about this, if I rightly comprehend what clairvoyance is. I think the clairvoyant professes to actually *see* concealed writing, and read it off word for word. This was not my case. I only seemed to know, and to know absolutely, the contents of the letter in detail and due order, but I had to *word* them myself. I translated them, so to speak, out of Wright's language into my own.

Wright's letter and the one which I had written to him but never sent were in substance the same.

Necessarily this could not come by accident; such elaborate accidents cannot happen. Chance might have duplicated one or two of the details, but she would have broken down on the rest. I could not doubt—there was no tenable reason for doubting—that Mr Wright's mind and mine had been in close and crystal-clear communication with each other across three thousand miles of mountain and desert on the morning of the 2d of March. I did not consider that both minds *originated* that succession of ideas, but that one mind originated them, and simply telegraphed them to the other. I was curious to know which brain was the telegrapher and which the receiver, so I wrote and asked for particulars. Mr Wright's reply showed that his mind had done the originating and telegraphing and mine the receiving. Mark that significant thing, now; consider for a moment how many a splendid 'original' idea has been unconsciously stolen from a man three thousand miles away! If one should question that this is so, let him look into the cyclopaedia and con once more that curious thing in the history of inventions which has puzzled every one so much—that is, the frequency with which the same machine or other contrivance has been invented at the same time by several persons in different quarters of the globe. The world was without an electric telegraph for several thousand years; then Professor Henry, the American, Wheatstone in England, Morse on the sea, and a German in Munich, all invented it at the same time.* The discovery of certain ways of applying steam was made in two or three countries in the same year. Is it not possible that inventors are constantly and unwittingly stealing each other's ideas whilst they stand thousands of miles asunder?

Last spring a literary friend of mine,* who lived a hundred miles away, paid me a visit, and in the course of our talk he said he had made a discovery—conceived an entirely new idea—one which certainly had never been used in literature. He told me what it was. I handed him a manuscript, and said he would find substantially the same idea in that—a manuscript which I had written a week before. The idea had been in my mind since the previous November; it had only entered his while I was putting it on paper, a week gone by. He had not yet written his; so he left it unwritten, and gracefully made over all his right and title in the idea to me.

The following statement, which I have clipped from a newspaper, is true. I had the facts from Mr Howells's lips when the episode was new:

'A remarkable story of a literary coincidence is told of Mr Howells's *Atlantic Monthly* serial "Dr Breen's Practice." A lady of Rochester, New York, contributed to the magazine, after "Dr Breen's Practice" was in type, a short story which so much resembled Mr Howells's that he felt it necessary to call upon her and explain the situation of affairs in order that no charge of plagiarism might be preferred against him. He showed her the proof-sheets of his story, and satisfied her that the similarity between her work and his was one of those strange coincidences which have from time to time occurred in the literary world.'

I had read portions of Mr Howells's story, both in MS and in proof, before the lady offered her contribution to the magazine.

Here is another case. I clip it from a newspaper:

'The republication of Miss Alcott's novel *Moods* recalls to a writer in the Boston *Post* a singular coincidence which was brought to light before the book was first published. "Miss Anna M. Crane, of Baltimore, published *Emily Chester*, a novel which was pronounced a very striking and strong story.* A comparison of this book with *Moods* showed that the two writers, though entire strangers to each other and living hundreds of miles apart, had both chosen the same subject for their novels, had followed almost the same line of treatment up to a certain point, where the parallel ceased and the dénouements were entirely opposite. And even more curious, the leading characters in both books had identically the same names, so that the names in Miss Alcott's novel had to be changed. Then the book was published by Loring."'

Four or five times within my recollection there has been a lively newspaper war in this country over poems whose authorship was claimed by two or three different people at the same time. There was a war of this kind over 'Nothing to Wear,' 'Beautiful Snow,' 'Rock Me to Sleep, Mother,' and also over one of Mr Will Carleton's* early ballads, I think. These were all blameless cases of unintentional and unwitting mental telegraphy, I judge.

RUDYARD KIPLING

The Deep-Sea Cables (1896)

The wrecks dissolve above us; their dust drops down from afar—
Down to the dark, to the utter dark, where the blind white sea-
　　snakes are.
There is no sound, no echo of sound, in the deserts of the deep,
Or the great gray level plains of ooze where the shell-burred cables
　　creep.

Here in the womb of the world—here on the tie-ribs of earth
　　Words, and the words of men, flicker and flutter and beat—
Warning, sorrow and gain, salutation and mirth—
　　For a Power troubles the Still that has neither voice nor feet.

They have wakened the timeless Things; they have killed their father
　　Time;
　　Joining hands in the gloom, a league from the last of the sun.
Hush! Men talk to-day o'er the waste of the ultimate slime,
　　And a new Word runs between: whispering, 'Let us be one!'

HENRY JAMES

In the Cage (1898)

In James's story, the unnamed protagonist is engaged to Mr Mudge, a
grocer. When she marries, she will be leaving her office and going to live in
Chalk Farm. Because telegraphy offers contact with upper-class clients
and stimulates her imagination, she is not looking forward to getting
married.

It had occurred to her early that in her position—that of a young
person spending, in framed and wired confinement, the life of a
guineapig or a magpie—she should know a great many persons
without their recognising the acquaintance. That made it an emotion
the more lively—though singularly rare and always, even then, with
opportunity still very much smothered—to see any one come in
whom she knew, as she called it, outside, and who could add

something to the poor identity of her function. Her function was to sit there with two young men—the other telegraphist and the counter-clerk; to mind the 'sounder,' which was always going, to dole out stamps and postal orders, weigh letters, answer stupid questions, give difficult change and, more than anything else, count words as numberless as the sands of the sea, the words of the telegrams thrust, from morning to night, through the gap left in the high lattice, across the encumbered shelf that her forearm ached with rubbing. This transparent screen fenced out or fenced in, according to the side of the narrow counter on which the human lot was cast, the duskiest corner of a shop pervaded not a little, in winter, by the poison of perpetual gas and at all times by the presence of hams, cheese, dried fish, soap, varnish, paraffin and other solids and fluids that she came to know perfectly by their smells without consenting to know them by their names.

The barrier that divided the little post-and-telegraph-office from the grocery was a frail structure of wood and wire; but the social, the professional separation was a gulf that fortune, by a stroke quite remarkable, had spared her the necessity of contributing at all publicly to bridge. When Mr Cocker's young men stepped over from behind the other counter to change a five-pound note—and Mr Cocker's situation, with the cream of the 'Court Guide' and the dearest furnished apartments, Simpkin's, Ladle's, Thrupp's, just round the corner, was so select that his place was quite pervaded by the crisp rustle of these emblems—she pushed out the sovereigns as if the applicant were no more to her than one of the momentary appearances in the great procession; and this perhaps all the more from the very fact of the connection—only recognised outside indeed—to which she had lent herself with ridiculous inconsequence. . . .

She was perfectly aware that her imaginative life was the life in which she spent most of her time; and she would have been ready, had it been at all worth while, to contend that, since her outward occupation didn't kill it, it must be strong indeed. Combinations of flowers and green stuff forsooth? What *she* could handle freely, she said to herself, was combinations of men and women. The only weakness in her faculty came from the positive abundance of her contact with the human herd; this was so constant, had the effect of becoming so cheap, that there were long stretches in which inspiration, divination and interest, quite dropped. The great thing was the flashes, the quick revivals, absolute accidents all and neither to be counted on nor to be resisted. Some one had only sometimes to put in a penny for a stamp, and the whole thing was upon her. She was so absurdly constructed that these were literally the moments that made up—made up for the long stiffness of sitting there in the stocks, made up for the cunning hostility of Mr Buckton and the importunate sympathy of the counter-clerk, made up for the daily, deadly, flourishy letter from Mr Mudge, made up even for the most haunting of her worries, the rage at moments of not knowing how her mother did 'get it.'

She had surrendered herself moreover, of late, to a certain expansion of her consciousness; something that seemed perhaps vulgarly accounted for by the fact that, as the blast of the season roared louder and the waves of fashion tossed their spray further over the counter, there were more impressions to be gathered and really—for it came to that—more life to be led. Definite, at any rate, it was that by the time May was well started the kind of company she kept at Cocker's had begun to strike her as a reason—a reason she might almost put forward for a policy of procrastination. It sounded silly, of course, as yet, to plead such a motive, especially as the fascination of the place was, after all, a sort of torment. But she liked her torment; it was a torment she should miss at Chalk Farm. She was ingenious and uncandid, therefore, about leaving the breadth of London a little longer between herself and that austerity. If she had not quite the courage, in short, to say to Mr Mudge that her actual chance for a play of mind was worth, any week, the three shillings he desired to help her to save, she yet saw something happen in the course of the month that, in her heart of hearts at least, answered the subtle question. This was connected precisely with the appearance of the memorable lady.

She pushed in three bescribbled forms which the girl's hand was quick to appropriate, Mr Buckton having so frequent a perverse instinct for catching first any eye that promised the sort of entertainment with which she had her peculiar affinity. The amusements of captives are full of a desperate contrivance, and one of our young friend's ha'pennyworths had been the charming tale of *Picciola*.* It was of course the law of the place that they were never to take no notice, as Mr Buckton said, whom they served; but this also never prevented, certainly on the same gentleman's own part, what he was fond of describing as the underhand game. Both her companions, for that matter, made no secret of the number of favourites they had among the ladies; sweet familiarities in spite of which she had repeatedly caught each of them in stupidities and mistakes, confusions of identity and lapses of observation that never failed to remind her how the cleverness of men ended where the cleverness of women began. 'Marguerite, Regent Street. Try on at six. All Spanish lace. Pearls. The full length.' That was the first; it had no signature. 'Lady Agnes Orme, Hyde Park Place. Impossible to-night, dining Haddon. Opera to-morrow, promised Fritz, but could do play Wednesday. Will try Haddon for Savoy, and anything in the world you like, if you can get Gussy. Sunday, Montenero. Sit Mason Monday, Tuesday. Marguerite awful. Cissy.' That was the second. The third, the girl noted when she took it, was on a foreign form: 'Everard, Hôtel Brighton, Paris. Only understand and believe. 22nd to 26th, and certainly 8th and 9th. Perhaps others. Come. Mary.'

Mary was very handsome, the handsomest woman, she felt in a moment, she had ever seen—or perhaps it was only Cissy. Perhaps it was both, for she had seen stranger things than that—ladies wiring to different persons under different names. She had seen all sorts of things and pieced together all sorts of mysteries. There had once been one—not long before—who, without winking, sent off five over five different signatures. Perhaps these represented five different friends who had asked her—all women, just as perhaps now Mary and Cissy, or one or other of them, were wiring by deputy. Sometimes she put in too much—too much of her own sense; sometimes she put in too little; and in either case this often came round to her afterwards, for she had an extraordinary way of keeping clues. When she noticed, she noticed; that was what it came to. There were days and days, there were weeks sometimes, of vacancy. This arose often from Mr Buckton's devilish and successful subterfuges for keeping her at the sounder whenever it looked as if anything might amuse; the sounder, which it was equally his business to mind, being the innermost cell of captivity, a cage within the cage, fenced off from the rest by a frame of ground glass. The counter-clerk would have played into her hands; but the counter-clerk was really reduced to idiocy by the effect of his passion for her. She flattered herself moreover, nobly, that with the unpleasant conspicuity of this passion she would never have consented to be obliged to him. The most she would ever do would be always to shove off on him whenever she could the registration of letters, a job she happened particularly to loathe. After the long stupors, at all events, there almost always suddenly would come a sharp taste of something; it was in her mouth before she knew it; it was in her mouth now.

To Cissy, to Mary, whichever it was, she found her curiosity going out with a rush, a mute effusion that floated back to her, like a returning tide, the living colour and splendour of the beautiful head, the light of eyes that seemed to reflect such utterly other things than the mean things actually before them; and, above all, the high, curt consideration of a manner that, even at bad moments, was a magnificent habit and of the very essence of the innumerable things—her beauty, her birth, her father and mother, her cousins and all her ancestors—that its possessor couldn't have got rid of if she had wished. How did our obscure little public servant know that, for the lady of the telegrams, this was a bad moment? How did she guess all sorts of impossible things, such as, almost on the very spot, the presence of drama, at a critical stage, and the nature of the tie with the gentleman at the Hôtel Brighton? More than ever before it floated to her through the bars of the cage that this at last was the high reality, the bristling truth that she had hitherto only patched up and eked out—one of the creatures, in fine, in whom all the conditions for happiness actually met and who, in the air they made, bloomed with an unwitting insolence. What came home to the girl was the way the insolence was tempered by something that was equally a part of the distinguished life, the custom of a flower-like bend to the less fortunate—a dropped fragrance, a mere quick breath, but which in fact pervaded and lingered. The apparition was very young, but certainly married, and our fatigued friend had a sufficient store of mythological comparison to recognise the port of Juno.* Marguerite might be 'awful,' but she knew how to dress a goddess.

Pearls and Spanish lace—she herself, with assurance, could see them, and the 'full length' too, and also red velvet bows, which, disposed on the lace in a particular manner (she could have placed them with the turn of a hand), were of course to adorn the front of a black brocade that would be like a dress in a picture. However, neither Marguerite, nor Lady Agnes, nor Haddon, nor Fritz, nor Gussy were what the wearer of this garment had really come in for. She had come in for Everard—and that was doubtless not *his* true name either. If our young lady had never taken such jumps before, it was simply that she had never before been so affected. She went all the way. Mary and Cissy had been round together, in their single superb person, to see him—he must live round the corner; they had found that, in consequence of something they had come, precisely, to make up for or to have another scene about, he had gone off—gone off just on purpose to make them feel it; on which they had come together to Cocker's as to the nearest place; where they had put in the three forms partly in order not to put in the one alone. The two others, in a manner, covered it, muffled it, passed it off. Oh yes, she went all the way, and this was a specimen of how she often went. She would know the hand again any time. It was as handsome and as everything else as the woman herself. The woman herself had, on learning his flight, pushed past Everard's servant and into his room; she had written her missive at his table and with his pen. All this, every inch of it, came in the waft that she blew through and left behind her, the influence that, as I have said, lingered. And among the things the girls was sure of, happily, was that she should see her again.

Bodies and Machines

CHARLES BABBAGE

From *On the Economy of Machinery and Manufactures* (1832)

ON THE DIVISION OF LABOUR

Perhaps the most important principle on which the economy of a manufacture depends, is the *division of labour* amongst the persons who perform the work. The first application of this principle must have been made in a very early stage of society; for it must soon have been apparent, that a larger number of comforts and conveniences could be acquired by each individual, if one man restricted his occupation to the art of making bows, another to that of building houses, a third boats, and so on. This division of labour into trades was not, however, the result of an opinion that the general riches of the community would be increased by such an arrangement; but it must have arisen from the circumstance of each individual so employed discovering that he himself could thus make a greater profit of his labour than by pursuing more varied occupations. Society must have made considerable advances before this principle could have been carried into the workshop; for it is only in countries which have attained a high degree of civilization, and in articles in which there is a great competition amongst the producers, that the most perfect system of the division of labour is to be observed. The various principles on which the advantages of this system depend, have been much the subject of discussion amongst writers on Political Economy; but the relative importance of their influence does not appear, in all cases, to have been estimated with sufficient precision. . . .

As the possibility of performing arithmetical calculations by machinery may appear to non-mathematical readers to be rather too large a postulate, and as it is connected with the subject of the *division of labour*, I shall here endeavour, in a few lines, to give some slight perception of the manner in which this can be done,—and thus to remove a small portion of the veil which covers that apparent mystery.

That nearly all tables of numbers which follow any law, however complicated, may be formed, to a greater or less extent, solely by the proper arrangement of the successive addition and subtraction of numbers befitting each table, is a general principle which can be demonstrated to those only who are well acquainted with mathematics; but the mind, even of the reader who is but very slightly acquainted with that science, will readily conceive that it is not impossible, by attending to the following example.

The subjoined table is the beginning of one in very extensive use, which has been printed and reprinted very frequently in many countries, and is called a *Table of Square Numbers*. Any number in the table, column A, may be obtained, by multiplying the number which expresses the distance of that term from the commencement of the table by itself; thus, 25 is the fifth term from the beginning of the table, and 5 multiplied by itself, or by 5, is equal to 25. Let us now

Terms of the Table	A Table	B First Difference	C Second Difference
1	1		
		3	
2	4		2
		5	
3	9		2
		7	
4	16		2
		9	
5	25		2
		11	
6	36		2
		13	
7	49		

subtract each term of this table from the next succeeding term, and place the results in another column (B), which may be called first-difference column. If we again subtract each term of this first difference from the succeeding term, we find the result is always the number 2, (column C;) and that the same number will always recur in that column, which may be called the second-difference, will appear to any person who takes the trouble to carry on the table a few terms further. Now when once this is admitted, it is quite clear that, provided the first term (1) of the Table, the first term (3) of the first differences, and the first term (2) of the second or constant difference, are originally given, we can continue the table of square numbers to any extent, merely by addition:—for the series of first differences may be formed by repeatedly adding the constant difference (2) to (3) the first number in column B, and we then have the series of numbers, 3, 5, 6, &c.: and again, by successively adding each of these to the first number (1) of the table, we produce the square numbers.

Having thus, I hope, thrown some light upon the theoretical part of the question, I shall endeavour to shew that the mechanical execution of such an engine, as would produce this series of numbers, is not so far removed from that of ordinary machinery as might be conceived. Let the reader imagine three clocks, placed on a table side by side, each having only one hand, and each having a thousand divisions instead of twelve hours marked on the face; and every time a string is pulled, let them strike on a bell the numbers of the divisions to which their hands point. Let him further suppose that two of the clocks, for the sake of distinction called B and C, have some mechanism by which the clock C advances the hand of the clock B one division, for each stroke it makes upon its own bell: and let the clock B by a similar contrivance advance the hand of the clock A one division, for each stroke it makes on its own bell. With such an arrangement, having set the hand of the clock A to the division I, that of B to III, and that of C to II, let the reader imagine the repeating parts of the clocks to be set in motion continually in the following order: viz.—pull the string of clock A; pull the string of clock B; pull the string of clock C.

The following table will then express the series of movements and their results. If now only those divisions struck or pointed at by the clock A be attended to and written down, it will be found that they produce the series of the squares of the natural numbers. Such a series could, of course, be carried by this mechanism only so far as the numbers which can be expressed by three figures; but this may be sufficient to give some idea of the construction,—and was, in fact, the point to which the first model of the calculating-engine, now in progress, extended.

We have seen, then, that the effect of the *division of labour*, both in mechanical and in mental operations, is, that it enables us to purchase and apply to each process precisely that quantity of skill and knowledge which is required for it: we avoid employing any part of the time of a man who can get eight or ten shillings a day by his skill in tempering needles, in turning a wheel, which can be done for sixpence a day; and we equally avoid the loss arising from the employment of an accomplished mathematician in performing the lowest processes of arithmetic. . . .

ON THE EFFECT OF MACHINERY IN REDUCING THE DEMAND FOR LABOUR

One of the objections most frequently urged against machinery is, that it has a tendency to supersede much of the hand-labour which was previously employed; and in fact unless a machine diminished the labour necessary to make an article, it could never come into use. But if it have that effect, its owner, in order to extend the sale of his

Repetitions of Process	Movements	CLOCK A — Hand set to I	CLOCK B — Hand set to III	CLOCK C — Hand set to II
		TABLE	*First difference*	*Second difference*
1	Pull A	A strikes 1	. . . . .	. . . . .
	— B	{ The hand is advanced (by B) 3 divisions . . }	B strikes 3	. . . . .
	— C	. . . .	{ The hand is advanced (by C) 2 divisions . . }	C strikes 2
2	Pull A	A strikes 4	. . . . .	. . . . .
	— B	{ The hand is advanced (by B) 5 divisions . . }	B strikes 5	. . . . .
	— C	. . . .	{ The hand is advanced (by C) 2 divisions . . }	C strikes 2
3	Pull A	A strikes 9	. . . . .	
	— B	{ The hand is advanced (by B) 7 divisions . . }	B strikes 7	
	— C	. . . .	{ The hand is advanced (by C) 2 divisions . . }	C strikes 2
4	Pull A	A strikes 16	. . . . .	
	— B	{ The hand is advanced (by B) 9 divisions . . }	B strikes 9	. . . . .
	— C	. . . .	{ The hand is advanced (by C) 2 divisions . . }	C strikes 2
5	Pull A	A strikes 25	. . . . .	
	— B	{ The hand is advanced (by B) 11 divisions . . }	B strikes 11	. . . . .
	— C	. . . .	{ The hand is advanced (by C) 2 divisions . . }	C strikes 2
6	Pull A	A strikes 36	. . . . .	
	— B	{ The hand is advanced (by B) 13 divisions . . }	B strikes 13	
	— C	. . . .	{ The hand is advanced (by C) 2 divisions . . }	C strikes 2

produce, will be obliged to undersell his competitors; this will induce them also to introduce the new machine, and the effect of this competition will soon cause the article to fall, until the profits on capital, under the new system, shall be reduced to the same rate as under the old. Although, therefore, the use of machinery has at first a tendency to throw labour out of employment, yet the increased demand consequent upon the reduced price, almost immediately absorbs a considerable portion of that labour, and perhaps, in some cases, the whole of what would otherwise have been displaced.

That the effect of a new machine is to diminish the labour required for the production of the *same* quantity of manufactured commodities may be clearly perceived, by imagining a society, in which occupations are not divided, each man himself manufacturing all the articles he consumes. Supposing each individual to labour during ten hours daily, one of which is devoted to making shoes, it is evident that if any tool or machine be introduced, by the use of which his shoes can be made in half the usual time, then each member of the community will enjoy the same comforts as before by only nine and one-half hours' labour.

If, therefore, we wish to prove that the total quantity of labour is not diminished by the introduction of machines, we must have recourse to some other principle of our nature. But the same motive which urges a man to activity will become additionally powerful, when he finds his comforts procured with diminished labour; and in such circumstances, it is probable, that many would employ the time thus redeemed in contriving new tools for other branches of their occupations. He who has habitually worked ten hours a day, will employ the half hour saved by the new machine in gratifying some other want; and as each new machine adds to these gratifications, new luxuries will open to his view, which continued enjoyment will as surely render necessary to his happiness.

In countries where occupations are divided, and where the division of labour is practised, the ultimate consequence of improvements in machinery is almost invariably to cause a greater demand for labour. Frequently the new labour requires, at its commencement, a higher degree of skill than the old; and, unfortunately, the class of persons driven out of the old employment are not always qualified for the new one; so that a certain interval must elapse before the whole of their labour is wanted. This, for a time, produces considerable suffering amongst the working classes; and it is of great importance for their happiness that they should be aware of these effects, and be enabled to foresee them at an early period, in order to diminish, as much as possible, the injury resulting from them.

One very important inquiry which this subject presents is the question,—*Whether it is more for the interest of the working classes, that improved machinery should be so perfect as to defy the competition of hand-labour; and that they should thus be at once driven out of the trade by it; or be gradually forced to quit it by the slow and successive advances of the machine?* The suffering which arises from a quick transition is undoubtedly more intense; but it is also much less permanent than that which results from the slower process: and if the competition is perceived to be perfectly hopeless, the workman will at once set himself to learn a new department of his art. On the other hand, although new machinery causes an increased demand for skill in those who make and repair it, and in those who first superintend its use; yet there are other cases in which it enables children and inferior workmen to execute work that previously required greater skill. In such circumstances, even though the increased demand for the article, produced by its diminished price, should speedily give occupation to all who were before employed, yet the very diminution of the skill required, would open a wider field of competition amongst the working classes themselves.

That machines do not, even at their first introduction, *invariably* throw human labour out of employment, must be admitted; and it has been maintained, by persons very competent to form an opinion on the subject, that they never produce that effect. The solution of this question depends on facts, which, unfortunately, have not yet been collected; and the circumstance of our not possessing the data necessary for the full examination of so important a subject, supplies an additional reason for impressing, upon the minds of all who are interested in such inquiries, the importance of procuring accurate registries, at various times, of the number of persons employed in particular branches of manufacture, of the number of machines used by them, and of the wages they receive.

CHARLES DICKENS

From *Dombey and Son* (1847–8)

Besides telling the story of proud Mr Dombey and his unscrupulous
business manager, Carker, *Dombey and Son* shows how the rapidly growing railways were affecting British society in the 1840s. In the first passage,
Mr Dombey is accompanying his friend, Major Bagstock, on a journey
shortly after the death of Dombey's only son, Paul. The second passage
describes Carker's demise.

He found no pleasure or relief in the journey. Tortured by these
thoughts he carried monotony with him, through the rushing landscape, and hurried headlong, not through a rich and varied country,
but a wilderness of blighted plans and gnawing jealousies. The very
speed at which the train was whirled along, mocked the swift course
of the young life that had been borne away so steadily and so inexor-
ably to its fore-doomed end. The power that forced itself upon its
iron way—its own—defiant of all paths and roads, piercing through
the heart of every obstacle, and dragging living creatures of all
classes, ages, and degrees behind it, was a type of the triumphant
monster, Death.

Away with a shriek, and a roar, and a rattle, from the town, bur-
rowing among the dwellings of men and making the streets hum,
flashing out into the meadows for a moment, mining in through the
damp earth, booming on in darkness and heavy air, bursting out
again into the sunny day so bright and wide; away, with a shriek, and
a roar, and a rattle, through the fields, through the woods, through
the corn, through the hay, through the chalk, through the mould,
through the clay, through the rock, among objects close at hand and
almost in the grasp, ever flying from the traveller, and a deceitful
distance ever moving slowly with him: like as in the track of the
remorseless monster, Death!

Through the hollow, on the height, by the heath, by the orchard,
by the park, by the garden, over the canal, across the river, where the
sheep are feeding, where the mill is going, where the barge is floating, where the dead are lying, where the factory is smoking, where
the stream is running, where the village clusters, where the great
cathedral rises, where the bleak moor lies, and the wild breeze
smooths or ruffles it at its inconstant will; away, with a shriek, and a

roar, and a rattle, and no trace to leave behind but dust and vapour: like as in the track of the remorseless monster, Death!

Breasting the wind and light, the shower and sunshine, away, and still away, it rolls and roars, fierce and rapid, smooth and certain, and great works and massive bridges crossing up above, fall like a beam of shadow an inch broad, upon the eye, and then are lost. Away, and still away, onward and onward ever: glimpses of cottage-homes, of houses, mansions, rich estates, of husbandry and handicraft, of people, of old roads and paths that look deserted, small, and insignificant as they are left behind: and so they do, and what else is there but such glimpses, in the track of the indomitable monster, Death!

Away, with a shriek, and a roar, and a rattle, plunging down into the earth again, and working on in such a storm of energy and perseverance, that amidst the darkness and whirlwind the motion seems reversed, and to tend furiously backward, until a ray of light upon the wet wall shows its surface flying past like a fierce stream. Away once more into the day, and through the day, with a shrill yell of exultation, roaring, rattling, tearing on, spurning everything with its dark breath, sometimes pausing for a minute where a crowd of faces are, that in a minute more are not: sometimes lapping water greedily, and before the spout at which it drinks has ceased to drip upon the ground, shrieking, roaring, rattling through the purple distance!

Louder and louder yet, it shrieks and cries as it comes tearing on resistless to the goal: and now its way, still like the way of Death, is strewn with ashes thickly. Everything around is blackened. There are dark pools of water, muddy lanes, and miserable habitations far below. There are jagged walls and falling houses close at hand, and through the battered roofs and broken windows, wretched rooms are seen, where want and fever hide themselves in many wretched shapes, while smoke, and crowded gables, and distorted chimneys, and deformity of brick and mortar penning up deformity of mind and body, choke the murky distance. As Mr Dombey looks out of his carriage window, it is never in his thoughts that the monster who has brought him there has let the light of day in on these things: not made or caused them. It was the journey's fitting end, and might have been the end of everything; it was so ruinous and dreary.

So, pursuing the one course of thought, he had the one relentless monster still before him. All things looked black, and cold, and deadly upon him, and he on them. He found a likeness to his misfortune everywhere. There was a remorseless triumph going on about him, and it galled and stung him in his pride and jealousy, whatever form it took: though most of all when it divided with him the love and memory of his lost boy. . . .

[Carker] had thought, in his dream, of going down into a remote Country-place he knew, and lying quiet there, while he secretly informed himself of what transpired, and determined how to act. Still in the same stunned condition, he remembered a certain station on the railway, where he would have to branch off to his place of destination, and where there was a quiet Inn. Here, he indistinctly resolved to tarry and rest.

With this purpose he slunk into a railway carriage as quickly as he could, and lying there wrapped in his cloak as if he were asleep, was soon borne far away from the sea, and deep into the inland green. Arrived at his destination he looked out, and surveyed it carefully. He was not mistaken in his impression of the place. It was a retired spot, on the borders of a little wood. Only one house, newly-built or altered for the purpose, stood there, surrounded by its neat garden; the small town that was nearest, was some miles away. Here he alighted then; and going straight into the tavern, unobserved by any one, secured two rooms up-stairs communicating with each other, and sufficiently retired.

His object was, to rest, and recover the command of himself, and the balance of his mind. Imbecile discomfiture and rage—so that, as he walked about his room, he ground his teeth—had complete possession of him. His thoughts, not to be stopped or directed, still wandered where they would, and dragged him after them. He was stupified, and he was wearied to death.

But, as if there were a curse upon him that he should never rest again, his drowsy senses would not lose their consciousness. He had no more influence with them, in this regard, than if they had been another man's. It was not that they forced him to take note of present sounds and objects, but that they would not be diverted from the whole hurried vision of his journey. It was constantly before him all at once. She stood there, with her dark disdainful eyes again upon him; and he was riding on nevertheless, through town and country, light and darkness, wet weather and dry, over road and pavement, hill and valley, height and hollow, jaded and scared by the monotony of bells, and wheels, and horses' feet, and no rest.

'What day is this?' he asked of the waiter, who was making preparations for his dinner.

'Day, Sir?'

'Is it Wednesday?'

'Wednesday, Sir! No, Sir. Thursday, Sir.'

'I forgot. How goes the time? My watch is unwound.'

'Wants a few minutes of five o'clock, Sir. Been travelling a long time, Sir, perhaps?'

'Yes.'

'By rail, Sir?'

'Yes.'

'Very confusing, Sir. Not much in the habit of travelling by rail myself, Sir, but gentlemen frequently say so.'

'Do many gentlemen come here?'

'Pretty well, Sir, in general. Nobody here at present. Rather slack just now, Sir. Everything *is* slack, Sir.'

He made no answer; but had risen into a sitting posture on the sofa where he had been lying, and leaned forward, with an arm on each knee, staring at the ground. He could not master his own attention for a minute together. It rushed away where it would, but it never, for an instant, lost itself in sleep.

He drank a quantity of wine after dinner, in vain. No such artificial means would bring sleep to his eyes. His thoughts, more incoherent, dragged him more unmercifully after them—as if a wretch, condemned to such expiation, were drawn at the heels of wild horses. No oblivion, and no rest.

How long he sat, drinking and brooding, and being dragged in imagination hither and thither, no one could have told less correctly than he. But he knew that he had been sitting a long time by candlelight, when he started up and listened, in a sudden terror.

For now, indeed, it was no fancy. The ground shook, the house rattled, the fierce impetuous rush was in the air! He felt it come up, and go darting by; and even when he had hurried to the window, and saw what it was, he stood, shrinking from it, as if it were not safe to look.

A curse upon the fiery devil, thundering along so smoothly,

tracked through the distant valley by a glare of light and lurid smoke, and gone! He felt as if he had been plucked out of its path, and saved from being torn asunder. It made him shrink and shudder even now, when its faintest hum was hushed, and when the lines of iron road he could trace in the moonlight, running to a point, were as empty and as silent as a desert.

Unable to rest, and irresistibly attracted—or he thought so—to this road, he went out, and lounged on the brink of it, marking the way the train had gone, by the yet smoking cinders that were lying in its track. After a lounge of some half-hour in the direction by which it had disappeared, he turned and walked the other way—still keeping to the brink of the road—past the inn garden, and a long way down; looking curiously at the bridges, signals, lamps, and wondering when another Devil would come by.

A trembling of the ground, and quick vibration in his ears; a distant shriek; a dull light advancing, quickly changed to two red eyes, and a fierce fire, dropping glowing coals; an irresistible bearing on of a great roaring and dilating mass; a high wind, and a rattle—another come and gone, and he holding to a gate, as if to save himself!

He waited for another, and for another. He walked back to his former point, and back again to that, and still, through the wearisome vision of his journey, looked for these approaching monsters. He loitered about the station, waiting until one should stay to call there; and when one did, and was detached for water, he stood parallel with it, watching its heavy wheels and brazen front, and thinking what a cruel power and might it had. Ugh! To see the great wheels slowly turning, and to think of being run down and crushed! . . .

The air struck chill and comfortless as it breathed upon him. There was a heavy dew; and, hot as he was, it made him shiver. After a glance at the place where he had walked last night, and at the signal-lights burning feebly in the morning, and bereft of their significance, he turned to where the sun was rising, and beheld it, in its glory, as it broke upon the scene.

So awful, so transcendent in its beauty, so divinely solemn. As he cast his faded eyes upon it, where it rose, tranquil and serene, unmoved by all the wrong and wickedness on which its beams had shone since the beginning of the world, who shall say that some weak sense of virtue upon Earth, and its reward in Heaven, did not manifest itself, even to him? If ever he remembered sister or brother with a touch of tenderness and remorse, who shall say it was not then?

He needed some such touch then. Death was on him. He was marked off from the living world, and going down into his grave.

He paid the money for his journey to the country-place he had thought of; and was walking to and fro, alone, looking along the lines of iron, across the valley in one direction, and towards a dark bridge near at hand in the other; when, turning in his walk, where it was bounded by one end of the wooden stage on which he paced up and down, he saw the man from whom he had fled, emerging from the door by which he himself had entered there. And their eyes met.

In the quick unsteadiness of the surprise, he staggered, and slipped on to the road below him. But recovering his feet immediately, he stepped back a pace or two upon that road, to interpose some wider space between them, and looked at his pursuer, breathing short and quick.

He heard a shout—another—saw the face change from its vindictive passion to a faint sickness and terror—felt the earth tremble—knew in a moment that the rush was come—uttered a shriek—looked round—saw the red eyes, bleared and dim, in the daylight, close upon him—was beaten down, caught up, and whirled away upon a jagged mill, that spun him round and round, and struck him limb from limb, and licked his stream of life up with its fiery heat, and cast his mutilated fragments in the air.

HERMANN VON HELMHOLTZ

On the Conservation of Force (1847)

Originally delivered as a lecture to the Berlin Physical Society on 23 July 1847.

Reason we call that faculty innate in us of discovering laws and applying them with thought. For the unfolding of the peculiar forces of pure reason in their entire certainty and in their entire bearing, there is no more suitable arena than inquiry into nature in the wider sense, the mathematics included. And it is not only the pleasure at the successful activity of one of our most essential mental powers; and the victorious subjections to the power of our thought and will of an external world, partly unfamiliar, and partly hostile, which is the reward of this labour; but there is a kind, I might almost say, of artistic satisfaction, when we are able to survey the enormous wealth of Nature as a regularly-ordered whole—a kosmos, an image of the logical thought of our own mind.

The last decades of scientific development have led us to the recognition of a new universal law of all natural phenomena, which, from its extraordinarily extended range, and from the connection which it constitutes between natural phenomena of all kinds, even of the remotest times and the most distant places, is especially fitted to give us an idea of what I have described as the character of the natural sciences, which I have chosen as the subject of this lecture.

This law is *the Law of the Conservation of Force*, a term the meaning of which I must first explain. It is not absolutely new; for individual domains of natural phenomena it was enunciated by Newton and Daniel Bernoulli; and Rumford and Humphry Davy* have recognised distinct features of its presence in the laws of heat.

The possibility that it was of universal application was first stated by Dr Julius Robert Mayer, a Schwabian physician (now living in Heilbronn) in the year 1842, while almost simultaneously with, and independently of him, James Prescot Joule,* an English manufacturer, made a series of important and difficult experiments on the relation of heat to mechanical force, which supplied the chief points in which the comparison of the new theory with experience was still wanting.

The law in question asserts, that the *quantity of force which can be brought into action in the whole of Nature is unchangeable*, and can neither be increased nor diminished. My first object will be to explain to you what is understood by *quantity of force*; or as the same idea is more popularly expressed with reference to its technical application, what we call *amount of work* in the mechanical sense of the word.

The idea of work for machines, or natural processes, is taken from comparison with the working power of man; and we can therefore best illustrate from human labour, the most important features of the question with which we are concerned. In speaking of the work of machines, and of natural forces, we must, of course, in this comparison eliminate anything in which activity of intelligence comes into play. The latter is also capable of the hard and intense work of thinking, which tries a man just as muscular exertion does. But whatever of the actions of intelligence is met with in the work of machines, of course is due to the mind of the constructor and cannot be assigned to the instrument at work.

Now, the external work of man is of the most varied kind as regards the force or ease, the form and rapidity, of the motions used on it, and the kind of work produced. But both the arm of the blacksmith who delivers his powerful blows with the heavy hammer, and that of the violinist who produces the most delicate variations in sound, and the hand of the lace-maker who works with threads so fine that they are on the verge of the invisible, all these acquire the force which moves them in the same manner and by the same organs, namely, the muscles of the arm. An arm the muscles of which are lamed is incapable of doing any work; the moving force of the muscle must be at work in it, and these must obey the nerves, which bring to them orders from the brain. That member is then capable of the greatest variety of motions; it can compel the most varied instruments to execute the most diverse tasks.

Just so is it with machines: they are used for the most diversified arrangements. We produce by their agency an infinite variety of movements, with the most various degrees of force and rapidity, from powerful steam-hammers and rolling-mills, where gigantic masses of iron are cut and shaped like butter, to spinning and weaving-frames, the work of which rivals that of the spider. Modern mechanism has the richest choice of means of transferring the motion of one set of rolling wheels to another with greater or less velocity; of changing the rotating motion of wheels into the up-and-down motion of the piston-rod, of the shuttle, of falling hammers and stamps; or, conversely, of changing the latter into the former; or it can, on the other hand, change movements of uniform into those of varying velocity, and so forth. Hence this extraordinarily rich utility of machines for so extremely varied branches of industry. But one thing is common to all these differences; they all need a *moving force*, which sets and keeps them in motion, just as the works of the human hand all need the moving force of the muscles.

Now, the work of the smith requires a far greater and more intense exertion of the muscles than that of the violin-player; and there are in machines corresponding differences in the power and duration of the moving force required. These differences, which correspond to the different degree of exertion of the muscles in human labour, are alone what we have to think of when we speak of the *amount of work* of a machine. We have nothing to do here with the manifold character of the actions and arrangements which the machines produce; we are only concerned with an expenditure of force.

This very expression which we use so fluently, 'expenditure of force,' which indicates that the force applied has been expended and lost, leads us to a further characteristic analogy between the effects of the human arm and those of machines. The greater the exertion, and the longer it lasts, the more is the arm *tired*, and the more *is the store of its moving force for the time exhausted*. We shall see that this peculiarity of becoming exhausted by work is also met with in the moving forces of inorganic nature; indeed, that this capacity of the human arm of being tired is only one of the consequences of the law with which we are now concerned. When fatigue sets in, recovery is needed, and this can only be effected by rest and nourishment. We shall find that also in the inorganic moving forces, when their capacity for work is spent, there is a possibility of reproduction, although in general other means must be used to this end than in the case of the human arm.

From the feeling of exertion and fatigue in our muscles, we can form a general idea of what we understand by amount of work; but we must endeavour, instead of the indefinite estimate afforded by this comparison, to form a clear and precise idea of the standard by which we have to measure the amount of work. This we can do better by the simplest inorganic moving forces than by the actions of our muscles, which are a very complicated apparatus, acting in an extremely intricate manner.

SAMUEL BUTLER

From *Erewhon* (1872)

'It can be answered that even though machines should hear never so well and speak never so wisely, they will still always do the one or the other for our advantage and not for their own; that man will be the ruling spirit and the machine the servant; that as soon as a machine fails to discharge the service which men expect from it, it is doomed to extinction; that the machines stand to man simply in the relation of lower animals, the vapour engine itself being only a more economical kind of horse; so that instead of being likely to be developed into a higher kind of life than man's, they owe their very existence and progress to their power of ministering to human wants, and must therefore both now and ever be man's inferiors.

'This is all very well. But the servant glides by imperceptible approaches into the master; and we have come to such a pass that even now man must suffer terribly on ceasing to benefit the machines. If all machines were to be annihilated at one moment, so that not a knife nor lever nor rag of clothing nor anything whatsoever were left to man but his bare body alone that he was born with, and if all knowledge of mechanical laws were taken from him so that he could make no more machines, and all machine-made food destroyed so that the race of man should be left as it were naked upon a desert island, we should become extinct in six weeks. A few miserable individuals might linger, but even these in a year or two would become worse than monkeys. Man's very soul is due to the machines; it is a machine-made thing: he thinks as he thinks and feels as he feels through the work that machines have wrought upon him, and their existence is quite as much a *sine quâ non* for his, as his for theirs. This fact precludes us from proposing the complete annihilation of machinery, but surely it indicates that we should destroy as many of them as we can possibly dispense with, lest they should tyrannise over us even more completely. It is true, from a low materialistic point of view, it would seem that those thrive best who use machinery wherever its use is possible with profit; but this is the art of the machines—they serve that they may rule. They bear no malice towards man for destroying a whole race of them provided he creates a better instead; on the contrary, they reward him liberally for having hastened their development. It is for neglecting them that he incurs their wrath, or for using inferior machines, or for not making sufficient exertions to invent new ones, or for destroying them without replacing them; yet this is what we must do, and do quickly; for though our rebellion against their infant power will cause infinite suffering, what will not things come to, if that rebellion is delayed?

'They have preyed upon man's grovelling preference for his

material over his spiritual interests, and have betrayed him into supplying that element of struggle and warfare without which no race
can advance. The lower animals progress because they struggle with
one another; the weaker die, the stronger breed and transmit their
strength. The machines being of themselves unable to struggle, have
got man to do their struggling for them: as long as he fulfils this
function duly, all goes well with him—at least he thinks so; but the
moment he fails to do his best for the advancement of machinery by
encouraging the good and destroying the bad, he is left behind in the
race of competition; and this means that he will be made uncomfortable in a variety of ways, and perhaps that he will die. So that even
now the machines will only serve on condition of being served, and
that too upon their own terms; the moment their terms are not
complied with, they jib, and either smash both themselves and all
whom they can reach, or turn churlish and refuse to work at all. How
many men at this hour are living in a state of bondage to the
machines? How many spend their whole lives, from the cradle to
the grave, in tending them by night and day? Is it not plain
that the machines are gaining ground upon us, when we reflect on
the increasing number of those who are bound down to them as
slaves, and of those who devote their whole souls to the advancement
of the mechanical kingdom?

'The vapour-engine must be fed with food and consume it by fire
even as man consumes it; it supports its combustion by air as man
supports it; it has a pulse and circulation as man has. It may be
granted that man's body is as yet the more versatile of the two, but
then man's body is an older thing; give the steam-engine but half the
time that man has had, give it also a continuance of our present
infatuation, and what may it not ere long attain to?

'There are certain functions indeed of the vapour-engine which
would probably remain unchanged for myriads of years—which in
fact would perhaps survive when the use of vapour had been super-
seded: the piston and cylinder, the beam, the fly-wheel, and other
parts of the machine would be probably permanent, just as we see
that man and many of the lower animals share like modes of eating,
drinking, and sleeping; thus they have hearts which beat as ours,
veins and arteries, eyes, ears, and noses; they sigh even in their sleep,
and weep and yawn; they are affected by their children; they feel
pleasure and pain, hope, fear, anger, shame; they have memory and

prescience, they know that if certain things happen to them they will die, and they fear death as much as we do: they communicate their thoughts to one another, and some of them deliberately act in concert. The comparison of similarities is endless: I only make it because some may say that the steam-engine not being likely to improve in the main particulars is unlikely to be henceforward extensively modified at all. This is too good to be true: it would be modified and suited for an infinite variety of purposes, as much as man has been modified so as to exceed the brutes in skill. In the meantime the stoker is almost as much a cook for his engine as our own cooks for ourselves. Consider also the colliers and pitmen and coal merchants and coal trains and the men who drive them and the ships that carry coals—what an army of servants do the machines thus employ! Are there not probably more men engaged in tending machinery than in tending men? Do not machines eat as it were by mannery? Are we not ourselves creating our successors in the supremacy of the earth? daily adding to the beauty and delicacy of their organisation, daily giving them greater skill and supplying more and more of that self-regulating self-acting power which will be better than intellect itself?

'What a new thing it is for a machine to feed at all! The plough, the spade, and the cart must eat through man's stomach; the fuel that sets them going must burn in the furnace of a man or of horses. Man must consume bread and meat or he cannot dig; the bread and meat are the fuel which drive the spade. If a plough be drawn by horses, the power is supplied by grass or beans or oats, which being burnt in the belly of the cattle give the power of working: without this fuel the work would cease, as an engine would stop if its furnaces were to go out. A man of science has demonstrated "that no animal has the power of originating mechanical energy, but that all the work done in its life by any animal, and all the heat that has been emitted from it, and the heat which would be obtained by burning the combustible matter which has been lost from its body during life, and by burning its body after death, make up altogether an exact equivalent to the heat which would be obtained by burning as much food as it has used during its life, and an amount of fuel which would generate as much heat as its body if burned immediately after death." How then can it be objected against the future vitality of the machines that they are, in their present infancy, at the beck and call of beings who are themselves incapable of originating mechanical energy?

'The main point however to be observed as affording cause for alarm is, that whereas animals were formerly the only stomachs of the machines, there are now many which have stomachs of their own, and consume their food themselves. This is a great step towards their becoming, if not animate, yet something so near akin to it, as not to differ more widely from our own life than animals do from vegetables. And though man should remain, in some respects, the higher creature, is not this in accordance with the practice of nature, which allows superiority in some things to animals which have, on the whole, been long surpassed? Has she not allowed the ant and the bee to retain superiority over man in the organisation of their communities and social arrangements, the bird in traversing the air, the fish in swimming, the horse in strength and fleetness, and the dog in self-sacrifice?'

WALT WHITMAN

To a Locomotive in Winter (1876)

Thee for my recitative,
Thee in the driving storm even as now, the snow, the winter-day declining,
Thee in thy panoply, thy measur'd dual throbbing and thy beat convulsive,
Thy black cylindric body, golden brass and silvery steel,
Thy ponderous side-bars, parallel and connecting rods, gyrating, shuttling at thy sides,
Thy metrical, now swelling pant and roar, now tapering in the distance,
Thy great protruding head-light fix'd in front,
Thy long, pale, floating vapor-pennants, tinged with delicate purple,
The dense and murky clouds out-belching from thy smoke-stack,
Thy knitted frame, thy springs and valves, the tremulous twinkle of thy wheels,
Thy train of cars behind, obedient, merrily following,
Through gale or calm, now swift, now slack, yet steadily careering;

Type of the modern—emblem of motion and power—pulse of the
    continent,
For once come serve the Muse and merge in verse, even as here I see
    thee,
With storm and buffeting gusts of wind and falling snow,
By day thy warning ringing bell to sound its notes,
By night thy silent signal lamps to swing.

Fierce-throated beauty!
Roll through my chant with all thy lawless music, thy swinging lamps
    at night,
Thy madly-whistled laughter, echoing, rumbling like an earthquake,
    rousing all,
Law of thyself complete, thine own track firmly holding,
(No sweetness debonair of tearful harp or glib piano thine,)
Thy trills of shrieks by rocks and hills return'd,
Launch'd o'er the prairies wide, across the lakes,
To the free skies unpent and glad and strong.

SCIENCES OF THE BODY

In 1882, when Frances Power Cobbe attacked the 'two-faced' advocates of vivisection, she accused scientists of writing one way for each other and quite another for the general public. According to Cobbe, scientists had intentionally developed two different styles for describing their experiments: a technical one that voiced their true motives (i.e. disproving Professor A's theory), and a more general one that stressed their usefulness to society. Written in different languages, their articles were telling vastly different stories.

During the nineteenth century, as the natural and physical sciences established themselves as fields, scientists valued their particular terms because their language helped to establish their identities as scholars. As a result, scientific writing became less accessible to lay readers. But how different is scientific from 'ordinary' or literary writing? Can people writing in the same culture, using the same inherited, highly connotative words to represent their thoughts, really tell such different stories?

These twenty-one accounts of the human body and its maladies illustrate the complex relationship between nineteenth-century scientific and literary writing. On the one hand, as Cobbe contends, their styles are undeniably different. Written in the same language, they appear to be *doing* very different things. But do texts written with the same vocabulary necessarily involve thinking of the same kind? On the other hand, both kinds of writers are trying to answer similar questions. They are disturbed by the same fears, and they are responding to the same cultural challenges, sometimes with the same images and metaphors. While their fields and experiences differ, they share goals as story-tellers: they are writing so that readers can see what they see.

In *The Physical Basis of Mind*, George Henry Lewes attacks 'imaginary anatomy'. He condemns scientists who argue for structures not because they have actually seen them but because these forms would support their theories about how nerves and muscles work. But while Lewes demanded that scientists base their theories on real observations, he agreed with his close friend, the physicist John Tyndall, and his partner, the novelist George Eliot, that imagination played a central role in scientific thinking.

Both the scientific and the literary writers represented here do their utmost to take readers into a scene so that the readers can experience it for themselves. The authors aim to convince, whether describing an unfamiliar situation or an experimental result few people would believe unless they saw it with their own eyes. When Luigi Galvani explains how the nervous system works, he offers vivid pictures of fluids circulating through tubes. He presents his hypothesis of animal electricity by making a comparison, asking readers to picture a muscle as 'an assemblage of Leyden jars'. Sir Edwin Chadwick demands that readers confront not just the sights but the nauseating smells of the slums in 1842, organizing his narrative so that the reader follows eye-witnesses into industrial cities' forbidding alleys. Like Galvani, he uses metaphor to turn his observations into an argument. Given the dungheaps of the slums, he submits, 'who can wonder' that disease spreads like their stench, or that people who live in such conditions are 'infected' with the moral filth of their environment? Chadwick's readers see, hear, and smell whatever the observer does, just as they might vicariously experience the sensations of a fictional character. H. G. Wells makes a similar move in 'The Stolen Bacillus', inviting readers to look through a microscope with his character so that they can see the cholera bacillus as a bacteriologist sees it.

Just as these writers show the importance of creative vision in literature and science, they demonstrate the need for alert, responsible reading. When George Eliot describes Dr Lydgate in *Middlemarch* (1871–2) as 'a cluster of signs for his neighbours' false suppositions', she foreshadows his own limited reading abilities as well as those of his townsmen. Set in the reform years of 1829–32, Eliot's novel suggests that hasty, self-centred readings can have disastrous social repercussions. Like people struggling to make sense of texts, nineteenth-century scientists were professional interpreters, relying on observations and imagined possibilities to make meaning.

When faced with the unknown, both literary and scientific writers created metaphors, not just so that their readers could understand them better, but so that they themselves could make sense of their encounters. To establish new meanings and convince readers of their legitimacy, writers must extrapolate from what is already known. Sir Humphry Davy persuaded readers of the importance of chemistry by showing its relation to better-known fields of knowledge, and Xavier Bichat convinced them that the body is composed of twenty-one tissues by comparing these tissues to chemical elements.

When describing Lydgate's anatomical research in *Middlemarch*, Eliot probes Bichat's metaphor, comparing the tissues first to building materials, then to different kinds of fabric derived from raw silk. By having Lydgate seek the origin of all tissues, Eliot challenges Bichat's comparison. Tissues are living, and one expects living things to have an origin, yet it made little sense—in 1801 or in 1871—to talk about the 'origin' of chemical elements. Getting the metaphor right, Eliot suggests, requires one to think through an idea. If metaphor has epistemological value, in literature or in science, it lies more in the thought the comparison stimulates than in its existence as a formula for future use. With deep irony, Eliot describes Lydgate's failure to 'put the question . . . in the way required by the awaiting answer'. As a whole, Eliot's study of literature and science suggests that there are no awaiting answers. Knowledge develops as one struggles to articulate the questions.

From the time of Bichat's anatomical studies at the century's outset, one intensely debated question was, 'what is the smallest functional unit of life?' Scientific and literary writers argued not just about the answer but about the value of the question. Bichat encouraged people to think of the body in terms of tissues, not organs, and in the late 1830s, German anatomists Mathias Schleiden and Theodor Schwann proposed that all living organisms were composed of semi-autonomous cells. By 1860 the German pathologist Rudolf Virchow had convinced many physicians to study disease at the cellular level, so that George Henry Lewes could protest in 1877 that 'the cell has usurped the place of the tissue'.

What does one gain epistemologically by breaking life down into smaller and smaller units? One can see from Virchow's phrasing, as well as Lewes's, that nineteenth-century scientists and literary writers considering the relationship between the cell and the body had another relationship in mind: that between the individual and society. For Virchow, the body is 'an arrangement of a social kind, in which a number of individual existences are mutually dependent'. While Lewes never denied that bodies were composed of cells, he challenged scientists' deplorable tendency to attribute qualities of entire organisms (consciousness, for instance) to individual sub-units. Like George Eliot, he viewed bodies and societies as highly interconnected webs in which one could explain events only by comprehending the relations among individuals. For Lewes, conceiving of life in terms of tiny sub-units and attributing life functions to these sub-units conveniently freed scientists from having to explain what life was.

But what was being 'usurped' by explanations of life at the cellular level? When nineteenth-century writers debated the relative independence of life's smallest units, they were arguing about the nature and definition of life itself. Did life depend on a non-corporeal vital force or soul, as traditional religious faith would have it, or was life simply a function of the natural body? As physiology gained prestige from the 1830s onward, the natural sciences increasingly claimed the authority to explain how living bodies differed from inanimate matter. Bichat had based his studies of living tissue on the premiss that to understand life, one must investigate death, and Mary Shelley's irresponsible scientist, Victor Frankenstein, takes Bichat literally as he 'dabbled among the unhallowed damps of the grave' to learn 'the principle of life'.

When scientific or literary writers described this principle, they usually did so metaphorically. Galvani had cautiously identified it with electricity—of which Frankenstein, again, makes literal use. The wide popularity of mesmerism, from the late 1830s onward, allowed people in all fields to discuss the body's unknown forces in the language of electromagnetism. In 1867 Walt Whitman attributed a new title to one of the poems in *Leaves of Grass*, originally published in 1855: 'I Sing the Body Electric'. By the 1860s electricity offered both scientists and poets a new way to describe the body's energy.

Like writers seeking to express the 'principle of life', those trying to distinguish its different forms relied upon comparisons. Visual metaphors arose with especially high frequency when writers confronted the problem of how people differed from animals. After the publication of Darwin's *The Origin of Species* in 1859, this issue took on a much greater urgency, and both scientists and literary writers addressed it. Wilkie Collins's and H. G. Wells's depictions of arrogant, sadistic scientists defy popular and scientific attempts to distinguish people from other animals. Both the fiendish Benjulia, who is a mere caricature, and Wells's more complex Moreau show themselves to be of a far lower moral order than the creatures on whom they experiment. Wells's *The Island of Dr Moreau* goes so far as to challenge the psychological criteria for human superiority. His violent, drunken characters display little reason, intelligence, or communicative ability, suggesting that people differ from animals only in degree, not in kind.

Neither Shelley's, nor Collins's, nor Wells's novel condemns science *per se*. To varying degrees, these stories of abusive scientists incorporate the language of contemporary studies, describing particular practitioners' errors in terms that emphasize their activities. In her attack on vivisectionists, Frances Power Cobbe quotes physiologists extensively, using the scientists' own metaphorical descriptions—such as that of a damaged brain as a 'lately-hoed potato field'—to alert readers to the 'real' nature of their experiments. Wilkie Collins describes a servant's memory of a vivisected dog as 'cut[ting] into his heart like a knife'. Like Wells's and Shelley's, Collins's novel condemns only certain kinds of scientists, those who fail to think ahead and consider the value and consequences of their experiments.

As embodied creatures, what right did people have to manipulate and control other organisms? Both scientific and literary writers considered this question. In 1802 Sir Humphry Davy criticized investigators who 'instead of slowly endeavouring to lift up the veil concealing the wonderful phenomena of living nature . . . vainly and presumptuously attempted to tear it asunder'. Even Claude Bernard, who argued eloquently for the value of vivisection, stipulated that experiments must be responsibly designed. Just as scientific and literary writers shared questions, they shared concerns about the ways these questions could be pursued.

The notion of individual rights and responsibilities, which emerged so frequently in debates about cell theory and vivisection, played an essential role in discussions of infectious diseases. As members of commercial, imperialistic cultures, nineteenth-century scientists and literary writers knew how quickly plagues could spread from one part of the world to another. Though written almost sixty years apart, Mary Shelley's *The Last Man* and *The Lancet*'s report about Robert Koch's lectures on cholera show that in a world united by global trade, a disease in any zone is a worldwide problem.

While many contagious diseases threatened Europe during the nineteenth century, I have focused on cholera because it inspired vivid scientific as well as literary descriptions and because these accounts often suggest the writers' prejudices about non-European cultures. Throughout the nineteenth century, cholera remained a dangerous disease. In two outbreaks, one six years after Shelley's narrative and the other eight years after Koch's, it would claim thousands of lives. When nineteenth-century writers tell stories about cholera, they combine traditional myths with realistic modern fears. Like Benjulia and Moreau, the disease is presented as a foreign import.

Mary Shelley, whose mother died of childbed fever, summarizes early nineteenth-century views of disease when she compares her imagined futuristic plague to a destructive fire. On the one hand, according to the classical tradition, fire is domesticated. As a gift from Prometheus—invoked in Shelley's *Frankenstein*—it symbolizes people's ability to tame and exploit natural forces. On the other, it frequently defies human control. By using fire to introduce her account of the plague in *The Last Man*, Shelley presents disease as something that both can and cannot be contained.

Chadwick, Holmes, and particularly Koch reject Shelley's representation of disease as an uncontrollable force of nature. Rather than disproving it, they simply ignore it, so that in their works, the notion that disease can be contained functions more as a premiss than a conclusion. Both in the writings of Chadwick, the traditional hygienist, and Koch, the bacteriologist, people become responsible for their diseases not because they have incurred divine wrath but because they have failed to follow hygienic laws. As the report on Koch's lecture repeats, 'cholera can only be spread by human intercourse'. This view, which slowly gained acceptance during the nineteenth century, gives individuals a new responsibility for disease in the sense that through ignorance or carelessness, they can transmit it to other people. Echoing thoughts that Dr Alexander Gordon had voiced as early as 1795, Oliver Wendell Holmes argued in 1843 that physicians themselves spread childbed fever. 'The existence of a *private pestilence* in the sphere of a single physician,' he wrote, 'should be looked upon, not as a misfortune, but a crime.'

In the 1860s, as Louis Pasteur and Joseph Lister described germs present in the air, they expressed a similar view. Evidence showed that infectious microbes were everywhere and could be transmitted between any two people at any time. H. G. Wells's humorous depiction of class differences in 'The Stolen Bacillus' is ironic considering that the cholera microbe—stolen by a would-be biological terrorist—recognizes no differences of speech or dress. At the same time, bacterial infections could be greatly reduced—though never completely eliminated—by covering wounds, sterilizing instruments, and washing one's hands. Once germ theory became publicly accepted in the mid-1880s, each individual became personally responsible for following hygienic measures. Those who ignorantly spread disease, Koch wrote, would be like the people he observed in India, who were daily performing experiments on one other.

While Edgar Allan Poe's 'The Mask of the Red Death' retains a mythological quality, it conveys this growing understanding of individual identity and responsibility. Certainly, when the 'red death' invades Prince Prospero's palace, it comes as a well-earned punishment. He and his revellers are being castigated for their hubris, but it is a hubris of a modern type. As Eliot and Lewes implied in their descriptions of the body and society, the greatest hubris depicted in nineteenth-century science was a denial of the connections between individuals—a denial that diseases relentlessly rebuked.

Animal Electricity

LUIGI GALVANI

From *De Viribus Electricitatis* (1791)

Although published in 1791, Galvani's *De Viribus Electricitatis* provoked debates that lasted until the mid-nineteenth century. In this work Galvani presented the first widely accepted, highly publicized evidence that living

organisms contained their own intrinsic electricity, a possibility that
inspired many nineteenth-century speculations about how bodies worked.

From what is known and explored thus far, I think it is sufficiently
established that there is electricity in animals, which, with Bartholinus* and others, we may be permitted to call by the general name of
animal electricity. This, if not in all, yet is contained in most parts of
animals; but manifests itself most conspicuously in muscles and
nerves. The peculiar and not previously recognized nature of this
seems to be that it flows from muscles to nerves, or rather from the
latter to the former, and that it traverses there either an arc or a series
of men* or any other conducting bodies which lead from nerves to
muscles by a shorter and quicker way, and flows most speedily
through them from the former to the latter.

From this, moreover, two consequences seem chiefly to ensue,
namely, that the electricity in these parts is, one positive, as we may
believe, the other negative, and that one is wholly distinct in nature
from the other; for when equilibrium is established, there is no
motion, no excursion of electricity, no phenomenon of muscular
contraction.

But forsooth, it is difficult to define in which of the designated
parts one electricity resides, in which the other; whether, for
example, one in muscle, the other in nerve, or both in one and the
same muscle, and from which part it flows. In this obscurity of
things, however, if it is permissible to have an opinion, my mind
inclines towards placing the location of both kinds of electricity in
muscle.

For to obtain muscular contractions grant that it is generally
necessary to apply one extremity of the arc outside of muscles, the
other to muscles, as we have said; but it does not seem to follow
thence, because nerves are rich in intrinsic electricity, that therefore
one kind has its seat in them and the other in muscles; just as in a
Leyden jar,* although it is customary that one extremity of the arc
should be applied to the external surface thereof, the other to its
conductor, in order that the excursion of electricity may be made
from one to the other, nevertheless it cannot be inferred therefrom
that the electricity which is produced in the conductor is peculiar,
and unlike that which collects within the bottom of the jar; nay even
it is established that that looks altogether towards the internal and

charged surface, and that both electricities, although contrary, are contained in the same flask.

Wherefore, if the great number of contractions obtained in the prepared animal be considered, for which surely the small quantity of electricity contained in the small part of the nerve remaining in the prepared muscles is adequate; if, moreover, the many arguments be considered which are sought from the animal functions, which openly declare that the nerve fluid,* already demonstrated by us is electric and flows freely and swiftly through the nerves; if finally the obvious and simple explanation of the phenomena from each electricity be sought residing in the muscle itself: it will not seem beside the point, as we shall show hereafter, that the muscle should be the proper seat of the electricity investigated by us, but that the nerve performs the function of a conductor.

These things being admitted, it would perhaps be a not inept hypothesis and conjecture, nor altogether deviating from the truth, which should compare a muscle fibre to a small Leyden jar, or other similar electric body, charged with two opposite kinds of electricity but should liken the nerve to the conductor, and therefore compare the whole muscle with an assemblage of Leyden jars. . . .

Now a few things about the nature of animal electricity chosen from those which it is permissible to infer from the described experiments.* This electricity, then, has some things in common with artificial and with ordinary electricity, some things with that of the torpedo* and other animals of this class.

Things in common with ordinary electricity are: First, free and easy passage through the same bodies through which common electricity is accustomed to pass, namely through metals, among the foremost, and, among these, through the more perfect and nobler, such as gold and silver, then through the less noble, namely copper, iron, tin and lead, moreover through the imperfect metals,* such as antimony, and finally through minerals; likewise free and easy passage through water and moist bodies; more difficult passage through stones, earth, and wood; finally, interrupted and completely cut off through glass, resin, and oily substances: wherefrom it results that if metals are laid on an insulating plane,* it is inevitable that common and artificial electricity should accumulate in them, and they would be wont to produce far greater effects, namely to excite more violent and longer contractions, than if the same metals communicated freely with other conducting bodies.

Second, the choice, in excursion, of a shorter and quicker way, an arc, for example, or angles, or points.

Third, a double and opposite nature, namely one positive, the other negative.

Fourth, daily and hourly constant attachment to muscles not otherwise than common electricity is wont by nature to electric bodies.

Fifth, spontaneous restoration, not lasting a short space of time.

Sixth, distinct increase of power by employment of the device of a so-called armature* made of the same metal with which the physicists are accustomed to surround resinous and vitreous bodies.*

Properties in common with electricity of the torpedo and other animals of this class are chiefly these:—

Namely, as it were, a sort of circulation of electricity from one part of the animal to another, and this either through an arc or through the fluid itself of the arc alternately, as the physicists have observed. Whereby forsooth it is established that such a circulation is characteristic, not of the torpedo alone or of similar animals but perhaps of animals generally when our devices are employed. Moreover, as in the latter so in the former, there are absent both sensation of a relatively gentle breeze, and attraction or repulsion of very light bodies, and finally indications of the slightest motion in electrometers hitherto invented.

But even our animal electricity has this in common with this kind of electricity, that it requires no previous device, friction for example, heat or other things of this sort, by which it should be excited, but it is ready as if by nature and continually prompt, and is produced on contact alone.

Nay, so great promptness for action is in this electricity of animals, which we have experienced, that if the vertebral column is allowed to be touched by an insulating body in a place where it is armatured, not rarely contractions are produced, particularly if the animal has been recently slaughtered and prepared. Moreover, they often occur if the same insulating body is so pressed against metallic foil that the contact of the foil with the nerve emerging from the vertebral column is either augmented or changed, but I know not whether this can be affirmed concerning the torpedo's electricity.

Moreover, this one thing seems particularly proper and peculiar of the torpedo and cognate animals that at their will and pleasure they can direct electricity outside the skin, and expel it so that it completes its circulation outside the body, and with such quantity and force that it exhibits a spark, if we heed the physicists, so that it produces a concussion and violent sensation and sometimes makes such an impact on the animalcules that fall into the path of its circulation, that it either kills or stupefies and terrifies them. But perhaps in animals of this class this indicates more abundant quantity and force, not really a different nature; and perhaps some time, devices can be found whereby effects of this sort can be obtained in other animals also.

Moreover, electric circulations of this sort, discovered and described by us in other animals, not only their strength and relations but also their ways and instruments, perhaps will be able to shed some light on the same circulation in the torpedo and cognate animals, and again from more diligent discussion and observation of these animal organs which are fitted for this function, these of ours will be able to receive light. The instruments perhaps will be similar, and the terminals of the electric circuit, namely muscles and nerves, the same.

These things concerning the nature and character of animal electricity: now a few things concerning its source. This I should think to be not dissimilar from that which physiologists, up to the present time, have indicated for animal spirits,* namely the cerebrum. For though we have indicated that electricity is inherent in muscles, yet we do not concur in the opinion that it emanates from them also, as from its proper and natural source.

For since all nerves, both those to the muscles and those which go to other parts of the body, seem to be altogether the same, as in kind so in nature, who will rightfully deny that all carry fluid of the same nature? But already we have shown above that electric fluid is carried through the nerves of muscles; therefore it will be carried through all: therefore from one common source, namely the cerebrum, they will drain it, from the source and origin of all: for otherwise there would be as many sources as there are parts in which nerves terminate; and although these are very different in nature and construction, they do not seem suited for the elaboration and secretion of one and the same fluid.

Therefore we believe it equally true that electricity is prepared by action of the cerebrum, and that it is extracted from the blood and that it enters the nerves, and that it runs through them within, whether they are hollow and free, or whether, as seems more probable, they carry a very thin lymph, or some other peculiar similar thin fluid, secreted, as many think, by the cortical cerebrum. If this prove so, the obscure nature of animal spirits, long sought in vain, may perhaps appear clearly. But as things are, certain no one of those hereafter, I think, after these experiments of ours, will call electricity into doubt. And although, led merely by reason and by some observations, we first brought this into our public Anatomical Amphitheater, and many illustrious men had already mentioned it before, yet never might we think fortune sufficiently favorable to us to grant to us perchance first to handle it, as it were with our hands, lurking in the nerves, and to draw it out of the nerves, and almost to place it under our eyes.

SIR HUMPHRY DAVY

From *Discourse, Introductory to a Course of Lectures on Chemistry* (1802)

Medicine and Physiology, those sciences which connect the preservation of the health of the human being with the abstruse philosophy of organized nature, will be found to have derived from chemistry most of their practical applications; and many of the analogies which have contributed to give to their scattered facts order and systematic arrangement. The art of preparing those substances, which operate powerfully upon animal bodies, and which, according to their different modes of exhibition, are either efficient remedies, or active poisons, is purely chemical. Indeed the want of an acquaintance with scientific principles in the processes of pharmacy has often been productive of dangerous consequences; and the study of the simple and unvarying agencies of dead matter ought surely to precede investigations concerning the mysterious and complicated powers of life. Knowing very little of the laws of his own existence, man has nevertheless derived some useful information from researches concerning the nature of respiration;* and the composition and properties of animal organs even in their dead state. And if the connexion of chemistry with physiology has given rise to some visionary and seductive theories; yet even this circumstance has been useful to the public mind in exciting it by doubt, and in leading it to new investigations. A reproach, to a certain degree just, has been thrown upon those doctrines known by the name of the chemical physiology; for in the applications of them speculative philosophers have been guided rather by the analogies of words than of facts. Instead of slowly endeavouring to lift up the veil concealing the wonderful phenomena of living nature; full of ardent imaginations, they have vainly and presumptuously attempted to tear it asunder. . . .

It is difficult to examine any of our common operations or labours without finding them more or less connected with chemistry. By means of this science man has employed almost all the substances in nature either for the satisfaction of his wants, or the gratification of his luxuries. Not contented with what is found upon the surface of the earth, he has penetrated into her bosom, and has even searched the bottom of the ocean, for the purpose of allaying the restlessness of his desires, or of extending and increasing his power. He is to a certain extent ruler of all the elements that surround him; and he is capable of using not only common matter according to his will and inclinations, but likewise of subjecting to his purposes the ethereal principles of heat and light. By his inventions they are elicited from the atmosphere; and under his control they become, according to circumstances, instruments of comfort and enjoyment, or of terror and destruction.

To be able indeed to form an accurate estimate of the effects of chemical philosophy, and the arts and sciences connected with it, upon the human mind, we ought to examine the history of society, to trace the progress of improvement, or more immediately to compare the uncultivated savage with the being of science and civilization.

Man, in what is called a state of nature, is a creature of almost pure sensation. Called into activity only by positive wants, his life is passed either in satisfying the cravings of the common appetites, or in apathy, or in slumber. Living only in moments, he calculates but little on futurity. He has no vivid feelings of hope, or thoughts of permanent and powerful action. And, unable to discover causes, he is either harassed by superstitious dreams, or quietly and passively submitted to the mercy of nature and the elements. How different is man informed through the beneficence of the Deity, by science, and the arts! Knowing his wants, and being able to provide for them, he is capable of anticipating future enjoyments, and of connecting hope with an infinite variety of ideas. He is in some measure independent of chance or accident for his pleasures. Science has given to him an acquaintance with the different relations of the parts of the external world; and more than that, it has bestowed upon him powers which may be almost called creative; which have enabled him to modify and change the beings surrounding him, and by his experiments to interrogate nature with power, not simply as a scholar, passive and seeking only to understand her operations, but rather as a master, active with his own instruments.

But, though improved and instructed by the sciences, we must not rest contented with what has been done; it is necessary that we should likewise do. Our enjoyment of the fruits of the labours of former times should be rather an enjoyment of activity than of indolence; and, instead of passively admiring, we ought to admire with that feeling which leads to emulation.

Science has done much for man, but it is capable of doing still more; its sources of improvement are not yet exhausted; the benefits that it has conferred ought to excite our hopes of its capability of conferring new benefits; and, in considering the progressiveness of our nature, we may reasonably look forwards to a state of greater cultivation and happiness than that which we at present enjoy.

As a branch of sublime philosophy,* chemistry is far from being perfect. It consists of a number of collections of facts, connected together by different relations; but as yet it is not furnished with a precise and beautiful theory. Though we can perceive, develope, and even produce, by means of our instruments of experiment, an almost infinite variety of minute phenomena, yet we are incapable of determining the general laws by which they are governed; and, in attempting to define them, we are lost in obscure, though sublime imaginations concerning unknown agencies. That they may be discovered, however, there is every reason to believe. And who would not be ambitious of becoming acquainted with the most profound secrets of nature; of ascertaining her hidden operations; and of exhibiting to men that system of knowledge which relates so intimately to their own physical and moral constitution?

The future is composed merely of images of the past, connected in new arrangements by analogy, and modified by the circumstances and feelings of the moment; our hopes are founded upon our experience; and in reasoning concerning what may be accomplished, we ought not only to consider the immense fields of research yet unexplored, but likewise to examine the latest operations of the human mind, and to ascertain the degree of its strength and activity.

At the beginning of the seventeenth century, very little was known concerning the philosophy of the intimate actions of bodies on each other: and before this time vague ideas, superstitious notions, and inaccurate practices, were the only effects of the first efforts of the mind to establish the foundations of chemistry. Men either were astonished and deluded by their first inventions, so as to become visionaries, and to institute researches after imaginary things, or they employed them as instruments for astonishing and deluding others, influenced by their dearest passions and interests, by ambition, or the love of money. Hence arose the dreams of Alchemy concerning the philosophers stone and the elixir of life. Hence for a long while the other metals were destroyed, or rendered useless, by experiments designed to transmute them into gold; and for a long while the means of obtaining earthly immortality were sought for amidst the unhealthy vapours of the laboratory. These views of things have passed away, and a new science has gradually arisen. The dim and uncertain twilight of discovery, which gave to objects false or indefinite appearances, has been succeeded by the steady light of truth, which has shown the external world in its distinct forms, and in its true relations to human powers. The composition of the atmosphere, and the properties of the gases, have been ascertained; the phenomena of electricity have been developed; the lightnings have been taken from the clouds; and, lastly, a new influence has been discovered, which has enabled man to produce from combinations of dead matter effects which were formerly occasioned only by animal organs.

MARY SHELLEY

From *Frankenstein* (1818)

None but those who have experienced them can conceive of the enticements of science. In other studies you go as far as others have gone before you, and there is nothing more to know; but in a scientific pursuit there is continual food for discovery and wonder. A mind of moderate capacity, which closely pursues one study, must infallibly arrive at great proficiency in that study; and I, who continually sought the attainment of one object of pursuit, and was solely wrapt up in this, improved so rapidly, that, at the end of two years, I made some discoveries in the improvement of some chemical instruments, which procured me great esteem and admiration at the university. When I had arrived at this point, and had become as well acquainted with the theory and practice of natural philosophy* as depended on the lessons of any of the professors at Ingolstadt, my residence there being no longer conducive to my improvements, I thought of returning to my friends and my native town, when an incident happened that protracted my stay.

One of the phaenonema which had peculiarly attracted my attention was the structure of the human frame, and, indeed, any animal endued with life. Whence, I often asked myself, did the principle of life proceed? It was a bold question, and one which has ever been considered as a mystery; yet with how many things are we upon the brink of becoming acquainted, if cowardice or carelessness did not restrain our inquiries. I revolved these circumstances in my mind, and determined thenceforth to apply myself more particularly to those branches of natural philosophy which relate to physiology. Unless I had been animated by an almost supernatural enthusiasm, my application to this study would have been irksome, and almost intolerable. To examine the causes of life, we must first have recourse to death. I became acquainted with the science of anatomy: but this was not sufficient; I must also observe the natural decay and corruption of the human body. In my education my father had taken the greatest precautions that my mind should be impressed with no supernatural horrors. I do not ever remember to have trembled at a tale of superstition, or to have feared the apparition of a spirit. Darkness had no effect upon my fancy; and a church-yard was to me merely the receptacle of bodies deprived of life, which, from being the seat of beauty and strength, had become food for the worm. Now I was led to examine the cause and progress of this decay, and forced to spend days and nights in vaults and charnel houses. My attention was fixed upon every object the most insupportable to the delicacy of the human feelings. I saw how the fine form of man was degraded and wasted; I beheld the corruption of death succeed to the blooming cheek of life; I saw how the worm inherited the wonders of the eye and brain. I paused, examining and analysing all the minutiae of causation, as exemplified in the change from life to death, and death to life, until from the midst of this darkness a sudden light broke in upon me—a light so brilliant and wondrous, yet so simple, that while I became dizzy with the immensity of the prospect which it illustrated, I was surprised that among so many men of genius, who had directed their inquiries towards the same science, that I alone should be reserved to discover so astonishing a secret.

Remember, I am not recording the vision of a madman. The sun does not more certainly shine in the heavens, than that which I now affirm is true. Some miracle might have produced it, yet the stages of the discovery were distinct and probable. After days and nights of incredible labour and fatigue, I succeeded in discovering the cause of generation and life; nay, more, I became myself capable of bestowing animation upon lifeless matter.

The astonishment which I had at first experienced on this discovery soon gave place to delight and rapture. After so much time spent in painful labour, to arrive at once at the summit of my desires, was the most gratifying consummation of my toils. But this discovery was so great and overwhelming, that all the steps by which I had been progressively led to it were obliterated, and I beheld only the result. What had been the study and desire of the wisest men since the creation of the world, was now within my grasp. Not that, like a magic scene, it all opened upon me at once: the information I had obtained was of a nature rather to direct my endeavours so soon as I should point them towards the object of my search, than to exhibit that object already accomplished. I was like the Arabian who had been buried with the dead, and found a passage to life aided only by one glimmering, and seemingly ineffectual, light.*

I see by your eagerness, and the wonder and hope which your eyes express, my friend, that you expect to be informed of the secret with which I am acquainted; that cannot be: listen patiently until the end of my story, and you will easily perceive why I am reserved upon that subject. 1 will not lead you on, unguarded and ardent as I then was, to your destruction and infallible misery. Learn from me, if not by my precepts, at least by my example, how dangerous is the acquirement of knowledge, and how much happier that man is who believes his native town to be the world, than he who aspires to become greater than his nature will allow.

When I found so astonishing a power placed within my hands, I hesitated a long time concerning the manner in which I should employ it. Although I possessed the capacity of bestowing animation, yet to prepare a frame for the reception of it, with all its intricacies of fibres, muscles, and veins, still remained a work of inconceivable difficulty and labour. I doubted at first whether I should attempt the creation of a being like myself or one of simpler organization; but my imagination was too much exalted by my first success to permit me to doubt of my ability to give life to an animal as complex and wonderful as man. The materials at present within my command hardly appeared adequate to so arduous an undertaking; but I doubted not that I should ultimately succeed. I prepared myself for a multitude of reverses; my operations might be incessantly baffled, and at last my work be imperfect: yet, when I considered the improvement which every day takes place in science and mechanics, I was encouraged to hope my present attempts would at least lay the foundations of future success. Nor could I consider the magnitude and complexity of my plan as any argument of its impracticability. It was with these feelings that I began the creation of a human being. As the minuteness of the parts formed a great hindrance to my speed, I resolved, contrary to my first intention, to make the being of a gigantic stature; that is to say, about eight feet in height, and proportionably large. After having formed this determination, and having spent some months in successfully collecting and arranging my materials, I began.

No one can conceive the variety of feelings which bore me onwards, like a hurricane, in the first enthusiasm of success. Life and death appeared to me ideal bounds, which I should first break through, and pour a torrent of light into our dark world. A new species would bless me as its creator and source; many happy and excellent natures would owe their being to me. No father could claim the gratitude of his child so completely as I should deserve their's. Pursuing these reflections, I thought, that if I could bestow animation upon lifeless matter, I might in process of time (although I now found it impossible) renew life where death had apparently devoted the body to corruption.

These thoughts supported my spirits, while I pursued my undertaking with unremitting ardour. My cheek had grown pale with study, and my person had become emaciated with confinement. Sometimes, on the very brink of certainty, I failed; yet still I clung to the hope which the next day or the next hour might realize. One secret which I alone possessed was the hope to which I had dedicated myself; and the moon gazed on my midnight labours, while, with unrelaxed and breathless eagerness, I pursued nature to her hiding places. Who shall conceive the horrors of my secret toil, as I dabbled among the unhallowed damps of the grave, or tortured the living animal to animate the lifeless clay? My limbs now tremble, and my eyes swim with the remembrance; but then a resistless, and almost frantic impulse, urged me forward; I seemed to have lost all soul or sensation but for this one pursuit. It was indeed but a passing trance, that only made me feel with renewed acuteness so soon as, the unnatural stimulus ceasing to operate, I had returned to my old habits. I collected bones from charnel houses; and disturbed, with profane fingers, the tremendous secrets of the human frame. In a solitary chamber, or rather cell, at the top of the house, and separated from all the other apartments by a gallery and staircase, I kept my workshop of filthy creation; my eyeballs were starting from their sockets in attending to the details of my employment. The dissecting room and the slaughter-house furnished many of my materials; and often did my human nature turn with loathing from my occupation, whilst, still urged on by an eagerness which perpetually increased, I brought my work near to a conclusion.

It was on a dreary night of November, that I beheld the accomplishment of my toils. With an anxiety that almost amounted to agony, I collected the instruments of life around me, that I might infuse a spark of being into the lifeless thing that lay at my feet. It was already one in the morning; the rain pattered dismally against the panes, and my candle was nearly burnt out, when, by the glimmer of the half-extinguished light, I saw the dull yellow eye of the creature open; it breathed hard, and a convulsive motion agitated its limbs.

How can I describe my emotions at this catastrophe, or how delineate the wretch whom with such infinite pains and care I had endeavoured to form? His limbs were in proportion, and I had selected his features as beautiful. Beautiful!—Great God! His yellow skin scarcely covered the work of muscles and arteries beneath; his hair was of a lustrous black, and flowing; his teeth of a pearly whiteness; but these luxuriances only formed a more horrid contrast with his watery eyes, that seemed almost of the same colour as the dun white sockets in which they were set, his shrivelled complexion, and straight black lips.

The different accidents of life are not so changeable as the feelings of human nature. I had worked hard for nearly two years, for the sole purpose of infusing life into an inanimate body. For this I had deprived myself of rest and health. I had desired it with an ardour that far exceeded moderation; but now that I had finished, the beauty of the dream vanished, and breathless horror and disgust filled my heart. Unable to endure the aspect of the being I had created, I rushed out of the room, and continued a long time traversing my bed-chamber, unable to compose my mind to sleep.

WALT WHITMAN

I Sing the Body Electric [1855] (1867)

I sing the Body electric;
The armies of those I love engirth me, and I engirth them;
They will not let me off till I go with them, respond to them,
And discorrupt them, and charge them full with the charge of the
    Soul.

Was it doubted that those who corrupt their own bodies conceal
    themselves?
And if those who defile the living are as bad as they who defile the
    dead?
And if the body does not do as much as the Soul?
And if the body were not the Soul, what is the Soul?

A man's Body at auction;
I help the auctioneer—the sloven does not half know his business.

Gentlemen, look on this wonder!
Whatever the bids of the bidders, they cannot be high enough for it;
For it the globe lay preparing quintillions of years, without one
    animal or plant;
For it the revolving cycles truly and steadily roll'd.

In this head the all-baffling brain;
In it and below it, the makings of heroes.

Examine these limbs, red, black, or white—they are so cunning in
    tendon and nerve;
They shall be stript, that you may see them.

Exquisite senses, life-lit eyes, pluck, volition,
Flakes of breast-muscle, pliant back-bone and neck, flesh not flabby,
    good sized arms and legs,
And wonders within there yet.

Within there runs blood,
The same old blood!
The same red-running blood!
There swells and jets a heart—there all passions, desires, reachings,
    aspirations;
Do you think they are not there because they are not express'd in
    parlors and lecture-rooms?

This is not only one man—this is the father of those who shall be
    fathers in their turns;
In him the start of populous states and rich republics;
Of him countless immortal lives, with countless embodiments and
    enjoyments.

How do you know who shall come from the offspring of his offspring
    through the centuries?
Who might you find you have come from yourself, if you could trace
    back through the centuries?

.   .   .   .

A woman's Body at auction!
She too is not only herself—she is the teeming mother of mothers;

She is the bearer of them that shall grow and be mates to the
mothers.

Have you ever loved the Body of a woman?
Have you ever loved the Body of a man?
Your father—where is your father?
Your mother—is she living? have you been much with her? and has
she been much with you?
Do you not see that these are exactly the same to all, in all nations
and times, all over the earth?

If any thing is sacred, the human body is sacred,
And the glory and sweet of a man, is the token of manhood
untainted;
And in man or woman, a clean, strong, firm-fibred body, is beautiful
as the most beautiful face.

Have you seen the fool that corrupted his own live body? or the fool
that corrupted her own live body?
For they do not conceal themselves, and cannot conceal themselves.

Cells and Tissues and Their Relation to the Body

XAVIER BICHAT

From *General Anatomy* (1801)

All animals are compounded of various organs, each of which exer-
cising a separate function, and in a manner peculiar to itself, concurs
to the preservation of the whole. These organs are so many distinct
and collateral machines, subordinate to the great, and general
machine. Each individual machine accordingly is itself composed of
several tissues differing in nature, and constituting the real elements
of these organs. Chemistry has its simple bodies, which by the various combinations they admit of, form the compound ones: these are
caloric, light, hydrogen, oxygen, carbon, azote,* phosphorus, &c.
Anatomy, in like manner, has its simple tissues, which, by their
combinations, form the organs, properly so called. These tissues are

1st. The cellular membrane. 2dly. The nerves of animal life. 3dly. The nerves of organic life.* 4thly. The arteries. 5thly. The veins. 6thly. The exhalants. 7thly. Absorbents and glands. 8thly. The bones. 9thly. The medulla. 10thly. Cartilage. 11th. Muscular fibre. 12th. Fibro-cartilaginous tissue. 13th. Muscles of organic life. 14th. Those of animal life.* 15th. The mucous membrane. 16th. The serous.* 17. The synovial* 18th. The Glands. 19th. The dermis. 20th. The epidermis. 21st. The cutis.

Such are the real organized elements of our frame. Whatever be the nature of those parts which are blended together, theirs remain uniformly the same; as in chemistry, simple substances do not vary, however the compounds they unite to may differ. We shall make these organized elements of man, the especial objects of this work. . . .

Much has been said since Bordieu's time,* of the peculiar life of each organ, or that particular character which distinguishes the whole of the vital properties of one organ, from the vital properties of another. Before these properties had been precisely and rigorously analysed, it was evidently impossible to form a correct idea of this peculiar life. From the sketch, therefore, that I have just drawn, it is obvious, that as the greatest part of the organs are formed of very different simple tissues, the idea of peculiar life can only be applied to these single tissues and by no means to the organs themselves.

Some striking examples will illustrate this very important part of my doctrine. The stomach is composed of serous, organic, muscular, and mucous tissues, and in addition to these common tissues, is furnished with arteries, veins, &c. which we must consider separately. Accordingly, if we take a confused and general view of the peculiar life of the stomach, it will be utterly impossible to form a correct and precise idea of it. In fact the mucous surface is so different from the serous, and both so distinct from the muscular, that we could form no clear judgment of them by confounding them in one general consideration. It is the same with the intestines, bladder, and uterus, &c.,—if we do not distinguish the fabric of the tissues that form these complicated organs, the term of peculiar life will offer vague and uncertain ideas. This is so unquestionably true, that we find tissues alternately absent and present in particular organs. Certain parts of the peritoneum,* for example, are either included or excluded, in the structure of the visceral organs, according as they are full or empty. Need I speak of the viscera of the thorax? What has the fleshy substance of the heart in common with the membrane that surrounds it? What concern has the pleura with the pulmonary structure? Or has this tissue in effect any concern with the membrane that lines the brouchia?* I might apply the same remark to the brain and its membranes, as well as to the ear, eye, and other organs.

When we study a function, we must consider the complicated organ which performs it in a general way; but if we would be instructed in the properties and life of that organ, we must absolutely resolve it into its constituent parts. So, too, if we are satisfied with general ideas in anatomy, we must examine every organ en masse, but it is imperiously necessary to separate their tissues one by one, if we purpose to go into a minute analysis of their intimate structure.

RUDOLF VIRCHOW

From *Cellular Pathology* (1858)

Rudolf Virchow's *Cellular Pathology* consists of a series of lectures 'taken down in short-hand, just as they were delivered' at the Berlin Pathological Institute in 1856–7. His audience consisted mainly of practising physicians, and he supported his claims with numerous microscopical preparations which he 'sent round' amongst his listeners.

Especial difficulty has been found in answering the question, from what parts of the body action really proceeds—what parts are active, what passive; and yet it is already quite possible to come to a definitive conclusion upon this point, even in the case of parts the structure of which is still disputed. The chief point in this application of histology to pathology is to obtain a recognition of the fact, that the cell is really the ultimate morphological element in which there is any manifestation of life, and that we must not transfer the seat of real action to any point beyond the cell. Before you, I shall have no particular reason to justify myself, if in this respect I make quite a special reservation in favour of life. In the course of these lectures you will be able to convince yourselves that it is almost impossible for any one to entertain more mechanical ideas in particular instances than I am wont to do, when called upon to interpret the individual processes of life. But I think that we must look upon this as certain, that, however much of the more delicate interchange of matter, which takes place within a cell, may not concern the material structure as a whole, yet the real action does proceed from the structure as such, and that the living element only maintains its activity as long as it really presents itself to us as an independent whole. . . .

According to my ideas, this is the only possible starting-point for all biological doctrines. If a definite correspondence in elementary form pervades the whole series of all living things, and if in this series something else which might be placed in the stead of the cell be in vain sought for, then must every more highly developed organism, whether vegetable or animal, necessarily, above all, be regarded as a progressive total, made up of larger or smaller number of similar or dissimilar cells. Just as a tree constitutes a mass arranged in a definite manner, in which, in every single part, in the leaves as in the root, in the trunk as in the blossom, cells are discovered to be the ultimate elements, so is it also with the forms of animal life. *Every animal presents itself as a sum of vital unities*, every one of which manifests all the characteristics of life. The characteristics and unity of life cannot be limited to any one particular spot in a highly developed organism (for example, to the brain of man), but are to be found only in the definite, constantly recurring structure, which every individual element displays. Hence it follows that the structural composition of a body of considerable size, a so-called individual, always represents a kind of social arrangement of parts, an arrangement of a social kind, in which a number of individual existences are mutually dependent, but in such a way, that every element has its own special action, and, even though it derive its stimulus to activity from other parts, yet alone effects the actual performance of its duties.

GEORGE ELIOT

From *Middlemarch* (1871–2)

Starting with some general reflections on history, Eliot offers readers the history of one of her main characters, Dr Tertius Lydgate, explaining what attracted him to the district of Middlemarch.

A great historian, as he insisted on calling himself, who had the happiness to be dead a hundred and twenty years ago, and so to take his place among the colossi whose huge legs our living pettiness is observed to walk under, glories in his copious remarks and digressions as the least imitable part of his work, and especially in those initial chapters to the successive books of his history, where he seems to bring his arm-chair to the proscenium and chat with us in all the lusty ease of his fine English. But Fielding* lived when the days were longer (for time, like money, is measured by our needs), when summer afternoons were spacious, and the clock ticked slowly in the winter evenings. We belated historians must not linger after his example; and if we did so, it is probable that our chat would be thin and eager, as if delivered from a camp-stool in a parrot-house. I at least have so much to do in unravelling certain human lots, and seeing how they were woven and interwoven, that all the light I can command must be concentrated on this particular web, and not dispersed over that tempting range of relevancies called the universe.

At present I have to make the new settler Lydgate better known to any one interested in him than he could possibly be even to those who had seen the most of him since his arrival in Middlemarch. For surely all must admit that a man may be puffed and belauded, envied, ridiculed, counted upon as a tool and fallen in love with, or at least selected as a future husband, and yet remain virtually unknown—known merely as a cluster of signs for his neighbours' false suppositions. There was a general impression, however, that Lydgate was not altogether a common country doctor, and in Middlemarch at that time such an impression was significant of great things being expected from him. For everybody's family doctor was remarkably clever, and was understood to have immeasurable skill in the management and training of the most skittish or vicious diseases. The evidence of his cleverness was of the higher intuitive order, lying in his lady-patients' immovable conviction, and was unassailable by any objection except that their intuitions were opposed by others equally strong; each lady who saw medical truth in Wrench and 'the strengthening treatment' regarding Toller and 'the lowering system' as medical perdition.* For the heroic times of copious bleeding and blistering had not yet departed, still less the times of thoroughgoing theory, when disease in general was called by some bad name, and treated accordingly without shilly-shally—as if, for example, it were to be called insurrection, which must not be fired on with blank-cartridge, but have its blood drawn at once. The strengtheners and the lowerers were all 'clever' men in somebody's opinion, which is really as much as can be said for any living talents. Nobody's imagination had gone so far as to conjecture that Mr Lydgate could know as much as Dr Sprague and Dr Minchin, the two physicians, who alone could offer any hope when danger was extreme, and when the smallest hope was worth a guinea. Still, I repeat, there was a general impression that Lydgate was something rather more uncommon than any general practitioner in Middlemarch. And this was true. He was but seven-and-twenty, an age at which many men are not quite common—at which they are hopeful of achievement, resolute in avoidance, thinking that Mammon shall never put a bit in their mouths and get astride their backs, but rather that Mammon, if they have anything to do with him, shall draw their chariot.

He had been left an orphan when he was fresh from a public school. His father, a military man, had made but little provision for three children, and when the boy Tertius asked to have a medical education, it seemed easier to his guardians to grant his request by apprenticing him to a country practitioner than to make any objections on the score of family dignity. He was one of the rarer lads who early get a decided bent and make up their minds that there is something particular in life which they would like to do for its own sake, and not because their fathers did it. Most of us who turn to any subject with love remember some morning or evening hour when we got on a high stool to reach down an untried volume, or sat with parted lips listening to a new talker, or for very lack of books began to listen to the voices within, as the first traceable beginning of our love. Something of that sort happened to Lydgate. . . . One vacation, a wet day sent him to the small home library to hunt once more for a book which might have some freshness for him: in vain! unless, indeed, he took down a dusty row of volumes with grey-paper backs and dingy labels—the volumes of an old Cyclopaedia which he had never disturbed. It would at least be a novelty to disturb them. They were on the highest shelf, and he stood on a chair to get them down. But he opened the volume he first took from the shelf: somehow, one is apt to read in a makeshift attitude, just where it might seem inconvenient to do so. The page he opened on was under the head of

Anatomy, and the first passage that drew his eyes was on the valves of the heart. He was not much acquainted with valves of any sort, but he knew that *valvae* were folding-doors, and through this crevice came a sudden light startling him with his first vivid notion of finely-adjusted mechanism in the human frame. A liberal education had of course left him free to read the indecent passages in the school classics, but beyond a general sense of secrecy and obscenity in connection with his internal structure, had left his imagination quite unbiassed, so that for anything he knew his brains lay in small bags at his temples, and he had no more thought of representing to himself how his blood circulated than how paper served instead of gold. But the moment of vocation had come, and before he got down from his chair, the world was made new to him by a presentiment of endless processes filling the vast spaces planked out of his sight by that wordy ignorance which he had supposed to be knowledge. From that hour Lydgate felt the growth of an intellectual passion.

We are not afraid of telling over and over again how a man comes to fall in love with a woman and be wedded to her, or else be fatally parted from her. Is it due to excess of poetry or of stupidity that we are never weary of describing what King James called a woman's 'makdom and her fairnesse,'* never weary of listening to the twanging of the old Troubadour strings, and are comparatively uninterested in that other kind of 'makdom and fairnesse' which must be wooed with industrious thought and patient renunciation of small desires? In the story of this passion, too, the development varies: sometimes it is the glorious marriage, sometimes frustration and final parting. And not seldom the catastrophe is wound up with the other passion, sung by the Troubadours. For in the multitude of middle-aged men who go about their vocations in a daily course determined for them much in the same way as the tie of their cravats, there is always a good number who once meant to shape their own deeds and alter the world a little. The story of their coming to be shapen after the average and fit to be packed by the gross, is hardly ever told even in their consciousness; for perhaps their ardour for generous unpaid toil cooled as imperceptibly as the ardour of other youthful loves, till one day their earlier self walked like a ghost in its old home and made the new furniture ghastly. Nothing in the world more subtle than the process of their gradual change! In the beginning they inhaled it unknowingly: you and I may have sent some of our breath towards infecting them, when we uttered our conforming falsities or drew our silly conclusions: or perhaps it came with the vibrations from a woman's glance.

Lydgate did not mean to be one of those failures, and there was the better hope of him because his scientific interest soon took the form of a professional enthusiasm: he had a youthful belief in his bread-winning work, not to be stifled by that initiation in makeshift called his 'prentice days; and he carried to his studies in London, Edinburgh, and Paris, the conviction that the medical profession as it might be was the finest in the world; presenting the most perfect interchange between science and art; offering the most direct alliance between intellectual conquest and the social good. Lydgate's nature demanded this combination: he was an emotional creature, with a flesh-and-blood sense of fellowship which withstood all the abstractions of special study. He cared not only for 'cases,' but for John and Elizabeth, especially Elizabeth.

There was another attraction in his profession: it wanted reform, and gave a man an opportunity for some indignant resolve to reject its venal decorations and other humbug, and to be the possessor of genuine though undemanded qualifications. He went to study in Paris with the determination that when he came home again he would settle in some provincial town as a general practitioner, and resist the irrational severance between medical and surgical knowledge in the interest of his own scientific pursuits, as well as of the general advance: he would keep away from the range of London intrigues, jealousies, and social truckling, and win celebrity, however slowly, as Jenner* had done, by the independent value of his work. For it must be remembered that this was a dark period; and in spite of venerable colleges which used great efforts to secure purity of knowledge by making it scarce, and to exclude error by a rigid exclusiveness in relation to fees and appointments, it happened that very ignorant young gentlemen were promoted in town, and many more got a legal right to practise over large areas in the country. Also, the high standard held up to the public mind by the College of Physicians, which gave its peculiar sanction to the expensive and highly-rarefied medical instruction obtained by graduates of Oxford and Cambridge, did not hinder quackery from having an excellent time of it; for since professional practice chiefly consisted in giving a great many drugs, the public inferred that it might be better off with more drugs still, if they could only be got cheaply, and hence swallowed large cubic measures of physic prescribed by unscrupulous ignorance which had taken no degrees. Considering that statistics had not yet embraced a calculation as to the number of ignorant or canting doctors which absolutely must exist in the teeth of all changes, it seemed to Lydgate that a change in the units was the most direct mode of changing the numbers. He meant to be a unit who would make a certain amount of difference towards that spreading change which would one day tell appreciably upon the averages, and in the mean time have the pleasure of making an advantageous difference to the viscera of his own patients. But he did not simply aim at a more genuine kind of practice than was common. He was ambitious of a wider effect: he was fired with the possibility that he might work out the proof of an anatomical conception and make a link in the chain of discovery.

Does it seem incongruous to you that a Middlemarch surgeon should dream of himself as a discoverer? Most of us, indeed, know little of the great originators until they have been lifted up among the constellations and already rule our fates. But that Herschel,* for example, who 'broke the barriers of the heavens'—did he not once play a provincial church-organ, and give music-lessons to stumbling pianists? Each of those Shining Ones had to walk on the earth among neighbours who perhaps thought much more of his gait and his garments than of anything which was to give him a title to everlasting fame: each of them had his little local personal history sprinkled with small temptations and sordid cares, which made the retarding friction of his course towards final companionship with the immortals. Lydgate was not blind to the dangers of such friction, but he had plenty of confidence in his resolution to avoid it as far as possible: being seven-and-twenty, he felt himself experienced. And he was not going to have his vanities provoked by contact with the showy worldly successes of the capital, but to live among people who could hold no rivalry with that pursuit of a great idea which was to be a twin object with the assiduous practice of his profession. There was fascination in the hope that the two purposes would illuminate each other: the careful observation and inference which was his daily work, the use of the lens to further his judgment in special cases, would further his thought as an instrument of larger inquiry. Was not this the typical pre-eminence of his profession? He would be a good Middlemarch doctor, and by that very means keep himself in the track of far-reaching investigation. On one point he may fairly claim approval at this particular stage of his career: he did not mean to imitate those philanthropic models who make a profit out of poisonous pickles to support themselves while they are exposing adulteration, or hold shares in a gambling-hell that they may have leisure to represent the cause of public morality. He intended to begin in his own case some particular reforms which were quite certainly within his reach, and much less of a problem than the demonstrating of an anatomical conception. One of these reforms was to act stoutly on the strength of a recent legal decision, and simply prescribe, without dispensing drugs or taking percentage from druggists. This was an innovation for one who had chosen to adopt the style of general practitioner in a country town, and would be felt as offensive criticism by his professional brethren. But Lydgate meant to innovate in his treatment also, and he was wise enough to see that the best security for his practising honestly according to his belief was to get rid of systematic temptations to the contrary.

Perhaps that was a more cheerful time for observers and theorisers than the present; we are apt to think it the finest era of the world when America was beginning to be discovered, when a bold sailor, even if he were wrecked, might alight on a new kingdom; and about 1829 the dark territories of Pathology were a fine America for a spirited young adventurer. Lydgate was ambitious above all to contribute towards enlarging the scientific, rational basis of his profession. The more he became interested in special questions of disease, such as the nature of fever or fevers, the more keenly he felt the need for that fundamental knowledge of structure which just at the beginning of the century had been illuminated by the brief and glorious career of Bichat, who died when he was only one-and-thirty, but, like another Alexander, left a realm large enough for many heirs. That great Frenchman first carried out the conception that living bodies, fundamentally considered, are not associations of organs which can be understood by studying them first apart, and then as it were federally; but must be regarded as consisting of certain primary webs or tissues, out of which the various organs—brain, heart, lungs, and so on—are compacted, as the various accommodations of a house are built up in various proportions of wood, iron, stone, brick, zinc, and the rest, each material having its

peculiar composition and proportions. No man, one sees, can understand and estimate the entire structure or its parts—what are its
frailties and what its repairs, without knowing the nature of the
materials. And the conception wrought out by Bichat, with his
detailed study of the different tissues, acted necessarily on medical
questions as the turning of gas-light would act on a dim, oil-lit
street, showing new connections and hitherto hidden facts of structure which must be taken into account in considering the symptoms
of maladies and the action of medicaments. But results which
depend on human conscience and intelligence work slowly, and now
at the end of 1829, most medical practice was still strutting or sham-
bling along the old paths, and there was still scientific work to be
done which might have seemed to be a direct sequence of Bichat's.
This great seer did not go beyond the consideration of the tissues as
ultimate facts in the living organism, marking the limit of anatomical
analysis; but it was open to another mind to say, have not these
structures some common basis from which they have all started, as
your sarsnet, gauze, net, satin and velvet from the raw cocoon? Here
would be another light, as of oxy-hydrogen, showing the very grain
of things, and revising all former explanations. Of this sequence to
Bichat's work, already vibrating along many currents of the European mind, Lydgate was enamoured; he longed to demonstrate the
more intimate relations of living structure, and help to define men's
thought more accurately after the true order. The work had not yet
been done, but only prepared for those who knew how to use the
preparation. What was the primitive tissue? In that way Lydgate put
the question—not quite in the way required by the awaiting answer;
but such missing of the right word befalls many seekers. And he
counted on quiet intervals to be watchfully seized, for taking up the
threads of investigation—on many hints to be won from diligent
application, not only of the scalpel, but of the microscope, which
research had begun to use again with new enthusiasm of reliance.
Such was Lydgate's plan of his future: to do good small work for
Middlemarch, and great work for the world.

GEORGE HENRY LEWES

From *The Physical Basis of Mind* (1877)

The progress of science involves an ever-increasing Analysis. Investigation is more and more directed towards the separated details of the phenomena previously studied as events: the observed facts are resolved into their component factors, complex wholes into their simpler elements, the organism into organs and tissues. But while the analytical process is thus indispensable, it is, as I have often to insist, beset with an attendant danger, namely, that in drawing the attention away from one group of factors to fix it exclusively on another, there is a tendency to forget this artifice, and instead of restoring the factors provisionally left out of account, we attempt a reconstruction in oblivion of these omitted factors. Hence, instead of studying the properties of a tissue in all the elements of that tissue, and the functions of an organ in the anatomical connections of that organ, a single element of the tissue is made to replace the whole, and very soon the function of the organ is assigned to this particular element. The 'superstition of the nerve-cell' is a striking illustration. The cell has usurped the place of the tissue, and has come to be credited with central functions; so that wherever anatomists have detected ganglionic cells,* physiologists have not hesitated to place central functions. By such interpretations the heart and intestines, the glands and blood-vessels, have, erroneously I think, their actions assigned to ganglionic cells.

It is unnecessary to point out the radical misconception which thus vitiates a great mass of anatomical exposition and physiological speculation. I only call the reader's attention to the point at the outset of the brief survey we have now to make of what is known respecting the elementary structure of the nervous system. . . .

In enumerating among the obstacles to research the tendency to substitute hypothetic deductions in place of objective facts, I had specially in my mind the wide-reaching influence of the reigning theories of the nerve-cell. Had we a solidly-established theory of the cell, equivalent, say, to our theory of gas-pressure, we should still need caution in allowing it to override exact observation; but insecure as our data are, and hypothetical as are the inferences respecting the part played by the cell, the reliance placed on deductions from such premisses is nothing less than superstition. Science will take a new start when the whole question is reinvestigated on a preliminary setting aside of all that has been precipitately accepted respecting the office of the cell. This exercise of the imagination, even should the reigning theories subsequently be confirmed, would not fail to bring many neglected facts into their rightful place.

I am old enough to remember when the cell held a very subordinate position in Neurology, and now my meditations have led me to return, if not to the old views of the cell, at least to something like the old estimate of its relative importance. Its existence was first brought prominently forward by Ehrenberg in 1834, who described its presence in the sympathetic ganglia; and by Remak in 1837, who described it in the spinal ganglia.* For some time afterwards the ganglia and centres were said to contain irregular masses of vesicular matter which were looked on as investing the fibres; what their office was, did not appear. But there rapidly arose the belief that the cells were minute batteries in which 'nerve-force' was developed, the fibres serving merely as conductors. Once started on this track, Hypothesis had free way, and a sort of fetichistic deification of the cell invested it with miraculous powers. In many works of repute we meet with statements which may fitly take their place beside the equally grave statements made by savages respecting the hidden virtues of sticks and stones. We find the nerve-cells credited with 'metabolic powers,' which enable them to 'spiritualise impressions, and materialise ideas,' to *transform* sensations into movements, and *elaborate* sensations into thoughts; not only have they this 'remarkable aptitude of metabolic local action,' they can also 'act at a distance.' The savage believes that one pebble will cure diseases, and another render him victorious in war; and there are physiologists who believe that one nerve-cell has sensibility, another motricity,* a third instinct, a fourth emotion, a fifth reflexion: they do not say this in so many words, but they assign to cells which differ only in size and shape, specific qualities. They describe sensational, emotional, ideational, sympathetic, reflex, and motor-cells; nay, Schröder van der Kolk* goes so far as to specify hunger-cells and thirst-cells. With what grace can these writers laugh at Scholasticism?

The hypothesis of the nerve-cell as the fountain of nerve-force is supported by the gratuitous hypothesis of cell-substance having greater chemical tension and molecular instability than nerve-fibre. No evidence has been furnished for this; indeed the only experimental evidence bearing on this point, if it has any force, seems directly adverse to the hypothesis. I allude to the experiments of Wundt,* which show that the faint stimulus capable of moving a muscle when applied directly to its nerve, must be increased if the excitation has to pass through the cells by stimulation of the sensory nerve. Wundt interprets this as proving that the cells retard every impulse, whereby they are enabled to store up latent force. The cells have thus the office of locks in a canal, which cause the shallow stream to deepen at particular places. I do not regard this interpretation as satisfactory; but the fact at any rate seems to prove that so far from the cells manifesting greater instability than the fibres, they manifest less.

The hypothesis of nerve-force being developed in the ganglia, gradually assumed a more precise expression when the nerve-cells were regarded as the only important elements of a ganglion. It has become the foundation-stone of Neurology, therefore very particular care should be taken to make sure that this foundation rests on clear and indisputable evidence. Instead of that, there is absolutely no evidence on which it can rest; and there is much evidence decidedly opposed to it. Neither structure nor experiment points out the cells as the chief agents in neural processes.

Hygiene, Germ Theory, and Infectious Diseases

MARY SHELLEY

From *The Last Man* (1826)

Set in the future, *The Last Man* depicts a plague that destroys all human life. In this passage Shelley's narrator, the self-educated shepherd Lionel Verney, begins describing the epidemic and its first consequences.

I remember, after having witnessed the destructive effects of a fire, I could not even behold a small one in a stove, without a sensation of fear. The mounting flames had curled round the building, as it fell, and was destroyed. They insinuated themselves into the substances about them, and the impediments to their progress yielded at their touch. Could we take integral parts of this power, and not be subject to its operation? Could we domesticate a cub of this wild beast, and not fear its growth and maturity?

Thus we began to feel, with regard to many-visaged death let loose on the chosen districts of our fair habitation, and above all, with regard to the plague. We feared the coming summer. Nations, bordering on the already infected countries, began to enter upon serious plans for the better keeping out of the enemy. We, a commercial people, were obliged to bring such schemes under consideration; and the question of contagion became matter of earnest disquisition.

That the plague was not what is commonly called contagious, like the scarlet fever, or extinct small-pox, was proved. It was called an epidemic. But the grand question was still unsettled of how this epidemic was generated and increased. If infection depended upon the air, the air was subject to infection. As for instance, a typhus fever* has been brought by ships to one sea-port town; yet the very people who brought it there, were incapable of communicating it in a town more fortunately situated. But how are we to judge of airs, and pronounce—in such a city plague will die unproductive; in such another, nature has provided for it a plentiful harvest? In the same way, individuals may escape ninety-nine times, and receive the death-blow at the hundredth; because bodies are sometimes in a state to reject the infection of malady, and at others, thirsty to imbibe it. These reflections made our legislators pause, before they could decide on the laws to be put in force. The evil was so wide-spreading, so violent and immedicable, that no care, no prevention could be judged superfluous, which even added a chance to our escape.

These were questions of prudence; there was no immediate necessity for an earnest caution. England was still secure. France, Germany, Italy and Spain, were interposed, walls yet without a breach, between us and the plague. Our vessels truly were the sport of winds and waves, even as Gulliver was the toy of the Brobdignagians;* but we on our stable abode could not be hurt in life or limb by these eruptions of nature. We could not fear—we did not. Yet a feeling of awe, a breathless sentiment of wonder, a painful sense of the degradation of humanity, was introduced into every heart.

Nature, our mother, and our friend, had turned on us a brow of menace. She shewed us plainly, that, though she permitted us to assign her laws and subdue her apparent powers, yet, if she put forth but a finger, we must quake. She could take our globe, fringed with mountains, girded by the atmosphere, containing the condition of our being, and all that man's mind could invent or his force achieve; she could take the ball in her hand, and cast it into space, where life would be drunk up, and man and all his efforts for ever annihilated.

These speculations were rife among us; yet not the less we proceeded in our daily occupations, and our plans, whose accomplishment demanded the lapse of many years. No voice was heard telling us to hold! When foreign distresses came to be felt by us through the channels of commerce, we set ourselves to apply remedies. Subscriptions were made for the emigrants, and merchants bankrupt by the failure of trade. The English spirit awoke to its full activity, and, as it had ever done, set itself to resist the evil, and to stand in the breach which diseased nature had suffered chaos and death to make in the bounds and banks which had hitherto kept them out.

At the commencement of summer, we began to feel, that the mischief which had taken place in distant countries was greater than we had at first suspected. Quito* was destroyed by an earthquake. Mexico laid waste by the united effects of storm, pestilence and famine. Crowds of emigrants inundated the west of Europe; and our island had become the refuge of thousands. In the mean time Ryland* had been chosen Protector. He had sought this office with eagerness, under the idea of turning his whole forces to the suppression of the privileged orders of our community. His measures were thwarted, and his schemes interrupted by this new state of things. Many of the foreigners were utterly destitute; and their increasing numbers at length forbade a recourse to the usual modes of relief. Trade was stopped by the failure of the interchange of cargoes usual between us, and America, India, Egypt and Greece. A sudden break was made in the routine of our lives. In vain our Protector and his partizans sought to conceal this truth; in vain, day after day, he appointed a period for the discussion of the new laws concerning hereditary rank and privilege; in vain he endeavoured to represent the evil as partial and temporary. These disasters came home to so many bosoms, and, through the various channels of commerce, were carried so entirely into every class and division of the community, that of necessity they became the first question in the state, the chief subjects to which we must turn our attention.

Can it be true, each asked the other with wonder and dismay, that whole countries are laid waste, whole nations annihilated, by these disorders in nature? The vast cities of America, the fertile plains of Hindostan, the crowded abodes of the Chinese, are menaced with utter ruin. Where late the busy multitudes assembled for pleasure or profit, now only the sound of wailing and misery is heard. The air is empoisoned, and each human being inhales death, even while in youth and health, their hopes are in the flower. We called to mind the plague of 1348, when it was calculated that a third of mankind had been destroyed. As yet western Europe was uninfected; would it always be so?

O, yes, it would—Countrymen, fear not! In the still uncultivated wilds of America, what wonder that among its other giant destroyers, Plague should be numbered! It is of old a native of the East, sister of the tornado, the earthquake, and the simoom. Child of the sun, and nursling of the tropics, it would expire in these climes. It drinks the dark blood of the inhabitant of the south, but it never feasts on the pale-faced Celt. If perchance some stricken Asiatic come among us, plague dies with him, uncommunicated and innoxious. Let us weep for our brethren, though we can never experience their reverse. Let us lament over and assist the children of the garden of the earth. Late we envied their abodes, their spicy groves, fertile plains, and abundant loveliness. But in this mortal life extremes are always matched; the thorn grows with the rose, the poison tree and the cinnamon mingle their boughs. Persia, with its cloth of gold, marble halls, and infinite wealth, is now a tomb. The tent of the Arab is fallen in the sands, and his horse spurns the ground unbridled and unsaddled. The voice of lamentation fills the valley of Cashmere; its dells and woods, its cool fountains, and gardens of roses, are polluted by the dead; in Circassia and Georgia the spirit of beauty weeps over the ruin of its favourite temple—the form of woman.

Our own distresses, though they were occasioned by the fictitious reciprocity of commerce, encreased in due proportion. Bankers, merchants, and manufacturers, whose trade depended on exports and interchange of wealth, became bankrupt. Such things, when they happen singly, affect only the immediate parties; but the prosperity of the nation was now shaken by frequent and extensive losses. Families, bred in opulence and luxury, were reduced to beggary. The very state of peace in which we gloried was injurious; there were no means of employing the idle, or of sending any overplus of population out of the country. Even the source of colonies was dried up, for in New Holland,* Van Diemen's Land,* and the Cape of Good Hope, plague raged. O, for some medicinal vial to purge unwholesome nature, and bring back the earth to its accustomed health!

SIR EDWIN CHADWICK

An Inquiry into the Sanitary Condition of the Labouring Population of Great Britain (1842)

The following extracts will serve to show, in the language chiefly of eye-witnesses, the varied forms in which disease attendant on removable circumstances appears from one end of the island to the other amidst the population of rural villages, and of the smaller towns, as well as amidst the population of the commercial cities and the most thronged of the manufacturing districts—in which last pestilence is frequently supposed to have its chief and almost exclusive residence.

Commencing with the reports on the sanitary condition of the population in Cornwall and Devon, *Mr Gilbert*,* when acting as Assistant Commissioner for those counties, reports, that he found the open drains and sewers the most prominent cause of malaria.* He gives the following as an instance of the common condition of the dwellings of the labouring classes in Devon, where it will be observed that the registered deaths from the four classes of disease amounted in one year to 5893 cases.

'In Tiverton there is a large district, from which I find numerous applications were made for relief to the Board of Guardians, in consequence of illness from fever. The expense in procuring the necessary attention and care, and the diet and comforts recommended by the medical officer, were in each case very high, and particularly attracted my attention.

'I requested the medical officer to accompany me through the district, and with him, and afterwards by myself, I visited the district, and examined the cottages and families living there. The land is nearly on a level with the water, the ground is marshy, and the sewers all open. Before reaching the district, I was assailed by a most disagreeable smell; and it was clear to the sense that the air was full of most injurious malaria. The inhabitants, easily distinguishable from the inhabitants of the other parts of the town, had all a sickly, miserable appearance. The open drains in some cases ran immediately before the doors of the houses, and some of the houses were surrounded by wide open drains, full of all the animal and vegetable refuse not only of the houses in that part, but of those in other parts of Tiverton. In many of the houses, persons were confined with fever and different diseases, and all I talked to either were ill or had been so: and the whole community presented a melancholy spectacle of disease and misery.

'Attempts have been made on various occasions by the local authorities to correct this state of things by compelling the occupants of the houses to remove nuisances, and to have the drains covered; but they find that in the present state of the law their powers are not sufficient, and the evil continues and is likely so to do, unless the legislature affords some redress in the nature of sanitary powers. Independently of this nuisance, Tiverton would be considered a fine healthy town, situate as it is on the slope of a hill, with a swift river running at its foot.

'It is not these unfortunate creatures only who choose this centre of disease for their living-place who are affected; but the whole town is more or less deteriorated by its vicinity to this pestilential mass, where the generation of those elements of disease and death is constantly going on.

'Another cause of disease is to be found in the state of the cottages. Many are built on the ground without flooring, or against a damp hill. Some have neither windows nor doors sufficient to keep out the weather, or to let in the rays of the sun, or supply the means of ventilation; and in others the roof is so constructed or so worn as not to be weather tight. The thatch roof frequently is saturated with wet, rotten, and in a state of decay, giving out malaria, as other decaying vegetable matter.'

The report of *Dr Barham*,* on the sanitary condition of the town of Truro, gives instances of the condition of the town population in that part of the country. He states—

'The perfect immunity from deaths by *febrile* and *acute* diseases, enjoyed by Lemon-street during the long period of three years and a half, is a strong testimony to the value of the breadth of its roadway, the openness of its site, and the judicious construction of the houses; for it has to contend with a great deficiency of sewerage. Fairmantle and Daniell-streets are modern, and are occupied by small traders, and by decent artisans and labourers; the *former* lies rather low, the *latter* is on a considerable elevation; both are fairly drained, and are healthy. Charles, Calenick, and Kenwyn-streets present some of the worst specimens of defective arrangement, rendered worse still by the recklessness of the very poor, which can be met with in Truro. The amount of *pauper sickness* is considerable, the deaths not few. The two latter streets are, in the greater part of their length, but little raised above high-water mark. Passing into *St Mary's* parish, the proportion of sickness and even of deaths in Castle-street and Castle-hill is, to their extent and population, as great, perhaps, as that of any part of Truro; yet their situation is elevated and favourable. There is, however, no mystery in the causation. Ill-constructed houses, many of them old, with decomposing refuse close upon their doors and windows, open drains bringing the oozings of pigsties and other filth to stagnate at the foot of a wall, between which and the entrances to a row of small dwellings there is only a very narrow passage; such are a few of the sources of disease which the breeze of the hill cannot always dissipate. Similar causes have produced like effects in the courts adjacent to Pyder-street, to the High Cross, and to St Clement's-streets, and in Bodmin-street and Good-wives'-lane, the situations being all more or less confined. The benefits, on the other hand, derived from open rows, and cottages of a better construction are evidenced in Boscawen and Paul's-row, and St Clement's-terrace, which are well ventilated, and consequently suffer less from the scanty provision of drains and other conveniences.

'A detailed account of the public sewers is given in the Appendix, and is believed to be nearly, if not quite, complete. Many of these are of recent date, and owe their existence to the alarm excited when the cholera was near at hand. Some of them are made to discharge themselves into the rivers; and such of these as are swept by a stream of water are unobjectionable in themselves. Several others stop short of this desirable termination, and, after collecting filth from various localities, deposit a portion in catchpits here and there, and finally open on the surface, frequently in some street or lane, where a neglected deposit of a mixed animal and vegetable nature is allowed to become a probable source of annoyance or mischief. Much of this incompleteness may be removed (as regards the main lines of sewerage) at no great expense; and it is said to be the intention of the commissioners of improvement to remedy the deficiency, when they are free from the debt with which they are now encumbered. Many of the smaller sewers are, however, much too narrow to be effective, and some of them are no better than covered drains. But the greatest evils in this department are unquestionably those which spring from the ignorance, cupidity, or negligence of landlords. It is useless to have a good sewer carried through the centre of a street, if the houses at the sides, and still more those situated in courts and lanes adjoining, have no communicating drains; and it is worse than useless to furnish these backlets with the mere semblance of drains—gutters forming pits here and there—then as they approach the street, perhaps slightly covered so as to produce obstruction more frequently than protection, a concentrated solution of all sorts of decomposing refuse being allowed to soak through and thoroughly impregnate the walls and ground adjoining. One or more of these mischievous conditions is to be found in connexion with a large proportion of the older houses in Truro, excepting the better class; and in many of the courts and backlets all these evils are in full operation. I have repeatedly noticed in the country that the occurrence of fever has been connected with *near proximity to even a small amount of decomposing organic matter*; and it is certain that all measures for effecting improvement in the sewerage of streets, the supply of water, and ventilation, may be rendered nearly inoperative for the obviating of the causes of disease, if a little nidus of morbific effluvia be permitted to remain in almost every corner of the confined court; where the poor man opens his narrow habitation in the hope of refreshing it with the breeze of summer, but gets instead a mixture of gases from reeking dunghills, or, what is worse, because more insidious, from a soil which has become impregnated with organic matters imbibed long before; and now, though, perhaps, to all appearance dry and clean, emitting the poisonous vapour in its most pernicious state. Nothing short of the placing in proper hands a peremptory authority for the removal of what is hurtful, and the supply of what is defective, making the exercise of that authority a duty, can remedy the existing evils.' . . .

The most wretched of the stationary population of which I have been able to obtain any account, or that I have ever seen, was that which I saw in company with *Dr Arnott*,* and others, in the wynds of Edinburgh and Glasgow.

I prefer citing his description of the residences we visited:—

'In the survey which I had the opportunity of making in September, 1840, of the state of Edinburgh and Glasgow, all appeared confirmatory of the view of the subject of fevers submitted to the Poor Law Commissioners by those who prepared the Report in London.

'In Glasgow, which I first visited, it was found that the great mass of the fever cases occurred in the low wynds and dirty narrow streets and courts, in which, because lodging was there cheapest, the poorest and most destitute naturally had their abodes. From one such locality, between Argyll-street and the river, 754 of about 5000 cases of fever which occurred in the previous year were carried to the hospitals. In a perambulation on the morning of September 24th, with Mr Chadwick, Dr Alison,* Dr Cowan (since deceased, who had laboured so meritoriously to alleviate the misery of the poor in Glasgow), the police magistrate, and others, we examined these wynds, and, to give an idea of the whole vicinity, I may state as follows:—

'We entered a dirty low passage like a house door, which led from the street through the first house to a square court immediately behind, which court, with the exception of a narrow path around it leading to another long passage through a second house, was occupied entirely as a dung receptacle of the most disgusting kind. Beyond this court the second passage led to a second square court, occupied in the same way by its dunghill; and from this court there was yet a third passage leading to a third court, and third dungheap. There were no privies or drains there, and the dungheaps received all filth which the swarm of wretched inhabitants could give; and we learned that a considerable part of the rent of the houses was paid by the produce of the dungheaps. Thus, worse off than wild animals, many of which withdraw to a distance and conceal their ordure, the dwellers in these courts had converted their shame into a kind of money by which their lodging was to be paid. The interiors of these houses and their inmates corresponded with the exteriors. We saw half-dressed wretches crowding together to be warm; and in one bed, although in the middle of the day, several women were imprisoned under a blanket, because as many others who had on their backs all the articles of dress that belonged to the party were then out of doors in the streets. This picture is so shocking that, without ocular proof, one would be disposed to doubt the possibility of the facts; and yet there is perhaps no old town in Europe that does not furnish parallel examples. London, before the great fire of 1666, had few drains and had many such scenes, and the consequence was, a pestilence occurring at intervals of about 12 years, each destroying at an average about a fourth of the inhabitants.

'Who can wonder that pestilential disease should originate and spread in such situations?'

EDGAR ALLAN POE

The Mask of the Red Death (1842)

A Fantasy

The 'Red Death' had long devastated the country. No pestilence had been ever so fatal, or so hideous. Blood was its Avator* and its seal—the redness and the horror of blood. There were sharp pains, and sudden dizziness, and then profuse bleedings at the pores, with dissolution. The scarlet stains upon the body and especially upon the face of the victim, were the pest-ban which shut him out from the aid and from the sympathy of his fellow-men. And the whole seizure, progress and termination of the disease were the incidents of half an hour.

But the Prince Prospero was happy and dauntless, and sagacious. When his dominions were half depopulated, he summoned to his presence a thousand hale and light-hearted friends from among the knights and dames of his court, and with these retired to the deep seclusion of one of his castellated abbeys. This was an extensive and magnificent structure, the creation of the prince's own eccentric yet august taste. A strong and lofty wall girdled it in. This wall had gates of iron. The courtiers, having entered brought furnaces and massy hammers and welded the bolts. They resolved to leave means neither of ingress or egress to the sudden impulses of despair from without or of frenzy from within. The abbey was amply provisioned. With such precautions the courtiers might bid defiance to contagion. The external world could take care of itself. In the meantime it was folly to grieve, or to think. The prince had provided all the appliances of pleasure. There were buffoons, there were improvisatori, there were ballet-dancers, there were musicians, there were cards, there was Beauty, there was wine. All these and security were within. Without was the 'Red Death.'

It was towards the close of the fifth or sixth month of his seclusion, and while the pestilence raged most furiously abroad, that the Prince Prospero entertained his thousand friends at a masked ball of the most unusual magnificence. It was a voluptuous scene that masquerade.

But first let me tell of the rooms in which it was held. There were seven—an imperial suite. In many palaces, however, such suites form a long and straight vista, while the folding doors slide back nearly to the walls on either hand, so that the view of the whole extent is scarcely impeded. Here the case was very different; as might have been expected from the duke's love of the *bizarre*. The apartments were so irregularly disposed that the vision embraced but little more than one at a time. There was a sharp turn at every twenty or thirty yards and at each turn a novel effect. To the right and left, in the middle of each wall, a tall and narrow Gothic window looked out upon a closed corridor which pursued the windings of the suite.

These windows were of stained glass whose color varied in accordance with the prevailing hue of the decorations of the chamber into which it opened. That at the eastern extremity was hung, for example, in blue—and vividly blue were its windows. The second chamber was purple in its ornaments and tapestries, and here the panes were purple. The third was green throughout, and so were the casements. The fourth was furnished and litten* with orange—the fifth with white—the sixth with violet. The seventh apartment was closely shrouded in black velvet tapestries that hung all over the ceiling and down the walls, falling in heavy folds upon a carpet of the same material and hue. But, in this chamber only, the color of the windows failed to correspond with the decorations. The panes here were scarlet—a deep blood color. Now in no one of the seven apartments was there any lamp or candelabrum, amid the profusion of golden ornaments that lay scattered to and fro or depended from the roof. There was no light of any kind emanating from lamp or candle within the suite of chambers. But in the corridors that followed the suite, there stood, opposite to each window, a heavy tripod, bearing a brasier of fire that projected its rays through the tinted glass and so glaringly illumined the room. And thus were produced a multitude of gaudy and fantastic appearances. But in the western or black chamber the effect of the fire-light that streamed upon the dark hangings through the blood-tinted panes, was ghastly in the extreme, and produced so wild a look upon the countenances of those who entered, that there were few of the company bold enough to set foot within its precincts at all.

It was in this apartment, also, that there stood against the western wall, a gigantic clock of ebony. Its pendulum swung to and fro with a dull, heavy, monotonous clang; and when its minute-hand made the circuit of the face, and the hour was to be stricken, there came forth from the brazen lungs of the clock a sound which was clear and loud and deep and exceedingly musical, but of so peculiar a note and emphasis that, at each lapse of an hour, the musicians in the orchestra were constrained to pause, momently, in their performance, to hearken to the sound; and thus the waltzers perforce ceased their evolutions; and there was a brief disconcert of the whole gay company; and, while the chimes of the clock yet rang, it was observed that the giddiest grew pale, and that the more aged and sedate passed their hands over their brows as if in confused reverie or meditation.

But when the echoes had fully ceased, a light laughter at once pervaded the assembly; the musicians looked at each other and smiled as if at their own nervousness and folly, and made whispering vows, each to the other, that the next chiming of the clock should produce in them no similar emotion; and then, after the lapse of sixty minutes, (which embrace three thousand and six hundred seconds of the Time that flies,) there came yet another chiming of the clock, and then there were the same disconcert and tremulousness and meditation as before.

But, in spite of these things, it was a gay and magnificent revel. The tastes of the duke were peculiar. He had a fine eye for colors and effects. He disregarded the *decora* of mere fashion. His plans were bold and fiery, and his conceptions glowed with barbaric lustre. There are some who would have thought him mad. His followers felt that he was not. It was necessary to hear and see and touch him to be *sure* that he was not.

He had directed, in great part, the moveable embellishments of the seven chambers, upon occasion of this great *fête*, and it was his own guiding taste which had given character to the costumes of the masqueraders. Be sure they were grotesque. There were much glare and glitter and piquancy and phantasm—much of what has been since seen in 'Hernani.'* There were arabesque figures with unsuited limbs and appointments. There were delirious fancies such as the madman fashions. There was much of the beautiful, much of the wanton, much of the *bizarre*, something of the terrible, and not a little of that which might have excited disgust. To and fro in the seven chambers there stalked, in fact, a multitude of dreams. And these, the dreams—writhed in and about, taking hue from the rooms, and causing the wild music of the orchestra to seem as the echo of their steps. And, anon, there strikes the ebony clock which stands in the hall of the velvet. And then, momently, all is still, and all is silent save the voice of the clock. The dreams are stiff-frozen as they stand. But the echoes of the chime die away—they have endured but an instant—and a light, half-subdued laughter floats after them as they depart. And now again the music swells, and the dreams live, and writhe to and fro more merrily than ever, taking hue from the many-tinted windows through which stream the rays from the tripods. But to the chamber which lies most westwardly of the seven there are now none of the maskers who venture; for the night is waning away; and there flows a ruddier light through the blood-colored panes; and the blackness of the sable drapery appals; and to him whose foot falls upon the sable carpet, there comes from the near clock of ebony a muffled peal more solemnly emphatic than any which reaches *their* ears who indulge in the more remote gaieties of the other apartments.

But these other apartments were densely crowded, and in them beat feverishly the heart of life. And the revel went whirlingly on, until at length was sounded the twelfth hour upon the clock. And then the music ceased, as I have told; and the evolutions of the waltzers were quieted; and there was an uneasy cessation of all things as before. But now there were twelve strokes to be sounded by the bell of the clock; and thus it happened, perhaps, that more of thought crept, with more of time, into the meditations of the thoughtful among those who revelled. And thus, again, it happened, perhaps, that before the last echoes of the last chime had utterly sunk into silence, there were many individuals in the crowd who had found leisure to become aware of the presence of a masked figure which had arrested the attention of no single individual before. And the rumor of this new presence having spread itself whisperingly around, there arose at length from the whole company a buzz, or murmur, expressive at first of disapprobation and surprise—then, finally, of terror, of horror, and of disgust.

In an assembly of phantasms such as I have painted, it may well be supposed that no ordinary appearance could have excited such sensation. In truth the masquerade license of the night was nearly unlimited; but the figure in question had out-Heroded Herod, and gone beyond the bounds of even the prince's indefinite decorum. There are chords in the hearts of the most reckless which cannot be touched without emotion. Even with the utterly lost, to whom life and death are equally jests, there *are* matters of which no jest can be properly made. The whole company, indeed, seemed now deeply to feel that in the costume and bearing of the stranger neither wit nor propriety existed. The figure was tall and gaunt, and shrouded from head to foot in the habiliments of the grave. The mask which concealed the visage was made so nearly to resemble the countenance of a stiffened corpse that the closest scrutiny must have had difficulty in detecting the cheat. And yet all this might have been endured, if not approved, by the mad revellers around. But the mummer had gone so far as to assume the type of the Red Death. His vesture was dabbled in *blood*—and his broad brow, with all the features of the face, was besprinkled with the scarlet horror.

When the eyes of the Prince Prospero fell upon this spectral image (which with a slow and solemn movement, as if more fully to sustain its *rôle*, stalked to and fro among the waltzers) he was seen to be convulsed, in the first moment, with a strong shudder either of terror or distaste; but, in the next, his brow reddened with rage.

'Who dares?' he demanded hoarsely of the group that stood around him, 'who dares thus to make mockery of our woes? Uncase the varlet that we may know whom we have to hang to-morrow at sunrise from the battlements. Will no one stir at my bidding?—stop him and strip him, I say, of those reddened vestures of sacrilege!'

It was in the eastern or blue chamber in which stood the Prince Prospero as he uttered these words. They rang throughout the seven rooms loudly and clearly—for the prince was a bold and robust man, and the music had become hushed at the waving of his hand.

It was in the blue room where stood the prince, with a group of pale courtiers by his side. At first, as he spoke, there was a slight rushing movement of this group in the direction of the intruder, who at the moment was also near at hand, and now, with deliberate and stately step, made closer approach to the speaker. But from a certain nameless awe with which the mad assumptions of the mummer had inspired the whole party, there were found none who put forth hand to seize him; so that, unimpeded, he passed within a yard of the prince's person; and, while the vast assembly, as if with one impulse, shrank from the centres of the rooms to the walls, he made his way uninterruptedly, but with the same solemn and measured step which had distinguished him from the first, through the blue chamber to the purple—through the purple to the green—through the green to the orange,—through this again to the white—and even thence to the violet, ere a decided movement had been made to arrest him. It was then, however, that the Prince Prospero, maddening with rage and the shame of his own momentary cowardice, rushed hurriedly through the six chambers—while none followed him on account of a deadly terror that had seized upon all. He bore aloft a drawn dagger, and had approached, in rapid impetuosity, to within three or four feet of the retreating figure, when the latter, having attained the extremity of the velvet apartment, turned suddenly round and confronted his pursuer. There was a sharp cry—and the dagger dropped gleaming upon the sable carpet, upon which instantly afterwards, fell prostrate in death the Prince Prospero. Then, summoning the wild courage of despair, a throng of the revellers at once threw themselves into the black apartment, and, seizing the mummer, whose tall figure stood erect and motionless within the shadow of the ebony clock, gasped in unutterable horror at finding the grave-cerements and corpse-like mask which they handled with so violent a rudeness, untenanted by any tangible form.

And now was acknowledged the presence of the Red Death. He had come like a thief in the night. And one by one dropped the revellers in the blood-bedewed halls of their revel, and died each in the despairing posture of his fall. And the life of the ebony clock went out with that of the last of the gay. And the flames of the tripods expired. And Darkness and Decay and the Red Death held illimitable dominion over all.

OLIVER WENDELL HOLMES

The Contagiousness of Puerperal Fever (1843)

Puerperal Fever, commonly known as 'childbed' or 'childbirth' fever, is a bacterial infection of the uterine lining spread by doctors who do not wash their hands between patients. In the early nineteenth century it was usually fatal. Holmes, who practised medicine in Boston 1836–46, published this essay on the disease in 1843, based on his own experiences with childbirth. In 1846, in Vienna hospital wards, the Hungarian physician Ignaz Semmelweiz (1818–65) began the definitive, statistical studies proving that the disease was transmitted by doctors, but he did not publish his results until 1861.

It has been long believed, by many competent observers, that Puerperal Fever (so called) is sometimes carried from patient to patient by medical assistants.

The express object of this Essay is to prove that it is so carried.

In order to prove this point, it is not necessary to consult any medical theorist as to whether or not it is consistent with his preconceived notions that such a mode of transfer should exist.

If the medical theorist insists on being consulted, and we see fit to indulge him, he cannot be allowed to assume that the alleged laws of contagion, *deduced from observation* in other diseases, shall be cited to disprove the alleged laws *deduced from observation* in this. Science would never make progress under such conditions. Neither the long incubation of hydrophobia,* nor the protecting power of vaccination, would ever have been admitted, if the results of observation in these affections had been rejected as contradictory to the previously ascertained laws of contagion.

The disease in question is not a common one; producing, on the average, about three deaths in a thousand births, according to the English Registration returns which I have examined.

When an unusually large number of cases of this disease occur about the same time, it is inferred, therefore, that there exists some special cause for this increased frequency. If the disease prevails extensively over a wide region of country, it is attributed without dispute to an *epidemic* influence. If it prevails in a single locality, as in a hospital, and not elsewhere, this is considered proof that some *local* cause is there active in its production.

When a large number of cases of this disease occur in rapid succession, in one individual's ordinary practice, and few or none elsewhere, these cases appearing in scattered localities, in patients of the same average condition as those who escape under the care of others, there is the same reason for connecting the cause of the disease with the *person* in this instance, as with the *place* in that last mentioned.

Many series of cases, answering to these conditions, are given in this Essay, and many others will be referred to which have occurred since it was written.

The alleged results of observation may be *set aside*; first, because the so-called facts are in their own nature equivocal; secondly, because they stand on insufficient authority; thirdly, because they are not sufficiently numerous. But, in this case, the disease is one of striking and well-marked character; the witnesses are experts, interested in denying and disbelieving the facts; the number of consecutive cases in many instances frightful, and the number of series of cases such that I have no room for many of them except by mere reference.

These results of observation, being admitted, may, we will suppose, be *interpreted* in different methods. Thus the coincidences may be considered the effect of *chance*. I have had the chances calculated by a competent person, that a given practitioner, A., shall have sixteen fatal cases in a month, on the following data: A. to average attendance upon two hundred and fifty births in a year; three deaths in one thousand births to be assumed as the average from puerperal fever; no epidemic to be at the time prevailing. It follows, from the answer given me, that if we suppose every one of the five hundred thousand annual births of England to have been recorded during the last half-century, there would not be one chance in a million million million millions that one such series should be noted. No possible fractional error in this calculation can render the chance a working probability. Applied to dozens of series of various lengths, it is obviously an absurdity. Chance, therefore, is out of the question as an explanation of the admitted coincidences.

There is, therefore, *some* relation of cause and effect between the physician's presence and the patient's disease.

Until it is proved to what *removable condition* attaching to the attendant the disease is owing, he is bound to stay away from his patients so soon as he finds himself singled out to be tracked by the disease. How long, and with what other precautions, I have suggested, without dictating, at the close of my Essay. If the physician does not at once act on any reasonable suspicion of his being the medium of transfer, the families where he is engaged, if they are allowed to know the facts, should decline his services for the time. His feelings on the occasion, however interesting to himself, should not be even named in this connection. A physician who talks about *ceremony* and *gratitude*, and *services rendered*, and the *treatment he got*, surely forgets himself; it is impossible that he should seriously think of these small matters where there is even a question whether he may not carry disease, and death, and bereavement into any one of 'his families,' as they are sometimes called. . . .

The treatise of Dr Gordon of Aberdeen* was published in the year 1795, being among the earlier special works upon the disease. A part of his testimony has been occasionally copied into other works, but his expressions are so clear, his experience is given with such manly distinctness and disinterested honesty, that it may be quoted as a model which might have been often followed with advantage.

'This disease seized such women only as were visited, or delivered by a practitioner, or taken care of by a nurse, who had previously attended patients affected with the disease.

'I had evident proofs of its infectious nature, and that the infection was as readily communicated as that of the small-pox or measles, and operated more speedily than any other infection with which I am acquainted.

'I had evident proofs that every person who had been with a patient in the puerperal fever became charged with an atmosphere of infection, which was communicated to every pregnant woman who happened to come within its sphere. This is not an assertion, but a fact, admitting of demonstration, as may be seen by a perusal of the foregoing table,'—referring to a table of seventy-seven cases, in many of which the channel of propagation was evident.

He adds, 'It is a disagreeable declaration for me to mention, that I myself was the means of carrying the infection to a great number of women.' He then enumerates a number of instances in which the disease was conveyed by midwives and others to the neighboring villages, and declares that 'these facts fully prove that the cause of the puerperal fever, of which I treat, was a specific contagion, or infection, altogether unconnected with a noxious constitution of the atmosphere.'

But his most terrible evidence is given in these words: 'I ARRIVED AT THAT CERTAINTY IN THE MATTER, THAT I COULD VENTURE TO FORETELL WHAT WOMEN WOULD BE AFFECTED WITH THE DISEASE, UPON HEARING BY WHAT MIDWIFE THEY WERE TO BE DELIVERED, OR BY WHAT NURSE THEY WERE TO BE ATTENDED, DURING THEIR LYING-IN: AND ALMOST IN EVERY INSTANCE, MY PREDICTION WAS VERIFIED.' . . .

If any should care to know my own conclusions, they are the following; and in taking the liberty to state them very freely and broadly, I would ask the inquirer to examine them as freely in the light of the evidence which has been laid before him.

1. A physician holding himself in readiness to attend cases of midwifery should never take any active part in the post-mortem examination of cases of puerperal fever.

2. If a physician is present at such autopsies, he should use thorough ablution, change every article of dress, and allow twenty-four hours or more to elapse before attending to any case of midwifery. It may be well to extend the same caution to cases of simple peritonitis.*

3. Similar precautions should be taken after the autopsy or surgical treatment of cases of erysipelas,* if the physician is obliged to

unite such offices with his obstetrical duties, which is in the highest degree inexpedient.

4. On the occurrence of a single case of puerperal fever in his practice, the physician is bound to consider the next female he attends in labor, unless some weeks at least have elapsed, as in danger of being infected by him, and it is his duty to take every precaution to diminish her risk of disease and death.

5. If within a short period two cases of puerperal fever happen close to each other, in the practice of the same physician, the disease not existing or prevailing in the neighborhood, he would do wisely to relinquish his obstetrical practice for at least one month, and endeavor to free himself by every available means from any noxious influence he may carry about with him.

6. The occurrence of three or more closely connected cases, in the practice of one individual, no others existing in the neighborhood, and no other sufficient cause being alleged for the coincidence, is *primâ facie* evidence that he is the vehicle of contagion.

7. It is the duty of the physician to take every precaution that the disease shall not be introduced by nurses or other assistants, by making proper inquiries concerning them, and giving timely warning of every suspected source of danger.

8. Whatever indulgence may be granted to those who have heretofore been the ignorant causes of so much misery, the time has come when the existence of a *private pestilence* in the sphere of a single physician should be looked upon, not as a misfortune, but a crime; and in the knowledge of such occurrences the duties of the practitioner to his profession should give way to his paramount obligations to society.

LOUIS PASTEUR

On the Organized Bodies Which Exist in the Atmosphere
(1861)

Translated by Thomas D. Brock.

Pasteur's 1861 memoir, delivered in May to the Chemical Society of Paris, is considered his most significant paper on fermentation and spontaneous generation. Trained as a chemist, Pasteur began studying fermentation in the mid-1850s and quickly became convinced that micro-organisms in the air caused fermentation and perhaps also infectious diseases. Here he describes experiments disproving spontaneous generation, the notion that micro-organisms can arise in inanimate matter, and demonstrating that substances cannot ferment when isolated from microbes in the air.

Chemists have discovered during the last twenty years a variety of really extraordinary phenomena which have been given the generic name of *fermentations*. All of these require the cooperation of two substances: one which is fermentable, such as sugar, and the other nitrogenous, which is always an albuminous* substance. But here is the universally accepted theory for this phenomenon: the albuminous material undergoes, when it comes in contact with air, an alteration, a particular oxidation of an unknown nature, which gives it the characteristics of a *ferment*. That is, it acquires the property of being able to cause fermentation upon contact with fermentable substances.

The oldest and the most remarkable ferment which has been known to be an organized being is the yeast of beer. But in all of the fermentations discovered since the beer yeast was shown to be organized, it has not been possible to demonstrate the existence of organized beings, even after careful study. Therefore, physiologists have gradually abandoned regretfully the hypothesis of M. Cagniard de Latour* concerning a probable relation between the organized nature of this ferment and its ability to cause the fermentation. Instead, to beer yeast has been applied the following general theory: 'It is not the fact that it is organized that makes the beer yeast active, rather it is because it has been in contact with air. It is the dead material of the yeast, that which has lived and is in the process of change, which acts on the sugar.'

My studies have lead me to entirely different conclusions. I have found that all true fermentations—viscous, lactic, butyric, or those of tartaric acid, malic acid, or urine* only occur with the presence and multiplication of an organized being. Therefore, the organized nature of the beer yeast is not a disadvantage for the theory of fermentation. Rather, this shows that it is no different than other ferments and fits the common rule. In my opinion, the albuminous materials were never the ferments, but the nutrients of the ferment. The true ferments were organized beings.

This granted, it was known that the ferments originate through the contact of albuminous materials with oxygen gas. If this is so, there are two possibilities to explain this. Since the ferments are organized, it is possible that oxygen, acting as itself, is able to induce the production of the ferments through its contact with the nitrogenous materials, and therefore the ferments have arisen spontaneously. But, if the ferments are not spontaneously generated beings, it is not the oxygen gas itself which is necessary for their formation, but the stimulation by oxygen of a germ which is either carried with it by the air, or which already exists preformed in the nitrogenous or fermentable materials. At this point in my studies on fermentations, I wanted to arrive at an opinion on the question of spontaneous generation. I would perhaps be able to uncover a powerful argument in favor of my ideas on the fermentation themselves . . .

My first problem was to develop a method which would permit me to collect in all seasons the solid particles that float in the air and examine them under the microscope. It was at first necessary to eliminate if possible the objections which the proponents of spontaneous generation have raised to the age-old hypothesis of the aerial dissemination of germs.

When the organic materials of infusions have been heated, they become populated with infusoria or molds. These organized bodies are in general neither so numerous nor so diverse as those that develop in infusions that have not been previously boiled, but they form nevertheless. But the germs of these infusoria and molds can only come from the air, if the liquid is boiled, because the boiling destroys all those that were present in the container or which had been brought there by the liquid. The first question to resolve is therefore: are there germs in the air? Are they there in sufficient numbers to explain the appearance of organized bodies in infusions which have been previously heated? Is it possible to obtain an approximate idea of the number of germs in a given volume of ordinary air? . . .

The procedure which I followed for collecting the suspended dust in the air and examining it under the microscope is very simple. A volume of the air to be examined is filtered through guncotton* which is soluble in a mixture of alcohol and ether. The fibers of the guncotton stop the solid particles. The cotton is then treated with the solvent until it is completely dissolved. All of the particles fall to the bottom of the liquid. After they have been washed several times, they are placed on the microscope stage where they are easily examined. . . .

These very simple manipulations provide a means of demonstrating that there exists in ordinary air continually a variable number of bodies. Their sizes range from extremely small up to 0.01 or more of a millimeter. Some are perfect spheres, while others are oval. Their shapes are more or less distinctly outlined. Many are completely translucent, but others are opaque with granules inside. Those which are translucent with distinct shapes resemble the spores of common molds, and could not be told from these by the most skillful microscopist. Among the other forms present, there are those which resemble spherical infusoria and may be their cysts or the globules which are generally regarded as the eggs of these small organisms. But I do not believe it is possible to state with certainty that a particular object is a spore, or more especially the spore of a particular species, or that another object is an egg, and the egg of a certain microzoan. I will limit myself to the statement that these bodies are obviously organized, resembling in all points the germs of the lowest organisms, and so diverse in size and structure that they obviously belong to a large number of species.

I believe I have rigorously established in the preceding chapters that all organized bodies in infusions which have been previously heated originate only from the solid particles carried by the air and which are constantly being deposited on all objects. In order to remove the slightest doubt in the reader, may I present the results of the following experiments.

In a glass flask I placed one of the following liquids which are extremely alterable through contact with ordinary air: yeast water, sugared yeast water, urine, sugar beet juice, pepper water. Then I drew out the neck of the flask under a flame, so that a number of curves were produced in it, as can be seen in the figure. I then boiled the liquid for several minutes until steam issued freely through the extremity of the neck. This end remained open without any other precautions. The flasks were then allowed to cool. Any one who is familiar with the delicacy of experiments concerning the so-called

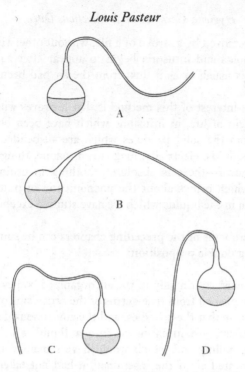

'spontaneous' generation will be astounded to observe that the liquid treated in this casual manner remains indefinitely without alteration. The flasks can be handled in any manner, can be transported from one place to another, can be allowed to undergo all the variations in temperature of the different seasons, the liquid does not undergo the slightest alteration. It retains its odor and flavor, and only, in certain cases, undergoes a direct oxidation, purely chemical in nature. *In no case is there the development of organized bodies in the liquid.*

It might seem that atmospheric air, entering with force during the first moments, might come in contact with the liquid in its original crude state. This is true, but it meets a liquid which is still close to the boiling point. The further entrance of air occurs much slower, and when the liquid has cooled to the point where it will not kill the germs, the entrance of air has slowed down enough so that the dust it carries which is able to act on the infusion and cause the development of organized bodies is deposited on the moist walls of the curved tube. At least, I can see no other explanation for these curious results. For, after one or more months in the incubator, if the neck of the flask is removed by a stroke of a file, without otherwise touching the flask, molds and infusoria begin to appear after 24, 36, or 48 hours, just as usual, or as if dust from the air had been inoculated into the flask. . . .

The great interest of this method is that it proves without doubt that the origin of life, in infusions which have been boiled, arises uniquely from the solid particles which are suspended in the air. Gas, various fluids, electricity, magnetism, ozone, things known or things unknown—there is absolutely nothing in ordinary atmospheric air which brings about the phenomenon of putrefaction or fermentation in the liquids which we have studied except these solid particles. . . .

The experiments of the preceding chapters can be summarized in the following double proposition:

1. There exist continually in the air organized bodies which cannot be distinguished from true germs of the organisms of infusions.

2. In the case that these bodies, and the amorphous debris associated with them, are inseminated into a liquid which has been subjected to boiling and which would have remained unaltered in previously heated air if the insemination had not taken place, the same beings appear in the liquid as those which develop when the liquid is exposed to the open air.

If we grant this, will a proponent of spontaneous generation continue to maintain his principles, even in the presence of this double proposition? This he can do, but he is forced to reason as follows, and I let the reader be the judge of it:

'There are solid particles present in the air,' he will say, 'such as calcium carbonate, silica, soot, wool and cotton fibers, starch grains, etc., and at the same time there are organized bodies with a perfect resemblance to the spores of molds and the eggs of infusoria. Well, I prefer to place the origin of the molds and infusoria in the first group of amorphous bodies, rather than in the second.'

In my opinion, the inconsistency of such reasoning is self-evident. The entire body of my research has placed the proponents of spontaneous generation in this predicament.

SIR JOSEPH LISTER

Illustrations of the Antiseptic System (1867)

Decomposition or putrefaction has long been known to be a source of great mischief in surgery, and antiseptic applications have for several years been employed by many surgeons. But the full extent of the evil, and the paramount importance of adopting effectual measures against it, are far from being generally recognised.

It is now six years* since I first publicly taught in the University of Glasgow that the occurrence of suppuration in a wound under ordinary circumstances, and its continuance on a healthy granulating sore* treated with water-dressing, are determined simply by the influence of decomposing organic matter. The subject has since received a large share of my attention, resulting in the system of treatment which I have been engaged for the last three years in elaborating. The benefits which attend this practice are so remarkable that I feel it incumbent upon me to do what I can to diffuse them; and with this view I propose to present to the readers of THE LANCET* a series of illustrative cases, prefacing them with a short notice of the principles which it is essential to bear in mind in order to attain success.

The cases in which this treatment is most signally beneficial are divisible into three great classes—incised wounds, of whatever form; contused or lacerated wounds, including compound fractures; and abscesses, acute or chronic—a list, indeed, which comprises the greater part of surgery. In each of these groups our aim is simply to prevent the occurrence of decomposition in the part, in order that its reparatory powers may be left undisturbed by the irritating and poisoning influence of putrid materials. In pursuing this object we are guided by the 'germ-theory,' which supplies us with a knowledge of the nature and habits of the subtle foe we have to contend with; and without a firm belief in the truth of that theory, perplexity and blunders must be of frequent occurrence. The facts upon which it is based appear sufficiently convincing. We know from the researches of Pasteur* that the atmosphere does contain among its floating particles the spores of minute vegetations and infusoria, and in greater numbers where animal and vegetable life abound, as in crowded cities or under the shade of trees, than where the opposite conditions prevail, as in unfrequented caves or on Alpine glaciers. Also, it appears that the septic energy of the air is directly proportioned to the abundance of the minute organisms in it, and is destroyed entirely by means calculated to kill its living germs—as, for example, by exposure for a while to a temperature of 212° Fahr., or a little higher, after which it may be kept for an indefinite time in contact with putrescible substances, such as urine, milk, or blood, without producing any effect upon them. It has further been shown, and this is particularly striking, that the atmosphere is deprived of its power of producing decomposition as well as organic growth by merely passing in a very gentle stream through a narrow and tortuous tube of glass, which, while it arrests all its solid particles, cannot possibly have any effect upon its gases; while conversely, 'air dust' collected by filtration rapidly gives rise simultaneously to the development of organisms and the putrefactive changes. Lastly, it seems to have been established that the character of the decomposition which occurs in a given fermentable substance is determined by the nature of the organism that develops in it. Thus the same saccharine solution may be made to undergo either the vinous or the butyric fermentation, according as the yeast plant or another organism, described by Pasteur, is introduced into it. Hence we cannot, I think, refuse to believe that the living beings invariably associated with the various fermentative and putrefactive changes are indeed their causes. And it is peculiarly in harmony with the extraordinary powers of self-diffusion and penetration exhibited by putrefaction that the chief agents in this process appear to the 'vibrios'* endowed with the faculty of locomotion, so that they are able to make their way speedily along a layer of fluid such as serum or pus.

Admitting, then, the truth of the germ theory, and proceeding in accordance with it, we must, when dealing with any case, destroy in the first instance once for all any septic organisms which may exist within the part concerned; and after this has been done, our efforts must be directed to the prevention of the entrance of others into it. And provided that these indications are really fulfilled, the less the antiseptic agent comes in contact with the living tissues the better, so that unnecessary disturbance from its irritating properties may be avoided.

The simplest conditions are presented by an unopened abscess. Here, as no septic particles are present in the contents, it is needless to apply the antiseptic directly to the part affected. All that is requisite is to guard securely against the possibility of the penetration of living germs from without, at the same time that free escape is afforded for the discharge from within. When this is done we witness an example of the unaided curative powers of Nature as beautiful as it is, I believe, entirely new. The pyogenic membrane,* freed from the operation of the stimulus derived from the presence of the pus pent up within it, without the substitution of the powerful stimulus of decomposition as has heretofore been the case after the opening of abscesses, ceases at once to develop pus-corpuscles, and, exuding merely a little clear serum, rapidly contracts and coalesces, discharging meanwhile its unirritating contents completely, whether the outlet be dependent in position or otherwise. At the same time the irritative fever and hectic hitherto so much dreaded in large abscesses are, with perfect security, entirely avoided.

In suppurations of the vertebrae or of the joints the results of this system are such as I ventured with trembling hope to anticipate; patient perseverance being rewarded by a spontaneous cure in cases where excision, amputation, or death must have resulted from any other known system of treatment. In short, the element of incurability has been eliminated from Caries.

In compound fractures and other severe contused wounds the antiseptic agent must in the first instance be applied freely and energetically to the injured parts themselves, the conditions being the opposite of those in unopened abscesses. The wound being of complicated form, with its interstices loaded with extravasated blood, into which septic organisms may have already insinuated themselves during the time that has elapsed before the patient is seen by the surgeon, mere guarding of the external orifice, however effectually, is not sufficient. After squeezing out as much as possible of the effused blood, a material calculated to kill the septic particles must be introduced into the recesses of the wound; and if the substance employed is of sufficient strength to operate to a certain extent as a caustic, this is regarded as a matter of little moment in comparison with the terrible evil of inefficiency in its antiseptic action. For experience has abundantly shown that parts killed in this way, including even portions of bone, become disposed of by absorption and organisation, provided that the subsequent part of the treatment is properly managed.

Sloughs, as ordinarily observed, are soaked with the acrid products of decomposition, and therefore produce disturbance upon the tissues around them, leading first to their gradual transformation into the rudimentary structure which, when met with at the surface of a sore, is termed 'granulations,' and afterwards to the formation of pus by the granulations. But a dead portion of tissue, if not altered by adventitious circumstances, is in its proper substance perfectly bland and unirritating, and causes no more disorder in its neighbourhood than a bullet or a piece of glass, which may remain imbedded in the living body for an indefinite period without inducing the formation of pus; while the dead tissue differs from the foreign bodies alluded to in the circumstance that the materials of which it is composed are susceptible of absorption.

Antiseptic substances, being, like the products of decomposition, chemically stimulating, will, like them, induce granulation and suppuration in tissues exposed for a sufficient length of time to their influence; but there is this all-important difference, that an antiseptic merely stimulates the surface to which it is applied, becoming dilated and weakened by the discharge which it excites; but the acrid salts which result from putrefaction are perpetually multiplied and intensified by self-propagating ferments, so that every drop of serum or pus effused through their agency becomes a drop of poison, extending its baleful influence both in the injured part and in the system generally.

These pathological considerations indicate the after-treatment in compound fracture, and explain the progress of the case. The antiseptic introduced into the wound is soon washed out by the discharge or carried away by the circulation, so that the blood and sloughs at first imbued with it become unstimulating and amenable to absorption, while at the same time they are prone to decomposition should any living atmospheric germs gain access to them. The further treatment, therefore, must consist in maintaining an efficient antiseptic guard over the orifice of the wound until sufficient time has elapsed to ensure complete consolidation of the injured parts.

The sanious* and serous discharge which occurs at the outset will give place in a few days to a small amount of pus, if the wound is dressed in such a way that the antiseptic continues to act upon the raw surface. This discharge, due to the stimulating nature of the application, being merely superficial, and involving no inflammatory or febrile disturbance, will occasion no anxiety to one who understands its cause; and I venture to repeat the caution given in a previous communication, that the surgeon must on no account be induced to explore the wound and pry into the source of the suppuration, so long as all is going on well otherwise; for such a course, by admitting germs into the interior, may produce the most disastrous consequences in an otherwise promising case.

But although suppuration resulting from the stimulating influence of the antiseptic is no cause for anxiety, it is more convenient that it should be avoided; and this may often be done entirely by leaving the lower layers of the dressing permanently on the limb and changing only its superficial parts—a plan which, while it protects the wound against the introduction of mischievous particles, permits the foreign body in contact with the tissues to part with its antiseptic material and become an unstimulating crust, under which complete healing by scabbing may occur in wounds of a size hitherto regarded as inconsistent with this process in the human subject.

Upon these principles a really trustworthy treatment for compound fractures and other severe contused wounds has been established for the first time, so far as I am aware, in the history of surgery. In an hospital which receives an unusually large number of patients suffering from machinery accidents, and in wards which, from circumstances to which I need not here allude, were peculiarly unhealthy, my experience of compound fracture in the lower limb was formerly far indeed from satisfactory, even in the selected cases in which alone I attempted to save the limb. But since the antiseptic principle has guided us, not only have ordinary cases of this formidable injury been treated by my successive house-surgeons with unvarying success, but limbs such as I should once have condemned without hesitation have gone on to complete recovery without either local or constitutional disturbance: a statement which might be suspected of exaggeration were it not that it refers to proceedings in a public hospital, witnessed not only by students, but by gentlemen once my pupils, and now practitioners in Glasgow.

ANONYMOUS

Dr Koch on the Cholera (1884)

Every week, *The Lancet* offered reports on European medical confer-
ences. Most, like this essay on Koch, were unsigned. This article
describes Robert Koch's presentation at a cholera conference sponsored
by the Imperial Board of Health in Berlin starting 26 July 1884 (two
weeks previously). The full German version of Koch's lecture can be
found in the *Berliner klinische Wochenschrift*, 4 and 11 August 1884. Having just returned from India where he had identified the comma bacillus
that caused cholera, Koch was considered the world's leading authority
on the disease.

Dr Koch commenced by remarking that what was required for the
prevention of cholera was a scientific basis. Many and diverse views
as to its mode of diffusion and infection prevailed, but they furnished no safe ground for prophylaxis. On the one hand, it was held
that cholera is a specific disease originating in India; on the other,
that it may arise spontaneously in any country and own no specific
cause. One view regards the infection to be conveyed only by the
patient and his surroundings; the other that it is spread by merchandise, by healthy individuals, and by atmospheric currents. There is a
like discrepancy in the views on the possibility of its diffusion by
drinking water, or the influence of conditions of soil, on the question
whether the dejecta contain the poison or not, and on the duration of
the incubation period. No progress was possible in combating the
disease until these root-questions of the aetiology of cholera are
decided.

*

Passing to speak of the microscopical characters of the contents of
the bowel, Dr Koch said that owing to the sanguinolent and putres-
cent character of these in the cases first examined, no conclusion was
arrived at for some time. Thus he found multitudes of bacteria of
various kinds, rendering it impossible to distinguish any special
forms; and it was not until he had examined two acute and
uncomplicated cases, before haemorrhage had occurred, and where
the evacuation had not decomposed, that he found more abundantly
the kind of organism which had been seen so richly in the intestinal

mucosa. He then proceeded to describe the characters of this bacterium. It is smaller than the tubercle bacillus,* being only about half or at most two-thirds the size of the latter, but much more plump, thicker, and slightly curved. As a rule, the curve is no more than that of a comma (,) but sometimes it assumes a semicircular shape, and he has seen it forming a double curve like an S; these two variations from the normal being suggestive of the junction of two individual bacilli. In cultures there always appears a remarkably free development of comma shaped bacilli. These bacilli often grow out to form long threads, not in the manner of anthrax* bacilli, nor with a simple undulating form, but assuming the shape of delicate long spirals, a corkscrew shape, reminding one very forcibly of the spirochaete of relapsing fever.* Indeed, it would be difficult to distinguish the two if placed side by side. On account of this developmental change, he doubted if the cholera organism should be ranked with bacilli; it is rather a transitional form between the bacillus and the spirillum.* Possibly it is a true spirillum, portions of which appear in the comma shape, much as in other spirilla—e.g., spirilla undula, which do not always form complete spirals, but consist only of more or less curved rods. The comma bacilli thrive well in meat infusion, growing in it with great rapidity. By examining microscopically a drop of this broth culture the bacilli are seen in active movement, swarming at the margins of the drop, interspersed with the spiral threads, which are also apparently mobile. They grow also in other fluids—e.g., very abundantly in milk, without coagulating it or changing its appearance. Also in blood serum they grow very richly. Another good nutrient medium is gelatine, wherein the comma bacilli form colonies of a perfectly characteristic kind, different from those of any other form of bacteria. The colony when very young appears as a pale and small spot, not completely spherical as other bacterial colonies in gelatine are wont to be, but with a more or less irregular protruding or jagged contour. It also very soon takes on a somewhat granular appearance. As the colony increases the granular character becomes more marked, until it seems to be made up of highly refractile granules, like a mass of particles of glass. In its further growth the gelatine is liquefied in the vicinity of the colony, which at the same time sinks down deeper into the gelatine mass, and makes a small thread-like excavation in the gelatine, in the centre of which the colony appears as a small white point. This, again, is peculiar; it is never seen, at least so marked, with any other bacterium.

*

Being thus convinced as to the distinctive characters of the common bacillus, the next thing was to determine the relation in which it stands to the cholera process, and whether it ever occurred in non-choleraic cases. In the ten examinations made in Egypt this point was only tested microscopically, no cultivations having then been made. In India the intestines were examined in forty-two cases, both microscopically and by cultivations, and in not one was the bacillus absent; in very acute cases it was found almost unmixed. Choleraic dejecta from thirty-two cases yielded similar results, but in only two out of many observations on vomited matter were bacilli found. It was probable that in these two cases the vomit contained faecal matter. Bacilli were also found in specimens from eight cases sent by Drs Kartulis and Schiess-Bey from Alexandria, and in two cases at Toulon in conjunction with Drs Strauss and Roux,* and in the choleraic dejecta of two other cases. One of these Toulon cases was that of a sailor attacked with cholera when convalescing from malarial fever; he died four hours after the seizure, and the autopsy was made half an hour after death, it being always an object to make such an examination as soon as possible. In this, as in other acute cases, the intestines contained almost a pure growth of the comma bacillus. The other Toulon case was similar; but in neither was the microbe found by Strauss in Egypt detected in the blood. Thus the comma bacillus has now been found in nearly one hundred cases of cholera, occurring in a constant relation to the cholera process, being most abundant in the lower end of the ileum, where the changes are most intense, and being most pure in the acute uncomplicated cases. On these grounds the comma bacillus may be considered as specific to cholera.

*

Three different views as to its relation to the cholera process are tenable. (1) That the disease favours the growth of these bacilli by affording them a suitable soil. If so, it would mean that the bacillus in question is most widely diffused, since it has been found in such different regions as Egypt, India, and France; whereas the contrary is the case, for the bacilli do not occur in other diseases, nor in the healthy, nor apart from human beings in localities most favourable to bacterial life. They only appear with the cholera. (2) It might be said that cholera produces conditions leading to a change in form and properties of the numerous intestinal bacteria—a pure hypothesis; the only instance of such a conversion refers to a change of physiological and pathogenic action, and not of form. Anthrax bacilli under certain conditions lose their pathogenic power, but undergo no change in shape; and that is an instance of a loss of pathogenic properties, whilst there is no analogy to support the view of the harmless intestinal bacteria becoming the deadly cholera bacilli. The more bacterial morphology is studied, the more certain is it that bacteria are constant in their form; moreover, the comma bacillus retains its special characters unchanged through many generations of culture. (3) Lastly, there is the view that the cholera process and the comma bacilli are intimately related, and there is no other conceivable relation but that the bacilli precede the disease and excite it. 'For my own part,' said Dr Koch, 'the matter is proved that the comma bacilli are the cause of cholera.'

*

In cholera we have instances amounting to actual experimental infection of man—e.g., the infection of those who are engaged in washing linen soiled by choleraic dejecta. Such linen contains the bacilli often in a pure form, and if infection occur through this medium, it must be by means of the comma bacilli, the only microorganism present. The hands may be soiled and the bacilli introduced into the mouth by direct contact or though the food, or drops of the washing water may come in contact with the lips, and thus in some way the human being is fed with a small quantity of a pure culture of comma bacilli. Another instance was found by Koch in the case of a tank of which the water was used for drinking and other purposes by many people among whom cholera was raging. He found the comma bacilli in this tank, and learned that the linen of the patients was washed in it. Around the tank were some thirty or forty huts, inhabited by 200 or 300 people; of these seventeen died, the number taken ill not being ascertained. The tank also received the refuse from the dwellings. The Hindoos bathe in the tank, wash their utensils in it, and deposit excreta on its shore; and if a hut has a latrine, its outflow is into the tank. Now, it was found that after a time the bacilli became less abundant in this water, and coincidentally the cholera declined; whereas, had the epidemic been the cause of their presence, and not the result, the number of bacilli should have increased it.

*

For the further dissemination of the disease it is necessary that the dejecta should be retained in the moist state, for drying destroys their potency; and this fact is borne out by the spread of the disease through the water-supply, or more directly by soiled hands, or even conveyance through insects, or blow-flies to food. Drains may be infected, and through them the water-supply. As the virus cannot be retained in the dry state, aerial infection seems impossible; nor has cholera ever been conveyed by merchandise or by letters, even if these are not disinfected and fumigated. Cholera can only be spread by human intercourse—a fact sometimes wanting in proof because it is overlooked, for the mildest case may be as infective as the most severe. The diagnosis of such mild cases by the detection of the comma bacillus becomes thus of much importance.

*

The diffusion of cholera in India depends on human intercourse, especially on pilgrimages, which are carried on to an inconceivable extent—e.g., hundreds of thousands flock yearly to Hurdivar and Puri,* remain there many weeks herded together, bathing in the tanks that supply them also with drinking-water. Over the borders of India the cholera is carried into Persia, and in the old caravan days thence to the south of Europe; but the route now is by the Red Sea and Suez Canal. Every year the danger to Europe by this route increases, for Bombay, which is seldom free from cholera, is but eleven days distant from Egypt, sixteen from Italy, and eighteen or twenty from France. It is also clear that the greatest danger lies in ships carrying large numbers of people, as troops, pilgrims, coolies, and emigrants, and not the merchant vessels with small crews, for in the former the outbreak of an epidemic would be likely to last till Europe was reached.

*

In conclusion, Dr Koch adverted to the subject of treatment, and reminded those who say that such discoveries do not enable us to cure the disease better than formerly, that a rational treatment of most diseases, and especially of infectious diseases, cannot be adopted until their cause and nature are known. But even yet the discovery of the cholera bacillus is important, as furnishing an aid in diagnosis which would facilitate the detection of the first case occurring in a district, and the adoption of measures to prevent its spread. Knowing also the nature and properties of the bacillus, and especially the readiness with which it is killed by drying, the right direction of prophylaxis is assured and the lavish expenditure of disinfectants checked, so that there will not be a repetition of what happened in the last epidemic, when millions of gallons were poured into the gutters and sewers without the slightest need. Even therapeutically the knowledge of the comma bacillus may be of value. Diagnosis will be possible in mild cases and in the early stages of the disease, when treatment is of most avail.

H. G. WELLS

The Stolen Bacillus (1895)

'This again,' said the Bacteriologist, slipping a glass slide under the microscope, 'is preparation of the celebrated Bacillus of cholera—the cholera germ.'

The pale-faced man peered down the microscope. He was evidently not accustomed to that kind of thing, and held a limp white hand over his disengaged eye. 'I see very little,' he said.

'Touch this screw,' said the Bacteriologist; 'perhaps the microscope is out of focus for you. Eyes vary so much. Just the fraction of a turn this way or that.'

'Ah! now I see,' said the visitor. 'Not so very much to see after all. Little streaks and shreds of pink. And yet those little particles, those mere atomies, might multiply and devastate a city! Wonderful!'

He stood up, and releasing the glass slip from the microscope, held it in his hand towards the window. 'Scarcely visible,' he said, scrutinising the preparation. He hesitated. 'Are these—alive? Are they dangerous now?'

'Those have been stained and killed,' said the Bacteriologist. 'I wish, for my own part, we could kill and stain every one of them in the universe.'

'I suppose,' the pale man said with a slight smile, 'that you scarcely care to have such things about you in the living—in the active state?'

'On the contrary, we are obliged to,' said the Bacteriologist. 'Here, for instance——' He walked across the room and took up one of several sealed tubes. 'Here is the living thing. This is a cultivation of the actual living disease bacteria.' He hesitated. 'Bottled cholera, so to speak.'

A slight gleam of satisfaction appeared momentarily in the face of the pale man. 'It's a deadly thing to have in your possession,' he said, devouring the little tube with his eyes. The Bacteriologist watched the morbid pleasure in his visitor's expression. This man, who had visited him that afternoon with a note of introduction from an old friend, interested him from the very contrast of their dispositions. The lank black hair and deep grey eyes, the haggard expression and nervous manner, the fitful yet keen interest of his visitor were a novel change from the phlegmatic deliberations of the ordinary scientific worker with whom the Bacteriologist chiefly associated. It was perhaps natural, with a hearer evidently so impressionable to the lethal nature of his topic, to take the most effective aspect of the matter.

He held the tube in his hand thoughtfully. 'Yes, here is the pestilence imprisoned. Only break such a little tube as this into a supply of drinking-water, say to these minute particles of life that one must needs stain and examine with the highest powers of the microscope even to see, and that one can neither smell nor taste—say to them, "Go forth, increase and multiply, and replenish the cisterns," and death—mysterious, untraceable death, death swift and terrible, death full of pain and indignity—would be released upon this city, and go hither and thither seeking his victims. Here he would take the husband from the wife, here the child from its mother, here the statesman from his duty, and here the toiler from his trouble. He would follow the water-mains, creeping along streets, picking out and punishing a house here and a house there where they did not boil their drinking-water, creeping into the wells of the mineral-water makers, getting washed into salad, and lying dormant in ices. He would wait ready to be drunk in the horse-troughs, and by unwary children in the public fountains. He would soak into the soil, to reappear in springs and wells at a thousand unexpected places. Once start him at the water supply, and before we could ring him in, and catch him again, he would have decimated the metropolis.'

He stopped abruptly. He had been told rhetoric was his weakness.

'But he is quite safe here, you know—quite safe.'

The pale-faced man nodded. His eyes shone. He cleared his throat. 'These Anarchist—rascals,' said he, 'are fools, blind fools—to use bombs when this kind of thing is attainable. I think——'

A gentle rap, a mere light touch of the finger-nails was heard at the door. The Bacteriologist opened it. 'Just a minute, dear,' whispered his wife.

When he re-entered the laboratory his visitor was looking at his watch. 'I had no idea I had wasted an hour of your time,' he said. 'Twelve minutes to four. I ought to have left here by half-past three. But your things were really too interesting. No, positively I cannot stop a moment longer. I have an engagement at four.'

He passed out of the room reiterating his thanks, and the Bacteriologist accompanied him to the door, and then returned thoughtfully along the passage to his laboratory. He was musing on the ethnology of his visitor. Certainly the man was not a Teutonic type nor a common Latin one. 'A morbid product, anyhow, I am afraid,' said the Bacteriologist to himself. 'How he gloated on those cultivations of disease-germs!' A disturbing thought struck him. He turned to the bench by the vapour-bath, and then very quickly to his writing-table. Then he felt hastily in his pockets, and then rushed to the door. 'I may have put it down on the hall table,' he said.

'Minnie!' he shouted hoarsely in the hall.

'Yes, dear,' came a remote voice.

'Had I anything in my hand when I spoke to you, dear, just now?'

Pause.

'Nothing, dear, because I remember——'

'Blue ruin!' cried the Bacteriologist, and incontinently ran to the front door and down the steps of his house to the street.

Minnie, hearing the door slam violently, ran in alarm to the window. Down the street a slender man was getting into a cab. The Bacteriologist, hatless, and in his carpet slippers, was running and gesticulating wildly towards this group. One slipper came off, but he did not wait for it. 'He has gone *mad*!' said Minnie; 'it's that horrid science of his'; and, opening the window, would have called after him. The slender man, suddenly glancing round, seemed struck with the same idea of mental disorder. He pointed hastily to the Bacteriologist, said something to the cabman, the apron of the cab slammed, the whip swished, the horse's feet clattered, and in a moment cab, and Bacteriologist hotly in pursuit, had receded up the vista of the roadway and disappeared round the corner.

Minnie remained straining out of the window for a minute. Then she drew her head back into the room again. She was dumbfounded. 'Of course he is eccentric,' she meditated. 'But running about London—in the height of the season, too—in his socks!' A happy thought struck her. She hastily put her bonnet on, seized his shoes, went into the hall, took down his hat and light overcoat from the pegs, emerged upon the doorstep, and hailed a cab that opportunely crawled by. 'Drive me up the road and round. Havelock Crescent, and see if we can find a gentleman running about in a velveteen coat and no hat.'

'Velveteen coat, ma'am, and no 'at. Very good, ma'am.' And the cabman whipped up at once in the most matter-of-fact way, as if he drove to this address every day in his life.

Some few minutes later the little group of cabmen and loafers that collects round the cabmen's shelter at Haverstock Hill were startled by the passing of a cab with a ginger-coloured screw of a horse, driven furiously.

They were silent as it went by, and then as it receded—'That's 'Arry 'Icks. Wot's *he* got?' said the stout gentleman known as Old Tootles.

'He's a-using his whip, he is, *to* rights,' said the ostler boy.

'Hullo!' said poor old Tommy Byles; 'here's another bloomin' loonatic. Blowed if there aint.'

'It's old George,' said old Tootles, 'and he's drivin' a loonatic, *as* you say. Aint he a-clawin' out of the keb? Wonder if he's after 'Arry 'Icks?'

The group round the cabmen's shelter became animated. Chorus: 'Go it, George!' 'It's a race.' 'You'll ketch 'em!' 'Whip up!'

'She's a goer, she is!' said the ostler boy.

'Strike me giddy!' cried old Tootles. 'Here! *I'm* a-goin' to begin in a minute. Here's another comin'. If all the kebs in Hampstead aint gone mad this morning!'

'It's a fieldmale this time,' said the ostler boy.

'She's a followin' *him*,' said old Tootles. 'Usually the other way about.'

'What's she got in her 'and?'

'Looks like a 'igh 'at.'

'What a bloomin' lark it is! Three to one on old George,' said the ostler boy. 'Nexst!'

Minnie went by in a perfect roar of applause. She did not like it but she felt that she was doing her duty, and whirled on down Haverstock Hill and Camden Town High Street with her eyes ever intent on the animated back view of old George, who was driving her vagrant husband so incomprehensibly away from her.

The man in the foremost cab sat crouched in the corner, his arms tightly folded, and the little tube that contained such vast possibilities of destruction gripped in his hand. His mood was a singular mixture of fear and exultation. Chiefly he was afraid of being caught before he could accomplish his purpose, but behind this was a vaguer but larger fear of the awfulness of his crime. But his exultation far exceeded his fear. No Anarchist before him had ever approached this conception of his. Ravachol, Vaillant,* all those distinguished persons whose fame he had envied dwindled into insignificance beside him. He had only to make sure of the water supply, and break the little tube into a reservoir. How brilliantly he had planned it, forged the letter of introduction and got into the laboratory, and how brilliantly he had seized his opportunity! The world should hear of him at last. All those people who had sneered at him, neglected him, preferred other people to him, found his company undesirable, should consider him at last. Death, death, death! They had always treated him as a man of no importance. All the world had been in a conspiracy to keep him under. He would teach them yet what it is to isolate a man. What was this familiar street? Great Saint Andrew's Street, of course! How fared the chase? He craned out of the cab. The Bacteriologist was scarcely fifty yards behind. That was bad. He would be caught and stopped yet. He felt in his pocket for money, and found half-a-sovereign. This he thrust up through the trap in the top of the cab into the man's face. 'More,' he shouted, 'if only we get away.'

The money was snatched out of his hand. 'Right you are,' said the cabman, and the trap slammed, and the lash lay along the glistening side of the horse. The cab swayed, and the Anarchist, half-standing under the trap, put the hand containing the little glass tube upon the apron to preserve his balance. He felt the brittle thing crack, and the broken half of it rang upon the floor of the cab. He fell back into the seat with a curse, and stared dismally at the two or three drops of moisture on the apron.

He shuddered.

'Well! I suppose I shall be the first. *Phew!* Anyhow, I shall be a Martyr. That's something. But it is a filthy death, nevertheless. I wonder if it hurts as much as they say.'

Presently a thought occurred to him—he groped between his feet. A little drop was still in the broken end of the tube, and he drank that to make sure. It was better to make sure. At any rate, he would not fail.

Then it dawned upon him that there was no further need to escape the Bacteriologist. In Wellington Street he told the cabman to stop, and got out. He slipped on the step, and his head felt queer. It was rapid stuff this cholera poison. He waved his cabman out of existence, so to speak, and stood on the pavement with his arms folded upon his breast awaiting the arrival of the Bacteriologist. There was something tragic in his pose. The sense of imminent death gave him a certain dignity. He greeted his pursuer with a defiant laugh.

'Vive l'Anarchie! You are too late, my friend. I have drunk it. The cholera is abroad!'

The Bacteriologist from his cab beamed curiously at him through his spectacles. 'You have drunk it! An Anarchist! I see now.' He was about to say something more, and then checked himself. A smile hung in the corner of his mouth. He opened the apron of his cab as if to descend, at which the Anarchist waved him a dramatic farewell and strode off towards Waterloo Bridge, carefully jostling his infected body against as many people as possible. The Bacteriologist was so preoccupied with the vision of him that he scarcely manifested the slightest surprise at the appearance of Minnie upon the pavement with his hat and shoes and overcoat. 'Very good of you to bring my things,' he said, and remained lost in contemplation of the receding figure of the Anarchist.

'You had better get in,' he said, still staring. Minnie felt absolutely convinced now that he was mad, and directed the cabman home on her own responsibility. 'Put on my shoes? Certainly dear,' said he, as the cab began to turn, and hid the strutting black figure, now small in the distance, from his eyes. Then suddenly something grotesque struck him, and he laughed. Then he remarked, 'It is really very serious, though.

'You see, that man came to my house to see me, and he is an Anarchist. No—don't faint, or I cannot possibly tell you the rest. And I wanted to astonish him, not knowing he was an Anarchist, and took up a cultivation of that new species of Bacterium I was telling you of, that infest, and I think cause, the blue patches upon various monkeys; and like a fool, I said it was Asiatic cholera. And he ran away with it to poison the water of London, and he certainly might have made things look blue for this civilised city. And now he has swallowed it. Of course, I cannot say what will happen, but you know it turned that kitten blue, and the three puppies—in patches, and the sparrow—bright blue. But the bother is, I shall have all the trouble and expense of preparing some more.

'Put on my coat on this hot day! Why? Because we might meet Mrs Jabber. My dear, Mrs Jabber is not a draught. But why should I wear a coat on a hot day because of Mrs ——. Oh! *very* well.'

Experimental Medicine and Vivisection

CLAUDE BERNARD

From *An Introduction to the Study of Experimental Medicine* (1865)

VIVISECTION

We have succeeded in discovering the laws of inorganic matter only by penetrating into inanimate bodies and machines; similarly we shall succeed in learning the laws and properties of living matter only by displacing living organs in order to get into their inner environment. After dissecting cadavers, then, we must necessarily dissect living beings, to uncover the inner or hidden parts of the organisms and see them work; to this sort of operation we give the name of vivisection, and without this mode of investigation, neither physiology nor scientific medicine is possible; to learn how man and animals live, we cannot avoid seeing great numbers of them die, because the mechanisms of life can be unveiled and proved only by knowledge of the mechanisms of death.

Men have felt this truth in all ages; and in medicine, from the earliest times, men have performed not only therapeutic experiments but even vivisection. We are told that the kings of Persia delivered men condemned to death to their physicians, so that they might perform on them vivisections useful to science. According to Galen, Attalus III (Philometor), who reigned at Pergamum, one hundred thirty-seven years before Jesus Christ, experimented with poisons and antidotes on criminals condemned to death.* Celsus recalls and approves the vivisection which Herophilus and Erasistratus performed on criminals with the Ptolemies' consent.* It is not cruel, he says, to inflict on a few criminals, sufferings which may benefit multitudes of innocent people throughout all centuries. The Grand Duke of Tuscany had a criminal given over to the professor of anatomy, Fallopius,* at Pisa, with permission to kill or dissect him at pleasure. As the criminal had a quartan fever, Fallopius wished to investigate the effects of opium on the paroxysms. He administered two drams of opium during an intermission; death occurred after the second experiment. Similar instances have occasionally recurred, and the story is well known of the archer of Meudon who was pardoned because a nephrotomy* was successfully performed on him. Vivisection of animals also goes very far back. Galen may be considered its founder. He performed his experiments especially on monkeys and on young pigs and described the instruments and methods used in experimenting. Galen performed almost no other kind of experiment than that which we call disturbing experiments, which consist in wounding, destroying or removing a part, so as to judge its function by the disturbance caused by its removal. He summarized earlier experiments and studied for himself the effects of destroying the spinal cord at different heights, of perforating the chest on one side or both sides at once; the effects of section of the nerves leading to the intercostal muscles and of section of the recurrent nerve. He tied arteries and performed experiments on the mechanism of deglutition. Since Galen, at long intervals in the midst of medical systems, eminent vivisectors have always appeared. As such, the names of Graaf, Harvey, Aselli, Pecquet, Haller, etc., have been handed down to us. In our time, and especially under the influence of Magendie,* vivisection has entered physiology and medicine once for all, as an habitual or indispensable method of study.

The prejudices clinging to respect for corpses long halted the progress of anatomy. In the same way, vivisection in all ages has met with prejudices and detractors. We cannot aspire to destroy all the prejudice in the world; neither shall we allow ourselves here to answer the arguments of detractors of vivisection; since they thereby deny experimental medicine, i.e., scientific medicine. However, we shall consider a few general questions, and then we shall set up the scientific goal which vivisection has in view.

First, have we a right to perform experiments and vivisections on man? Physicians make therapeutic experiments daily on their patients, and surgeons perform vivisections daily on their subjects. Experiments, then, may be performed on man, but within what limits? It is our duty and our right to perform an experiment on man whenever it can save his life, cure him or gain him some personal benefit. The principle of medical and surgical morality, therefore, consists in never performing on man an experiment which might be harmful to him to any extent, even though the result might be highly advantageous to science, i.e., to the health of others. But performing experiments and operations exclusively from the point of view of the patient's own advantage does not prevent their turning out profitably to science. It cannot indeed be otherwise; an old physician who has often administered drugs and treated many patients is more experienced, that is, he will experiment better on new patients, because he has learned from experiments made on others. A surgeon who has performed operations on different kinds of patients learns and perfects himself experimentally. Instruction comes only through experience; and that fits perfectly into the definitions given at the beginning of this introduction.

May we make experiments on men condemned to death or vivisect them? Instances have been cited, analogous to the one recalled above, in which men have permitted themselves to perform dangerous operations on condemned criminals, granting them pardon in exchange. Modern ideas of morals condemn such actions; I completely agree with these ideas; I consider it wholly permissible, however, and useful to science, to make investigations on the properties of tissues immediately after the decapitations of criminals. A helminthologist* had a condemned woman without her knowledge swallow larvae of intestinal worms, so as to see whether the worms developed in the intestines after her death. Others have made analogous experiments on patients with phthisis* doomed to an early death; some men have made experiments on themselves. As experiments of this kind are of great interest to science and can be conclusive only on man, they seem to be wholly permissible when they involve no suffering or harm to the subject of the experiment. For we must not deceive ourselves, morals do not forbid making experiments on one's neighbour or on one's self; in everyday life men do nothing but experiment on one another. Christian morals forbid only one thing, doing ill to one's neighbour. So, among the experiments that may be tried on man, those that can only harm are forbidden, those that are innocent are permissible, and those that may do good are obligatory.

Another question presents itself. Have we the right to make experiments on animals and vivisect them? As for me, I think we have this right, wholly and absolutely. It would be strange indeed if we recognized man's right to make use of animals in every walk of life, for domestic service, for food, and then forbade him to make use of them for his own instruction in one of the sciences most useful to humanity. No hesitation is possible; the science of life can be established only through experiment, and we can save living beings from death only after sacrificing others. Experiments must be made either on man or on animals. Now I think that physicians already make too many dangerous experiments on man, before carefully studying them on animals. I do not admit that it is moral to try more or less dangerous or active remedies on patients in hospitals, without first experimenting with them on dogs; for I shall prove, further on, that results obtained on animals may all be conclusive for man when we know how to experiment properly. If it is immoral, then, to make an experiment on man when it is dangerous to him, even though the result may be useful to others, it is essentially moral to make experiments on an animal, even though painful and dangerous to him, if they may be useful to man.

After all this, should we let ourselves be moved by the sensitive cries of people of fashion or by the objections of men unfamiliar with scientific ideas? All feelings deserve respect, and I shall be very careful never to offend anyone's. I easily explain them to myself, and that is why they cannot stop me. I understand perfectly how physicians under the influence of false ideas, and lacking the scientific sense, fail to appreciate the necessity of experiment and vivisection in establishing biological science. I also understand perfectly how people of fashion, moved by ideas wholly different from those that animate physiologists, judge vivisection quite differently. It cannot be otherwise. Somewhere in this introduction we said that, in science, ideas are what give facts their value and meaning. It is the same in morals, it is everywhere the same. Facts materially alike may have opposite scientific meanings, according to the ideas with which they are connected. A cowardly assassin, a hero and a warrior each plunges a dagger into the breast of his fellow. What differentiates them, unless it be the ideas which guide their hands? A surgeon, a physiologist and Nero* give themselves up alike to mutilation of living beings. What differentiates them also, if not ideas? I therefore shall not follow the example of LeGallois,* in trying to justify physiologists in the eyes of strangers to science who reproach them with cruelty; the difference in ideas explains everything. A physiologist is not a man of fashion, he is a man of science, absorbed by the scientific idea which he pursues: he no longer hears the cry of animals, he no longer sees the blood that flows, he sees only his idea and perceives only organisms concealing problems which he intends to solve. Similarly, no surgeon is stopped by the most moving cries and sobs, because he sees only his idea and the purpose of his operation. Similarly again, no anatomist feels himself in a horrible slaughter house; under the influence of a scientific idea, he delightedly follows a nervous filament through stinking livid flesh, which to any other man would be an object of disgust and horror. After what has gone before we shall deem all discussion of vivisection futile or absurd. It is impossible for men, judging facts by such different ideas, ever to agree; and as it is impossible to satisfy everybody, a man of science should attend only to the opinion of men of science who understand him, and should derive rules of conduct only from his own conscience.

The scientific principle of vivisection is easy, moreover, to grasp. It is always a question of separating or altering certain parts of the living machine, so as to study them and thus to decide how they function and for what. Vivisection, considered as an analytic method of investigation of the living, includes many successive steps, for we may need to act either on organic apparatus, or on organs, or on tissue, or on the histological units themselves. In extemporized and other vivisections, we produce mutilations whose results we study by preserving the animals. At other times, vivisection is only an autopsy on the living, or a study of properties of tissues immediately after death. The various processes of analytic study of the mechanisms of life in living animals are indispensable, as we shall see, to physiology, to pathology and to therapeutics. However, it would not do to believe that vivisection in itself can constitute the whole experimental method as applied to the study of vital phenomena. Vivisection is only anatomical dissection of the living; it is necessarily combined with all the other physico-chemical means of investigation which must be carried into the organism. Reduced to itself, vivisection would have only a limited range and in certain cases must even mislead us as to the actual rôle of organs. By these reservations I do not deny the usefulness or even the necessity of vivisection in the study of vital phenomena. I merely declare it insufficient. Our instruments for vivisection are indeed so coarse and our senses so imperfect that we can reach only the coarse and complex parts of an organism. Vivisection under the microscope would make much finer analysis possible, but it presents much greater difficulties and is applicable only to very small animals.

But when we reach the limits of vivisection we have other means of going deeper and dealing with the elementary parts of organisms where the elementary properties of vital phenomena have their seat. We may introduce poisons into the circulation, which carry their specific action to one or another histological unit. Localized poisonings, as Fontana and J. Müller* have already used them, are valuable means of physiological analysis. Poisons are veritable reagents of life, extremely delicate instruments which dissect vital units. I believe myself the first to consider the study of poisons from this point of view, for I am of the opinion that studious attention to agents which alter histological units should form the common foundation of general physiology, pathology and therapeutics. We must always, indeed, go back to the organs to find the simplest explanations of life.

To sum up, dissection is a displacing of a living organism by means of instruments and methods capable of isolating its different parts. It is easy to understand that such dissection of the living presupposes dissection of the dead.

SIR JAMES PAGET

Vivisection: Its Pains and Its Uses (1881)

It seems fair to demand that those who inflict pain or other distress on animals, for the purpose of acquiring knowledge, should be judged by the same rules as those who, for any other purposes, do the same.

The rules by which these are judged may be read in the customs by which a very great majority of sensible and humane persons encourage or permit the infliction of pain and death on large numbers of animals, for purposes far short of great utility, necessity, or self-defence.

It seems in these customs an admitted rule that, for the sake of certain quantities of utility or pleasure, or both, men may inflict great pain on animals without incurring the blame of cruelty. Can it be shown, for those who make painful scientific experiments, that the pain of their experiments is less and the utility more than in the majority of the practices permitted or encouraged by the great majority of reasonable and humane persons among the educated classes in this country?

In enumerating some of the instances of pain-giving which are generally and, as I think, for the most part rightly allowed, I am aware that some may seem trivial, and some nearly necessary to human welfare; however, they are not cited for the purpose of speaking ill of them, but as examples of practices which, not being deemed blameworthy or restrained by law (unless in respect of the seasons in which they are allowed), may serve as measures with which to compare the pain-giving experiments of scientific inquirers.

Among such practices are the painful restraint and training of our horses and other domestic animals; the caging of birds for the sake of their beauty or their song; the imprisonment of animals of all kinds in zoological gardens and aquaria for study or for amusement. In all these instances animals are compelled or restrained from the happiness of natural life; they have to endure what might be inflicted as severe punishment on criminals—slavery or imprisonment for life. But the inflictions are justified by the utility which men derive from them.

In another large group of painful customs generally encouraged are those inflicting death and often great suffering on birds and beasts for obtaining ornamental fur or feathers; the mutilation of sheep and oxen for the sake of their better or quicker fattening; the multiplication of pains and deaths in the killing of small birds and small fish, such as larks, quails, whitebait, and the like; although, so far as mere sustenance of life is concerned, any weight of food in one large fish or one large bird would serve as well as an equal weight in a hundred small ones. Still, the pleasure of delicious food, or of beautiful decoration, or, in some instances, the utility of better nutriment, seems sufficient to a vast majority of civilised men and women to justify these customs.

In another group may be named all the pain-giving sports—shooting, hunting, stalking, fishing, and the rest—various in the pleasure that they give, various in utility. And in yet another, the trapping, hunting, and killing of mice, rats, stoats, frogs, and toads invading cultivated land—worms, and slugs, and the whole class of what we call vermin—creatures generally troublesome and sometimes injurious.

From a list such as this, which might easily be enlarged, a rough estimate may be formed of the quantity of pain or distress, imprisonment or death, which, in the opinion of great majorities of persons entitled to judge, may be inflicted on animals for purposes of utility or of pleasure, or from other motives far less than those of necessary self-defence or maintenance of human life. The list may thus serve as a standard with which to compare the pains and the utilities of vivisections. Doubtless many persons would find in it some practices which they would forbid; some would hunt or shoot, but would not keep parrots or larks in confinement; some would eat whitebait or small birds, and wear sealskin, and order the destruction (anyhow) of all the rats and mice in their houses, but would put down fox-hunting and salmon-fishing. But there are very few, even among the generally most sensible and humane, who do not allow or encourage, even if they do not practise, many things of which I think it certain that the pain is greater and the utility less than that of many experiments on living animals. They may do it thoughtlessly, but they may find that they do it, if they will make a careful survey of their furniture, clothes, and ornaments, their food, amusements, and habits of life for a year, and then estimate the pains which in providing all these have been inflicted upon animals. Let them estimate them, if they can, with the same measure as that with which they estimate the pain of vivisection.

Such an estimate will probably seem the more easy the less the subject of pain has been studied. If we reflect on the evidence on which we believe that, from any given injury or disease, anyone must suffer less or more pain, we find that we are generally guessing, or saying to ourselves, 'It must be so,' without any clear evidence that 'It is so.' At most, if we have ourselves had any injury or disease, we may believe that another in the same condition would suffer just as we did. But few beliefs would be more fallacious. The sensibility to pain is as various as is the 'ear for music'; the disease which by one is described, and very truly according to that one's sensations, as a source of agony only to be compared with the rack or some such torture, is by another described as not very distressing; and the accounts given of it by others imply that between these extremes there are all intermediate degrees. To those who study them in surgical practice it is sure that degrees of pain depend on differences of personality much more than on different intensities or quantities of disease or injury. And there are abundant cases to prove that the general sensibility to pain is far greater among the more than among the less cultivated races of mankind; that savages, as they are called, endure with comparative indifference inflictions which to most persons of the higher races would be terrible. Mental cultivation continued through many generations has not only increased the general keenness of our senses, so that we discern far wider and minuter varieties and combinations of form, colour, sound, and flavour, than can be discriminated by lower races; it seems to have increased equally our sensibility to pain and our power of directing our attention to it. This seems to be especially true among persons with poetic and artistic minds: and, as we may be sure of the contrast between the higher and the lower races of men, so we may believe that the contrast must be yet greater between ourselves and any of the animals lower than man. It is as nearly certain as anything of the kind can be that with every degree of diminution of the proportion which the nervous system bears to the rest of the body there is an equal diminution of the sensibility to pain—the lower in the scale of nature the less the sensibility; so the pain inflicted by a deer-stalker, a salmon-fisher, or a vivisector is certainly less than would be inflicted in a similar injury on any man. . . .

[In many cases, vivisection causes less pain to animals than socially accepted sports like hunting and fishing.] If it may thus be justly held that the pain and other miseries inflicted by vivisection are less than those inflicted in many practices encouraged by sensible and humane persons, it may next be considered whether their utility be as great. It might justly be asked whether their utility and pleasure be as great, for it will not be denied that pleasure is a considerable motive in most of the sports, and in the wearing of decorative dresses such as cannot be procured without giving pain. But I would rather not argue that man's pleasure can ever be reason enough for his giving pain. It seems impossible to define even nearly the 'when,' or the how much pain for how much pleasure. But, if any will hold the contrary, and that in the pursuit of pleasure pain may be inflicted, even without considerations of probable utility, then it may certainly be maintained that there are no pleasures more intense than the pursuit of new knowledge, nor any for which, if for any, greater pain might be given.

But, omitting the pleasures of both, may the utilities of the two groups of pain-giving pursuits be estimated? Looking back at the list, it is clear that one method of utility cannot be pleaded for all. Sports may well be justified by the skill, patience, self-control, and endurance which may be trained in them; by the recreation which they provide for tired men; by their great social advantages; by their satisfaction of a desire which, in many minds, has the force of a natural instinct that cannot justly be repressed. As for the restraints, and imprisonments, and fattenings of animals, their utility is in most instances so evident that the whole course of quiet social life and trade would need to be changed if they were forbidden. Besides, for most of these, as well as for most field sports, the creatures would have no opportunity of living at all if it were not given on condition of their submitting to restraint or death at the will of men. There would be no more foxes than wolves in this country if they were not kept to be hunted; pheasants, partridges, and other game would soon be extinct if they were not preserved on purpose to be shot.

The destruction of vermin has, no doubt, utility—is sometimes even necessary for the safety of our food and property; but one must regret that it is so often pursued in a very merciless manner—left to cats or dogs, or slowly-acting poisons, or starvings in traps. The procuring of decorative furs and other parts of dress and furniture, attended as it often is with great suffering to the creatures hunted, may, I suppose, be justified by some utility. But I am not a fair judge of it. I can speak more certainly of the utility of vivisection.

Speaking generally, it is certain that there are few portions of useful medical knowledge to which experiments on animals have not contributed. The knowledge may be now so familiar that the sources from which parts of it were derived may be forgotten; or what was first found by experiments may now have other evidences; or, experiments may only have made sure that which, without them, was believed: but the whole history of medicine would show that, whatever useful or accurate knowledge we possess, we owe some parts of it to experiments on animals.

To different parts of knowledge they have contributed very different proportions; and it is often difficult to assign to them their just proportion. They have never been the sole means of study. Chemists, physicists, practitioners, all have worked as well as physiologists; and the work of each has guided and strengthened that of others. The whole value of experiments on animals, therefore, cannot be estimated by a few examples; it may be made evident in them, and they may indicate how it stands alone in the utility of saving life; but no one can measure it who is not able to analyse the whole progress of medical knowledge during at least the last century.

A clear instance of its utility may be found in the tying of arteries whether for the cure of aneurism or for the stopping of bleeding. Before Hunter's time*—that is, about a hundred years ago—it is nearly certain that ninety-five out of a hundred persons who had aneurism of the principal artery of a lower limb died of it: a few more may have been saved by amputation above the knee, but at that time about half the patients who submitted to that operation died. At the present time, it is as certain that of a hundred persons with the same disease less than ten die. At that time all patients with aneurisms of arteries between the thigh and spine or in the neck or arm-pit, died, unless by some strange course of the disease one or two in a hundred went on living. Now, among all such patients, from fifty to seventy in every hundred are saved by operations. In the same time there has been a great diminution in the deaths from bleeding after large operations: I remember when such bleeding might be called common; it is now very rare. . . .

Looking back over the improvements of practical medicine and surgery during my own observation of them in nearly fifty years, I see great numbers of means effectual for the saving of lives and for the detection, prevention, or quicker remedy of diseases and physical disabilities, all obtained by means of knowledge to the acquirement or safe use of which experiments on animals have contributed. There is scarcely an operation in surgery of which the mortality is now more than half as great as it was forty years ago; scarcely a serious injury of which the consequences are more than half as serious; several diseases are remediable which used to be nearly always fatal; potent medicines have been introduced and safely used; altogether such a quantity of life and of working power has been saved by lately-acquired knowledge as is truly past counting. And in these advantages our domestic animals have had due share by the improvement of veterinary medicine. What proportion is due to experiments on animals no one can tell; it would be as hard to estimate the proportion contributed by each national means of education to the general intellectual improvement of our population. Let it be guessed at a tenth or a twentieth of the whole, and in either case the utility of vivisection must far surpass that of the great majority of pain-giving practices permitted or encouraged by thousands of persons of recognised humanity and good sense. And it is by these, when duly informed on the facts, that the question should be judged, for it is eminently one of those in which sentiment is predominant on one side, reason on the other; in which the arguments on one side are mainly based on kindly feeling and sympathy with sufferings of which the amount is guessed at, while on the other they rest mainly on facts observed, on considerations of utility, and on the desire for knowledge. The only competent judges in such a case are those in whom sentiment and intellectual power are fairly balanced, and who will dispassionately study the facts and compare the pain-giving and the utility of experiments on animals with those of any generally allowed or encouraged pursuit.

FRANCES POWER COBBE

Vivisection and Its Two-Faced Advocates (1882)

The position in which we, the opponents of Vivisection, find ourselves at present is this:—

We seek to stop certain practices which appear to us to involve gross cruelty, and to be contrary to the spirit of English law. Our knowledge of them is derived almost exclusively from the published reports and treatises prepared and issued by the actual individuals who carry out those practices; and our arguments are grounded upon *verbatim* citations from those published and accessible reports and treatises.

The persons whose practices we desire to stop, and their immediate associates, now meet our charges of cruelty by articles in the leading periodicals, wherein the proceedings in question are invested with a character not only diverse from, but opposite to, that which they wear in the scientific treatises and reports containing the original accounts. . . .

In the first place, the *purpose* of the great majority of experiments is differently described in the scientific treatises and in the popular articles. In the former, the *raison d'être* of most experiments appears to be the elucidation of points of purely scientific interest. It is only occasionally that we meet with allusions to diseases or their remedies, but the experiments are generally described as showing that one organ acts in one way and another in another—that such a lesion, or such an irritation, produces such and such results and reactions; and (especially) that Professor A.'s theory has been disproved and that of Professor B. (temporarily) established. In short, every page of these books corroborates the honest statement of Professor Hermann of Zurich.* 'The advancement of science, and not practical utility to medicine, is the true and straightforward object of all vivisection. No true investigator in his researches thinks of the practical utilization. Science can afford to despise this justification with which vivisection has been defended in England.'—*Die Vivisectionsfrage* p. 16.

We now turn to such articles as the six which have appeared in the *Nineteenth Century* and the two in the *Fortnightly Review** in defence of vivisection, and, *mirabile dictu*! not a solitary vivisection is mentioned of which the direct advancement of the healing art does not appear as the single-minded object.

Again, the *severity* of the experiments in common use, appears from the Treatises and Reports (always including the English 'Handbook [of the Physiological Laboratory],' *Transactions [of the Royal Society]*, and *Journal of Physiology*) to be truly frightful. Sawing across the backbone, dissecting out and irritating all the great nerves, driving catheters along the veins and arteries, inoculating with the most dreadful diseases, cutting out pieces of the intestine, baking, stewing, pouring boiling water into the stomach, freezing to death, reducing the brain to the condition of a 'lately-hoed potato field;' these and similarly terrible experiments form the staple of some of them, and a significant feature in all.

But turning now to the popular articles, we find Dr Lauder Brunton* assuring the readers of the *Nineteenth Century* that 'he has calculated that about twenty-four out of every 100 of the experiments (in the Parliamentary Returns), might have given pain. But of these twenty-four, four-fifths are like vaccination, the pain of which is of no great moment. In about one-seventh of the cases the animal only suffered from the healing of a wound.' Sir James Paget afforded us a still more *couleur de rose* view of the subject. He said: 'I believe that, with these few exceptions, there are no physiological experiments which are not matched or far surpassed in painfulness by common practices permitted or encouraged by the most humane persons.'*

Again, in reading these terrible Treatises (the English 'Handbook' included), we do not meet with one solitary appeal against the repetition of painful experiments, one caution to the student to forbear from the extremity of torture, one expression of pity or regret—even when the keenest suffering had been inflicted. On the contrary, we find frequent repetitions of such phrases as 'interesting experiments,' 'very interesting experiments,' 'beautiful' (*schöne*) cerebral inflammation, and so on. In short, the writers, frankly, seem pleased with their work, and exemplify Claude Bernard's description* of the ideal Vivisector—the man who 'does not hear the animal's cries of pain, and is blind to the blood that flows, and who sees nothing but his idea and organisms which conceal from him the secrets he is resolved to discover.' Or, still more advanced, they realized Cyon's* yet stronger picture in his great book of the 'Methodik,' of which, by the way, he has lately told us in the *Gaulois*, that when the book was coming out his English colleagues implored him not to allow it to be advertised in England.

In this great treatise M. Cyon tells us:—

'The true vivisector must approach a difficult vivisection with *joyful excitement*. . . . . He who shrinks from cutting into a living animal, he who approaches a vivisection as a disagreeable necessity, may be able to repeat one or two vivisections, but he will never be an artist in vivisection. . . . . The sensation of the physiologist when, from a gruesome wound, full of blood and mangled tissue, he draws forth some delicate nerve thread . . . . has much in common with that of a sculptor.'—*Methodik*, p. 15.

This is the somewhat startling self-revelation of the Vivisector, made by himself to his colleagues. The picture of him in the *Nineteenth Century* and *Fortnightly Review* is almost as different as one face of Janus from the other. We find him talking of the power of 'controlling one's emotions,' 'disregarding one's own feelings at the sight of suffering,' 'subordinating feeling to judgment,' and much more in the same strain, whereby the Vivisector is made to appear a martyr to the Enthusiasm of Humanity.

Again, as to the *number* of animals dissected alive, the Treatises make us suppose it to be enormous. M. Paul Bert* gives cases of terrible experiments on dogs placed under the compression of eight atmospheres and coming out stiffened, 'so that the animal may be carried by one paw just as a piece of wood'—and cats which, when dissected after death, showed a 'marrow which flowed like cream;' and of these experiments he gives the public instances up to No. 286. Schiff* is calculated to have 'used' 14,000 dogs and nearly 50,000 other animals during his ten years' work in Florence. Flourens told Blatin that Magendie had sacrificed 4,000 dogs to prove Bell's* theory of the nerves, and 4,000 more to disprove the same; and that he, Flourens, had proved Bell was right by sacrificing some thousand more. Dr Lauder-Brunton himself told the Royal Commission (Q. 5,721) that in one series, out of three on one subject, he had sacrificed (without result) ninety cats in an experiment during which they lingered four or five hours after the chloroform (Q. 5,724), with their intestines 'operated upon.' He also carried on another series of 150 experiments on various animals, very painful, and notoriously without results (Q. 5,748). This is the scale on which vivisections abroad and at home are carried on, if we are to be guided by the Treatises.

Turn we now to the popular Articles; and we find mention only of the very smallest numbers. Sir William Gull* minimizes Bernard's stove-baked dogs to six and Professor Yeo brings down those of Professor Rutherford's victims* to twelve every reference to numbers being apparently, like those of the Fuegians,* limited to the digits of physiologists.

Again, as regards Anaesthetics, throughout the Treatises I cannot recall having once seen them mentioned as *means of allaying the sufferings of the animals*, but very often as convenient applications for *keeping them quiet*. Claude Bernard in his 'Physiologie Opératoire,' and Cyon in his great 'Methodik,' each devote a section to them as MEANS OF RESTRAINT ('*contention*'), and describe their merits from that point of view. Morphia, for example, Bernard recommends because it keeps the animal still, though '*il souffre la douleur*;' and of curare* (which, he says, causes 'the most atrocious sufferings which the imagination can conceive'), he remarks, without an expression of regret, that its use in vivisection is so universal that it may always be assumed to have been used in experiments not otherwise described. Nor can haste explain this omission to treat anaesthetics from the humanitarian point of view, for the Treatises contain long chapters of advice to the neophyte in vivisection, how he may ingeniously avoid being bitten by the dogs, or scratched by the yet more '*terrible*' cats, which are, Bernard pathetically complains, '*indocile*' when lifted on the torture trough.

Turning to our *Nineteenth Century* essayists, we find chloroform is everywhere, and curare nowhere.

Lastly, there is not a trace in the Treatises—even in the English 'Handbook'—of the supposed Wall of China which guards the Flowery Land of English Vivisection from the hordes of outer barbarians who practise in Paris, Leipsic, Florence, Strasbourg, and Vienna. We find, on the contrary, a frequent and cordial interchange of experiments and compliments. Our English vivisectionists study in the schools of the Continent, and in several cases have brought over foreigners to be their assistants at home. When Claude Bernard died, so little did English physiologists think of repudiating him, that a letter appeared in the *Times* of March 20, 1878, inviting subscriptions to raise a monument to his honour, signed by Sir James Paget, Dr Burdon-Sanderson, Professor Humphry, Professor Gerald Yeo, Mr Ernest Hart, Mr Romanes, and Dr Michael Foster.*

Even last autumn, when Professors Goltz, Flint, Brown-Séquard, Béclard, and Chauveau joined the International Congress in London, they were received with the warmest welcome from their English colleagues, one hundred of whom accompanied Professors Goltz and Ferrier* to inspect the dogs of the former and the monkeys of the latter (I beg pardon, of Professor Yeo); and when Professor Goltz returned to Germany, he published a volume containing beautiful coloured pictures of the mutilated brains of his dogs, and dedicated it—to whom does the reader think? To—

'HIS ENGLISH FRIENDS!'

All this does not look exactly like hearty disgust and repudiation of the foreign system.

But turn we to the *Nineteenth Century* and *Fortnightly Review*, and lo! the garments of our English physiologists are drawn closely around them, and we are assured they have 'no connection whatever with the establishment over the way.' I am even rebuked for placing on the same page (in my article 'Four Replies') certain English experiments and 'the disgusting details of foreign atrocities, which excite a persistent feeling of repugnance.' Professor Yeo says he 'regards with pain and loathing such work as that of Mantegazza,' and asks me bitterly, 'Why repeat the oft-told tale of horrors contained in the works of Claude Bernard, Paul Bert, Brown-Séquard, and Richet in France, of Goltz in Germany, Mantegazza in Italy,* and Flint in America?'

Surely this is a cargo of Jonahs thrown overboard together! Claude Bernard, the prince of physiologists, to whom this same Professor Gerald Yeo, four years ago, wished to raise a statue! Brown-Séquard, the honoured of Professor Huxley! Professor Flint, who, six months since, was the favoured guest of every scientific throng in London, and who, I presume, is of Anglo-Saxon race, only corrupted from humane British vivisection by evil American communications! And lastly, Goltz!—poor Professor Goltz, who had so many cordial hand-shakes on quitting perfidious Albion, while the autumn leaves were falling, and who is now flung down the Gemonian stairs* a sacrifice to the rabble of anti-vivisectors, even while the ink is scarcely dry on his touching dedication of his book:—

'SEINEN
FREUNDEN IN ENGLAND
GEWIDMET
VON DEM VERFASSER.'*

May not this new Raleigh* fitly cry, not, 'O the friendship of Princes!' but 'O the friendship of Physiologists?'

Thus we see that, as regards, first, the *purpose* of the majority of vivisections; second, their severity; third, their number; fourth, the caution of the experimenters; fifth, the use of anaesthetics; sixth, the difference between English and foreign vivisection,—in short, on every one of the points of importance in the controversy,—there is contradiction on the broadest scale between the scientific Treatises and Reports prepared for 'brethren of the craft' and in the articles written in lay periodicals for the edification of the British public.

It is for the reader to judge which class of statement may, with the greater probability, be held to represent the genuine doings and feelings of the writers.

WILKIE COLLINS

From *Heart and Science* (1883)

In the first scene included here, Dr Nathan Benjulia has summoned his younger brother, Lemuel, because he has learned that Mr Morphew has written Lemuel a detailed letter about Ovid Vere. Vere, a young doctor known to both brothers, has travelled to Canada to regain his health. Benjulia is hoping Vere is suffering from a disease of the brain. He longs to study people as well as animals, and he is particularly interested in neurophysiology. When Benjulia learns that another scientist has pre-empted him in describing Vere's disease, he feels that all his experiments have been conducted in vain and vows to destroy his laboratory.

Between one and two o'clock, the next afternoon, Benjulia (at work in his laboratory) heard the bell which announced the arrival of a visitor at the house. No matter what the circumstances might be, the servants were forbidden to disturb him at his studies in any other way.

Very unwillingly he obeyed the call, locking the door behind him. . . . Getting within view of the front of the house, he saw a man standing on the door-step. Advancing a little nearer, he recognized Lemuel.

'Hullo!' cried the elder brother.

'Hullo!' answered the younger, like an echo.

They stood looking at each other with the suspicious curiosity of two strange cats. Between Nathan Benjulia, the famous doctor, and Lemuel Benjulia, the publisher's clerk, there was just family resemblance enough to suggest that they were relations. The younger brother was only a little over the ordinary height; he was rather fat than thin; he wore a moustache and whiskers; he dressed smartly — and his prevailing expression announced that he was thoroughly well satisfied with himself. But he inherited Benjulia's gipsy complexion; and, in form and colour, he had Benjulia's eyes. . . .

The distant barking of a dog became audible from the lane by which the house was approached. The sound seemed to annoy Benjulia. 'What's that?' he asked.

Lemuel saw his way to making some return for his brother's reception of him.

'It's my dog,' he said; 'and it's lucky for you that I have left him in the cab.'

'Why?'

'Well, he's as sweet-tempered a dog as ever lived. But he has one fault. He doesn't take kindly to scientific gentlemen in your line of business.' Lemuel paused, and pointed to his brother's hands. 'If he smelt *that*, he might try his teeth at vivisecting You.'

The spots of blood which Ovid had once seen on Benjulia's stick, were on his hands now. With unruffled composure he looked at the horrid stains, silently telling their tale of torture.

'What's the use of washing my hands,' he answered, 'when I am going back to my work?'

He wiped his finger and thumb on the tail of his coat. . . .

The distant dog barked again . . . 'Please excuse my dear old dog,' he said with maudlin tenderness; 'the poor dumb animal seems to know that I'm taking his side in the controversy. *Bow-wow* means, in his language, Fie upon the cruel hands that bore holes in our heads and use saws on our backs. Ah, Nathan, if you have got any dogs in that horrid place of yours, pat them and give them their dinner! You never heard me talk like this before—did you? I'm a new man since I joined the Society for suppressing you. Oh, if I only had the gift of writing!'

The effect of this experiment on his brother's temper, failed to fulfil Lemuel's expectations. The doctor's curiosity was roused on the doctor's own subject of inquiry. . . .

'Now,' said Benjulia, 'what is it to be. The favourite public bugbear? Vivisection?'

'Yes.'

'Very well. What can I do for you?'

'Tell me first,' said Lemuel, 'what is Law?'

'Nobody knows.'

'Well, then, what *ought* it to be?'

'Justice, I suppose.'

'Let me wait a bit, Nathan, and get that into my mind.' Benjulia waited with exemplary patience.

'Now about yourself;' Lemuel continued. 'You won't be offended—will you? Should I be right, if I called you a dissector of living creatures?'

Benjulia was reminded of the day when he had discovered his brother in the laboratory. His dark complexion deepened into hue. His cold grey eyes seemed to promise a coming outbreak. Lemuel went on.

'Does the law forbid you to make your experiments on a man,' he asked.

'Of course it does!'

'Why doesn't the law forbid you to make your experiments on a dog?'

Benjulia's face cleared again. The one penetrable point in his ironclad nature had not been reached yet. That apparently childish question about the dog appeared, not only to have interested him, but to have taken him by surprise. His attention wandered away from his brother. His clear intellect put Lemuel's objection in closer logical form, and asked if there was any answer to it, thus:

The law which forbids you to dissect a living man, allows you to dissect a living dog. Why?

There was positively no answer to this.

Suppose he said, Because a dog is an animal? Could he, as a physiologist, deny that a man is an animal too?

Suppose he said, Because the dog is the inferior creature in intellect? The obvious answer to this would be, But the lower order of savage, or the lower order of lunatic, compared with the dog, is the inferior creature in intellect; and, in these cases, the dog has, on your own showing, the better right to protection of the two.

Suppose he said, Because a man is a creature with a soul, and a dog is a creature without a soul? This would be simply inviting another unanswerable question: How do you know?

Honestly accepting the dilemma which thus presented itself, the conclusion that followed seemed to be beyond dispute.

If the Law, in the matter of Vivisection, asserts the principle of interference, the Law has barred its right to place arbitrary limits on its own action. If it protects any living creatures, it is bound in reason and in justice, to protect all.

'Well,' said Lemuel, 'am I to have an answer?'

'I'm not a lawyer.'

With this convenient reply, Benjulia opened Mr Morphew's letter, and read the forbidden part of it which began on the second page. There he found the very questions with which his brother had puzzled him—followed by the conclusion at which he had himself arrived!

'You interpreted the language of your dog just now,' he said quietly to Lemuel, 'and I naturally supposed your brain might be softening. Such as it is, I perceive your memory is in working order. Accept my excuses for feeling your pulse. You have ceased to be an object of interest to me.'

He returned to his reading. Lemuel watched him—still confidently waiting for results.

The letter proceeded in these terms:

'Your employer may perhaps be inclined to publish my work, if I can satisfy him that it will address itself to the general reader.

'We all know what are the false pretences, under which English physiologists practise their cruelties. I want to expose those false pretences in the simplest and plainest way, by appealing to my own experience as an ordinary working member of the medical profession.

'Take the pretence of increasing our knowledge of the action of drugs and poisons, by trying them on animals. The very drugs, the action of which dogs and cats have been needlessly tortured to demonstrate, I have successfully used on my human patients in the practice of a lifetime.

'I should also like to ask what proof there is that the effect of a poison on an animal may be trusted to inform us, with certainty, of the effect of the same poison on a man. To quote two instances only which justify doubt—and to take birds this time, by way of a change—a pigeon will swallow opium enough to kill a man, and will not be in the least affected by it; and parsley, which is an innocent herb in the stomach of a human being, is deadly poison to a parrot.

'I should deal in the same way, with the other pretence, of improving our practice of surgery by experiment on living animals.

'Not long since, I saw the diseased leg of a dog cut off at the hip joint. When the limb was removed, not a single vessel bled. Try the same operation on a man—and twelve or fifteen vessels must be tied as a matter of absolute necessity.

'Again. We are told by a great authority that the baking of dogs in ovens has led to new discoveries in treating fever. I have always supposed that the heat, in fever, is not a cause of disease, but a consequence. However, let that be, and let us still stick to experience. Has this infernal cruelty produced results which help us to cure scarlet fever? Our bedside practice tells us that scarlet fever runs its course as it always did. I can multiply such examples as these by hundreds when I write my book.

'Briefly stated, you now have the method by which I propose to drag the scientific English Savage from his shelter behind the medical interests of humanity, and to show him in his true character,—as plainly as the Scientific Foreign savage shows himself of his own accord. *He* doesn't shrink behind false pretences. *He* doesn't add cant to cruelty. *He* boldly proclaims the truth:—*I* do it, because I like it!'

Benjulia rose, and threw the letter on the floor.

'*I* proclaim the truth,' he said; '*I* do it because I like it. There are some few Englishmen who treat ignorant public opinion with the contempt that it deserves—and I am one of them.' He pointed scornfully to the letter. 'That wordy old fool is right about the false pretences. Publish his book, and I'll buy a copy of it.'

'That's odd,' said Lemuel.

'What's odd?'

'Well, Nathan, I'm only a fool—but if you talk in that way of false pretences and public opinion, why do you tell everybody that your horrid cutting and carving is harmless chemistry? And why were you in such a rage when I got into your workshop, and found you out! Answer me that!'

'Let me congratulate you first,' said Benjulia. 'It isn't every fool who knows that he *is* a fool. Now you shall have your answer. Before the end of the year, all the world will be welcome to come into my workshop, and see me at the employment of my life. Brother Lemuel, when you stole your way through my unlocked door, you found me travelling on the road to the grandest medical discovery of this century. You stupid ass, do you think I cared about what *you* could find out? I am in such perpetual terror of being forestalled by my colleagues, that I am not master of myself, even when such eyes as yours look at my work. In a month or two more—perhaps in a week or two—I shall have solved the grand problem. I labour at it all day. I think of it, I dream of it, all night. It will kill me. Strong as I am, it will kill me. What do you say? Am I working myself into my grave, in the medical interests of humanity? *That* for humanity! I am working for my own satisfaction—for my own pride—for my own unutterable pleasure in beating other men—for the fame that will keep my name living hundreds of years hence. Humanity! I say with my foreign brethren—Knowledge for its own sake, is the one god I worship. Knowledge is its own justification and its own reward. The roaring mob follows us with its cry of Cruelty. We pity their ignorance. Knowledge sanctifies cruelty. The old anatomist stole dead bodies for Knowledge. In that sacred cause, if I could steal a living man without being found out, I would tie him on my table, and grasp my grand discovery in days, instead of months. Where are you going? What! You're afraid to be in the same room with me! A man who can talk as I do, is a man who would stick at nothing? Is that the light in which you lower order of creatures look at us? Look a little higher—and you will see that a man who talks as I do is a man set above you by Knowledge. Exert yourself, and try to understand me. Have I no virtues, even from your point of view? Am I not a good citizen? Don't I pay my debts? Don't I serve my friends? You miserable creature, you have had my money when you wanted it. Look at that letter on the floor. The man mentioned in it is one of those colleagues whom I distrust. I did my duty by him for all that. I gave him the information he wanted; I introduced him to a friend in a land of strangers. Have I no feeling, as you call it? My last experiments on a monkey horrified me. His cries of suffering, his gestures of entreaty were like the cries and gestures of a child. I would have given the world to put him out of his misery. But I went on. In the glorious cause I went on. My hands turned cold—my heart ached—I thought of a child I sometimes play with—I suffered—I resisted—I went on. All for Knowledge! all for knowledge!'

His brother's presence was forgotten. His dark face turned livid; his gigantic frame shuddered; his breath came and went in deep sobbing gasps—it was terrible to see him and hear him.

Lemuel slunk out of the room. The jackal had roused the lion; the mean spirit of mischief in him had not bargained for this. 'I begin to believe in the devil,' he said to himself when he got to the house door. . . .

After waiting until the short winter daylight was at an end, the footman ventured to knock, and ask if the master wanted lights. He replied that he had lit the candles for himself. No smell of tobacco smoke came from the room; and he had let the day pass without going to the laboratory. These were portentous signs. The footman said to his fellow servants, 'There's something wrong.' The women looked at each other in vague terror. One of them said, 'Hadn't we better give notice to leave?' And the other whispered a question: 'Do you think he's committed a crime?'

Towards ten o'clock, the bell rang at last. Immediately afterwards they heard him calling to them from the hall. 'I want you, all three, up here.'

They went up together—the two women anticipating a sight of horror, and keeping close to the footman.

[*Benjulia dismisses his servants, offering each a month's wages and letter of reference and telling them he is going away. He then asks them to witness the signature of his will.*]

'I am going to the laboratory,' the master said; 'and I want a few things carried to the door.'

The big basket for waste paper, three times filled with letters and manuscripts; the books; the medicine chest; and the stone jar of oil from the kitchen—these, the master and the man removed together; setting them down at the laboratory door. It was a still cold starlight winter's night. The intermittent shriek of a railway whistle in the distance, was the only sound that disturbed the quiet of the time.

'Good night!' said the master.

The man returned the salute, and walked back to the house, closing the front door. He was now more firmly persuaded than ever that something was wrong. In the hall, the women were waiting for him. 'What *does* it mean?' they asked. 'Keep quiet,' he said; 'I'm going to see.'

In another minute he was posted at the back of the house, behind the edge of the wall. Looking out from this place, he could see the light of the lamps in the laboratory streaming through the open door, and the dark figure of the master coming and going, as he removed the objects left outside into the building. Then the door was shut, and nothing was visible but the dim glow that found its way to the skylight, through the white blind inside.

He boldly crossed the open space of ground, resolved to try what his ears might discover, now that his eyes were useless. He posted himself at the back of the laboratory, close to one of the side walls.

Now and then, he heard,—what had reached his ears when he had been listening on former occasions—the faint whining cries of animals. These were followed by new sounds. Three smothered shrieks, succeeding each other at irregular intervals, made his blood run cold. Had three death-strokes been dealt on some suffering creatures,with the same sudden and terrible certainty? Silence, horrible silence, was all that answered. In the distant railway there was an interval of peace.

The door was opened again; the flood of light streamed out on the darkness. Suddenly the yellow glow was spotted by the black figures of small swiftly-running creatures—perhaps cats, perhaps rabbits— escaping from the laboratory. The tall form of the master followed slowly, and stood revealed watching the flight of the animals. In a moment more, the last of the liberated creatures came out—a large dog, limping as if one of its legs was injured. It stopped as it passed the master, and tried to fawn on him. He threatened it with his hand. 'Be off with you, like the rest!' he said. The dog slowly crossed the flow of light, and was swallowed up in darkness.

The last of them that could move was gone. The death shrieks of the others had told their fate.

But still, there stood the master alone—a grand black figure, with its head turned up to the stars. The minutes followed one another: the servant waited, and watched him. The solitary man had a habit, well known to those about him, of speaking to himself; not a word escaped him now; his upturned head never moved; the bright wintry heaven held him spell-bound.

At last, the change came. Once more the silence was broken by the scream of the railway whistle.

He started like a person suddenly roused from deep sleep, and went back into the laboratory. The last sound then followed—the locking and bolting of the door.

The servant left his hiding-place: his master's secret, was no secret now. He hated himself for eating that master's bread, and earning that master's money. One of the ignorant masses, this man! Mere sentiment had a strange hold on his stupid mind; the remembrance of the poor wounded dog, companionable and forgiving under cruel injuries, cut into his heart like a knife. His thought, at that moment, was an act of treason to the royalty of Knowledge,—'I wish to God I could lame *him*, as he has lamed the dog!' Another fanatic! another fool! Oh, Science, be merciful to the fanatics, and the fools!

When he got back to the house, the women were still on the look-out for him. 'Don't speak to me now,' he said. 'Get to your beds. And, mind this—let's be off to-morrow morning before *he* can see us.'

There was no sleep for him when he went to his own bed.

The remembrance of the dog tormented him. The other lesser animals were active; capable of enjoying their liberty and finding shelter for themselves. Where had the maimed creature found a refuge, on that bitter night? Again, and again, and again, the question forced its way into his mind. He could endure it no longer. Cautiously and quickly—in dread of his extraordinary conduct being perhaps discovered by the women—he dressed himself, and opened the house door to look for the dog.

Out of the darkness on the step, there rose something dark. He put out his hand. A persuasive tongue, gently licking it, pleaded for a word of welcome. The crippled animal could only have got to the door in one way; the gate which protected the house-enclosure must have been left open. First giving the dog a refuge in the kitchen, the footman—rigidly performing his last duties—went to close the gate.

At his first step into the enclosure he stopped panic-stricken.

The starlit sky over the laboratory was veiled in murky red. Roaring flame, and spouting showers of sparks, poured through

the broken skylight. Voices from the farm raised the first cry—'Fire!
fire!'

*

At the inquest, the evidence suggested suspicion of incendiarism and
suicide. The papers, the books, the oil betrayed themselves as combustible materials, carried into the place for a purpose. The medicine
chest was known (by its use in cases of illness among the servants) to
contain opium. Adjourned inquiry elicited that the laboratory was
not insured, and that the deceased was in comfortable circumstances.
Where were the motives? One intelligent man, who had drifted into
the jury, was satisfied with the evidence. He held that the desperate
wretch had some reason of his own for first poisoning himself, and
then setting fire to the scene of his labours. Having a majority of
eleven against him, the wise juryman consented to a merciful verdict
of death by misadventure. The hideous remains of what had once
been Benjulia, found Christian burial. His brethren of the torture-
table, attended the funeral in large numbers. Vivisection had been
beaten on its own field of discovery. They honoured the martyr who
had fallen in their cause.

H. G. WELLS

From *The Island of Dr Moreau* (1896)

'And now, Prendick, I will explain,' said Doctor Moreau, so soon as
we had eaten and drunk. 'I must confess you are the most dictatorial
guest I ever entertained. I warn you that this is the last I do to oblige
you. The next thing you threaten to commit suicide about I shan't
do—even at some personal inconvenience.' . . .

'You admit that vivisected human being, as you called it, is, after
all, only the puma?' said Moreau. He had made me visit that horror
in the inner room to assure myself of its inhumanity.

'It is the puma,' I said, 'still alive, but so cut and mutilated as I
pray I may never see living flesh again. Of all vile——'

'Never mind that,' said Moreau. 'At least spare me those youthful
horrors. Montgomery used to be just the same. You admit it is the
puma. Now be quiet while I reel off my physiological lecture to you.'

And forthwith, beginning in the tone of a man supremely bored, but presently warming a little, he explained his work to me. He was very simple and convincing. Now and then there was a touch of sarcasm in his voice. Presently I found myself hot with shame at our mutual positions.

The creatures I had seen were not men, had never been men. They were animals—humanised animals—triumphs of vivisection.

'You forget all that a skilled vivisector can do with living things,' said Moreau. 'For my own part I'm puzzled why the things I have done here have not been done before. Small efforts of course have been made—amputation, tongue-cutting, excisions. Of course you know a squint may be induced or cured by surgery? Then in the case of excisions you have all kinds of secondary changes, pigmentary disturbances, modifications of the passions, alterations in the secretion of fatty tissue. I have no doubt you have heard of these things?'

'Of course,' said I. 'But these foul creatures of yours——'

'All in good time,' said he, waving his hand at me; 'I am only beginning. Those are trivial cases of alteration. Surgery can do better things than that. There is building up as well as breaking down and changing. You have heard, perhaps, of a common surgical operation resorted to in cases where the nose has been destroyed. A flap of skin is cut from the forehead, turned down on the nose, and heals in the new position. This is a kind of grafting in a new position of part of an animal upon itself. Grafting of freshly obtained material from another animal is also possible, —the case of teeth, for example. The grafting of skin and bone is done to facilitate healing. The surgeon places in the middle of the wound pieces of skin snipped from another animal, or fragments of bone from a victim freshly killed. Hunter's cockspur—possibly you have heard of that—flourished on the bull's neck. And the rhinoceros rats of the Algerian zouaves are also to be thought of,—monsters manufactured by transferring a slip from the tail of an ordinary rat to its snout, and allowing it to heal in that position.'

'Monsters manufactured!' said I. 'Then you mean to tell me——'

'Yes. These creatures you have seen are animals carven and wrought into new shapes. To that—to the study of the plasticity of living forms—my life has been devoted. I have studied for years, gaining in knowledge as I go. I see you look horrified, and yet I am telling you nothing new. It all lay in the surface of practical anatomy years ago, but no one had the temerity to touch it. It's not simply the outward form of an animal I can change. The physiology, the chemical rhythm of the creature, may also be made to undergo an enduring modification, of which vaccination and other methods of inoculation with living or dead matter are examples that will, no doubt, be familiar to you. A similar operation is the transfusion of blood, with which subject indeed I began. These are all familiar cases. Less so, and probably far more extensive, were the operations of those mediaeval practitioners who made dwarfs and beggar cripples and show-monsters; some vestiges of whose art still remain in the preliminary manipulation of the young mountebank or contortionist. Victor Hugo gives an account of them in *L'Homme qui Rit*.* . . . But perhaps my meaning grows plain now. You begin to see that it is a possible thing to transplant tissue from one part of an animal to another, or from one animal to another, to alter its chemical reactions and methods of growth, to modify the articulations of its limbs, and indeed to change it in its most intimate structure?

'And yet this extraordinary branch of knowledge has never been sought as an end, and systematically, by modern investigators, until I took it up! Some such things have been hit upon in the last resort of surgery; most of the kindred evidence that will recur to your mind has been demonstrated, as it were, by accident—by tyrants, by criminals, by the breeders of horses and dogs, by all kinds of untrained clumsy-handed men working for their own immediate ends. I was the first man to take up this question armed with antiseptic surgery, and with a really scientific knowledge of the laws of growth.

'Yet one would imagine it must have been practised in secret before. Such creatures as the Siamese Twins. . . . And in the vaults of the Inquisition. No doubt their chief aim was artistic torture, but some, at least, of the inquisitors must have had a touch of scientific curiosity. . . .'

'But,' said I, 'These things—these animals *talk*!'

He said that was so, and proceeded to point out that the possibilities of vivisection do not stop at a mere physical metamorphosis. A pig may be educated. The mental structure is even less determinate than the bodily. In our growing science of hypnotism we find the promise of a possibility of replacing old inherent instincts by new suggestions, grafting upon or replacing the inherited fixed ideas.

Very much, indeed, of what we call moral education is such an artificial modification and perversion of instinct; pugnacity is trained into courageous self-sacrifice, and suppressed sexuality into religious emotion. And the great difference between man and monkey is in the larynx, he said, in the incapacity to frame delicately different sound-symbols by which thought could be sustained. In this I failed to agree with him, but with a certain incivility he declined to notice my objection. He repeated that the thing was so, and continued his account of his work.

But I asked him why he had taken the human form as a model. There seemed to me then, and there still seems to me now, a strange wickedness in that choice.

He confessed that he had chosen that form by chance. 'I might just as well have worked to form sheep into llamas, and llamas into sheep. I suppose there is something in the human form that appeals to the artistic turn of mind more powerfully than any animal shape can. But I've not confined myself to man-making. Once or twice . . .' He was silent, for a minute perhaps. 'These years! How they have slipped by! And here I have wasted a day saving your life, and am now wasting an hour explaining myself!'

'But,' said I, 'I still do not understand. Where is your justification for inflicting all this pain? The only thing that could excuse vivisection to me would be some application——'

'Precisely,' said he. 'But you see I am differently constituted. We are on different platforms. You are a materialist.'

'I am *not* a materialist,' I began hotly.

'In my view—in my view. For it is just this question of pain that parts us. So long as visible or audible pain turns you sick, so long as your own pains drive you, so long as pain underlies your propositions about sin, so long, I tell you, you are an animal, thinking a little less obscurely what an animal feels. This pain——'

I gave an impatient shrug at such sophistry.

'Oh! but it is such a little thing. A mind truly opened to what science has to teach must see that it is a little thing. It may be that, save in this little planet, this speck of cosmic dust, invisible long before the nearest star could be attained—it may be, I say, that nowhere else does this thing called pain occur. But the laws we feel our way towards . . . Why, even on this earth, even among living things, what pain is there?'

He drew a little penknife as he spoke from his pocket, opened the smaller blade and moved his chair so that I could see his thigh. Then, choosing the place deliberately, he drove the blade into his leg and withdrew it.

'No doubt you have seen that before. It does not hurt a pin-prick. But what does it show? The capacity for pain is not needed in the muscle, and it is not placed there; it is but little needed in the skin, and only here and there over the thigh is a spot capable of feeling pain. Pain is simply our intrinsic medical adviser to warn us and stimulate us. All living flesh is not painful, nor is all nerve, nor even all sensory nerve. There's no taint of pain, real pain, in the sensations of the optic nerve. If you wound the optic nerve you merely see flashes of light, just as disease of the auditory nerve merely means a humming in our ears. Plants do not feel pain; the lower animals—it's possible that such animals as the starfish and crayfish do not feel pain. Then with men, the more intelligent they become the more intelligently they will see after their own welfare, and the less they will need the goad to keep them out of danger. I never yet heard of a useless thing that was not ground out of existence by evolution sooner or later. Did you? And pain gets needless.

'Then I am a religious man, Prendick, as every sane man must be. It may be I fancy I have seen more of the ways of this world's Maker than you—for I have sought his laws, in *my* way, all my life, while you, I understand, have been collecting butterflies. And I tell you, pleasure and pain have nothing to do with heaven or hell. Pleasure and pain—Bah! What is your theologian's ecstasy but Mahomet's houri* in the dark? This store men and women set on pleasure and pain, Prendick, is the mark of the beast upon them, the mark of the beast from which they came. Pain! Pain and pleasure—they are for us, only so long as we wriggle in the dust. . . .

'You see, I went on with this research just the way it led me. That is the only way I ever heard of research going. I asked a question, devised some method of getting an answer, and got—a fresh question. Was this possible, or that possible? You cannot imagine what this means to an investigator, what an intellectual passion grows upon him. You cannot imagine the strange colourless delight of these intellectual desires. The thing before you is no longer an animal, a fellow-creature, but a problem. Sympathetic pain—all I know of it I remember as a thing I used to suffer from years ago. I wanted—it was the only thing I wanted—to find out the extreme limit of plasticity in a living shape.'

'But,' said I, 'the thing is an abomination——'

'To this day I have never troubled about the ethics of the matter. The study of Nature makes a man at last as remorseless as Nature.'

EVOLUTION

Forced to describe an inaccessible past, scientists and literary writers recreating natural history appealed to their readers' imaginations. In *The Origin of Species*, Darwin tried to convince his audience of the evolution of species by reminding them how breeders produced new animals. Summoning images from their memories, he encouraged them to construct new ones of events they had never seen. Darwin offered readers large numbers of his own observations, but he knew he would never win adherents for the natural selection hypothesis unless he also succeeded as a narrator, telling readers a story they would accept as real.

In the nineteenth century writers called on readers' imaginations to reveal the way small changes could produce transformations over long periods of time. The challenge was to make readers picture a thousand, ten thousand, or a million years of gradual change, periods that for most people were almost unimaginable. Here metaphor proved valuable to literary and scientific writers, both of whom thought consciously about the comparisons they were making. Both struggled with their metaphors, for the alignments language invited often worked against the ideas writers were trying to express. In *Philosophy of the Inductive Sciences*, William Whewell pointed out that the English language conveys time in terms of space, creating a false impression that the two are fundamentally similar. To explain the concept of time—which unlike that of space, he believed, did not come from experience—he asked readers to think about familiar verses. For Whewell, the rhythm and metre of language suggested time's passage far better than the spatial metaphors that language offered.

Scientists used metaphors not just to help readers picture invisible forces but to explain why they could not see evidence they should have been seeing. The German embryologist Ernst Haeckel, who argued that developing organisms recapitulated their species' development, used the alphabet to explain why these recapitulations were imperfect. Even if a growing embryo 'spelled out' A, B, F, H, instead of A, B, C, D, he proposed, it was still passing through its ancestors' forms. The theory held true if one could just read the evidence right. For Haeckel and other biologists, developing organisms were texts in which one could read the past.

Like biologists, geologists needed to prove that the world had changed gradually as a result of small, accumulated alterations. Both needed to explain (1) that the past could be read, and (2) why gaps in the record made the past so difficult to read. Until the early 1860s the geologist

Charles Lyell opposed the zoologist Jean Baptiste de Lamarck's ideas that animals had evolved, protesting that Lamarck had developed his theories through imagination, not observation. In *Principles of Geology*, Lyell compared himself to a historian, criticizing his opponents' theories in terms that echo reviews of bad fiction. 'Such a portion of history would immediately assume the air of a romance,' he protested. 'The events would seem devoid of credibility, and inconsistent with the present course of human affairs.' Lyell was always conscious that he was telling a story, and he knew that he must use every resource to make it more convincing than rival versions of the past.

As a liberal reformer horrified by the French revolution, Lyell hoped to steer readers away from Neptunist and Vulcanist theories, for their cataclysmic floods and explosions made political upheaval seem 'natural'. Anxious to appeal to conservative readers, Lyell wrote his story in the language of educated gentlemen, illustrating his ideas with quotations from Virgil, Horace, Shakespeare, and Milton. Because his history was so readable, it sold very well, convincing readers that violent change was implausible and geology was worthy of gentlemen's attention.

With its biblical roots, the image of the destructive flood was easily transposed from popular culture to scientific theory. George Eliot's depiction of a flood in *The Mill on the Floss* shows the power of this image and suggests why Lyell had to work so hard to oppose it. Until the final pages, Eliot's novel is one of slow, careful development, describing Maggie and Tom Tulliver's complex relationship by telling stories of their childhood and family connections. Like geologists and naturalists, Eliot suggests, novelists are retelling lost tales, recovering lives and events whose traces have been obliterated. When the flood comes, it 'uproots' the narrative structure along with much of the setting. For the most part, Eliot presents the relations between present and past in a manner quite similar to Lyell's, as in her emphasis on gaps in the record. As a narrative device, however, the catastrophic flood proved hard to resist.

For both scientists and novelists, the idea that people might have evolved from other life forms made it all the more essential to tell their stories. In the intense debates that evolutionary theory provoked, the consequences for individual identity became immediately apparent. For those who believed people had evolved, the notion of individuality changed. Samuel Butler and the Austrian biologist Ewald Hering described an individual as a 'link in a chain', a body that contained and often re-enacted the past. The idea that complex organisms had developed out of unicellular ones affected the ways people viewed cells in human bodies. Evolutionary theory reinforced earlier proposals, like Rudolf Virchow's, that people were societies, associations of partly independent beings.

Studying the notion of individuality from a broad, biological perspective, Herbert Spencer concluded in *Principles of Biology* that people's understanding of selfhood made no sense on an evolutionary scale. When many strawberry plants are connected to one long rhizoid, he proposed, and many organisms pass through different forms in their life cycles, the idea of a unique, representative individual loses its meaning. One can talk about an individual only in a relative fashion, selecting a representative unit after studying the ways organisms function and interact. The human concept of individuality had no basis in nature. It was rooted in culture and was being imposed on nature by writers who failed to see humanity from a broader, evolutionary perspective. Years before Spencer, Alfred, Lord Tennyson had achieved the same insight. It was not necessary to dissect animals to see that nature was 'careless of the single life'. Striving for decades to accept his closest friend's death, Tennyson used language to immortalize a life that nature threatened to obliterate.

Both scientists and literary writers knew that relationships between people and their ancestors were complex. Even Haeckel, who argued hardest that the past was accessible through contemporary individuals, admitted that it could be extraordinarily difficult to see. In the prologue to *The Princess*, Tennyson challenged the idea that random traces constituted a coherent history. In his poem, his visitor confronts a confused jumble of fossils, weapons, and cultural relics, and Tennyson's juxtaposition suggests that his hosts' lives are related to their ancestors' as these random objects are related to human history. Like the portraits of ancestors, fossils alone can tell no story. It takes imagination, not just memories, to create a meaningful narrative.

Many scientific and literary writers would challenge the idea that gradual, cumulative changes could leave a legible record. If one rejected this idea, the individual life looked even less significant. Until the end of the nineteenth century Lamarck's hypothesis of the inheritance of acquired characters enjoyed more adherents than Darwin's theory of natural selection, for Lamarck's idea that individual actions had lasting effects appealed to people's sense of self-worth. According to Lamarck, valuable new traits and habits could be directly transmitted to the next generation. Of course, if the experiences of all individuals could be recorded and passed on to their offspring, then all individuals born inherited their ancestors' memories and served as palimpsests of their species' development. Samuel Butler joined numerous scientists and literary writers in arguing for organic memory, the notion that all individuals inherited traces of their ancestors' knowledge.

Organic memory was only possible if individuals could transmit newly acquired traits to their descendants, and according to Darwin, they could not. Natural selection dictated that variations could change a species only by allowing their bearers to survive longer and produce more offspring. German biologist August Weismann took an even harder line against Lamarck's idea than did Darwin himself. According to Weismann, individual organisms lived and died without influencing their 'immortal' germ plasm.

The novelist Thomas Hardy, who read Weismann's essays in the late 1880s, shared his view that individual habits made no direct change to the hereditary material. While Weismann's *Essays on Heredity* were widely read in the early 1890s, Hardy's novels offered the public more accessible stories of individuals enslaved by inherited drives. Throughout his works, Hardy depicts the impact of evolution on individual human lives, challenging a growing body of evolutionary theory that did not yet deal with human consciousness. In *A Pair of Blue Eyes*, a young geologist looks into the eyes of a dead trilobite. Faced with his own death, the scientist wonders what his own life is worth, considering that his knowledge and intelligence cannot keep him from suffering the trilobite's fate. According to the theories he supports, the individual must be sacrificed for the good of the species, but it is rarely clear why particular lives are destroyed. In her ironic poem, 'Lay of the Trilobite', May Kendall adds her voice to Hardy's, questioning the meaning of human consciousness. Like Hardy's novel, her poem invites the reader to imagine life from the perspective of an extinct animal. Kendall's narrator declares the trilobite to have been 'happy', but his claim is as absurd as the creature's litany of human achievements. In the end, the fossils impress their viewers not because of their biological remoteness but because of what they and the scientists have in common.

Whether or not readers believed they had inherited their ancestors' memories, cultural debates about evolution encouraged observations of people's similarity to animals. If people had descended from non-human ancestors, it seemed likely that they retained traces of these ancient animals within them. Both scientists and fiction writers explored people's animal-like tendencies, stressing not just people's bestiality but animals' 'human' traits. In *The Story of an African Farm*, Olive Schreiner juxtaposes the creative potential of the human mind with a senseless, destructive impulse she calls 'play'. Describing natural drives in Shakespearian terms, she presents a scenario in which noble labour ends 'in nothing' because of an urge people and animals share. George John Romanes's *Mental Evolution in Man*, though very different in style, uses similar images to argue that people and animals differ only in degree. Challenging the notion that human emotion and intellect distinguish them from horses or dogs, Schreiner and Romanes question the uniqueness of the human soul.

In their poems *In Memoriam* and 'Nature is a Heraclitean Fire', Tennyson and Gerard Manley Hopkins resist science's claim to replace religion as a provider of inspiration and enlightenment. Science deprives people of a sense of purpose, they suggested, promising true knowledge but delivering neither knowledge nor justice. Nine years before Darwin published *The Origin of Species*, Tennyson pictured a relentless nature 'red in tooth and claw', and Emily Pfeiffer saw 'dread Force', pure irrational hunger. In 'Hap', Hardy subversively suggests that it is more comforting to think of a world directed by a vengeful god than a world without direction or purpose. Even science's offer of steadily increasing knowledge provides no comfort to those who see their loved ones' lives snuffed out. Despite his great respect for the natural sciences, Hardy implies that such knowledge will only lead to greater unhappiness. Caught between natural drives and social demands, individuals are crushed despite their awareness of the forces crushing them.

Chief among the natural drives—and socially, one of the most carefully regulated—is the urge to reproduce, and in their depictions of sexuality, nineteenth-century scientists and literary writers combined cultural and biological understandings of mating. Novelists had always depicted the quest for a mate as a fierce, though sometimes comic struggle. More than four decades before Darwin published *The Origin of Species*, Jane Austen suggested how much was at stake—socially and economically—in the search for a wealthy husband. In 1871, when Darwin introduced the idea of sexual selection, he offered literary writers a new language in which to formulate a problem they had long been describing. In *The Descent of Man*, he attributed considerable power to female organisms, providing anthropomorphic descriptions in which females choose their mates based on the males' ostentatious displays. In Darwin's account, active males sing, fight, and perform for observant females, who then select the most promising partners. Constance Naden's 'Natural Selection' offers an ironic parody of Darwin's tale, describing a woman who scorns the narrator's learning in favour of his rival's singing and dancing abilities. With such forces in effect, readers might wonder, how did higher consciousness ever evolve?

Darwin, however, did not see female choice as a universal law of sexual selection. Human beings differed from all other animals, he believed, in leaving sexual choice to the males. Darwin's account reinforced cultural readings of female desire as a dangerous force that threatened the social order. When women did take the active role and select their mates, they were acting in a primitive fashion, revealing people's animal origins.

Henry Rider Haggard's fantasy novel *She* depicts a fictional society in which women choose their husbands. 'Thou art my chosen,' one woman proclaims to the attractive young hero, Vincey. The violence of this matri archal culture, where women make all the choices, affirms the convictions of any reader who regards female sexual choice as uncivilized. By contrast, Hardy's *Tess of the D'Urbervilles* supports Darwin's cultural reading with tragic force, illustrating the impact of sexual selection on individual lives. Despite unmistakable natural urges, working-class girls—of whom there are always too many—cannot even consider marrying the middle-class men to whom they are attracted. As both natural and social creatures, people suffer when their instincts and customs clash.

As scientists told stories using well-known strategies, images, and metaphors, they changed the rules about how stories could be told. Evolutionary theory presented individuality in a new light, emphasizing people's links to their past and, more importantly, to other people. Darwin's and Lyell's stories suggested new possibilities to novelists, and cultural debates about evolution offered story-tellers ways to recast their narratives of descent and social bonds. At the same time, the realist novel preceded and influenced evolutionary stories with its webs of interrelated characters. In this complex interplay of literary and scientific representations, the single life came to be seen as an intersection of forces, influenced by other lives in the present and the past.

The Present and the Past

JEAN BAPTISTE DE LAMARCK

From *Zoological Philosophy* (1809)

We are not here concerned with an argument, but with the examination of a positive fact—a fact which is of more general application than is supposed, and which has not received the attention that it deserves, no doubt because it is usually very difficult to recognise. This fact consists in the influence that is exerted by the environment on the various living bodies exposed to it.

It is indeed long since the influence of the various states of our organisation on our character, inclinations, activities and even ideas has been recognised; but I do not think that anyone has yet drawn attention to the influence of our activities and habits even on our organisation. Now since these activities and habits depend entirely on the environment in which we are habitually placed, I shall endeavour to show how great is the influence exerted by that environment on the general shape, state of the parts and even organisation of living bodies. It is, then, with this very positive fact that we have to do in the present chapter.

If we had not had many opportunities of clearly recognising the result of this influence on certain living bodies that we have transported into an environment altogether new and very different from that in which they were previously placed, and if we had not seen the resulting effects and alterations take place almost under our very eyes, the important fact in question would have remained for ever unknown to us.

The influence of the environment as a matter of fact is in all times and places operative on living bodies; but what makes this influence difficult to perceive is that its effects only become perceptible or recognisable (especially in animals) after a long period of time.

Before setting forth to examine the proofs of this fact, which deserves our attention and is so important for zoological philosophy, let us sum up the thread of the discussions that we have already begun.

In the preceding chapter* we saw that it is now an unquestionable fact that on passing along the animal scale in the opposite direction from that of nature, we discover the existence, in the groups composing this scale, of a continuous but irregular degradation in the organisation of animals, an increasing simplification in their organisation and, lastly, a corresponding diminution in the number of their faculties.

This well-ascertained fact may throw the strongest light over the actual order followed by nature in the production of all the animals that she has brought into existence, but it does not show us why the increasing complexity of the organisation of animals from the most imperfect to the most perfect exhibits only an *irregular gradation*, in the course of which there occur numerous anomalies or deviations with a variety in which no order is apparent.

Now on seeking the reason of this strange irregularity in the increasing complexity of animal organisation, if we consider the influence that is exerted by the infinitely varied environments of all

parts of the world on the general shape, structure and even organisation of these animals, all will then be clearly explained.

It will in fact become clear that the state in which we find any
animal, is, on the one hand, the result of the increasing complexity of
organisation tending to form a regular gradation; and, on the other
hand, of the influence of a multitude of very various conditions ever
tending to destroy the regularity in the gradation of the increasing
complexity of organisation.

I must now explain what I mean by this statement: *the environment
affects the shape and organisation of animals*, that is to say that when
the environment becomes very different, it produces in course of
time corresponding modifications in the shape and organisation of
animals.

It is true if this statement were to be taken literally, I should be
convicted of an error; for, whatever the environment may do, it
does not work any direct modification whatever in the shape and
organisation of animals.

But great alterations in the environment of animals lead to great
alterations in their needs, and these alterations in their needs necessarily lead to others in their activities. Now if the new needs become
permanent, the animals then adopt new habits which last as long as
the needs that evoked them. This is easy to demonstrate, and indeed
requires no amplification.

It is then obvious that a great and permanent alteration in the
environment of any race of animals induces new habits in these
animals.

Now, if a new environment, which has become permanent for
some race of animals, induces new habits in these animals, that is to
say, leads them to new activities which become habitual, the result
will be the use of some one part in preference to some other part, and
in some cases the total disuse of some part no longer necessary.

Nothing of all this can be considered as hypothesis or private
opinion; on the contrary, they are truths which, in order to be made
clear, only require attention and the observation of facts.

We shall shortly see by the citation of known facts in evidence, in
the first place, that new needs which establish a necessity for some
part really bring about the existence of that part, as a result of
efforts; and that subsequently its continued use gradually strengthens, develops and finally greatly enlarges it; in the second place,

we shall see that in some cases, when the new environment and the new needs have altogether destroyed the utility of some part, the total disuse of that part has resulted in its gradually ceasing to share in the development of the other parts of the animal; it shrinks and wastes little by little, and ultimately, when there has been total disuse for a long period, the part in question ends by disappearing. All this is positive; I propose to furnish the most convincing proofs of it. . . .

Nothing is more remarkable than the effects of habit in herbivorous mammals.

A quadruped, whose environment and consequent needs have for long past inculcated the habit of browsing on grass, does nothing but walk about on the ground; and for the greater part of its life is obliged to stand on its four feet, generally making only few or moderate movements. The large portion of each day that this kind of animal has to pass in filling itself with the only kind of food that it cares for, has the result that it moves but little and only uses its feet for support in walking or running on the ground, and never for holding on, or climbing trees.

From this habit of continually consuming large quantities of food-material, which distend the organs receiving it, and from the habit of making only moderate movements, it has come about that the body of these animals has greatly thickened, become heavy and massive and acquired a very great size: as is seen in elephants, rhinoceroses, oxen, buffaloes, horses, etc.

The habit of standing on their four feet during the greater part of the day, for the purpose of browsing, has brought into existence a thick horn which invests the extremity of their digits; and since these digits have no exercise and are never moved and serve no other purpose than that of support like the rest of the foot, most of them have become shortened, dwindled and, finally, even disappeared.

Thus in the pachyderms, some have five digits on their feet invested in horn, and their hoof is consequently divided into five parts; others have only four, and others again not more than three; but in the ruminants, which are apparently the oldest of the mammals that are permanently confined to the ground, there are not more than two digits on the feet and indeed, in the solipeds,* there is only one (horse, donkey).

Nevertheless some of these herbivorous animals, especially the ruminants, are incessantly exposed to the attacks of carnivorous animals in the desert countries that they inhabit, and they can only find safety in headlong flight. Necessity has in these cases forced them to exert themselves in swift running, and from this habit their body has become more slender and their legs much finer; instances are furnished by the antelopes, gazelles, etc.

In our own climates, there are other dangers, such as those constituted by man, with his continual pursuit of red deer, roe deer and fallow deer; this has reduced them to the same necessity, has impelled them into similar habits, and had corresponding effects.

Since ruminants can only use their feet for support, and have little strength in their jaws, which only obtain exercise by cutting and browsing on the grass, they can only fight by blows with their heads, attacking one another with their crowns.

In the frequent fits of anger to which the males especially are subject, the efforts of their inner feeling cause the fluids to flow more strongly towards that part of their head; in some there is hence deposited a secretion of horny matter, and in others of bony matter mixed with horny matter, which gives rise to solid protuberances: thus we have the origin of horns and antlers, with which the head of most of these animals is armed.

It is interesting to observe the result of habit in the peculiar shape and size of the giraffe (*Camelo-pardalis*): this animal, the largest of the mammals, is known to live in the interior of Africa in places where the soil is nearly always arid and barren, so that it is obliged to browse on the leaves of trees and to make constant efforts to reach them. From this habit long maintained in all its race, it has resulted that the animal's fore-legs have become longer than its hind legs, and that its neck is lengthened to such a degree that the giraffe, without standing up on its hind legs, attains a height of six metres (nearly 20 feet). . . .

It is a fact that all animals have special habits corresponding to their genus and species, and always possess an organisation that is completely in harmony with those habits.

It seems from the study of this fact that we may adopt one or other of the two following conclusions, and that neither of them can be verified.

Conclusion adopted hitherto: Nature (or her Author) in creating animals, foresaw all the possible kinds of environment in which they would have to live, and endowed each species with a fixed organisation and with a definite and invariable shape, which compel each species to live in the places and climates where we actually find them, and there to maintain the habits which we know in them.

My individual conclusion: Nature has produced all the species of animals in succession, beginning with the most imperfect or simplest, and ending her work with the most perfect, so as to create a gradually increasing complexity in their organisation; these animals have spread at large throughout all the habitable regions of the globe, and every species has derived from its environment the habits that we find in it and the structural modifications which observation shows us.

The former of these two conclusions is that which has been drawn hitherto, at least by nearly everyone: it attributes to every animal a fixed organisation and structure which never have varied and never do vary; it assumes, moreover, that none of the localities inhabited by animals ever vary; for if they were to vary, the same animals could no longer survive, and the possibility of finding other localities and transporting themselves thither would not be open to them.

The second conclusion is my own: it assumes that by the influence of environment on habit, and thereafter by that of habit on the state of the parts and even on organisation, the structure and organisation of any animal may undergo modifications, possibly very great, and capable of accounting for the actual condition in which all animals are found.

In order to show that this second conclusion is baseless, it must first be proved that no point on the surface of the earth ever undergoes variation as to its nature, exposure, high or low situation, climate, etc., etc.; it must then be proved that no part of animals undergoes even after long periods of time any modification due to a change of environment or to the necessity which forces them into a different kind of life and activity from what has been customary to them.

Now if a single case is sufficient to prove that an animal which has long been in domestication differs from the wild species whence it sprang, and if in any such domesticated species, great differences of conformation are found between the individuals exposed to such a habit and those which are forced into different habits, it will then be certain that the first conclusion is not consistent with the laws of nature, while the second, on the contrary, is entirely in accordance with them.

Everything then combines to prove my statement, namely: that it is not the shape either of the body or its parts which gives rise to the habits of animals and their mode of life; but that it is, on the contrary, the habits, mode of life and all the other influences of the environment which have in course of time built up the shape of the body and of the parts of animals. With new shapes, new faculties have been acquired, and little by little nature has succeeded in fashioning animals such as we actually see them.

Can there be any more important conclusion in the range of natural history, or any to which more attention should be paid than that which I have just set forth?

SIR CHARLES LYELL

From *Principles of Geology* (1830–3)

We have seen that, during the progress of geology, there have been great fluctuations of opinion respecting the nature of the causes to which all former changes of the earth's surface are referrible. The first observers conceived that the monuments which the geologist endeavours to decipher, relate to a period when the physical constitution of the earth differed entirely from the present, and that, even after the creation of living beings, there have been causes in action distinct in kind or degree from those now forming part of the economy of nature. These views have been gradually modified, and some of them entirely abandoned in proportion as observations have been multiplied, and the signs of former mutations more skilfully interpreted. Many appearances, which for a long time were regarded as indicating mysterious and extraordinary agency, are finally recognized as the necessary result of the laws now governing the material world; and the discovery of this unlooked for conformity has induced some geologists to infer that there has never been any interruption to the same uniform order of physical events. The same assemblage of general causes, they conceive, may have been sufficient to produce, by their various combinations, the endless diversity of effects, of which the shell of the earth has preserved the memorials, and, consistently with these principles, the recurrence of analogous changes is expected by them in time to come.

Whether we coincide or not in this doctrine, we must admit that the gradual progress of opinion concerning the succession of phenomena in remote eras, resembles in a singular manner that which accompanies the growing intelligence of every people, in regard to the economy of nature in modern times. In an early stage of advancement, when a great number of natural appearances are unintelligible, an eclipse, an earthquake, a flood, or the approach of a comet, with many other occurrences afterwards found to belong to the regular course of events, are regarded as prodigies. The same delusion prevails as to moral phenomena, and many of these are ascribed to the intervention of demons, ghosts, witches, and other immaterial and supernatural agents. By degrees, many of the enigmas of the moral and physical world are explained, and, instead of being due to extrinsic and irregular causes, they are found to depend on fixed and invariable laws. The philosopher at last becomes convinced of the undeviating uniformity of secondary causes, and, guided by his faith in this principle, he determines the probability of accounts transmitted to him of former occurrences, and often rejects the fabulous tales of former ages, on the ground of their being irreconcilable with the experience of more enlightened ages.

As a belief in want of conformity in the physical constitution of the earth, in ancient and modern times, was for a long time universally prevalent, and that too amongst men who were convinced that the order of nature is *now* uniform, and has continued so for several thousand years; every circumstance which could have influenced their minds and given an undue bias to their opinions deserves particular attention. Now the reader may easily satisfy himself, that, however undeviating the course of nature may have been from the earliest epochs, it was impossible for the first cultivators of geology to come to such a conclusion, so long as they were under a delusion as to the age of the world, and the date of the first creation of animate beings. However fantastical some theories of the sixteenth century may now appear to us,—however unworthy of men of great talent and sound judgment, we may rest assured that, if the same misconceptions now prevailed in regard to the memorials of human transactions, it would give rise to a similar train of absurdities. Let us imagine, for example, that Champollion,* and the French and Tuscan literati now engaged in exploring the antiquities of Egypt, had visited that country with a firm belief that the banks of the Nile were never peopled by the human race before the beginning of the nineteenth century, and that their faith in this dogma was as difficult to shake as the opinion of our ancestors, that the earth was never the abode of living beings until the creation of the present continents, and of the species now existing,—it is easy to perceive what extravagant systems they would frame, while under the influence of this delusion, to account for the monuments discovered in Egypt. The sight of the pyramids, obelisks, colossal statues, and ruined temples, would fill them with such astonishment, that for a time they would be as men spell-bound—wholly incapacitated to reason with sobriety. They might incline at first to refer the construction of such stupendous works to some superhuman powers of a primeval world. A system might be invented resembling that so gravely advanced by Manetho,* who relates that a dynasty of gods originally ruled in Egypt, of whom Vulcan, the first monarch, reigned nine thousand years. After them came Hercules and other demi-gods, who were at last succeeded by human kings. When some fanciful speculations of this kind had amused the imagination for a time, some vast repository of mummies would be discovered and would immediately undeceive those antiquaries who enjoyed an opportunity of personally examining them, but the prejudices of others at a distance, who were not eye-witnesses of the whole phenomena, would not be so easily overcome. The concurrent report of many travellers would indeed render it necessary for them to accommodate ancient theories to some of the new facts, and much wit and ingenuity would be required to modify and defend their old positions. Each new invention would violate a greater number of known analogies; for if a theory be required to embrace some false principle, it becomes more visionary in proportion as facts are multiplied, as would be the case if geometers were now required to form an astronomical system on the assumption of the immobility of the earth.

Amongst other fanciful conjectures concerning the history of Egypt, we may suppose some of the following to be started. 'As the banks of the Nile have been so recently colonized, the curious substances called mummies could never in reality have belonged to men. They may have been generated by some *plastic virtue* residing in the interior of the earth, or they may be abortions of nature produced by her incipient efforts in the work of creation. For if deformed beings are sometimes born even now, when the scheme of the universe is fully developed, many more may have been "sent before their time, scarce half made up," when the planet itself was in the embryo state. But if these notions appear to derogate from the perfection of the Divine attributes, and if these mummies be in all their parts true representations of the human form, may we not refer them to the future rather than the past? May we not be looking into the womb of nature, and not her grave? may not these images be like the shades of the unborn in Virgil's Elysium*—the archetypes of men not yet called into existence?'

These speculations, if advocated by eloquent writers, would not fail to attract many zealous votaries, for they would relieve men from the painful necessity of renouncing preconceived opinions. Incredible as such scepticism may appear, it would be rivalled by many systems of the sixteenth and seventeenth centuries, and among others by that of the learned Falloppio,* who regarded the tusks of fossil elephants as earthy concretions, and the vases of Monte Testaceo, near Rome, as works of nature, and not of art. But when one generation had passed away, and another not compromised to the support of antiquated dogmas had succeeded, they would review the evidence afforded by mummies more impartially, and would no longer controvert the preliminary question, that human beings had lived in Egypt before the nineteenth century: so that when a hundred years perhaps had been lost, the industry and talents of the philosopher would be at last directed to the elucidation of points of real historical importance.

But we have adverted to one only of many prejudices with which the earlier geologists had to contend. Even when they conceded that the earth had been peopled with animate beings at an earlier period than was at first supposed, they had no conception that the quantity of time bore so great a proportion to the historical era as is now generally conceded. How fatal every error as to the quantity of time must prove to the introduction of rational views concerning the state of things in former ages, may be conceived by supposing that the annals of the civil and military transactions of a great nation were perused under the impression that they occurred in a period of one hundred instead of two thousand years. Such a portion of history would immediately assume the air of a romance; the events would seem devoid of credibility, and inconsistent with the present course of human affairs. A crowd of incidents would follow each other in thick succession. Armies and fleets would appear to be assembled only to be destroyed, and cities built merely to fall in ruins. There would be the most violent transitions from foreign or intestine war to periods of profound peace, and the works effected during the years of disorder or tranquillity would be alike superhuman in magnitude.

He who should study the monuments of the natural world under the influence of a similar infatuation, must draw a no less exaggerated picture of the energy and violence of causes, and must experience the same insurmountable difficulty in reconciling the former and present state of nature. If we could behold in one view all the volcanic cones thrown up in Iceland, Italy, Sicily, and other parts of Europe, during the last five thousand years, and could see the lavas which have flowed during the same period; the dislocations, subsidences and elevations caused by earthquakes; the lands added to various deltas, or devoured by the sea, together with the effects of devastation by floods, and imagine that all these events had happened in one year, we must form most exalted ideas of the activity of the agents, and the suddenness of the revolutions. Were an equal amount of change to pass before our eyes in the next year, could we avoid the conclusion that some great crisis of nature was at hand? If geologists, therefore, have misinterpreted the signs of a succession of events, so as to conclude that centuries were implied where the characters imported thousands of years, and thousands of years where the language of nature signified millions, they could not, if they reasoned logically from such false premises, come to any other conclusion, than that the system of the natural world had undergone a complete revolution. . . .

In our first volume we merely described that part of Etna* which has been formed during the historical era; an insignificant portion of the whole mass. Nearly all the remainder may be referred to the tertiary period immediately antecedent to the *recent* epoch. We before stated, that the great cone is, in general, of a very symmetrical form, but is broken, on its eastern side, by a deep valley, called the Val del Bove[1], which, commencing near the summit of the mountain, descends into the woody region, and is then continued, on one side, by a second and narrower valley, called the Val di Calanna. . . .

---

[1] In the provincial dialect of the peasants called 'Val del Bué,' for here the herdsman

——'in reductâ valle *mugientium*
Prospectat errantes greges.—'*

Scenery of the Val del Bove.—Without entering at present into any further discussions respecting the origin of the Val del Bove, we shall proceed to describe some of its most remarkable features. Let the reader picture to himself a large amphitheatre, five miles in diameter, and surrounded on three sides by precipices from two thousand to three thousand feet in height. If he has beheld that most picturesque scene in the chain of the Pyrenees, the celebrated 'cirque of Gavarnie,'* he may form some conception of the magnificent circle of precipitous rocks which inclose, on three sides, the great plain of the Val del Bove. This plain has been deluged by repeated streams of lava, and although it appears almost level when viewed from a distance, it is, in fact, more uneven than the surface of the most tempestuous sea. Besides the minor irregularities of the lava, the valley is in one part interrupted by a ridge of rocks, two of which, Musara and Capra, are very prominent. It can hardly be said that they

> ——'like giants stand
> To sentinel enchanted land;'

for although, like the Trosachs,* they are of gigantic dimensions, and appear almost isolated as seen from many points, yet the stern and severe grandeur of the scenery which they adorn is not such as would be selected by a poet for a vale of enchantment. The character of the scene would accord far better with Milton's picture of the infernal world; and if we imagine ourselves to behold in motion, in the darkness of the night, one of those fiery currents, which have so often traversed the great valley, we may well recall

> ——'yon dreary plain, forlorn and wild,
> The seat of desolation, void of light
> Save what the glimmering of these livid flames
> Cast pale and dreadful.'*

The face of the precipices already mentioned is broken in the most picturesque manner by the vertical walls of lava which traverse them. These masses usually stand out in relief, are exceedingly diversified in form, and often of immense altitude. In the autumn, their black outline may often be seen relieved by clouds of fleecy vapour which settle behind them, and do not disperse until midday, continuing to fill the valley while the sun is shining on every other part of Sicily, and on the higher regions of Etna.

As soon as the vapours begin to rise, the changes of scene are varied in the highest degree, different rocks being unveiled and hidden by turns, and the summit of Etna often breaking through the clouds for a moment with its dazzling snows, and being then as suddenly withdrawn from the view.

An unusual silence prevails, for there are no torrents dashing from the rocks, nor any movement of running water in this valley, such as may almost invariably be heard in mountainous regions. Every drop of water that falls from the heavens, or flows from the melting ice and snow, is instantly absorbed by the porous lava; and such is the dearth of springs, that the herdsman is compelled to supply his flocks, during the hot season, from stores of snow laid up in hollows of the mountain during winter.

The strips of green herbage and forest-land, which have here and there escaped the burning lavas, serve, by contrast, to heighten the desolation of the scene. When I visited the valley, nine years after the eruption of 1819, I saw hundreds of trees, or rather the white skeletons of trees, on the borders of the black lava, the trunks and branches being all leafless, and deprived of their bark by the scorching heat emitted from the melted rock; an image recalling those beautiful lines—

> ——'As when heaven's fire
> Hath scath'd the forest oaks, or mountain pines,
> With singed top their stately growth, though bare,
> Stands on the blasted heath.'*

WILLIAM WHEWELL

From *Philosophy of the Inductive Sciences* (1840)

The Idea of Time, like the Idea of Space, offers to our notice some characters which do not belong to our fundamental ideas generally, but which are deserving of remark. These characters are, in some respects, closely similar with regard to time and to space, while, in other respects, the peculiarities of these two ideas are widely different. We shall point out some of these characters.

Time is not a general *abstract* notion collected from experience; as, for example, a certain general conception of the relations of things.

For we do not consider particular *times* as examples of Time in general, (as we consider particular causes to be examples of Cause,) but we conceive all particular times to be parts of a single and endless Time. This continually-flowing and endless time is what offers itself to us when we contemplate any series of occurrences. All actual and possible times exist as Parts, in this original and general Time. And since all particular times are considered as derivable from time in general, it is manifest that the notion of time in general cannot be derived from the notions of particular times. The notion of time in general is therefore not a general conception gathered from experience.

Time is infinite. Since all actual and possible times exist in the general course of time, this general time must be infinite. All limitation merely divides, and does not terminate, the extent of absolute time. Time has no beginning and no end; but the beginning and the end of every other existence takes place in it.

Time, like space, is not only a form of perception, but of *intuition*. We contemplate events as taking place *in* time. We consider its parts as added to one another, and events as filling a larger or smaller extent of such parts. The time which any event takes up is the sum of all such parts, and the relation of the same to time is fully understood when we can clearly see what portions of time it occupies, and what it does not. Thus the relation of known occurrences to time is perceived by intuition; and time is a form of intuition of the external world.

Time is conceived as a quantity of one dimension; it has great analogy with a line, but none at all with a surface or solid. Time may be considered as consisting of a series of instants, which are before and after one another; and they have no other relation than this, of *before* and *after*. Just the same would be the case with a series of points taken along a line; each would be after those on one side of it, and before those on another. Indeed the analogy between time, and space of one dimension, is so close, that the same terms are applied to both ideas, and we hardly know to which they originally belong. Times and lines are alike called *long* and *short*; we speak of the *beginning* and *end* of a line; of a *point* of time, and of the *limits* of a portion of duration.

But, as has been said, there is nothing in time which corresponds to more than one dimension in space, and hence nothing which has any obvious analogy with figure. Time resembles a line indefinitely extended both ways; all partial times are portions of this line; and no mode of conceiving time suggests to us a line making any angle with the original line, or any other combination which might give rise to figures of any kind. The analogy between time and space, which in many circumstances is so clear, here disappears altogether. Spaces of two and of three dimensions, planes and solids, have nothing to which we can compare them in the conceptions arising out of time.

As figure is a conception solely appropriate to space, there is also a conception which peculiarly belongs to time, namely, the conception of recurrence of times similarly marked; or, as it may be termed, *rhythm*, using this word in a general sense. The term rhythm is most commonly used to designate the recurrence of times marked by the syllables of a verse, or the notes of a melody: but it is easy to see that the general conception of such a recurrence does not depend on the mode in which it is impressed upon the sense. The forms of such recurrence are innumerable. Thus in such a line as

> Quádrupedánte putrém sonitú quatit úngula cámpum,*

we have alternately one long or forcible syllable, and two short or light ones, recurring over and over. In like manner in our own language, in the line

> At the clóse of the dáy when the hámlet is still,

we have two light and one strong syllable repeated four times over. Such repetition is the essence of versification. The same kind of rhythm is one of the main elements of music, with this difference only, that in music the forcible syllables are made so for the purposes of rhythm by their length only or principally; for example, if either of the above lines were imitated by a melody in the most simple and obvious manner, each strong syllable would occupy exactly twice as much time as two of the weaker ones. Something very analogous to such rhythm may be traced in other parts of poetry and art, which we need not here dwell upon. But in reference to our present subject, we may remark that by the introduction of such rhythm, the flow of time, which appears otherwise so perfectly simple and homogeneous, admits of an infinite number of varied yet regular modes of progress. All the kinds of versification which occur in all languages, and the still more varied forms of recurrence of notes of different lengths, which are heard in all the varied strains of melodies, are only examples of such modifications, or configurations as we may call them, of time. They involve relations of various portions of time, as figures involve relations of various portions of space. But yet the analogy between rhythm and figure is by no means very close; for in rhythm we have relations of quantity alone in the parts of time, whereas in figure we have relations not only of quantity, but of a kind altogether different,—namely, of position. On the other hand, a *repetition* of similar elements, which does not necessarily occur in figures, is quite essential in order to impress upon us that measured progress of time of which we here speak. And thus the ideas of time and space have each its peculiar and exclusive relations; position and figure belonging only to space, while repetition and rhythm are appropriate to time.

One of the simplest forms of recurrence is *alternation*, as when we have alternate strong and slight syllables. For instance,—

> Awáke, arise, or bé for éver fáll'n.

Or without any subordination, as when we reckon numbers, and call them in succession, *odd, even, odd, even*.

But the simplest of all forms of recurrence is that which has no variety;—in which a series of units, each considered as exactly similar to the rest, succeed each other; as *one, one, one*, and so on. In this case, however, we are led to consider each unit with reference to all that have preceded; and thus the series *one, one, one*, and so forth, becomes *one, two, three, four, five*, and so on; a series with which all are familiar, and which may be continued without limit.

We thus collect from that repetition of which time admits, the conception of *Number*.

ALFRED, LORD TENNYSON

From *The Princess* (1847)

Sir Walter Vivian all a summer's day
Gave his broad lawns until the set of sun
Up to the people: thither flock'd at noon
His tenants, wife and child, and thither half

The neighbouring borough with their Institute
Of which he was the patron. I was there
From college, visiting the son,—the son
A Walter too,—with others of our set.

And me that morning Walter show'd the house,
Greek, set with busts: from vases in the hall
Flowers of all heavens, and lovelier than their names,
Grew side by side; and on the pavement lay
Carved stones of the Abbey-ruin in the park,
Huge Ammonites,* and the first bones of Time;
And on the tables every clime and age
Jumbled together; celts and calumets,*
Claymore* and snowshoe, toys in lava, fans
Of sandal, amber, ancient rosaries,
Laborious orient ivory sphere in sphere,
The cursed Malayan crease,* and battle-clubs
From the isles of palm: and higher on the walls,
Betwixt the monstrous horns of elk and deer,
His own forefathers' arms and armour hung.

And 'this' he said 'was Hugh's at Agincourt;
And that was old Sir Ralph's at Ascalon:*
A good knight he! we keep a chronicle
With all about him'—which he brought, and I
Dived in a hoard of tales that dealt with knights
Half-legend, half-historic, counts and kings
Who laid about them at their wills and died;
And mixt with these, a lady, one that arm'd
Her own fair head, and sallying thro' the gate,
Had beat her foes with slaughter from her walls.

And, I all rapt in this, 'Come out,' he said,
'To the Abbey: there is Aunt Elizabeth
And sister Lilia with the rest.' We went
(I kept the book and had my finger in it)
Down thro' the park: strange was the sight to me;
For all the sloping pasture murmur'd sown
With happy faces and with holiday.
There moved the multitude, a thousand heads:

The patient leaders of their Institute
Taught them with facts. One rear'd a font of stone
And drew, from butts of water on the slope,
The fountain of the moment, playing now
A twisted snake, and now a rain of pearls,
Or steep-up spout whereon the gilded ball
Danced like a wisp: and somewhat lower down
A man with knobs and wires and vials fired
A cannon: Echo answer'd in her sleep
From hollow fields: and here were telescopes
For azure views; and there a group of girls
In circle waited, whom the electric shock
Dislink'd with shrieks and laughter: round the lake
A little clock-work steamer paddling plied
And shook the lilies: perch'd about the knolls
A dozen angry models jetted steam:
A petty railway ran: a fire-balloon
Rose gem-like up before the dusky groves
And dropt a fairy parachute and past:
And there thro' twenty posts of telegraph
They flash'd a saucy message to and fro
Between the mimic stations; so that sport
With Science hand in hand went; otherwhere
Pure sport: a herd of boys with clamour bowl'd
And stump'd the wicket; babies roll'd about
Like tumbled fruit in grass; and men and maids
Arranged a country dance, and flew thro' light
And shadow, while the twangling violin
Struck up with Soldier-laddie, and overhead
The broad ambrosial aisles of lofty lime
Made noise with bees and breeze from end to end.

CHARLES DARWIN

From *The Origin of Species* (1859)

STRUGGLE FOR EXISTENCE

Before entering on the subject of this chapter, I must make a few preliminary remarks, to show how the struggle for existence bears on Natural Selection. It has been seen in the last chapter that amongst organic beings in a state of nature there is some individual variability; indeed I am not aware that this has ever been disputed. It is immaterial for us whether a multitude of doubtful forms be called species or sub-species or varieties; what rank, for instance, the two or three hundred doubtful forms of British plants are entitled to hold, if the existence of any well-marked varieties be admitted. But the mere existence of individual variability and of some few well-marked varieties, though necessary as the foundation for the work, helps us but little in understanding how species arise in nature. How have all those exquisite adaptations of one part of the organisation to another part, and to the conditions of life, and of one distinct organic being to another being, been perfected? We see these beautiful co-adaptations most plainly in the woodpecker and missletoe; and only a little less plainly in the humblest parasite which clings to the hairs of a quadruped or feathers of a bird; in the structure of the beetle which dives through the water; in the plumed seed which is wafted by the gentlest breeze; in short, we see beautiful adaptations everywhere and in every part of the organic world.

Again, it may be asked, how is it that varieties, which I have called incipient species, become ultimately converted into good and distinct species, which in most cases obviously differ from each other far more than do the varieties of the same species? How do those groups of species, which constitute what are called distinct genera, and which differ from each other more than do the species of the same genus, arise? All these results, as we shall more fully see in the next chapter, follow inevitably from the struggle for life. Owing to this struggle for life, any variation, however slight and from whatever cause proceeding, if it be in any degree profitable to an individual of any species, in its infinitely complex relations to other organic beings and to external nature, will tend to the preservation of that individual, and will generally be inherited by its offspring. The offspring, also, will thus have a better chance of surviving, for, of the many individuals of any species which are periodically born, but a small number can survive. I have called this principle, by which each slight variation, if useful, is preserved, by the term of Natural Selection, in order to mark its relation to man's power of selection. We have seen that man by selection can certainly produce great results, and can adapt organic beings to his own uses, through the accumulation of slight but useful variations, given to him by the hand of Nature. But Natural Selection, as we shall hereafter see, is a power incessantly ready for action, and is as immeasurably superior to man's feeble efforts, as the works of Nature are to those of Art.

We will now discuss in a little more detail the struggle for existence. In my future work this subject shall be treated, as it well deserves, at much greater length. The elder De Candolle* and Lyell have largely and philosophically shown that all organic beings are exposed to severe competition. In regard to plants, no one has treated this subject with more spirit and ability than W. Herbert, Dean of Manchester,* evidently the result of his great horticultural knowledge. Nothing is easier than to admit in words the truth of the universal struggle for life, or more difficult—at least I have found it so—than constantly to bear this conclusion in mind. Yet unless it be thoroughly engrained in the mind, I am convinced that the whole economy of nature, with every fact on distribution, rarity, abundance, extinction, and variation, will be dimly seen or quite misunderstood. We behold the face of nature bright with gladness, we often see superabundance of food; we do not see, or we forget, that the birds which are idly singing round us mostly live on insects or seeds, and are thus constantly destroying life; or we forget how largely these songsters, or their eggs, or their nestlings, are destroyed by birds and beasts of prey; we do not always bear in mind, that though food may be now superabundant, it is not so at all seasons of each recurring year.

I should premise that I use the term Struggle for Existence in a large and metaphorical sense, including dependence of one being on another, and including (which is more important) not only the life of the individual, but success in leaving progeny. Two canine animals in a time of dearth, may be truly said to struggle with each other which shall get food and live. But a plant on the edge of a desert is said to struggle for life against the drought, though more properly it should be said to be dependent on the moisture. A plant which annually produces a thousand seeds, of which on an average only one comes to maturity, may be more truly said to struggle with the plants of the same and other kinds which already clothe the ground. The missletoe is dependent on the apple and a few other trees, but can only in a far-fetched sense be said to struggle with these trees, for if too many of these parasites grow on the same tree, it will languish and die. But several seedling missletoes, growing close together on the same branch, may more truly be said to struggle with each other. As the missletoe is disseminated by birds, its existence depends on birds; and it may metaphorically be said to struggle with other fruit-bearing plants, in order to tempt birds to devour and thus disseminate its seeds rather than those of other plants. In these several senses, which pass into each other, I use for convenience sake the general term of struggle for existence.

A struggle for existence inevitably follows from the high rate at which all organic beings tend to increase. Every being, which during its natural lifetime produces several eggs or seeds, must suffer destruction during some period of its life, and during some season or occasional year, otherwise, on the principle of geometrical increase, its numbers would quickly become so inordinately great that no country could support the product. Hence, as more individuals are produced than can possibly survive, there must in every case be a struggle for existence, either one individual with another of the same species, or with the individuals of distinct species, or with the physical conditions of life. It is the doctrine of Malthus applied with manifold force to the whole animal and vegetable kingdoms; for in this case there can be no artificial increase of food, and no prudential restraint from marriage. Although some species may be now increasing, more or less rapidly, in numbers, all cannot do so, for the world would not hold them. . . .

NATURAL SELECTION

How will the struggle for existence . . . act in regard to variation? Can the principle of selection, which we have seen is so potent in the hands of man, apply in nature? I think we shall see that it can act most effectually. Let it be borne in mind in what an endless number of strange peculiarities our domestic productions, and, in a lesser degree, those under nature, vary; and how strong the hereditary tendency is. Under domestication, it may be truly said that the whole organisation becomes in some degree plastic. Let it be borne in mind how infinitely complex and close-fitting are the mutual relations of all organic beings to each other and to their physical conditions of life. Can it, then, be thought improbable, seeing that variations useful to man have undoubtedly occurred, that other variations useful in some way to each being in the great and complex battle of life, should sometimes occur in the course of thousands of generations? If such do occur, can we doubt (remembering that many more individuals are born than can possibly survive) that individuals having any advantage, however slight, over others, would have the best chance of surviving and of procreating their kind? On the other hand, we may feel sure that any variation in the least degree injurious would be rigidly destroyed. This preservation of favourable variations and the rejection of injurious variations, I call Natural Selection. Variations neither useful nor injurious would not be affected by natural selection, and would be left a fluctuating element, as perhaps we see in the species called polymorphic.

We shall best understand the probable course of natural selection by taking the case of a country undergoing some physical change, for instance, of climate. The proportional numbers of its inhabitants would almost immediately undergo a change, and some species might become extinct. We may conclude, from what we have seen of the intimate and complex manner in which the inhabitants of each country are bound together, that any change in the numerical proportions of some of the inhabitants, independently of the change of climate itself, would most seriously affect many of the others. If the country were open on its borders, new forms would certainly immigrate, and this also would seriously disturb the relations of some of the former inhabitants. Let it be remembered how powerful the influence of a single introduced tree or mammal has been shown to be. But in the case of an island, or of a country partly surrounded by barriers, into which new and better adapted forms could not freely enter, we should then have places in the economy of nature which would assuredly be better filled up, if some of the original inhabitants were in some manner modified; for, had the area been open to immigration, these same places would have been seized on by intruders. In such case, every slight modification, which in the course of ages chanced to arise, and which in any way favoured the individuals of any of the species, by better adapting them to their altered conditions, would tend to be preserved; and natural selection would thus have free scope for the work of improvement.

We have reason to believe, as stated in the first chapter, that a change in the conditions of life, by specially acting on the reproductive system, causes or increases variability; and in the foregoing case the conditions of life are supposed to have undergone a change, and this would manifestly be favourable to natural selection, by giving a better chance of profitable variations occurring; and unless profitable variations do occur, natural selection can do nothing. Not that, as I believe, any extreme amount of variability is necessary; as man can certainly produce great results by adding up in any given direction mere individual differences, so could Nature, but far more easily, from having incomparably longer time at her disposal. Nor do I believe that any great physical change, as of climate, or any unusual degree of isolation to check immigration, is actually necessary to produce new and unoccupied places for natural selection to fill up by modifying and improving some of the varying inhabitants. For as all the inhabitants of each country are struggling together with nicely balanced forces, extremely slight modifications in the structure or habits of one inhabitant would often give it an advantage over others; and still further modifications of the same kind would often still further increase the advantage. No country can be named in which all the native inhabitants are now so perfectly adapted to each other and to the physical conditions under which they live, that none of them could anyhow be improved; for in all countries, the natives have been so far conquered by naturalised productions, that they have allowed foreigners to take firm possession of the land. And as foreigners have thus everywhere beaten some of the natives, we may safely conclude that the natives might have been modified with advantage, so as to have better resisted such intruders.

As man can produce and certainly has produced a great result by his methodical and unconscious means of selection, what may not nature effect? Man can act only on external and visible characters: nature cares nothing for appearances, except in so far as they may be useful to any being. She can act on every internal organ, on every shade of constitutional difference, on the whole machinery of life.

Man selects only for his own good; Nature only for that of the being which she tends. Every selected character is fully exercised by her; and the being is placed under well-suited conditions of life. Man keeps the natives of many climates in the same country; he seldom exercises each selected character in some peculiar and fitting manner; he feeds a long and a short beaked pigeon on the same food; he does not exercise a long-backed or long-legged quadruped in any peculiar manner; he exposes sheep with long and short wool to the same climate. He does not allow the most vigorous males to struggle for the females. He does not rigidly destroy all inferior animals, but protects during each varying season, as far as lies in his power, all his productions. He often begins his selection by some half-monstrous form; or at least by some modification prominent enough to catch his eye, or to be plainly useful to him. Under nature, the slightest difference of structure or constitution may well turn the nicely-balanced scale in the struggle for life, and so be preserved. How fleeting are the wishes and efforts of man! how short his time! and consequently how poor will his products be, compared with those accumulated by nature during whole geological periods. Can we wonder, then, that nature's productions should be far 'truer' in character than man's productions; that they should be infinitely better adapted to the most complex conditions of life, and should plainly bear the stamp of far higher workmanship?

It may be said that natural selection is daily and hourly scrutinising, throughout the world, every variation, even the slightest; rejecting that which is bad, preserving and adding up all that is good; silently and insensibly working, whenever and wherever opportunity offers, at the improvement of each organic being in relation to its organic and inorganic conditions of life. We see nothing of these slow changes in progress, until the hand of time has marked the long lapse of ages, and then so imperfect is our view into long past geological ages, that we only see that the forms of life are now different from what they formerly were. . . .

DIFFICULTIES ON THEORY

Organs of extreme perfection and complication.—To suppose that the eye, with all its inimitable contrivances for adjusting the focus to different distances, for admitting different amounts of light, and for the correction of spherical and chromatic aberration, could have been formed by natural selection, seems, I freely confess, absurd in the highest possible degree. Yet reason tells me, that if numerous gradations from a perfect and complex eye to one very imperfect and simple, each grade being useful to its possessor, can be shown to exist; if further, the eye does vary ever so slightly, and the variations be inherited, which is certainly the case; and if any variation or modification in the organ be ever useful to an animal under changing conditions of life, then the difficulty of believing that a perfect and complex eye could be formed by natural selection, though insuperable by our imagination, can hardly be considered real. How a nerve comes to be sensitive to light, hardly concerns us more than how life itself first originated; but I may remark that several facts make me suspect that any sensitive nerve may be rendered sensitive to light, and likewise to those coarser vibrations of the air which produce sound.

In looking for the gradations by which an organ in any species has been perfected, we ought to look exclusively to its lineal ancestors; but this is scarcely ever possible, and we are forced in each case to look to species of the same group, that is to the collateral descendants from the same original parent-form, in order to see what gradations are possible, and for the chance of some gradations having been transmitted from the earlier stages of descent, in an unaltered or little altered condition. Amongst existing Vertebrata, we find but a small amount of gradation in the structure of the eye, and from fossil species we can learn nothing on this head. In this great class we should probably have to descend far beneath the lowest known fossiliferous stratum to discover the earlier stages, by which the eye has been perfected.

In the Articulata* we can commence a series with an optic nerve merely coated with pigment, and without any other mechanism; and from this low stage, numerous gradations of structure, branching off in two fundamentally different lines, can be shown to exist, until we reach a moderately high stage of perfection. In certain crustaceans, for instance, there is a double cornea, the inner one divided into facets, within each of which there is a lens-shaped swelling. In other crustaceans the transparent cones which are coated by pigment, and which properly act only by excluding lateral pencils of light, are convex at their upper ends and must act by convergence; and at their lower ends there seems to be an imperfect vitreous substance. With these facts, here far too briefly and imperfectly given, which show that there is much graduated diversity in the eyes of living crust-aceans, and bearing in mind how small the number of living animals is in proportion to those which have become extinct, I can see no very great difficulty (not more than in the case of many other struc-tures) in believing that natural selection has converted the simple apparatus of an optic nerve merely coated with pigment and invested by transparent membrane, into an optical instrument as perfect as is possessed by any member of the great Articulate class.

He who will go thus far, if he find on finishing this treatise that large bodies of facts, otherwise inexplicable, can be explained by the theory of descent, ought not to hesitate to go further, and to admit that a structure even as perfect as the eye of an eagle might be formed by natural selection, although in this case he does not know any of the transitional grades. His reason ought to conquer his imagination; though I have felt the difficulty far too keenly to be surprised at any degree of hesitation in extending the principle of natural selection to such startling lengths.

It is scarcely possible to avoid comparing the eye to a telescope. We know that this instrument has been perfected by the long-continued efforts of the highest human intellects; and we naturally infer that the eye has been formed by a somewhat analogous process. But may not this inference be presumptuous? Have we any right to assume that the Creator works by intellectual powers like those of man? If we must compare the eye to an optical instrument, we ought in imagination to take a thick layer of transparent tissue, with a nerve sensitive to light beneath, and then suppose every part of this layer to be continually changing slowly in density, so as to separate into layers of different densities and thicknesses, placed at different dis-tances from each other, and with the surfaces of each layer slowly changing in form. Further we must suppose that there is a power always intently watching each slight accidental alteration in the transparent layers; and carefully selecting each alteration which, under varied circumstances, may in any way, or in any degree, tend to produce a distincter image. We must suppose each new state of the instrument to be multiplied by the million; and each to be preserved till a better be produced, and then the old ones to be destroyed. In living bodies, variation will cause the slight alterations, generation will multiply them almost infinitely, and natural selection will pick out with unerring skill each improvement. Let this process go on for millions on millions of years; and during each year on millions of individuals of many kinds; and may we not believe that a living optical instrument might thus be formed as superior to one of glass, as the works of the Creator are to those of man?

If it could be demonstrated that any complex organ existed, which could not possibly have been formed by numerous, successive, slight modifications, my theory would absolutely break down. But I can find out no such case. No doubt many organs exist of which we do not know the transitional grades, more especially if we look to much-isolated species, round which, according to my theory, there has been much extinction. Or again, if we look to an organ common to all the members of a large class, for in this latter case the organ must have been first formed at an extremely remote period, since which all the many members of the class have been developed; and in order to discover the early transitional grades through which the organ has passed, we should have to look to very ancient ancestral forms, long since become extinct. . . .

CONCLUSION

Authors of the highest eminence seem to be fully satisfied with the view that each species has been independently created. To my mind it accords better with what we know of the laws impressed on matter by the Creator, that the production and extinction of the past and present inhabitants of the world should have been due to secondary causes, like those determining the birth and death of the individual. When I view all beings not as special creations, but as the lineal descendants of some few beings which lived long before the first bed of the Silurian* system was deposited, they seem to me to become ennobled. Judging from the past, we may safely infer that not one living species will transmit its unaltered likeness to a distant futurity. And of the species now living very few will transmit progeny of any kind to a far distant futurity; for the manner in which all organic beings are grouped, shows that the greater number of species of each genus, and all the species of many genera, have left no descendants, but have become utterly extinct. We can so far take a prophetic glance into futurity as to foretel that it will be the common and widely-spread species, belonging to the larger and dominant groups, which will ultimately prevail and procreate new and dominant species. As all the living forms of life are the lineal descendants of those which lived long before the Silurian epoch, we may feel certain that the ordinary succession by generation has never once been broken, and that no cataclysm has desolated the whole world. Hence we may look with some confidence to a secure future of equally inappreciable length. And as natural selection works solely by and for the good of each being, all corporeal and mental endowments will tend to progress towards perfection.

It is interesting to contemplate an entangled bank, clothed with many plants of many kinds, with birds singing on the bushes, with various insects flitting about, and with worms crawling through the damp earth, and to reflect that these elaborately constructed forms, so different from each other, and dependent on each other in so complex a manner, have all been produced by laws acting around us. These laws, taken in the largest sense, being Growth with Reproduction; Inheritance which is almost implied by reproduction; Variability from the indirect and direct action of the external conditions of life, and from use and disuse; a Ratio of Increase so high as to lead to a Struggle for Life, and as a consequence to Natural Selection, entailing Divergence of Character and the Extinction of less-improved forms. Thus, from the war of nature, from famine and death, the most exalted object which we are capable of conceiving, namely, the production of the higher animals, directly follows. There is grandeur in this view of life, with its several powers, having been originally breathed into a few forms or into one; and that, whilst this planet has gone cycling on according to the fixed law of gravity, from so simple a beginning endless forms most beautiful and most wonderful have been, and are being, evolved.

GEORGE ELIOT

From *The Mill on the Floss* (1860)

At that moment Maggie felt a startling sensation of sudden cold about her knees and feet—it was water flowing under her. She started up: the stream was flowing under the door that led into the passage. She was not bewildered for an instant: she knew it was the flood!

The tumult of emotion she had been enduring for the last twelve hours seemed to have left a great calm in her. Without screaming, she hurried with the candle up stairs to Bob Jakin's bedroom. The door was ajar. She went in and shook him by the shoulder.

'Bob, the flood is come—it is in the house: let us see if we can make the boats safe.'

She lighted his candle, while the poor wife, snatching up her baby, burst into screams, and then she hurried down again to see if the waters were rising fast. There was a step down into the room at the door leading from the staircase: she saw that the water was already on a level with the step. While she was looking, something came with a tremendous crash against the window, and sent the leaded panes and the old wooden framework inward in shivers, the water pouring in after it.

'It is the boat!' cried Maggie. 'Bob, come down to get the boats!'

And without a moment's shudder of fear she plunged through the water, which was rising fast to her knees, and by the glimmering light of the candle she had left on the stairs she mounted on to the window-sill and crept into the boat, which was left with the prow lodging and protruding through the window. Bob was not long after her, hurrying without shoes or stockings, but with the lantern in his hand.

'Why, they're both here—both the boats,' said Bob, as he got into the one where Maggie was. 'It's wonderful this fastening isn't broke too, as well as the mooring.'

In the excitement of getting into the other boat, unfastening it and mastering an oar, Bob was not struck with the danger Maggie incurred. We are not apt to fear for the fearless when we are companions in their danger, and Bob's mind was absorbed in possible expedients for the safety of the helpless in-doors. The fact that Maggie had been up, had waked him, and had taken the lead in activity, gave Bob a vague impression of her as one who would help to protect, not need to be protected. She too had got possession of an oar, and had pushed off, so as to release the boat from the overhanging window-frame.

'The water's rising so fast,' said Bob, 'I doubt it'll be in at the chambers before long, th' house is so low. I've more mind to get

Prissy and the child and the mother into the boat, if I could, and trusten to the water, for the old house is none so safe. And if I let go the boat . . . . but *you*!' he exclaimed, suddenly lifting the light of his lantern on Maggie, as she stood in the rain with the oar in her hand and her black hair streaming.

Maggie had no time to answer, for a new tidal current swept along the line of the houses, and drove both the boats out on to the wide water with a force that carried them far past the meeting current of the river.

In the first moments Maggie felt nothing, thought of nothing but that she had suddenly passed away from that life which she had been dreading: it was the transition of death without its agony, and she was alone in the darkness with God.

The whole thing had been so rapid—so dream-like, that the threads of ordinary association were broken. She sank down on the seat clutching the oar mechanically, and for a long while had no distinct conception of her position. The first thing that waked her to fuller consciousness was the cessation of the rain, and a perception that the darkness was divided by the faintest light, which parted the overhanging gloom from the immeasurable watery level below. She was driven out upon the flood—that awful visitation of God which her father used to talk of—which had made the nightmare of her childish dreams. And with that thought there rushed in the vision of the old home—and Tom—and her mother—they had all listened together.

'O God, where am I? Which is the way home?' she cried out, in the dim loneliness.

What was happening to them at the Mill? The floods had once nearly destroyed it. They might be in danger—in distress; her mother and her brother, alone there, beyond reach of help! Her whole soul was strained now on that thought; and she saw the long-loved faces looking for help into the darkness, and finding none.

She was floating in smooth water now—perhaps far on the over-flooded fields. There was no sense of present danger to check the outgoing of her mind to the old home, and she strained her eyes against the curtain of gloom that she might seize the first sight of her whereabout—that she might catch some faint suggestion of the spot toward which all her anxieties tended.

Oh how welcome, the widening of that dismal watery level—the gradual uplifting of the cloudy firmament—the slowly defining blackness of objects above the glossy dark! Yes, she must be out on the fields: those were the tops of hedgerow trees. Which way did the river lie? Looking behind her, she saw the lines of black trees; looking before her, there were none: then the river lay before her. She seized an oar, and began to paddle the boat forward with the energy of wakening hope: the dawning seemed to advance more swiftly now she was in action, and she could soon see the poor dumb beasts crowding piteously on a mound where they had taken refuge. Onward she paddled and rowed by turns in the growing twilight; her wet clothes clung round her, and her streaming hair was dashed about by the wind, but she was hardly conscious of any bodily sensations except a sensation of strength inspired by a mighty emotion. Along with the sense of danger and possible rescue for those long-remembered beings at the old home, there was an undefined sense of reconcilement with her brother: what quarrel, what harshness, what unbelief in each other can subsist in the presence of a great calamity, when all the artificial vesture of our life is gone, and we are all one with each other in primitive mortal needs? Vaguely Maggie felt that; in the strong resurgent love toward her brother that swept away all the later impressions of hard, cruel offense and misunderstanding, and left only the deep, underlying, unshakable memories of early union.

But now there was a large dark mass in the distance, and near to her Maggie could discern the current of the river. The dark mass must be—yes, it was—St Ogg's. Ah! now she knew which way to look for the first glimpse of the well-known trees—the gray willows, the now yellowing chestnuts—and above them the old roof! But there was no colour, no shape yet; all was faint and dim. More and more strongly the energies seemed to come and put themselves forth, as if her life were a stored-up force that was being spent in this hour, unneeded for any future.

She must get her boat into the current of the Floss, else she would never be able to pass the Ripple and approach the house: this was the thought that occurred to her as she imagined with more and more vividness the state of things round the old home. But then she might be carried very far down, and be unable to guide her boat out of the current again. For the first time distinct ideas of danger began to press upon her; but there was no choice of courses, no room for hesitation, and she floated into the current. Swiftly she went now, without effort; more and more clearly in the lessening distance and the growing light she began to discern the objects that she knew must be the well-known trees and roofs; nay, she was not far off a rushing muddy current that must be the strangely altered Ripple.

Great God! there were floating masses in it, that might dash against her boat as she passed, and cause her to perish too soon. What were those masses?

For the first time Maggie's heart began to beat in an agony of dread. She sat helpless, dimly conscious that she was being floated along—more intensely conscious of the anticipated clash. But the horror was transient; it passed away before the oncoming warehouses of St Ogg's. She had passed the mouth of the Ripple, then; *now* she must use all her skill and power to manage the boat, and get it, if possible, out of the current. She could see now that the bridge was broken down; she could see the masts of a stranded vessel far out over the watery field; but no boats were to be seen moving on the river; such as had been laid hands on were employed in the flooded streets.

With new resolution Maggie seized her oar, and stood up again to paddle; but the now ebbing tide added to the swiftness of the river, and she was carried along beyond the bridge. She could hear shouts from the windows overlooking the river, as if the people there were calling to her. It was not till she had passed on nearly to Tofton that she could get the boat clear of the current. Then, with one yearning look toward her uncle Deane's house, that lay farther down the river, she took to both her oars, and rowed with all her might across the watery fields back toward the Mill. Colour was beginning to awake now, and as she approached the Dorlcote fields she could discern the tints of the trees—could see the old Scotch firs far to the right, and the home chestnuts—oh how deep they lay in the water—deeper than the trees on this side the hill. And the roof of the Mill—where was it? Those heavy fragments hurrying down the Ripple—what had they meant? But it was not the house—the house stood firm: drowned up to the first story, but still firm—or was it broken in at the end toward the Mill?

With panting joy that she was there at last—joy that overcame all distress, Maggie neared the front of the house. At first she heard no sound—she saw no object moving. Her boat was on a level with the up-stairs windows. She called out in a loud, piercing voice,

'Tom, where are you? Mother, where are you? Here is Maggie!'

Soon, from the window of the attic in the central gable, she heard Tom's voice:

'Who is it? Have you brought a boat?'

'It is I, Tom—Maggie. Where is mother?'

'She is not here; she went to Garum the day before yesterday. I'll come down to the lower window.'

'Alone, Maggie?' said Tom, in a voice of deep astonishment, as he opened the middle window on a level with the boat.

'Yes, Tom: God has taken care of me to bring me to you. Get in quickly. Is there no one else?'

'No,' said Tom, stepping into the boat, 'I fear the man is drowned: he was carried down the Ripple, I think, when part of the mill fell with the crash of trees and stones against it. I've shouted again and again, and there has been no answer. Give me the oars, Maggie.' . . .

Tom rowed with untired vigour, and with a different speed from poor Maggie's. The boat was soon in the current of the river again, and soon they would be at Tofton.

'Park House stands high up out of the flood,' said Maggie. 'Perhaps they have got Lucy there.'

Nothing else was said; now a new danger was being carried toward them by the river. Some wooden machinery had just given way on one of the wharves, and huge fragments were being floated along. The sun was rising now, and the wide area of watery desolation was spread out in dreadful clearness around them—in dreadful clearness floated onward the hurrying, threatening masses. A large company in a boat that was working its way along under the Tofton houses observed their danger, and shouted, 'Get out of the current!'

But that could not be done at once, and Tom, looking before him, saw death rushing on them. Huge fragments, clinging together in fatal fellowship, made one wide mass across the stream.

'It is coming, Maggie!' Tom said, in a deep hoarse voice, loosing the oars and clasping her.

The next instant the boat was no longer seen upon the water, and the huge mass was hurrying on in hideous triumph.

But soon the keel of the boat reappeared, a black speck on the golden water.

The boat reappeared, but brother and sister had gone down in an embrace never to be parted; living through again in one supreme moment the days when they had clasped their little hands in love, and roamed the daisied fields together.

Nature repairs her ravages—repairs them with her sunshine and with human labour. The desolation wrought by that flood had left but little visible trace on the face of the earth five years after. The fifth autumn was rich in golden cornstacks, rising in thick clusters among the distant hedgerows; the wharves and warehouses on the Floss were busy again, with echoes of eager voices, with hopeful lading and unlading.

And every man and woman mentioned in this history was still living, except those whose end we know.

Nature repairs her ravages, but not all. The uptorn trees are not rooted again; the parted hills are left scarred: if there is a new growth, the trees are not the same as the old, and the hills underneath their green vesture bear the marks of the past rending. To the eyes that have dwelt on the past there is no thorough repair.

THOMAS HENRY HUXLEY

On the Physical Basis of Life (1869)

In order to make the title of this discourse generally intelligible, I have translated the term 'Protoplasm,' which is the scientific name of the substance of which I am about to speak, by the words 'the physical basis of life.' I suppose that, to many, the idea that there is such a thing as a physical basis, or matter, of life may be novel—so widely spread is the conception of life as a something which works through matter, but is independent of it; and even those who are aware that matter and life are inseparably connected; may not be prepared for the conclusion plainly suggested by the phrase, '*the* physical basis or matter of life,' that there is some one kind of matter which is common to all living beings, and that their endless diversities are bound together by a physical, as well as an ideal, unity. In fact, when first apprehended, such a doctrine as this appears almost shocking to common sense.

What, truly, can seem to be more obviously different from one another in faculty, in form, and in substance, than the various kinds of living beings? What community of faculty can there be between the brightly-coloured lichen, which so nearly resembles a mere mineral incrustation of the bare rock on which it grows, and the painter, to whom it is instinct with beauty, or the botanist, whom it feeds with knowledge? . . .

No very abstruse argumentation is needed, in the first place, to prove that the powers, or faculties, of all kinds of living matter, diverse as they may be in degree, are substantially similar in kind.

Goethe has condensed a survey of all the powers of mankind into the well known epigram:—

> 'Warum treibt sich das Volk so und schreit? Es will sich ernähren
> Kinder zeugen, und die nähren so gut es vermag.
>
> .   .   .   .
>
> Weiter bringt es kein Mensch, stell' er sich wie er auch will.'*

In physiological language this means, that all the multifarious and complicated activities of man are comprehensible under three categories. Either they are immediately directed towards the maintenance and development of the body, or they effect transitory changes in the relative positions of parts of the body, or they tend towards the continuance of the species. Even those manifestations of intellect, of feeling, and of will, which we rightly name the higher faculties, are not excluded from this classification, inasmuch as to every one but the subject of them, they are known only as transitory changes in the relative positions of parts of the body. Speech, gesture, and every other form of human action are, in the long run, resolvable into muscular contraction, and muscular contraction is but a transitory change in the relative positions of the parts of a muscle. But the scheme which is large enough to embrace the activities of the highest form of life, covers all those of the lower creatures. The lowest plant, or animalcule, feeds, grows, and reproduces its kind. In addition, all animals manifest those transitory changes of form which we class under irritability and contractility; and, it is more than probable, that when the vegetable world is thoroughly explored, we shall find all plants in possession of the same powers, at one time or other of their existence. . . .

Enough has, perhaps, been said to prove the existence of a general uniformity in the character of the protoplasm, or physical basis, of life, in whatever group of living beings it may be studied. But it will be understood that this general uniformity by no means excludes any amount of special modifications of the fundamental substance. The mineral, carbonate of lime, assumes an immense diversity of characters, though no one doubts that under all these Protean changes it is one and the same thing.

And now, what is the ultimate fate, and what the origin, of the matter of life?

Is it, as some of the older naturalists supposed, diffused throughout the universe in molecules, which are indestructible and unchangeable in themselves; but, in endless transmigration, unite in innumerable permutations, into the diversified forms of life we know? Or, is the matter of life composed of ordinary matter, differing from it only in the manner in which its atoms are aggregated. Is it built up of ordinary matter, and again resolved into ordinary matter when its work is done?

Modern science does not hesitate a moment between these alternatives. Physiology writes over the portals of life—

'Debemur morti nos nostraque,'*

with a profounder meaning than the Roman poet attached to that melancholy line. Under whatever disguise it takes refuge, whether fungus or oak, worm or man, the living protoplasm not only ultimately dies and is resolved into its mineral and lifeless constituents, but is always dying, and, strange as the paradox may sound, could not live unless it died.

In the wonderful story of the 'Peau de Chagrin,'* the hero becomes possessed of a magical wild ass' skin, which yields him the means of gratifying all his wishes. But its surface represents the duration of the proprietor's life; and for every satisfied desire the skin shrinks in proportion to the intensity of fruition, until at length life and the last handbreadth of the *peau de chagrin* disappear with the gratification of a last wish.

Balzac's studies had led him over a wide range of thought and speculation, and his shadowing forth of physiological truth in this strange story may have been intentional. At any rate, the matter of life is a veritable *peau de chagrin*, and for every vital act it is somewhat the smaller. All work implies waste, and the work of life results, directly or indirectly, in the waste of protoplasm.

Every word uttered by a speaker costs him some physical loss, and, in the strictest sense, he burns that others may have light—so much eloquence, so much of his body resolved into carbonic acid, water, and urea. It is clear that this process of expenditure cannot go on for ever. But, happily, the protoplasmic *peau de chagrin* differs from Balzac's in its capacity of being repaired, and brought back to its full size, after every exertion.

OLIVE SCHREINER

From *The Story of an African Farm* (1883)

Bonaparte Blenkins, a wandering con-artist, has just gained control of a South African farm by convincing its owner, 'the Boer-woman' Tant' Sannie, to marry him. Bonaparte has driven off its deeply religious German overseer, who until that time cared for the 14-year-old orphan Waldo. Blenkins particularly dislikes Waldo, believing the boy suspects his true nature.

Doss [the dog] sat among the karroo bushes, one yellow ear drawn over his wicked little eye, ready to flap away any adventurous fly that might settle on his nose. Around him in the morning sunlight fed the sheep; behind him lay his master polishing his machine. He found much comfort in handling it that morning. A dozen philosophical essays, or angelically attuned songs for the consolation of the bereaved, could never have been to him what that little sheep-shearing machine was that day.

After struggling to see the unseeable, growing drunk with the endeavour to span the infinite, and writhing before the inscrutable mystery, it is a renovating relief to turn to some simple, feelable, weighable substance; to something which has a smell and colour, which may be handled and turned over this way and that. Whether there be or be not a hereafter, whether there be any use in calling aloud to the Unseen power, whether there be an Unseen power to call to, whatever be the true nature of the *I* who call and of the objects around me, whatever be our meaning, our internal essence, our cause (and in a certain order of minds death and the agony of loss inevitably awaken the wild desire, at other times smothered, to look into these things), whatever be the nature of that which the limits of the human intellect build up on every hand, this thing is certain—a knife will cut wood, and one cogged wheel will turn another. This is sure.

Waldo found an immeasurable satisfaction in the handling of his machine; but Doss winked and blinked, and thought it all frightfully monotonous out there on the flat, and presently dropped asleep, sitting bolt upright. Suddenly his eyes opened wide; something was coming from the direction of the homestead. Winking his eyes and looking intently, he perceived it was the grey mare. Now Doss had wondered much of late what had become of her master. Seeing she carried someone on her back, he now came to his own conclusion, and began to move his tail violently up and down. Presently he pricked up one ear and let the other hang; his tail became motionless, and the expression of his mouth was one of decided disapproval bordering on scorn. He wrinkled his lips up on each side into little lines.

The sand was soft, and the grey mare came on so noiselessly that the boy heard nothing till Bonaparte dismounted. Then Doss got up and moved back a step. He did not approve of Bonaparte's appearance. His costume, in truth, was of a unique kind. It was a combination of the town and country. The tails of his black cloth coat were pinned up behind to keep them from rubbing; he had on a pair of moleskin trousers and leather gaiters, and in his hand he carried a little whip of rhinoceros hide.

Waldo started and looked up. Had there been a moment's time he would have dug a hole in the sand with his hands and buried his treasure. It was only a toy of wood, but he loved it, as one of necessity loves what has been born of him, whether of the flesh or spirit. When cold eyes have looked at it, the feathers are rubbed off our butterfly's wing for ever.

'What have you here, my lad?' said Bonaparte, standing by him, and pointing with the end of his whip to the medley of wheels and hinges.

The boy muttered something inaudible, and half-spread his hand over the thing.

'But this seems to be a very ingenious little machine,' said Bonaparte, seating himself on the ant-heap, and bending down over it with deep interest. 'What is it for, my lad?'

'Shearing sheep.'

'It is a very nice little machine,' said Bonaparte. 'How does it work, now? I have never seen anything so ingenious!'

There was never a parent who heard deception in the voice that praised his child—his first-born. Here was one who liked the thing that had been created in him. He forgot everything. He showed how the shears would work with a little guidance, how the sheep would be held, and the wool fall into the trough. A flush burst over his face as he spoke.

'I tell you what, my lad,' said Bonaparte emphatically, when the explanation was finished, 'we must get you a patent. Your fortune is made. In three years' time there'll not be a farm in this colony where it isn't working. You're a genius, that's what *you* are!' said Bonaparte, rising.

'If it were made larger,' said the boy, raising his eyes, 'it would work more smoothly. Do you think there would be anyone in this colony would be able to make it?'

'I'm sure they could,' said Bonaparte; 'and if not, why I'll do my best for you. I'll send it to England. It must be done somehow. How long have you worked at it?'

'Nine months,' said the boy.

'Oh, it is such a nice little machine,' said Bonaparte, 'one can't help feeling an interest in it. There is only *one* little improvement, one very little improvement, I should like to make.'

Bonaparte put his foot on the machine and crushed it into the sand. The boy looked up into his face.

'Looks better now,' said Bonaparte, 'doesn't it? If we can't have it made in England we'll send it to America. Good-bye; ta-ta,' he added. 'You're a great genius, a born genius, my dear boy, there's no doubt about it.'

He mounted the grey mare and rode off. The dog watched his retreat with cynical satisfaction; but his master lay on the ground with his head on his arms in the sand, and the little wheels and chips of wood lay on the ground around him. The dog jumped on to his back and snapped at the black curls, till, finding that no notice was taken, he walked off to play with a black beetle. The beetle was hard at work trying to roll home a great ball of dung it had been collecting all the morning; but Doss broke the ball, and ate the beetle's hind legs, and then bit off its head. And it was all play, and no one could tell what it had lived and worked for. A striving, and a striving, and an ending in nothing.

GEORGE JOHN ROMANES

From *Mental Evolution in Man* (1888)

The present work being thus a treatise on human psychology in relation to the theory of descent, the first question which it must seek to attack is clearly that as to the evidence of the mind of man having been derived from mind as we meet with it in the lower animals. And here, I think, it is not too much to say that we approach a problem which is not merely the most interesting of those that have fallen within the scope of my own works; but perhaps the most interesting that has ever been submitted to the contemplation of our race. If it is true that 'the proper study of mankind is man',* assuredly the study of nature has never before reached a territory of thought so important in all its aspects as that which in our own generation it is for the first time approaching. After centuries of intellectual conquest in all regions of the phenomenal universe, man has at last begun to find that he may apply in a new and most unexpected manner the adage of antiquity—*Know thyself.* For he has begun to perceive a strong probability, if not an actual certainty, that his own living nature is identical in kind with the nature of all other life, and that even the most amazing side of this his own nature—nay, the most amazing of all things within the reach of his knowledge—the human mind itself, is but the topmost inflorescence of one mighty growth, whose roots and stem and many branches are sunk in the abyss of planetary time. . . .

If we have regard to Emotions as these occur in the brute, we cannot fail to be struck by the broad fact that the area of psychology which they cover is so nearly co-extensive with that which is covered by the emotional faculties of man. In my previous works* I have given what I consider unquestionable evidence of all the following emotions, which I here name in the order of their appearance through the psychological scale,—fear, surprise, affection, pugnacity, curiosity, jealousy, anger, play, sympathy, emulation, pride, resentment, emotion of the beautiful, grief, hate, cruelty, benevolence, revenge, rage, shame, regret, deceitfulness, emotion of the ludicrous.

Now, this list exhausts all the human emotions, with the exception of those which refer to religion, moral sense, and perception of the sublime. Therefore I think we are fully entitled to conclude that, so far as emotions are concerned, it cannot be said that the facts of animal psychology raise any difficulties against the theory of descent. On the contrary, the emotional life of animals is so strikingly similar to the emotional life of man—and especially of young children—that I think the similarity ought fairly to be taken as direct evidence of a genetic continuity between them.

And so it is with regard to Instinct. Understanding this term in the sense previously defined, it is unquestionably true that in man— especially during the periods of infancy and youth—sundry well-marked instincts are presented, which have reference chiefly to nutrition, self-preservation, reproduction, and the rearing of progeny. No one has ventured to dispute that all these instincts are identical with those which we observe in the lower animals; nor, on the other hand, has any one ventured to suggest that there is any instinct which can be said to be peculiar to man, unless the moral and religious sentiments are taken to be of the nature of instincts. And although it is true that instinct plays a larger part in the psychology of many animals than it does in the psychology of man, this fact is plainly of no importance in the present connection, where we are concerned only with identity of principle. If any one were childish enough to argue that the mind of a man differs in kind from that of a brute because it does not display any particular instinct—such, for example, as the spinning of webs, the building of nests, or the incubation of eggs,—the answer of course would be that, by parity of reasoning, the mind of a spider must be held to differ in kind from that of a bird. So far, then, as instincts and emotions are concerned, the parallel before us is much too close to admit of any argument on the opposite side.

With regard to Volition more will be said in a future instalment of this work. Here, therefore, it is enough to say, in general terms, that no one has seriously questioned the identity of kind between the animal and the human will, up to the point at which so-called freedom is supposed by some dissentients to supervene and characterize the latter. Now, of course, if the human will differs from the animal will in any important feature or attribute such as this, the fact must be duly taken into account during the course of our subsequent analysis. At present, however, we are only engaged upon a preliminary sketch of the points of resemblance between animal and human psychology. So far, therefore, as we are now concerned with the will, we have only to note that up to the point where the volitions of a man begin to surpass those of a brute in respect of complexity, refinement, and foresight, no one disputes identity of kind.

Lastly, the same remark applies to the faculties of Intellect. Enormous as the difference undoubtedly is between these faculties in the two cases, the difference is conceded not to be one of kind *ab initio.** On the contrary, it is conceded that up to a certain point—namely, as far as the highest degree of intelligence to which an animal attains—there is not merely a similarity of kind, but an identity of correspondence. . . . Now, it belongs to the very essence of evolution, considered as a process, that when one order of existence passes on to higher grades of excellence, it does so upon the foundation already laid by the previous course of its progress; so that when compared with any allied order of existence which has not been carried so far in this upward course, a more or less close parallel admits of being traced between the two, up to the point at which the one begins to distance the other, where all further comparison admittedly ends. Therefore, upon the face of them, the facts of comparative psychology now before us are, to say the least, strongly suggestive of the superadded powers of the human intellect having been due to a process of evolution. . . .

Another distinction between the man and the brute which we often find asserted is, that the latter shows no signs of mental progress in successive generations. On this alleged distinction I may remark, first of all, that it begs the whole question of mental evolution in animals, and, therefore, is directly opposed to the whole body of facts presented in my work upon this subject. In the next place, I may remark that the alleged distinction comes with an ill grace from opponents of evolution, seeing that it depends upon a recognition of the principles of evolution in the history of mankind. But, leaving aside these considerations, I meet the alleged distinction with a plain denial of both the statements of fact on which it rests. That is to say, I deny on the one hand that mental progress from generation to generation is an invariable peculiarity of human intelligence; and, on the other hand, I deny that such progress is never found to occur in the case of animal intelligence.

Taking these two points separately, I hold it to be a statement opposed to fact to say, or to imply, that all existing savages, when not brought into contact with civilized man, undergo intellectual development from generation to generation. On the contrary, one of the most generally applicable statements we can make with reference to the psychology of uncivilized man is that it shows, in a remarkable degree, what we may term a *vis inertiae** as regards upward movement. Even so highly developed a type of mind as that of the Negro*—submitted, too, as it has been in millions of individual cases to close contact with minds of the most progressive type, and enjoying as it has in many thousands of individual cases all the advantages of liberal education—has never, so far as I can ascertain, executed one single stroke of original work in any single department of intellectual activity. . . .

On the whole, then, I cannot see that there is any valid distinction to be drawn between human and brute psychology with respect to improvement from generation to generation. Indeed, I should deem it almost more philosophical in any opponent of the theory of evolution, who happened to be acquainted with the facts bearing upon the subject, if he were to adopt the converse position, and argue that for the purposes of this theory there is *not a sufficient* distinction between human and brute psychology in this respect. For when we remember the great advance which, according to the theory of evolution, the mind of palaeolithic man must already have made upon that of the higher apes, and when we remember that all races of existing men have the immense advantage of some form of language whereby to transmit to progeny the results of individual experience,—when we remember these things, the difficulty appears to me to lie on the side of explaining why, with such a start and with such advantages, the human species, both when it first appears upon the pages of geological history, and as it now appears in the great majority of its constituent races, should so far resemble animal species in the prolonged stagnation of its intellectual life.

The Individual and the Species

ALFRED, LORD TENNYSON

From *In Memoriam* (1850)

LIII

Oh yet we trust that somehow good
　　Will be the final goal of ill,
　　To pangs of nature, sins of will,
Defects of doubt, and taints of blood;

That nothing walks with aimless feet;
　　That not one life shall be destroy'd,
　　Or cast as rubbish to the void,
When God hath made the pile complete;

That not a worm is cloven in vain;
　　That not a moth with vain desire
　　Is shrivel'd in a fruitless fire,
Or but subserves another's gain.

Behold, we know not anything;
　　I can but trust that good shall fall
　　At last—far off—at last, to all,
And every winter change to spring.

So runs my dream: but what am I?
　　An infant crying in the night:
　　An infant crying for the light:
And with no language but a cry.

LIV

The wish, that of the living whole
　　No life may fail beyond the grave;
　　Derives it not from what we have
The likest God within the soul?

Are God and Nature then at strife,
　　That Nature lends such evil dreams?

So careful of the type she seems,
So careless of the single life:

That I, considering everywhere
   Her secret meaning in her deeds,
   And finding that of fifty seeds
She often brings but one to bear;

I falter where I firmly trod,
   And falling with my weight of cares
   Upon the great world's altar-stairs
That slope thro' darkness up to God;

I stretch lame hands of faith, and grope,
   And gather dust and chaff, and call
   To what I feel is Lord of all,
And faintly trust the larger hope.

LV

'So careful of the type?' but no.
   From scarped cliff and quarried stone
   She cries 'a thousand types are gone:
I care for nothing, all shall go.

Thou makest thine appeal to me:
   I bring to life, I bring to death:
   The spirit does but mean the breath:
I know no more.' And he, shall he,

Man, her last work, who seem'd so fair,
   Such splendid purpose in his eyes,
   Who roll'd the psalm to wintry skies,
Who built him fanes* of fruitless prayer,

Who trusted God was love indeed
   And love Creation's final law—
   Tho' Nature, red in tooth and claw
With ravine, shriek'd against his creed—

Who loved, who suffer'd countless ills,
   Who battled for the True, the Just,
   Be blown about the desert dust,
Or seal'd within the iron hills?

No more? A monster then, a dream,
　　A discord. Dragons of the prime,
　　That tare each other in their slime,
Were mellow music match'd with him.

O life as futile, then, as frail!
　　O for thy voice to soothe and bless!
　　What hope of answer, or redress?
Behind the veil, behind the veil.

CXVIII

I trust I have not wasted breath:
　　I think we are not wholly brain,
　　Magnetic mockeries; not in vain,
Like Paul with beasts,* I fought with Death;

Not only cunning casts in clay:
　　Let Science prove we are, and then
　　What matters Science unto men,
At least to me? I would not stay.

Let him, the wiser man who springs
　　Hereafter, up from childhood shape
　　His action like the greater ape,
But I was born to other things.

HERBERT SPENCER

From *Principles of Biology* (1864–7)

What is an individual? is a question which many readers will think it
easy to answer. Yet it is a question that has led to much controversy
among Zoologists and Botanists; and no quite satisfactory reply to it
seems possible. As applied to a man, or to any one of the higher
animals, which are all sharply-defined and independent, the word
individual has a clear meaning; though even here, when we turn
from average cases to exceptional cases—as a calf with two heads and
two pairs of fore-limbs—we find ourselves in doubt whether to
predicate one individuality or two. But when we extend our range of

observation to the organic world at large, we find that difficulties allied to this exceptional one, meet us everywhere under every variety of form.

Each uniaxial plant may perhaps fairly be regarded as a distinct individual; though there are botanists who do not make even this admission. What, however, are we to say of a multiaxial plant?* It is, indeed, usual to speak of a tree with its many branches and shoots, as singular; but strong reasons may be urged for considering it as plural. Every one of its axes has a more or less independent life, and when cut off and planted, may grow into the likeness of its parent; or by grafting and budding, parts of this tree may be developed upon another tree, and there manifest their specific peculiarities. Shall we regard all the growing axes thus resulting from slips and grafts and buds, as parts of one individual, or as distinct individuals? If a strawberry-plant sends out runners carrying buds at their ends, which strike root and grow into independent plants, that separate from the original one by decay of the runners, must we not say that they possess separate individualities; and yet if we do this, are we not at a loss to say when their separate individualities were established, unless we admit that each bud was from the beginning an individual? Commenting on such perplexities, Schleiden* says—'Much has been written and disputed concerning the conception of the individual, without, however, elucidating the subject, principally owing to the misconception that still exists as to the origin of the conception. Now the individual is no conception, but the mere subjective comprehension of an actual object, presented to us under some given specific conception, and on this latter it alone depends whether the object is or is not an individual. Under the specific conception of the solar system, ours is an individual: in relation to the specific conception of a planetary body, it is an aggregate of many individuals. . . . I think, however, that looking at the indubitable facts already mentioned, and the relations treated of in the course of these considerations, it will appear most advantageous and most useful, in a scientific point of view, to consider the vegetable cell as the general type of the plant (simple plant of the first order). Under this conception, *Protococcus** and other plants consisting of only one cell, and the spore and pollen-granule, will appear as individuals. Such individuals may, however, again, with a partial renunciation of their individual independence, combine under definite laws into definite forms (somewhat as the individual animals do in the globe of the *Volvox globator**). These again appear empirically as individual beings, under a conception of a species (simple plants of the second order) derived from the form of the normal connexion of the elementary individuals. But we cannot stop here, since nature herself combines these individuals, under a definite form, into larger associations, whence we draw the third conception of the plant, from a connexion, as it were, of the second power (compound plants—plants of the third order). The simple plant proceeding from the combination of the elementary individuals is then termed a bud (*gemma*), in the composition of plants of the third order.'

The animal kingdom presents still greater difficulties. When, from sundry points on the body of a common polype,* there bud-out young polypes, which, after acquiring mouths and tentacles and closing up the communications between their stomachs and the stomach of the parent, finally separate from the parent; we may with propriety regard them as distinct individuals. But when, in the allied compound *Hydrozoa*,* we find that these young polypes continue permanently connected with the parent; and when, by this continuous budding-out, there is presently produced a tree-like aggregation, having a common alimentary canal into which the digestive cavity of each polype opens; it is no longer so clear that these little sacs furnished with mouths and tentacles, are severally to be regarded as distinct individuals. We cannot deny a certain individuality to the polypedom. And on discovering that some of the buds, instead of unfolding in the same manner as the rest, are transformed into capsules in which eggs are developed—on discovering that certain of the incipient polypes thus become wholly dependent on the aggregate for their nutrition, and discharge functions which have nothing to do with their own maintenance, we have still clearer proof that the individualities of the members are partially merged in the individuality of the group. . . .

On the hypothesis of Evolution, perplexities of this nature are just such as we might anticipate. If Life in general, commenced with minute and simple forms, like those out of which all individual organisms, however complex, now originate; and if the transitions from these primordial units to organisms made up of groups of such units, and to higher organisms made up of groups of such groups, took place by degrees; it is clear that individualities of the first and simplest order, would merge gradually in those of a larger and more complex order, and these again in others of an order having still greater bulk and organization; and that hence it would be impossible to say where the lower individualities ceased, and the higher individualities commenced.

To meet these difficulties, it has been proposed that the whole product of a single fertilized germ, shall be regarded as a single individual: whether such whole product be organized into one mass, or whether it be organized into many masses, that are partially or completely separate. It is urged that whether the development of the fertilized germ be continuous or discontinuous is a matter of secondary importance; that the totality of living tissue to which the fertilized germ gives rise in any one case, is the equivalent of the totality to which it gives rise in any other case; and that we must recognize this equivalence, whether such totality of living tissue takes a concrete or a discrete arrangement. In pursuance of this view, a zoological individual is constituted either by any such single animal as a mammal or bird, which may properly claim the title of a *zoon*, or by any such group of animals as the numerous *Medusae** that have been developed from the same egg, which are to be severally distinguished as *zooids*.

Admitting it to be very desirable that there should be words for expressing these relations and this equivalence, it may still be objected, that to apply the word individual to a number of separate living bodies, is inconvenient: conflicting so much, as it does, with the ordinary conception which this word suggests. It seems a questionable use of language to say that the countless masses of *Anacharis Alsinastrum*,* which, within these few years, have grown up in our rivers, canals, and ponds, are all parts of one individual; and yet as this plant does not seed in England, these countless masses, having arisen by discontinuous development, must be so regarded, if we accept the above definition. . . .

There is, indeed, as already implied, no definition of individuality that is unobjectionable. All we can do is to make the best practicable compromise.

As applied either to an animate or an inanimate object, the word individual ordinarily connotes union among the parts of the object, and separateness from other objects. This fundamental element in the conception of individuality, we cannot with propriety ignore in the biological application of the word. That which we call an individual plant or animal, must, therefore, be some concrete whole, and not a discrete whole. If, however, we say that each concrete living whole is to be regarded as an individual, we are still met by the question—What constitutes a concrete living whole? A young organism arising by internal or external gemmation* from a parent organism, passes gradually from a state in which it is an indistinguishable part of the parent organism, to a state in which it is a separate organism of like structure with the parent. At what stage does it become an individual? And if its individuality be conceded only when it completely separates from the parent, must we deny individuality to all organisms thus produced, which permanently retain their connexions with their parents? Or again, what must we say of the *Hectocotylus*,* which is an arm of the Cuttle-fish that undergoes a special development, and then detaching itself, lives independently for a considerable period? And what must we say of that larval *Echinus*,* which is left to move about awhile after being robbed of its viscera by the young *Echinus* developed within it?

To answer such questions, we must revert to the definition of Life. The distinction between individual in its biological sense, and individual in its more general sense, must consist in the manifestation of Life, properly so called. Life we have seen to be, 'the definite combination of heterogeneous changes, both simultaneous and successive, in correspondence with external co-existences and sequences.' Hence, a biological individual is any concrete whole having a structure which enables it, when placed in appropriate conditions, to continuously adjust its internal relations to external relations, so as to maintain the equilibrium of its functions.

THOMAS HARDY

Hap (1866)

If but some vengeful god would call to me
  From up the sky, and laugh: 'Thou suffering thing,
Know that thy sorrow is my ecstasy,
  That thy love's loss is my hate's profiting!'

Then would I bear, and clench myself, and die,
   Steeled by the sense of ire unmerited;
Half-eased, too, that a Powerfuller than I
   Had willed and meted me the tears I shed.

But not so. How arrives it joy lies slain,
   And why unblooms the best hope ever sown?
—Crass Casualty obstructs the sun and rain,
   And dicing Time for gladness casts a moan. . . .
   These purblind Doomsters had as readily strown
Blisses about my pilgrimage as pain.

From *A Pair of Blue Eyes* (1873)

Haggard cliffs, of every ugly altitude, are as common as sea-fowl along the line of coast between Exmoor and Land's End; but this outflanked and encompassed specimen was the ugliest of them all. Their summits are not safe places for scientific experiment on the principles of air-currents, as Knight had now found, to his dismay.

He still clutched the face of the escarpment—not with the frenzied hold of despair, but with a dogged determination to make the most of his every jot of endurance, and so give the longest possible scope to Elfride's intentions, whatever they might be.

He reclined hand in hand with the world in its infancy. Not a blade, not an insect, which spoke of the present, was between him and the past. The inveterate antagonism of these black precipices to all strugglers for life is in no way more forcibly suggested than by the absence of the minutest tufts of grass, lichens, or confervae* from their outermost ledges.

Knight pondered on the meaning of Elfride's hasty disappearance, but could not avoid an instinctive conclusion that there existed but a doubtful hope for him. As far as he could judge, his sole chance of deliverance lay in the possibility of a rope or pole being brought; and this possibility was remote indeed. The soil upon these high downs was left so untended that they were unenclosed for miles, except by a casual bank or dry wall, and were rarely visited but for the purpose of collecting or counting the flock which found a scanty means of subsistence thereon.

At first, when death appeared improbable, because it had never visited him before, Knight could think of no future, nor of anything connected with his past. He could only look sternly at Nature's treacherous attempt to put an end to him, and strive to thwart her.

From the fact that the cliff formed the inner face of the segment of a huge cylinder, having the sky for a top and the sea for a bottom, which enclosed the cove to the extent of more than a semicircle, he could see the vertical face curving round on each side of him. He looked far down the façade, and realised more thoroughly how it threatened him. Grimness was in every feature, and to its very bowels the inimical shape was desolation.

By one of those familiar conjunctions in which the inanimate world baits the mind of man when he pauses in moments of suspense, opposite Knight's eyes was an imbedded fossil, standing forth in low relief from the rock. It was a creature with eyes. The eyes, dead and turned to stone, were even now regarding him. It was one of the early crustaceans called Trilobites.* Separated by millions of years in their lives, Knight and this underling seemed to have met in their death. It was the single instance within reach of his vision of anything that had ever been alive and had had a body to save, as he himself had now.

The creature represented but a low type of animal existence, for never in their vernal years had the plains indicated by those numberless slaty layers been traversed by an intelligence worthy of the name. Zoophytes,* mollusca, shell-fish, were the highest developments of those ancient dates. The immense lapses of time each formation represented had known nothing of the dignity of man. They were grand times, but they were mean times too, and mean were their relics. He was to be with the small in his death.

Knight was a geologist; and such is the supremacy of habit over occasion, as a pioneer of the thoughts of men, that at this dreadful juncture his mind found time to take in, by a momentary sweep, the varied scenes that had had their day between this creature's epoch and his own. There is no place like a cleft landscape for bringing home such imaginings as these.

Time closed up like a fan before him. He saw himself at one extremity of the years, face to face with the beginning and all the intermediate centuries simultaneously. Fierce men, clothed in the hides of beasts, and carrying, for defence and attack, huge clubs and pointed spears, rose from the rock, like the phantoms before the doomed Macbeth. They lived in hollows, woods, and mud huts— perhaps in caves of the neighbouring rocks. Behind them stood an earlier band. No man was there. Huge elephantine forms, the mastodon, the hippopotamus, the tapir, antelopes of monstrous size, the megatherium, and the mylodon*—all, for the moment, in juxtaposition. Farther back, and overlapped by these, were perched hugebilled birds and swinish creatures as large as horses. Still more shadowy were the sinister crocodilian outlines—alligators and other horrible reptiles, culminating in the colossal lizard, the iguanodon.* Folded behind were dragon forms and clouds of flying reptiles: still underneath were fishy beings of lower development; and so on, till the life-time scenes of the fossil confronting him were a present and modern condition of things.

These images passed before Knight's inner eye in less than half a minute, and he was again considering the actual present. Was he to die? The mental picture of Elfride in the world, without himself to cherish her, smote his heart like a whip. He had hoped for deliverance, but what could a girl do? He dared not move an inch. Was Death really stretching out his hand? The previous sensation, that it was improbable he would die, was fainter now. . . .

Knight perseveringly held on. Had he any faith in Elfride? Perhaps. Love is faith, and faith, like a gathered flower, will live on a long time after nutriment has ceased.

Nobody would have expected the sun to shine on such an evening as this. Yet it appeared, low down upon the sea. Not with its natural golden fringe, sweeping the farthest ends of the landscape, not with the strange glare of whiteness which it sometimes puts on as an alternative with colour, but as a splotch of vermilion red upon a leaden ground—a red face looking on with a drunken leer.

Most men who have brains know it, and few are so foolish as to disguise this fact from themselves or others, even though an ostentatious display may be called self-conceit. Knight, without showing it much, knew that his intellect was above the average. And he thought—he could not help thinking—that his death would be a deliberate loss to earth of good material; that such an experiment in killing might have been practised upon some less developed life.

A fancy some people hold, when in a bitter mood, is that

inexorable circumstance only tries to prevent what intelligence attempts. Renounce a desire for a long contested position, and go on another tack, and after a while the prize is thrown at you, seemingly in disappointment that no more tantalising is possible.

Knight gave up thoughts of life utterly and entirely, and turned to contemplate the Dark Valley and the unknown future beyond. Into the solemn depths of these reflections we will not pry. Let it suffice to state what followed.

At that moment of taking no more thought for this life, something disturbed the outline of the bank above him. A spot appeared.

It was the head of Elfride.

Knight immediately prepared to welcome life again.

ERNST HAECKEL

From *The Evolution of Man* (1874)

The History of the Evolution of Man, as it has been usually treated in lectures for medical students at the universities, has only concerned itself with Embryology, so-called, or more correctly with Ontogeny, in other words, with the history of the evolution of individual human organisms. This, however, is only the first part of the task before us, only the first half of the History of the Evolution of Man in the wider sense which will here be attributed to the term. The second part, equal in importance and interest, is Phylogeny, which is the history of the evolution of the descent of man, that is, of the evolution of the various animal forms through which, in the course of countless ages, mankind has gradually passed into its present form. All my readers know of the very important scientific movement which Charles Darwin caused fifteen years ago, by his book on the Origin of Species. The most important direct consequence of this work, which marks a fresh epoch, has been to cause new inquiries to be made into the origin of the human race, which have proved the natural evolution of man through lower animal forms. The Science which treats of the development of the human race from the animal kingdom is called Phylogeny, or the tribal history of man. The most important source from which the science derives its material, is Ontogeny, or the history of germs, in other words, of the evolution of the individual. Palaeontology, or the science of petrifactions, and, in a yet greater degree, Comparative Anatomy, also afford most important aid to Phylogeny.

These two divisions of our science, Ontogeny, or the history of the germ, Phylogeny, or the history of the tribe, are most intimately connected, and the one cannot be understood without the other. The close intertwining of both branches, the increased proportions which germ-history and tribal history lend to each other, alone raise Biogeny (or the history of organic evolution, in the widest sense) to the rank of a philosophic natural science. The connection between the two is not external and superficial, but deeply internal and causal. Our knowledge of this connection has been but very recently obtained; it is most clearly and accurately expressed in the comprehensive statement which I call '*the fundamental law of organic evolution*,' or more briefly, '*the first principle of Biogeny*.'

This fundamental law, to which we shall recur again and again, and on the recognition of which depends the thorough understanding of the history of evolution, is briefly expressed in the proposition: that the History of the Germ is an epitome of the History of the Descent; or, in other words: that Ontogeny is a recapitulation of Phylogeny; or, somewhat more explicitly: that the series of forms through which the Individual Organism passes during its progress from the egg cell to its fully developed state, is a brief, compressed reproduction of the long series of forms through which the animal ancestors of that organism (or the ancestral forms of its species) have passed from the earliest periods of so-called organic creation down to the present time.

The causal nature of the relation which connects the History of the Germ (Embryology, or Ontogeny) with that of the tribe (Phylogeny) is dependent on the phenomena of Heredity and Adaptation. When these are properly understood, and their fundamental importance in determining the forms of organisms recognized, we may go a step further, and say: Phylogenesis is the mechanical cause of Ontogenesis. The Evolution of the Tribe, which is dependent on the laws of Heredity and Adaptation, effects all the events which take place in the course of the Evolution of the Germ or Embryo.

The chain of different animal forms which, according to the Theory of Descent, constitutes the series of ancestors, or chain of forefathers of every higher organism, and hence also of man, always forms a connected whole. This unbroken succession of forms may be represented by the letters of the Alphabet A, B, C, D, E, etc., down to Z, in their alphabetical order. In apparent contradiction to this, the history of the individual evolution, or the Ontogeny of most organisms show us only a fragment of this series of forms, so that the interrupted chain of embryonic forms would be represented by something like: A, B, F, H, I, K, L, etc.; or, in other cases, thus: B, D, H, L, M, N, etc. Several evolutionary forms have, therefore, usually dropped out of the originally unbroken chain of forms. In many cases also (retaining the figure of the repeated alphabet) one or more letters, representing ancestral forms, are replaced in the corresponding places among the embryonic forms by equivalent letters of another alphabet. Thus, for example, in place of the Latin B or D, a Greek β or Δ is often found. Here, therefore, the text of the biogenetic first principle is vitiated, while in the former case it was epitomized. This gives more importance to the fact that, notwithstanding this, the sequence remains the same, so that we are enabled to recognize its original order.

Indeed, there is always a complete parallelism between the two series of evolution. This is, however, vitiated by the fact that in most cases many forms which formerly existed and actually lived in the phylogenetic series are now wanting, and have been lost from the ontogenetic series of evolution. If the parallelism between the two series were perfect, and if this great fundamental law of the causal connection between Ontogeny and Phylogeny, in the strict sense of the word, had full and unconditional sway, we should only have to ascertain, with the aid of microscope and scalpel, the series of forms through which the fertilized human egg passes before it attains its complete development. Such an examination would at once give us a complete picture of the remarkable series of forms through which the animal ancestors of the human race have passed, from the beginning of organic creation to the first appearance of man. But this reproduction of the Phylogeny in the Ontogeny is complete only in rare instances, and seldom corresponds to the entire series of the letters of the alphabet. In fact, in most cases the epitome is very incomplete, and greatly altered and perverted by causes which we shall investigate hereafter. Hence we are seldom able to determine directly, by means of its Ontogeny, the different forms through which the ancestry of each organism has passed; on the contrary, we commonly find,—and not less so in the Phylogeny of man,—a number of gaps. We are, however, able to bridge over the greater part of these gaps satisfactorily by the help of Comparative Anatomy, though not to fill them up directly by ontogenetic research. It is therefore all the more important that we are acquainted with a considerable number of lower animal forms which still find place in the history of the individual evolution of man. In such cases, from the nature of the transient individual form, we may quite safely infer the nature of the ancestral animal form.

For example, from the fact that the human egg is a simple cell, we may at once infer that there has been at a very remote time a unicellular ancestor of the human race resembling an Amoeba. Again, from the fact that the human embryo originally consists merely of two simple germ-layers, we may at once safely infer that a very ancient ancestral form is represented by the two-layered Gastraea.* A later embryonic form of the human being points with equal certainty to a primitive worm-like ancestral form which is related to the sea-squirts or Ascidians* of the present day. But the low animal forms which constitute the ancestral line between the unicellular amoeba and the gastraea, and further between the gastraea and the ascidian form, can only be approximately conjectured with the aid of Comparative Anatomy and Ontogeny. On account of a shortened process of Heredity, various ontogenetic intermediate forms, which must have existed phylogenetically, or in the ancestral lineage, have in the course of historic evolution gradually dropped out from these gaps. But notwithstanding these numerous and sometimes very considerable gaps, there is, on the whole, complete agreement between the two series of evolution. Indeed, it will be one of my principal objects to prove the deep harmony, and original parallelism, between the two series. By adducing numerous facts, I hope to convince my readers that from the actually existing series of embryonic forms which can be shown at any time, we are able to draw the most important conclusions as to the genealogical tree of the human species. We shall thus be able to form a general picture of the series of animal forms which succeeded each other as the direct ancestors of man, in the long course of the history of the organic world.

SAMUEL BUTLER

From *Unconscious Memory* (1880)

The passage included here is Butler's translation of Ewald Hering's published lecture, 'Über das Gedächtnis als eine allgemeine Function der organisierten Materie' ('On Memory as a General Function of Organized Matter', 1876). Butler admired Hering's ideas so much that he incorporated the entire 20-page essay into his book, *Unconscious Memory*.

What is the descent of special peculiarities but a reproduction on the part of organised matter of processes in which it once took part as a germ in the germ-containing organs of its parent, and of which it seems still to retain a recollection that reappears when time and the occasion serve, inasmuch as it responds to the same or like stimuli in a like way to that in which the parent organism responded, of which it was once part, and in the events of whose history it was itself also an accomplice? When an action through long habit or continual practice has become so much a second nature to any organisation that its effects will penetrate, though ever so faintly, into the germ that lies within it, and when this last comes to find itself in a new sphere, to extend itself, and develop into a new creature—(the individual parts of which are still always the creature itself and flesh of its flesh, so that what is reproduced is the same being as that in company with which the germ once lived, and of which it was once actually a part)—all this is as wonderful as when a greyhaired man remembers the events of his own childhood; but it is not more so. Whether we say that the same organised substance is again reproducing its past experience, or whether we prefer to hold that an offshoot or part of the original substance has waxed and developed itself since separation from the parent stock, it is plain that this will constitute a difference of degree, not kind.

When we reflect upon the fact that unimportant acquired characteristics can be reproduced in offspring, we are apt to forget that offspring is only a full-sized reproduction of the parent—a reproduction, moreover, that goes as far as possible into detail. We are so accustomed to consider family resemblance a matter of course, that we are sometimes surprised when a child is in some respect unlike its parent; surely, however, the infinite number of points in respect of which parents and children resemble one another is a more reasonable ground for our surprise.

But if the substance of the germ can reproduce characteristics acquired by the parent during its single life, how much more will it not be able to reproduce those that were congenital to the parent, and which have happened through countless generations to the organised matter of which the germ of to-day is a fragment? We cannot wonder that action already taken on innumerable past occasions by organised matter is more deeply impressed upon the recollection of the germ to which it gives rise than action taken once only during a single lifetime.

We must bear in mind that every organised being now in existence represents the last link of an inconceivably long series of organisms, which come down in a direct line of descent, and of which each has inherited a part of the acquired characteristics of its predecessor. Everything, furthermore, points in the direction of our believing that at the beginning of this chain there existed an organism of the very simplest kind, something, in fact, like those which we call organised germs. The chain of living beings thus appears to be the magnificent achievement of the reproductive power of the original organic structure from which they have all descended. As this sub-divided itself and transmitted its characteristics to its descendants, these acquired new ones, and in their turn transmitted them—all new germs transmitting the chief part of what had happened to their predecessors, while the remaining part lapsed out of their memory, circumstances not stimulating it to reproduce itself.

An organised being, therefore, stands before us a product of the unconscious memory of organised matter, which, ever increasing and ever dividing itself, ever assimilating new matter and returning it in changed shape to the inorganic world, ever receiving some new thing into its memory, and transmitting its acquisitions by way of reproduction, grows continually richer and richer the longer it lives.

EMILY PFEIFFER

Evolution (1880)

Hunger that strivest in the restless arms
   Of the sea-flower, that drivest rooted things
   To break their moorings, that unfoldest wings
In creatures to be rapt above thy harms;
Hunger, of whom the hungry-seeming waves
   Were the first ministers, till, free to range,
   Thou mad'st the Universe thy park and grange,
What is it thine insatiate heart still craves?

Sacred disquietude, divine unrest!
   Maker of all that breathes the breath of life,
No unthrift greed spurs thine unflagging zest,
   No lust self-slaying hounds thee to the strife;
Thou art the Unknown God on whom we wait:
Thy path the course of our unfolding fate.

To Nature

Dread Force, in whom of old we loved to see
   A nursing mother, clothing with her life
   The seeds of Love divine,—with what sore strife
We hold or yield our thoughts of Love and thee!
Thou art not 'calm,' but restless as the ocean,
   Filling with aimless toil the endless years—
   Stumbling on thought, and throwing off the spheres,
Churning the Universe with mindless motion.

Dull fount of joy, unhallowed source of tears,
   Cold motor of our fervid faith and song,
Dead, but engendering life, love, pangs, and fears,
   Thou crownedst thy wild work with foulest wrong
When first thou lightedst on a seeming goal,
And darkly blundered on man's suffering soul.

AUGUST WEISMANN

From *Essays on Heredity* (1881–5)

THE CONTINUITY OF THE GERM-PLASM AS THE
FOUNDATION OF A THEORY OF HEREDITY

When we see that, in the higher organisms, the smallest structural
details, and the most minute peculiarities of bodily and mental disposition, are transmitted from one generation to another; when we
find in all species of plants and animals a thousand characteristic
peculiarities of structure continued unchanged through long series
of generations; when we even see them in many cases unchanged
throughout whole geological periods; we very naturally ask for the
causes of such a striking phenomenon: and enquire how it is that
such facts become possible, how it is that the individual is able to
transmit its structural features to its offspring with such precision.
And the immediate answer to such a question must be given in the
following terms:—'A single cell out of the millions of diversely differentiated cells which compose the body, becomes specialized as a
sexual cell; it is thrown off from the organism and is capable of
reproducing all the peculiarities of the parent body, in the new individual which springs from it by cell-division and the complex process of differentiation.' Then the more precise question follows:
'How is it that such a single cell can reproduce the *tout ensemble** of
the parent with all the faithfulness of a portrait?' . . .

If, according to the received physiological and morphological ideas
of the day, it is impossible to imagine that gemmules* produced by
each cell of the organism are at all times to be found in all parts of
the body, and furthermore that these gemmules are collected in the
sexual cells, which are then able to again reproduce in a certain order
each separate cell of the organism, so that each sexual cell is capable
of developing into the likeness of the parent body; if all this is
inconceivable, we must enquire for some other way in which we can
arrive at a foundation for the true understanding of heredity. My
present task is not to deal with the whole question of heredity, but
only with the single although fundamental question—'How is it that
a single cell of the body can contain within itself all the hereditary tendencies of the whole organism?' I am here leaving out of account the

further question as to the forces and the mechanism by which these tendencies are developed in the building-up of the organism. . . .

Now if it is impossible for the germ-cell* to be, as it were, an extract of the whole body, and for all the cells of the organism to despatch small particles to the germ-cells, from which the latter derive their power of heredity; then there remain, as it seems to me, only two other possible, physiologically conceivable, theories as to the origin of germ-cells, manifesting such powers as we know they possess. Either the substance of the parent germ-cell is capable of undergoing a series of changes which, after the building-up of a new individual, leads back again to identical germ-cells; or the germ-cells are not derived at all, as far as their essential and characteristic substance is concerned, from the body of the individual, but they are derived directly from the parent germ-cell.

I believe that the latter view is the true one: I have expounded it for a number of years, and have attempted to defend it, and to work out its further details in various publications. I propose to call it the theory of 'The Continuity of the Germ-plasm,' for it is founded upon the idea that heredity is brought about by the transference from one generation to another, of a substance with a definite chemical, and above all, molecular constitution. I have called this substance 'germ-plasm,' and have assumed that it possesses a highly complex structure, conferring upon it the power of developing into a complex organism. I have attempted to explain heredity by supposing that in each ontogeny,* a part of the specific germ-plasm contained in the parent egg-cell is not used up in the construction of the body of the offspring, but is reserved unchanged for the formation of the germ-cells of the following generation.

It is clear that this view of the origin of germ-cells explains the phenomena of heredity very simply, inasmuch as heredity becomes thus a question of growth and of assimilation,—the most fundamental of all vital phenomena. If the germ-cells of successive generations are directly continuous, and thus only form, as it were, different parts of the same substance, it follows that these cells must, or at any rate may, possess the same molecular constitution, and that they would therefore pass through exactly the same stages under certain conditions of development, and would form the same final product. The hypothesis of the continuity of the germ-plasm gives an identical starting-point to each successive generation, and thus explains how it is that an identical product arises from all of them. In other words, the hypothesis explains heredity as part of the underlying problems of assimilation and of the causes which act directly during ontogeny: it therefore builds a foundation from which the explanation of these phenomena can be attempted.

It is true that this theory also meets with difficulties, for it seems to be unable to do justice to a certain class of phenomena, viz. the transmission of so-called acquired characters.* I therefore gave immediate and special attention to this point in my first publication on heredity, and I believe that I have shown that the hypothesis of the transmission of acquired characters—up to that time generally accepted—is, to say the least, very far from being proved, and that entire classes of facts which have been interpreted under this hypothesis may be quite as well interpreted otherwise, while in many cases they must be explained differently. I have shown that there is no ascertained fact, which, at least up to the present time, remains in irrevocable conflict with the hypothesis of the continuity of the germ-plasm; and I do not know any reason why I should modify this opinion to-day, for I have not heard of any objection which appears to be feasible. E. Roth* has objected that in pathology we everywhere meet with the fact that acquired local disease may be transmitted to the offspring as a predisposition; but all such cases are exposed to the serious criticism that the very point that first needs to be placed on a secure footing is incapable of proof, viz. the hypothesis that the causes which in each particular case led to the predisposition were really acquired. It is not my intention, on the present occasion, to enter fully into the question of acquired characters; I hope to be able to consider the subject in greater detail at a future date. But in the meantime I should wish to point out that we ought, above all, to be clear as to what we really mean by the expression 'acquired character.' An organism cannot acquire anything unless it already possesses the predisposition to acquire it: acquired characters are therefore no more than local or sometimes general variations which arise under the stimulus provided by certain external influences. If by the long-continued handling of a rifle, the so-called 'Exercierknochen' (a bony growth caused by the pressure of the weapon in drilling) is developed, such a result depends upon the fact that the bone in question, like every other bone, contains within itself a predisposition to react upon certain mechanical stimuli, by growth in a certain direction and to a certain extent. The predisposition towards an 'Exercierknochen' is therefore already present, or else the growth could not be formed; and the same reasoning applies to all other 'acquired characters.'

Nothing can arise in an organism unless the predisposition to it is pre-existent, for every acquired character is simply the reaction of the organism upon a certain stimulus.

MAY KENDALL

Lay of the Trilobite (1885)

A mountain's giddy height I sought,
   Because I could not find
Sufficient vague and mighty thought
   To fill my mighty mind;
And as I wandered ill at ease,
   There chanced upon my sight
A native of Silurian seas,
   An ancient Trilobite.

So calm, so peacefully he lay,
   I watched him even with tears:
I thought of Monads* far away
   In the forgotten years.
How wonderful it seemed and right,
   The providential plan,
That he should be a Trilobite,
   And I should be a Man!

And then, quite natural and free
   Out of his rocky bed,
That Trilobite he spoke to me,
   And this is what he said:
'I don't know how the thing was done,
   Although I cannot doubt it;
But Huxley—he if anyone
   Can tell you all about it;

'How all your faiths are ghosts and dreams,
    How in the silent sea
Your ancestors were Monotremes*—
    Whatever these may be;
How you evolved your shining lights
    Of wisdom and perfection
From Jelly-fish and Trilobites
    By Natural Selection.

'You've Kant to make your brains go round,
    Hegel you have to clear them,
You've Mr Browning to confound,
    And Mr Punch* to cheer them!
The native of an alien land
    You call a man and brother,
And greet with hymn-book in one hand
    And pistol in the other!

'You've Politics to make you fight
    As if you were possessed:
You've cannon and you've dynamite
    To give the nations rest:
The side that makes the loudest din
    Is surest to be right,
And oh, a pretty fix you're in!'
    Remarked the Trilobite.

'But gentle, stupid, free from woe
    I lived among my nation,
I didn't care—I didn't know
    That I was a Crustacean.
I didn't grumble, didn't steal,
    I *never* took to rhyme:
Salt water was my frugal meal,
    And carbonate of lime.'

Reluctantly I turned away,
    No other word he said;
An ancient Trilobite, he lay
    Within his rocky bed.

I did not answer him, for that
    Would have annoyed my pride:
I merely bowed, and raised my hat,
    But in my heart I cried:—

'I wish our brains were not so good,
    I wish our skulls were thicker,
I wish that Evolution could
    Have stopped a little quicker;
For oh, it was a happy plight,
    Of liberty and case,
To be a simple Trilobite
    In the Silurian seas!'

GERARD MANLEY HOPKINS

Nature is a Heraclitean Fire (1888)

THAT NATURE IS A HERACLITEAN FIRE AND OF THE COMFORT OF THE RESURRECTION

Cloud-puffball, torn tufts, tossed pillows ¦ flaunt forth, then chevy* on an air-
built thoroughfare: heaven-roysterers, in gay-gangs ¦ they throng; they glitter in marches.
Down roughcast, down dazzling whitewash, ¦ wherever an elm arches,
Shivelights* and shadowtackle in long ¦ lashes lace, lance, and pair.
Delightfully the bright wind boisterous ¦ ropes, wrestles, beats earth bare
Of yestertempest's creases; in pool and rut peel parches
Squandering ooze to squeezed ¦ dough, crust, dust; stanches, starches
Squadroned masks and manmarks ¦ treadmire toil there
Footfretted in it.   Million-fuelèd, ¦ nature's bonfire burns on.
But quench her bonniest, dearest ¦ to her, her clearest-selvèd spark
Man, how fast his firedint, ¦ his mark on mind, is gone!
Both are in an unfathomable, all is in an enormous dark
Drowned.   O pity and indig ¦ nation!   Manshape, that shone

Sheer off, disseveral, a star, ¹ death blots black out; nor mark
                    Is any of him at all so stark
But vastness blurs and time ¹ beats level. Enough! the Resur-
        rection,
A heart's-clarion! Away grief's gasping, ¹ joyless days, dejection.
                    Across my foundering deck shone
A beacon, an eternal beam. ¹ Flesh fade, and mortal trash
Fall to the residuary worm; ¹ world's wildfire, leave but ash:
                    In a flash, at a trumpet crash,
I am all at once what Christ is, ¹ since he was what I am, and
This Jack, joke, poor potsherd,* ¹ patch, matchwood, immortal
        diamond,
                    Is immortal diamond.

Sexual Selection

JANE AUSTEN

From *Pride and Prejudice* (1813)

It is a truth universally acknowledged that a single man in possession
of a good fortune must be in want of a wife.

However little known the feelings or views of such a man may be
on his first entering a neighbourhood, this truth is so well fixed in
the minds of the surrounding families, that he is considered as the
rightful property of some one or other of their daughters.

'My dear Mr Bennet,' said his lady to him one day, 'have you
heard that Netherfield Park is let at last?'

Mr Bennet replied that he had not.

'But it is,' returned she; 'for Mrs Long has just been here, and
she told me all about it.'

Mr Bennet made no answer.

'Do you not want to know who has taken it?' cried his wife
impatiently.

'*You* want to tell me, and I have no objection to hearing it.'

This was invitation enough.

'Why, my dear, you must know, Mrs Long says that Netherfield is taken by a young man of large fortune from the north of England; that he came down on Monday in a chaise and four to see the place, and was so much delighted with it that he agreed with Mr Morris immediately; that he is to take possession before Michaelmas, and some of his servants are to be in the house by the end of next week.'

'What is his name?'

'Bingley.'

'Is he married or single?'

'Oh, single, my dear, to be sure! A single man of large fortune; four or five thousand a year. What a fine thing for our girls!'

'How so? how can it affect them?'

'My dear Mr Bennet,' replied his wife, 'how can you be so tiresome? You must know that I am thinking of his marrying one of them.'

'Is that his design in settling here?'

'Design? nonsense, how can you talk so! But it is very likely that he *may* fall in love with one of them, and therefore you must visit him as soon as he comes.'

'I see no occasion for that. You and the girls may go, or you may send them by themselves, which perhaps will be still better; for as you are as handsome as any of them, Mr Bingley might like you the best of the party.'

'My dear, you flatter me. I certainly *have* had my share of beauty, but I do not pretend to be anything extraordinary now. When a woman has five grown-up daughters, she ought to give over thinking of her own beauty.'

'In such cases a woman has not often much beauty to think of.'

'But, my dear, you must indeed go and see Mr Bingley when he comes into the neighbourhood.'

'It is more than I engage for, I assure you.'

'But consider your daughters. Only think what an establishment it would be for one of them. Sir William and Lady Lucas are determined to go, merely on that account; for in general, you know, they visit no newcomers. Indeed you must go, for it will be impossible for *us* to visit him if you do not.'

'You are over-scrupulous, surely. I daresay Mr Bingley will be very glad to see you; and I will send a few lines by you to assure him of my hearty consent to his marrying whichever he chooses of the girls; though I must throw in a good word for my little Lizzy.'

'I desire you will do no such thing. Lizzy is not a bit better than the others; and I am sure she is not half so handsome as Jane, nor half so good-humoured as Lydia. But you are always giving *her* the preference.'

'They have none of them much to recommend them,' replied he—'they are all silly and ignorant like other girls; but Lizzy has something more of quickness than her sisters.'

'Mr Bennet, how can you abuse your own children in such a way? You take delight in vexing me. You have no compassion on my poor nerves.'

'You mistake me, my dear. I have a high respect for your nerves. They are my old friends. I have heard you mention them with consideration these twenty years at least.'

'Ah, you do not know what I suffer.'

'But I hope you will get over it, and live to see many young men of four thousand a year come into the neighbourhood.'

'It will be no use to us if twenty such should come, since you will not visit them.'

'Depend upon it, my dear, that when there are twenty I will visit them all.'

Mr Bennet was so odd a mixture of quick parts, sarcastic humour, reserve, and caprice, that the experience of three-and-twenty years had been insufficient to make his wife understand his character. *Her* mind was less difficult to develop. She was a woman of mean understanding, little information, and uncertain temper. When she was discontented, she fancied herself nervous. The business of her life was to get her daughters married; its solace was visiting and news.

CHARLES DARWIN

From *The Descent of Man and Selection in Relation to Sex* (1871)

Our difficulty in regard to sexual selection lies in understanding how it is that the males which conquer other males, or those which prove the most attractive to the females, leave a greater number of offspring to inherit their superiority than the beaten and less attractive males. Unless this result followed, the characters which gave to certain males an advantage over others, could not be perfected and augmented through sexual selection. When the sexes exist in exactly equal numbers, the worst-endowed males will ultimately find females (excepting where polygamy prevails), and leave as many off-spring, equally well fitted for their general habits of life, as the best-endowed males. From various facts and considerations, I formerly inferred that with most animals, in which secondary sexual characters were well developed, the males considerably exceeded the females in number; and this does hold good in some few cases. If the males were to the females as two to one, or as three to two, or even in a somewhat lower ratio, the whole affair would be simple: for the better-armed or more attractive males would leave the largest number of offspring. But after investigating, as far as possible, the numerical proportions of the sexes, I do not believe that any great inequality in number commonly exists. In most cases sexual selection appears to have been effective in the following manner:

Let us take any species, a bird for instance, and divide the females inhabiting a district into two equal bodies: the one consisting of the more vigorous and better-nourished individuals, and the other of the less vigorous and healthy. The former, there can be little doubt, would be ready to breed in the spring before the others; and this is the opinion of Mr Jenner Weir, who has during many years carefully attended to the habits of birds. There can also be no doubt that the most vigorous, healthy, and best-nourished females would on an average succeed in rearing the largest number of offspring. The males, as we have seen, are generally ready to breed before the females; of the males the strongest, and with some species the best armed, drive away the weaker males; and the former would then unite with the more vigorous and best-nourished females, as these are the first to breed. Such vigorous pairs would surely rear a larger number of offspring than the retarded females, which would be compelled, supposing the sexes to be numerically equal, to unite with the conquered and less powerful males; and this is all that is wanted to add, in the course of successive generations, to the size, strength, and courage of the males, or to improve their weapons.

But in a multitude of cases the males which conquer other males do not obtain possession of the females, independently of choice on the part of the latter. The courtship of animals is by no means so simple and short an affair as might be thought. The females are most excited by, or prefer pairing with, the more ornamented males, or those which are the best songsters, or play the best antics; but it is obviously probable, as has been actually observed in some cases, that they would at the same time prefer the more vigorous and lively males. Thus the more vigorous females, which are the first to breed, will have the choice of many males; and though they may not always select the strongest or best armed, they will select those which are vigorous and well armed, and in other respects the most attractive. Such early pairs would have the same advantage in rearing offspring on the female side as above explained, and nearly the same advantage on the male side. And this apparently has sufficed during a long course of generations to add not only to the strength and fighting-powers of the males, but likewise to their various ornaments or other attractions. . . .

In various classes of animals a few exceptional cases occur, in which the female instead of the male has acquired well-pronounced secondary sexual characters, such as brighter colours, greater size, strength, or pugnacity. With birds, as we shall hereafter see, there has sometimes been a complete transposition of the ordinary characters proper to each sex; the females having become the more eager in courtship, the males remaining comparatively passive, but apparently selecting, as we may infer from the results, the more attractive females. Certain female birds have thus been rendered more highly coloured or otherwise ornamented, as well as more powerful and pugnacious, than the males, these characters being transmitted to the female offspring alone.

It may be suggested that in some cases a double process of selection has been carried on; the males having selected the more attractive females, and the latter the more attractive males. This process, however, though it might lead to the modification of both sexes, would not make the one sex different from the other, unless indeed their taste for the beautiful differed; but this is a supposition too improbable in the case of any animal, excepting man, to be worth considering. There are, however, many animals, in which the sexes resemble each other, both being furnished with the same ornaments, which analogy would lead us to attribute to the agency of sexual selection. In such cases it may be suggested with more plausibility, that there has been a double or mutual process of sexual selection; the more vigorous and precocious females having selected the more attractive and vigorous males, the latter having rejected all except the more attractive females. But, from what we know of the habits of animals, this view is hardly probable, the male being generally eager to pair with any female. It is more probable that the ornaments common to both sexes were acquired by one sex, generally the male, and then transmitted to the offspring of both sexes. If, indeed, during a lengthened period the males of any species were greatly to exceed the females in number, and then during another lengthened period under different conditions the reverse were to occur, a double, but not simultaneous, process of sexual selection might easily be carried on, by which the two sexes might be rendered widely different.

We shall hereafter see that many animals exist, of which neither sex is brilliantly coloured or provided with special ornaments, and yet the members of both sexes or of one alone have probably been modified through sexual selection. The absence of bright tints or other ornaments may be the result of variations of the right kind never having occurred, or of the animals themselves preferring simple colours, such as plain black or white. Obscure colours have often been acquired through natural selection for the sake of protection, and the acquirement through sexual selection of conspicuous colours, may have been checked from the danger thus incurred. But in other cases the males have probably struggled together during long ages, through brute force, or by the display of their charms, or by both means combined, and yet no effect will have been produced unless a larger number of offspring were left by the more successful males to inherit their superiority, than by the less successful males; and this, as previously shown, depends on various complex contingencies.

Sexual selection acts in a less rigorous manner than natural selection. The latter produces its effects by the life or death at all ages of the more or less successful individuals. Death, indeed, not rarely ensues from the conflicts of rival males. But generally the less successful male merely fails to obtain a female, or obtains later in the season a retarded and less vigorous female, or, if polygamous, obtains fewer females; so that they leave fewer, or less vigorous, or no offspring. In regard to structures acquired through ordinary or natural selection, there is in most cases, as long as the conditions of life remain the same, a limit to the amount of advantageous modification in relation to certain special ends; but in regard to structures adapted to make one male victorious over another, either in fighting or in charming the female, there is no definite limit to the amount of advantageous modification; so that as long as the proper variations arise the work of sexual selection will go on. This circumstance may partly account for the frequent and extraordinary amount of variability presented by secondary sexual characters. Nevertheless, natural selection will determine that characters of this kind shall not be acquired by the victorious males, which would be injurious to them in any high degree, either by expending too much of their vital powers, or by exposing them to any great danger. The development, however, of certain structures—of the horns, for instance, in certain stags—has been carried to a wonderful extreme; and in some instances to an extreme which, as far as the general conditions of life are concerned, must be slightly injurious to the male. From this fact we learn that the advantages which favoured males have derived from conquering other males in battle or courtship, and thus leaving a numerous progeny, have been in the long-run greater than those derived from rather more perfect adaptation to the external conditions of life. We shall further see, and this could never have been anticipated, that the power to charm the female has been in some few instances more important than the power to conquer other males in battle.

HENRY RIDER HAGGARD

From *She* (1887)

There were also some women among them, who, instead of the leopard-skin, wore a tanned hide of a small red buck, something like that of the oribé,* only rather darker in colour. These woman were, as a class, exceedingly good-looking, with large, dark eyes, well-cut features, and a thick bush of curling hair—not crisped like a negro's—ranging from black to chestnut in hue, with all shades of intermediate colour. Some, but very few of them, wore a yellowish linen garment, such as I have described as worn by Billali,* but this, as we afterwards discovered, was a mark of rank, rather than an attempt at clothing. For the rest, their appearance was not quite so terrifying as that of the men, and they sometimes, though rarely, smiled. As soon as we had alighted they gathered round us and examined us with curiosity, but without excitement. Leo's tall, athletic form and clear-cut Grecian face, however, evidently excited their attention, and when he politely lifted his hat to them, and showed his curling yellow hair, there was a slight murmur of admiration. Nor did it stop there; for, after regarding him critically from head to foot, the handsomest of the young women—one wearing a robe, and with hair of a shade between brown and chestnut—deliberately advanced to him, and, in a way that would have been winning had it not been so determined, quietly put her arm round his neck, bent forward, and kissed him on the lips.

I gave a gasp, expecting to see Leo instantly speared; and Job ejaculated, 'The hussy—well, I never!' As for Leo, he looked slightly astonished; and then, remarking that we had got into a country where they clearly followed the customs of the early Christians, deliberately returned the embrace.

Again I gasped, thinking that something would happen; but to my surprise, though some of the young women showed traces of vexation, the older ones and the men only smiled slightly. When we came to understand the customs of this extraordinary people the mystery was explained. It then appeared that, in direct opposition to the habits of almost every other savage race in the world, women among the Amahagger are not only upon terms of perfect equality with the men, but are not held to them by any binding ties. Descent is traced only through the line of the mother, and while individuals are as proud of a long and superior female ancestry as we are of our families in Europe, they never pay attention to, or even acknowledge, any man as their father, even when their male parentage is perfectly well known. There is but one titular male parent of each tribe, or, as they call it, 'Household,' and he is its elected and immediate ruler, with the title of 'Father.' For instance, the man Billali was the father of this 'household,' which consisted of about seven thousand individuals all told, and no other man was ever called by that name. When a woman took a fancy to a man she signified her preference by advancing and embracing him publicly, in the same way that this handsome and exceedingly prompt young lady, who was called Ustane, had embraced Leo. If he kissed her back it was a token that he accepted her, and the arrangement continued till one of them wearied of it. I am bound, however, to say that the change of husbands was not nearly so frequent as might have been expected. Nor did quarrels arise out of it, at least among the men, who, when their wives deserted them in favour of a rival, accepted the whole thing much as we accept the income-tax or our marriage laws, as something not to be disputed, and as tending to the good of the community, however disagreeable they may in particular instances prove to the individual.

It is very curious to observe how the customs of mankind on this matter vary in different countries, making morality an affair of latitude, and what is right and proper in one place wrong and improper in another. It must, however, be understood that, as all civilised nations appear to accept it as an axiom that ceremony is the touchstone of morality, there is, even according to our canons, nothing immoral about this Amahagger custom, seeing that the interchange of the embrace answers to our ceremony of marriage, which, as we know, justifies most things.

At breakfast one of the women, no longer quite young, advanced, and publicly kissed Job. I think it was in its way the most delightful thing (putting its impropriety aside for a moment) that I ever saw. Never shall I forget the respectable Job's abject terror and disgust. Job, like myself, is a bit of a misogynist—I fancy chiefly owing to the fact of his having been one of a family of seventeen—and the feelings expressed upon his countenance when he realised that he was not only being embraced publicly, and without authorisation on his own part, but also in the presence of his masters, were too mixed and painful to admit of accurate description. He sprang to his feet, and pushed the woman, a buxom person of about thirty, from him.

'Well, I never!' he gasped, whereupon probably thinking that he was only coy, she embraced him again.

'Be off with you! Get away, you minx!' he shouted, waving the wooden spoon, with which he was eating his breakfast, up and down before the lady's face. 'Beg your pardon, gentlemen, I am sure I haven't encouraged her. Oh, Lord! she's coming for me again. Hold her, Mr Holly! please hold her! I can't stand it; I can't, indeed. This has never happened to me before, gentlemen, never. There's nothing against my character,' and here he broke off, and ran as hard as he could go down the cave, and for once I saw the Amahagger laugh. As for the woman, however, she did not laugh. On the contrary, she seemed to bristle with fury, which the mockery of the other women about only served to intensify. She stood there literally snarling and shaking with indignation . . .

At first we were much puzzled as to the origin and constitution of this extraordinary race, points upon which they were singularly uncommunicative. As the time went on—for the next four days passed without any striking event—we learnt something from Leo's lady friend Ustane, who, by the way, stuck to that young gentleman like his own shadow. As to origin, they had none, at least, so far as she was aware. There were, however, she informed us, mounds of masonry and many pillars near the place where *She* lived, which was called Kôr, and which the wise said had once been houses wherein men lived, and it was suggested that they were descended from these men. No one, however, dared go near these great ruins, because they were haunted: they only looked on them from a distance. Other similar ruins were to be seen, she had heard, in various parts of the country, that is, wherever one of the mountains rose above the level of the swamp. Also the caves in which they lived had been hollowed out of the rocks by men, perhaps the same who built the cities. They themselves had no written laws, only custom, which was, however, quite as binding as law. If any man offended against the custom, he was put to death by order of the Father of the 'Household.' I asked how he was put to death, and she only smiled, and said that I might see one day soon.

They had a Queen, however. *She* was their Queen, but she was very rarely seen, perhaps once in two or three years, when she came forth to pass sentence on some offenders, and when seen was muffled up in a big cloak, so that nobody could look upon her face. Those who waited upon her were deaf and dumb, and therefore could tell no tales, but it was reported that she was lovely as no other woman was lovely, or ever had been. It was rumoured also that she was immortal, and had power over all things, but she, Ustane, could say nothing of all that. What she believed was that the Queen chose a husband from time to time, and as soon as a female child was born this husband, who was never again seen, was put to death. Then the female child grew up and took the place of the Queen when its mother died, and had been buried in the great caves. But of these matters none could speak for certain. Only *She* was obeyed throughout the length and breadth of the land, and to question her command was certain death. She kept a guard, but had no regular army, and to disobey her was to die. . . .

We three and Ustane were sitting round a fire in the cave just before bedtime, when suddenly the woman, who had been brooding in silence, rose, and laid her hand upon Leo's golden curls, and addressed him. Even now, when I shut my eyes, I can see her proud, imperial form, clothed alternately in dense shadow and the red flickering of the fire, as she stood, the wild centre of as weird a scene as I ever witnessed, and delivered herself of the burden of her thoughts and forebodings in a kind of rhythmical speech that ran something as follows:—

Thou art my chosen—I have waited for thee from the beginning!

Thou art very beautiful. Who hath hair like unto thee, or skin so white?

Who hath so strong an arm, who is so much a man?

Thine eyes are the sky, and the light in them is the stars.

Thou art perfect and of a happy face, and my heart turned itself towards thee.

Ay, when mine eyes fell on thee I did desire thee,—

Then did I take thee to me—thou, my Beloved,

And hold thee fast, lest harm should come unto thee.

Ay, I did cover thine head with mine hair, lest the sun should strike it;

And altogether was I thine, and thou wast altogether mine.

And so it went for a little space, till Time was in labour with an evil Day;

And then what befell on that day? Alas! my Beloved, I know not!

But I, I saw thee no more—I, I was lost in the blackness.

And she who is stronger did take thee; ay, she who is fairer than Ustane.

Yet didst thou turn and call upon me, and let thine eyes wander in the darkness.

But, nevertheless, she prevailed by Beauty, and led thee down horrible places,

And then, ah! then my Beloved——

Here this extraordinary woman broke off her speech, or chant, which was so much musical gibberish to us, for all that we understood of what she was talking about, and seemed to fix her flashing eyes upon the deep shadow before her. Then in a moment they acquired a vacant, terrified stare, as though they were striving to realise some half-seen horror. She lifted her hand from Leo's head, and pointed into the darkness. We all looked, and could see nothing; but she saw something, or thought she did, and something evidently that affected even her iron nerves, for, without another sound, down she fell senseless between us.

CONSTANCE NADEN

Natural Selection (1887)

I had found out a gift for my fair,
 I had found where the cave-men were laid;
Skull, femur, and pelvis were there,
 And spears, that of silex* they made.

But he ne'er could be true, she averred,
 Who would dig up an ancestor's grave—
And I loved her the more when I heard
 Such filial regard for the Cave.

My shelves, they are furnished with stones
 All sorted and labelled with care,
And a splendid collection of bones,
 Each one of them ancient and rare;

One would think she might like to retire
 To my study—she calls it a 'hole!'
Not a fossil I heard her admire,
 But I begged it, or borrowed, or stole.

But there comes an idealess lad,
 With a strut, and a stare, and a smirk;
And I watch, scientific though sad,
 The Law of Selection at work.

Of Science he hasn't a trace,
 He seeks not the How and the Why,
But he sings with an amateur's grace,
 And he dances much better than I.

And we know the more dandified males
  By dance and by song win their wives—
'Tis a law that with *Aves** prevails,
  And even in *Homo* survives.

Shall I rage as they whirl in the valse?
  Shall I sneer as they carol and coo?
Ah no! for since Chloe is false,
  I'm certain that Darwin is true!

THOMAS HARDY

From *Tess of the D'Urbervilles* (1891)

The hot weather of July had crept upon them unawares, and the atmosphere of the flat vale hung heavy as an opiate over the dairy-folk, the cows, and the trees. Hot steaming rains fell frequently, making the grass where the cows fed yet more rank, and hindering the late haymaking in the other meads.

It was Sunday morning; the milking was done; the outdoor milkers had gone home. Tess and the other three were dressing themselves rapidly, the whole bevy having agreed to go together to Mellstock Church, which lay some three or four miles distant from the dairy-house. She had now been two months at Talbothays, and this was her first excursion.

All the preceding afternoon and night heavy thunderstorms had hissed down upon the meads, and washed some of the hay into the river; but this morning the sun shone out all the more brilliantly for the deluge, and the air was balmy and clear.

The crooked lane leading from their own parish to Mellstock ran along the lowest levels in a portion of its length, and when the girls reached the most depressed spot they found that the result of the rain had been to flood the lane over-shoe to a distance of some fifty yards. This would have been no serious hindrance on a week-day; they would have clicked through it in their high pattens and boots quite unconcerned; but on this day of vanity, this Sun's-day, when flesh went forth to coquet with flesh while hypocritically affecting business with spiritual things; on this occasion for wearing their white stockings and thin shoes, and their pink, white, and buff gowns, on which every mud spot would be visible, the pool was an awkward impediment. They could hear the church-bell calling—as yet nearly a mile off.

'Who would have expected such a rise in the river in summer-time!' said Marian, from the top of the roadside bank on which they had climbed, and were maintaining a precarious footing in the hope of creeping along its slope till they were past the pool.

'We can't get there anyhow, without walking right through it, or else going round Stone Bridge way; and that would make us so very late!' said Retty, pausing hopelessly.

'And I do colour up so hot, walking into church late, and all the people staring round,' said Marian, 'that I hardly cool down again till we get into the That-it-may-please-Thees.'

While they stood clinging to the bank they heard a splashing round the bend of the road, and presently appeared Angel Clare, advancing along the lane towards them through the water.

Four hearts gave a big throb simultaneously.

His aspect was probably as un-Sabbatarian a one as a dogmatic parson's son often presented; his attire being his dairy clothes, long wading boots, a cabbage-leaf inside his hat to keep his head cool, with a thistle-spud to finish him off.

'He's not going to church,' said Marian.

'No—I wish he was!' murmured Tess.

Angel, in fact, rightly or wrongly (to adopt the safe phrase of evasive controversialists), preferred sermons in stones to sermons in churches and chapels on fine summer days. This morning, moreover, he had gone out to see if the damage to the hay by the flood was considerable or not. On his walk he observed the girls from a long distance, though they had been so occupied with their difficulties of passage as not to notice him. He knew that the water had risen at that spot, and that it would quite check their progress. So he had hastened on, with a dim idea of how he could help them—one of them in particular.

The rosy-cheeked, bright-eyed quartet looked so charming in their light summer attire, clinging to the roadside bank like pigeons on a roof-slope, that he stopped a moment to regard them before coming close. Their gauzy skirts had brushed up from the grass innumerable flies and butterflies which, unable to escape, remained caged in the transparent tissue as in an aviary. Angel's eye at last fell upon Tess, the hindmost of the four; she, being full of suppressed laughter at their dilemma, could not help meeting his glance radiantly.

He came beneath them in the water, which did not rise over his long boots; and stood looking at the entrapped flies and butterflies.

'Are you trying to get to church?' he said to Marian, who was in front, including the next two in his remark, but avoiding Tess.

'Yes, sir; and 'tis getting late; and my colour do come up so——'

'I'll carry you through the pool—every Jill of you.'

The whole four flushed as if one heart beat through them.

'I think you can't, sir,' said Marian.

'It is the only way for you to get past. Stand still. Nonsense—you are not too heavy! I'd carry you all four together. Now, Marian, attend,' he continued, 'and put your arms round my shoulders, so. Now! Hold on. That's well done.'

Marian had lowered herself upon his arm and shoulder as directed, and Angel strode off with her, his slim figure, as viewed from behind, looking like the mere stem to the great nosegay suggested by hers. They disappeared round the curve of the road, and only his sousing footsteps and the top ribbon of Marian's bonnet told where they were. In a few minutes he reappeared. Izz Huett was the next in order upon the bank.

'Here he comes,' she murmured, and they could hear that her lips were dry with emotion. 'And I have to put my arms round his neck and look into his face as Marian did.'

'There's nothing in that,' said Tess quickly.

'There's a time for everything,' continued Izz, unheeding. 'A time to embrace, and a time to refrain from embracing; the first is now going to be mine.'

'Fie—it is Scripture, Izz!'

'Yes,' said Izz, 'I've always a' ear at church for pretty verses.'

Angel Clare, to whom three-quarters of this performance was a commonplace act of kindness, now approached Izz. She quietly and dreamily lowered herself into his arms, and Angel methodically marched off with her. When he was heard returning for the third time Retty's throbbing heart could be almost seen to shake her. He went up to the red-haired girl, and while he was seizing her he glanced at Tess. His lips could not have pronounced more plainly, 'It will soon be you and I.' Her comprehension appeared in her face; she could not help it. There was an understanding between them.

Poor little Retty, though by far the lightest weight, was the most troublesome of Clare's burdens. Marian had been like a sack of meal, a dead weight of plumpness under which he had literally staggered. Izz had ridden sensibly and calmly. Retty was a bunch of hysterics.

However, he got through with the disquieted creature, deposited her, and returned. Tess could see over the hedge the distant three in a group, standing as he had placed them on the next rising ground. It was now her turn. She was embarrassed to discover that excitement at the proximity of Mr Clare's breath and eyes, which she had contemned in her companions, was intensified in herself; and as if fearful of betraying her secret she paltered with him at the last moment.

'I may be able to clim' along the bank perhaps—I can clim' better than they. You must be so tired, Mr Clare!'

'No, no, Tess,' said he quickly. And almost before she was aware she was seated in his arms and resting against his shoulder.

'Three Leahs to get one Rachel,' he whispered.

'They are better women than I,' she replied, magnanimously sticking to her resolve.

'Not to me,' said Angel.

He saw her grow warm at this; and they went some steps in silence.

'I hope I am not too heavy?' she said timidly.

'Oh no. You should lift Marian! Such a lump. You are like an undulating billow warmed by the sun. And all this fluff of muslin about you is the froth.'

'It is very pretty—if I seem like that to you.'

'Do you know that I have undergone three-quarters of this labour entirely for the sake of the fourth quarter?'

'No.'

'I did not expect such an event to-day.'

'Nor I. . . . The water came up so sudden.'

That the rise in the water was what she understood him to refer to, the state of her breathing belied. Clare stood still, and inclined his face towards hers.

'O Tessy!' he exclaimed.

The girl's cheeks burned to the breeze, and she could not look into his eyes for her emotion. It reminded Angel that he was somewhat unfairly taking advantage of an accidental position; and he went no further with it. No definite words of love had crossed their lips as yet, and suspension at this point was desirable now. However, he walked slowly, to make the remainder of the distance as long as possible; but at last they came to the bend, and the rest of their progress was in full view of the other three. The dry land was reached, and he set her down.

Her friends were looking with round thoughtful eyes at her and him, and she could see that they had been talking of her. He hastily bade them farewell, and splashed back along the stretch of submerged road.

The four moved on together as before, till Marian broke the silence by saying—

'No—in all truth; we have no chance against her!' She looked joylessly at Tess.

'What do you mean?' asked the latter.

'He likes 'ee best—the very best! We could see it as he brought 'ee. He would have kissed 'ee, if you had encouraged him to do it, ever so little.'

'No, no,' said she.

The gaiety with which they had set out had somehow vanished; and yet there was no enmity or malice between them. They were generous young souls; they had been reared in the lonely country nooks where fatalism is a strong sentiment, and they did not blame her. Such supplanting was to be.

Tess's heart ached. There was no concealing from herself the fact that she loved Angel Clare, perhaps all the more passionately from knowing that the others had also lost their hearts to him. There is contagion in this sentiment, especially among women. And yet that same hungry heart of hers compassionated her friends. Tess's honest nature had fought against this, but too feebly, and the natural result had followed.

'I will never stand in your way, nor in the way of either of 'ee!' she declared to Retty that night in the bedroom (her tears running down). 'I can't help this, my dear! I don't think marrying is in his mind at all; but if he were even to ask me I should refuse him, as I should refuse any man.'

'Oh! would you? Why?' said wondering Retty.

'It cannot be! But I will be plain. Putting myself quite on one side, I don't think he will choose either of you.'

'I have never expected it—thought of it!' moaned Retty. 'But O! I wish I was dead!'

The poor child, torn by a feeling which she hardly understood, turned to the two other girls who came upstairs just then.

'We be friends with her again,' she said to them. 'She thinks no more of his choosing her than we do.'

So the reserve went off, and they were confiding and warm.

'I don't seem to care what I do now,' said Marian, whose mood was tuned to its lowest bass. 'I was going to marry a dairyman at Stickleford, who's asked me twice; but—my soul—I would put an end to myself rather'n be his wife now! Why don't ye speak, Izz?'

'To confess, then,' said Izz, 'I made sure today that he was going to kiss me as he held me; and I stayed still against his breast, hoping and hoping, and never moved at all. But he did not. I don't like biding here at Talbothays any longer! I shall go home.'

The air of the sleeping-chamber seemed to palpitate with the hopeless passion of the girls. They writhed feverishly under the oppressiveness of an emotion thrust on them by cruel Nature's law—an emotion which they had neither expected nor desired. The incident of the day had fanned the flame that was burning the inside of their hearts out, and the torture was almost more than they could endure. The differences which distinguished them as individuals were abstracted by this passion, and each was but portion of one organism called sex. There was little jealousy because there was no hope. Each one was a girl of fair common-sense, and she did not delude herself with any vain conceits, or dress herself up, or give herself airs, in the idea of outshining the others. The full recognition of the futility of their infatuation, from a social point of view; its purposeless beginning; its self-bounded outlook; its lack of everything to justify its existence in the eye of civilization (while lacking nothing in the eye of Nature); the one fact that it did exist, ecstasizing them to a killing joy; all this imparted to them a resignation, a dignity, which a practical and sordid expectation of winning him as a husband would have destroyed.

They tossed and turned on their little beds, and the cheese-wring dripped monotonously downstairs.

'B' you awake, Tess?' whispered one, half-an-hour later.

It was Izz Huett's voice.

Tess replied in the affirmative, whereupon also Retty and Marian suddenly flung the bed-clothes off them, and sighed—

'So be we!'

'I wonder what she is like—the lady they say his family have looked out for him!'

'I wonder,' said Izz.

'Some lady looked out for him?' gasped Tess, starting. 'I have never heard o' that!'

'Oh yes—'tis whispered; a young lady of his own rank, chosen by his family; a Doctor of Divinity's daughter near his father's parish of Emminster; he don't much care for her, they say. But he is sure to marry her.'

They had heard so very little of this; yet it was enough to build up wretched dolorous dreams upon, there in the shade of the night. They pictured all the details of his being won round to consent, of the wedding preparations, of the bride's happiness, of her dress and veil, of her blissful home with him, when oblivion would have fallen upon themselves as far as he and their love were concerned. Thus they talked, and ached, and wept till sleep charmed their sorrow away.

After this disclosure Tess nourished no further foolish thought that there lurked any grave and deliberate import in Clare's attentions to her. It was a passing summer love of her face, for love's own temporary sake—nothing more. And the thorny crown of this sad conception was that she whom he really did prefer in a cursory way to the rest, she who knew herself to be more impassioned in nature, cleverer, more beautiful than they, was in the eyes of propriety far less worthy of him than the homelier ones whom he ignored.

SCIENCES OF THE MIND

Until the 1830s, the study of the human mind was a division of philosophy. The emergence of mental science (the terms 'psychology' and 'psychiatry' were not widely used until the early twentieth century) proceeded slowly, amid much controversy, and studies of the mind retained their philosophical roots. Associationism, the belief that all complex ideas arise from associations among simpler ones and can ultimately be traced to sensory perceptions, was regarded as a philosophy, not a scientific theory, although its adherents ranged from social theorists like John Stuart Mill to physiologists like William Carpenter. Many, like Herbert Spencer and George Henry Lewes, relied on neurophysiology to develop their theories of mind. The main tenet of nineteenth-century mental physiology, the conviction that the mind and body were interdependent so that any understanding of the mind must be based on neuroanatomical and neurophysiological knowledge, owes a great deal to John Locke's belief that true knowledge must be gained through experience, and David Hume's insistence that philosophy be inductive. The mind, asserted William James, is built from the bottom up.

Over the course of the nineteenth century, several factors combined to encourage the emergence of mental science: an increasing respect for knowledge gained through experimentation; a conviction that the methods of the physical sciences could be applied to other fields; and an idea that minds, like bodies, had evolved and could be scanned for traces of ancestral forms. But as physiologists of mind struggled to establish the new field, they encountered considerable resistance. Their subject matter—human perceptions, thoughts, and behaviour—was inherently subjective. How could one study subjective phenomena objectively? Even within the field, scientists and physicians debated which of their activities could be considered 'scientific'. As late as the 1860s, the physiologist Henry Maudsley joined many writers in questioning whether 'alienism', the branch of medicine devoted to mental illness, could ever be a science.

Mental scientists' efforts to convey states of consciousness created a special affinity between their task and that of literary writers. Trying to capture human thought in scientific terms, they endeavoured to persuade readers that their language was more truthful than that of their precursors or rivals for knowledge in this sphere. In their effort to create an authoritative voice, they quoted poets whose insights into the mind were culturally respected. In his treatise on mesmerism, Chauncey Hare Townsend quoted Coleridge and Newton side by side.

To justify their task, these writers needed to change readers' understanding of what constituted scientific 'evidence'. If the sciences of the mind were to win credibility, personal testimony needed to achieve the status of fact. Writers like Harriet Martineau, who described her experiences with mesmerism, and John Elliotson, who recorded his patients' perceptions of anaesthesia, offered their own observations as evidence for controversial phenomena. When Thomas De Quincey described his sensations while under the influence of opium, he showed how a substance taken into the body could transform the mind. Like mesmerists and psychologists, De Quincey relied on his own personal testimony as 'evidence'—here, in a literary work—of how changes to the body could alter one's perceptions. When describing altered states of consciousness, scientific and literary writers alike relied on 'case studies' to convey subjective feelings to readers.

Like literary texts, scientific studies achieved credibility through consistency, vivid description, and narrative force. James Cowles Prichard's detailed portraits of morally insane individuals offered histories, personal idiosyncrasies, and detailed narratives similar to those associated with fictional characters, so that readers got to 'know' Prichard's patients as they knew Oliver Twist. Not surprisingly, physicians who wrote compelling case studies—Oliver Wendell Holmes and S. Weir Mitchell, for instance—often wrote very readable fiction. When they wanted to offer unsubstantiated ideas too speculative for scientific journals, some physicians turned to literature, where they could create imaginary case histories and suggest appropriate therapies.

Since classical times, writers had observed that one's physical state affects one's mental outlook and one's mental state shapes one's perceptions of physical experiences. In the nineteenth century the growing prestige of scientific studies encouraged a new interpretation of these observations. They were easily explicable if people had no 'souls' independent of their bodies and mental phenomena depended instead on the brain's participation in the bodily economy. As part of the nervous system, the brain was inseparable from the body.

But the interdependence of mind and body was not something literary writers 'learned' from mental scientists. On the contrary, stories like 'Bartleby the Scrivener' suggested ways to describe the effects of food and alcohol on behaviour, illustrating the complex interplay of constitution and environment. The physiologist and alienist Henry Maudsley, who took a particular interest in the mental disorders of women, also found himself describing patterns of human irritability when he noted the ways menstrual cycles affected his patients' moods. According to his observations, their reproductive systems powerfully influenced their mental states.

If the mind and body were so closely linked, then selfhood could only be the product of the entire 'economy'. During the American Civil War, the neurologist S. Weir Mitchell explored the mental and physical roots of personal identity by studying his patients' phantom limb experiences. The fact that amputees felt pain in limbs that were no longer present suggested not just that mental perceptions were the result of bodily processes but that bodily processes might have an impact on perception. Mitchell published his observations in two neurological textbooks, but to explore his studies' broader implications, he illustrated the links between mind and body in an anonymous story, 'The Case of George Dedlow'. Here his fictional patient—who has had all four limbs amputated—explains how his bodily changes have altered his sense of self. So vividly did Mitchell present the case, which is narrated by the protagonist, that readers of the *Atlantic Monthly* thought it was an actual case history and took up a collection for Dedlow.

In examining people's mental and physical interdependence, nineteenth-century writers also studied the way the mind could affect the body. In 'The Birthmark', Nathaniel Hawthorne reminded readers that 'the body' is a mental construct, subject to the projections—though not always to the control—of the mind. William Carpenter, by contrast, one of England's most respected physiologists, contended that the mind's power over the body was as yet underestimated. Their interplay was extremely complex, he observed, so that one could define no clear boundary between voluntary and involuntary phenomena. Like many nineteenth-century authors, Carpenter was fascinated by the human will, a cultural as well as a physiological concept. When scientists analysed it, they carried all its existing connotations to their new fields, but Carpenter did not see this as a threat to mental physiology. By opening his chapter on the will with a series of verbs (I am, I ought, I can, I will), Carpenter tied his classification of mental faculties to ordinary language, while establishing definitional discriminations within that language.

If the human mind was housed in a bodily organ, the brain, then structural studies of that organ might yield valuable information about its function. In the late eighteenth century the Protestant minister Johann Caspar Lavater developed the science of physiognomy, seeking evidence of the divine in the human form. Like phrenology, which concentrated more specifically on the human skull's shape, physiognomy was a science of reading. Its practitioners functioned as skilled interpreters of bodily texts, warning against irresponsible inferences by lay practitioners.

Johann Gaspar Spurzheim saw physiognomy as the study of relations between formal attributes. One could learn nothing from the overall size of a head, he argued, only from the relative sizes of its component parts. George Combe, one of Scotland's leading phrenologists, concurred, distinguishing power from activity and presenting phrenological readings as indicators of potential, not destiny.

As the associations drawn by phrenologists became known to the public, literary writers—who had always used corporeality to suggest character traits—integrated the language of phrenology into physical descriptions of their characters so as to play on readers' assumptions. At the same time, they challenged the inferences being drawn, depicting phrenological readings as questionable interpretations. Charlotte Brontë, who was well informed in phrenology, juxtaposed face-reading (scientific observation) with palm-reading (superstition) in *Jane Eyre*. Her ironic representation of a phrenological reading ('well said, forehead') suggests that Jane's face itself is speaking—or declining to speak—and that Rochester is reading—or misreading—a story written upon it. Readers of *Jane Eyre* have every reason to believe his tale—except that the context entirely undermines it. Rochester, who claims that features cannot lie, is disguised in this scene as an old gypsy woman, a fact clear to the narrator (an older, wiser Jane) though not initially to Jane, the character, or perhaps to the reader. The scene, in which Rochester deceives Jane and the narrator deceives the reader, urges one to mistrust all physical appearances.

George Eliot's 'The Lifted Veil' offers an equally sceptical picture of phrenology. Here, the sickly young narrator who is the object of analysis protests against a determinative reading, one that defines his strengths and weaknesses and demands that he remedy his 'defects'. As a result of this authoritative assessment, he is subjected to an education which any personal knowledge of him would deem inappropriate. As in *Jane Eyre*, the context of the reading undermines the interpretive process. The ailing narrator, whose capacity for physical movement is limited, tries to control his life—and the reader's experience of it—by telling his own story, but in this scene he is objectified by a science that reads his story in his face.

Mesmerism, another technique for exploring the mind, gave the subject's own testimony much greater importance. On the one hand, as Alison Winter has shown, physicians like John Elliotson—one of the chief promoters of mesmerism in England—viewed their patients as laboratory instruments with which they could perform valuable experiments. On the other, the data produced in these experiments relied largely on the patient's own perceptions. Mesmerized people were both objects and subjects, yielding valuable information and authorized to describe their own feelings.

When the respected writer Harriet Martineau turned to mesmerism to relieve her chronic pain, she did her best to convince readers that mesmerism provided valid, effective therapy. In her *Letters on Mesmerism*, she made her sensations 'real' by using the precise visual descriptions and innovative metaphors her readers would have encountered in good realist fiction. When literary writers used the same kind of detail, they sometimes convinced readers their imaginary patients were real. With its scientific references and suspenseful dialogue between mesmerist and subject, Edgar Allan Poe's 'Mesmeric Revelation' appears to be an actual case history. In the 1840s actual and fictional accounts of mesmerism inspired one another with their strategies to win readers' belief.

As Robert Browning suggests in his poem 'Mesmerism' both imagination and mesmerism offered opportunities for controlling the world around one. To some degree, fiction and mesmeric trances suspended ordinary behaviour, turning a person into the character an 'author' wanted him or her to be. While many mesmerists and subjects denied that subjects could be controlled against their wills, the public feared being manipulated by magnetic figures. Reports like James Esdaile's, about incidences of kidnapping by means of mesmerism, reinforced anxieties about mind control. Some readers doubted that Esdaile's mesmeric studies would hold true in England, since India, where he conducted them, was regarded as a primitive, superstitious country. Wilkie Collins's enormously popular mystery, *The Moonstone*, brought Esdaile's findings home, however. Playing on public concerns about foreign influence or 'invasion', Collins inverts Esdaile's case studies (in which British or British-trained physicians mesmerized Indian patients) and depicts a British boy used as an instrument by Indians.

Mesmerism was known and accepted by the public decades before scientists developed the idea of the unconscious. Novelists had always used physical descriptions to suggest thoughts which their characters did not reveal in words, but only when physiologists systematically studied nervous reflexes did the unconscious mind become an area of scientific study. In 1833, when Marshall Hall demonstrated that the body could respond to stimuli through spinal reflexes alone, his study provoked wide interest. Writers from every field saw the implications of his finding: movement was produced not by a soul but by the body itself. A body could perform any number of functions independent of the brain's control and possibly even of its awareness. Studies of muscular reflexes offered a new vocabulary for discussing unconscious phenomena, so that in nineteenth-century stories about inaccessible parts of the mind, these new fields merged with an ongoing literary tradition.

For the chemist August Kekulé, who fell asleep while pondering the structure of benzene, the unconscious offered a specific solution to a scientific problem. In Kekulé's 1890 address to the German Chemical Society—at a meeting commemorating the twenty-fifth anniversary of his discovery of the structure of benzene—he recreated two moments of inspiration, both of which, he claimed, had occurred while he was half asleep. Kekulé concluded his story by advising listeners to 'learn to dream', suggesting that rather than forging scientific ideas, reason might destroy them in the process of emergence.

Frances Power Cobbe's argument for unconscious cerebration also combines scientific and literary accounts of dreams and sleep. For the lay reader, her examples from literature, philosophy, mythology, and everyday life provide convincing evidence that 'matter can think'. Cobbe proposes that people can commit immoral actions in their dreams without any apparent attacks of conscience because consciousness is not needed for thought and mental activity continues when the will is suspended. This hypothesis comforted readers and supported the claims of physiologists, who saw the will as a civilized person's means of controlling primitive impulses.

The existence of an unconscious mind that spoke when the will was relaxed suggested the potential for struggle between different parts of human consciousness. In *The Strange Case of Dr Jekyll and Mr Hyde*, Robert Louis Stevenson offered the public a fictional case study, a thought experiment in which the hypothetical split in consciousness becomes destructively literal. So powerful is Stevenson's depiction of Jekyll—who as a scientist thinks actively about the issues his experience raises—that it is easy to accept him as an actual 'case'. For over a century Stevenson's novel has been read as 'evidence' for a painful division of human consciousness.

Both scientific and literary depictions of the human will convinced the public they were vulnerable when the will was suspended. In the 1860s the popularity—and suspected danger—of 'sensation novels' made the relations between the *reader's* mind and body an issue of social concern. Mary Elizabeth Braddon's *Lady Audley's Secret* depicts a woman tainted by hereditary madness and is at times so suspenseful that it nearly maddens the reader. Appealing directly to readers' emotions, novels like Braddon's were believed to bypass their wills, threatening their mental health by exciting their nerves directly.

In an exhausted mind, nineteenth-century scientists contended, the will could no longer control emotional impulses, so that one might fall victim to hysteria. The American neurologist S. Weir Mitchell warned readers that the stress of late-nineteenth-century life was literally 'wearing out' their nerves. Inspired by physiologists like Maudsley and centuries of cultural tradition, Mitchell maintained that women were especially vulnerable to nervous exhaustion. Writing and study taxed the female brain more heavily than the male, he asserted, leaving women unfit for their primary social role of motherhood. Both Mitchell and his mentor, Oliver Wendell Holmes, wrote fictional as well as actual case studies to illustrate these views.

Holmes's psychological novel *Elsie Venner* makes a plea for better treatment of the mentally disturbed, suggesting that most mental illness results from constitutional factors over which individuals have no control. In his far-fetched tale, fierce, solitary Elsie develops snake-like qualities because her mother, while pregnant, was bitten by a rattlesnake. In his depiction of minor characters, however, such as Elsie's overworked teacher, Holmes shows how overwhelming environmental pressures can wear out a mind. Exhausted, the lonely young schoolmistress becomes hysterical when she encounters the 'animal-like' frankness of Elsie's essay.

While literature provided physicians with an opportunity to present their theories to the public, it offered dissatisfied patients a chance to reply to their doctors. Charlotte Perkins Gilman's 'The Yellow Wall-paper' gives the patient narrative—if not actual—power. In her story, Gilman, who was herself a patient of Mitchell, speaks back to her husband-doctor, depicting a character who manages to express herself even when her doctor denies her interpretation of her illness. In her story of a woman forbidden to write, Gilman uses personal experience to challenge a scientific theory that denied her creativity. In nineteenth-century accounts of mental illness, both scientists and literary writers used their personal perceptions to shape readers' understanding of the mind.

The Relationship between Mind and Body

THOMAS DE QUINCEY

From *Confessions of an English Opium-Eater* (1822)

Arrived at my lodgings, it may be supposed that I lost not a moment in taking the quantity prescribed. I was necessarily ignorant of the whole art and mystery of opium-taking: and, what I took, I took under every disadvantage. But I took it:—and in an hour, oh! heavens! what a revulsion! what an upheaving, from its lowest depths, of the inner spirit! what an apocalypse of the world within me! That my pains had vanished, was now a trifle in my eyes:—this negative effect was swallowed up in the immensity of those positive effects which had opened before me—in the abyss of divine enjoyment thus suddenly revealed. Here was a panacea—a *φαρμακον νηπενθες*,* for all human woes: here was the secret of happiness, about which philosophers had disputed for so many ages, at once discovered: happiness might now be bought for a penny, and carried in the waistcoat pocket: portable ecstasies might be had corked up in a pint bottle: and peace of mind could be sent down in gallons by the mail coach. But, if I talk in this way, the reader will think I am laughing: and I can assure him, that nobody will laugh long who deals much with opium: its pleasures even are of a grave and solemn complexion; and in his happiest state, the opium-eater cannot present himself in the character of *l'Allegro*: even then, he speaks and thinks as becomes *Il Penseroso*.* Nevertheless, I have a very reprehensible way of jesting at times in the midst of my own misery: and, unless when I am checked by some more powerful feelings, I am afraid I shall be guilty of this indecent practice even in these annals of suffering or enjoyment. The reader must allow a little to my infirm nature in this respect: and with a few indulgences of that sort, I shall endeavour to be as grave, if not drowsy, as fits a theme like opium, so anti-mercurial as it really is, and so drowsy as it is falsely reputed.

And, first, one word with respect to its bodily effects: for upon all that has been hitherto written on the subject of opium, whether by travellers in Turkey (who may plead their privilege of lying as an old immemorial right), or by professors of medicine, writing *ex cathedrâ*,*—I have but one emphatic criticism to pronounce—Lies! lies! lies! I remember once, in passing a book-stall, to have caught these words from a page of some satiric author:—'By this time I became convinced that the London newspapers spoke truth at least twice a week, viz. on Tuesday and Saturday, and might safely be depended upon for——the list of bankrupts.' In like manner, I do by no means deny that some truths have been delivered to the world in regard to opium: thus it has been repeatedly affirmed by the learned, that opium is a dusky brown in colour; and this, take notice, I grant: secondly, that it is rather dear; which also I grant: for in my time, East-India opium has been three guineas a pound, and Turkey eight: and, thirdly, that if you eat a good deal of it, most probably you must——do what is particularly disagreeable to any man of regular habits, viz. die. These weighty propositions are, all and singular, true: I cannot gainsay them: and truth ever was, and will be, commendable. But in these three theorems, I believe we have exhausted the stock of knowledge as yet accumulated by man on the subject of opium. And therefore, worthy doctors, as there seems to be room for further discoveries, stand aside, and allow me to come forward and lecture on this matter.

First, then, it is not so much affirmed as taken for granted, by all who ever mention opium, formally or incidentally, that it does, or can, produce intoxication. Now, reader, assure yourself, *meo periculo,** that no quantity of opium ever did, or could intoxicate. As to the tincture of opium (commonly called laudanum) *that* might certainly intoxicate if a man could bear to take enough of it; but why? because it contains so much proof spirit, and not because it contains so much opium. But crude opium, I affirm peremptorily, is incapable of producing any state of body at all resembling that which is produced by alcohol: and not in *degree* only incapable, but even in *kind*: it is not in the quantity of its effects merely, but in the quality, that it differs altogether. The pleasure given by wine is always mounting, and tending to a crisis, after which it declines: that from opium, when once generated, is stationary for eight or ten hours: the first, to borrow a technical distinction from medicine, is a case of acute—the second, of chronic pleasure: the one is a flame, the other a steady and equable glow. But the main distinction lies in this, that whereas wine disorders the mental faculties, opium, on the contrary (if taken in a proper manner), introduces amongst them the most exquisite order, legislation, and harmony. Wine robs a man of his self-possession: opium greatly invigorates it. Wine unsettles and clouds the judgment, and gives a preternatural brightness, and a vivid exaltation to the contempts and the admirations, the loves and the hatreds, of the drinker: opium, on the contrary, communicates serenity and equipoise to all the faculties, active or passive: and with respect to the temper and moral feelings in general, it gives simply that sort of vital warmth which is approved by the judgment, and which would probably always accompany a bodily constitution of primeval or antediluvian health. Thus, for instance, opium, like wine, gives an expansion to the heart and the benevolent affections: but then, with this remarkable difference, that in the sudden development of kindheartedness which accompanies inebriation, there is always more or less of a maudlin character, which exposes it to the contempt of the by-stander. Men shake hands, swear eternal friendship, and shed tears—no mortal knows why: and the sensual creature is clearly uppermost. But the expansion of the benigner feelings, incident to opium, is no febrile access, but a healthy restoration to that state which the mind would naturally recover upon the removal of any deep-seated irritation of pain that had disturbed and quarrelled with the impulses of a heart originally just and good. True it is, that even wine, up to a certain point, and with certain men, rather tends to exalt and to steady the intellect: I myself, who have never been a great wine-drinker, used to find that half a dozen glasses of wine advantageously affected the faculties—brightened and intensified the consciousness—and gave to the mind a feeling of being ponderibus librata suis:* and certainly it is most absurdly said, in popular language, of any man, that he is *disguised* in liquor: for, on the contrary, most men are disguised by sobriety; and it is when they are drinking (as some old gentleman says in Athenaeus), that men ἐαυτοὺς ἐμφανίζουσιν οἵτινες εἰσίν—display themselves in their true complexion of character; which surely is not disguising themselves. But still, wine constantly leads a man to the brink of absurdity and extravagance; and, beyond a certain point, it is sure to volatilize and to disperse the intellectual energies: whereas opium always seems to compose what had been agitated, and to concentrate what had been distracted. In short, to sum up all in one word, a man who is inebriated, or tending to inebriation, is, and feels that he is, in a condition which calls up into supremacy the merely human, too often the brutal, part of his nature: but the opium-eater (I speak of him who is not suffering from any disease, or other remote effects of opium,) feels that the diviner part of his nature is paramount; that is, the moral affections are in a state of cloudless serenity; and over all is the great light of the majestic intellect.

MARSHALL HALL

On the Reflex Function (1833)

The English physiologist and physician Marshall Hall (1790–1857) conducted his experiments and successful private practice in his own London home. He began studying animal reflexes (especially those of frogs, toads, lizards, and newts) in 1832. The following selection is taken from his second major paper on the subject, read in 1833 before the Royal Society. Hall's work was received much more enthusiastically by German and French physiologists than it was by the British scientific community. Although Hall avoided discussing the consequences of his theory for human consciousness, it later became a topic of debate in popular journals, due partly to Continental responses.

In the entire animal, sensation and voluntary motion, functions of the cerebrum, combine with the functions of the medulla oblongata and medulla spinalis,* and may therefore render it difficult or impossible to determine those which are peculiar to each; if, in an animal deprived of the brain, the spinal marrow, or the nerves supplying the muscles, be stimulated, those muscles, whether voluntary or respiratory, are equally thrown into contraction, and, it may be added, equally in the complete and in the mutilated animal; and, in the case of the nerves, equally in limbs connected with and detached from the spinal marrow.

The operation of all these various causes of muscular contraction may be designated *centric*, as taking place *at*, or at least in a direction *from*, central parts of the nervous system. But there is another function the phenomena of which are of a totally different order and obey totally different laws, being excited by causes in a situation which is *eccentric* in the nervous system, that is, distant from the nervous centres. This mode of action has not, I think, been hitherto distinctly understood by physiologists. It is involved in the question which Baron CUVIER* considers as so full of interest, and is that treated of in the following pages.

Many of the phenomena of this principle of action, as they occur in the limbs, have certainly been observed. But, in the first place, this function is by no means confined to the limbs: for, whilst it imparts to each muscle its appropriate tone, and to each system of muscles its appropriate equilibrium or balance, it performs the still more important office of presiding over the orifices and terminations of each of the internal canals in the animal economy, giving to them their due form and action; and, in the second place, in the instances in which the phenomena of this function have been noticed, they have been confounded, as I have stated, with those of sensation and volition; or, if they have been distinguished from these, they have been too indefinitely denominated instinctive, or automatic. I have been compelled, therefore, to adopt some new designation for them, and I shall now give the reasons for my choice of that which is given in the title of this paper.

This property is characterized by being *excited* in its action, and *reflex* in its course: in every instance in which it is exerted, an impression made upon the extremities of certain nerves is conveyed to the medulla oblongata or the medulla spinalis, and is reflected along other nerves to parts adjacent to, or remote from, that which has received the impression.

It is by this reflex character that the function to which I have alluded is to be distinguished from every other. There are, in the animal economy, four modes of muscular action, of muscular contraction. The *first* is that designated *voluntary*: volition, originating in the cerebrum, and spontaneous in its acts, extends its influence along the spinal marrow and the motor nerves, in a *direct line*, to the voluntary muscles. The *second* is that of the *respiration*: like volition, the motive influence in respiration passes in a *direct line* from one point of the nervous system to certain muscles; but as voluntary motion seems to originate in the cerebrum, so the respiratory motions originate in the medulla oblongata: like the voluntary motions, the motions of respiration are spontaneous; they continue, at least, after the eighth pair of nerves has been divided. The *third* kind of muscular action in the animal economy is that termed *involuntary*: it depends upon the principle of irritability, and requires the *immediate* application of a stimulus to the nervo-muscular fibre itself. These three kinds of muscular motion are well known to physiologists; and I believe they are all which have been hitherto pointed out. There is, however, a *fourth*, which subsists, in part, after the voluntary and respiratory motions have ceased, by the removal of the cerebrum and medulla oblongata, and which is attached to the medulla spinalis, ceasing itself when this is removed, and leaving the irritability undiminished. In this kind of muscular motion, the motive influence does not originate in any central part of the nervous system, but at a distance from that centre: it is neither spontaneous in its action, nor direct in its course; it is, on the contrary, *excited* by the application of appropriate stimuli, which are not, however, applied immediately to the muscular or nervo-muscular fibre, but to certain membranous parts, whence the impression is carried to the medulla, *reflected*, and reconducted to the part impressed, or conducted to a part remote from it, in which muscular contraction is effected.

The first three modes of muscular action are known only by actual movements or muscular contractions. But the reflex function exists as a continuous muscular action, as a power presiding over organs not actually in a state of motion, preserving in some, as the glottis, an open, in others, as the sphincters, a closed form, and in the limbs, a due degree of equilibrium, or balanced muscular action,—a function, not, I think, hitherto recognised by physiologists.

The three kinds of muscular motion hitherto known may be distinguished in another way. The muscles of voluntary motion and of respiration may be excited by stimulating the nerves which supply them, in any part of their course, whether at their source, as a part of the medulla oblongata or medulla spinalis, or exterior to the spinal canal: the muscles of involuntary motion are chiefly excited by the actual contact of stimuli. In the case of the reflex function alone, the muscles are excited by a stimulus acting mediately and indirectly in a curved and reflex course, along superficial sub-cutaneous or submucous nerves proceeding to the medulla, and muscular nerves proceeding from the medulla. The first three of these causes of muscular motion may act on detached limbs or muscles. The last requires the connexion with the medulla to be preserved entire.

All the kinds of muscular motion may be unduly excited. But the reflex function is peculiar in being excitable into modes of action not previously subsisting in the animal economy, as in the cases of sneezing, coughing, vomiting, &c. The reflex function also admits of being permanently diminished or augmented, and of taking on some other morbid forms.

JAMES COWLES PRICHARD

From *A Treatise on Insanity* (1835)

MORAL INSANITY

This form of mental derangement has been described as consisting in a morbid perversion of the feelings, affections, and active powers, without any illusion or erroneous conviction impressed upon the understanding: it sometimes co-exists with an apparently un-impaired state of the intellectual faculties.

There are many individuals living at large, and not entirely separated from society, who are affected in a certain degree with this modification of insanity. They are reputed persons of a singular, wayward, and eccentric character. An attentive observer will often recognize something remarkable in their manners and habits, which may lead him to entertain doubts as to their entire sanity; and circumstances are sometimes discovered, on inquiry, which add strength to his suspicion. In many instances it has been found that an hereditary tendency to madness has existed in the family, or that several relatives of the person affected have laboured under other diseases of the brain. The individual himself has been discovered to have suffered, in a former period of life, an attack of madness of a decided character. His temper and dispositions are found to have undergone a change; to be not what they were previously to a certain time: he has become an altered man, and the difference has, perhaps, been noted from the period when he sustained some reverse of fortune, which deeply affected him, or the loss of some beloved relative. In other instances, an alteration in the character of the individual has ensued immediately on some severe shock which his bodily constitution has undergone. This has been either a disorder affecting the head, a slight attack of paralysis, a fit of epilepsy, or some febrile or inflammatory disorder, which has produced a perceptible change in the habitual state of the constitution. In some cases the alteration in temper and habits has been gradual and imperceptible, and it seems only to have consisted in an exaltation and increase of peculiarities, which were always more or less natural and habitual.

In a state like that above described, many persons have continued for years to be the sources of apprehension and solicitude to their friends and relatives. The latter, in many instances, cannot bring themselves to admit the real nature of the case. The individual follows the bent of his inclinations; he is continually engaging in new pursuits, and soon relinquishing them without any other inducement than mere caprice and fickleness. At length the total perversion of his affections, the dislike, and perhaps even enmity, manifested towards his dearest friends, excite greater alarm. When it happens that the head of a family labours under this ambiguous modification of insanity, it is sometimes thought necessary, from prudential motives, and to prevent absolute ruin from thoughtless and absurd extravagance, or from the results of wild projects and speculations, in the pursuit of which the individual has always a plausible reason to offer for his conduct, to make some attempt with a view to take the management of his affairs out of his hands. The laws have made inadequate provision for such contingencies, and the endeavour is often unsuccessful. If the matter is brought before a jury, and the individual gives pertinent replies to the questions that are put to him, and displays no particular mental illusion,—a feature which is commonly looked upon as essential to madness,—it is most probable that the suit will be rejected.

Persons labouring under this disorder are capable of reasoning or supporting an argument upon any subject within their sphere of knowledge that may be presented to them; and they often display great ingenuity in giving reasons for the eccentricities of their conduct, and in accounting for and justifying the state of moral feeling under which they appear to exist. In one sense, indeed, their intellectual faculties may be termed unsound; they think and act under the influence of strongly-excited feelings, and persons accounted sane are, under such circumstances, proverbially liable to error both in judgement and conduct. . . .

CASES EXEMPLIFYING THE DESCRIPTION OF MORAL INSANITY AND THAT OF MONOMANIA, OR ILLUSTRATING THE RELATION BETWEEN THESE FORMS OF DISEASE, AND THE TRANSITION FROM ONE INTO THE OTHER

The first case that I shall relate, is one which for some years bore precisely the character attributed to moral insanity. During this period many of the friends of the individual affected supposed him to be only *very eccentric*; while some, who had opportunities of observing him closely, were convinced that he was deranged. His disorder at length broke out in a form which admitted of no doubt, viz., that of monomania accompanied with great distress of mind, and it terminated in suicide. I give the details of this case as I received them from an intimate friend of the individual affected.

Case 1.—A.B., a gentleman remarkable for the warmth of his affections, and the amiable simplicity of his character, possessed of great intellectual capacity, strong powers of reasoning, and a lively imagination, married a lady of high mental endowments, and who was long well known in the literary world. He was devotedly attached to her, but entertained the greatest jealousy lest the world should suppose that, in consequence of her talents, she exercised an undue influence over his judgement, or dictated his compositions. He accordingly set out with a determination of never consulting her, or yielding to her influence, and was always careful, when engaged in writing, that she should be ignorant of the subject which occupied his thoughts. His wife has been often heard to lament that want of sympathy and union of mind which are so desirable in married life. This peculiarity, however, in the husband so much increased, that in after years the most trifling proposition on her part was canvassed and discussed by every kind of argument. In the meantime he acquired strange peculiarities of habits. His love of order, or placing things in what he considered order or regularity, was remarkable. He was continually putting chairs, &c. in their places; and if articles of ladies' work or books were left upon a table, he would take an opportunity *unobserved* of putting them in order, generally spreading the work smooth, and putting the other articles in rows. He would steal into rooms belonging to other persons for the purpose of arranging the various articles. So much time did he consume in trifles, placing and replacing, and running from one room to another, that he was rarely dressed by dinner-time, and often apologised for dining in his dressing-gown, when it was well known that he had done nothing the whole morning but dress. And he would often take a walk in a winter's evening with a lanthorn, because he had not been able to get ready earlier in the day. He would run up and down the garden a certain number of times, rinsing his mouth with water, and spitting alternately on one side and then on the other in regular succession. He employed a good deal of time in rolling up little pieces of writing-paper which he used for cleaning his nose. In short his peculiarities were innumerable, but he concealed them as much as possible from the observation of his wife, whom he knew to be vexed at his habits, and to whom he always behaved with the most respectful and affectionate attention, although she could not influence him in the slightest degree. He would, however, occasionally break through these habits; as on Sundays, though he rose early for the purpose, he was always ready to perform service at a chapel a mile and a half distant from his house. It was a mystery to his intimate friends when and how he prepared these services. It did not at all surprise those who were best acquainted with his peculiarities, to hear that in a short time he became notoriously insane. He fancied his wife's affections were alienated from him, continually affirming that it was quite impossible she could have any regard for a person who had rendered himself so contemptible. He committed several acts of violence, argued vehemently in favour of suicide, and was shortly afterwards found drowned in a canal near his house. It must not be omitted that this individual derived a predisposition to madness by hereditary transmission: his father had been insane.

NATHANIEL HAWTHORNE

The Birthmark (1846)

In the latter part of the last century there lived a man of science, an eminent proficient in every branch of natural philosophy, who not long before our story opens had made experience of a spiritual affinity more attractive than any chemical one. He had left his laboratory to the care of an assistant, cleared his fine countenance from the furnace-smoke, washed the stain of acids from his fingers, and persuaded a beautiful woman to become his wife. In those days, when the comparatively recent discovery of electricity and other kindred mysteries of Nature seemed to open paths into the region of miracle, it was not unusual for the love of science to rival the love of woman in its depths and absorbing energy. The higher intellect, the imagination, the spirit, and even the heart might all find their congenial aliment in pursuits which, as some of their ardent votaries believed, would ascend from one step of powerful intelligence to another, until the philosopher should lay his hand on the secret of creative force and perhaps make new worlds for himself. We know not whether Aylmer possessed this degree of faith in man's ultimate control over nature. He had devoted himself, however, too unreservedly to scientific studies ever to be weaned from them by any second passion. His love for his young wife might prove the stronger of the two; but it could only be by intertwining itself with his love of science and uniting the strength of the latter to his own.

Such a union accordingly took place, and was attended with truly remarkable consequences and a deeply impressive moral. One day, very soon after their marriage Aylmer sat gazing at his wife with a trouble in his countenance that grew stronger until he spoke.

'Georgiana,' said he, 'has it never occurred to you that the mark upon your cheek might be removed?'

'No, indeed,' said she, smiling; but, perceiving the seriousness of his manner, she blushed deeply. 'To tell you the truth, it has been so often called a charm, that I was simple enough to imagine it might be so.'

'Ah, upon another face perhaps it might,' replied her husband; 'but never on yours. No, dearest Georgiana, you came so nearly perfect from the hand of Nature, that this slightest possible defect, which we hesitate whether to term a defect or a beauty, shocks me, as being the visible mark of earthly imperfection.'

'Shocks you, my husband!' cried Georgiana, deeply hurt; at first reddening with momentary anger, but then bursting into tears. 'Then why did you take me from my mother's side? You cannot love what shocks you!'

To explain this conversation, it must be mentioned that in the centre of Georgiana's left cheek there was a singular mark, deeply interwoven, as it were, with the texture and substance of her face. In the usual state of her complexion—a healthy though delicate bloom—the mark wore a tint of deeper crimson, which imperfectly defined its shape amid the surrounding rosiness. When she blushed it gradually became more indistinct, and finally vanished amid the triumphant rush of blood that bathed the whole cheek with its brilliant glow. But if any shifting motion caused her to turn pale there was the mark again, a crimson stain upon the snow, in what Aylmer sometimes deemed an almost fearful distinctness. Its shape bore not a little similarity to the human hand, though of the smallest pygmy size. Georgiana's lovers were wont to say that some fairy at her birth-hour had laid her tiny hand upon the infant's cheek, and left this impress there in token of the magic endowments that were to give her such sway over all hearts. Many a desperate swain would have risked life for the privilege of pressing his lips to the mysterious hand. It must not be concealed, however, that the impression wrought by this fairy sign-manual varied exceedingly according to the difference of temperament in the beholders. Some fastidious persons—but they were exclusively of her own sex—affirmed that the bloody hand, as they chose to call it, quite destroyed the effect of Georgiana's beauty and rendered her countenance even hideous. But it would be as reasonable to say that one of those small blue stains which sometimes occur in the purest statuary marble would convert the Eve of Powers* to a monster. Masculine observers, if the birthmark did not heighten their admiration, contented themselves with wishing it away, that the world might possess one living specimen of ideal loveliness without the semblance of a flaw. After his marriage,—for he thought little or nothing of the matter before,—Aylmer discovered that this was the case with himself.

Had she been less beautiful,—if Envy's self could have found aught else to sneer at,—he might have felt his affection heightened by the prettiness of this mimic hand, now vaguely portrayed, now lost, now stealing forth again and glimmering to and fro with every pulse of emotion that throbbed within her heart; but, seeing her otherwise so perfect, he found this one defect grow more and more intolerable with every moment of their united lives. It was the fatal flaw of humanity which Nature, in one shape or another, stamps ineffaceably on all her productions, either to imply that they are temporary and finite, or that their perfection must be wrought by toil and pain. The crimson hand expressed the ineludible grip in which mortality clutches the highest and purest of earthly mould, degrading them into kindred with the lowest, and even with the very brutes, like whom their visible frames return to dust. In this manner, selecting it as the symbol of his wife's liability to sin, sorrow, decay, and death, Aylmer's sombre imagination was not long in rendering the birthmark a frightful object, causing him more trouble and horror than ever Georgiana's beauty, whether of soul or sense, had given him delight. . . .

[*Finally, Aylmer persuades Georgiana that the birthmark must be removed, and he prepares a potion.*]

The sound of her husband's footsteps aroused her. He bore a crystal goblet containing a liquor colourless as water, but bright enough to be the draught of immortality. Aylmer was pale; but it seemed rather the consequence of a highly wrought state of mind and tension of spirit than of fear or doubt.

'The concoction of the draught has been perfect,' said he, in answer to Georgiana's look. 'Unless all my science have deceived me, it cannot fail.'

'Save on your account, my dearest Aylmer,' observed his wife, 'I might wish to put off this birthmark of mortality by relinquishing mortality itself in preference to any other mode. Life is but a sad possession to those who have attained precisely the degree of moral advancement at which I stand. Were I weaker and blinder, it might be happiness. Were I stronger, it might be endured hopefully. But, being what I find myself, methinks I am of all mortals the most fit to die.'

'You are fit for heaven without tasting death!' replied her husband. 'But why do we speak of dying? The draught cannot fail. Behold its effect upon this plant.'

On the window-seat there stood a geranium diseased with yellow blotches, which had overspread all its leaves. Aylmer poured a small quantity of the liquid upon the soil in which it grew. In a little time, when the roots of the plant had taken up the moisture, the unsightly blotches began to be extinguished in a living verdure.

'There needed no proof,' said Georgiana, quietly. 'Give me the goblet. I joyfully stake all upon your word.'

'Drink, then, thou lofty creature!' exclaimed Aylmer, with fervid admiration. 'There is no taint of imperfection on thy spirit. Thy sensible frame, too, shall soon be all perfect.'

She quaffed the liquid and returned the goblet to his hand.

'It is grateful,' said she, with a placid smile. 'Methinks it is like water from a heavenly fountain; for it contains I know not what of unobtrusive fragrance and deliciousness. It allays a feverish thirst that had parched me for many days. Now, dearest, let me sleep. My earthly senses are closing over my spirit like the leaves around the heart of a rose at sunset.'

She spoke the last words with a gentle reluctance, as if it required almost more energy than she could command to pronounce the faint and lingering syllables. Scarcely had they loitered through her lips ere she was lost in slumber. Aylmer sat by her side, watching her aspect with the emotions proper to a man the whole value of whose existence was involved in the process now to be tested. Mingled with this mood, however, was the philosophic investigation characteristic of the man of science. Not the minutest symptom escaped him. A heightened flush of the cheek, a slight irregularity of breath, a quiver of the eyelid, a hardly perceptible tremor through the frame,—such were the details which, as the moments passed, he wrote down in his folio volume. Intense thought had set its stamp upon every previous page of that volume; but the thoughts of years were all concentrated upon the last.

While thus employed, he failed not to gaze often at the fatal hand, and not without a shudder. Yet once, by a strange and unaccountable impulse, he pressed it with his lips. His spirit recoiled, however, in the very act; and Georgiana, out of the midst of her deep sleep, moved uneasily and murmured, as if in remonstrance. Again Aylmer resumed his watch. Nor was it without avail. The crimson hand, which at first had been strongly visible upon the marble paleness of Georgiana's cheek, now grew more faintly outlined. She remained not less pale than ever; but the birthmark, with every breath that came and went, lost somewhat of its former distinctness. Its presence had been awful; its departure was more awful still. Watch the stain of the rainbow fading out of the sky, and you will know how that mysterious symbol passed away.

'By Heaven! it is wellnigh gone!' said Aylmer to himself, in almost irrepressible ecstasy. 'I can scarcely trace it now. Success! success! And now it is like the faintest rose colour. The lightest flush of blood across her cheek would overcome it. But she is so pale!'

He drew aside the window-curtain and suffered the light of natural day to fall into the room and rest upon her cheek. At the same time he heard a gross, hoarse chuckle, which he had long known as his servant Aminadab's expression of delight.

'Ah, clod! ah, earthly mass!' cried Aylmer, laughing in a sort of frenzy, 'you have served me well! Matter and spirit—earth and heaven—have both done their part in this! Laugh, thing of the senses! You have earned the right to laugh.'

These exclamations broke Georgiana's sleep. She slowly unclosed her eyes and gazed into the mirror which her husband had arranged for that purpose. A faint smile flitted over her lips when she recognized how barely perceptible was now that crimson hand which had once blazed forth with such disastrous brilliancy as to scare away all their happiness. But then her eyes sought Aylmer's face with a trouble and anxiety that he could by no means account for.

'My poor Aylmer!' murmured she.

'Poor? Nay, richest, happiest, most favoured!' exclaimed he. 'My peerless bride, it is successful! You are perfect!'

'My poor Aylmer,' she repeated, with a more than human tenderness, 'you have aimed loftily; you have done nobly. Do not repent that, with so high and pure a feeling, you have rejected the best the earth could offer. Aylmer, dearest Aylmer, I am dying!'

Alas! it was too true! The fatal hand had grappled with the mystery of life, and was the bond by which an angelic spirit kept itself in union with a mortal frame. As the last crimson tint of the birthmark—that sole token of human imperfection—faded from her cheek, the parting breath of the now perfect woman passed into the atmosphere, and her soul, lingering a moment near her husband, took its heavenward flight.

HERMAN MELVILLE

From *Bartleby the Scrivener* (1856)

At the period just preceding the advent of Bartleby, I had two persons as copyists in my employment, and a promising lad as an office-boy. First, Turkey; second, Nippers; third, Ginger Nut. These may seem names, the like of which are not usually found in the Directory. In truth they were nicknames, mutually conferred upon each other by my three clerks, and were deemed expressive of their respective persons or characters. Turkey was a short, pursy Englishman of about my own age, that is, somewhere not far from sixty. In the morning, one might say, his face was of a fine florid hue, but after twelve o'clock, meridian—his dinner hour—it blazed like a grate full of Christmas coals; and continued blazing—but, as it were, with a gradual wane—till 6 o'clock P.M. or thereabouts, after which I saw no more of the proprietor of the face, which, gaining its meridian with the sun, seemed to set with it, to rise, culminate, and decline the following day, with the like regularity and undiminished glory. There are many singular coincidences I have known in the course of my life, not the least among which was the fact, that exactly when Turkey displayed his fullest beams from his red and radiant countenance, just then, too, at that critical moment, began the daily period when I considered his business capacities as seriously disturbed for the remainder of the twenty-four hours. Not that he was absolutely idle, or averse to business then; far from it. The difficulty was, he was apt to be altogether too energetic. There was a strange, inflamed, flurried, flighty recklessness of activity about him. He would be incautious in dipping his pen into his inkstand. All his blots upon my documents, were dropped there after twelve o'clock, meridian. Indeed, not only would he be reckless and sadly given to making blots in the afternoon, but some days he went further, and was rather noisy. At such times, too, his face flamed with augmented blazonry, as if cannel coal had been heaped on anthracite.* He made an unpleasant racket with his chair; spilled his sand-box; in mending his pens, impatiently split them all to pieces, and threw them on the floor in a sudden passion; stood up and leaned over his table, boxing his papers about in a most indecorous manner, very sad to behold in an elderly man like him. Nevertheless, as he was in many ways a most valuable person to me, and all the time before twelve o'clock, meridian, was the quickest, steadiest creature, too, accomplishing a great deal of work in a style not easy to be matched—for these reasons, I was willing to overlook his eccentricities, though indeed, occasionally, I remonstrated with him. I did this very gently, how-ever, because, though the civilest, nay, the blandest and most rever-ential of men in the morning, yet in the afternoon he was disposed, upon provocation, to be slightly rash with his tongue, in fact, inso-lent. Now, valuing his morning services as I did, and resolving not to lose them—yet, at the same time, made uncomfortable by his inflamed ways after twelve o'clock; and being a man of peace, unwill-ing by my admonitions to call forth unseemly retorts from him—I took upon me, one Saturday noon (he was always worse on Satur-days), to hint to him, very kindly, that perhaps now that he was growing old, it might be well to abridge his labours; in short, he need not come to my chambers after twelve o'clock, but, dinner over, had best go home to his lodgings and rest himself till tea-time. But no; he insisted upon his afternoon devotions. His countenance became intolerably fervid, as he oratorically assured me—gesticulating, with a long ruler, at the other side of the room—that if his services in the morning were useful, how indispensable, then, in the afternoon?

'With submission, sir,' said Turkey on this occasion, 'I consider myself your right-hand man. In the morning I but marshal and deploy my columns; but in the afternoon I put myself at their head, and gallantly charge the foe, thus!'—and he made a violent thrust with the ruler. . . .

Nippers, the second on my list, was a whiskered, sallow, and, upon the whole, rather piratical-looking young man of about five and twenty. I always deemed him the victim of two evil powers—ambition and indigestion. The ambition was evinced by a certain impatience of the duties of a mere copyist—an unwarrantable usurpation of strictly professional affairs, such as the original drawing up of legal documents. The indigestion seemed betokened in an occasional nervous testiness and grinning irritability, causing the teeth to audibly grind together over mistakes committed in copying; unnecessary maledictions, hissed, rather than spoken, in the heat of business; and especially by a continual discontent with the height of the table where he worked. Though of a very ingenious mechanical turn, Nippers could never get this table to suit him. He put chips under it, blocks of various sorts, bits of pasteboard, and at last went so far as to attempt an exquisite adjustment by final pieces of folded blotting-paper. But no invention would answer. If, for the sake of easing his back, he brought the table lid at a sharp angle well up toward his chin, and wrote there like a man using the steep roof of a Dutch house for his desk—then he declared that it stopped the circulation in his arms. If now he lowered the table to his waistbands, and stooped over it in writing, then there was a sore aching in his back. In short, the truth of the matter was, Nippers knew not what he wanted. Or, if he wanted anything, it was to be rid of a scrivener's table altogether. . . .

Though concerning the self-indulgent habits of Turkey I had my own private surmises, yet touching Nippers I was well persuaded that whatever might be his faults in other respects, he was, at least, a temperate young man. But, indeed, nature herself seemed to have been his vintner, and at his birth charged him so thoroughly with an irritable, brandy-like disposition, that all subsequent potations were needless. When I consider how, amid the stillness of my chambers, Nippers would sometimes impatiently rise from his seat, and stooping over his table, spread his arms wide apart, seize the whole desk, and move it, and jerk it, with a grim, grinding motion on the floor, as if the table were a perverse voluntary agent, intent on thwarting and vexing him; I plainly perceive that for Nippers, brandy and water were altogether superfluous.

It was fortunate for me that, owing to its peculiar cause—indigestion—the irritability and consequent nervousness of Nippers, were mainly observable in the morning, while in the afternoon he was comparatively mild. So that Turkey's paroxysms only coming on about twelve o'clock, I never had to do with their eccentricities at one time. Their fits relieved each other like guards. When Nipper's was on, Turkey's was off; and *vice versa*. This was a good natural arrangement under the circumstances.

THOMAS LAYCOCK

From *Mind and Brain* (1860)

The hemispheres of the brain are now generally held to be the seat of those teleorganic* processes which are coincident with noetic* ideas and the active faculties of the mind. It follows, therefore, that in them, in co-operation with the other encephalic structures, to which they are closely bound by the most intimate connections, all the various modes of mental energy of which they are the seat—whether they be those of attention, memory, will, association of ideas, or the feelings—directly influence not only the voluntary and involuntary systems of muscles, and the secretions and excretions in general, but also all those more hidden and minute changes in the living tissues known as growth, nutrition, repair, and the like. Or, in other words, the functions of the hemispherical ganglia, as the organs of thought and mental action proper, are in unity with all the processes of life whatever, whether they be termed vegetative or animal.

If this view of the encephalic functions be correct, it is obvious that it is much more than the common centre of conscious activity, and that consequently those physiologists who have limited their inquiries to its relations to consciousness alone, or to the relations of its parts to a common centre or seat of consciousness—*i.e.*, a *sensorium commune*—have taken too limited a view of its function. For probably there is not any tissue of the body, nor the functions of any of its parts, which are not influenced directly or indirectly by this unifying energy of the encephalon. It follows, therefore, that in this structure we have the final evolution in organisation of the fundamental teleiotic* idea of unity, and that it is in truth a differentiation of the properties of all tissues whatever.

From this point of view it appears that a true method of inquiry into the laws of the cerebral functions, and into the structure and mutual relations of the parts of the encephalon, can only be based upon an inquiry into the laws of life and organisation, as manifested in the most general mode and in the simplest tissues, whether of plant or animal. To adopt the usual method, and begin the inquiry with the ganglia of the nervous system, is to commence with the complex; the proper commencement is with the phenomena of *irritability* as to adapted acts, and with the phenomena of histological change, as to the processes coincident with adaptation to ends. To set animal-life in opposition to plant-life, or the functions of the nerves and ganglia in opposition to the functions of simpler cell-tissues, is to embarrass the whole subject and render successful inquiry impossible. The tissues subservient to the reflex acts of animal organisms are but differentiations of those tissues which are the seat of plant and animal adaptations to ends; and the brain itself, as the organ of conscious design, is but a special structure evolved, like all other vital structures in adaptation to ends, according to the law of design. Being thus the final expression of the archetypal idea upon which the organism is constructed, both as to its parts and as a whole, its function is necessarily that of bringing into unity all the organs and functions subservient to the ends for which the organism exists.

But even this would be an imperfect conception of the law by which the encephalon is evolved, for it is necessary to bear in mind that the unifying cause is general in its operation, and that while its most intense form of manifestation is seen in integration of parts of a unit into an organism, it is seen equally in the combination of distinct units into harmonious relation. Thus the teleiotic idea manifested in the integration of the sperm-cell and germ-cell, so that another integer or organism results, is equally active in the combination of distinct integers or organisms into a community. This form of manifestation is seen in organisation in plants generally, and in the lower forms of animal life, such as the Protozoa, Radiata, and lower Articulata and Mollusca.* These organisms are societies or communities of individuals. It is this social character, indeed, which gives the plant-like form to the Hydrozoa and Polyzoa, the Polypes and Zoophytes* of the older naturalists. The objects of the combination of this social class of organisms are identical with those of the individual. They co-operate—1. To secure a common supply of nutriment through a common system of organs of acquisition or prehension, and digestion, as roots, leaves, tentacula, mouths, stomach.

2. To provide means in common for protection and defence against injurious agencies. 3. To attain most effectually the reproduction and continuance of the species. Hence it is obvious, from the teleiotic point of view, that all the composite plants, the Zoophytes, or plant-like animals, as the Hydrozoa, the Molluscoid Polyzoa, and the lower Articulata, are rather analogous to the social republics of higher animals (as the hymenoptera* amongst insects, and man amongst vertebrates) than to individual organisms. We must therefore examine the unifying cause from this double point of view—viz., of integration and combination.

Perhaps the best idea of this unity of organisation will be obtained by examining the structure and function of a zoophyte; and for this purpose we will take the Hydrozoa, or Polypes, recently investigated by Mr Huxley.* The body of every hydrozoon is essentially a living sac or animal cell, composed of two membranes, an external and internal, conveniently designated by Professor Allman the *ectoderm* and *endoderm*. The cavity of the sac (the *somatic cavity*) contains a fluid, the *somatic fluid*, charged with nutritive matter in solution, and sometimes, if not always, with suspended solid particles, which seem to perform the functions of the blood in animals of higher organisation. . . .

Now, the interesting point in these simple animals is the homology of their existence (if the phrase may be permitted), both as to their social and individual conditions, to higher animals. As to their social conditions, they offer (after composite plants) the typical form of a community or society of organisms; as to their individual life, they are the analogies of the highest form of teleiotic development. 'For it is well known,' as Mr Huxley observes, 'that in a very early state, the germ even of the highest animals is a more or less complete sac, whose thin wall is divisible into two membranes, an inner and an outer; the latter turned towards the external world, the former in relation with the nutritive fluid—the yolk. The inner layer, as Remak* has more particularly shown, undergoes but little histological change, and throughout life remains more particularly devoted to the function of alimentation; while the outer gives rise, by manifold differentiations of its tissue, to those complex structures which we know as integument, bones, muscles, nerves, and sensory apparatus, and which especially subserve the functions of relation. At the same time, the various organs are produced by a process of budding from one or other or both of these primary layers of the germ.'

Now, if we conceive clearly the operation of the telciotic idea of unity in these simple organisms, we can apply it to the conception of the fundamental laws of union of body and mind—the encephalon being considered as the organ in which the teleiotic idea of unity is fully manifested both in Life and Thought. In the Hydra there is no nerve, no nerve-centre, no brain, no spinal cord; yet the various parts are combined into a perfect organism, and co-operate in function to attain the ends for which it was created, whatever these may be. Here, then, the unifying function can be nowhere else than in the relations which the two membranes hold to each other, to the nutrient fluid, and to the external world. They are in synthesis as the relative and correlative. Everything which touches the apparatus of external relation of the simple hydra, if appropriate thereto, or in biotic affinity, is in external relation to the other parts, but only in common with the external apparatus. And here we discover the first type of that act of consciousness which refers all corporeal sensations or feelings of external things, derived through the sense of touch, to the surface of the body, and, in the case of the other senses, to the external source of the impression, although the teleorganic changes upon which the sensation or state of consciousness depends are wholly internal—*i.e.*, take place in the encephalon.

Again, we see in these phenomena the first type of those animal movements which, taking place by the intervention of a conducting or internuncial apparatus, stretching between the nerve-centres and the muscles in higher animals, and termed reflex acts, cause the various organs of the body, the functions of which are essentially motor, to move in adaptation to the multitudinous wants of the organism. These variously formed organs are but differentiations of the simple ectoderm and endoderm; and the apparatus of nerves and nerve-centres, which minister to the reception of impressions, to their combination, and their transmission to the proper muscular apparatus, are only differentiations of that unifying element in the simpler tissue which enables the hydrozoon to seize fit alimentary materials, and reject the unfit, to grasp the fitting things with the tentacula in the appropriate way, and to perform all those other acts which are necessary for the continuance of the animal or its species in Time and Space. In like manner the apparatus of bones and muscles—of assimilating, excreting, and secreting viscera—together with their nervous apparatus and their common action to a common end, are nothing more than evolutions, in other forms of structure and function, of the fundamental teleiotic idea, thus manifested in its most general way in the hydrozoon. These doctrines are not limited, however, to animal organisms; for it is obvious that plant-life in its simplest forms, as in the locomotive Algae, and throughout its most complex developments, manifests itself according to the same general laws.

MARY ELIZABETH BRADDON
From *Lady Audley's Secret* (1862)

Lady Audley, who carries a taint of hereditary madness, is doing her best to conceal her bigamy. She had married Sir Michael Audley after having received no word from her husband, George Talboys, for three years. Hearing of Talboys's return, she feigned her own death, and attempted to murder him, but she has been discovered by her husband's nephew, Robert Audley. She is also being blackmailed by her maid's husband, Luke Marks, who runs the Castle Inn and is being harassed by creditors. In this scene, she attempts to rid herself of Robert Audley and Luke Marks simultaneously by burning them as they sleep.

Lady Audley set the lamp upon a table near the fireplace, and went to the window. She removed the iron bar and the light wooden shutter, and then opened the glass door. The March night was black and moonless, and a gust of wind blew in upon her as she opened this door, and filled the room with its chilly breath, extinguishing the lamp upon the table.

'No matter,' my lady muttered, 'I could not have left it burning. I shall know how to find my way through the house when I come back. I have left all the doors ajar.'

She stepped quickly out upon the smooth gravel, and closed the glass-door behind her. She was afraid lest that treacherous wind should blow-to the door opening into the library, and thus betray her.

She was in the quadrangle now, with that chill wind sweeping against her, and swirling her silken garments round her with a shrill rustling noise, like the whistling of a sharp breeze against the sails of a yacht. She crossed the quadrangle and looked back—looked back for a moment at the fire-light gleaming through the rosy-tinted curtains in her boudoir, and the dim gleam of the lamp behind the mullioned windows in the room where Sir Michael Audley lay asleep.

'I feel as if I was running away,' she thought. 'I feel as if I was running away secretly in the dead of the night, to lose myself and be forgotten. Perhaps it would be wiser in me to run away, to take this man's warning, and escape out of his power for ever. If I were to run away and disappear—as George Talboys disappeared. But where could I go? What would become of me? I have no money: my jewels are not worth a couple of hundred pounds, now that I have got rid of the best part of them. What could I do? I must go back to the old life, the old, hard, cruel, wretched life—the life of poverty, and humiliation, and vexation, and discontent. I should have to go back and wear myself out in that long struggle, and die—as my mother died, perhaps.'

My lady stood still for a moment on the smooth lawn between the quadrangle and the archway, with her head drooping upon her breast and her hands locked together, debating this question in the unnatural activity of her mind. Her attitude reflected the state of that mind—it expressed irresolution and perplexity. But presently a sudden change came over her; she lifted her head—lifted it with an action of defiance and determination.

'No, Mr Robert Audley,' she said aloud, in a low, clear voice; 'I will not go back—I will not go back. If the struggle between us is to be a duel to the death, you shall not find me drop my weapon.'

She walked with a firm and rapid step under the archway. As she passed under that massive arch, it seemed as if she disappeared into some black gulf that had waited open to receive her. The stupid clock struck twelve, and the solid masonry seemed to vibrate under its heavy strokes, as Lady Audley emerged upon the other side, and joined Phoebe Marks, who had waited for her late mistress very near the gateway of the Court.

'Now, Phoebe,' she said, 'it is three miles from here to Mount Stanning, isn't it?'

'Yes, my lady.'

'Then we can walk it in an hour.'

Lady Audley had not stopped to say this: she was walking quickly along the avenue with her humble companion by her side. Fragile and delicate as she was in appearance, she was a very good walker. She had been in the habit of taking long country rambles with Mr Dawson's children in her old days of dependence, and she thought very little of a distance of three miles.

'Your beautiful husband will sit up for you, I suppose, Phoebe?' she said, as they struck across an open field that was used as a short cut from Audley Court to the high road.

'Oh, yes, my lady; he's sure to sit up. He'll be drinking with the man, I dare say.'

'The man! What man?'

'The man that's in possession, my lady.'

'Ah, to be sure,' said Lady Audley, indifferently.

It was strange that Phoebe's domestic troubles should seem so very far away from her thoughts at the time she was taking such an extraordinary step towards setting things right at the Castle Inn. . . .

Mr Marks gave a discontented growl, and set his empty glass down upon the table, with an impatient gesture.

'You might have given the money to Phoebe,' he said, 'as well as have brought it yourself. We don't want no fine ladies up here, pryin' and pokin' their precious noses into everythink.'

'Luke, Luke,' remonstrated Phoebe, 'when my lady has been so kind!'

'Oh, damn her kindness!' cried Mr Marks; 'it ain't her kindness as we want, gal, it's her money. She won't get no snivellin' gratitood from me. Whatever she does for us she does because she is obliged, and if she warn't obliged she wouldn't do it—'

Heaven knows how much more Luke Marks might have said, had not my lady turned upon him suddenly, and awed him into silence by the unearthly glitter of her beauty. Her hair had been blown away from her face, and, being of a light, feathery quality, had spread itself into a tangled mass that surrounded her forehead like a yellow flame. There was another flame in her eyes—a greenish light, such as might flash from the changing hued orbs of an angry mermaid.

'Stop,' she cried. 'I didn't come up here in the dead of the night to listen to your insolence. How much is this debt?'

'Nine pound.'

Lady Audley produced her purse—a toy of ivory, silver, and

turquoise—and took from it a bank-note and four sovereigns. She laid these upon the table.

'Let that man give me a receipt for the money,' she said, 'before I go.'

It was some time before the man could be roused into sufficient consciousness for the performance of this simple duty, and it was only by dipping a pen into the ink and pushing it between his clumsy fingers, that he was at last made to comprehend that his autograph was wanted at the bottom of the receipt which had been made out by Phoebe Marks. Lady Audley took the document as soon as the ink was dry, and turned to leave the parlour. Phoebe followed her.

'You musn't go home alone, my lady,' she said. 'You'll let me go with you?'

'Yes, yes, you shall go home with me.'

The two women were standing near the door of the inn as my lady said this. Phoebe stared wonderingly at her patroness. She had expected that Lady Audley would be in a hurry to return home after settling this business which she had capriciously taken upon herself; but it was not so; my lady stood leaning against the inn door and staring into vacancy, and again Mrs Marks began to fear that trouble had driven her late mistress mad.

A little Dutch clock in the bar struck one while Lady Audley lingered in this irresolute, absent manner.

She started at the sound and began to tremble violently.

'I think I am going to faint, Phoebe,' she said; 'where can I get some cold water?'

'The pump is in the washhouse, my lady, I'll run and get you a glass of water.'

'No, no, no,' cried my lady, clutching Phoebe's arm as she was about to run away upon this errand, 'I'll get it myself. I must dip my head in a basin of water if I want to save myself from fainting. In which room does Mr Audley sleep?'

There was something so irrelevant in this question that Phoebe Marks stared aghast at her mistress before she answered it

'It was number three that I got ready, my lady—the front room—the room next to ours,' she replied, after that pause of astonishment.

'Give me a candle,' said my lady; 'I'll go into your room, and get some water for my head. Stay where you are,' she added authoritatively, as Phoebe Marks was about to show the way—'stay where you are, and see that that brute of a husband of yours doesn't follow me!'

She snatched the candle which Phoebe had lighted, from the girl's hand; and ran up the rickety, winding staircase which led to the narrow corridor upon the upper floor. Five bed-rooms opened out of this low-ceilinged, close-smelling corridor: the numbers of these rooms were indicated by squat black figures painted upon the upper panels of the doors. Lady Audley had driven to Mount Stanning to inspect the house, when she had bought the business for her servant's bridegroom, and she knew her way about the dilapidated old place; she knew where to find Phoebe's bed-room; but she stopped before the door of that other chamber which had been prepared for Mr Robert Audley.

She stopped and looked at the number on the door. The key was in the lock, and her hand dropped upon it as if unconsciously. Then she suddenly began to tremble again, as she had trembled a few minutes before at the striking of the clock. She stood for a few moments trembling thus; with her hand still upon the key; then a horrible expression came over her face, and she turned the key in the lock; she turned it twice, double locking the door.

There was no sound from within; the occupant of the chamber made no sign of having heard that ominous creaking of the rusty key in the rusty lock.

Lady Audley hurried into the next room. She set the candle on the dressing-table, flung off her bonnet and slung it loosely across her arm; she went to the wash-hand-stand and filled the basin with water. She plunged her golden hair into this water, and then stood for a few moments in the centre of the room looking about her, with a white earnest face, and an eager gaze that seemed to take in every object in the poorly-furnished chamber. Phoebe's bedroom was certainly very shabbily furnished; she had been compelled to select all the most decent things for those best bedrooms which were set apart for any chance traveller who might stop for a night's lodging at the Castle Inn. But Mrs Marks had done her best to atone for the lack of substantial furniture in her apartment by a superabundance of drapery. Crisp curtains of cheap chintz hung from the tent-bedstead; festooned draperies of the same material shrouded the narrow window, shutting out the light of day, and affording a pleasant harbour for tribes of flies and predatory bands of spiders. Even the looking-glass, a miserably cheap construction which distorted every face whose owner had the hardihood to look into it, stood upon a draperied altar of starched muslin and pink glazed calico, and was adorned with frills of lace and knitted work.

My lady smiled as she looked at the festoons and furbelows which met her eye upon every side. She had reason, perhaps, to smile, remembering the costly elegance of her own apartments; but there was something in that sardonic smile that seemed to have a deeper meaning than any natural contempt for Phoebe's poor attempts at decoration. She went to the dressing-table and smoothed her wet hair before the looking-glass, and then put on her bonnet. She was obliged to place the flaming tallow candle very close to the lace furbelows about the glass, so close that the starched muslin seemed to draw the flame towards it by some power of attraction in its fragile tissue.

S. WEIR MITCHELL

The Case of George Dedlow (1866)

On the 19th of September, 1863, occurred the battle of Chicka-mauga,* in which my regiment took a conspicuous part. The close of our own share in this contest is, as it were, burnt into my memory with every least detail. It was about six P.M., when we found our-selves in line, under cover of a long, thin row of scrubby trees, beyond which lay a gentle slope, from which, again, rose a hill rather more abrupt, and crowned with an earthwork. We received orders to cross this space, and take the fort in front, while a brigade on our right was to make a like movement on its flank.

Just before we emerged into the open ground, we noticed what, I think, was common in many fights,—that the enemy had begun to bowl round-shot at us, probably from failure of shell. We passed across the valley in good order, although the men fell rapidly all along the line. As we climbed the hill, our pace slackened, and the fire grew heavier. At this moment a battery opened on our left,—the shots crossing our heads obliquely. It is this moment which is so printed on my recollection. I can see now, as if through a window, the gray smoke, lit with red flashes,—the long, wavering line,—the sky blue above,—the trodden furrows, blotted with blue blouses. Then it was as if the window closed, and I knew and saw no more. No other scene in my life is thus scarred, if I may say so, into my memory. I have a fancy that the horrible shock which suddenly fell upon me must have had something to do with thus intensifying the momentary image then before my eyes.

When I awakened, I was lying under a tree somewhere at the rear. The ground was covered with wounded, and the doctors were busy at an operating-table, improvised from two barrels and a plank. At length two of them who were examining the wounded about me came up to where I lay. A hospital steward raised my head, and poured down some brandy and water, while another cut loose my pantaloons. The doctors exchanged looks, and walked away. I asked the steward where I was hit.

'Both thighs,' said he; 'the Doc's won't do nothing.'

'No use?' said I.

'Not much,' said he.

'Not much means none at all,' I answered. . . .

No more passed, and I saw this man no longer, for another set of doctors were handling my legs, for the first time causing pain. A moment after, a steward put a towel over my mouth, and I smelt the familiar odor of chloroform, which I was glad enough to breathe. In a moment the trees began to move around from left to right,—then faster and faster; then a universal grayness came before me, and I recall nothing further until I awoke to consciousness in a hospital-tent. I got hold of my own identity in a moment or two; and was suddenly aware of a sharp cramp in my left leg. I tried to get at it to rub it with my single arm, but, finding myself too weak, hailed an attendant. 'Just rub my left calf,' said I, 'if you please.'

'Calf?' said he, 'you ain't none, pardner. It's took off.'

'I know better,' said I. 'I have pain in both legs.'

'Wall, I never!' said he. 'You ain't got nary leg.'

As I did not believe him, he threw off the covers, and, to my horror, showed me that I had suffered amputation of both thighs, very high up.

'That will do,' said I, faintly.

A month later, to the amazement of every one, I was so well as to be moved from the crowded hospital at Chattanooga to Nashville, where I filled one of the ten thousand beds of that vast metropolis of hospitals. Of the sufferings which then began I shall presently speak. It will be best just now to detail the final misfortune which here fell upon me. Hospital No. 2, in which I lay, was inconveniently crowded with severely wounded officers. After my third week, an epidemic of hospital gangrene broke out in my ward. In three days it attacked twenty persons Then an inspector came out, and we were transferred at once to the open air, and placed in tents. Strangely enough, the wound in my remaining arm, which still suppurated, was seized with gangrene. The usual remedy, bromine, was used locally, but the main artery opened, was tied, bled again and again, and at last, as a final resort, the remaining arm was amputated at the shoulder-joint. Against all chances I recovered, to find myself a useless torso, more like some strange larval creature than anything of human shape. Of my anguish and horror of myself I dare not speak. I have dictated these pages, not to shock my readers, but to possess them with facts in regard to the relation of the mind to the body; and I hasten, therefore, to such portions of my case as best illustrate these views.

In January, 1864, I was forwarded to Philadelphia, in order to enter what was then known as the Stump Hospital, South Street. This favor was obtained through the influence of my father's friend, the late Governor Anderson, who has always manifested an interest in my case, for which I am deeply grateful. It was thought, at the time, that Mr Palmer, the leg-maker, might be able to adapt some form of arm to my left shoulder, as on that side there remained five inches of the arm bone, which I could move to a moderate extent. The hope proved illusory, as the stump was always too tender to bear any pressure. The hospital referred to was in charge of several surgeons while I was an inmate, and was at all times a clean and pleasant home. It was filled with men who had lost one arm or leg, or one of each, as happened now and then. I saw one man who had lost both legs, and one who had parted with both arms; but none, like myself, stripped of every limb. There were collected in this place hundreds of these cases, which gave to it, with reason enough, the not very pleasing title of Stump Hospital.

I spent here three and a half months, before my transfer to the United States Army Hospital for nervous diseases.* Every morning I was carried out in an arm-chair, and placed in the library, where some one was always ready to write or read for me, or to fill my pipe. The doctors lent me medical books; the ladies brought me luxuries, and fed me; and, save that I was helpless to a degree which was humiliating, I was as comfortable as kindness could make me.

I amused myself, at this time, by noting in my mind all that I could learn from other limbless folk, and from myself, as to the peculiar feelings which were noticed in regard to lost members. I found that the great mass of men who had undergone amputations, for many months felt the usual consciousness that they still had the lost limb. It itched or pained, or was cramped, but never felt hot or cold. If they had painful sensations referred to it, the conviction of its existence continued unaltered for long periods; but where no pain was felt in it, then, by degrees, the sense of having that limb faded away entirely. I think we may to some extent explain this. The knowledge we possess of any part is made up of the numberless impressions from without which affect its sensitive surfaces, and which are transmitted through its nerves to the spinal nerve-cells, and through them, again, to the brain. We are thus kept endlessly informed as to the existence of parts, because the impressions which reach the brain are, by a law of our being, referred by us to the part from which they came. Now, when the part is cut off, the nerve-trunks which led to it and from it, remaining capable of being impressed by irritations, are made to convey to the brain from the stump impressions which are as usual referred by the brain to the lost parts, to which these nerve-threads belonged. In other words, the nerve is like a bell-wire. You may pull it at any part of its course, and thus ring the bell as well as if you pulled at the end of the wire; but, in any case, the intelligent servant will refer the pull to the front door, and obey it accordingly. The impressions made on the cut ends of the nerve, or on its sides, are due often to the changes in the stump during healing, and consequently cease as it heals, so that finally, in a very healthy stump, no such impressions arise; the brain ceases to correspond with the lost leg, and, as *les absents ont toujours tort,** it is no longer remembered or recognized. But in some cases, such as mine proved at last to my sorrow, the ends of the nerves undergo a curious alteration, and get to be enlarged and altered. This change, as I have seen in my practice of medicine, passes up the nerves towards the centres, and occasions a more or less constant irritation of the nerve-fibres, producing neuralgia, which is usually referred to that part of the lost limb to which the affected nerve belongs. This pain keeps the brain ever mindful of the missing part, and, imperfectly at least, preserves to the man a consciousness of possessing that which he has not.

Where the pains come and go, as they do in certain cases, the subjective sensations thus occasioned are very curious, since in such cases the man loses and gains, and loses and regains, the consciousness of the presence of lost parts, so that he will tell you, 'Now I feel my thumb,—now I feel my little finger.' I should also add, that nearly every person who has lost an arm above the elbow feels as though the lost member were bent at the elbow, and at times is vividly impressed with the notion that his fingers are strongly flexed.

Another set of cases present a peculiarity which I am at a loss to account for. Where the leg, for instance, has been lost, they feel as if the foot was present, but as though the leg were shortened. If the thigh has been taken off, there seems to them to be a foot at the knee; if the arm, a hand seems to be at the elbow, or attached to the stump itself. . . .

Notwithstanding these drawbacks, my physical health was good, which I confess surprised me, for this among other reasons. It is said that a burn of two thirds of the surface destroys life, because then all the excretory matters which this portion of the glands of the skin evolved are thrown upon the blood, and poison the man, just as happens in an animal whose skin the physiologist has varnished, so as in this way to destroy its function. Yet here was I, having lost at least a third of my skin, and apparently none the worse for it.

Still more remarkable, however, were the physical changes which I now began to perceive. I found to my horror that at times I was less conscious of myself, of my own existence, than used to be the case. This sensation was so novel, that at first it quite bewildered me. I felt like asking some one constantly if I were really George Dedlow or not; but, well aware how absurd I should seem after such a question, I refrained from speaking of my case, and strove more keenly to analyze my feelings. At times the conviction of my want of being myself was overwhelming, and most painful. It was, as well as I can describe it, a deficiency in the egoistic sentiment of individuality. About one half of the sensitive surface of my skin was gone, and thus much of relation to the outer world destroyed. As a consequence, a large part of the receptive central organs must be out of employ, and, like other idle things, degenerating rapidly. Moreover, all the great central ganglia, which give rise to movements in the limbs, were also eternally at rest. Thus one half of me was absent or functionally dead. This set me to thinking how much a man might lose and yet live. If I were unhappy enough to survive, I might part with my spleen at least, as many a dog has done, and grown fat afterwards. The other organs, with which we breathe and circulate the blood, would be essential; so also would the liver; but at least half of the intestines might be dispensed with, and of course all of the limbs. And as to the nervous system, the only parts really necessary to life are a few small ganglia. Were the rest absent or inactive, we should have a man reduced, as it were, to the lowest terms, and leading an almost vegetative existence. Would such a being, I asked myself, possess the sense of individuality in its usual completeness,—even if his organs of sensation remained, and he were capable of consciousness? Of course, without them, he could not have it any more than a dahlia, or a tulip. But with it—how then? I concluded that it would be at a minimum, and that, if utter loss of relation to the outer world were capable of destroying a man's consciousness of himself, the destruction of half of his sensitive surfaces might well occasion, in a less degree, a like result, and so diminish his sense of individual existence.

I thus reached the conclusion that a man is not his brain, or any one part of it, but all of his economy, and that to lose any part must lessen this sense of his own existence. I found but one person who properly appreciated this great truth. She was a New England lady, from Hartford,—an agent, I think, for some commission, perhaps the Sanitary. After I had told her my views and feelings, she said: 'Yes, I comprehend. The fractional entities of vitality are embraced in the oneness of the unitary Ego. Life,' she added, 'is the garnered condensation of objective impressions; and, as the objective is the remote father of the subjective, so must individuality, which is but focused subjectivity, suffer and fade when the sensation lenses, by which the rays of impression are condensed, become destroyed.' I am not quite clear that I fully understood her, but I think she appreciated my ideas, and I felt grateful for her kindly interest.

HENRY MAUDSLEY

From *Body and Mind* (1870)

The British alienist Henry Maudsley (1835–1918) was one of the strongest advocates of the idea that mental illnesses had biological causes. His textbook *Body and Mind* went through numerous editions, and he was widely cited in popular journals.

I pass on now to exhibit the effects of organic sympathies in the causation of mental disorders, or rather the specific effects of particular organs upon the features of different forms of insanity. In my first lecture I pointed out that there is the closest physiological consent of functions between the different organs; that the brain, as the organ of mind, joins in this consent; and that our ideas and feelings are obtained by the concurrence of impressions from the internal organs of the body and the external organs of the senses. The consequence is, that derangement of an internal organ, acting upon the brain, may engender, by pathological sympathy, morbid feelings and their related ideas. The mental effects may be general or specific: a general emotional depression through which all ideas loom gloomy, of which every one's experience testifies; and a special morbid feeling with its particular sympathetic ideas, of which the phenomena of dreaming and insanity yield illustrations.

The slight shades of this kind of morbid influence we cannot venture to trace; but it is easy to recognize the most marked effects. Take, for example, the irritation of ovaries or uterus, which is sometimes the direct occasion of *nymphomania*—a disease by which the most chaste and modest woman is transformed into a raging fury of lust. Some observers have, without sufficient reason I think, made of *nymphomania* a special variety, grouping under the term cases in which it was a prominent symptom. But it certainly occurs in forms of mania that are quite distinct—in puerperal mania, for example, in epileptic mania, and in the mania sometimes met with in old women; and the cases in which it does occur have not such characteristic features as warrant the formation of a definite group. We have, indeed, to note and bear in mind how often sexual ideas and feelings arise and display themselves in all sorts of insanity; how they connect themselves with ideas which in a normal mental state have no known relation to them; so that it seems as inexplicable that a virtuous person should ever have learned, as it is distressing that she should manifest, so much obscenity of thought and feeling. Perhaps it is that such ideas are excited sympathetically in a morbidly active brain by unrelated ideas, just as, in other nervous disorders, sympathetic morbid sensations and movements occur in parts distant from the seat of the primary irritation. Considering, too, what an important agent in the evolution of mind the sexual feeling is, how much of thought, feeling, and energy it remotely inspires, there is less cause for wonder at the naked intervention of its simple impulses in the phenomena of mania, when coördination of function is abolished in the supreme centres, and the mind resolved, as it were, into its primitive animal elements. This should teach us to take care not to attribute too hastily the sexual feelings to a morbid irritation of the sexual organs. It is plain that they may have a purely central origin, just as the excitation of them in health may proceed from the mind. Here, in fact, as in other cases, we must bear in mind the reciprocal influence of mind on organ, and of organ on mind. . . .

The monthly activity of the ovaries which marks the advent of puberty in women has a notable effect upon the mind and body; wherefore it may become an important cause of mental and physical derangement. Most women at that time are susceptible, irritable, and capricious, any cause of vexation affecting them more seriously than usual; and some who have the insane neurosis exhibit a disturbance of mind which amounts almost to disease. A sudden suppression of the menses has produced a direct explosion of insanity; or, occurring some time before an outbreak, it may be an important link in its causation. It is a matter also of common experience in asylums, that exacerbations of insanity often take place at the menstrual periods; but whether there is a particular variety of mental derangement connected with disordered menstruation, and, if so, what are its special features, we are not yet in a position to say positively. There is certainly a recurrent mania, which seems sometimes to have, in regard to its origin and the times of its attacks, a relation to the menstrual function, suppression or irregularity of which often accompanies it; and it is an obvious presumption that the mania may be a sympathetic morbid effect of the ovarian and uterine excitement, and may represent an exaggeration of the mental irritability which is natural to women at that period. The patient becomes elated, hilarious, talkative, passing soon from that condition into a state of acute and noisy mania, which may last for two or three weeks or longer, and then sinking into a brief stage of more or less depression or confusion of mind, from which she awakens to calmness and clearness of mind. In vain we flatter ourselves with the hope of a complete recovery; after an interval of perfect lucidity, of varying duration in different cases, the attack recurs, goes through the same stages, and ends in the same way, only to be followed by other attacks, until at last, the mind being permanently weakened, there are no longer intervals of entire lucidity. Could we stop the attacks, the patient might still regain by degrees mental power; but we cannot. All the resources of our art fail to touch them, and I know no other form of insanity which, having so much the air of being curable, thus far defies all efforts to stay its course. We should be apt to conclude that it was connected with the menstrual function, were it not that periodicity is more or less the law of all nervous diseases, that its attacks often recur at uncertain intervals, and, more decisive still, that it is not confined to women, but occurs perhaps as often in men. Whether connected or not, however, in any way with the generative functions, it certainly presents features of relationship to epilepsy, and occurs where the insane neurosis exists; and, if I were to describe it in a few words, I should designate it an epilepsy of the mind. Its recurrence more or less regularly; the uniformity of the prodromata* and of the symptoms of the attack, each being almost an exact image of the other; its comparatively brief duration; the mental torpor or confusion which follows it, and the ignorance or denial sometimes, on the part of the patient, of his having had the attack; the temporary recovery; and the undoubted fact that it often occurs where there is evidence of an insane neurosis produced by epilepsy, or insanity, or both, in the family; these are facts which support the opinion of its kinship to epilepsy. I have under my care an unmarried lady who for many years has been subject to these recurrent attacks of mania, and whose intelligence has now been destroyed by them; ultimately true epileptic fits supervened, but they only occur, at long intervals, usually not oftener than twice a year, while the maniacal attacks recur regularly every three or four weeks. It is of some interest, in regard to the question of its nature, that the age of its most frequent outbreak is, as it is with epilepsy, the years that cover the development of puberty. Irregularity or suppression of menstruation may or may not be present, so that we are not warranted in attributing the disease to amenorrhoea or dysmenorrhoea; we are the less warranted in doing so, as any form of insanity, however caused, may occasion a suppression of the menses.

The natural cessation of menstruation at the change of life is accompanied by a revolution in the economy which is often trying to the mental stability of those who have a predisposition to insanity. The age of pleasing is past, but not always the desire, which, indeed, sometimes grows then more exacting; there are all sorts of anomalous sensations of bodily distress, attesting the disturbance of circulation and of nerve functions; and it is now that an insane jealousy and a propensity to stimulants are apt to appear, especially where there have been no children. When positive insanity breaks out, it usually has the form of profound melancholia, with vague delusions of an extreme character, as that the world is in flames, that it is turned upside down, that every thing is changed, or that some very dreadful but undefined calamity has happened or is about to happen. The countenance has the expression of a vague terror and apprehension. In some cases short and transient paroxysms of excitement break the melancholy gloom. These usually occur at the menstrual periods, and may continue to do so for some time after the function has ceased. It is not an unfavourable form of insanity as regards probability of recovery under suitable treatment.

Continuing the consideration of the influence of the generative organs in the production of insanity, I come now to puerperal insanity. Under this name are sometimes confounded three distinct varieties of disease—that which occurs during pregnancy, that which follows parturition and is properly puerperal, and that which comes on months afterward during lactation. The insanity of pregnancy is, as a rule, of a marked melancholic type, with suicidal tendency; a degree of mental weakness or apparent dementia being sometimes conjoined with it. Other cases, however, exhibit much moral perversion, perhaps an uncontrollable craving for stimulants, which we may regard as an exaggerated display of the fanciful cravings from which women suffer in the earlier months of pregnancy. We can hardly fail, indeed, to recognize a connection between the features of this form of insanity and the strange longings, the capriciousness, and the morbid fears, of the pregnant woman. The patient may be treated successfully by removal from home; but, if the disease be allowed to go on, there is no good ground to expect that parturition will have a beneficial effect upon it; on the contrary, the probability is, that it will run into a severe puerperal insanity, and from that into dementia.

Puerperal insanity proper comes on within one month of parturition; and, like the insanity of pregnancy, occurs most often in primiparae.* The statistics of the Edinburgh Asylum show that in all the cases occurring before the sixteenth day after labour, as most cases do, the symptoms were those of acute mania; but in all the cases which occurred after the sixteenth day they were those of melancholia. In both forms, but especially in the latter, there is sometimes a mixture of childishness and apparent dementia. The mania is more likely than the melancholia to get well. It is of an acute and extremely incoherent character, a delirious rather than a systematized mania, marked by noisy restlessness, sleeplessness, tearing of clothes, hallucinations, and in some cases by great salacity, which is probably the direct mental effect of the irritation of the generative organs. Suicide may be attempted in an excited, purposeless way. The bodily symptoms, contradicting the violence of the mental excitement, indicate feebleness; the features are pinched; the skin is pale, cold, and clammy; and the pulse is quick, small, and irritable. We may safely say that recovery takes place in three out of four cases of puerperal mania, usually in a few weeks; the patient, after the acute symptoms have subsided, sinking into a temporary state of confusion and feebleness of mind, and then waking up as from a dream. I may add the expression of a conviction that no good, but rather harm, is done by attempting to stifle this or any other form of acute insanity by the administration of large doses of opium.

The insanity of lactation does not come under the scheme of this lecture for it is an asthenic* insanity, produced by bodily exhaustion and the depression of mental worries. The time of its occurrence seems to show that the longer the child is suckled the greater is the liability to it; and in the majority of cases it has the form of melancholia, often with determined suicidal tendency.

So frequently is hereditary predisposition more or less distinctly traceable in these three forms of insanity occurring in connection with child-bearing, that we are warranted in declaring it quite exceptional for any one of them to be met with where it is entirely absent.

I have now enumerated all the forms of insanity which, being specially connected with the generative organs, present characteristic features. It is certain, however, that disease of them may act as a powerful coöperating cause in the production of insanity, without giving rise, so far as we know, to a special group of symptoms.

WILLIAM B. CARPENTER

From *Principles of Mental Physiology* (1874)

INFLUENCE OF THE WILL ON BODILY MOVEMENT

'I am, I ought, I can, I will,' are (as has been recently well said) the only firm foundation-stones on which we can base our attempt to climb into a higher sphere of existence. The *first* implies that we have a faculty of *Introspection*, which converts a simple state of consciousness into *self*-consciousness, and thus makes it the object of our own contemplation:—the *second*, that we have submitted that state of consciousness (whether Thought or Feeling) to our *moral judgment*, which has pronounced its verdict upon it:—the *third*, that we are conscious of a *freedom* and a *power* to act in accordance with that judgment, though drawn by cogent motives in some different direction;—and the *fourth*, that we *determinately exercise* that power. Hence we may define *Volition* or *Will* as *a determinate effort to carry out a purpose previously conceived*; and this effort may be directed to the performance of either the Mental or the Bodily acts which are adapted to carry that purpose into execution.—The manner in which this Volitional power is exerted in either case, and the conditions of its exercise, constitute our present subject of enquiry.

In our examination of the different forms of Nervous activity presented to us in the ascending series of Animal life, we have found, as we approach Man, blind unreasoning Instinct gradually giving place as a spring of action to rational Intelligence. But neither the performance of Reasoning processes, nor the execution of their results, necessarily involves the exercise of Will—at least in the sense in which it is here defined. For we have seen that, even in Man, intellectual operations of a high order may go on *automatically*,—one state of consciousness calling forth another in strict accordance with the 'laws of thought,' without any Volitional interference; and also that *ideational* as well as *emotional* states may express themselves in Muscular action, not only without any exertion of the Will, but even in opposition to it. And this will hereafter become still more obvious, when we investigate the phenomena of those abnormal states in which the Will is in more or less complete abeyance.—Now if, under the light afforded by this principle, we carefully study the actions of even those among brutes whose nature has been most completely shaped into accordance with that of Man by habitual association with him, we see that they afford no indication of the existence of any other spring, than the Idea or Feeling with which the mind of the animal may be at the moment possessed; in this respect corresponding closely with those of the young Child, in whom the power of *self*-control has not yet come into exercise, and whose conduct is entirely determined by the 'preponderance of motives.' ...

Now the Man in full possession of his Volitional power can use it (1) in giving bodily effect to his mental decision, by either putting in action the Muscles which will execute the movement he has determined-on, or by restraining them from the action to which they are prompted by some other impulse; and (2) in controlling and directing that succession of Mental operations, by which the determination is arrived at.—In the prosecution of our enquiry as to the mechanism of Mental self-direction, we shall find ourselves greatly aided by the indications we may draw from the study of the mode in which the Will operates on the Bodily organism.—The distinction between voluntary and involuntary *movements*, is recognized by every Physiologist; but it has been customary to assign these characters to the *muscles* by which certain of these two classes of movements are respectively performed. Thus the Heart, the Muscular coat of the Stomach and Intestines, the Iris, &c., are said to be 'involuntary' muscles, because no *intentional effort* of the conscious Ego can either excite or check their contractions, although some of them may be acted on by Emotional states. On the other hand, the muscles of our limbs are termed 'voluntary,' because we can use them to carry out the purposive determinations of the Will. But the muscles which are concerned in the act of Respiration, are both 'voluntary' and 'involuntary;' for while the ordinary movements of breathing are as 'automatic' as are those of the Heart, we yet have a certain measure of Volitional control over them, by which we can regulate their actions in subservience to the purposes of Speech. And, further, there is not a single one of the so-called 'voluntary' muscles, which may not be automatically thrown into violent contraction (as in cramp or tetanus), which the Will vainly attempts to restrain; whilst a large part of their ordinary sequential actions are performed 'mechanically,' without anything more than an *initiation* by the Will, which, though it can *cheek* them at any time, is *not* exercised in constantly sustaining them.—Hence we see that the distinction between voluntary and involuntary Muscles is good only to this extent, that there are certain muscles which are *entirely* removed from the control of the Will, their contractions being altogether involuntary; while the actions of all others may be either voluntary or involuntary, according as they are called into exercise by the Will, or by an automatic prompting of which we may or may not be conscious. And we must, therefore, look *higher*—that is, to the *sources* and the *channels* of the Nerve-force that excites the Muscles to contraction,—for the real distinction between their several modes of activity. . . .

Carrying back our inquiry, now, to the nature of the Cerebral change which initiates a Volitional action, we find reason for attributing this also to a local *hyperaemia** of some part of that cortical layer which constitutes the instrument of Ideation.* For all Volitional action, it will be remembered, is based on an *idea* of what is to be done, whether this have reference to Bodily movements; or to Mental exertion. And it seems clear that the same Vaso-motor action which is the condition of the state of *attention* to that idea, will, if exerted to produce a still greater local *hyperaemia*, give effect to it in a spontaneous motorial discharge. And thus we are led to regard the immediate source of *ideo-motor* and of *volitional* movements as the same; and the Volitional effort as really exerted in augmenting the nervous tension of the part of the cortical substance of the Cerebrum, which is concerned in the formation of the Idea of the thing to be done. This doctrine finds a remarkable confirmation in two orders of facts;—(1) that there is practically every gradation between those *voluntary* actions, which (under *permission* of the Will) simply express dominant ideas, and those actions which proceed from distinct and cogent *volitional* determinations;—and (2) that *emotional* states have a most powerful influence either in augmenting or in diminishing the motor force which the Will can call forth. For the known influence of the Emotions on the Vaso-motor system of nerves, and the manner in which they intensify those Ideational states which express themselves in movement, afford a strong indication that they exert their effect on Volitional action by increasing the local hyperaemia of the cortical substance. And this conclusion will be shown to derive yet stronger confirmation from the remarkable result of Dr Ferrier's recent experiments.*—The *restraining* influence of the Will on bodily movement (as when we make an effort to stifle a cough, to resist a yawn, to repress laughter, or to keep down the expression of some passionate impulse) seems really to consist in putting the antagonist Muscles into action; and we experience just the same sense of effort in doing this, that we do in trying to stop a horse that is running away, or to check the rotation of a wheel.

Now the strongest Volitional effort may be inoperative, through some defect of the apparatus by which the Nerve-force is transmitted to the muscles which are to execute the behests of the Will; as happens in paralysis. But there are states of absolute incapacity for such effort; the mental *desire* existing, while the energy needed to carry it into effect is deficient. That this incapacity arises from deficient supply of blood to the ideational (Cerebral) nerve-centre, appears probable from the familiar fact, that a general deficiency of Volitional power over the muscles is a marked feature of the physical depression which betokens feebleness of the circulation, being especially noticeable in sea-sickness; while a defect in the distributive action of the Vaso-motor system of nerves (such as that of which we have evidence in many local congestions) might very well account for such cases as the two following, which are recorded by Professor J. H. Bennett (*Mesmeric Mania* of 1851) on the authority of Sir Robert Christison:*—

a. 'The first was that of a gentleman who frequently could not carry out what he *wished* to perform. Often, on endeavouring to undress, he was two hours before he could get off his coat, all his mental faculties, Volition excepted, being perfect. On one occasion, having ordered a glass of water, it was presented to him on a tray, but he could not take it, though anxious to do so; and he kept the servant standing before him half an hour, when the obstruction was overcome.'

b. 'In the other case the peculiarity was limited. If, when walking in the street, this individual came to a gap in the line of houses, his will suddenly became inoperative, and he could not proceed. An unbuilt-on space in the street was sure to stop him. Crossing a street also was very difficult; and on going in or out of a door, he was always arrested for some minutes. Both these gentlemen graphically described their feelings to be "As if another person had taken possession of their will."'

This state seems akin to that form of *hysterical paralysis*, in which the defect lies not so much in the *want of power*, as in the want of that *belief in the possession of the power*, which is essential to its exercise. A strong motive will here sometimes take the place of Volition; and no motive is so efficacious, as that *confident expectation* of cure, which is awakened either by Religious faith, or by the belief in the occult powers of Mesmerism, Spiritualism, &c. Thus it has been that numberless pseudo-miracles have been worked on patients of this class by Religious Enthusiasts; whilst they furnish to Mesmerists and Spiritualists the subjects of 'wonderful cures,' effected by the agencies which they profess to wield.—Such cases are peculiarly interesting to the Psychologist, from their parallelism to those in which there is a like suspension of volitional control over the course of Thought.

WILLIAM JAMES

From *Principles of Psychology* (1890)

Psychology is the Science of Mental Life, both of its phenomena and of their conditions. The phenomena are such things as we call feelings, desires, cognitions, reasonings, decisions, and the like; and, superficially considered, their variety and complexity is such as to leave a chaotic impression on the observer. The most natural and consequently the earliest way of unifying the material was, first, to classify it as well as might be, and, secondly, to affiliate the diverse mental modes thus found, upon a simple entity, the personal Soul, of which they are taken to be so many facultative manifestations. Now, for instance, the Soul manifests its faculty of Memory, now of Reasoning, now of Volition, or again its Imagination or its Appetite. This is the orthodox 'spiritualistic'* theory of scholasticism and of common-sense. Another and a less obvious way of unifying the chaos is to seek common elements *in* the divers mental facts rather than a common agent behind them, and to explain them constructively by the various forms of arrangement of these elements, as one explains houses by stones and bricks. The 'associationist' schools of Herbart in Germany, and of Hume the Mills and Bain in Britain* have thus constructed a *psychology without a soul* by taking discrete 'ideas,' faint or vivid, and showing how, by their cohesions, repulsions, and forms of succession, such things as reminiscences, perceptions, emotions, volitions, passions, theories, and all the other furnishings of an individual's mind may be engendered. The very Self or *ego* of the individual comes in this way to be viewed no longer as the pre-existing source of the representations, but rather as their last and most complicated fruit.

Now, if we strive rigorously to simplify the phenomena in either of these ways, we soon become aware of inadequacies in our method. Any particular cognition, for example, or recollection, is accounted for on the soul-theory by being referred to the spiritual faculties of Cognition or of Memory. These faculties themselves are thought of as absolute properties of the soul; that is, to take the case of memory, no reason is given why we should remember a fact as it happened, except that so to remember it constitutes the essence of our Recollective Power. We may, as spiritualists, try to explain our memory's failures and blunders by secondary causes. But its *successes* can invoke no factors save the existence of certain objective things to be remembered on the one hand, and of our faculty of memory on the other. When, for instance, I recall my graduation-day, and drag all its incidents and emotions up from death's dateless night, no mechanical cause can explain this process, nor can any analysis reduce it to lower terms or make its nature seem other than an ultimate *datum*, which, whether we rebel or not at its mysteriousness, must simply be taken for granted if we are to psychologize at all. However the associationist may represent the present ideas as thronging and arranging themselves, still, the spiritualist insists, he has in the end to admit that *something*, be it brain, be it 'ideas,' be it 'association,' *knows* past time *as* past, and fills it out with this or that event. And when the spiritualist calls memory an 'irreducible faculty,' he says no more than this admission of the associationist already grants.

And yet the admission is far from being a satisfactory simplification of the concrete facts. For why should this absolute god-given Faculty retain so much better the events of yesterday than those of last year, and, best of all, those of an hour ago? Why, again, in old age should its grasp of childhood's events seem firmest? Why should illness and exhaustion enfeeble it? Why should repeating an experience strengthen our recollection of it? Why should drugs, fevers, asphyxia, and excitement resuscitate things long since forgotten? If we content ourselves with merely affirming that the faculty of memory is so peculiarly constituted by nature as to exhibit just these oddities, we seem little the better for having invoked it, for our explanation becomes as complicated as that of the crude facts with which we started. Moreover there is something grotesque and irrational in the supposition that the soul is equipped with elementary powers of such an ingeniously intricate sort. Why *should* our memory cling more easily to the near than the remote? Why should it lose its grasp of proper sooner than of abstract names? Such peculiarities seem quite fantastic; and might, for aught we can see *a priori*, be the precise opposites of what they are. Evidently, then, *the faculty does not exist absolutely, but works under conditions*; and *the quest of the conditions* becomes the psychologist's most interesting task.

However firmly he may hold to the soul and her remembering faculty, he must acknowledge that she never exerts the latter without a *cue*, and that something must always precede and *remind* us of whatever we are to recollect. 'An *idea*!' says the associationist, 'an idea associated with the remembered thing; and this explains also why things repeatedly met with are more easily recollected, for their associates on the various occasions furnish so many distinct avenues of recall.' But this does not explain the effects of fever, exhaustion, hypnotism, old age, and the like. And in general, the pure associationist's account of our mental life is almost as bewildering as that of the pure spiritualist. This multitude of ideas, existing absolutely, yet clinging together, and weaving an endless carpet of themselves, like dominoes in ceaseless change, or the bits of glass in a kaleidoscope,—whence do they get their fantastic laws of clinging, and why do they cling in just the shapes they do?

For this the associationist must introduce the order of experience in the outer world. The dance of the ideas is a copy, somewhat mutilated and altered, of the order of phenomena. But the slightest reflection shows that phenomena have absolutely no power to influence our ideas until they have first impressed our senses and our brain. The bare existence of a past fact is no ground for our remembering it. Unless we have seen it, or somehow *undergone* it, we shall never know of its having been. The experiences of the body are thus one of the conditions of the faculty of memory being what it is. And a very small amount of reflection on facts shows that one part of the body, namely, the brain, is the part whose experiences are directly concerned. If the nervous communication be cut off between the brain and other parts, the experiences of those other parts are non-existent for the mind. The eye is blind, the ear deaf, the hand insensible and motionless. And conversely, if the brain be injured, consciousness is abolished or altered, even although every other organ in the body be ready to play its normal part. A blow on the head, a sudden subtraction of blood, the pressure of an apoplectic hemorrhage, may have the first effect; whilst a very few ounces of alcohol or grains of opium or hasheesh, or a whiff of chloroform or nitrous oxide gas, are sure to have the second. The delirium of fever, the altered self of insanity, are all due to foreign matters circulating through the brain, or to pathological changes in that organ's substance. The fact that the brain is the one immediate bodily condition of the mental operations is indeed so universally admitted nowadays that I need spend no more time in illustrating it, but will simply postulate it and pass on. The whole remainder of the book will be more or less of a proof that the postulate was correct.

Bodily experiences, therefore, and more particularly brain-experiences, must take a place amongst those conditions of the mentallife of which Psychology need take account. *The spiritualist and the associationist must both be 'cerebralists,'* to the extent at least of admitting that certain peculiarities in the way of working of their own favorite principles are explicable only by the fact that the brain laws are a codeterminant of the result.

Our first conclusion, then, is that a certain amount of brain-physiology must be presupposed or included in Psychology.

In still another way the psychologist is forced to be something of a nerve-physiologist. Mental phenomena are not only conditioned *a parte ante* by bodily processes; but they lead to them *a parte post*.* That they lead to *acts* is of course the most familiar of truths, but I do not merely mean acts in the sense of voluntary and deliberate muscular performances. Mental states occasion also changes in the calibre of blood-vessels, or alteration in the heart-beats, or processes more subtle still, in glands and viscera. If these are taken into account, as well as acts which follow at some *remote period* because the mental state was once there, it will be safe to lay down the general law that *no mental modification ever occurs which is not accompanied or followed by a bodily change*. The ideas and feelings, *e.g.*, which these present printed characters excite in the reader's mind not only occasion movements of his eyes and nascent movements of articulation in him, but will some day make him speak, or take sides in a discussion, or give advice, or choose a book to read, differently from what would have been the case had they never impressed his retina. Our psychology must therefore take account not only of the conditions antecedent to mental states, but of their resultant consequences as well.

Physiognomy and Phrenology

GEORGE COMBE

From *Elements of Phrenology* (1824)

It is ascertained by experiment and observation, that the form of the brain can be discovered, in individuals, in perfect health, and under the middle period of life, by inspecting the cranium.

The Phrenologist compares cerebral development with the manifestations of mental power, for the purpose of discovering the functions of the brain, and the organs of the mind; and this method of investigation is conform to the principles of the inductive philosophy, and free from the objections attending the anatomical and metaphysical modes of research. . . .

EFFECTS OF SIZE AND ACTIVITY IN THE ORGANS, AND PRACTICAL DIRECTIONS FOR OBSERVING DEVELOPMENT

As 'self-conviction can be obtained only by self-observation,' every one who desires to become a Phrenologist should learn to observe. A healthy brain, at a vigorous period of life, is the proper subject for observation; and as the fundamental principle of the science is, that the *power* or *energy* of mental manifestation bears a uniform relation, *caeteris paribus*,* to the *size* of the organs, we must be careful not to confound this quality of mind with that of mere *activity* in the faculties, as size in the organ is an indication of the former, and not at all of the latter.

In physics, power is quite distinguishable from activity. The balance-wheel of a watch moves with much rapidity, but so slight is its impetus, that a hair would suffice to stop it; the beam of a steam-engine traverses slowly and ponderously through space, but its *power* is prodigiously great.

In muscular action, these qualities are recognized with equal facility as different. The greyhound bounds over hill and dale with animated agility; but a slight obstacle would counterbalance his momentum and arrest his progress. The elephant, on the other hand, rolls slowly and heavily along; but the impetus of his motion would sweep away an impediment sufficient to resist fifty greyhounds at the summit of their speed.

In mental manifestations (considered apart from organization) the distinction between power and activity is equally palpable. On the stage, Mrs SIDDONS *senior* and Mr JOHN KEMBLE were remarkable for the solemn deliberation of their manner, both in declamation and action, and yet they were splendidly gifted in power. They carried captive at once the sympathies and understanding of the audience, and made every man feel his faculties expanding, and his whole mind becoming greater under the influence of their energies. This was a display of power. Other performers, again, are remarkable for vivacity of action and elocution, who nevertheless are felt to be feeble and ineffective in rousing an audience to emotion. *Activity* is their distinguishing attribute, with an absence of power. At the bar, in the pulpit, and in the senate, the same distinction prevails. Many members of the learned professions display great felicity of illustration and fluency of elocution, surprising us with the quickness of their parts, who nevertheless are felt to be neither impressive nor profound. They possess acuteness without power, and ingenuity without comprehensiveness and depth of understanding. This also proceeds from activity, with little vigour. There are other public speakers, again, who open heavily in debate, their faculties acting slowly but deeply, like the first heave of a mountain-wave. Their words fall like minute-guns upon the ear, and to the superficial they appear about to terminate ere they have begun their efforts. But even their first accent is one of power; it rouses and arrests attention; their very pauses are expressive, and indicate gathering energy to be embodied

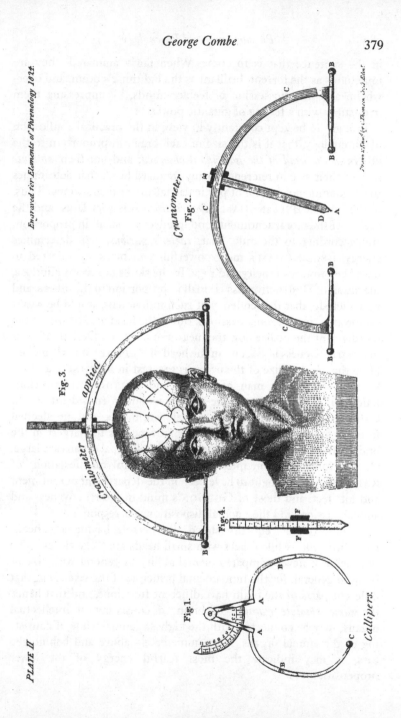

PLATE II

Engraved for Elements of Phrenology 1824.

Fig. 3.

applied

Craniometer

Fig. 2.

Craniometer

Fig. 4.

Fig. 1.

Callipers

in the sentence that is to come. When fairly animated, they are impetuous as the torrent, brilliant as the lightning's beam, and overwhelm and take possession of feebler minds, by impressing them irresistibly with a feeling of gigantic power. . . .

It ought to be kept constantly in view, in the practical application of Phrenology, that it is the size of each organ in proportion to the others *in the head of the individual observed*; and not their *absolute size*; or their size in reference to any standard head, that determines the predominance in him of particular talents or dispositions. Thus, in the head of BELLINGHAM,* *Destructiveness* is very large, and the organs of the moral sentiments and intellect are small in proportion; and according to the rule, that, *caeteris paribus*, size determines energy, BELLINGHAM's most powerful tendencies are inferred to have been towards cruelty and rage. In the skulls of several Hindoos, the organ of Destructiveness is small in proportion to the others, and we conclude, that the tendency of such individuals, would be weakest towards the foregoing passions. But in the head of GORDON,* the murderer of the pedlar boy, the measurement from Destructiveness to Destructiveness is 5⅛, and in the head of RAPHAEL it is 5⅝ inches. Here the *absolute* size of the organ is greatest in RAPHAEL, and yet he was an amiable man of genius, and GORDON an atrocious murderer. This illustrates the rule now under consideration. In GORDON, the organs of the moral sentiments and intellectual faculties are small, and that of Destructiveness is the largest in the brain; while in RAPHAEL, the moral and intellectual organs are large. On the foregoing principle, the most powerful manifestations of RAPHAEL's mind ought to have been in the department of sentiment and intellect, and those of GORDON's mind in Destructiveness and animal passion; and their actual dispositions corresponded.

An objection is frequently stated, that persons having large heads have 'little wit,' while others with small heads are 'very clever.' The Phrenologist never compares mental ability in general with size of brain in general; for the fundamental principle of the science is, that different parts of the brain have different functions, and that hence the *same absolute quantity* of brain, if consisting of intellectual organs, may be connected with the highest genius, while, if consisting of the animal organs, lying immediately above and behind the ears, it may indicate the most fearful energy of the lower propensities. . . .

Suppose that two individuals possess an organization exactly similar, but that one is highly educated and the other left entirely to the impulses of nature; the former will manifest his faculties with higher *power* than the latter; and hence it is argued, that size is not in all cases a measure of energy.

Here, however, the requisite of *caeteris paribus* does not hold. An important condition is altered, and the Phrenologist uniformly allows for the effects of education, before drawing positive conclusions. The objector may perhaps push his argument farther, and maintain, that if exercise thus increases power, it is impossible to draw the line of distinction between energy derived from this cause and that which proceeds from size in the organs, and hence that the real effects of size can never be determined. In reply, it may be observed, that education may cause the faculties to manifest themselves with the highest degree of energy *which the size of the organs will permit*, but that size fixes a limit which education cannot surpass. DENNIS, we may presume, received some improvement from education, but it did not render him equal to POPE,* much less to SHAKESPEARE or MILTON: therefore, if we take two individuals whose brains are equally healthy, but whose organs differ in size, and educate them alike, the advantages in power and attainment will be greatest in the direct ratio of the size in favour of the largest brain. Thus the objection ends in this, that if we compare brains in opposite conditions, we may be led into error—which is granted; but this is not in opposition to the doctrine that, *caeteris paribus*, size determines power. Finally—extreme deficiency in size produces incapacity for education, as in idiots; while extreme development, if healthy, as in SHAKESPEARE, BURNS, MOZART,* anticipates its effects in so far that the individuals educate themselves.

In saying, then, that *caeteris paribus*, size is a measure of power, Phrenologists demand no concessions which are not made to physiologists in general, among whom, in this instance, they rank themselves.

JOHANN GASPAR SPURZHEIM

From *Phrenology in Connection with the Study of
Physiognomy* (1826)

In 1800 Johann Gaspar Spurzheim (1776–1832), then a medical student,
travelled to Vienna to work with Franz Joseph Gall (1758–1828), one of
the founders of phrenology. Spurzheim became Gall's research assistant,
and the two toured Germany in 1805–7. Rivalry and differences of opinion later ended their collaboration; the younger Spurzheim favoured using
the classificatory system of botany to describe the structure of the mind.
After receiving his medical degree in 1813, Spurzheim travelled to
England and the United States. Spurzheim's theories were well known to
British phrenologists.

Lavater,* who wrote fragments on physiognomy, and who styles
himself a fragment of a physiognomist, maintains that physiognomy
exists as a true science. With this opinion of Lavater I agree entirely.

Let us, therefore, begin by determining wherein the study of the
physiognomical signs of the affective and intellectual faculties of
man consists. Whether, for instance, the respective signs are to be
sought for in the size and configuration of the hard parts, or in the
motions of the soft and flexible ones? This distinction between signs
dependent on configuration and organic constitution, and those
emanating from gestures and motions, is essential to the establishment of principles. Signs of the first kind proclaim innate dispositions and capacities of action. They constitute the study of
physiognomy, strictly speaking. Signs of the second kind, again,
indicate powers in action, and constitute what is called *pathognomy*,
or natural language. The latter description of signs is not included
in the plan of this work; it will be examined in a separate treatise: at
present I treat of the physiognomical signs alone.

Whilst some who cultivate physiognomy look for signs over the
whole of the body, others search for them in particular parts of it
only. Lavater conceived it possible to discover physiognomical signs
of the affective and intellectual powers in the whole body. He
declares positively, that the same force builds up every part; that
such an eye supposes such a forehead and such a beard; in short, that
each isolated part indicates the configuration of the whole, as, for

example, that all parts are oval if the head present that form: hence that man is a unit, and that his size, form, colour, hair, nose, mouth, skin, ears, hands, feet, bones, muscles, arteries, veins, nerves, voice, affections, passions, &c., are all and ever in harmony with each other.

According to this hypothesis, an unsightly person ought to be the concomitant of an unenviable soul. The contrary of this, however, is observed every day. Esop and Socrates* are proofs that a fine form is not necessary to greatness of talent and to generosity of feeling. Indeed, Euripides, Plutarch, and Seneca* have long ago maintained the inaccuracy of such an opinion. Lavater himself was obliged to acknowledge, that ungainly forms are sometimes combined with honesty of character, and that individuals, beautiful and well-proportioned, are occasionally deceitful. 'I have often seen (says he) a contradiction between the solid and flexible parts, and every one may possess certain qualities, without the respective signs.' He, therefore, admits exceptions, and his assertions contradict each other.

This, however, is not the case in nature. She makes no exceptions from her laws, and is never in contradiction with herself. Moreover, the individual parts of the body are not proportionate to each other. The head of Pericles* was too large for his body, hence the ancient artists who made his bust thought it necessary to conceal this disproportion by covering the head with a helmet. On the other hand, small heads are often found upon large bodies. There is occasionally a resemblance observable between the nose, mouth, or some other part of different individuals, whilst all the rest of their persons is extremely unlike. Now, as every part has its particular function, and as each part indicates its special dispositions, it is impossible to find in any one part physiognomical sign of the functions performed by any other part whatever.

It will be sufficient for my purpose merely to mention the error committed by those writers who, after La Porte, Lebrun,* and others, compare the human face with that of certain animals. These comparisons, like fortune-telling and chiromancy, or the interpretation of moral dispositions from the form of the hand, are to be classed among the aberrations of the human understanding.

Innumerable observations have proved, that the affective and intellectual faculties, as innate dispositions, are manifested by various parts of the brain. Hence the physiognomical signs of these faculties are to be sought for in the size and organic constitution of the cerebral parts. Several physiognomists, particularly Lavater, have already pointed out a few general signs of this kind in the configuration of the whole head, and in that of the forehead; but it is necessary to do more than this, *viz.*, to determine individually the parts appropriated to, and the signs of, the special faculties, and also of the several combinations of these which constitute determinate characters.

From numerous observations it further results, that not the size only, but also the organic constitution of the cerebral parts, must be taken into consideration before physiognomical signs of the mental operations can be established. They who attend to the mere size of the organs, and they who derive all from the influence of bodily constitution, or temperament, as it is called, are equally in error. . . .

I have given figs. 1 and 2 to show that the whole face, the forehead inclusive, is not sufficient to convey a likeness, nor to indicate a character. Both figures were intended to have been drawn with the same face and forehead, the latter part, however, in fig. 2, is not exactly of the same form as in fig. 1; but supposing it the same, every one will certainly judge differently of their characters, on account of the difference in the rest of their heads. Fig. 1 I consider as the portrait of a person religiously inclined, whose moral inclinations, however, find great obstacles, in his self-esteem, and in his unbending disposition. He will be apt to espouse Calvinistic principles. He has pretty good intellectual powers, but his judgment will not be of the deepest kind. His verbal memory is moderate. The physiognomical signs which make me judge in this way, are as follows. The temperament is nervous; the sincipital is large, compared with the basilar* region, and the occipital part of the sincipital region is much greater than its frontal portion. Such a character is severe, and inclined to acknowledge the immutable and eternal laws of nature as dictates of the Creator; to these he will at no time hesitate to subject his benevolence. Both portions of the forehead are of middling size; the eyes are small, and lie deep in their sockets.

In fig. 2 a moral character of a very different description. He is modest, indulgent, and places charity above every other virtue. His religion consists in good works. He is not indifferent to distinctions and worldly pleasures, but he acknowledges the law according to which feelings and their actions must all be directed by moral principles. He will, however, never take the lead in any profession he may choose. I form this opinion from the large size of the sincipital

FIG. I

FIG. 2

region generally, and from observing that its frontal portion out-measures its occipital one. The basilar region is not actually small, but it is inferior in size to the sincipital. Self-esteem is not large enough to push forward and take up a conspicuous position.

Thus it is very far from a matter of indifference what form of head is joined to a given face; artists, therefore, err when they imitate the face only of the individual whose portrait they would paint.

CHARLOTTE BRONTË

From *Jane Eyre* (1847)

The Library looked tranquil enough as I entered it, and the Sybil—if Sybil she were, was seated snugly enough in an easy chair at the chimney-corner. She had on a red cloak and a black bonnet; or rather, a broad-brimmed gipsy hat, tied down with a striped hand-kerchief under her chin. An extinguished candle stood on the table; she was bending over the fire, and seemed reading in a little black book, like a prayer-book, by the light of the blaze: she muttered the words to herself, as most old women do, while she read; she did not desist immediately on my entrance: it appeared she wished to finish a paragraph.

I stood on the rug and warmed my hands, which were rather cold with sitting at a distance from the drawing-room fire. I felt now as composed as ever I did in my life: there was nothing indeed in the gipsy's appearance to trouble one's calm. She shut her book and slowly looked up; her hat-brim partially shaded her face, yet I could see, as she raised it, that it was a strange one. It looked all brown and black: elf-locks bristled out from beneath a white band which passed under her chin, and came half over her cheeks or rather jaws; her eye confronted me at once, with a bold and direct gaze.

'Well, and you want your fortune told?' she said in a voice as decided as her glance, as harsh as her features.

'I don't care about it, mother; you may please yourself: but I ought to warn you, I have no faith.' . . .

'If you wish me to speak plainly, show me your palm.'

'And I must cross it with silver, I suppose?'

'To be sure.'

I gave her a shilling: she put it into an old stocking-foot which she took out of her pocket, and having tied it round and returned it, she told me to hold out my hand. I did. She approached her face to the palm, and pored over it without touching it.

'It is too fine;' said she. 'I can make nothing of such a hand as that; almost without lines: besides, what is in a palm? Destiny is not written there.'

'I believe you,' said I.

'No;' she continued, 'It is in the face: on the forehead, about the eyes, in the eyes themselves, in the lines of the mouth. Kneel, and lift up your head.' . . .

I knelt. She did not stoop towards me, but only gazed, leaning back in her chair. She began muttering:

'The flame flickers in the eye; the eye shines like dew; it looks soft and full of feeling; it smiles at my jargon: it is susceptible; impression follows impression through its clear sphere; when it ceases to smile, it is sad; an unconscious lassitude weighs on the lid: that signifies melancholy resulting from loneliness. It turns from me; it will not suffer farther scrutiny; it seems to deny, by a mocking glance, the truth of the discoveries I have already made,—to disown the charge both of sensibility and chagrin: its pride and reserve only confirm me in my opinion. The eye is favourable.

'As to the mouth, it delights at times in laughter: it is disposed to impart all that the brain conceives; though I dare say it would be silent on much the heart experiences. Mobile and flexible, it was never intended to be compressed in the eternal silence of solitude: it is a mouth which should speak much and smile often, and have human affection for its interlocutor. That feature, too, is propitious.

'I see no enemy to a fortunate issue but in the brow; and that brow professes to say,— "I can live alone, if self-respect and circumstances require me so to do. I need not sell my soul to buy bliss. I have an inward treasure, born with me, which can keep me alive if all extraneous delights should be withheld; or offered only at a price I cannot afford to give." The forehead declares, "Reason sits firm and holds the reins, and she will not let the feelings burst away and hurry her to wild chasms. The passions may rage furiously, like true heathens, as they are; and the desires may imagine all sorts of vain things: but judgment shall still have the last word in every argument, and the casting vote in every decision. Strong wind, earthquake, shock, and fire may pass by: I shall follow the guiding but of that still small voice which interprets the dictates of conscience."

'Well said, forehead; your declaration shall be respected. I have formed my plans—right plans I deem them—and in them I have attended to the claims of conscience, the counsels of reason. I know how soon youth would fade and bloom perish, if, in the cup of bliss offered, but one dreg of shame, or one flavour of remorse were detected; and I do not want sacrifice, sorrow, dissolution—such is not my taste. I wish to foster, not to blight—to earn gratitude, not to wring tears of blood—no, nor of brine: my harvest must be in smiles, in endearments, in sweet. That will do. I think I rave in a kind of exquisite delirium. I should wish now to protract this moment *ad infinitum*; but I dare not. So far I have governed myself thoroughly. I have acted as I inwardly swore I would act; but farther might try me beyond my strength. Rise, Miss Eyre: leave me; "the play is played out."'

Where was I? Did I wake or sleep? Had I been dreaming? Did I dream still? The old woman's voice had changed: her accent, her gesture, and all, were familiar to me as my own face in the glass—as the speech of my own tongue. I got up, but did not go. I looked; I stirred the fire, and I looked again: but she drew her bonnet and her bandage closer about her face, and again beckoned me to depart. The flame illuminated her hand stretched out: roused now, and on the alert for discoveries, I at once noticed that hand. It was no more the withered limb of eld than my own: it was a rounded supple member, with smooth fingers, symmetrically turned; a broad ring flashed on the little finger, and stooping forward, I looked at it, and saw a gem I had seen a hundred times before. Again I looked at the face; which was no longer turned from me—on the contrary, the bonnet was doffed, the bandage displaced, the head advanced.

'Well, Jane, do you know me?' asked the familiar voice.

'Only take off the red cloak, sir, and then——'

'But the string is in a knot—help me.'

'Break it, sir.'

'There, then—"Off, ye lendings!"' And Mr Rochester stepped out of his disguise.

GEORGE ELIOT

From *The Lifted Veil* (1859)

I fancy my father thought me an odd child, and had little fondness for me, though he was very careful in fulfilling what he regarded as a parent's duties. But he was already past the middle of life, and I was not his only son. My mother had been his second wife, and he was five-and-forty when he married her. He was a firm, unbending, intense, orderly man, in root and stem a banker, but with a flourishing graft of the active landholder, aspiring to county influence: one of those people who are always like themselves from day to day, who are uninfluenced by the weather, and neither know melancholy nor high spirits. I held him in great awe, and appeared more timid and sensitive in his presence than at other times—a circumstance which, perhaps, helped to confirm him in the intention to educate me on a different plan from the prescriptive one with which he had complied in the case of my elder brother, already a tall youth at Eton. My brother was to be his representative and successor; he must go to Eton and Oxford, for the sake of making connections, of course. My father was not a man to underrate the bearing of Latin satirists or Greek dramatists on the attainment of an aristocratic position. But intrinsically he had slight esteem for 'those dead but sceptered spirits,' having qualified himself for forming an independent opinion by reading Potter's 'Aeschylus' and dipping into Francis's 'Horace.'* To this negative view he added a positive one, derived from a recent connection with mining speculations—namely, that a scientific education was the really useful training for a younger son. Moreover, it was clear that a shy, sensitive boy like me was not fit to encounter the rough experience of a public school. Mr Letherall had said so very decidedly. Mr Letherall was a large man in spectacles, who one day took my small head between his large hands, and pressed it here and there in an exploratory, suspicious manner, then placed each of his great thumbs on my temples, and pushed me a little way from him, and stared at me with glittering spectacles. The contemplation appeared to displease him, for he frowned sternly, and said to my father, drawing his thumbs across my eyebrows,

'The deficiency is there, sir—there; and here,' he added—

touching the upper sides of my head—'here is the excess. That must be brought out, sir, and this must be laid to sleep.'

I was in a state of tremor, partly at the vague idea that I was the object of reprobation, partly in the agitation of my first hatred—hatred of this big spectacled man, who pulled my head about as if he wanted to buy and cheapen it.

I am not aware how much Mr Letherall had to do with the system afterwards adopted towards me, but it was presently clear that private tutors, natural history, science, and the modern languages were the appliances by which the defects of my organization were to be remedied. I was very stupid about machines, so I was to be greatly occupied with them; I had no memory for classification, so it was particularly necessary that I should study systematic zoology and botany; I was hungry for human deeds and human emotions, so I was to be plentifully crammed with the mechanical powers, the elementary bodies, and the phenomena of electricity and magnetism. A better-constituted boy would certainly have profited under my intelligent tutors, with their scientific apparatus, and would doubtless have found the phenomena of electricity and magnetism as fascinating as I was every Thursday assured they were. As it was, I could have paired off, for ignorance of whatever was taught me, with the worst Latin scholar that was ever turned out of a classical academy. I read Plutarch and Shakespeare and 'Don Quixote' by the sly, and supplied myself in that way with wandering thoughts, while my tutor was assuring me that 'an improved man, as distinguished from an ignorant one, was a man who knew the reason why water ran down hill.' I had no desire to be this improved man. I was glad of the running water; I could watch it and listen to it gurgling among the pebbles and bathing the bright green water-plants by the hour together. I did not want to know *why* it ran; I had perfect confidence that there were good reasons for what was so very beautiful.

Mesmerism and Magnetism

CHAUNCEY HARE TOWNSEND

From *Facts in Mesmerism* (1840)

'To every form of being is assign'd
An active principle:—howe'er remov'd
From sense and observation, it subsists
In all things, in all natures, in the stars
Of azure heaven, the unenduring clouds,
In flower and tree, in every pebbly stone
That paves the brooks, the stationary rocks,
The moving waters, and the invisible air.'

WORDSWORTH*

THE MESMERIC MEDIUM

Having, as I trust, shown the conformity of mesmerism, in all essential points, with the principles of nature and the inferences of reason, I now proceed to exhibit it in connexion with such a cause as its peculiar manifestations indicate and demand.

First, I affirm that, productive of the effects called mesmeric, there is an action of matter as distinct and specific as that of light, heat, electricity, or any other of the imponderable agents, as they are called;—that, when the mesmeriser influences his patient, he does this by a medium, either known already in another guise, or altogether new to our experience.

What proofs, it will be asked, can I bring forward of this assertion? I answer, such proofs as are considered available in all cases where an impalpable imponderable medium is to be considered; facts, namely, or certain appearances, which, bearing a peculiar character, irresistibly suggest a peculiar cause.

Let us take only one of these.

Standing at some yards distant from a person who is in the mesmeric state (that person being perfectly stationary, and with his back to me), I, by a slight motion of my hand (far too slight to be felt by the patient, through any disturbance of the air), draw him towards me, as if I actually grasped him.

What is the chain of facts which is here presented to me? First, an action of my mind, without which I could not have moved my hand; secondly, my hand's motion; thirdly, motion produced in a body altogether external to, and distant from myself. But it will at once be perceived, that, in the chain of events, as thus stated, there is a deficient link. The communication between me and the distant body is not accounted for. How could an act of my mind originate in an effect so unusual?

That which is immaterial cannot, by its very definition, move masses of water. It is only when mysteriously united to a body that spirit is brought into relationship with place or extension, and under such a condition alone, and only through such a medium, can it propagate motion. Now, in some wondrous way, spirit is in us incorporate. Our bodies are its medium of action. By them, and only by them, as far as our experience reaches, are we enabled to move masses of foreign matter. I may sit and may will for ever that yonder chair come to me, but without the direct agency of my body it must remain where it is. All the willing in the world cannot stir it an inch. I must bring myself into absolute contact with the body which I desire to move. But, in the case before us, I will—I extend my hands; I move them hither and thither, and I see the body of another person—a mass of matter external to myself, yet not in apparent contact with me—moved and swayed by the same action which stirs my own body. Am I thence to conclude that a miracle has been performed—that the laws of nature are reversed—that I can move foreign matter without contact, or intermediate agency? Or must I not rather be certain that, if I am able to sway a distant body, it is by means of some unseen lever—that volition is employing something that is equivalent to a body—something, which may be likened to an extended corporeity, which has become the organ of my will?

Surely there is no effect without a cause; and from actions we may infer the existence of an agent. We do this a thousand times in other cases,—in that of mesmerism, for instance. We never behold this power but in its results. It cannot even be made evident, like the electric spark, or felt in our own persons, like the galvanic concussion. The needle that has become a magnet, has undergone no change which any mortal sight is fine enough to appreciate, has acquired no weight which can be detected by our earthly senses. Yet, solely because we are sure that we behold certain phenomena, we allow that there is a distinct form of electricity, to which we have given the name of magnetism. Why should we refuse to mesmerism that which we grant to magnetism? It is true that as yet we have no balance of torsion, whereby the mesmeric force can be measured; but in the human body itself we do possess an instrument whereby its presence may be ascertained; nor would it be reasonable to insist upon separate agencies being detected by the same test. Why, then, but from the force of prejudice, should we call the mesmeric medium a gratuitous assumption? That such a medium exists is not a gratuitous assumption, but an unavoidable deduction of reason. But there is a class of persons who refuse to admit of anything which they cannot see, taste, or handle; with such it is difficult to argue. Should proofs by experiment be exhibited to them again and again, they still return to their cuckoo note—'Show me the agent.' One of these practical men, as they are called, actually said to me on one occasion, 'I never will believe that what you call mesmerism exists, unless you can put it in a bottle, and submit it to analysis.'

To what end, then, is reason given us, if not to judge of things invisible by those which are clearly seen? For what purpose possess we the irresistible propensity to supply deficient links in a chain of causation, if not to prompt us where our senses fail? We move a magnet over a needle; the needle moves in a corresponding manner; and the human mind is so constituted that we cannot behold these two facts, in seeming connexion, without uniting them by a third, which we consider as *proved* by them, since it is in truth their necessary consequence. We infer that the effect is produced by means of a magnetic current or medium,—a something which propagates motion from the magnet to the needle. This something we cannot indeed behold;—yet do we believe in it,—and with justice, for that which reason perceives to be necessary is *not* an invention, and can never be superfluous: on the contrary, the *only* immutable and essential truths come out of the mould of the intuitive reason, which, as Coleridge* observes, stops not at 'This *will* be so,' but at once decides, 'This *must* be so.'

Now, in all cases where motion is communicated from one body to another, the line of communication must be maintained unbroken. The first impulse gives motion to certain atoms, which in their turn propel others, and so on, till the whole series between the active body and the body which is to receive the original impulse is set in motion, and then, at length, the sequence of events is complete, and the body, towards which motion tended, is set vibrating. If the medium that propagates the first impulsion be undulatory and elastic, its atoms only oscillate on either side a fixed point of rest; but, if it be composed of travelling atoms, there is an actual progression of the medium. In either case, motion is propagated by a real action of matter till it reach its final destination. This is the history of all communicated motion, and it is plain that this holds good whether we behold the collection of atoms, in a bodily shape, that transmits the motion, as in the case of one billiard ball propelling another, or whether we behold them not, as in the case of sound being communicated to the ear from a vibrating body, by means of the intervening air. I grant that the old axiom, 'A body cannot act where it is not,' is very properly exploded; but for it we must substitute another; namely, 'A body cannot act where it is not, save by deputy, or transmissive means.' Yet some have overlooked this truth, and in their zeal to avoid theories, when they behold two sensible actions, evidently dependent the one on the other, and yet apparently disjoined, fear to unite them properly by suggesting the presence of an unseen link, which nevertheless cannot but occur between the visible antecedent and the visible consequent; for motion is not an entity that can go through void spaces independently and alone; it is merely a property which has no existence out of the subject that manifests it; and, where matter fails, there motion fails also. It is vain, then, to hold such language as if it were possible for one body to produce motion in another without something intermediate,—that is, miraculously and without means; yet your good hater of theories will even dare to blame Newton* for having suggested an ether to account for that action which one body produces on another, and even, in many cases, from vast distances, and which we call attraction. It is true that Newton may be wrong in the manner in which he manages his ether, and accounts for impulsion and re-impulsion by differences of dense and rare; but he cannot be wrong in preserving an unbroken series of atoms between separate bodies which manifestly influence each other,—between the sun and the earth for instance,— since, in this case, there is mutual action, and motion communicated from a distance. Extending the principle, and perceiving that all the heavenly bodies were in mutual relationship, and the whole celestial system harmoniously bound together, Newton supposed his ether to be of universal action, and to fill and pervade creation, establishing a means of communication between all its several parts. Were this allowed, there would be but little difficulty in explaining mesmerism; but a sublime divination of this kind is too vast for the general understanding. Accordingly, even Newton's name has failed to render the theory palateable, and men of small views have dared to call even this suggestion of a mighty mind *gratuitous*, treating its author with a levity which can only lessen one's respect for the objectors. Have these cavillers an intellect superior to Newton's own? If they have, let them give us something better than Newton's suggestions (better, not only in their own opinion but in ours) respecting the great problems of creation; some theory more solid and sublime to satisfy the cravings of humanity after pure and lofty generalisation: till then let them, at least by silence, acquiesce in Professor Playfair's beautifully expressed opinion of the queries:*—'Such enlarged and comprehensive views, so many new and bold conceptions, were never before combined with the sobriety and caution of philosophical induction. The anticipation of future discoveries, the assemblage of so many facts from the most distant regions of human research, all brought to bear on the same points, and to elucidate the same questions, are never to be sufficiently admired.' In recalling this to the reader's mind, I trust that I seem not to stray from my subject, which is, in truth, so deeply implicated in the truth or falsehood of Newton's principal suggestions. But I might leave this great man's defence to time, which already has 'brought in its revenges,' science being even now occupied in developing Newton's ideas, and in establishing as undoubted truths the greater part of all which he so modestly advanced as queries. Facts relative to the acceleration observed in the mean motion of comets have demonstrated, to the satisfaction of men of science, the existence of a resisting medium, undulatory and elastic, which pervades the known universe.

JOHN ELLIOTSON

From *Surgical Operations without Pain in the Mesmeric State* (1843)

CASE OF AMPUTATION OF A LEG ABOVE THE KNEE,
WITHOUT PAIN, IN THE MESMERIC STATE:
DESCRIPTION OF THE CASE

'I never said it was possible. I only said it was true.'
—M. G. LEWIS
'Le vrai n'est pas toujours vraisemblable.'
—FONTENELLE*

On the 22nd of November last, the Royal Medical and Chirurgical Society of London assembled to hear read an 'Account of a case of successful amputation of the thigh, during the mesmeric state, without the knowledge of the patient,' in the District Hospital of Wellow, Nottinghamshire: and voted thanks for it *without a dissentient voice*.

The mesmeriser was W. Topham, Esq., Barrister, of the Middle Temple: the operator, W. Squire Ward, Esq., Surgeon, of Wellow Hall.* The patient was a labourer, six feet high and forty-two years of age, named James Wombell. He had suffered for nearly five years from neglected disease of the left knee, the interior of the joint of which was found after the amputation deeply and extensively ulcerated. '*The* SLIGHTEST *motion of the joint was attended by the* MOST EXCRUCIATING *agony*; his nights were almost wholly sleepless, in consequence of the *painful startings of the limb*; his pulse weak and rapid; his face constantly marked with a hectic flush; his tongue foul; appetite gone;' in truth, when Mr Topham first saw him, on the 9th of September, 'he was sitting upright upon a bed in the hospital; *the only position which he could bear*: he complained of great pain from his knee and of *much excitability* and loss of strength, from his constant restlessness and deprivation of sleep, for *he had not, during the* THREE *previous weeks, slept more than* TWO *hours in* SEVENTY.'

On this day he was first mesmerised by Mr Topham, and for five and thirty minutes. 'The only effect produced was a closing of the eyelids, with that quivering appearance which so commonly results from the process; and, though awake and speaking, he could not raise them until after a lapse of a minute and a half.'

On the 10th he was sent to sleep in twenty minutes. On the 11th 'he was suffering *great agony, and distressed even to tears.*' Mr Topham 'commenced by making passes longitudinally, over the diseased knee: in *five minutes* he was *comparatively easy*; and, on proceeding further to mesmerise him, at the expiration of *ten minutes* more he was *sleeping like an infant*. Not only his arms were then *violently pinched*, but also *the diseased leg itself*, without his exhibiting *any sensation*: yet his limb was so sensitive to pain, in his natural state, he *could not bear even the* LIGHTEST *covering* to rest upon it. *That night he slept* SEVEN *hours* WITHOUT INTERRUPTION.'

'After constantly mesmerising him for ten or twelve days, a great change was observed in his appearance. *The hue of health returned; he became cheerful; felt much stronger; was easier, both in mind and body; slept well, and recovered his appetite.*' So great was the change, that Mr Ward, after having been absent from indisposition, 'was as much *astonished*, on his return on the 27th of September, about three weeks after the commencement of the mesmerism,' as he 'was *delighted* to observe the *improved condition* of the man;' and, had he 'not known the previous history of the case, *much doubt must have arisen in his mind, as to the propriety of immediately amputating the limb.*'

'On the 22nd of September the patient was first apprised of the necessity of an early amputation. The communication seemed almost unexpected, and *affected him considerably*, and *destroyed his natural sleep that night.*' The next day he was still 'fretting, restless, and in consequent pain.' Yet he was put to sleep mesmerically in four minutes and a half.

Like many other susceptible patients, he could now be affected locally when in his natural state,—without coma. For example, passes without contact along his extended extremities would render them so rigid as not to be bent by mechanical force short of danger, though breathing upon them constantly caused them to relax and drop to his sides.

Although in this mesmeric coma the sensibility to mechanical causes of pain was so far lessened that violent pinching, and sudden pricking, and of even the diseased limb, produced no evidence of sensation, and he lost all pain in his knee while this was in perfect rest, the exquisitely sensitive interior of the diseased joint was not proof against the torture of motion, which, however slight, agonized and awoke him. In many cases I have seen excruciating internal pain of nerves, inflamed or otherwise under disease, give evidence of its fierce shootings by the sudden agitation of the frame, expression of the countenance, and catching of the breath, when there was not sensibility enough for sensation from pinching, pricking, cutting, tearing, or even burning; the excruciating internal pain not awaking them unless when at the very highest intensity, or when the coma was not at the greatest depth. When there is exquisite tenderness of a part, as in the knee-joint of this poor man, the coma must indeed be profound,—more profound than it seems ever to have been in this case, except perhaps when the precaution was taken of keeping the fingers on the eyes after the operation was begun,—for motion of the part not to cause anguish. At the time of the operation, the 1st of October, it was found *impossible, without such torture as aroused him from his mesmeric coma, to remove him from his bed to the table.* Indeed, his coma was not so deep but that it *was dissipated by attempting to converse with him*; and in general it ceased spontaneously in half an hour, his waking being 'slow and gradual and without the least start.' Instead of being placed upon a table, he was therefore lifted with his low bed upon a temporary platform, and 'he was soon put into the mesmeric sleep, *although he was considerably excited* by hearing the cries of another patient upon whom Mr Ward had been performing a tedious and painful operation.' He was then 'drawn by means of the bed clothes beneath him towards the end of the bed.' Even his movement excited the pain and awoke him. But the pain soon ceased, and, his limb being 'raised about two inches from the mattress' by a surgeon present (Mr Wood), who 'rested the heel upon his shoulder and supported the joint with his hand,' he was mesmerised into coma again in four minutes.

Mr Topham continued to mesmerise him for fifteen minutes, and then informed Mr Ward that the operation might be begun, and '*brought two fingers of each hand gently in contact with the patient's closed eyelids; and there kept them, still further to deepen the sleep.*' This is a circumstance of no little importance to remember. Of all parts of the body, the eyes are the most ready receivers and transmitters of mesmerism. I noticed this first in the cases of the Okeys,* and I may remark that all the exquisitely interesting phenomena which occurred in the *perfectly genuine and wonderful cases* of those two sisters,—I repeat it as emphatically as I can, and hope my words will be read by the uninformed, and presumptuous, and cruel writer of an article in the present number (CXLI) of the Quarterly Review, who exclaims, 'how many grave persons were deceived by the impostures of the Miss Okeys of St Pancras,'—the *perfectly genuine and wonderful phenomena* of those two sisters, I have verified again and again in numerous other cases, some in one, some in another. The moist mucous membranes are more susceptible than the skin; and of membranes, the surface of the eye and inner surface of the eyelid, to say nothing of the nervous interior of the eye to which there is admission through the pupil to projected mesmeric influence, are the most susceptible. Intervening bodies impede mesmerism, and *caeteris paribus*,* in proportion to their substance; the eyelids therefore prevent so strong an effect as would result if the mesmerising body were applied to the eye itself. Still the points of the fingers placed upon the eyelids would have a great effect. The pointed parts of the body, as the ends of the fingers and the point of the nose, I, in the same Okeys and subsequently in others, ascertained to be more powerful in mesmerising as well as in being mesmerised, *caeteris paribus*, than other parts. If the fingers had been kept on the eyelids before the patient was moved at all, he probably would have suffered no more while he was moved than during the operation.

The operation was now commenced. 'Mr Ward, after one earnest look at the man,' in the words of Mr Topham, 'slowly plunged his knife into the centre of the outside of the thigh, directly to the bone, and then made a clear incision round the bone, to the opposite point on the inside of the thigh. The stillness at this moment was something awful; the *calm* respiration of the sleeping man alone was heard, for all other seemed suspended. In making the second incision, the position of the leg was found more inconvenient than it appeared to be;' and Mr Ward, to use his own words, 'having made the anterior flap,' 'was under the necessity of completing the posterior one in *three* stages. First, by *dividing a portion of the flap on the inside*; then a *similar portion on the outside*. This proceeding, which was of course far more tedious and painful than the ordinary one, was necessary to enable me to *pass the knife through under the bone and thus complete the whole*, as I could not sufficiently depress the handle to do so, without the two lateral cuts.' Yet, notwithstanding all this, the patient's 'sleep continued as profound as ever. *The* PLACID *look of his countenance never changed for* AN INSTANT; his whole frame rested, *uncontrolled*, in *perfect stillness* and repose; *not a muscle was seen to twitch*. To the end of the operation, including the sawing of the bone, securing the arteries, and applying the bandages, occupying a period of upwards of twenty minutes, he *lay like a statue.*' . . .

The mesmeric state of the patient usually lasted half an hour; and, after this lapse of time, the operation having been commenced in rather more than a quarter of an hour subsequently to its production, and having occupied, inclusively of applying the bandages, above twenty minutes, he '*gradually and calmly*,' as usual, awoke. Some sal volatile* and water had just been given to him, and might have contributed to his waking, because his coma, according to its usual course, was probably near its end, and at this period stimuli which proved inert previously might take more or less effect. This, however, is exceedingly doubtful, as the usual duration of his coma was completed, and as he was not suddenly aroused by the sal volatile and gave no sign of irritation from it, but, on the contrary, awoke 'gradually and calmly.' In fact Mr Wood, who mixed the sal volatile and water, assures me that it was very weak, and is persuaded equally with myself that the man awoke independently of it.

'At first, he uttered no exclamation; and for some moments seemed lost and bewildered,'—a characteristic and striking phenomenon so familiar to mesmerists when any visible change in external circumstances has occurred while the patient was asleep. But, after looking around, he exclaimed 'I bless the Lord to find it's all over.'

'He was then removed to another room; and, following immediately,' Mr Topham 'asked him in the presence of all assembled to describe all he felt or knew after he was mesmerised. His reply was "*I never knew anything more; and never felt any pain at all: I, once, felt as if I heard a kind of crunching.*"' Mr Topham 'asked if that were painful? He replied, "*No pain at all; I never had any; and knew nothing till I was awakened by that strong stuff*" (the sal volatile).' Of course the moment he became sensible he must have tasted the sal volatile, and would fancy that it awoke him, and he must have continued to taste it for some time after he was awake. When mesmeric patients awake spontaneously, they continually ascribe their waking to their first sensation, or even to something imagined.

'The crunching no doubt was the sawing his own thigh bone.' It is not uncommon for patients in the mesmeric coma, although insensible to mechanical causes of irritation, yet to hear more or less. As there are in mesmerism various degrees of insensibility to mechanical causes of irritation, from perfect to but slightly impaired sensibility, in different cases; sometimes in the same case at different mesmerisations; and sometimes at different periods of the same mesmerisation; and sometimes one part is insensible and another sensible: so there are various degrees of affection of hearing. In some cases patients hear not the loudest sounds; in others, they hear and answer questions; and it is very common for them to hear well at one moment and appear perfectly deaf at another, as the mesmeric conditions fluctuate in intensity: and the state of sensibility to mechanical causes of irritation and of hearing may bear no relation to each other. It would be wonderful were all this not to happen, since the very same observations hold in similar affections of a functional character independent of mesmerism. I have no doubt that the man did confusedly hear the sawing of the bone in his coma.

'He was left easy and comfortable; and still found so at nine o'clock that night: about which time' Mr Topham 'again mesmerised him (in a minute and three quarters) and he slept an hour and a half.'

Two days afterwards, when he was put into the mesmeric coma, Mr Topham proposed to Mr Ward, who intended to dress the wound that day for the first time, to take this opportunity; and *the wound was accordingly dressed without the man's knowledge, and therefore without the least pain.*

The man has done perfectly well. Within twenty-four hours after the operation he was singing. In three weeks he sat up to dinner, 'and had not a single bad symptom: *none even of the nervous excitement, so frequently observed in patients who have undergone painful operations, and who have suffered much previous anxiety in making up their minds.*'

Such was the artless tale; beautifully true to nature in every incident, and at once recognised as pure truth by all who are not ignorant of mesmeric phenomena, or who do not unphilosophically allow unworthy feelings to supplant their judgment.

EDGAR ALLAN POE

Mesmeric Revelation (1844)

Whatever doubt may still envelop the *rationale* of mesmerism, its startling *facts* are now almost universally admitted. Of these latter, those who doubt are your mere doubters by profession—an unprofitable and disreputable tribe. There can be no more absolute waste of time than the attempt to *prove*, at the present day, that man, by mere exercise of will, can so impress his fellow as to cast him into an abnormal condition, whose phenomena resemble very closely those of *death*, or at least resemble them more nearly than they do the phenomena of any other normal condition within our cognizance; that, while in this state, the person so impressed employs only with effort, and then feebly, the external organs of sense, yet perceives, with keenly refined perception, and through channels supposed unknown, matters beyond the scope of the physical organs; that, moreover, his intellectual faculties are wonderfully exalted and invigorated; that his sympathies with the person so impressing him are profound; and, finally, that his susceptibility to the impression increases with its frequency, while, in the same proportion, the peculiar phenomena elicited are more extended and more *pronounced*.

I say that these—which are the laws of mesmerism in its general features—it would be supererogation to demonstrate; nor shall I inflict upon my readers so needless a demonstration to-day. My purpose at present is a very different one indeed. I am impelled, even in the teeth of a world of prejudice, to detail without comment the very remarkable substance of a colloquy, occurring not many days ago between a sleep-waker and myself.

I had been long in the habit of mesmerizing the person in question, (Mr Vankirk,) and the usual acute susceptibility and exaltation of the mesmeric perception had supervened. For many months he had been laboring under confirmed phthisis,* the more distressing effects of which had been relieved by my manipulations; and on the night of Wednesday, the fifteenth instant, I was summoned to his bedside.

The invalid was suffering with acute pain in the region of the heart, and breathed with great difficulty, having all the ordinary symptoms of asthma. In spasms such as these he had usually found relief from the application of mustard to the nervous centres, but to-night this had been attempted in vain.

As I entered his room he greeted me with a cheerful smile, and although evidently in much bodily pain, appeared to be, mentally, quite at ease.

'I sent for you to-night,' he said, 'not so much to administer to my bodily ailment as to satisfy me concerning certain psychal impressions which, of late, have occasioned me much anxiety and surprise. I need not tell you how sceptical I have hitherto been on the topic of the soul's immortality. I cannot deny that there has always existed, as if in that very soul which I have been denying, a vague, half sentiment of its own existence. But this half sentiment at no time amounted to conviction. With it my reason had nothing to do. All attempts at logical inquiry resulted, indeed, in leaving me more sceptical than before. I had been advised to study Cousin.* I studied him in his own works as well as in those of his European and American echoes. The "Charles Elwood" of Mr Brownson,* for example, was placed in my hands. I read it with profound attention. Throughout I found it logical, but the portions which were not *merely* logical were unhappily the initial arguments of the disbelieving hero of the book. In his summing up it seemed evident to me that the reasoner had not even succeeded in convincing himself. His end had plainly forgotten his beginning, like the government of Trinculo.* In short, I was not long in perceiving that if man is to be intellectually convinced of his own immortality, he will never be so convinced by the mere *abstractions* which have been so long the fashion of the moralists of England, of France and of Germany. Abstractions may amuse and exercise, but take no hold upon the mind. Here upon earth, at least, philosophy, I am persuaded, will always in vain call upon us to look upon qualities as things. The will may assent—the soul—the intellect, never.

'I repeat, then, that I only half felt, and never intellectually believed. But latterly there has been a certain deepening of the feeling, until it has come so nearly to resemble the acquiescence of reason, that I find it difficult to distinguish between the two. I am enabled, too, plainly to trace this effect to the mesmeric influence. I cannot better explain my meaning than by the hypothesis that the mesmeric exaltation enables me to perceive a train of convincing ratiocination—a train which, in my abnormal existence, convinces, but which, in full accordance with the mesmeric phenomena, does not extend, except through its *effect*, into my normal condition. In sleep-waking, the reasoning and its conclusion—the cause and its effect—are present together. In my natural state, the cause vanishing, the effect only, and perhaps only partially, remains.

'These considerations have led me to think that some good results might ensue from a series of well directed questions propounded to me while mesmerized. You have often observed the profound self-cognizance evinced by the sleep-waker, the extensive knowledge he displays upon all points relating to the mesmeric condition itself; and from this self-cognizance may be deduced hints for the proper conduct of a catechism.'

I consented of course to make this experiment. A few passes threw Mr Vankirk into the mesmeric sleep. His breathing became immediately more easy, and he seemed to suffer no physical uneasiness. The following conversation then ensued. V. In the dialogue representing Mr Vankirk, and P. myself.

P. Are you asleep?

V. Yes—no; I would rather sleep more soundly.

P. (*After a few more passes.*) Do you sleep now?

V. Yes.

P. Do you still feel the pain in your heart?

V. No.

P. How do you think your present illness will result?

V. (*After long hesitation and speaking as if with effort.*) I must die.

P. Does the idea of death afflict you?

V. (*Very quickly.*) No—no!

P. Are you pleased with the prospect?

V. If I were awake I should like to die, but now it is no matter. The mesmeric condition is so near death as to content me. . . .

P. You have often said that the mesmeric state very nearly resembled death. How is this?

V. When I say that it resembles death, I mean that it resembles the ultimate life; for the senses of my rudimental life are in abeyance, and I perceive external things directly, without organs, through a medium which I shall employ in the ultimate, unorganized life.

P. Unorganized?

V. Yes; organs are contrivances by which the individual is brought into sensible relation with particular classes and forms of matter, to the exclusion of other classes and forms. The organs of man are adapted to his rudimental condition, and to that only; his ultimate condition, being unorganized, is of unlimited comprehension in all points but one—the nature of the volition, or motion, of the unparticled matter. You will have a distinct idea of the ultimate body by conceiving it to be entire brain. This it is *not*; but a conception of this nature will bring you near to a comprehension of what it *is*. A luminous body imparts vibration to the luminiferous ether.* The vibrations generate similar ones within the retina, which again communicate similar ones to the optic nerve. The nerve conveys similar ones to the brain; the brain, also, similar ones to the unparticled matter which permeates it. The motion of this latter is thought, of which perception is the first undulation. This is the mode by which the mind of the rudimental life communicates with the external world; and this external world is limited, through the idiosyncrasy of the organs. But in the ultimate, unorganized life, the external world reaches the whole body, (which is of a substance having affinity to brain, as I have said,) with no other intervention than that of an infinitely rarer ether than even the luminiferous; and to this ether—in unison with it—the whole body vibrates, setting in motion the unparticled matter which permeates it. It is to the absence of idiosyncratic organs, therefore, that we must attribute the nearly unlimited perception of the ultimate life. To rudimental beings, organs are the cages necessary to confine them until fledged.

P. You speak of rudimental 'beings.' Are there other rudimental thinking beings than man?

V. The multitudinous conglomeration of rare matter into nebulae, planets, suns and other bodies which are neither nebulae, suns, nor planets, is for the sole purpose of supplying *pabulum* for the idiosyncrasy of the organs of an infinity of rudimental beings. But for the necessity of the rudimental, prior to the ultimate life, there would have been no bodies such as these. Each of these is tenanted by a distinct variety of organic, rudimental, thinking creatures. In all, the organs vary with the features of the place tenanted. At death, or metamorphosis, these creatures, enjoying the ultimate life, and cognizant of all secrets but *the one*, pervade at pleasure the weird dominions of the infinite.

As the sleep-waker pronounced these latter words, in a feeble tone, I observed upon his countenance a singular expression, which somewhat alarmed me, and induced me to awake him at once. No sooner had I done this, than, with a bright smile irradiating all his features, he fell back upon his pillow and expired. I noticed that in less than a minute afterward his corpse had all the stern rigidity of stone.

HARRIET MARTINEAU

From *Letters on Mesmerism* (1845)

From the early summer of 1839, I was, till this autumn, a prisoner from illness.* My recovery now, by means of mesmeric treatment alone, has given me the most thorough knowledge possible that Mesmerism is true.

This is not the place in which to give any details of disease. It will be sufficient to explain briefly, in order to render my story intelligible, that the internal disease, under which I have suffered, appears to have been coming on for many years; that after warnings of failing health, which I carelessly overlooked, I broke down, while travelling abroad, in June 1839;—that I sank lower and lower for three years after my return, and remained nearly stationary for two more, preceding last June. During these five years, I never felt wholly at ease for one single hour. I seldom had severe pain; but never entire comfort. A besetting sickness, almost disabling me from taking food for two years, brought me very low; and, together with other evils, it confined me to a condition of almost entire stillness,—to a life passed between my bed and my sofa. It was not till after many attempts at gentle exercise that my friends agreed with me that the cost was too great for any advantage gained: and at length it was clear that even going down one flight of stairs was imprudent. From that time, I lay still; and by means of this undisturbed quiet, and such an increase of opiates as kept down my most urgent discomforts, I passed the last two years with less suffering than the three preceding. There was, however, no favourable change in the disease. Everything was done for me that the best medical skill and science could suggest, and the most indefatigable humanity and family affection devise: but nothing could avail beyond mere alleviation. My dependence on opiates was desperate. My kind and vigilant medical friend,—the most sanguine man I know, and the most bent upon keeping his patients hopeful,—avowed to me last Christmas, and twice afterwards, that he found himself compelled to give up all hope of affecting the disease,—of doing more than keeping me up, in collateral respects, to the highest practicable point. This was no surprise to me; for when any specific medicine is taken for above two years without affecting the disease, there is no more ground for hope in reason than in feeling. In June last, I suffered more than usual, and new measures of alleviation were resorted to. As to all the essential points of the disease, I was never lower than immediately before I made trial of Mesmerism. . . .

On Saturday, June 22nd, Mr Spencer Hall* and my medical friend came, as arranged, at my worst hour of the day, between the expiration of one opiate and the taking of another. By an accident, the gentlemen were rather in a hurry,—a circumstance unfavourable to a first experiment. But result enough was obtained to encourage a further trial, though it was of a nature entirely unanticipated by me. I had no other idea than that I should either drop asleep or feel nothing. I did not drop asleep, and I did feel something very strange. Various passes were tried by Mr Hall; the first that appeared effectual, and the most so for some time after, were passes over the head, made from behind,—passes from the forehead to the back of the head, and a little way down the spine. A very short time after these were tried, and twenty minutes from the beginning of the *séance*, I became sensible of an extraordinary appearance, most unexpected, and wholly unlike anything I had ever conceived of. Something seemed to diffuse itself through the atmosphere,—not like smoke, nor steam, nor haze,—but most like a clear twilight, closing in from the windows and down from the ceiling, and in which one object after another melted away, till scarcely anything was left visible before my wide-open eyes. First, the outlines of all objects were blurred; then a bust, standing on a pedestal in a strong light, melted quite away; then the opposite bust; then the table with its gay cover, then the floor, and the ceiling, till one small picture, high up on the opposite wall, only remained visible,—like a patch of phosphoric light. I feared to move my eyes, lest the singular appearance should vanish; and I cried out, 'O! deepen it! deepen it!' supposing this the precursor of the sleep. It could not be deepened, however; and when I glanced aside from the luminous point, I found that I need not fear the return of objects to their ordinary appearance while the passes were continued. The busts reappeared, ghost-like, in the dim atmosphere, like faint shadows, except that their outlines, and the parts in the highest relief, burned with the same phosphoric light. The features of one, an Isis* with bent head, seemed to be illumined by a fire on the floor, though this bust has its back to the windows. Wherever I glanced, all outlines were dressed in this beautiful light; and so they have been, at every _séance_, without exception, to this day; though the appearance has rather given way to drowsiness since I left off opiates entirely. This appearance continued during the remaining twenty minutes before the gentlemen were obliged to leave me. The other effects produced were, first, heat, oppression and sickness, and, for a few hours after, disordered stomach; followed, in the course of the evening, by a feeling of lightness and relief, in which I thought I could hardly be mistaken.

On occasions of a perfectly new experience, however, scepticism and self-distrust are very strong. I was aware of this beforehand, and also, of course, of the common sneer—that mesmeric effects are 'all imagination.' When the singular appearances presented themselves, I thought to myself,—'Now, shall I ever believe that this was all fancy? When it is gone, and when people laugh, shall I ever doubt having seen what is now as distinct to my waking eyes as the rolling waves of yonder sea, or the faces round my sofa?' I did a little doubt it in the course of the evening: I had some misgivings even so soon as that; and yet more the next morning, when it appeared like a dream.

Great was the comfort, therefore, of recognising the appearances on the second afternoon. 'Now,' thought I, 'can I again doubt?' I did, more faintly; but, before a week was over, I was certain of the fidelity of my own senses in regard to this, and more.

There was no other agreeable experience on this second afternoon. Mr Hall was exhausted and unwell, from having mesmerised many patients; and I was more oppressed and disordered than on the preceding day, and the disorder continued for a longer time; but again, towards night, I felt refreshed and relieved. How much of my ease was to be attributed to Mesmerism, and how much to my accustomed opiate, there was no saying, in the then uncertain state of my mind.

The next day, however, left no doubt. Mr Hall was prevented by illness from coming over, too late to let me know. Unwilling to take my opiate while in expectation of his arrival, and too wretched to do without some resource, I rang for my maid, and asked whether she had any objection to attempt what she saw Mr Hall do the day before. With the greatest alacrity she complied. Within one minute the twilight and phosphoric lights appeared; and in two or three more, a delicious sensation of ease spread through me,—a cool comfort, before which all pain and distress gave way, oozing out, as it were, at the soles of my feet. During that hour, and almost the whole evening, I could no more help exclaiming with pleasure than a person in torture crying out with pain. I became hungry, and ate with relish, for the first time for five years. There was no heat, oppression, or sickness during the *séance*, nor any disorder afterwards. During the whole evening, instead of the lazy hot ease of opiates, under which pain is felt to lie in wait, I experienced something of the indescribable sensation of health, which I had quite lost and forgotten. I walked about my rooms, and was gay and talkative. Something of this relief remained till the next morning; and then there was no reaction. I was no worse than usual; and perhaps rather better. . . .

Another thing, however, was also becoming clear: that more aid was necessary. My maid did for me whatever, under my own instruction, good-will and affection could do. But the patience and strenuous purpose required in a case of such long and deep-seated disease can only be looked for in an educated person, so familiar with the practice of Mesmerism as to be able to keep a steady eye on the end, through all delays and doubtful incidents. And it is also important, if not necessary, that the predominance of will should be in the Mesmerist, not the patient. The offices of an untrained servant may avail perfectly in a short case,—for the removal of sudden pain, or a brief illness; but, from the subordination being in the wrong party, we found ourselves coming to a stand.

This difficulty was abolished by the kindness and sagacity of Mr Atkinson,* who had been my adviser throughout. He explained my position to a friend of his—a lady, the widow of a clergyman, deeply and practically interested in Mesmerism—possessed of great mesmeric power, and of those high qualities of mind and heart which fortify and sanctify its influence. In pure zeal and benevolence, this lady came to me, and has been with me ever since. When I found myself able to repose on the knowledge and power (mental and moral) of my Mesmerist, the last impediments to my progress were cleared away, and I improved accordingly.

Under her hands the visual appearances and other immediate sensations were much the same as before; but the experience of recovery was more rapid. I can describe it only by saying, that I felt as if my life were fed from day to day. The vital force infused or induced was as clear and certain as the strength given by food to those who are faint from hunger. I am careful to avoid theorising at present on a subject which has not yet furnished me with a sufficiency of facts; but it can hardly be called theorising to say (while silent as to the nature of the agency) that the principle of life itself—that principle which is antagonistic to disease—appears to be fortified by the mesmeric influence; and thus far we may account for Mesmerism being no specific, but successful through the widest range of diseases that are not hereditary, and have not caused disorganisation. No mistake about Mesmerism is more prevalent than the supposition that it can avail only in nervous disease. The numerous cases recorded of cure of rheumatism, dropsy, cancer, and the whole class of tumours,— cases as distinct, and almost as numerous as those of cure of paralysis, epilepsy, and other diseases of the brain and nerves, must make any inquirer cautious of limiting his anticipations and experiments by any theory of exclusive action on the nervous system. Whether Mesmerism, and, indeed, any influence whatever, acts exclusively through the nervous system, is another question.

JAMES ESDAILE

From *Mesmerism in India* (1847)

Before submitting to the reader the results of my observations on somnambulism, I beg leave to prefix the following summary of the appearances recognised as distinctive of the somnambulistic state in Europe. It is given in the British and Foreign Medical Review, already quoted:—'Somnambulism is a condition in which certain senses and faculties are suppressed, or rendered thoroughly impassive, whilst others prevail in most unwonted exultation; in which an individual, though asleep, feels and acts most energetically, holding an anomalous species of communication with the external world, awake to objects of attention, and most profoundly torpid to things at the time indifferent; a condition respecting which, most commonly, the patient on awaking retains no recollection; but, on any relapse into which, a train of thought and feeling related to, and associated with, the antecedent paroxysm, will very often be developed.'

I intended to have reserved this branch of the subject till I had examined it in all its purely medical bearings; but I was forced, by most extraordinary circumstances, to enter prematurely into this difficult and obscure field of experiment, in order to enable me to give my evidence in a court of justice; and in describing my experiments, I hope it will be borne in mind, that I had never seen a somnambulist, or thought of making one, up to this date. My first essay was as extemporaneous and accidental as the production of mesmeric coma, on the first occasion I tried to mesmerise:—the facts are simply these.

June 17th.—About a fortnight ago, I was driving through Hooghly Bazaar, and saw a crowd collected before the police office. On asking what was the matter, I was told that a man had been apprehended in the act of stealing a boy, and that the parties were inside the guard-house. Upon hearing this, I entered the house, and found a boy of ten or twelve years old, sitting on the lap of a man who was said to have rescued him. The boy was half stupid, and one of his eyes was swollen; I therefore ordered him to be taken to the hospital. The culprit was then shown to me. He said he was a barber; and a bundle containing his implements of trade, was produced: this I carefully examined, but only found the usual barber's tools. The boy soon recovered his senses, and told me, readily and consistently, the following tale, which I again heard him repeat before the magistrate, in a different sequence, but without a tittle of variation. He said, that early in the morning he went into a field close to a house, and that shortly after, a strange man left the road, and came up to him: as soon as he was near him, he began to mutter charms, and then took hold of his hand; very soon after, he passed his hand across his eyes, and that thereupon he lost his senses, and only recollected that the man led him away, but without force, and that he felt compelled to follow him. When he came to his senses, it was at the gate of Chandernagore, two miles from where he had met the man; and this was all he had to say. He had not eaten, drunk, or smoked, in company with the man; and his master and friends all said he was a clever, well-behaved boy, and had never been known to have fits, or walk in his sleep. I then examined the man who was said to have rescued him: his evidence was to this effect; that on the morning in question, he saw the boy, whom he knew very well, following a strange man; that he stopped him, and asked what he was doing there? The boy made no answer, and appeared to be idiotic: upon seeing this, he became alarmed, brought water to throw on his face, and used other means to revive him; in which he at last succeeded. On again questioning him, he said that he did not know why he was there; that he was obliged to follow that man, though he did not know him, and after saying this, he fell down, and bruised his eye on the ground. In the mean time, the man was making off, but was apprehended, and brought to Hooghly. I then called in the barber; and this was his story: he met the boy on the road crying and looking stupid, and on asking him what ailed him he said that he had lost his way. Upon hearing this, he desired the boy to accompany him to the police station, and that a policeman would take him home. The strange nature of the transaction, whichever side was true, strongly arrested my attention, and the trade of the man roused my suspicions; as I had heard that barbers in this country, while performing their tedious processes, could put people to sleep; and reports are rife, all over the country, of people having been obliged to follow persons who had charmed them; and the victims are said to be usually women. The barbers, all over the world, are a shrewd, observing race; their occupation brings them into close contact with the surfaces most sensitive to the mesmeric influence; and they are, therefore, very likely to have become possessed of the secret of Mesmerism at an early period, and perhaps it has descended to them as a mystery of their craft. I could only see two roads out of the dilemma: it was either a case of natural, or artificial somnambulism; and if the latter, how could it be brought about unless by Mesmerism? As accident had made me a witness in the case, I anticipated that I should be called upon to speak as to the possibility of such a mode of abduction; and as I was completely ignorant of the subject, I determined to make experiments, to satisfy myself. I thought it probable, that if this could be done by Mesmerism, I should perhaps be able to imitate it, as the greater power includes the less; and that I had only to stop short in the progress to insensibility, in order to produce like effects, if obtainable by this means.

I therefore repaired to the Jail Hospital, and mesmerised a man; in whom I had subdued inflammation of the eye, by entrancing him several times; but only went to the extent of inducing the cataleptic tendency, and leaving him the power of moving and hearing, but very imperfectly. At this point, I led him away, and then letting him go, he stalked to the other end of the enclosure, till brought up by the wall; being turned, he walked in a straight line till some obstacle obstructed him, and then stood helplessly still. If allowed to stand motionless for some minutes, the trance deepened, and he became insensible to sounds; by blowing in his eyes, and addressing him all the time, he revived, and repeated after me, with great exactness, both English and Hindostanee; on awakening him, he had no recollection of any part of his proceedings, and said that he had never stirred from the spot, although he was at the opposite end of the enclosure from where we commenced. Being summoned to the Magistrate's Court as a witness, I was asked, 'if I thought it practicable to carry off a person in the way described in the evidence?' I replied, that 'I thought it possible, because I had just done something very like it, by making a prisoner follow me round the hospital enclosure, without his knowing it.' The magistrate committed the case; but when it came to be tried before the judge, it was found to be utterly impossible to convey even a glimpse of my meaning in the minds of the native law officers who had to try the case; and the judge therefore asked me if I had any objection to show the Moulavies* in court that it was possible for one person to make another follow him involuntarily, as I said. I answered, that I was willing to make the experiment, but would engage to do nothing: if he would order three men, whom I named, to be sent for to Court, I would try what could be done,—the men to be kept in total ignorance of our intentions.

In a day or two after, I was requested to attend the judge's court, which was crowded with Europeans and natives. Nazir Mahomed was brought in, and placed at the bar: I mesmerised him in a few minutes, and led him, with his arms catalepsed, out of the court, and set him walking down the road for some distance, making his arms rigid in any position, as long as I pleased. I then replaced him at the bar, where the judge and Moulavies all loudly addressed him, without his paying any attention to them; and they were obliged to ask me to awake him. This I did, and on being asked from the bench, if he had left the room since he first entered it, he confidently answered, 'No.' While they were speaking to him in front, I approached, unperceived, behind, and entranced him on the spot, in the act of speaking. The words died on his lips, and he became insensible to all voices that addressed him; he was again awoke by blowing in his eyes. Madub was put in the dock, and he did not see me on entering. The judge and Moulavies engaged him in conversation, and while he was speaking with animation and intelligence, I catalepsed him from behind, while in the usual praying attitude of a prisoner at the bar, and, in a moment, he ceased to speak or hear: I was told by those in front, that his lips moved as if in the act of speaking, after he ceased to be heard. He was so deeply affected that all motive power was nearly extinguished, and I had to push him from behind with my finger, to make him walk: he walked a few yards with difficulty, and then becoming suddenly rigid from head to foot, a slight push sent him down headlong upon the floor, in a most alarming manner: the fit of rigidity was so instantaneous that I was not aware of it. He was revived with some difficulty, and fortunately was not injured by his fall.

Sooroop Chund was next brought in, and, as I had not seen him for a month, I began asking him about his health, &c., mesmerising him all the time. In a few minutes, he ceased to answer, and I took him out of the dock, turned him round like a teetotum,* his arms rigidly fixed all the time, and then restored him to his former place in a state of complete insensibility: no one could make him hear, or show the slightest sign of life. When I blew in his eyes, he instantly recovered his senses, and declared he had never left the spot.

Whether the barber stole the boy mesmerically or not, I will not pretend to decide, but it gave me an opportunity of proving, in the most public manner, that the thing could be done, and no one has ventured to deny publicly that I stole the men; and, with the facilities of a native barber, I could almost engage to steal a man, woman, or child, daily. From the moment that I witnessed the extreme degrees of Mesmerism, I became deeply impressed with a conviction of its power for evil us well as good; and I have driven it thus far, in the hope of rousing the public mind to a sense of the dangers, as well as benefits, that may be expected from it; and I trust the day is not distant, when public opinion will strongly condemn all those who practise the art, except for philosophic and medical purposes.

ROBERT BROWNING
Mesmerism (1855)

I

All I believe is true!
 I am able yet
 All I want, to get
By a method as strange as new:
Dare I trust the same to you?

II

If at night, when doors are shut,
 And the wood-worm picks,
 And the death watch ticks,
And the bar has a flag of smut,
And a cat's in the water-butt*—

III.

And the socket floats and flares,
 And the house beams groans,
 And a foot unknown
Is surmised on the garret stairs,
And the locks slip unawares—

IV

And the spider, to serve his ends,
 By a sudden thread,
 Arms and legs outspread,
On the table's midst descends,
Comes to find, God knows what friends!—

V

If since eve drew in, I say,
 I have sat and brought
 (So to speak) my thought
To bear on the woman away,
Till I felt my hair turn gray—

VI

Till I seemed to have and hold,
    In the vacancy
    'Twixt the wall and me
From the hair-plait's chestnut-gold
To the foot in its muslin fold—

VII

Have and hold, then and there,
    Her, from head to foot,
    Breathing and mute,
Passive, and yet aware,
In the grasp of my steady stare—

VIII

Hold and have, there and then,
    All her body and soul
    That completes my whole,
All that women add to men,
In the clutch of my steady ken—

IX

Having and holding, till
    I imprint her fast
    On the void at last
As the sun does whom he will
By the calotypist's* skill—

X

Then,—if my heart's strength serve,
    And through all and each
    Of the veils I reach
To her soul and never swerve,
Knitting an iron nerve—

XI

Command her soul to advance
    And inform the shape
    Which has made escape
And before my countenance
Answers me glance for glance—

XII

I, still with a gesture fit
   Of my hands that best
   Do my soul's behest,
Pointing the power from it,
While myself do steadfast sit—

XIII

Steadfast and still the same
   On my object bent,
   While the hands give vent
To my ardor and my aim
And break into very flame—

XIV

Then I reach, I must believe,
   Not her soul in vain,
   For to me again
It reaches, and past retrieve
Its wound in the toils I weave;

XV

And must follow as I require,
   As befits a thrall,
   Bringing flesh and all,
Essence and earth-attire,
To the source of the tractile fire:

XVI

Till the house called hers, not mine,
   With a growing weight
   Seems to suffocate
If she break not its leaden line
And escape from its close confine.

XVII

Out of doors into the night!
   On to the maze
   Of the wild wood-ways,
Not turning to left or right
From the pathway, blind with sight—

XVIII

Making thro' rain and wind
    O'er the broken shrubs,
    'Twixt the stems and stubs,
With a still, composed, strong mind,
Not a care for the world behind—

XIX

Swifter and still more swift,
    As the crowding peace
    Doth to joy increase
In the wide blind eyes uplift
Thro' the darkness and the drift!

XX

While I—to the shape, I too
    Feel my soul dilate:
    Nor with abate,
And relax not a gesture due,
And I see my belief come true.

XXI

For, there! have I drawn or no
    Life to that lip?
    Do my fingers dip
In aflame which again they throw
On the cheek that breaks a-glow?

XXII

Ha! was the hair so first?
    What, unfilleted,
    Made alive, and spread
Through the void with a rich outburst,
Chestnut gold-interspersed?

XXIII

Like the doors of a casket-shrine,
    See, on either side,
    Her two arms divide
Till the heart betwixt make signs,
'Take me for I am thine!'

XXIV

'Now—now'—the door is heard!
Hark, the stairs! and near—
Nearer—and here—
'Now!' and, at call the third,
She enters without a word.

XXV

On doth she march and on
To the fancied shape;
It is, past escape,
Herself, now: the dream is done
And the shadow and she are one.

XXVI

First, I will pray. Do Thou
That ownest the soul,
Yet wilt grant control
To another, nor disallow
For a time, restrain me now!

XXVII

I admonish me while I may,
Not to squander guilt,
Since require Thou wilt
At my hand its price one day!
What the price is, who can say?

WILKIE COLLINS

From *The Moonstone* (1868)

Going round to the terrace, I found three mahogany-colored Indians, in white linen frocks and trowsers, looking up at the house.

The Indians, as I saw on looking closer, had small hand-drums slung in front of them. Behind them stood a little, delicate-looking, light-haired, English boy carrying a bag. I judged the fellows to be strolling conjurors, and the boy with the bag to be carrying the tools of their trade. One of the three, who spoke English, and who exhibited, I must own, the most elegant manners, presently informed me that my judgment was right. He requested permission to show his tricks in the presence of the lady of the house.

Now I am not a sour old man. I am generally all for amusement, and the last person in the world to distrust another person because he happens to be a few shades darker than myself. But the best of us have our weaknesses—and my weakness, when I know a family plate-basket to be out on a pantry-table, is to be instantly reminded of that basket by the sight of a strolling stranger whose manners are superior to my own. I accordingly informed the Indian that the lady of the house was out; and I warned him and his party off the premises. He made me a beautiful bow in return; and he and his party went off the premises. On my side, I returned to my bee-hive chair, and set myself down on the sunny side of the court, and fell (if the truth must be owned) not exactly into a sleep, but into the next best thing to it.

I was roused up by my daughter Penelope running out at me as if the house was on fire. What do you think she wanted? She wanted to have the three Indian jugglers instantly taken up; for this reason, namely, that they knew who was coming from London to visit us, and that they meant some mischief to Mr Franklin Blake.

Mr Franklin's name roused me. I opened my eyes, and made my girl explain herself.

It appeared that Penelope had just come from our lodge, where she had been having a gossip with the lodge-keeper's daughter. The two girls had seen the Indians pass out, after I had warned them off, followed by their little boy. Taking it into their heads that the boy was ill used by the foreigners—for no reason that I could discover, except that he was pretty and delicate-looking—the girls had stolen along the inner side of the hedge between us and the road, and had watched the proceedings of the foreigners on the outer side. These proceedings resulted in the performance of the following extraordinary tricks:

They first looked up the road and down the road, and made sure that they were alone. Then they all three faced about, and stared hard in the direction of our house. Then they jabbered and disputed in their own language, and looked at each other like men in doubt.

Then they all turned to their little English boy, as if they expected *him* to help them. And then the chief Indian, who spoke English, said to the boy, 'Hold out your hand.'

On hearing those dreadful words, my daughter Penelope said she didn't know what prevented her heart from flying straight out of her. I thought privately that it might have been her stays. All I said, however, was, 'You make my flesh creep.' (*Nota bene*: women like these little compliments.)

Well, when the Indian said 'Hold out your hand,' the boy shrunk back, and shook his head, and said he didn't like it. The Indian thereupon asked him (not at all unkindly) whether he would like to be sent back to London, and left where they had found him, sleeping in an empty basket in a market—a hungry, ragged, and forsaken little boy. This, it seems, ended the difficulty. The little chap unwillingly held out his hand. Upon that the Indian took a bottle from his bosom, and poured out of it some black stuff, like ink, into the palm of the boy's hand. The Indian—first touching the boy's head, and making signs over it in the air—then said, 'Look.' The boy became quite stiff, and stood like a statue, looking into the ink in the hollow of his hand.

(So far, it seemed to me to be juggling, accompanied by a foolish waste of ink. I was beginning to feel sleepy again, when Penelope's next words stirred me up.)

The Indians looked up the road and down the road once more— and then the chief Indian said these words to the boy: 'See the English gentleman from foreign parts.'

The boy said, 'I see him.'

The Indian said, 'Is it on the road to this house, and on no other, that the English gentleman will pass by us to-day?'

The boy said, 'It is on the road to this house, and on no other, that the English gentleman will pass by you to-day.'

The Indian put a second question—after waiting a little first. He said: 'Has the English gentleman got It about him?'

The boy answered—also, after waiting a little first—'Yes.'

The Indian put a third and last question: 'Will the English gentleman come here, as he has promised to come, at the close of day?'

The boy said, 'I can't tell.'

The Indian asked why.

The boy said, 'I am tired. The mist rises in my head, and puzzles me. I can see no more to-day.'

With that the catechism ended. The chief Indian said something in his own language to the other two, pointing to the boy, and pointing toward the town, in which (as we afterward discovered) they were lodged. He then, after making more signs on the boy's head, blew on his forehead, and so woke him up with a start. After that they all went on their way toward the town, and the girls saw them no more.

Dreams and the Unconscious

CHARLOTTE BRONTË

When Thou Sleepest (1837)

When thou sleepest, lulled in night,
   Art thou lost in vacancy?
Does no silent inward light,
   Softly breaking, fall on thee?
Does no dream on quiet wing
   Float a moment mid that ray,
Touch some answering mental string,
   Wake a note and pass away?

When thou watchest, as the hours
   Mute and blind are speeding on,
O'er that rayless path, where lowers
   Muffled midnight, black and lone;
Comes there nothing hovering near,
   Thought or half reality,
Whispering marvels in thine ear,
   Every word a mystery,

Chanting low an ancient lay,
   Every plaintive note a spell,
Clearing memory's clouds away,
   Showing scenes thy heart loves well?

Songs forgot, in childhood sung,
    Airs in youth beloved and known,
Whispered by that airy tongue,
    Once again are made thine own.

Be it dream in haunted sleep,
    Be it thought in vigil lone,
Drink'st thou not a rapture deep
    From the feeling, 'tis thine own?
All thine own; thou need'st not tell
    What bright form thy slumber blest;—
All thine own; remember well
    Night and shade were round thy rest.

Nothing looked upon thy bed,
    Save the lonely watch-light's gleam;
Not a whisper, not a tread
    Scared thy spirit's glorious dream.
Sometimes, when the midnight gale
    Breathed a moan and then was still,
Seemed the spell of thought to fail,
    Checked by one ecstatic thrill;

Felt as all external things,
    Robed in moonlight, smote thine eye;
Then thy spirit's waiting wings
    Quivered, trembled, spread to fly;
Then th' aspirer wildly swelling
    Looked, where mid transcendency
Star to star was mutely telling
    Heaven's resolve and fate's decree.

Oh! it longed for holier fire
    Than this spark in earthly shrine;
Oh! it soared, and higher, higher,
    Sought to reach a home divine.
Hopeless quest! soon weak and weary
    Flagged the pinion, drooped the plume,
And again in sadness dreary
    Came the baffled wanderer home.

And again it turned for soothing
    To th' unfinished, broken dream;
While, the ruffled current smoothing,
    Thought rolled on her startled stream.
I have felt this cherished feeling,
    Sweet and known to none but me;
Still I felt it nightly healing
    Each dark day's despondency.

FRANCES POWER COBBE

Unconscious Cerebration: A Psychological Study (1871)

The laws which govern dreams are still half unexplained, but the most obvious of them singularly illustrate the nature of the processes of the unconscious brain-work which causes them. Much of the labour of our minds, conscious and unconscious, consists in transmuting Sentiments into Ideas. It is not in this little essay that the subject can be developed in its various branches, the ordinary passions of life,—the religious and moral sentiments (wherein our translations are the source of all our myths and half our errors),—and lastly, insanity, wherein the false sentiment usually creates the intellectual delusion. Suffice it that our conscious brains are for ever at work of the kind, 'giving to airy nothing' (or at least to what is a merely subjective feeling) 'a local habitation and a name.' Our unconscious brains accordingly, after their wont, proceed on the same track during sleep. Our sentiments of love, hate, fear, anxiety, are each one of them the fertile source of whole series of illustrative dreams. Our bodily sensations of heat, cold, hunger, and suffocation, supply another series often full of the quaintest suggestions,—such as those of the poor gentleman who slept over a cheesemonger's shop, and dreamt he was shut up in a cheese to be eaten by rats; and that of the lady whose hot bottle scorched her feet, and who imagined she was walking into Vesuvius. In all such dreams we find our brains with infinite play of fancy merely adding illustrations like those of M. Doré* to the page of life which we have turned the day before, or to that which lies upon our beds as we sleep.

Again, the small share occupied by the Moral Law in the dream world is a significant fact. So far as I have been able to learn, it is the rarest thing possible for any check of conscience to be felt in a dream, even by persons whose waking hours are profoundly imbued with moral feeling. We commit in dreams acts for which we should weep tears of blood were they real, and yet never feel the slightest remorse. On the most trifling provocation we cram an offending urchin into a lion's cage (if we happen to have recently visited the Zoological Gardens), or we set fire to a house merely to warm ourselves with the blaze, and all the time feel no pang of compunction. The familiar check of waking hours, 'I must not do it, because it would be unjust or unkind,' never once seems to arrest us in the satisfaction of any whim which may blow about our wayward fancies in sleep. Nay, I think that if ever we do feel a sentiment like Repentance in dreams, it is not the legitimate sequel to the crime we have previously imagined, but a wave of feeling rolled on from the real sentiment experienced in former hours of consciousness. Our dream-selves, like the Undines* of German folk-lore, have no Souls, no Responsibility and no Hereafter. Of course this observation does not touch the fact that a person who in his conscious life has committed a great crime may be haunted with its hideous shadow in his sleep, and that Lady Macbeth may in vain try and wash the stain from her 'little hand.'* It is the imaginary acts of sleeping fancy which are devoid of moral character. But this immoral character of unconscious cerebration precisely tallies with the Kantian doctrine, that the moral will is the true *Homo Noumenon*, the Self of man.* This conscious Self being dormant in dreams, it is obvious that the true phenomena of Conscience cannot be developed in them, Plutarch says that Zeno ordered his followers to regard dreams as a test of virtue, and to note it as a dangerous sign if they did not recoil, even in their sleep, from vice;* and Sir Thomas Browne* talks solemnly of 'Sinful Dreams' which ecclesiastical history abundantly shows have proved terrible stumbling blocks to the saints. But the doctrine of Unconscious Cerebration explains clearly enough how, in the absence of the controlling Will, the animal elements of our nature assert themselves—generally in the ratio of their unnatural suppression at other times—and abstinence is made up for by hungry Fancy spreading a glutton's feast. The *want* of sense of sin in such dreams is, I think, the most natural and most healthful symptom about them. . . .

Somnambulism is an unmistakeable form of unconscious cerebration. Here while consciousness is wholly dormant, the brain performs occasionally the most brilliant operations. Coleridge's poem of Kubla Khan,* composed in opiate sleep, is an instance of its achievements in the realm of pure imagination. Many cases are recorded of students rising at night, seeking their desks, and there writing down whole columns of algebraic calculations; solutions of geometric problems, and opinions on difficult cases of law. Cabanis says that Condillac* brought continually to a conclusion at night in his sleep the reasonings of the day. In all such cases the work done asleep seems better than that done in waking hours, nay there is no lack of anecdotes which would point to the possibility of persons in an unconscious state accomplishing things beyond their ordinary powers altogether. The muscular strength of men in somnambulism and delirium, their power of balancing themselves on roofs, of finding their way in the dark, are physical advantages reserved for such conditions. Abnormal acuteness of hearing is also a well-known accompaniment of them, and in this relation we must, I conclude, understand the marvellous story vouched for by the late Sir Edward Codrington.* The captain in command of a man-of-war was one night sleeping in his cabin, with a sentinel as usual posted at his door. In the middle of the night the captain rang his bell, called suddenly to the sentinel, and sharply desired him to tell the lieutenant of the watch to alter the ship's course by so many points. Next morning the officer, on greeting the captain, observed that it was most fortunate he had been aware of their position and had given such an order, as there had been a mistake in the reckoning, and the ship was in shoal water, on the point of striking a reef. 'I!' said the astonished captain, 'I gave no order; I slept soundly all night.' The sentinel was summoned, and of course testified that the experienced commander had in some unknown way learned the peril of his ship, and saved it, even while in a state of absolute unconsciousness. . . .

When we place the phenomena of Unconscious Thought on one side, and over against them our conscious personality, we obtain, I think, a new and vivid sense of the separation, not to say the antithesis, which exists between the two; close as is their mutual interdependence. Not to talk about the distinction between object and subject, or dwell on the absurdity (as it seems to us) of the proposition that we ourselves are only the sum-total of a series of cerebrations—the recognition of the fact *that our brains sometimes think without us*, seems to enable us to view our connection with them in quite a new light. So long as all our attention was given to Conscious Thought, and philosophers eagerly argued the question, whether the Soul did or did not ever sleep or cease to think, it was easy to confound the organ of thought with the Conscious Self who was supposed to set it in action. But the moment we mass together for review the long array of the phenomena of Unconscious Cerebration, the case is altered; the severance becomes not only cogitable, but manifest.

Let us then accept cheerfully the possibility, perhaps the probability, that science ere long will proclaim the dogma, 'Matter can think.' Having humbly bowed to the decree, we shall find ourselves none the worse. Admitting that our brains accomplish much without our conscious guidance, will help us to realize that our relation to them is of a variable—an intermittent—and (we may venture to hope) of a *terminable* kind.

That such a conclusion, if reached, will have afforded us any *direct* argument for human immortality, cannot be pretended. Though we may succeed in proving 'that the Brain can think without the Conscious Man,' the great converse theorem, 'that the Conscious Man can think without a Brain,' has as yet received no jot of direct evidence; nor ever will do so, I hold, while we walk by faith and not by sight, and Heaven remains 'a part of our religion, and not a branch of our geography'!

But it is something, nay it is surely much, if, by groping among the obscurer facts of consciousness, we may attain the certainty that whatever be the final conclusions of science regarding our mental nature, the one which we have most dreaded, if reached at last, will militate not at all against the hope, written on the heart of the nations, by that Hand which writes no falsehoods—that 'when the dust returns to the dust whence it was taken, the Spirit—the Conscious Self of Man—shall return to God who gave it.'

ROBERT LOUIS STEVENSON

From *The Strange Case of Dr Jekyll and Mr Hyde* (1886)

HENRY JEKYLL'S FULL STATEMENT OF THE CASE

I was born in the year 18— to a large fortune, endowed besides with excellent parts, inclined by nature to industry, fond of the respect of the wise and good among my fellow-men, and thus, as might have been supposed, with every guarantee of an honourable and distinguished future. And indeed the worst of my faults was a certain impatient gaiety of disposition, such as has made the happiness of many, but such as I found it hard to reconcile with my imperious desire to carry my head high, and wear a more than commonly grave countenance before the public. Hence it came about that I concealed my pleasures; and that when I reached years of reflection, and began to look round me and take stock of my progress and position in the world, I stood already committed to a profound duplicity of life. Many a man would have even blazoned such irregularities as I was guilty of; but from the high views that I had set before me, I regarded and hid them with an almost morbid sense of shame. It was thus rather the exacting nature of my aspirations than any particular degradation in my faults, that made me what I was and, with even a deeper trench than in the majority of men, severed in me those provinces of good and ill which divide and compound man's dual nature. In this case, I was driven to reflect deeply and inveterately on that hard law of life, which lies at the root of religion and is one of the most plentiful springs of distress. Though so profound a double-dealer, I was in no sense a hypocrite; both sides of me were in dead earnest; I was no more myself when I laid aside restraint and plunged in shame, than when I laboured, in the eye of day, at the furtherance of knowledge or the relief of sorrow and suffering. And it chanced that the direction of my scientific studies, which led wholly towards the mystic and the transcendental, rëacted and shed a strong light on this consciousness of the perennial war among my members. With every day, and from both sides of my intelligence, the moral and the intellectual, I thus drew steadily nearer to that truth, by whose partial discovery I have been doomed to such a dreadful shipwreck: that man is not truly one, but truly two. I say two, because the state of my own knowledge does not pass beyond that point. Others will follow, others will outstrip me on the same lines; and I hazard the guess that man will be ultimately known for a mere polity of multifarious, incongruous and independent denizens. I for my part, from the nature of my life, advanced infallibly in one direction and in one direction only. It was on the moral side, and in my own person, that I learned to recognise the thorough and primitive duality of man; I saw that, of the two natures that contended in the field of my consciousness, even if I could rightly be said to be either, it was only because I was radically both; and from an early date, even before the course of my scientific discoveries had begun to suggest the most naked possibility of such a miracle, I had learned to dwell with pleasure, as a beloved daydream, on the thought of the separation of these elements. If each, I told myself, could but be housed in separate identities, life would be relieved of all that was unbearable; the unjust might go his way, delivered from the aspirations and remorse of his more upright twin; and the just could walk steadfastly and securely on his upward path, doing the good things in which he found his pleasure, and no longer exposed to disgrace and penitence by the hands of this extraneous evil. It was the curse of mankind that these incongruous faggots were thus bound together— that in the agonised womb of consciousness, these polar twins should be continuously struggling. How, then, were they dissociated?

I was so far in my reflections when, as I have said, a side light began to shine upon the subject from the laboratory table. I began to perceive more deeply than it has ever yet been stated, the trembling immateriality, the mist-like transience, of this seemingly so solid body in which we walk attired. Certain agents I found to have the power to shake and to pluck back that fleshly vestment, even as a wind might toss the curtains of a pavilion. For two good reasons, I will not enter deeply into this scientific branch of my confession. First, because I have been made to learn that the doom and burthen of our life is bound forever on man's shoulders, and when the attempt is made to cast it off, it but returns upon us with more unfamiliar and more awful pressure. Second, because as my narrative will make alas! too evident, my discoveries were incomplete. Enough, then, that I not only recognised my natural body for the mere aura and effulgence of certain of the powers that made up my spirit, but managed to compound a drug by which these powers should be dethroned from their supremacy, and a second form and countenance substituted, none the less natural to me because they were the expression, and bore the stamp, of lower elements in my soul.

I hesitated long before I put this theory to the test of practice. I knew well that I risked death; for any drug that so potently controlled and shook the very fortress of identity, might by the least scruple of an overdose or at the least inopportunity in the moment of exhibition, utterly blot out that immaterial tabernacle which I looked to it to change. But the temptation of a discovery so singular and profound, at last overcame the suggestions of alarm. I had long since prepared my tincture; I purchased at once, from a firm of wholesale chemists, a large quantity of a particular salt which I knew, from my experiments, to be the last ingredient required; and late one accursed night, I compounded the elements, watched them boil and smoke together in the glass, and when the ebullition had subsided, with a strong glow of courage, drank off the potion.

The most racking pangs succeeded: a grinding in the bones, deadly nausea, and a horror of the spirit that cannot be exceeded at the hour of birth or death. Then these agonies began swiftly to subside, and I came to myself as if out of a great sickness. There was something strange in my sensations, something indescribably new and, from its very novelty, incredibly sweet. I felt younger, lighter, happier in body; within I was conscious of a heady recklessness, a current of disordered sensual images running like a mill race in my fancy, a solution of the bonds of obligation, an unknown but not an innocent freedom of the soul. I knew myself, at the first breath of this new life, to be more wicked, tenfold more wicked, sold a slave to my original evil; and the thought, in that moment, braced and delighted me like wine. I stretched out my hands, exulting in the freshness of these sensations; and in the act, I was suddenly aware that I had lost in stature.

There was no mirror, at that date, in my room; that which stands beside me as I write, was brought there later on and for the very purpose of these transformations. The night, however, was far gone into the morning—the morning, black as it was, was nearly ripe for the conception of the day—the inmates of my house were locked in the most rigorous hours of slumber; and I determined, flushed as I was with hope and triumph, to venture in my new shape as far as to my bedroom. I crossed the yard, wherein the constellations looked down upon me, I could have thought, with wonder, the first creature of that sort that their unsleeping vigilance had yet disclosed to them; I stole through the corridors, a stranger in my own house; and coming to my room, I saw for the first time the appearance of Edward Hyde.

I must here speak by theory alone, saying not that which I know, but that which I suppose to be most probable. The evil side of my nature, to which I had now transferred the stamping efficacy, was less robust and less developed than the good which I had just deposed. Again, in the course of my life, which had been, after all, nine tenths a life of effort, virtue and control, it had been much less exercised and much less exhausted. And hence, as I think, it came about that Edward Hyde was so much smaller, slighter and younger than Henry Jekyll. Even as good shone upon the countenance of the one, evil was written broadly and plainly on the face of the other. Evil besides (which I must still believe to be the lethal side of man) had left on that body an imprint of deformity and decay. And yet when I looked upon that ugly idol in the glass, I was conscious of no repugnance, rather of a leap of welcome. This, too, was myself. It seemed natural and human. In my eyes it bore a livelier image of the spirit, it seemed more express and single, than the imperfect and divided countenance, I had been hitherto accustomed to call mine. And in so far I was doubtless right. I have observed that when I wore the semblance of Edward Hyde, none could come near to me at first without a visible misgiving of the flesh. This, as I take it, was because all human beings, as we meet them, are commingled out of good and evil: and Edward Hyde, alone in the ranks of mankind, was pure evil.

AUGUST KEKULÉ

Address to the German Chemical Society (1890)

They say that genius thinks in leaps. Gentlemen, the waking mind does not think in leaps. It is not in its power to do so.

Perhaps it would be of interest if I lay out for you, through some highly indiscreet disclosures of my mental life, how I came upon some of my ideas.

During my stay in London I lived for a long time in Clapham Road near the Common. Often, though, I spent my evenings with my friend Hugo Müller in Islington, at the opposite end of that gigantic city. We spoke there of many things, but mostly of our beloved chemistry. On one beautiful summer evening I was riding home again on the last omnibus through the by then desolate streets of that usually so lively cosmopolitan city. I was riding 'outside,' on the roof of the omnibus, as always. I sank into a state of reverie. The atoms were being juggled before my eyes. I had always seen them in motion, those small entities, but I had never been able to sense the nature of their movement. On that day I saw how often two of the smaller ones clung together in pairs; how the larger ones took hold of the smaller ones, how the larger ones held three or sometimes four of the smaller in place, and how all of it rotated in whirling rings. I saw how the larger ones formed a row and carried the smaller ones along only at the ends of the chain. I saw what Altmeister Kopp, my esteemed teacher and friend, sketched out for us in his 'Molecular World' in such an exciting way, but I saw it long before he did. The cry of the conductor, 'Clapham Road!' woke me out of my reverie, but I spent part of the night rendering at least sketches of my dream images on paper. That is how the theory of structure emerged.

With the theory of benzene, it happened in a similar way. During my stay in Ghent in Belgium I lived in an elegant bachelor apartment on the main street. My work room, though, lay on a narrow side street and during the day got hardly any light. For the chemist who spends his days in the laboratory, this was not a disadvantage. I was sitting there writing my textbook, but it was not going well; my mind was on other things. I turned my chair toward the fireplace and sank into a semi-slumber. Once again the atoms were being juggled before my eyes. This time small groups of them remained modestly in the background. My mind's eye, sharpened by repeated visions of this nature, now distinguished larger shapes of many different forms. Long rows, often densely pressed together: all of it was moving, wriggling and turning like a snake. And look, what was that? One of the snakes seized its own tail, and the shape whirled tauntingly before my eyes. As though struck by lightning, I awoke; this time, too, I spent the rest of the night working out the consequences of this hypothesis.

Let us learn to dream, gentlemen, for then, perhaps, we may find the truth:

> Und wer nicht denkt,
> Dem wird sie geschenkt,
> Er hat sie ohne Sorgen*

but let us take care to publish our dreams, before they are put to the test by waking reason.

Nervous Exhaustion

OLIVER WENDELL HOLMES

From *Elsie Venner* (1861)

It was the old story. A poor country-clergyman dies, and leaves a widow and a daughter. In Old England the daughter would have eaten the bitter bread of a governess in some rich family. In New England she must keep a school. So, rising from one sphere to another, she at length finds herself the *prima donna* in the department of Instruction in Mr Silas Peckham's educational establishment.

What a miserable thing it is to be poor! She was dependent, frail, sensitive, conscientious. She was in the power of a hard, grasping, thin-blooded, tough-fibred, trading educator, who neither knew nor cared for a tender woman's sensibilities, but who paid her and meant to have his money's worth out of her brains, and as latter, more than his money's worth could get. She was consequently, in plain English, overworked, and an overworked woman is always a sad sight,— sadder a great deal than an overworked man, because she is so much more fertile in capacities of suffering than a man. She has so many varieties of headache,—sometimes as if Jael were driving the nail that knifed Sisera* into her temples,—sometimes letting her work with half her brain while the other half throbs as if it would go to pieces,—sometimes tightening round the brows as if her cap-band were a ring of iron,—and then her neuralgias, and her back-aches, and her fits of depression, when she thinks she is nothing and less than nothing, and those paroxysms which men speak slightingly of as hysterical,—convulsions, that is all, only not commonly fatal ones,— so many trials which belong to her fine and mobile structure, that she is always entitled to pity, when she is placed in conditions which develop her nervous tendencies.

The poor young lady's work had, of course, been doubled since the departure of Master Langdon's predecessor. Nobody knows what the weariness of instruction is, as soon as the teacher's faculties begin to be overtasked, but those who have tried it. The relays of fresh pupils, each new set with its exhausting powers in full action, coming one after another, take out all the reserved forces and faculties of resistance from the subject of their draining process.

The day's work was over, and it was late in the evening, when she sat down, tired and faint, with a great bundle of girls' themes or compositions to read over before she could rest her weary head on the pillow of her narrow trundle-bed, and forget for a while the treadmill stair of labor she was daily climbing.

How she dreaded this most forlorn of all a teacher's tasks! She was conscientious in her duties, and would insist on reading every sentence,—there was no saying where she might find faults of grammar or bad spelling. There might have been twenty or thirty of these themes in the bundle before her. Of course she knew pretty well the leading sentiments they could contain: that beauty was subject to the accidents of time; that wealth was inconstant, and existence uncertain; that virtue was its own reward; that youth exhaled, like the dewdrop from the flower, ere the sun had reached its meridian; that life was o'ershadowed with trials; that the lessons of virtue instilled by our beloved teachers were to be our guides through all our future career. The imagery employed consisted principally of roses, lilies, birds, clouds, and brooks, with the celebrated comparison of wayward genius to a meteor. Who does not know the small, slanted, Italian hand of these girls'-compositions,—their stringing together of the good old traditional copy-book phrases, their occasional gushes of sentiment, their profound estimates of the world, sounding to the old folks that read them as the experience of a bantam-pullet's last-hatched young one with the chips of its shell on its head would sound to a Mother Cary's chicken,* who knew the great ocean with all its typhoons and tornadoes? Yet every now and then one is liable to be surprised with strange clairvoyant flashes, that can hardly be explained, except by the mysterious inspiration which every now and then seizes a young girl and exalts her intelligence, just as hysteria in other instances exalts the sensibility,—a little something of that which made Joan of Arc, and the Burney girl who prophesied 'Evelina,'* and the Davidson sisters. In the midst of these commonplace exercises which Miss Darley read over so carefully were two or three that had something of individual flavor about them, and here and there there was an image or an epithet which showed the footprint of a passionate nature, as a fallen scarlet feather marks the path the wild flamingo has trodden.

The young lady teacher read them with a certain indifference of manner, as one reads proofs,—noting defects of detail, but not commonly arrested by the matters treated of. Even Miss Charlotte Ann Wood's poem, beginning

'How sweet at evening's balmy hour,'

did not excite her. She marked the inevitable false rhyme of Cockney and Yankee beginners, morn and dawn, and tossed the verses on the pile of papers she had finished. She was looking over some of the last of them in a rather listless way—for the poor thing was getting sleepy in spite of herself,—when she came to one which seemed to rouse her attention, and lifted her drooping lids. She looked at it a moment before she would touch it. Then she took hold of it by one corner and slid it off from the rest. One would have said she was afraid of it, or had some undefined antipathy which made it hateful to her. Such odd fancies are common enough in young persons in her nervous state. Many of these young people will jump up twenty times a day and run to dabble the tips of their fingers in water, after touching the most inoffensive objects.

The composition was written in a singular, sharp-pointed, long, slender hand, on a kind of wavy, ribbed paper. There was something strangely suggestive about the look of it,—but exactly of what, Miss Darley either could not or did not try to think. The subject of the paper was The Mountain,—the composition being a sort of descriptive rhapsody. It showed a startling familiarity with some of the savage scenery of the region. One would have said that the writer must have threaded its wildest solitudes by the light of the moon and stars as well as by day. As the teacher read on, her color changed, and a kind of tremulous agitation came over her. There were hints in this strange paper she did not know what to make of. There was something in its descriptions and imagery that recalled,—Miss Darley could not say what, —but it made her frightfully nervous. Still she could not help reading, till she came to one passage which so agitated her, that the tired and overwearied girl's self-control left her entirely. She sobbed once or twice, then laughed convulsively, and flung herself on the bed, where she worked out a set hysteric spasm as she best might, without anybody to rub her hands and see that she did not hurt herself. By-and-by she got quiet, rose and went to her bookcase, took down a volume of Coleridge, and read a short time, and so to bed, to sleep and wake from time to time with a sudden start out of uneasy dreams.

S. WEIR MITCHELL

From *Wear and Tear, or Hints for the Overworked* (1872)

In studying this subject, it will not answer to look only at the causes of sickness and weakness which affect the male sex. If the mothers of a people are sickly and weak, the sad inheritance falls upon their offspring, and this is why I must deal first, however briefly, with the health of our girls, because it is here, as the doctor well knows, that the trouble begins. Ask any physician of your acquaintance to sum up thoughtfully the young girls he knows, and to tell you how many in each score are fit to be healthy wives and mothers or in fact to be wives and mothers at all. I have been asked this question myself very often, and I have heard it asked of others. The answers I am not going to give, chiefly because I should not be believed—a disagreeable position, in which I shall not deliberately place myself. Perhaps I ought to add that the replies I have heard given by others were appalling.

Next, I ask you to note carefully the expression and figures of the young girls whom you may chance to meet in your walks, or whom you may observe at a concert or in the ball-room. You will see many very charming faces, the like of which the world cannot match— figures somewhat too spare of flesh, and, especially south of Rhode Island, a marvellous littleness of hand and foot. But look further, and especially among New England young girls: you will be struck with a certain hardness of line in form and feature which should not be seen between thirteen and eighteen, at least; and if you have an eye which rejoices in the tints of health, you will too often miss them on the cheeks we are now so daringly criticising. I do not want to do more than is needed of this ungracious talk: suffice it to say that multitudes of our young girls are merely pretty to look at, or not that; that their destiny is the shawl and the sofa, neuralgia, weak backs, and the varied forms of hysteria,—that domestic demon which has produced untold discomfort in many a household, and, I am almost ready to say, as much unhappiness as the husband's dram. My phrase may seem outrageously strong, but only the doctor knows what one of these self-made invalids can do to make a household wretched. Mrs Gradgrind* is, in fiction, the only successful portrait of this type of misery, of the woman who wears out and destroys generations of nursing relatives, and who, as Wendell Holmes has said, is like a vampire, sucking slowly the blood of every healthy, helpful creature within reach of her demands. . . .

The time taken for the more serious instruction of girls extends to the age of nineteen, and rarely over this. During some of these years they are undergoing such organic development as renders them remarkably sensitive. At seventeen I presume that healthy girls are as well able to study *with proper precautions*, as men; but before this time overuse, or even a very steady use, of the brain is in many dangerous to health and to every probability of future womanly usefulness.

In most of our schools the hours are too many, for both girls and boys. From nine until two is, with us, the common school-time in private seminaries. The usual recess is twenty minutes or half an hour, and it is not as a rule filled by enforced exercise. In certain schools—would it were common!—ten minutes' recess is given after every hour; and in the Blind Asylum of Philadelphia this time is taken up by light gymnastics, which are obligatory. To these hours we must add the time spent in study out of school. This, for some reason, nearly always exceeds the time stated by teachers to be necessary; and most girls of our common schools and normal schools between the ages of thirteen and seventeen thus expend two or three hours. Does any physician believe that it is good for a growing girl to be so occupied seven or eight hours a day? or that it is right for her to use her brains as long a time as the mechanic employs his muscles?

But this is only a part of the evil. The multiplicity of studies, the number of teachers,—each eager to get the most he can out of his pupil,—the severer drill of our day, and the greater intensity of application demanded, produce effects on the growing brain which, in a vast number of cases, can be only disastrous. . . .

In private schools for girls of what I may call the leisure class of society overwork is of course much more rare than in our normal schools for girls, but the precocious claims of social life and the indifference of parents as to hours and systematic living needlessly add to the ever-present difficulties of the school-teacher, whose control ceases when the pupil passes out of her house.

As to the school in which both sexes are educated together a word may be said. Surely no system can be worse than that which complicates a difficult problem by taking two sets of beings of different gifts, and of unlike physiological needs and construction, and forcing them into the same educational mould.

It is a wrong for both sexes. Not much unlike the boy in childhood, there comes a time when in the rapid evolution of puberty the girl becomes for a while more than the equal of the lad, and, owing to her conscientiousness, his moral superior, but at this era of her life she is weighted by periodical disabilities which become needlessly hard to consider in a school meant to be both home and school for both sexes. Finally, there comes a time when the matured man certainly surpasses the woman in persistent energy and capacity for unbroken brain-work. If then she matches herself against him, it will be, with some exceptions, at bitter cost.

It is sad to think that the demands of civilised life are making this contest almost unavoidable. Even if we admit equality of intellect, the struggle with man is cruelly unequal and is to be avoided whenever it is possible.

CHARLOTTE PERKINS GILMAN

The Yellow Wall-Paper (1892)

It is very seldom that mere ordinary people like John and myself secure ancestral halls for the summer.

A colonial mansion, a hereditary estate, I would say a haunted house, and reach the height of romantic felicity—but that would be asking too much of fate!

Still I will proudly declare that there is something queer about it.

Else, why should it be let so cheaply? And why have stood so long untenanted?

John laughs at me, of course, but one expects that in marriage.

John is practical in the extreme. He has no patience with faith, an intense horror of superstition, and he scoffs openly at any talk of things not to be felt and seen and put down in figures.

John is a physician, and *perhaps*—(I would not say it to a living soul, of course, but this is dead paper and a great relief to my mind—) *perhaps* that is one reason I do not get well faster.

You see he does not believe I am sick!

And what can one do?

If a physician of high standing, and one's own husband, assures friends and relatives that there is really nothing the matter with one but temporary nervous depression—a slight hysterical tendency— what is one to do?

My brother is also a physician, and also of high standing, and he says the same thing.

So I take phosphates or phosphites—whichever it is, and tonics, and journeys, and air, and exercise, and am absolutely forbidden to 'work' until I am well again.

Personally, I disagree with their ideas.

Personally, I believe that congenial work, with excitement and change, would do me good.

But what is one to do?

I did write for a while in spite of them; but it *does* exhaust me a good deal—having to be so sly about it, or else meet with heavy opposition.

I sometimes fancy that in my condition if I had less opposition and more society and stimulus—but John says the very worst thing I can do is to think about my condition, and I confess it always makes me feel bad.

So I will let it alone and talk about the house.

The most beautiful place! It is quite alone, standing well back from the road, quite three miles from the village. It makes me think of English places that you read about, for there are hedges and walls and gates that lock, and lots of separate little houses for the gardeners and people.

There is a *delicious* garden! I never saw such a garden—large and shady, full of box-bordered paths, and lined with long grape-covered arbors with seats under them.

There were greenhouses, too, but they are all broken now.

There was some legal trouble, I believe, something about the heirs and co-heirs; anyhow, the place has been empty for years.

That spoils my ghostliness, I am afraid, but I don't care—there is something strange about the house—I can feel it.

I even said so to John one moonlight evening, but he said what I felt was a *draught*, and shut the window.

I get unreasonably angry with John sometimes. I'm sure I never used to be so sensitive. I think it is due to this nervous condition.

But John says if I feel so, I shall neglect proper self-control; so I take pains to control myself—before him, at least, and that makes me very tired.

I don't like our room a bit. I wanted one downstairs that opened on the piazza and had roses all over the window, and such pretty old-fashioned chintz hangings! but John would not hear of it.

He said there was only one window and not room for two beds, and no near room for him if he took another.

He is very careful and loving, and hardly lets me stir without special direction.

I have a schedule prescription for each hour in the day; he takes all care from me, and so I feel basely ungrateful not to value it more.

He said we came here solely on my account, that I was to have perfect rest and all the air I could get. 'Your exercise depends on your strength, my dear,' said he, 'and your food somewhat on your appetite; but air you can absorb all the time.' So we took the nursery at the top of the house.

It is a big, airy room, the whole floor nearly, with windows that look all ways, and air and sunshine galore. It was nursery first and then playroom and gymnasium, I should judge; for the windows are barred for little children, and there are rings and things in the walls.

The paint and paper look as if a boys' school had used it. It is stripped off—the paper—in great patches all around the head of my bed, about as far as I can reach, and in a great place on the other side of the room low down. I never saw a worse paper in my life.

One of those sprawling flamboyant patterns committing every artistic sin.

It is dull enough to confuse the eye in following, pronounced enough to constantly irritate and provoke study, and when you follow the lame uncertain curves for a little distance they suddenly commit suicide—plunge off at outrageous angles, destroy themselves in unheard of contradictions.

The color is repellant, almost revolting; a smouldering unclean yellow, strangely faded by the slow-turning sunlight.

It is a dull yet lurid orange in some places, a sickly sulphur tint in others.

No wonder the children hated it! I should hate it myself if I had to live in this room long.

There comes John, and I must put this away,—he hates to have me write a word. . . .

It is so hard to talk with John about my case, because he is so wise, and because he loves me so.

But I tried it last night.

It was moonlight. The moon shines in all around just as the sun does.

I hate to see it sometimes, it creeps so slowly, and always comes in by one window or another.

John was asleep and I hated to waken him, so I kept still and watched the moonlight on that undulating wallpaper till I felt creepy.

The faint figure behind seemed to shake the pattern, just as if she wanted to get out.

I got up softly and went to feel and see if the paper *did* move, and when I came back John was awake.

'What is it, little girl?' he said. 'Don't go walking about like that— you'll get cold.'

I thought it was a good time to talk, so I told him that I really was not gaining here, and that I wished he would take me away.

'Why, darling!' said he, 'our lease will be up in three weeks, and I can't see how to leave before.

'The repairs are not done at home, and I cannot possibly leave town just now. Of course if you were in any danger, I could and would, but you really are better, dear, whether you can see it or not. I am a doctor, dear, and I know. You are gaining flesh and color, your appetite is better, I feel really much easier about you.'

'I don't weigh a bit more,' said I, 'nor as much; and my appetite may be better in the evening when you are here, but it is worse in the morning when you are away!'

'Bless her little heart!' said he with a big hug, 'she shall be as sick as she pleases! But now let's improve the shining hours by going to sleep, and talk about it in the morning!'

'And you won't go away?' I asked gloomily.

'Why, how can I, dear? It is only three weeks more and then we will take a nice little trip of a few days while Jennie is getting the house ready. Really dear you are better!'

'Better in body perhaps—' I began, and stopped short, for he sat up straight and looked at me with such a stern, reproachful look that I could not say another word.

'My darling,' said he, 'I beg of you, for my sake and for our child's sake, as well as for your own, that you will never for one instant let that idea enter your mind! There is nothing so dangerous, so fascinating, to a temperament like yours. It is a false and foolish fancy. Can you not trust me as a physician when I tell you so?'

So of course I said no more on that score, and we went to sleep before long. He thought I was asleep first, but I wasn't, and lay there for hours trying to decide whether that front pattern and the back pattern really did move together or separately.

SOCIAL SCIENCES

Over the course of the nineteenth century, new discoveries and theories increasingly indicated that human beings were subject to natural laws, so that the societies and legal systems they created might be seen to have a foundation in nature. The relationship between nature and society was an issue of intense debate. Were human systems of justice verifiable by reference to natural law, or was social justice a necessary recourse against the fundamental injustice of nature?

Before Darwin offered a mechanism for biological evolution, the French philosopher Auguste Comte proposed that human thought had developed in distinct stages, progressing from the theological to the metaphysical to the scientific. Positivism, the philosophy his works inspired, dictated that steady advances in human knowledge would underpin moral and social progress. Comte's positivism, presented in lectures over the period 1826–40, differed significantly from Darwin's concept of evolution, for Darwin avoided references to 'progress' and discouraged teleological thinking. To some degree, however, Comte's hierarchy of knowledge suggests Darwin's great tree of nature, for he arranged its fields in the order in which they had become 'scientific'.

The newest and youngest of these fields was social science, and Comte had to argue persuasively to convince readers that the name was not a contradiction in terms. Until the mid-nineteenth century, social phenomena had been a subject for philosophers, and it was by no means obvious that social growth followed any recognizable laws. To make sociology a science, scholars would need quantifiable data documenting social processes. From the facts observed, they would need to generate hypotheses, then test these hypotheses in controlled experiments. Like natural scientists, they hoped to learn to predict phenomena so that eventually they would be able to control them.

While struggling to legitimize their field, early sociologists relied heavily on literary techniques. Like naturalists, they needed to convey original visions but also make the public see familiar sights in new ways. Social commentators like Henry Mayhew and Walter Besant described urban problems by creating semi-fictional protagonists, inviting readers to hear the poor 'speak with their own voices'. J. W. Horsley, who in 1879 offered the readers of *Macmillan's* an 'Autobiography of a Thief in Thieves' Language', envisioned himself as a translator, converting the argot of the very poor into a language his readers would understand. Like novelists, these reformers suspected that middle–class readers would never grasp unfamiliar situations if they were described in general terms. Instead, the public needed to hear about them from individual characters who engaged their imaginations.

From the beginning, social science was marked by a profound contradiction. It originated not in the field's scientific and literary allegiances, whose interplay stimulated its growth, but in the issue of government interference. If social laws were an extension of natural ones, then poverty was a natural phenomenon and could be viewed as inevitable, perhaps even necessary to civilization. Thomas Malthus argued along these lines, proposing that charity, however well-intended, only added to human suffering. While Charles Dickens usually challenged such wholesale rejections of social aid, his fictional portrait of 'telescopic philanthropy' in *Bleak House* reinforced the utilitarian belief that charity begins at home. Thomas Hardy's depiction of a young boy's radical solution presents overpopulation in a tragic, despairing light, as a biological fact that no social initiative can overcome. From an economic perspective, contended the political economist Jeremy Bentham, the best strategy a government could follow was to 'be quiet'. If, on the other hand, human society was not governed by natural laws, then people and governments were responsible for eliminating social problems.

The social sciences attempted to build knowledge in order to control and improve societies. Interestingly, Bentham, who advised governments not to interfere in economic matters, also designed the architectural panopticon which allowed government supervisors to control every aspect of their subjects' lives. Intended for prisons, workhouses, hospitals, and schools, the panopticon offered a physical space in which unseen observers could oversee everyone in their charge. Subjects would follow prescribed rules, understanding that at any moment they might be watched. Despite the apparent contradiction, this desire for both freedom and control makes sense when one considers whose freedom was being advocated. Early social scientists sought to legitimize a system in which wealthy subjects managed their lives as they chose, but troublesome paupers were managed for their own good.

John Stuart Mill, who, along with Bentham, developed the philosophy of utilitarianism, urged readers to think in practical terms, advocating a society that would please as many members as possible. Mill defined 'pleasure' not as physical enjoyment but as intellectual wealth achieved through reason and knowledge. Inspired by this ideal, writers like J. R. M'Culloch offered readers volumes of facts, inscribing knowledge in terms of practical use rather than intellectual value. In his *Dictionary*,

Practical, Theoretical, and Historical, M'Culloch defined the horse as 'a domestic quadruped of the highest utility'.

When Charles Dickens parodied utilitarian educational philosophies in *Hard Times* he was not attacking Bentham or Mill; he was challenging the cruder directness of popular utilitarianism. Dickens, who openly stated he hoped to stimulate social reform through his fiction, condemned reformers who banned imaginative vision from the social sciences. 'You mustn't fancy,' a visiting school inspector tells the sensitive, intelligent student Sissy Jupe, outdoing M'Culloch in his passion for facts. By associating an objectionable attitude with an unforgettable personality, Dickens uses the same kind of characterization employed by social commentators against one of contemporary social science's main tenets. Through a dialogue in his fictional classroom, Dickens makes readers wonder whether utility is the best goal of knowledge, and whether scientific knowledge can ever comprehend human behaviour. Like the naturalist Darwin, he suggests that 'fancy' is indispensable to any system of knowledge.

In the 1850s race became one of the social issues that most invited systematic study. Since the seventeenth century imperial expansion had stimulated naturalists' efforts to classify unknown plants and animals. As European imperial growth reached its peak, it encouraged anthropologists to categorize human beings, carefully defining their differences from the new peoples they were encountering. Not surprisingly, these racial hierarchies placed Europeans on top, justifying their attempts to dominate foreign cultures. Robert Knox's racial science and, later, Francis Galton's eugenics present the supplanting of one people by another as a natural, even a compassionate process. While Galton never advocated genocide, he argued that 'breeding down' an inferior race (gradually reducing their population by discouraging early marriage) ultimately alleviated human suffering. Some novelists, like Sarah Grand, were prepared to go further and propose that unfit Europeans should be forbidden from breeding, in the interest of maintaining an intelligent, physically healthy population.

While incorporating some nineteenth-century assumptions about race, Arthur Conan Doyle's 'The Yellow Face' questions the validity of race science. When a white mother masks her black daughter—who has reverted, as Galton predicted, to the 'norms' of her father's race—she blocks not just any glimpse of the girl's skin, but also any assumptions viewers might make about her. The truth eludes even Sherlock Holmes in this one shameful case in which his deductive method fails him. By depicting a literal unmasking, Doyle suggests how many 'racial' characteristics are projected onto subjects by observers.

According to Friedrich Engels, metaphorical 'masking' was an essential strategy of middle- and upper-class life, allowing the wealthy to maintain their ideas about society by hiding the facts that undermined them. As Elizabeth Gaskell's descriptions reveal, impoverished workers frightened members of the middle classes. In Engels's detailed descriptions of Manchester, he proposes that the rich have consciously constructed their city so that its leading citizens never see the slums in which their employees live. Like a naturalist, Engels asks readers to take a close look at their environment, then consider how its inhabitants have adapted themselves to it.

Central to nineteenth-century social science was the desire to make middle-class readers see and hear the poor. Matthew Arnold's 'East London' and 'West London' suggest that the rich and poor were in constant contact, yet both poems rely on a presumed distance between the readers and the poverty described. In nineteenth-century fiction and social science, this gap was often bridged by a narrator from the upper classes. Poets' and scientists' attempts to 'translate' show just how convinced readers were that they and the subjects of social studies lived in different worlds.

While facts and statistics lent sociology prestige, they did not make the poor any more visible, nor could they answer social science's most persistent question: How might one reduce or end urban poverty? The central issue was to determine how extensively the environment could affect an individual. If it was all-determining, as the sanitary reformer Edwin Chadwick suggested, then all of society was responsible for poverty. If it was not, then crime, disease, and urban misery might be blamed on the 'nature' of the poor. Reformers who believed in the overpowering force of the environment held that the slums corrupted their inhabitants. Often, they found that the best way to educate the literate classes was to let the poor speak for themselves.

Here fiction, with its art of creating personas, offered the best methods for depicting reality. Henry Mayhew published his interviews with England's 'nomads' as letters to the influential reformist journal the *Morning Chronicle*, presenting the poor as a traveller might describe foreigners in his log. Mayhew's interviewees show signs of being prompted, their 'candid' remarks suggesting responses to repeated questions. Unfailingly, they reveal the ways their environments have corrupted them. The novelist and social reformer Walter Besant also created personas to voice general messages, while relying on an omniscient narrator from the upper classes. 'I introduce you to a baby,' he begins in *East London*, asking genteel readers to accept the innocent representative of a class they would probably never intentionally have encountered.

It would be misleading, of course, to call Mayhew's or Besant's writing 'scientific'. Some nineteenth-century readers may have regarded their writing as little more than descriptive journalism and turned to quantitative studies like Lombroso's or Nordau's for a more 'objective' analysis of social problems. But the criterion of objectivity was not yet as entrenched as it would become in the twentieth century. The most vivid depictions of the poor as individuals came from reformers like Elizabeth Gaskell, who made no pretence of being analytical and whose insights were valued precisely for their subjectivity. In Gaskell's *North and South*, the poor are never guided by leading questions: They defy the wealthy characters who cross-examine them, thwarting any attempt to define them as the passive recipients of charity. While Matthew Arnold's 'East London' suggests that the human spirit can triumph over any physical hardship, Gaskell remains sceptical. Her characters scorn the advice of those who 'preach on what [they] know naught about'.

George Bernard Shaw's characters present an even more direct challenge to conservative ideology, reinforcing Engels's claim that poverty sustains the wealth of the élite. Like Gaskell, Shaw focused on the situation of female workers, many of whom could not support themselves with low-paying factory jobs and were forced to sell themselves to survive. Vivie Warren's dependence on her mother—a madam and ex-prostitute—suggests the unbreakable bond between the rich and the poor, implying that even the highest intellectual work is sustained by the sale of human flesh. Depicting a fictional family with powerful verisimilitude, Shaw's play offers 'evidence' for Karl Marx's contention that workers selling their labour are in the position of prostitutes.

As a Lamarckian, Shaw believed that organisms were shaped by their environments. If an enterprising girl became a prostitute, it was because her surroundings offered her no better way to survive. When social scientists appropriated Darwin's natural selection hypothesis, however, many began to attribute vice to hereditary factors. In 1876 the anthropologist Cesare Lombroso argued that a third of all criminals were physical and moral degenerates who had reverted to earlier stages in human development. While their moral atavism made them vicious, their physical degeneracy made them detectable to an informed observer. These 'born criminals' could be spotted by their thick black hair, attached earlobes, coarse features, and other physical characteristics of 'primitive' people. Lombroso's theories, summarized by his daughter Gina Lombroso Ferrero in the extract below, encouraged scientists all over the world to look for signs of inborn criminality.

Most social scientists and novelists who wrote about degeneration attributed it to both environmental and hereditary factors. In the 1860s the French psychologist Benedict Morel argued that many mental illnesses resulted from degeneration, mental and physical damage that had accumulated over successive generations. According to Morel, each generation of poor urban dwellers subjected to malnutrition, bad air, alcohol, tobacco, or syphilis produced sicklier children. Some of these were neurotic, insane, or severely retarded. Morel's degeneration involved heredity as well as environment, for it relied on Lamarck's notion that acquired changes could be transmitted. While Gissing wrote his novels largely to illustrate the way poverty destroyed lives, his descriptions of characters in *The Nether World* reinforce Morel's portrayal of degeneration. The environmental effects seem to have been registered over more than one lifetime. Toward the end of the century both scientific and literary writers depicted degeneration as a gradual loss of manhood. In *Dracula*, Bram Stoker depicts this dreaded emasculation as a literal draining. Transfusions from 'four strong men' fail to sustain Lucy, who is herself being drained by the invasive Count. Their vain efforts imply that increasing weakness is making England vulnerable to outside forces.

While nineteenth-century writers associated degeneracy with the stressful urban environment, they never believed it was restricted to the very poor. Oscar Wilde's *The Picture of Dorian Gray* depicts degeneracy among society's most privileged members. His wealthy characters advocate an aestheticism many readers found decadent, but Dorian's degeneracy is never tied to any kind of artistic taste. Instead, his most immoral act is the rejection of responsibility, his determination to satisfy his appetites while refusing to accept the consequences. Like *Mrs Warren's Profession*, Wilde's novel suggests that the most uncivilized behaviour is refusing to accept one's connection to others.

The German physician Max Nordau, who shared Wilde's interest in the development of art, 'diagnosed' *fin de siècle* artwork as degenerate, the result of a slow cultural poisoning. According to Nordau, modern stresses like railway travel and urban crowding were overtaxing people's nervous systems, leaving them unfit for the demands of everyday life. When accumulated over many generations, this exhaustion was undermining the physical foundation of the human mind. Along with tables of statistics, Nordau presented readers with the same metaphor employed by Thomas Hardy and Sarah Grand: that of the degenerate individual as prematurely old.

Like Nordau's study, Grand's controversial novel *The Heavenly Twins* depicts degeneration as an avoidable process, offering a diagnosis and a warning. A eugenicist and feminist, Grand left her physician husband in 1893, changed her name, and dedicated herself to writing and lecturing. Like Lombroso, she told readers stories of physical decay, confronting them with the pathetic image of a syphilitic baby. Grand believed that degeneracy could be prevented through intelligently planned

reproduction, but as an advocate of women's rights, she associated unfit-
ness with poor education and irresponsible choices more than with any
racial qualities. Men who acquired syphilis through sexual promiscuity
were passing it on to their ignorant wives, leaving their descendants unfit
to survive. By protecting women from unseemly realities, modern society
was contributing to its own undoing.

Like *Hard Times*, *The Heavenly Twins* suggests that the way to social
reform lies through rethinking education. Hereditary and environmental
factors could only destroy lives if people were prevented from making
informed choices. As writers determined to show readers other people's
lives, social scientists shared novelists' faith in metaphor and characterization. Future reformers would need to develop their imaginations
along with their capacities for facts. An education that told students
'you mustn't fancy' would be as deadly to science as it would be to
literature.

Creating the Social Sciences

JEREMY BENTHAM

From *Panopticon,*
or,
The Inspection-House, &c (1791)

PREFACE

*Morals reformed—health preserved—industry invigorated—instruction
diffused—public burthens lightened—Economy seated, as it were, upon a
rock—the gordian knot of the Poor-Laws not cut, but untied—all by a
simple idea in Architecture!*——Thus much I ventured to say on laying
down the pen—and thus much I should perhaps have said on taking
it up, if at that early period I had seen the whole of the way before
me. A new mode of obtaining power of mind over mind, in a quantity hitherto without example: and that, to a degree equally without
example, secured by whoever chooses to have it so, against abuse. —
Such is the engine: such the work that may be done with it. How far
the expectations thus held out have been fulfilled, the reader will
decide. . . .

PLAN FOR A PENITENTIARY INSPECTION-HOUSE

Before you look at the plan, take in words the general idea of it.

The building is circular.

The apartments of the prisoners occupy the circumference. You may call them, if you please, the *cells*.

These *cells* are divided from one another, and the prisoners by that means secluded from all communication with each other, by *partitions* in the form of *radii* issuing from the circumference towards the centre, and extending as many feet as shall be thought necessary to form the largest dimension of the cell.

The apartment of the inspector occupies the centre; you may call it if you please the *inspector's lodge*.

It will be convenient in most, if not in all cases, to have a vacant space or *area* all round, between such centre and such circumference. You may call it if you please the *intermediate* or *annular* area.

About the width of a cell may be sufficient for a *passage* from the outside of the building to the lodge.

Each cell has in the outward circumference, a *window*, large enough, not only to light the cell, but, through the cell, to afford light enough to the correspondent part of the lodge.

The inner circumference of the cell is formed by an iron *grating*, so light as not to screen any part of the cell from the inspector's view. ·

Of this grating, a part sufficiently large opens, in form of a *door*, to admit the prisoner at his first entrance; and to give admission at any time to the inspector or any of his attendants.

To cut off from each prisoner the view of every other, the partitions are carried on a few feet beyond the grating into the intermediate area: such projecting parts I call the *protracted partitions*.

It is conceived, that the light, coming in in this manner through the cells, and so across the intermediate area, will be sufficient for the inspector's lodge. But, for this purpose, both the windows in the cells, and those corresponding to them in the lodge, should be as large as the strength of the building, and what shall be deemed a necessary attention to economy, will permit.

To the windows of the lodge there are *blinds*, as high up as the eyes of the prisoners in their cells can, by any means they can employ, be made to reach.

To prevent *thorough light*, whereby, notwithstanding the blinds, the prisoners would see from the cells whether or no any person was in the lodge, that apartment is divided into quarters, by *partitions* formed by two diameters to the circle, crossing each other at right angles. For these partitions the thinnest materials might serve; and they might be made removeable at pleasure; their height, sufficient to prevent the prisoners seeing over them from the cells. Doors to these partitions, if left open at any time, might produce the thorough light. To prevent this, divide each partition into two, at any part required, setting down the one-half at such distance from the other as shall be equal to the aperature of a door. . . .

ESSENTIAL POINTS OF THE PLAN

It may be of use, that among all the particulars you have seen, it should be clearly understood what circumstances are, and what are not, essential to the plan. The essence of it consists, then, in the *centrality* of the inspector's situation, combined with the well-known and most effectual contrivances for *seeing without being seen*. As to the *general form* of the building, the most commodious for most purposes seems to be the circular but this is not an absolutely essential circumstance. Of all figures, however, this, you will observe, is the only one that affords a perfect view, and the same view, of an indefinite number of apartments of the same dimensions: that affords a spot from which, without any change of situation, a man may survey, in the same perfection, the whole number, and without so much as a change of posture, the half of the whole number, at the same time: that, within a boundary of a given extent, contains the greatest quantity of room:—that places the centre at the least distance from the light:—that gives the cells most width, at the part where, on account of the light, most light may, for the purposes of work, be wanted:— and that reduces to the greatest possible shortness, the path taken by the inspector, in passing from each part of the field of inspection to every other.

You will please to observe, that though perhaps it is the most important point, that the persons to be inspected should always feel themselves as if under inspection, at least as standing a great chance of being so, yet it is not by any means the *only* one. If it were, the same advantage might be given to buildings of almost any form.

What is also of importance is, that for the greatest proportion of time possible, each man should actually *be* under inspection. This is matcrial in *all* cases, that the inspector may have the satisfaction of knowing, that the discipline actually has the effect which it is designed to have: and it is more particularly material in such cases where the inspector, besides seeing that they conform to such standing rules as are prescribed, has more or less frequent occasion to give them such transient and incidental directions as will require to be given and enforced, at the commencement at least of every course of industry. And I think, it needs not much argument to prove, that the business of inspection, like every other, will be performed to a greater degree of perfection, the less trouble the performance of it requires.

Not only so, but the greater chance there is, of a given person's being at a given time actually under inspection, the more strong will be the persuasion—the more *intense*, if I may say so, the *feeling*, he has of his being so. How little turn soever the greater number of persons so circumstanced may be supposed to have for calculation, some rough sort of calculation can scarcely, under such circumstances, avoid forcing itself upon the rudest mind. Experiment, venturing first upon slight trangressions, and so on, in proportion to success, upon more and more considerable ones, will not fail to teach him the difference between a loose inspection and a strict one.

From *Manual of Political Economy* (1793)

Political Economy is at once a *science* and an *art*. The value of the science has for its efficient cause and measure, its subserviency to the art.

According to the principle of utility in every branch of the art of legislation, the object or end in view should be the production of the maximum of happiness in a given time in the community in question.

In the instance of this branch of the art, the object or end in view should be the production of that maximum of happiness, in so far as this more general end is promoted by the production of the maximum of wealth and the maximum of population.

The practical questions, therefore, are—How far the measures respectively suggested by these two branches of the common end agree?—how far they differ, and which requires the preference?—how far the end in view is best promoted by individuals acting for themselves? and in what cases these ends may be best promoted by the hands of government. . . .

With the view of causing an increase to take place in the mass of national wealth, or with a view to increase of the means either of subsistence or enjoyment, without some special reason, the general rule is, that nothing ought to be done or attempted by government. The motto, or watchword of government, on these occasions, ought to be—*Be quiet.*

For this quietism there are two main reasons:—1. Generally speaking, any interference for this purpose on the part of government is *needless.* The wealth of the whole community is composed of the wealth of the several individuals belonging to it taken together. But to increase his particular portion is, generally speaking, among the constant objects of each individual's exertions and care. Generally speaking, there is no one who knows what is for your interest, so well as yourself—no one who is disposed with so much ardour and constancy to pursue it.

2. Generally speaking, it is moreover likely to be pernicious, viz. by being unconducive, or even obstructive, with reference to the attainment of the end in view. Each individual bestowing more time and attention upon the means of preserving and increasing his portion of wealth, than is or can be bestowed by government, is likely to take a more effectual course than what, in his instance and on his behalf, would be taken by government.

It is, moreover, universally and constantly pernicious in another way, by the restraint or constraint imposed on the free agency of the individual. Pain is the general concomitant of the sense of such restraint, wherever it is experienced.

THOMAS MALTHUS

From *An Essay on the Principle of Population* (1798)

I think I may fairly make two postulata.

First, That food is necessary to the existence of man.

Secondly, That the passion between the sexes is necessary, and will remain nearly in its present state.

These two laws ever since we have had any knowledge of mankind, appear to have been fixed laws of our nature; and, as we have not hitherto seen any alteration in them, we have no right to conclude that they will ever cease to be what they now are, without an immediate act of power in that Being who first arranged the system of the universe; and for the advantage of his creatures, still executes, according to fixed laws, all its various operations. . . .

Assuming then, my postulata as granted, I say, that the power of population is indefinitely greater than the power in the earth to produce subsistence for man.

Population, when unchecked, increases in a geometrical ratio. Subsistence increases only in an arithmetical ratio. A slight acquaintance with numbers will shew the immensity of the first power in comparison of the second.

By that law of our nature which makes food necessary to the life of man, the effects of these two unequal powers must be kept equal.

This implies a strong and constantly operating check on population from the difficulty of subsistence. This difficulty must fall some where; and must necessarily be severely felt by a large portion of mankind.

Through the animal and vegetable kingdoms, nature has scattered the seeds of life abroad with the most profuse and liberal hand. She has been comparatively sparing in the room, and the nourishment necessary to rear them. The germs of existence contained in this spot of earth, with ample food, and ample room to expand in, would fill millions of worlds in the course of a few thousand years. Necessity, that imperious all pervading law of nature, restrains them within the prescribed bounds. The race of plants, and the race of animals shrink under this great restrictive law. And the race of man cannot, by any efforts of reason, escape from it. Among plants and animals its effects are waste of seed, sickness, and premature death. Among mankind, misery and vice. The former, misery, is an absolutely necessary consequence of it. Vice is a highly probable consequence, and we therefore see it abundantly prevail; but it ought not, perhaps, to be called an absolutely necessary consequence. The ordeal of virtue is to resist all temptation to evil.

This natural inequality of the two powers of population, and of production in the earth, and that great law of our nature which must constantly keep their effects equal, form the great difficulty that to me appears insurmountable in the way to the perfectibility of society. All other arguments are of slight and subordinate consideration in comparison of this. I see no way by which man can escape from the weight of this law which pervades all animated nature. No fancied equality, no agrarian regulations in their utmost extent, could remove the pressure of it even for a single century. And it appears, therefore, to be decisive against the possible existence of a society, all the members of which, should live in ease; happiness, and comparative leisure; and feel no anxiety about providing the means of subsistence for themselves and families.

Consequently, if the premises are just, the argument is conclusive against the perfectibility of the mass of mankind. . . .

The poor-laws of England tend to depress the general condition of the poor in these two ways. Their first obvious tendency is to increase population without increasing the food for its support. A poor man may marry with little or no prospect of being able to support a family in independence. They may be said therefore in some measure to create the poor which they maintain; and as the provisions of the country must, in consequence of the increased population, be distributed to every man in smaller proportions, it is evident that the labour of those who are not supported by parish assistance, will purchase a smaller quantity of provisions than before, and consequently, more of them must be driven to ask for support.

Secondly, the quantity of provisions consumed in workhouses upon a part of the society, that cannot in general be considered as the most valuable part, diminishes the shares that would otherwise belong to more industrious, and more worthy members; and thus in the same manner forces more to become dependent. If the poor in the workhouses were to live better than they now do this new distribution of the money of the society would tend more conspicuously to depress the condition of those out of the workhouses, by occasioning a rise in the price of provisions.

Fortunately for England, a spirit of independence still remains among the peasantry. The poor-laws are strongly calculated to eradicate this spirit. They have succeeded in part; but had they succeeded as completely as might have been expected, their pernicious tendency would not have been so long concealed.

Hard as it may appear in individual instances, dependent poverty ought to be held disgraceful. Such a stimulus seems to be absolutely necessary to promote the happiness of the great mass of mankind; and every general attempt to weaken this stimulus, however benevolent its apparent intention, will always defeat its own purpose. If men are induced to marry from a prospect of parish provision, with little or no chance of maintaining their families in independence, they are not only unjustly tempted to bring unhappiness and dependence upon themselves and children; but they are tempted, without knowing it, to injure all in the same class with themselves. A labourer who marries without being able to support a family, may in some respects be considered as an enemy to all his fellow-labourers.

I feel no doubt whatever, that the parish laws of England have contributed to raise the price of provisions, and to lower the real price of labour. They have therefore contributed to impoverish that class of people whose only possession is their labour. It is also difficult to suppose that they have not powerfully contributed to generate that carelessness, and want of frugality observable among the poor, so contrary to the disposition frequently to be remarked among petty tradesmen and small farmers. The labouring poor, to use a vulgar expression, seem always to live from hand to mouth. Their present wants employ their whole attention, and they seldom think of the future. Even when they have an opportunity of saving they seldom exercise it; but all that is beyond their present necessities goes, generally speaking, to the ale-house. The poor-laws of England may therefore be said to diminish both the power and the will to save, among the common people, and thus to weaken one of the strongest incentives to sobriety and industry, and consequently to happiness.

J. R. M'CULLOCH

From *A Dictionary, Practical, Theoretical, and Historical of Commerce and Commercial Navigation* (1832)

HORSE, a domestic quadruped of the highest utility, being by far the most valuable acquisition made by man among the lower animals. There is a great variety of horses in Britain. The frequent introduction of foreign breeds, and their judicious mixture, having greatly improved the native stocks. Our race horses are the fleetest in the world; our carriage and cavalry horses are amongst the handsomest and most active of those employed for these purposes; and our heavy draught horses are the most powerful, beautiful, and docile of any of the large breeds.

Number and Value of Horses in Great Britain.—The number of horses used in Great Britain for different purposes is very great, although less so, perhaps, than has been generally supposed. Mr Middleton (*Survey of Middlesex*, 2d ed. p. 639) estimated the total number of horses in England and Wales, employed in husbandry, at 1,200,000, and those employed for other purposes at 600,000. Dr Colquhoun,* contrary to his usual practice, reduces this estimate to 1,500,000 for Great Britain: and in this instance we are inclined to think his guess is pretty near the mark. The subjoined official statements give the numbers of the various descriptions of horses in England and Wales, which paid duty in 1814, when those used in husbandry were taxed; and the numbers, when summed up, amount to 1,204,307. But this account does not include stage coach, mail coach, and hackney coach horses, nor does it include those used in posting. Poor persons keeping only one horse were also exempted from the duty; as were all horses employed in the regular regiments of cavalry and artillery, and in the volunteer cavalry. In Mr Middleton's estimate, already referred to, he calculated the number of post chaise, mail, stage, and hackney coach horses, at 100,000; and from the inquiries we have made, we are satisfied that if we estimate the number of such horses in Great Britain, at this moment, at 125,000, we shall be decidedly beyond the mark.

On the whole, therefore, it may be fairly estimated that there are in Great Britain from 1,400,000 to 1,500,000 horses employed for various purposes of pleasure and utility. They may, probably, be worth at an average from 12*l.*, to 15*l.*, making their total value from 18,000,000*l.* to 22,500,000*l.* sterling, exclusive of the young horses.

CHARLES DICKENS

From *Bleak House* (1852–3)

In this scene, Richard Carstone, Ada Clare, and her companion, Esther Summerson (the narrator), visit the Jellyby family, to whom they have been sent by their protector, John Jarndyce.

There was a confused little crowd of people, principally children, gathered about the house at which we stopped, which had a tarnished brass plate on the door, with the inscription, JELLYBY.

'Don't be frightened!' said Mr Guppy, looking in at the coach-window. 'One of the young Jellybys been and got his head through the area railings!'

'O poor child,' said I, 'let me out, if you please!'

'Pray be careful of yourself, miss. The young Jellybys are always up to something,' said Mr Guppy.

I made my way to the poor child, who was one of the dirtiest little unfortunates I ever saw, and found him very hot and frightened, and crying loudly, fixed by the neck between two iron railings, while a milkman and a beadle, with the kindest intentions possible, were endeavouring to drag him back by the legs, under a general impression that his skull was compressible by those means. As I found (after pacifying him), that he was a little boy, with a naturally large head, I thought that, perhaps, where his head could go, his body could follow, and mentioned that the best mode of extrication might be to push him forward. This was so favourably received by the milkman and beadle, that he would immediately have been pushed into the area, if I had not held his pinafore, while Richard and Mr Guppy ran down through the kitchen, to catch him when he should be released. At last he was happily got down without any accident, and then he began to beat Mr Guppy with a hoop-stick in quite a frantic manner.

Nobody had appeared belonging to the house, except a person in pattens, who had been poking at the child from below with a broom; I don't know with what object, and I don't think she did. I therefore supposed that Mrs Jellyby was not at home; and was quite surprised when the person appeared in the passage without the pattens, and going up to the back room on the first floor, before Ada and me, announced us as, 'Them two young ladies, Missis Jellyby!' We passed several more children on the way up, whom it was difficult to avoid treading on in the dark; and as we came into Mrs Jellyby's presence, one of the poor little things fell down stairs—down a whole flight (as it sounded to me), with a great noise.

Mrs Jellyby, whose face reflected none of the uneasiness which we could not help showing in our own faces, as the dear child's head recorded its passage with a bump on every stair—Richard afterwards said he counted seven, besides one for the landing—received us with perfect equanimity. She was a pretty, very diminutive, plump woman, of from forty to fifty, with handsome eyes, though they had a curious habit of seeming to look a long way off. As if—I am quoting Richard again—they could see nothing nearer than Africa!

'I am very glad indeed,' said Mrs Jellyby, in an agreeable voice, 'to have the pleasure of receiving you. I have a great respect for Mr Jarndyce; and no one in whom he is interested can be an object of indifference to me.'

We expressed our acknowledgments, and sat down behind the door where there was a lame invalid of a sofa. Mrs Jellyby had very good hair, but was too much occupied with her African duties to brush it. The shawl in which she had been loosely muffled, dropped on to her chair when she advanced to us; and as she turned to resume her seat, we could not help noticing that her dress didn't nearly meet up the back, and that the open space was railed across with a lattice-work of stay-lace—like a summer-house.

The room, which was strewn with papers and nearly filled by a great writing-table covered with similar litter, was, I must say, not only very untidy, but very dirty. We were obliged to take notice of that with our sense of sight, even while, with our sense of hearing, we followed the poor child who had tumbled down stairs: I think into the back kitchen, where somebody seemed to stifle him.

But what principally struck us was a jaded, and unhealthy-looking, though by no means plain girl, at the writing-table, who sat biting the feather of her pen, and staring at us. I suppose nobody ever was in such a state of ink. And, from her tumbled hair to her pretty feet, which were disfigured with frayed and broken satin slippers trodden down at heel, she really seemed to have no article of dress upon her, from a pin upwards, that was in its proper condition or its right place.

'You find me, my dears,' said Mrs Jellyby, snuffing the two great office candles in tin candlesticks which made the room taste strongly of hot tallow (the fire had gone out, and there was nothing in the grate but ashes, a bundle of wood, and a poker), 'you find me, my dears, as usual, very busy; but that you will excuse. The African project at present employs my whole time. It involves me in correspondence with public bodies, and with private individuals anxious for the welfare of their species all over the country. I am happy to say it is advancing. We hope by this time next year to have from a hundred and fifty to two hundred healthy families cultivating coffee and educating the natives of Borrioboola-Gha, on the left bank of the Niger.'

As Ada said nothing, but looked at me, I said it must be very gratifying.

'It *is* gratifying,' said Mrs Jellyby. 'It involves the devotion of all my energies, such as they are; but that is nothing, so that it succeeds; and I am more confident of success every day. Do you know, Miss Summerson, I almost wonder that *you* never turned your thoughts to Africa?'

This application of the subject was really so unexpected to me, that I was quite at a loss how to receive it. I hinted that the climate——

'The finest climate in the world!' said Mrs Jellyby.

'Indeed, ma'am?'

'Certainly. With precaution,' said Mrs Jellyby. 'You may go into Holborn, without precaution, and be run over. You may go into Holborn, with precaution, and never be run over. Just so with Africa.'

I said, 'No doubt.'—I meant as to Holborn.

'If you would like,' said Mrs Jellyby, putting a number of papers towards us, 'to look over some remarks on that head, and on the general subject (which have been extensively circulated), while I finish a letter I am now dictating—to my eldest daughter, who is my amanuensis——'

The girl at the table left off biting her pen, and made a return to our recognition, which was half bashful and half sulky.

'—I shall then have finished for the present,' proceeded Mrs Jellyby, with a sweet smile; 'though my work is never done. Where are you, Caddy?'

' "Presents her compliments to Mr Swallow, and begs——" ' said Caddy.

' "—And begs," ' said Mrs Jellyby, dictating, ' "to inform him, in reference to his letter of inquiry on the African project."—No, Peepy! Not on any account!'

Peepy (so self-named) was the unfortunate child who had fallen down stairs, who now interrupted the correspondence by presenting himself, with a strip of plaister on his forehead, to exhibit his wounded knees, in which Ada and I did not know which to pity most—the bruises or the dirt. Mrs Jellyby merely added, with the serene composure with which she said everything, 'Go along, you naughty Peepy!' and fixed her fine eyes on Africa again.

However, as she at once proceeded with her dictation, and as I interrupted nothing by doing it, I ventured quietly to stop poor Peepy as he was going out, and to take him up to nurse. He looked very much astonished at it, and at Ada's kissing him; but soon fell fast asleep in my arms, sobbing at longer and longer intervals, until he was quiet. I was so occupied with Peepy that I lost the letter in detail, though I derived such a general impression from it of the momentous importance of Africa, and the utter insignificance of all other places and things, that I felt quite ashamed to have thought so little about it.

'Six o'clock!' said Mrs Jellyby. 'And our dinner hour is nominally (for we dine at all hours) five! Caddy, show Miss Clare and Miss Summerson their rooms. You will like to make some change, perhaps? You will excuse me, I know, being so much occupied. O, that very bad child! Pray put him down, Miss Summerson!' . . .

Soon after seven o'clock we went down to dinner; carefully, by Mrs Jellyby's advice; for the stair-carpets, besides being very deficient in stair-wires, were so torn as to be absolute traps. We had a fine cod-fish, a piece of roast beef, a dish of cutlets, and a pudding; an excellent dinner, if it had had any cooking to speak of, but it was almost raw. The young woman with the flannel bandage waited, and dropped everything on the table wherever it happened to go, and never moved it again until she put it on the stairs. The person I had seen in pattens (who I suppose to have been the cook), frequently came and skirmished with her at the door, and there appeared to be ill-will between them.

All through dinner; which was long, in consequence of such

accidents as the dish of potatoes being mislaid in the coal scuttle, and the handle of the corkscrew coming off, and striking the young woman in the chin; Mrs Jellyby preserved the evenness of her disposition. She told us a great deal that was interesting about Borrioboola-Gha and the natives; and received so many letters that Richard, who sat by her, saw four envelopes in the gravy at once. Some of the letters were proceedings of ladies' committees, or resolutions of ladies' meetings, which she read to us; others were applications from people excited in various ways about the cultivation of coffee, and natives; others required answers, and these she sent her eldest daughter from the table three or four times to write. She was full of business, and undoubtedly was, as she had told us, devoted to the cause.

I was a little curious to know who a mild bald gentleman in spectacles was, who dropped into a vacant chair (there was no top or bottom in particular) after the fish was taken away, and seemed passively to submit himself to Borrioboola-Gha, but not to be actively interested in that settlement. As he never spoke a word, he might have been a native, but for his complexion. It was not until we left the table, and he remained alone with Richard, that the possibility of his being Mr Jellyby ever entered my head. But he *was* Mr Jellyby; and a loquacious young man called Mr Quale, with large shining knobs for temples, and his hair all brushed to the back of his head, who came in the evening, and told Ada he was a philanthropist, also informed her that he called the matrimonial alliance of Mrs Jellyby with Mr Jellyby the union of mind and matter.

This young man, besides having a great deal to say for himself about Africa, and a project of his for teaching the coffee colonists to teach the natives to turn piano-forte legs and establish an export trade, delighted in drawing Mrs Jellyby out by saying, 'I believe now, Mrs Jellyby, you have received as many as from one hundred and fifty to two hundred letters respecting Africa in a single day, have you not?' or, 'If my memory does not deceive me, Mrs Jellyby, you once mentioned that you had sent off five thousand circulars from one post-office at one time?'—always repeating Mrs Jellyby's answer to us like an interpreter. During the whole evening, Mr Jellyby sat in a corner with his head against the wall, as if he were subject to low spirits. It seemed that he had several times opened his mouth when alone with Richard, after dinner, as if he had something on his mind;

but had always shut it again, to Richard's extreme confusion, without saying anything.

Mrs Jellyby, sitting in quite a nest of waste paper, drank coffee all the evening, and dictated at intervals to her eldest daughter. She also held a discussion with Mr Quale; of which the subject seemed to be—if I understood it—the Brotherhood of Humanity; and gave utterance to some beautiful sentiments. I was not so attentive an auditor as I might have wished to be, however, for Peepy and the other children came flocking about Ada and me in a corner of the drawing-room to ask for another story: so we sat down among them, and told them in whispers Puss in Boots and I don't know what else, until Mrs Jellyby, accidentally remembering them, sent them to bed. As Peepy cried for me to take him to bed, I carried him upstairs; where the young woman with the flannel bandage charged into the midst of the little family like a dragoon, and overturned them into cribs.

After that, I occupied myself in making our room a little tidy, and in coaxing a very cross fire that had been lighted, to burn; which at last it did, quite brightly. On my return downstairs, I felt that Mrs Jellyby looked down upon me rather, for being so frivolous; and I was sorry for it; though at the same time I knew that I had no higher pretensions.

It was nearly midnight before we found an opportunity of going to bed; and even then we left Mrs Jellyby among her papers drinking coffee, and Miss Jellyby biting the feather of her pen.

'What a strange house!' said Ada, when we got upstairs. 'How curious of my cousin Jarndyce to send us here!'

'My love,' said I, 'it quite confuses me. I want to understand it, and I can't understand it at all.'

'What?' asked Ada, with her pretty smile.

'All this, my dear,' said I. 'It *must* be very good of Mrs Jellyby to take such pains about a scheme for the benefit of Natives—and yet— Peepy and the housekeeping!'

Ada laughed; and put her arm about my neck, as I stood looking at the fire; and told me I was a quiet, dear, good creature, and had won her heart. 'You are so thoughtful, Esther,' she said, 'and yet so cheerful! and you do so much, so unpretendingly! You would make a home out of even this house.'

AUGUSTE COMTE

From *Positive Philosophy* (1853)

The first characteristic of the Positive Philosophy is that it regards all phenomena as subjected to invariable natural *Laws*. Our business is,—seeing how vain is any research into what are called *Causes*, whether first or final,—to pursue an accurate discovery of these Laws, with a view to reducing them to the smallest possible number. By speculating upon causes, we could solve no difficulty about origin and purpose. Our real business is to analyse accurately the circumstances of phenomena, and to connect them by the natural relations of succession and resemblance. The best illustration of this is in the case of the doctrine of Gravitation. We say that the general phenomena of the universe are *explained* by it, because it connects under one head the whole immense variety of astronomical facts; exhibiting the constant tendency of atoms towards each other in direct proportion to their masses, and in inverse proportion to the squares of their distances; whilst the general fact itself is a mere extension of one which is perfectly familiar to us, and which we therefore say that we know;—the weight of bodies on the surface of the earth. As to what weight and attraction are, we have nothing to do with that, for it is not a matter of knowledge at all. Theologians and metaphysicians may imagine and refine about such questions; but positive philosophy rejects them. When any attempt has been made to explain them, it has ended only in saying that attraction is universal weight, and that weight is terrestrial attraction: that is, that the two orders of phenomena are identical; which is the point from which the question set out. Again, M. Fourier,* in his fine series of researches on Heat, has given us all the most important and precise laws of the phenomena of heat, and many large and new truths, without once inquiring into its nature, as his predecessors had done when they disputed about calorific matter and the action of an universal ether. In treating his subject in the Positive method, he finds inexhaustible material for all his activity of research, without betaking himself to insoluble questions.

Before ascertaining the stage which the Positive Philosophy has reached, we must bear in mind that the different kinds of our knowledge have passed through the three stages of progress at different rates, and have not therefore arrived at the same time. The rate of advance depends on the nature of the knowledge in question, so distinctly that, as we shall see hereafter, this consideration constitutes an accessary to the fundamental law of progress. Any kind of knowledge reaches the positive stage early in proportion to its generality, simplicity, and independence of other departments. Astronomical science, which is above all made up of facts that are general, simple, and independent of other sciences, arrived first; then terrestrial Physics; then Chemistry; and, at length, Physiology.

It is difficult to assign any precise date to this revolution in science. It may be said, like everything else, to have been always going on; and especially since the labours of Aristotle and the school of Alexandria;* and then from the introduction of natural science into the West of Europe by the Arabs. But, if we must fix upon some marked period, to serve as a rallying point, it must be that,—about two centuries ago,—when the human mind was astir under the precepts of Bacon, the conceptions of Descartes, and the discoveries of Galileo.* Then it was that the spirit of the Positive philosophy rose up in opposition to that of the superstitious and scholastic systems which had hitherto obscured the true character of all science. Since that date, the progress of the Positive philosophy, and the decline of the other two, have been so marked that no rational mind now doubts that the revolution is destined to go on to its completion,—every branch of knowledge being, sooner or later, brought within the operation of Positive philosophy. This is not yet the case. Some are still lying outside: and not till they are brought in will the Positive philosophy possess that character of universality which is necessary to its definitive constitution.

In mentioning just now the four principal categories of phenomena,—astronomical, physical, chemical, and physiological,— there was an omission which will have been noticed. Nothing was said of Social phenomena. Though involved with the physiological, Social phenomena demand a distinct classification, both on account of their importance and of their difficulty. They are the most individual, the most complicated, the most dependent on all others; and therefore they must be the latest,—even if they had no special obstacle to encounter. This branch of science has not hitherto entered into the domain of Positive philosophy. Theological and metaphysical methods, exploded in other departments, are as yet exclusively applied, both in the way of inquiry and discussion, in all treatment of Social subjects, though the best minds are heartily weary of eternal disputes about divine right and the sovereignty of the people. This is the great, while it is evidently the only gap which has to be filled, to constitute, solid and entire, the Positive Philosophy. Now that the human mind has grasped celestial and terrestrial physics,—mechanical and chemical; organic physics, both vegetable and animal,—there remains one science, to fill up the series of sciences of observation,—Social physics. This is what men have now most need of: and this it is the principal aim of the present work to establish.

It would be absurd to pretend to offer this new science at once in a complete state. Others, less new, are in very unequal conditions of forwardness. But the same character of positivity which is impressed on all the others will be shown to belong to this. This once done, the philosophical system of the moderns will be in fact complete, as there will then be no phenomenon which does not naturally enter into some one of the five great categories. All our fundamental conceptions having become homogeneous, the Positive state will be fully established. It can never again change its character, though it will be for ever in course of development by additions of new knowledge. Having acquired the character of universality which has hitherto been the only advantage resting with the two preceding systems, it will supersede them by its natural superiority, and leave to them only an historical existence.

CHARLES DICKENS

From *Hard Times* (1854)

'Now, what I want is, Facts. Teach these boys and girls nothing but Facts. Facts alone are wanted in life. Plant nothing else, and root out everything else. You can only form the minds of reasoning animals upon Facts: nothing else will ever be of any service to them. This is the principle on which I bring up my own children, and this is the principle on which I bring up these children. Stick to Facts, sir!'

The scene was a plain, bare, monotonous vault of a school-room, and the speaker's square forefinger emphasised his observations by underscoring every sentence with a line on the schoolmaster's sleeve. The emphasis was helped by the speaker's square wall of a forehead, which had his eyebrows for its base, while his eyes found commodious cellarage in two dark caves, overshadowed by the wall. The emphasis was helped by the speaker's mouth, which was wide, thin, and hard set. The emphasis was helped by the speaker's voice, which was inflexible, dry, and dictatorial. The emphasis was helped by the speaker's hair, which bristled on the skirts of his bald head, a plantation of firs to keep the wind from its shining surface, all covered with knobs, like the crust of a plum pie, as if the head had scarcely warehouse-room for the hard facts stored inside. The speaker's obstinate carriage, square coat, square legs, square shoulders,—nay, his very neckcloth, trained to take him by the throat with an unaccommodating grasp, like a stubborn fact, as it was,—all helped the emphasis.

'In this life, we want nothing but Facts, sir; nothing but Facts!'

The speaker, and the schoolmaster, and the third grown person present, all backed a little, and swept with their eyes the inclined plane of little vessels then and there arranged in order, ready to have imperial gallons of facts poured into them until they were full to the brim.

Thomas Gradgrind, sir. A man of realities. A man of facts and calculations. A man who proceeds upon the principle that two and two are four, and nothing over, and who is not to be talked into allowing for anything over. Thomas Gradgrind, sir—peremptorily Thomas—Thomas Gradgrind. With a rule and a pair of scales, and the multiplication table always in his pocket, sir, ready to weigh and measure any parcel of human nature, and tell you exactly what it comes to. It is a mere question of figures, a case of simple arithmetic. You might hope to get some other nonsensical belief into the head of George Gradgrind, or Augustus Gradgrind, or John Gradgrind, or Joseph Gradgrind (all suppositious, nonexistent persons), but into the head of Thomas Gradgrind—no, sir!

In such terms Mr Gradgrind always mentally introduced himself, whether to his private circle of acquaintance, or to the public in general. In such terms, no doubt, substituting the words 'boys and girls,' for 'sir,' Thomas Gradgrind now presented Thomas

Gradgrind to the little pitchers before him, who were to be filled so full of facts.

Indeed, as he eagerly sparkled at them from the cellarage before mentioned, he seemed a kind of cannon loaded to the muzzle with facts, and prepared to blow them clean out of the regions of child-hood at one discharge. He seemed a galvanising apparatus,* too, charged with a grim mechanical substitute for the tender young imaginations that were to be stormed away.

'Girl number twenty,' said Mr Gradgrind, squarely pointing with his square forefinger, 'I don't know that girl. Who is that girl?'

'Sissy Jupe, sir,' explained number twenty, blushing, standing up, and curtseying.

'Sissy is not a name,' said Mr Gradgrind. 'Don't call yourself Sissy. Call yourself Cecilia.'

'It's father as calls me Sissy, sir,' returned the young girl in a trembling voice, and with another curtsey.

'Then he has no business to do it,' said Mr Gradgrind. 'Tell him he mustn't. Cecilia Jupe. Let me see. What is your father?'

'He belongs to the horse-riding, if you please, sir.'

Mr Gradgrind frowned, and waved off the objectionable calling with his hand.

'We don't want to know anything about that, here. You mustn't tell us about that, here. Your father breaks horses, don't he?'

'If you please, sir, when they can get any to break, they do break horses in the ring, sir.'

'You mustn't tell us about the ring, here. Very well, then. Describe your father as a horsebreaker. He doctors sick horses, I dare say?'

'Oh yes, sir.'

'Very well, then. He is a veterinary surgeon, a farrier and horse-breaker. Give me your definition of a horse.'

(Sissy Jupe thrown into the greatest alarm by this demand.)

'Girl number twenty unable to define a horse!' said Mr Gradgrind, for the general behoof of all the little pitchers. 'Girl number twenty possessed of no facts, in reference to one of the commonest of animals! Some boy's definition of a horse. Bitzer, yours.'

The square finger, moving here and there, lighted suddenly on Bitzer, perhaps because he chanced to sit in the same ray of sunlight which, darting in at one of the bare windows of the intensely whitewashed room, irradiated Sissy. For, the boys and girls sat on the face of the inclined plane in two compact bodies, divided up the centre by a narrow interval; and Sissy, being at the corner of a row on the sunny side, came in for the beginning of a sunbeam, of which Bitzer, being at the corner of a row on the other side, a few rows in advance, caught the end. But, whereas the girl was so dark-eyed and dark-haired, that she seemed to receive a deeper and more lustrous colour from the sun when it shone upon her, the boy was so light-eyed and light-haired that the self-same rays appeared to draw out of him what little colour he ever possessed. His cold eyes would hardly have been eyes, but for the short ends of lashes which, by bringing them into immediate contrast with something paler than themselves, expressed their form. His short-cropped hair might have been a mere continuation of the sandy freckles on his forehead and face. His skin was so unwholesomely deficient in the natural tinge, that he looked as though, if he were cut, he would bleed white.

'Bitzer,' said Thomas Gradgrind. 'Your definition of a horse.'

'Quadruped. Graminivorous.* Forty teeth, namely twenty-four grinders, four eye-teeth, and twelve incisive. Sheds coat in the spring; in marshy countries, sheds hoofs, too. Hoofs hard, but requiring to be shod with iron. Age known by marks in mouth.' Thus (and much more) Bitzer.

'Now girl number twenty,' said Mr Gradgrind. 'You know what a horse is.'

JOHN STUART MILL

From *Utilitarianism* (1861)

A passing remark is all that needs be given to the ignorant blunder of supposing that those who stand up for utility, as the test of right and wrong, use the term in that restricted and merely colloquial sense in which utility is opposed to pleasure. An apology is due to the philosophical opponents of utilitarianism for even the momentary appearance of confounding them with any one capable of so absurd a misconception; which is the more extraordinary, inasmuch as the contrary accusation, of referring every thing to pleasure, and that, too, in its grossest form, is another of the common charges against utilitarianism: and, as has been pointedly remarked by an able writer, the same sort of persons, and often the very same persons, denounce the theory 'as impracticably dry when the word "utility" precedes the word "pleasure," and as too practicably voluptuous when the word "pleasure" precedes the word "utility."' Those who know any thing about the matter are aware, that every writer, from Epicurus* to Bentham, who maintained the theory of utility, meant by it, not something to be contradistinguished from pleasure, but pleasure itself, together with exemption from pain; and, instead of opposing the useful to the agreeable or the ornamental, have always declared that the useful means these, among other things. Yet the common herd, including the herd of writers, not only in newspapers and periodicals, but in books of weight and pretension, are perpetually falling into this shallow mistake. Having caught up the word 'utilitarian,' while knowing nothing whatever about it but its sound, they habitually express by it the rejection or the neglect of pleasure in some of its forms; of beauty, of ornament, or of amusement. Nor is the term thus ignorantly misapplied solely in disparagement, but occasionally in compliment; as though it implied superiority to frivolity and the mere pleasures of the moment. And this perverted use is the only one in which the word is popularly known, and the one from which the new generation are acquiring their sole notion of its meaning. Those who introduced the word, but who had for many years discontinued it as a distinctive appellation, may well feel themselves called upon to resume it, if by doing so they can hope to contribute any thing towards rescuing it from this utter degradation.

The creed which accepts, as the foundation of morals, Utility, or the Greatest-happiness Principle, holds that actions are right in proportion as they tend to promote happiness, wrong as they tend to produce the reverse of happiness. By happiness is intended pleasure and the absence of pain; by unhappiness, pain and the privation of pleasure. To give a clear view of the moral standard set up by the theory, much more requires to be said; in particular, what things it includes in the ideas of pain and pleasure, and to what extent this is left an open question. But these supplementary explanations do not affect the theory of life on which this theory of morality is grounded,—namely, that pleasure, and freedom from pain, are the only things desirable as ends; and that all desirable things (which are as numerous in the utilitarian as in any other scheme) are desirable either for the pleasure inherent in themselves, or as means to the promotion of pleasure and the prevention of pain.

Now, such a theory of life excites in many minds, and among them in some of the most estimable in feeling and purpose, inveterate dislike. To suppose that life has (as they express it) no higher end than pleasure,—no better and nobler object of desire and pursuit,— they designate as utterly mean and grovelling; as a doctrine worthy only of swine, to whom the followers of Epicurus were, at a very early period, contemptuously likened: and modern holders of the doctrine are occasionally made the subject of equally polite comparisons by its German, French, and English assailants.

When thus attacked, the Epicureans have always answered, that it is not they, but their accusers, who represent human nature in a degrading light, since the accusation supposes human beings to be capable of no pleasures except those of which swine are capable. If this supposition were true, the charge could not be gainsaid, but would then be no longer an imputation; for, if the sources of pleasure were precisely the same to human beings and to swine, the rule of life which is good enough for the one would be good enough for the other. The comparison of the Epicurean life to that of beasts is felt as degrading, precisely because a beast's pleasures do not satisfy a human being's conceptions of happiness. Human beings have faculties more elevated than the animal appetites; and, when once made conscious of them, do not regard any thing as happiness which does not include their gratification. . . .

In the golden rule of Jesus of Nazareth, we read the complete spirit of the ethics of utility. To do as you would be done by, and to love your neighbour as yourself, constitute the ideal perfection of utilitarian morality. As the means of making the nearest approach to this ideal, utility would enjoin, first, that laws and social arrangements should place the happiness or (as, speaking practically, it may be called) the interest of every individual as nearly as possible in harmony with the interest of the whole; and, secondly, that education and opinion, which have so vast a power over human character, should so use that power as to establish in the mind of every individual an indissoluble association between his own happiness and the good of the whole,—especially between his own happiness, and the practice of such modes of conduct, negative and positive, as regard for the universal happiness prescribes,—so that not only he may be unable to conceive the possibility of happiness to himself, consistently with conduct opposed to the general good, but also that a direct impulse to promote the general good may be in every individual one of the habitual motives of action, and the sentiments connected therewith may fill a large and prominent place in every human being's sentient existence. If the impugners of the utilitarian morality represented it to their own minds in this its true character, I know not what recommendation possessed by any other morality they could possibly affirm to be wanting to it; what more beautiful or more exalted developments of human nature any other ethical system can be supposed to foster; or what springs of action, not accessible to the utilitarian, such systems rely on for giving effect to their mandates.

THOMAS HARDY

From *Jude the Obscure* (1895)

Physically and intellectually attracted, Jude Fawley and Sue Bridehead decide to live as husband and wife after withdrawing from unhappy marriages: he, to the barmaid Arabella Donn; she, to the schoolmaster Phillotson. Their gloomy eldest child, referred to here simply as 'the boy', is actually the son of Jude and Arabella. In this scene, Jude and Sue have been forced to seek separate lodgings because Sue has impulsively revealed to their innkeeper that they were married, but not to each other.

The failure to find another lodging, and the lack of room in this house for his father, had made a deep impression on the boy;—a brooding undemonstrative horror seemed to have seized upon him. The silence was broken by his saying: 'Mother, *what* shall we do to-morrow!'

'I don't know!' said Sue despondently. 'I am afraid this will trouble your father.'

'I wish father was quite well, and there had been room for him! Then it wouldn't matter so much! Poor father!'

'It wouldn't!'

'Can I do anything?'

'No! All is trouble, adversity and suffering!'

'Father went away to give us children room, didn't he?'

'Partly.'

'It would be better to be out o' the world than in it, wouldn't it?'

'It would almost, dear.'

' 'Tis because of us children, too, isn't it, that you can't get a good lodging?'

'Well—people do object to children sometimes.'

'Then if children make so much trouble, why do people have 'em?'

'O—because it is a law of nature.'

'But we don't ask to be born?'

'No indeed.'

'And what makes it worse with me is that you are not my real mother, and you needn't have had me unless you liked. I oughtn't to have come to 'ee—that's the real truth! I troubled 'em in Australia, and I trouble folk here. I wish I hadn't been born!'

'You couldn't help it, my dear.'

'I think that whenever children be born that are not wanted they should be killed directly, before their souls come to 'em, and not allowed to grow big and walk about!'

Sue did not reply. She was doubtfully pondering how to treat this too reflective child.

She at last concluded that, so far as circumstances permitted, she would be honest and candid with one who entered into her difficulties like an aged friend.

'There is going to be another in our family soon,' she hesitatingly remarked.

'How?'

'There is going to be another baby.'

'What!' The boy jumped up wildly. 'O God, mother, you've never a-sent for another; and such trouble with what you've got!'

'Yes, I have, I am sorry to say!' murmured Sue, her eyes glistening with suspended tears.

The boy burst out weeping. 'O you don't care, you don't care!' he cried in bitter reproach. 'How *ever* could you, mother, be so wicked and cruel as this, when you needn't have done it till we was better off, and father well!—To bring us all into *more* trouble! No room for us, and father a-forced to go away, and we turned out to-morrow; and yet you be going to have another of us soon! . . . 'Tis done o' purpose!—'tis—'tis!' He walked up and down sobbing.

'Y-you must forgive me, little Jude!' she pleaded, her bosom heaving now as much as the boy's. 'I can't explain—I will when you are older. It does seem—as if I had done it on purpose, now we are in these difficulties! I can't explain, dear! But it—is not quite on purpose—I can't help it!'

'Yes it is—it must be! For nobody would interfere with us, like that, unless you agreed! I won't forgive you, ever, ever! I'll never believe you care for me, or father, or any of us any more!'

He got up, and went away into the closet adjoining her room, in which a bed had been spread on the floor. There she heard him say: 'If we children was gone there'd be no trouble at all!'

'Don't think that, dear,' she cried, rather peremptorily. 'But go to sleep!'

The following morning she awoke at a little past six, and decided to get up and run across before breakfast to the inn which Jude had informed her to be his quarters, to tell him what had happened before he went out. She arose softly, to avoid disturbing the children, who, as she knew, must be fatigued by their exertions of yesterday. . . .

She joined Jude in a hasty meal, and in a quarter of an hour they started together, resolving to clear out from Sue's too respectable lodging immediately. On reaching the place and going upstairs she found that all was quiet in the children's room, and called to the landlady in timorous tones to please bring up the tea-kettle and something for their breakfast. This was perfunctorily done, and producing a couple of eggs which she had brought with her she put them into the boiling kettle, and summoned Jude to watch them for the youngsters, while she went to call them, it being now half-past eight o'clock.

Jude stood bending over the kettle, with his watch in his hand, timing the eggs, so that his back was turned to the little inner chamber where the children lay. A shriek from Sue suddenly caused him to start round. He saw that the door of the room, or rather closet—which had seemed to go heavily upon its hinges as she pushed it back—was open, and that Sue had sunk to the floor just within it. Hastening forward to pick her up he turned his eyes to the little bed spread on the boards; no children were there. He looked in bewilderment round the room. At the back of the door were fixed two hooks for hanging garments, and from these the forms of the two youngest children were suspended, by a piece of box-cord round each of their necks, while from a nail a few yards off the body of little Jude was hanging in a like manner. An overturned chair was near the elder boy, and his glazed eyes were staring into the room; but those of the girl and the baby boy were closed.

Half paralysed by the sudden and hideous horror of the scene he let Sue lie, cut the cords with his pocket-knife and threw the three children on the bed; but the feel of their bodies in the momentary handling seemed to say that they were dead. He caught up Sue, who was in fainting fits, and put her on the bed in the other room, after which he breathlessly summoned the landlady and ran out for a doctor.

When he got back Sue had come to herself, and the two helpless women, bending over the children in wild efforts to restore them, and the triplet of little corpses, formed a scene which overthrew his self-command. The nearest surgeon came in, but, as Jude had inferred, his presence was superfluous. The children were past saving, for though their bodies were still barely cold it was conjectured that they had been hanging more than an hour. The probability held by the parents later on, when they were able to reason on the case, was that the elder boy, on waking, looked into the outer room for Sue, and, finding her absent, was thrown into a fit of aggravated despondency that the events and information of the evening before had induced in his morbid temperament. Moreover a piece of paper was found upon the floor, on which was written, in the boy's hand, with the bit of lead pencil that he carried:

'Done because we are too menny.'

Race Science

ROBERT KNOX

From *The Races of Men* (1850)

Knox began his career as an anatomist, lecturing at the University of Edinburgh in the late 1820s. He left his position after his name was linked to a scandal involving the source of cadavers for medical students' dissections. He supported himself by writing and translating anatomy texts before turning to studies of race in the late 1840s. Knox approached race as an anatomist, conceiving of racial characteristics as inborn and permanent. In the 1840s many prominent comparative anatomists were establishing museums of all known specimens. Knox followed suit by collecting the skulls of members of different races. This practice later became central to nineteenth-century anthropology. See Nancy Stepan, *The Idea of Race in Science: Great Britain, 1800–1960* (Hamden, Conn.: Archon, 1982).

Since the earliest times, then, the dark races have been the slaves of their fairer brethren. Now, how is this? Mr Gibbon* solves the question in his usual dogmatic way; he speaks of the obvious physical inferiority of the Negro; he means, no doubt, the dark races generally, for the remark applies to all. But, notwithstanding the contrary opinion professed by Dr Tiedemann* respecting the great size of some African skulls, which he found in my own museum, sent to me from the western coast of Africa, I feel disposed to think that there must be a physical and, consequently, a psychological inferiority in the dark races generally. This may not depend altogether on deficiency in the size of the brain *en masse*, nor on any partial defects; to which, however, I shall advert presently; but rather, perhaps, to specific characters in the quality of the brain itself. It may, perhaps, be right to consider first the different obvious physical qualities of the dark races, before we enter on the history of their position as regards the mass of mankind, and especially as regards those races which seem destined, if not to destroy them altogether, at least to limit their position to those regions of the earth where the fair races can neither labour nor live—the equatorial regions and the regions adjoining the tropics, usually termed by romancists and travellers, and not unfairly, the grave of Europeans.

First, as regards mere physical strength, the dark races are generally much inferior to the Saxon and Celt; the bracelets worn by the Kaffirs,* when placed on our own arms, prove this. Secondly, in size of brain they seem also considerably inferior to the above races, and no doubt also to the Sarmatian* and the Slavonic. Thirdly, the form of the skull differs from ours, and is placed differently on the neck; the texture of the brain is I think generally darker, and the white part more strongly fibrous; but I speak from extremely limited experience. Mr Tiedemann, I think it is, who says that the convolutions of the upper surface of the two hemispheres of the brain are nearly symmetrical; in our brain the reverse always happens. Lastly, the whole shape of the skeleton differs from ours, and so also I find do the forms of almost every muscle of the body. The upper jaw is uniformly of extraordinary size, and this, together with a peculiarity in the setting on of the face, I find to constitute the most striking differences. I at one time thought that the bones of the nose were peculiar in some races, as in the Bosjeman and Hottentot.* In these races, or race, for perhaps they are but one, I fancied that, more frequently at least than in others, the bones of the nose are remark-ably narrow, run together to form but one bone, and show even an additional thin germ mesially;* perhaps merely the anterior margin of another bone, or an extension of the spine of the frontal. Still the specimens are so few in Europe, that I feel disinclined to attach much importance to this sufficiently singular fact. I think I have seen one of the nasal bones so short and thin as not to reach the frontal.

In the Peruvian skull, at twelve years of age, Von Tchudi* thinks he has detected a new germ of bone, an interparietal bone,* in fact, peculiar to the native American race; the physical differences in the structure of the Boschjiee women* and Hottentots are unmistakeable. Still be it remembered that we have no accurate account of the structural differences of the races of *men* on which we can depend— mere scraps of observations scarcely worthy of notice. The Negro muscles are differently shaped from ours; the curly, corkscrew locks of the Hottentot bear no resemblance to the lank, black hair of the Esquimaux. The Tasmanian and Australian races are said to show many peculiarities in structure.

Let it be remembered, however, that, after all, it is to the exterior we must look for the more remarkable characteristics of animals; it is it alone which nature loves to decorate and to vary: the interior organs of animals, not far removed from each other, vary but little. To this fact I shall advert more particularly in the lecture on tran-scendental anatomy,* the internal structures of animals present details which we read imperfectly, connected as they are, on the one hand, with mechanical arrangements, and on the other with the primitive laws of creation.

There is one thing obvious in the history of the dark races, that they all, more or less, exhibit the outline of the interior more strongly marked than in the fair races generally. Thus the face of the adult Negro or Hottentot resembles, from the want of flesh, a skeleton, over which has been drawn a blackened skin.

But who are the dark races of ancient and modern times? It would not be easy to answer this question. Were the Copts* a dark race? Are the Jews a dark race? The Gipsies? The Chinese, &c.? Dark they are to a certain extent; so are all the Mongol tribes—the American Indian and Esquimaux—the inhabitants of nearly all Africa—of the East—of Australia. What a field of extermination lies before the Saxon Celtic and Sarmatian races! The Saxon will not mingle with any dark race, nor will he allow him to hold an acre of land in the country occupied by him; this, at least, is the law of Anglo-Saxon America. The fate, then, of the Mexicans, Peruvians, and Chilians, is in no shape doubtful. Extinction of the race—sure extinction—it is not even denied.

Already, in a few years, we have cleared Van Diemen's Land* of every *human* aboriginal; Australia, of course, follows, and New Zealand next; there is no denying the fact, that the Saxon, call him by what name you will, has a perfect horror for his darker brethren. Hence the folly of the war carried on by the philanthropists of Britain against nature: of these persons some are honest, some not. I venture to recommend the honest ones—to try their strength in a practical measure. Let them demand for the natives of Hindostan, of Ceylon, or even of the Cape or New Zealand, the privileges and rights wholly and fairly of Britons; I predict a refusal on the part of the Colonial-office. The office will appoint you as many aborigines protectors as you like—that is, spies; but the extension of equal rights and privileges to all colours is quite another question.

SIR FRANCIS GALTON

From *Inquiries into Human Faculty and Its Development* (1883)

SELECTION AND RACE

The fact of an individual being naturally gifted with high qualities, may be due either to his being an exceptionally good specimen of a poor race, or an average specimen of a high one. The difference of origin would betray itself in his descendants; they would revert towards the typical centre of their race, deteriorating in the first case but not in the second. The two cases, though theoretically distinct, are confused in reality, owing to the frequency with which exceptional personal qualities connote the departure of the entire nature of the individual from his ancestral type, and the formation of a new strain having its own typical centre. It is hardly necessary to add that it is in this indirect way that natural selection improves a race. The two events of selection and difference of race ought, however, to be carefully distinguished in broad practical considerations, while the frequency of their concurrence is borne in mind and allowed for.

So long as the race remains radically the same, the stringent selection of the best specimens to rear and breed from, can never lead to any permanent result. The attempt to raise the standard of such a race is like the labour of Sisyphus* in rolling his stone uphill; let the effort be relaxed for a moment, and the stone will roll back. Whenever a new typical centre appears, it is as though there was a facet upon the lower surface of the stone, on which it is capable of resting without rolling back. It affords a temporary sticking point in the forward progress of evolution. . . .

Whenever a low race is preserved under conditions of life that exact a high level of efficiency, it must be subjected to rigorous selection. The few best specimens of that race can alone be allowed to become parents, and not many of their descendants can be allowed to live. On the other hand, if a higher race be substituted for the low one, all this terrible misery disappears. The most merciful form of what I ventured to call 'eugenics' would consist in watching for the indications of superior strains or races, and in so favouring them that their progeny shall outnumber and gradually replace that of the old one. Such strains are of no infrequent occurrence. It is easy to specify families who are characterised by strong resemblances, and whose features and character are usually prepotent over those of their wives or husbands in their joint offspring, and who are at the same time as prolific as the average of their class. These strains can be conveniently studied in the families of exiles, which, for obvious reasons, are easy to trace in their various branches.

The debt that most countries owe to the race of men whom they received from one another as immigrants, whether leaving their native country of their own free will, or as exiles on political or religious grounds, has been often pointed out, and may, I think, be accounted for as follows:—The fact of a man leaving his compatriots, or so irritating them that they compel him to go, is fair evidence that either he or they, or both, feel that his character is alien to theirs. Exiles are also on the whole men of considerable force of character; a quiet man would endure and succumb, he would not have energy to transplant himself or to become so conspicuous as to be an object of general attack. We may justly infer from this, that exiles are on the whole men of exceptional and energetic natures, and it is especially from such men as these that new strains of race are likely to proceed.

INFLUENCE OF MAN UPON RACE

The influence of man upon the nature of his own race has already been very large, but it has not been intelligently directed, and has in many instances done great harm. Its action has been by invasions and migration of races, by war and massacre, by wholesale deportation of population, by emigration, and by many social customs which have a silent but widespread effect.

There exists a sentiment, for the most part quite unreasonable, against the gradual extinction of an inferior race. It rests on some confusion between the race and the individual, as if the destruction of a race was equivalent to the destruction of a large number of men. It is nothing of the kind when the process of extinction works silently and slowly through the earlier marriage of members of the superior race, through their greater vitality under equal stress, through their better chances of getting a livelihood, or through their prepotency in mixed marriages. That the members of an inferior class should dislike being elbowed out of the way is another matter; but it may be somewhat brutally argued that whenever two individuals struggle for a single place, one must yield, and that there will be no more unhappiness on the whole, if the inferior yield to the superior than conversely, whereas the world will be permanently enriched by the success of the superior. The conditions of happiness are, however, too complex to be disposed of by *à priori* argument, it is safest to appeal to observation. I think it could be easily shown that when the differences between the races is not so great as to divide them into obviously different classes, and where their language, education, and general interests are the same, the substitution may take place gradually without any unhappiness. Thus the movements of commerce have introduced fresh and vigorous blood into various parts of England, the new-comers have intermarried with the residents, and their characteristics have been prepotent in the descendants of the mixed marriages. I have referred in the earlier part of the book to the changes of type in the English nature that have occurred during the last few hundred years. These have been effected so silently that we only know of them by the results. . . .

EARLY AND LATE MARRIAGES

It is important to obtain a just idea of the relative effects of early and late marriages. I attempted this in *Hereditary Genius*,* but I think the following is a better estimate. We are unhappily still deficient in collected data as regards the fertility of the upper and middle classes at different ages; but the facts collected by Dr Matthews Duncan* as regards the lower orders will serve our purpose approximately, by furnishing the required *ratios*, though not the absolute values. The following are his results, from returns kept at the Lying-in Hospital of St Georges-in-the-East:—

Age of Mother at her Marriage	Average Fertility
15–19	9.12
20–24	7.92
25–29	6.30
30–34	4.60

The meaning of this Table will be more clearly grasped after a little modification of its contents. We may consider the fertility of each group to refer to the medium age of that group, as by writing 17 instead of 15–19, and we may slightly smooth the figures, then we have

Age of Mother at her Marriage	Approximate average Fertility
17	$9.00 = 6 \times 1.5$
22	$7.50 = 5 \times 1.5$
27	$6.00 = 4 \times 1.5$
32	$4.50 = 3 \times 1.5$

which shows that the relative fertility of mothers married at the ages of 17, 22, 27, and 32 respectively is as 6, 5, 4, and 3 approximately.

The increase in population by a habit of early marriages is further augmented by the greater rapidity with which the generations follow each other. By the joint effect of these two causes, a large effect is in time produced.

Let us compute a single example. Taking a group of 100 mothers married at the age of 20, whom we will designate as A, and another group of 100 mothers married at the age of 29, whom we will call B, we shall find by interpolation that the fertility of A and B respectively would be about 8.2 and 5.4. We need not, however, regard their absolute fertility, which would differ in different classes of society, but will only consider their relative production of such female children as may live and become mothers, and we will suppose the number of such descendants in the first generation to be the same as that of the A and B mothers together—namely, 200. Then the number of such children in the A and B classes respectively, being in the proportion of 8.2 to 5.4, will be 115 and 85.

We have next to determine the average lengths of the A and B generations, which may be roughly done by basing it on the usual estimate of an average generation, irrespectively of sex, at a third of a century, or say of an average female generation at 31.5 years. We will further take 20 years as being 4.5 years earlier than the average time of marriage, and 29 years as 4.5 years later than it, so that the length of each generation of the A group will be 27 years, and that of the B group will be 36 years. All these suppositions appear to be perfectly fair and reasonable, while it may easily be shown that any other suppositions within the bounds of probability would lead to results of the same general order.

The least common multiple of 27 and 36 is 108, at the end of which term of years A will have been multiplied four times over by the factor 1.5, and B three times over by the factor 0.85. The results are given in the Table (opposite). The general result is that the group B gradually disappears, and the group A more than supplants it. Hence if the races best fitted to occupy the land are encouraged to marry early, they will breed down the others in a very few generations.

	A	B
	Number of Female Descendants who themselves become Mothers	
After Number of Years as below	*Of 100 Mothers whose Marriages and those of their Daughters all take place at the Age of 20 Years*	*Of 100 Mothers whose Marriages and those of their Daughters all take place at the Age of 29 Years*
	(Ratio of Increase in each successive Generation being 1.15)	*(Ratio of Decrease in each successive Generation being 0.85)*
108	175	61
216	299	38
324	535	23

ARTHUR CONAN DOYLE

The Yellow Face (1894)

In the first part of the story, the desperate Mr Grant Munro has come to Sherlock Holmes, asking him to account for his wife's strange behaviour. Effie, Munro's wife of three years, has asked him for £100 of the money she brought to the marriage. She has been making unexplained visits to a nearby cottage at whose window an unnaturally white face sometimes appears.

'I am afraid that this is a bad business, Watson,' said my companion, as he returned after accompanying Mr Grant Munro to the door. 'What do you make of it?'

'It has an ugly sound,' I answered.

'Yes. There's blackmail in it, or I am much mistaken.'

'And who is the blackmailer?'

'Well, it must be this creature who lives in the only comfortable room in the place, and has her photograph above his fireplace. Upon my word, Watson, there's something very attractive about that livid face at the window, and I would not have missed the case for worlds.'

'You have a theory?'

'Yes, a provisional one. But I shall be surprised if it does not turn out to be correct. This woman's first husband is in that cottage.'

'Why do you think so?'

'How else can we explain her frenzied anxiety that her second one should not enter it? The facts, as I read them, are something like this: This woman was married in America. Her husband developed some hateful qualities, or, shall we say, that he contracted some loathsome disease, and became a leper or an imbecile. She fled from him at last, returned to England, changed her name, and started her life, as she thought, afresh. She had been married three years, and believed that her position was quite secure—having shown her husband the death certificate of some man whose name she had assumed—when suddenly her whereabouts was discovered by her first husband, or, we may suppose, by some unscrupulous woman, who had attached herself to the invalid. They write to the wife and threaten to come and expose her. She asks for a hundred pounds and endeavours to buy them off. They come in spite of it, and when the husband mentions casually to the wife that there are new-comers in the cottage, she knows in some way that they are her pursuers. She waits until her husband is asleep, and then she rushes down to endeavour to persuade them to leave her in peace. Having no success, she goes again next morning, and her husband meets her, as he has told us, as she came out. She promises him then not to go there again, but two days afterwards, the hope of getting rid of those dreadful neighbours is too strong for her, and she makes another attempt, taking down with her the photograph which had probably been demanded from her. In the midst of this interview the maid rushes in to say that the master has come home, on which the wife, knowing that he would come straight down to the cottage, hurries the inmates out at the back door, into that grove of fir trees probably which was mentioned as standing near. In this way he finds the place deserted. I shall be very much surprised, however, if it is still so when he reconnoitres it this evening. What do you think of my theory?'

'It is all surmise.'

'But at least it covers all the facts. When new facts come to our knowledge which cannot be covered by it, it will be time enough to reconsider it. At present we can do nothing until we have a fresh message from our friend at Norbury.'

But we had not very long to wait. It came just as we had finished our tea. 'The cottage is still tenanted,' it said. 'Have seen the face again at the window. I'll meet the seven o'clock train, and take no steps until you arrive.'

He was waiting on the platform when we stepped out, and we could see in the light of the station lamps that he was very pale, and quivering with agitation.

'They are still there, Mr Holmes,' said he, laying his hand upon my friend's sleeve. 'I saw lights in the cottage as I came down. We shall settle it now, once and for all.'

'What is your plan, then?' asked Holmes, as we walked down the dark, tree-lined road.

'I am going to force my way in and see for myself who is in the house. I wish you both to be there as witnesses.'

'You are quite determined to do this, in spite of your wife's warning that it is better that you should not solve the mystery?'

'Yes, I am determined.'

'Well, I think that you are in the right. Any truth is better than indefinite doubt. We had better go up at once. Of course, legally we are putting ourselves hopelessly in the wrong, but I think that it is worth it.'

It was a very dark night, and a thin rain began to fall as we turned from the high road into a narrow lane, deeply rutted, with hedges on either side. Mr Grant Munro pushed impatiently forward, however, and we stumbled after him as best we could.

'There are the lights of my house,' he murmured, pointing to a glimmer among the trees, 'and here is the cottage which I am going to enter.'

We turned a corner in the lane as he spoke, and there was the building close beside us. A yellow bar falling across the black foreground showed that the door was not quite closed, and one window in the upper story was brightly illuminated. As we looked we saw a dark blurr moving across the blind.

'There is that creature,' cried Grant Munro; 'you can see for yourselves that someone is there. Now follow me, and we shall soon know all.'

We approached the door, but suddenly a woman appeared out of the shadow and stood in the golden track of the lamp-light. I could not see her face in the darkness, but her arms were thrown out in an attitude of entreaty.

'For God's sake, don't, Jack!' she cried. 'I had a presentiment that you would come this evening. Think better of it, dear! Trust me again, and you will never have cause to regret it.'

'I have trusted you too long, Effie!' he cried, sternly. 'Leave go of me! I must pass you. My friends and I are going to settle this matter once and for ever.' He pushed her to one side and we followed closely after him. As he threw the door open an elderly woman ran out in front of him and tried to bar his passage, but he thrust her back, and an instant afterwards we were all upon the stairs. Grant Munro rushed into the lighted room at the top, and we entered it at his heels.

It was a cosy, well-furnished apartment, with two candles burning upon the table and two upon the mantelpiece. In the corner, stooping over a desk, there sat what appeared to be a little girl. Her face was turned away as we entered, but we could see that she was dressed in a red frock, and that she had long white gloves on. As she whisked round to us I gave a cry of surprise and horror. The face which she turned towards us was of the strangest livid tint, and the features were absolutely devoid of any expression. An instant later the mystery was explained. Holmes, with a laugh, passed his hand behind the child's ear, a mask peeled off from her countenance, and there was a little coal-black negress with all her white teeth flashing in amusement at our amazed faces. I burst out laughing out of sympathy with her merriment, but Grant Munro stood staring, with his hand clutching at his throat.

'My God!' he cried, 'what can be the meaning of this?'

'I will tell you the meaning of it,' cried the lady, sweeping into the room with a proud, set face. 'You have forced me against my own judgment to tell you, and now we must both make the best of it. My husband died at Atlanta. My child survived.'

'Your child!'

She drew a large silver locket from her bosom. 'You have never seen this open.'

'I understood that it did not open.'

She touched a spring, and the front hinged back. There was a portrait within of a man, strikingly handsome and intelligent, but bearing unmistakable signs upon his features of his African descent.

'That is John Hebron, of Atlanta,' said the lady, 'and a nobler man never walked the earth. I cut myself off from my race in order to wed him; but never once while he lived did I for one instant regret it. It was our misfortune that our only child took after his people rather than mine. It is often so in such matches, and little Lucy is darker far than ever her father was. But, dark or fair, she is my own dear little girlie, and her mother's pet.' The little creature ran across at the words and nestled up against the lady's dress.

'When I left her in America,' she continued, 'it was only because her health was weak, and the change might have done her harm. She was given to the care of a faithful Scotchwoman who had once been our servant. Never for an instant did I dream of disowning her as my child. But when chance threw you in my way, Jack, and I learned to love you, I feared to tell you about my child. God forgive me, I feared that I should lose you, and I had not the courage to tell you. I had to choose between you, and in my weakness I turned away from my own little girl. For three years I have kept her existence a secret from you, but I heard from the nurse, and I knew that all was well with her. At last, however, there came an overwhelming desire to see the child once more. I struggled against it, but in vain. Though I knew the danger, I determined to have the child over, if it were but for a few weeks. I sent a hundred pounds to the nurse, and I gave her instructions about this cottage, so that she might come as a neighbour without my appearing to be in any way connected with her. I pushed my precautions so far as to order her to keep the child in the house during the daytime, and to cover up her little face and hands, so that even those who might see her at the window should not gossip about there being a black child in the neighbourhood. If I had been less cautious I might have been more wise, but I was half crazy with fear lest you should learn the truth.

'It was you who told me first that the cottage was occupied. I should have waited for the morning, but I could not sleep for excitement, and so at last I slipped out, knowing how difficult it is to awaken you. But you saw me go, and that was the beginning of my troubles. Next day you had my secret at your mercy, but you nobly refrained from pursuing your advantage. Three days later, however, the nurse and child only just escaped from the back door as you rushed in at the front one. And now to-night you at last know all, and I ask you what is to become of us, my child and me?' She clasped her hands and waited for an answer.

It was a long two minutes before Grant Munro broke the silence, and when his answer came it was one of which I love to think. He lifted the little child, kissed her, and then, still carrying her, he held his other hand out to his wife and turned towards the door.

'We can talk it over more comfortably at home,' said he. 'I am not a very good man, Effie, but I think I am a better one than you have given me credit for being.'

Holmes and I followed them down to the lane, and my friend plucked at my sleeve as we came out. 'I think,' said he, 'that we shall be of more use in London than in Norbury.'

Not another word did he say of the case until late that night when he was turning away, with his lighted candle, for his bedroom.

'Watson,' said he, 'if it should ever strike you that I am getting a little over-confident in my powers, or giving less pains to a case than it deserves, kindly whisper "Norbury" in my ear, and I shall be infinitely obliged to you.'

Urban Poverty

FRIEDRICH ENGELS

From *The Condition of the Working Class in England* (1845)

Manchester lies at the foot of the southern slope of a range of hills, which stretch hither from Oldham, their last peak Kersall-moor, being at once the race-course and the Mons Sacer* of Manchester. Manchester proper lies on the left bank of the Irwell, between that stream and the two smaller ones, the Irk and the Medlock, which here empty into the Irwell. On the left bank of the Irwell, bounded by a sharp curve of the river, lies Salford, and further westward Pendleton; northward from the Irwell lie Upper and Lower Broughton, northward of the Irk, Cheetham Hill; south of the Medlock lies Hulme, further east Chorlton on Medlock; still further, pretty well to the east of Manchester, Ardwick. The whole assemblage of buildings is commonly called Manchester, and contains about four hundred thousand inhabitants, rather more than less. The town itself is peculiarly built, so that a person may live in it for years, and go in and out daily without coming into contact with a working people's quarter or even with workers, that is, so long as he confines himself to his business or to pleasure walks. This arises chiefly from the fact, that by unconscious tacit agreement as well as with out-spoken conscious determination, the working people's quarters are sharply separated from the sections of the city reserved for the middle class; or if this does not succeed, they are concealed with the cloak of charity. Manchester contains, at its heart, a rather extended commercial district, perhaps half a mile long and about as broad, and consisting almost wholly of offices and warehouses. Nearly the whole district is abandoned by dwellers and is lonely and deserted at night; only watchmen and policemen traverse its narrow lanes with their dark lanterns. This district is cut through by certain main thorough-fares upon which the vast traffic concentrates, and in which the ground level is lined with brilliant shops. In these streets the upper floors are occupied, here and there, and there is a good deal of life upon them until late at night. With the exception of this commercial district, all Manchester proper, all Salford and Hulme, a great part of Pendleton and Chorlton, two-thirds of Ardwick, and single stretches of Cheetham Hill and Broughton are all unmixed working people's quarters, stretching like a girdle averaging a mile and a half in breadth, around the commercial district. Outside, beyond this girdle, lives the upper and middle bourgeoisie, the middle bourgeoisie in regularly laid out streets in the vicinity of the working quarters, especially in Chorlton and the lower lying portions of Cheetham Hill, the upper bourgeoisie in remoter villas with gardens in Chorl-ton and Ardwick, or on the breezy heights of Cheetham Hill, Broughton and Pendleton, in free, wholesome country air, in fine comfortable homes, passed once every half or quarter hour by omni-buses going into the city. And the finest part of the arrangement is this, that the members of this money aristocracy can take the short-est road through the middle of all the labouring districts to their places of business, without ever seeing that they are in the midst of the grimy misery that lurks to the right and the left. For the thoroughfares leading from the Exchange in all directions out of the city are lined, on both sides with an almost unbroken series of shops,

and are so kept in the hands of the middle and lower bourgeoisie,
which, out of self-interest, cares for a decent and cleanly external
appearance and *can* care for it. True, these shops bear some relation
to the districts which lie behind them and are more elegant in the
commercial and residential quarters than when they hide grimy
workingmen's dwellings; but they suffice to conceal from the eyes of
the wealthy men and women of strong stomachs and weak nerves the
misery and grime which form the complement of their wealth. So,
for instance, Deansgate, which leads from the old church directly
southward, is lined first with mills and warehouses, then with
second-rate shops and alehouses; further south, when it leaves the
commercial district, with less inviting shops, which grow dirtier and
more interrupted by alehouses and gin palaces the farther one goes,
until at the southern end the appearance of the shops leaves no doubt
that workers and workers only are their customers. So Market Street
running southeast from the Exchange; at first brilliant shops of the
best sort with counting houses or warehouses above; in the
continuation, Piccadilly, immense hotels and warehouses; in the farther continuation, London Road, in the neighbourhood of the Medlock, factories, alehouses, shops for the humbler bourgeoisie and the
working population, and from this point onward, great gardens and
country seats of the wealthier merchants and manufacturers. In this
way any one who knows Manchester can infer the adjoining districts,
from the appearance of the thoroughfare, but one is seldom in a
position to catch from the street a glimpse of the real labouring
districts. I know very well that this hypocritical plan is more or less
common to all great cities; I know, too, that the retail dealers are
forced by the nature of their business to take possession of the
great highways; I know that there are more good buildings than
bad ones upon such streets everywhere, and that the value of land
is greater near them than in remoter districts; but at the same
time I have never seen so systematic a shutting out of the working
class from the thoroughfares, so tender a concealment of everything which might affront the eye and the nerves of the bourgeoisie, as in Manchester. And yet, in other respects, Manchester
is less built according to a plan, after official regulations, is more
an outgrowth of accident, than any other city; and when I consider in this connection the eager assurances of the middle class,
that the working class is doing famously, I cannot help feeling that

the liberal manufacturers, the 'Big Whigs' of Manchester are not so innocent, after all, in the matter of this sensitive method of construction. . . .

At the bottom flows, or rather stagnates the Irk, a narrow, coal-black, foul-smelling stream, full of débris and refuse which it deposits on the shallower right bank. In dry weather, a long string of the most disgusting blackish-green slime pools are left standing on this bank, from the depths of which bubbles of miasmatic gas* constantly arise and give forth a stench unendurable even on the bridge forty or fifty feet above the surface of the stream. But besides this, the stream itself is checked every few paces by high weirs, behind which slime and refuse accumulate and rot in thick masses. Above the bridge are tanneries, bonemills and gasworks, from which all drains and refuse find their way into the Irk, which receives further the contents of all the neighbouring sewers and privies. It may be easily imagined, therefore, what sort of residue the stream deposits. Below the bridge you look upon the piles of débris, the refuse, filth and offal from the courts on the steep left bank; here each house is packed close behind its neighbour and a piece of each is visible, all black, smoky, crumbling, ancient, with broken panes and window frames. The background is furnished by old barrack-like factory buildings. On the lower right bank stands a long row of houses and mills; the second house being a ruin without a roof, piled with débris; the third stands so low that the lowest floor is uninhabitable, and therefore without windows or doors. Here the background embraces the pauper burial ground, the station of the Liverpool and Leeds railway, and, in the rear of this, the Workhouse, the 'Poor-Law Bastille'* of Manchester, which, like a citadel, looks threateningly down from behind its high walls and parapets on the hill top, upon the working people's quarter below.

Above Ducie Bridge, the left bank grows more flat and the right bank steeper, but the condition of the dwellings on both banks grows worse rather than better. He who turns to the left here from the main street, Long Millgate, is lost; he wanders from one court to another, turns countless corners, passes nothing but narrow, filthy nooks and alleys, until after a few minutes he has lost all clues, and knows not whither to turn. Everywhere half or wholly ruined buildings, some of them actually uninhabited, which means a great deal here; rarely a wooden or stone floor to be seen in the houses, almost uniformly broken, ill-fitting windows and doors, and a state of filth! Everywhere heaps of débris, refuse and offal; standing pools for gutters, and a stench which alone would make it impossible for a human being in any degree civilized to live in such a district. The newly-built extension of the Leeds railway* which crosses the Irk here, has swept away some of these courts and lanes, laying others completely open to view. Immediately under the railway bridge there stands a court, the filth and horrors of which surpass all the others by far, just because it was hitherto so shut off, so secluded that the way to it could not be found without a good deal of trouble. I should never have discovered it myself, without the breaks made by the railway, though I thought I knew this whole region thoroughly. Passing along a rough bank, among stakes and washing-lines, one penetrates into this chaos of small one-storied, one-roomed huts, in most of which there is no artificial floor, kitchen, living and sleeping-room all in one. In such a hole, scarcely five feet long by six broad, I found two beds—and such bedsteads and beds!—which, with a staircase and chimney-place, exactly filled the room. In several others I found absolutely nothing, while the door stood open, and the inhabitants leaned against it. Everywhere before the doors refuse and offal; that any sort of pavement lay underneath could not be seen but only felt, here and there, with the feet. This whole collection of cattle-sheds for human beings was surrounded on two sides by houses and a factory, and on the third by the river, and besides the narrow stair up the bank, a narrow doorway alone led out into another almost equally ill-built, ill-kept labyrinth of dwellings.

Enough! The whole side of the Irk is built in this way, a planless, knotted chaos of houses, more or less on the verge of uninhabitableness, whose unclean interiors fully correspond with their filthy external surroundings. And how could the people be clean with no proper opportunity for satisfying the most natural and ordinary wants? Privies are so rare here that they are either filled up every day, or are too remote for most of the inhabitants to use. How can people wash when they have only the dirty Irk water at hand, while pumps and water pipes can be found in decent parts of the city alone? In truth, it cannot be charged to the account of these helots* of modern society if their dwellings are not more cleanly than the pig-pens which are here and there to be seen among them.

HENRY MAYHEW

From *London Labour and the London Poor* (1851)

OF THE WANDERING TRIBES OF THIS COUNTRY

The nomadic races of England are of many distinct kinds—from the habitual vagrant—half-beggar, half-thief—sleeping in barns, tents, and casual wards—to the mechanic on tramp, obtaining his bed and supper from the trade societies in the different towns, on his way to seek work. Between these two extremes there are several mediate varieties—consisting of pedlars, showmen, harvest-men, and all that large class who live by either selling, showing, or doing something through the country. These are, so to speak, the rural nomads—not confining their wanderings to any one particular locality, but ranging often from one end of the land to the other. Besides these, there are the urban and suburban wanderers, or those who follow some itinerant occupation in and round about the large towns. Such are, in the metropolis more particularly, the pickpockets—the beggars—the prostitutes—the street-sellers—the street-performers—the cabmen—the coachmen—the watermen—the sailors and such like. In each of these classes—according as they partake more or less of the purely vagabond, doing nothing whatsoever for their living, but moving from place to place preying upon the earnings of the more industrious portion of the community, so will the attributes of the nomade tribes be found to be more or less marked in them. Whether it be that in the mere act of wandering, there is a greater determination of blood to the surface of the body, and consequently a less quantity sent to the brain, the muscles being thus nourished at the expense of the mind, I leave physiologists to say. But certainly be the physical cause what it may, we must all allow that in each of the classes above-mentioned, there is a greater development of the animal than of the intellectual or moral nature of man, and that they are all more or less distinguished for their high cheek-bones and protruding jaws—for their use of a slang language—for their lax ideas of property—for their general improvidence—their repugnance to continuous labour—their disregard of female honour—their love of cruelty—their pugnacity—and their utter want of religion. . . .

OF THE LOW LODGING-HOUSES

[*To demonstrate the ill effects of cheap lodging-houses on innocent young people, Mayhew quotes 'a man of superior education and intelligence . . . whom circumstances . . . had reduced from affluence to beggary, so that he was compelled to be a constant resident in those places.'*]

'The influence of the lodging-house society on boys who have run away from their parents, and have got thither, either separately or in company with lads who have joined them in the streets, is this:— Boys there, after paying their lodgings, may exercise the some freedom from every restraint as they see the persons of maturer years enjoy. This is often pleasant to a boy, especially if he has been severely treated by his parents or master; he apes, and often outdoes, all the men's ways, both in swearing and lewd talk, and so he gets a relish for that sort of life. After he has resorted to such places—the sharper boys for three, and the duller for six months—they are adepts at any thieving or vice. Drunkenness, and even moderate drinking, is very rare among them. I seldom or never see the boys drink—indeed, thieves of all ages are generally sober men. Once get to like a lodging-house life, and a boy can hardly be got out of it. I said the other day to a youth, "I wish I could get out of these haunts and never see a lodging-house again;" and he replied, "If I had ever so much money I would never live anywhere else." I have seen the boys in a lodging-house sit together telling stories, but paid no attention to them.'

STATEMENT OF A YOUNG PICKPOCKET

To show the class of characters usually frequenting these lodging houses, I will now give the statement of a boy—a young pickpocket—without shoes or stockings. He wore a ragged, dirty, and very thin great coat, of some dark jean or linen, under which was another thin coat, so arranged that what appeared rents—and, indeed, were rents, but designedly made—in the outer garment, were slits through which the hand readily reached the pockets of the inner garment, and could there deposit any booty. He was a slim, agile lad, with a sharp but not vulgar expression, and small features. His hands were of singular delicacy and beauty. His fingers were very long, and no lady's could have been more taper. A burglar told me that with such a hand he ought to have made his fortune. He was worth 20*l.* a week, he said, as a '*wire*,' that is, a picker of ladies' pockets. When engaged 'for a turn,' as he told me he once was by an old pickpocket, the man looked minutely at his fingers, and approved of them highly. . . . I asked him what he, as a sharp lad, thought was the cause of so many boys becoming vagrant pickpockets? He answered, 'Why, sir, if boys runs away, and has to shelter in low lodging-houses—and many runs away from cruel treatment at home—they meet there with boys such as me, or as bad, and the devil soon lays his hand on them. If there wasn't so many lodging-houses there wouldn't be so many bad boys—there couldn't. Lately a boy came down to Billingsgate, and said he wouldn't stay at home to be knocked about any longer. He said it to some boys like me; and he was asked if he could get anything from his mother, and he said "yes, he could." So he went back, and brought a brooch and some other things with him to a place fixed on, and then he and some of the boys set off for the country; and that's the way boys is trapped. I think the fathers of such boys either ill-treat them, or neglect them; and so they run away. My father used to beat me shocking; so I hated home. I stood hard licking well, and was called "the plucked one."' This boy first stole flowers, currants, and gooseberries out of the clergyman's garden, more by way of bravado, and to ensure the approbation of his comrades, than for anything else. He answered readily to my inquiry, as to what he thought would become of him?—'Transportation.* If a boy has great luck he may carry on for eight years. Three or four years is the common run, but transportation is what he's sure to come to in the end.' This lad picked my pocket at my request, and so dexterously did he do his 'work,' that though I was alive to what he was trying to do, it was impossible for me to detect the least movement of my coat. To see him pick the pockets, as he did, of some of the gentlemen who were present on the occasion, was a curious sight. He crept behind much like a cat with his claws out, and while in the act held his breath with suspense; but immediately the handkerchief was safe in his hand, the change in the expression of his countenance was most marked. He then seemed almost to be convulsed with delight at the success of his perilous adventure, and, turning his back, held up the handkerchief to discover the value of his prize, with intense glee evident in every feature.

ELIZABETH GASKELL

From *North and South* (1855)

The side of the town on which Crampton* lay was especially a thoroughfare for the factory people. In the back streets around them there were many mills, out of which poured streams of men and women two or three times a day. Until Margaret had learnt the times of their ingress and egress, she was very unfortunate in constantly falling in with them. They came rushing along, with bold, fearless faces, and loud laughs and jests, particularly aimed at all those who appeared to be above them in rank or station. The tones of their unrestrained voices, and their carelessness of all common rules of street politeness, frightened Margaret a little at first. The girls, with their rough, but not unfriendly freedom, would comment on her dress, even touch her shawl or gown to ascertain the exact material; nay, once or twice she was asked questions relative to some article which they particularly admired. There was such a simple reliance on her womanly sympathy with their love of dress, and on her kindliness, that she gladly replied to these inquiries, as soon as she understood them; and half smiled back at their remarks. She did not mind meeting any number of girls, loud spoken and boisterous though they might be. But she alternately dreaded and fired up against the workmen, who commented not on her dress, but on her looks, in the same open fearless manner. She, who had hitherto felt that even the most refined remark on her personal appearance was an impertinence, had to endure undisguised admiration from these outspoken men. But the very out-spokenness marked their innocence of any intention to hurt her delicacy, as she would have perceived if she had been less frightened by the disorderly tumult. Out of her fright came a flash of indignation which made her face scarlet, and her dark eyes gather flame, as she heard some of their speeches. Yet there were other sayings of theirs, which, when she reached the quiet safety of home, amused her even while they irritated her.

For instance, one day, after she had passed a number of men, several of whom had paid her the not unusual compliment of wishing she was their sweetheart, one of the lingerers added, 'Your bonny face, my lass, makes the day look brighter.' And another day, as she was unconsciously smiling at some passing thought, she was addressed by a poorly-dressed, middle-aged workman, with 'You may well smile, my lass; many a one would smile to have such a bonny face.' This man looked so careworn that Margaret could not help giving him an answering smile, glad to think that her looks, such as they were, should have had the power to call up a pleasant thought. He seemed to understand her acknowledging glance, and a silent recognition was established between them whenever the chances of the day brought them across each other's paths. They had never exchanged a word; nothing had been said but that first compliment; yet somehow Margaret looked upon this man with more interest than upon any one else in Milton.* Once or twice, on Sundays, she saw him walking with a girl, evidently his daughter, and, if possible, still more unhealthy than he was himself.

One day Margaret and her father had been as far as the fields that lay around the town; it was early spring, and she had gathered some of the hedge and ditch flowers, dog-violets, lesser celandines, and the like, with an unspoken lament in her heart for the sweet profusion of the South. Her father had left her to go into Milton upon some business; and on the road home she met her humble friends. The girl looked wistfully at the flowers, and, acting on a sudden impulse, Margaret offered them to her. Her pale blue eyes lightened up as she took them, and her father spoke for her.

'Thank yo, Miss. Bessy 'll think a deal o' them flowers; that hoo will; and I shall think a deal o' yor kindness. Yo're not of this country, I reckon?'

'No!' said Margaret, half sighing. 'I come from the South—from Hampshire,' she continued, a little afraid of wounding his consciousness of ignorance, if she used a name which he did not understand.

'That's beyond London, I reckon? And I come fro' Burnley-ways, and forty mile to th' North, And yet, yo see, North and South has both met and made kind o'friends in this big smoky place.'

Margaret had slackened her pace to walk alongside of the man and his daughter, whose steps were regulated by the feebleness of the latter. She now spoke to the girl, and there was a sound of tender pity in the tone of her voice as she did so that went right to the heart of the father.

'I'm afraid you are not very strong.'

'No,' said the girl, 'nor never will be.'

'Spring is coming,' said Margaret, as if to suggest pleasant, hopeful thoughts.

'Spring nor summer will do me good,' said the girl quietly.

Margaret looked up at the man, almost expecting some contradiction from him, or at least some remark that would modify his daughter's utter hopelessness. But, instead, he added—

'I'm afeared hoo speaks truth. I'm afeared hoo's too far gone in a waste.'

'I shall have a spring where I'm boun to, and flowers, and amaranths, and shining robes besides.'

'Poor lass, poor lass!' said her father in a low tone. 'I'm none so sure o' that; but it's a comfort to thee, poor lass, poor lass. Poor father! it'll be soon.'

Margaret was shocked by his words—shocked but not repelled; rather attracted and interested.

'Where do you live? I think we must be neighbours, we meet so often on this road.'

'We put up at nine Frances Street, second turn to th' left at after yo've past th' Goulden Dragon.'

'And your name? I must not forget that.'

'I'm none ashamed o' my name. It's Nicholas Higgins. Hoo's called Bessy Higgins. Whatten yo' asking for?'

Margaret was surprised at this last question, for at Helstone* it would have been an understood thing, after the inquiries she had made, that she intended to come and call upon any poor neighbour whose name and habitation she had asked for.

'I thought—I meant to come and see you.' She suddenly felt rather shy of offering the visit, without having any reason to give for her wish to make it, beyond a kindly interest in a stranger. It seemed all at once to take the shape of an impertinence on her part; she read this meaning too in the man's eyes.

'I'm none so fond of having strange folk in my house.' But then relenting, as he saw her heightened colour, he added, 'Yo're a foreigner, as one may say, and maybe don't know many folk here, and yo've given my wench here flowers out of yo'r own hand;—yo may come if yo like.'

Margaret was half-amused, half-nettled at this answer. She was not sure if she would go where permission was given so like a favour conferred. But when they came to the town into Frances Street, the girl stopped a minute, and said,

'Yo'll not forget yo're to come and see us.'

'Aye, aye,' said the father, impatiently, 'hoo'll come. Hoo's a bit set up now, because hoo thinks I might ha' spoken more civilly; but hoo'll think better on it, and come. I can read her proud bonny face like a book. Come along, Bess; there's the mill bell ringing.'

Margaret went home, wondering at her new friends, and smiling at the man's insight into what had been passing in her mind. From that day Milton became a brighter place to her. It was not the long, bleak sunny days of spring, nor yet was it that time was reconciling her to the town of her habitation. It was that in it she had found a human interest.

Visiting register offices, seeing all manner of unlikely people, and very few in the least likely, absorbed Margaret's time and thoughts for several days. One afternoon she met Bessy Higgins in the street, and stopped to speak to her.

'Well, Bessy, how are you? Better, I hope, now the wind has changed.'

'Better and not better, if yo' know what that means.'

'Not exactly,' replied Margaret, smiling.

'I'm better in not being torn to pieces by coughing o' nights, but I'm weary and tired o' Milton, and longing to get away to the land o' Beulah,* and when I think I'm farther and farther off, my heart sinks, and I'm no better; I'm worse.'

Margaret turned round to walk alongside of the girl in her feeble progress homeward. But for a minute or two she did not speak. At last she said in a low voice.

'Bessy, do you wish to die?' For she shrank from death herself, with all the clinging to life so natural to the young and healthy.

Bessy was silent in her turn for a minute or two. Then she replied,

'If yo'd led the life I have, and getten as weary of it as I have, and thought at times, "maybe it'll last for fifty or sixty years—it does wi' some,"—and got dizzy and dazed, and sick, as each of them sixty years seemed to spin about me, and mock me with its length of hours and minutes, and endless bits o' time—oh, wench! I tell thee thou'd been glad enough when th' doctor said he feared thou'd never see another winter.'

'Why, Bessy, what kind of a life has yours been?'

'Nought worse than many others', I reckon. Only I fretted again it, and they didn't.'

'But what was it? You know, I'm a stranger here, so perhaps I'm not so quick at understanding what you mean as if I'd lived all my life at Milton.'

'If yo'd ha' come to our house when yo' said yo' would, I could maybe ha' told you. But father says yo're just like th' rest on 'em; its out o' sight out o' mind wi' you.'

'I don't know who the rest are; and I've been very busy; and, to tell the truth, I had forgotten my promise—'

'Yo' offered it; we asked none of it.'

'I had forgotten what I said for the time,' continued Margaret quietly. 'I should have thought of it again when I was less busy. May I go with you now?'

Bessy gave a quick glance at Margaret's face, to see if the wish expressed was really felt. The sharpness in her eye turned to a wistful longing as she met Margaret's soft and friendly gaze.

'I ha' none so many to care for me; if yo' care yo' may come.'

So they walked on together in silence. As they turned up into a small court, opening out of a squalid street, Bessy said,

'Yo'll not be daunted if father's at home, and speaks a bit gruffish at first. He took a mind to ye, yo' see, and he thought a deal o' your coming to see us; and just because he liked yo' he were vexed and put about.'

'Don't fear, Bessy.'

But Nicholas was not at home when they entered. A great slatternly girl, not so old as Bessy, but taller and stronger, was busy at the wash-tub, knocking about the furniture in a rough capable way, but altogether making so much noise that Margaret shrunk, out of sympathy with poor Bessy, who had sat down on the first chair, as if completely tired out with her walk. Margaret asked the sister for a cup of water, and while she ran to fetch it (knocking down the fire-irons, and tumbling over a chair in her way), she unloosed Bessy's bonnet strings, to relieve her catching breath.

'Do you think such life as this is worth caring for?' gasped Bessy, at last. Margaret did not speak, but held the water to her lips. Bessy took a long and feverish draught, and then fell back and shut her eyes. Margaret heard her murmur to herself: 'They shall hunger no more, neither thirst any more; neither shall the sun light on them, nor any heat.'*

Margaret bent over and said, 'Bessy, don't be impatient with your life, whatever it is—or may have been. Remember who gave it you, and made it what it is!'

She was startled by hearing Nicholas speak behind her; he had come in without her noticing him.

'Now, I'll not have my wench preached to. She's bad enough as it is, with her dreams and her methodee* fancies, and her visions of cities with goulden gates and precious stones. But if it amuses her I let it abe, but I'm none going to have more stuff poured into her.'

'But surely,' said Margaret, facing round, 'you believe in what I said, that God gave her life, and ordered what kind of life it was to be?'

'I believe what I see, and no more. That's what I believe, young woman. I don't believe all I hear—no! not by a big deal. I did hear a young lass make an ado about knowing where we lived, and coming to see us. And my wench here thought a deal about it, and flushed up many a time, when hoo little knew as I was looking at her, at the sound of a strange step. But hoo's come at last,—and hoo's welcome, as long as hoo'll keep from preaching on what hoo knows nought about.'

MATTHEW ARNOLD

East London (1867)

'Twas August, and the fierce sun overhead
Smote on the squalid streets of Bethnal Green,
And the pale weaver, through his windows seen
In Spitalfields,* look'd thrice dispirited.

I met a preacher there I knew, and said:
'Ill and o'erwork'd, how fare you in this scene?'—
'Bravely!' said he; 'for I of late have been
Much cheer'd with thoughts of Christ, *the living bread*.'

O human soul! as long as thou canst so
Set up a mark of everlasting light,
Above the howling senses' ebb and flow,

To cheer thee, and to right thee if thou roam—
Not with lost toil thou labourest through the night!
Thou mak'st the heaven thou hop'st indeed thy home.

West London (1867)

Crouch'd on the pavement, close by Belgrave Square,*
A tramp I saw, ill, moody, and tongue-tied.
A babe was in her arms, and at her side
A girl; their clothes were rags, their feet were bare.

Some labouring men, whose work lay somewhere there,
Pass'd opposite; she touch'd her girl, who hied
Across, and begg'd, and came back satisfied.
The rich she had let pass with frozen stare.

Thought I: 'Above her state this spirit towers;
She will not ask of aliens, but of friends,
Of sharers in a common human fate.

She turns from that cold succour, which attends
The unknown little from the unknowing great,
And points us to a better time than ours.'

J. W. HORSLEY

Autobiography of a Thief in Thieves' Language (1879)

The following autobiography is both authentic and true. I have had
many opportunities of testing its truth in various ways during a
friendship of some eighteen months, during which the writer has
been pursuing the less exciting and less lucrative occupation of a
teetotal costermonger. I leave it to speak for itself, and confine my
function to that of an interpreter of what will be to many an
unknown tongue. It is a typical career that might be that of dozens or
even hundreds in East London.

J. W. HORSLEY,
Chaplain H.M. Prison, Clerkenwell.

I was born in 1853 at Stamford Hill, Middlesex. My parents removed from there to Stoke Newington, when I was sent to an infant school. Some time afterwards I was taken by two pals (companions) to an orchard to cop (steal) some fruit, me being a mug (inexperienced) at the game. This got to my father's ears; when I went home he set about me with a strap until he was tired. He thought that was not enough, but tied me to a bedstead—you may be sure what followed. I got loose, tied a blanket and a counterpane together, fastened it to the bedstead, and let myself out of the window, and did not go home that night, but met my two pals and dossed (slept) in a haystack. Early next morning my pals said they knew where we could get some toke (food), and took me to a terrace; we went down the dancers (steps) to a safe, and cleared it out. Two or three days after I met my mother, who in tears begged of me to go home, so I went home. My parents moved to Clapton; when they sent me to school, my pals used to send stiffs (notes) to the schoolmaster, saying that I was wanted at home; but instead of that we used to go and smug snowy (steal linen) that was hung out to dry, or rob the bakers' barrows. Things went from bad to worse, so I was obliged to leave home again. This time I palled in with some older hands at the game, who used to take me a parlour-jumping (robbing rooms), putting me in where the windows was open. I used to take anything there was to steal, and at last they told me all about wedge (silverplate), how I should know it by the ramp (hallmark—rampant lion?); we used to break it up in small pieces and sell it to watchmakers, and afterwards to a fence (buyer of stolen goods) down the Lane (Petticoat Lane). Two or three times a week I used to go to the Brit. (Britannia Theatre) in Hoxton, or the Gaff (penny music-room) in Shoreditch. I used to steal anything to make money to go to these places. Some nights I used to sleep at my pals' houses, sometimes in a shed where there was a fire kept burning night and day. All this time I had escaped the hands of the reelers (police), but one day I was taken for robbing a baker's cart, and got twenty-one days. While there I made pals with another one who came from Shoreditch, and promised to meet him when we got out, which I did, and we used to go together, and left the other pals at Clapton.

At last, one day we was at St John's Wood, I went in after some wedge; while picking some up off the table, I frightened a cat, which upset a lot of plates when jumping out of the window. So I was taken and tried at Marylebone Police Court, and sent to Feltham Industrial School. I had not been there a month before I planned with another boy to guy (run away), and so we did, but was stopped at Brentford, and took back to the school, for which we got twelve strokes with the birch. I thought when I first went there that I knew a great deal about thieving, but I found there was some there that knew more, and I used to pal in with those that knew the most. One day while talking with a boy he told me he was going home in a day or so; he said his friends was going to claim him out because he was more than sixteen years old. When my friends came to see me I told them that they could claim me out, and with a good many fair promises that I would lead a new life if they did so, they got me out of the school. When I got home I found a great change in my father, who had taken to drink, and he did not take so much notice of what I done as he used. I went on all straight the first few moons (months) at costering. One day there was a *fête* at Clapton, and I was coming home with my kipsy (basket). I had just sold all my goods out, I just stopped to pipe (see) what was going on, when a reeler came up to me and rapped (said), 'Now —— you had better guy, or else I shall give you a drag (three months in prison).' So I said all right, but he rapped, 'It is not all right, I don't want any sauce from you, or else I shall set about (beat) you myself;' so I said 'What for? I have done nothing; do you want to get it up for me?' Then he began to push me about, so I said I would not go at all if he put his dukes (hands) on me. Then he rammed my nut (head) against the wall, and shook the very life out of me. This got a scuff (crowd) round us, and the people ask him what he was knocking me about for, so he said, 'This is young —— just come home from a schooling' (a term in a reformatory). So he did not touch me again; so I went home, turned into kip (bed), and could not get up for two or three days because he had given me such a shaking, him being a great powerful man, and me only a little fellow. I still went on all straight until things got very dear at the market. I had been down three or four days running, and could not buy any-thing to earn a deaner (shilling) out of. So one morning I found I did not have more than a caser (5s.) for stock-pieces (stock-money). So I thought to myself, What shall I do? I said, 'I know what I will do. I will go to London Bridge rattler (railway), and take a deaner ride and go a wedge-hunting (stealing plate).' So I took a ducat (ticket) for Sutton in Surrey, and went a wedge-hunting. I had not been at

Sutton very long before I piped a slavey (servant) come out of a chat (house), so when she had got a little way up the double (turning), I pratted (went) in the house. When inside I could not see any wedge laying about in the kitchen, so I screwed my nut into the washhouse, and I piped three or four pair of daisy-roots (boots). So I claimed (stole) them and took off the lid of my kipsy and put them inside, put a cloth over them, and then put the lid on again, put the kipsy on my back as though it was empty, and guyed to the rattler and took a brief (ticket) to London Bridge, and took the daisies to a sheney (Jew) down the Gaff, and done them for thirty blow (shillings). The next day I took the rattler to Forest Hill, and touched for (succeeded in getting) some wedge, and a kipsy full of clobber (clothes). You may be sure this gave me a little pluck, so I kept on at the old game, only with this difference, that I got more pieces (money) for the wedge. I got three and a sprat (3s. 6d.) an ounce. But afterwards I got 3s. 9d., and then four blow. I used to get a good many pieces about this time, so I used to clobber myself up and go to the concert-rooms. But although I used to go to these places I never used to drink any beer for some time afterwards. It was while using one of these places I first met a sparring bloke (pugilist), who taught me how to spar, and showed me the way to put my dukes up. But after a time I gave him best (left him) because he used to want to bite my ear (borrow) too often. It was while I was with him that I got in company with some of the widest (cleverest) people in London. They used to use at (frequent) a pub in Shoreditch. The following people used to go in there—toy-getters (watch-stealers), magsmen (confidence-trick men), men at the mace (sham loan offices), broadsmen (card-sharpers), peter-claimers (box-stealers), busters and screwsmen (burglars), snide-pitchers (utterers of false coin), men at the duff (passing false jewellery), welshers (turf-swindlers), and skittle-sharps. Being with this nice mob (gang) you may be sure what I learned. I went out at the game three or four times a week, and used to touch almost every time. I went on like this for very near a stretch (year) without being smugged (apprehended). One night I was with the mob, I got canon (drunk), this being the first time. After this, when I used to go to concert-rooms, I used to drink beer. It was at one of these places down Whitechapel I palled in with a trip and staid with her until I got smugged. One day I was at Blackheath I got very near canon, and when I went into a place I claimed two wedge spoons, and was just going up the dancers, a slavey piped the spoons sticking out of my skyrocket (pocket), so I got smugged. While at the station they asked me what my monarch (name) was. A reeler came to the cell and cross-kidded (questioned) me, but I was too wide for him. I was tried at Greenwich; they ask the reeler if I was known, and he said no. So I was sent to Maidstone Stir (prison) for two moon.

GEORGE BERNARD SHAW

From *Mrs Warren's Profession* (1898)

Vivie Warren, a strong-minded mathematician educated at Cambridge, has been brought up in ignorance of the real source of her mother's income, prostitution.

MRS WARREN. You! you've no heart. (*She suddenly breaks out vehemently in her natural tongue—the dialect of a woman of the people—with all her affectations of maternal authority and conventional manners gone, and an overwhelming inspiration of true conviction and scorn in her.*) Oh, I won't bear it: I won't put up with the injustice of it. What right have you to set yourself up above me like this? You boast of what you are to me—to me, who gave you the chance of being what you are. What chance had I? Shame on you for a bad daughter and a stuck-up prude!

VIVIE (*cool and determined, but no longer confident; for her replies, which have sounded convincingly sensible and strong to her so far, now begin to ring rather woodenly and even priggishly against the new tone of her mother*). Don't think for a moment I set myself above you in any way. You attacked me with the conventional authority of a mother: I defended myself with the conventional superiority of a respectable woman. Frankly, I am not going to stand any of your nonsense; and when you drop it I shall not expect you to stand any of mine. I shall always respect your right to your own opinions and your own way of life.

MRS WARREN. My own opinions and my own way of life! Listen to her talking! Do you think I was brought up like you—able to pick and choose my own way of life? Do you think I did what I did because I liked it, or thought it right, or wouldn't rather have gone to college and been a lady if I'd had the chance?

VIVIE. Everybody has some choice, mother. The poorest girl alive may not be able to choose between being Queen of England or Principal of Newnham;* but she can choose between ragpicking and flowerselling, according to her taste. People are always blaming their circumstances for what they are. I don't believe in circumstances. The people who get on in this world are the people who get up and look for the circumstances they want, and, if they can't find them, make them.

MRS WARREN. Oh, it's easy to talk, very easy, isn't it? Here!—would you like to know what my circumstances were?

VIVIE. Yes: you had better tell me. Won't you sit down?

MRS WARREN. Oh, I'll sit down: don't you be afraid. (*She plants her chair farther forward with brazen energy, and sits down. Vivie is impressed in spite of herself.*) D'you known what your gran'mother was?

VIVIE. No.

MRS WARREN. No, you don't. I do. She called herself a widow and had a fried-fish shop down by the Mint, and kept herself and four daughters out of it. Two of us were sisters: that was me and Liz; and we were both good-looking and well made. I suppose our father was a well-fed man: mother pretended he was a gentleman; but I don't know. The other two were only half sisters—undersized, ugly, starved looking, hard working, honest poor creatures: Liz and I would have half-murdered them if mother hadn't half-murdered us to keep our hands off them. They were the respectable ones. Well, what did they get by their respectability? I'll tell you. One of them worked in a whitelead* factory twelve hours a day for nine shillings a week until she died of lead poisoning. She only expected to get her hands a little paralyzed; but she died. The other was always held up to us as a model because she married a Government labourer in the Deptford victualling yard, and kept his room and the three children neat and tidy on eighteen shillings a week—until he took to drink. That was worth being respectable for, wasn't it?

VIVIE (*now thoughtfully attentive*). Did you and your sister think so?

MRS WARREN. Liz didn't, I can tell you: she had more spirit. We both went to a church school—that was part of the ladylike airs we gave ourselves to be superior to the children that knew nothing and went nowhere—and we stayed there until Liz went out one night and never came back. I know the schoolmistress thought I'd soon follow her example; for the clergyman was always warning me that Lizzie'd end by jumping off Waterloo Bridge. Poor fool: that was all he knew about it! But I was more afraid of the whitelead factory than I was of the river; and so would you have been in my place. That clergyman got me a situation as scullery maid in a temperance restaurant where they sent out for anything you liked. Then I was waitress; and then I went to the bar at Waterloo station—fourteen hours a day serving drinks and washing glasses for four shillings a week and my board. That was considered a great promotion for me. Well, one cold, wretched night, when I was so tired I could hardly keep myself awake, who should come up for a half of Scotch but Lizzie, in a long fur cloak, elegant and comfortable, with a lot of sovereigns in her purse.

VIVIE (*grimly*). My aunt Lizzie!

MRS WARREN. Yes: and a very good aunt to have, too. She's living down at Winchester now, close to the cathedral, one of the most respectable ladies there—chaperones girls at the county ball, if you please. No river for Liz, thank you! You remind me of Liz a little: she was a first-rate business woman—saved money from the beginning—never let herself look too like what she was—never lost her head or threw away a chance. When she saw I'd grown up good-looking she said to me across the bar: 'What are you doing there, you little fool? wearing out your health and your appearance for other people's profit!' Liz was saving money then to take a house for herself in Brussels: and she thought we two could save faster than one. So she lent me some money and gave me a start; and I saved steadily and first paid her back, and then went into business with her as her partner. Why shouldn't I have done it? The house in Brussels was real high class—a much better place for a woman to be in than the factory where Anne Jane got poisoned. None of our girls were ever treated as I was treated in the scullery of that temperance place, or at the Waterloo bar, or at home. Would you have had me stay in them and become a worn out old drudge before I was forty?

VIVIE (*intensely interested by this time*). No; but why did you choose that business? Saving money and good management will succeed in any business.

MRS WARREN. Yes, saving money. But where can a woman get the money to save in any other business? Could you save out of four shillings a week and keep yourself dressed as well? Not you. Of course, if you're a plain woman and can't earn anything more; or if you have a turn for music, or the stage, or newspaper-writing: that's different. But neither Liz nor I had any turn for such things: all we had was our appearance and our turn for pleasing men. Do you think we were such fools as to let other people trade in our good looks by employing us as shopgirls, or barmaids, or waitresses, when we could trade in them ourselves and get all the profits instead of starvation wages? Not likely.

VIVIE. You were certainly quite justified—from the business point of view.

MRS WARREN. Yes; or any other point of view. What is any respectable girl brought up to do but to catch some rich man's fancy and get the benefit of his money by marrying him?—as if a marriage ceremony could make any difference in the right or wrong of the thing! Oh, the hypocrisy of the world makes me sick! Liz and I had to work and save and calculate just like other people; elseways we should be as poor as any good-for-nothing, drunken waster of a woman that thinks her luck will last for ever. (*With great energy.*) I despise such people: they've no character; and if there's a thing I hate in a woman, it's want of character.

VIVIE. Come, now, mother: frankly! Isn't it part of what you call character in a woman that she should greatly dislike such a way of making money?

MRS WARREN. Why, of course. Everybody dislikes having to work and make money; but they have to do it all the same. I'm sure I've often pitied a poor girl, tired out and in low spirits, having to try to please some man that she doesn't care two straws for—some half-drunken fool that thinks he's making himself agreeable when he's teasing and worrying and disgusting a woman so that hardly any money could pay her for putting up with it. But she has to bear with disagreeables and take the rough with the smooth, just like a nurse in a hospital or anyone else. It's not work that any woman would do for pleasure, goodness knows; though to hear the pious people talk you would suppose it was a bed of roses.

VIVIE. Still you consider it worth while. It pays.

MRS WARREN. Of course it's worth while to a poor girl, if she can resist temptation and is good-looking and well conducted and sensible. It's far better than any other employment open to her. I always thought that oughtn't to be. It can't be right, Vivie, that there shouldn't be better opportunities for women. I stick to that: it's wrong. But it's so, right or wrong; and a girl must make the best of it. But, of course, it's not worth while for a lady. If you took to it you'd be a fool; but I should have been a fool if I'd taken to anything else.

VIVIE (*more and more deeply moved*). Mother: suppose we were both as poor as you were in those wretched old days, are you quite sure that you wouldn't advise me to try the Waterloo bar, or marry a labourer, or even go into the factory?

MRS WARREN (*indignantly*). Of course not. What sort of mother do you take me for! How could you keep your self-respect in such starvation and slavery? And what's a woman worth? what's life worth? without self-respect! Why am I independent and able to give my daughter a first-rate education, when other women that had just as good opportunities are in the gutter? Because I always knew how to respect myself and control myself. Why is Liz looked up to in a cathedral town? The same reason. Where would we be now if we'd minded the clergyman's foolishness? Scrubbing floors for one and sixpence a day and nothing to look forward to but the workhouse infirmary. Don't you be led astray by people who don't know the world, my girl. The only way for a woman to provide for herself decently is for her to be good to some man that can afford to be good to her. If she's in his own station of life, let her make him marry her; but if she's far beneath him she can't expect it—why should she? It wouldn't be for her own happiness. Ask any lady in London society that has daughters; and she'll tell you the same, except that I tell you straight and she'll tell you crooked. That's all the difference.

VIVIE (*fascinated, gazing at her*). My dear mother: you are a wonderful woman—you are stronger than all England. And are you really and truly not one wee bit doubtful—or—or—ashamed?

MRS WARREN. Well, of course, dearie, it's only good manners to be ashamed of it; it's expected from a woman. Women have to pretend to feel a great deal that they don't feel. Liz used to be angry with me for plumping out the truth about it. She used to say that when every woman could learn enough from what was going on in the world before her eyes, there was no need to talk about it to her. But then Liz was such a perfect lady! She had the true instinct of it;

while I was always a bit of a vulgarian. I used to be so pleased when you sent me your photographs to see that you were growing up like Liz: you've just her ladylike, determined way. But I can't stand saying one thing when everyone knows I mean another. What's the use in such hypocrisy? If people arrange the world that way for women, there's no good pretending that it's arranged the other way. I never was a bit ashamed really. I consider that I had a right to be proud that we managed everything so respectably, and never had a word against us, and that the girls were so well taken care of. Some of them did very well: one of them married an ambassador. But of course now I daren't talk about such things: whatever would they think of us! (*She yawns.*) Oh, dear! I do believe I'm getting sleepy after all. (*She stretches herself lazily, thoroughly relieved by her explosion, and placidly ready for her night's rest.*)

WALTER BESANT

From *East London* (1899)

In *East London*, novelist and social reformer Walter Besant (1836–1901) offers middle-class readers fictional portraits of social 'types'. While none are intended to represent actual persons, Besant attempts to make them as realistic as possible, based on his own contacts with London's poor. In the 1880s Besant had founded the Society of Authors and Mile End, organizations to promote the education, particularly the writing, of working people.

I introduce you to a baby. Her name is Liz. She has as yet but a few days of life behind her. She is hardly conscious of hunger, cold, or uneasiness, or any of the things with which life first makes its beginning apparent to the half-awakened brain. She opens eyes that understand nothing—neither form, nor distance, nor colour, nor any differences; she sees men, like trees, walking. When she is hungry she wails; when she is not hungry she sleeps. We will leave the child with her mother, and we will stand aside and watch while the springs and summers pass, and while she grows from an infant to a child, a girl, a woman.

The room where the baby lies is a first-floor front, in a house of four rooms and a ruinous garret, belonging to a street which is occupied, like all the streets in this quarter, wholly by the people of the lower working-class. This is London Street, Ratcliffe.* It is a real street, with a real name and it is in a way typical of East London of the lower kind. . . .

You will perceive, however, that this child is not born of the very poor; her parents are not in destitution; her father is, in fact, a docker, and, being a big, burly fellow, born and brought up in the country, he gets tolerably regular employment and very fair wages. If he would spend less than the third or the half of his wages in drink his wife might have a four-roomed cottage. But we must take him as he is. His children suffer no serious privation. They are clothed and fed; they have the chance of living respectably, and with such decencies as belong to their ideals and their standards. In a word, Liz will be quite a commonplace, average girl of the lower working-class. . . .

Liz remained at school from three to fourteen years of age. What she learned I do not exactly know. Some years ago I looked through some 'readers' for Board-schools,* and came to the conclusion that nothing at all could be learned from them, counting scraps as worth nothing. But I hear that they have altered their 'readers.' Still, if you remember that no one has any books at all in London Street, that even a halfpenny paper is not often seen there, that no talk goes on which can instruct a child in anything, you will own that a child may be at school even for eleven years and yet learn very little. And since she found no means of carrying on her education after she left school, no free libraries, no encouragement from her companions, you will not be surprised to hear that all she had learned from books presently dropped from her like a cloak or wrapper for which she had no further use. Let us be reasonable. The Board-school taught her, besides a certain small amount of temporary and short-lived book-lore, some kind of elementary manners—a respect, at least, for manners; the knowledge of what manners may mean. The clergy and the machinery of the parish cannot teach these things. It can be done only at the Board-school. It is the school, and not the church, which softens manners and banishes some of the old brutality, because, you see, they do not go to church, and they must go to school. How rough, how rude, the average girl of Ratcliffe was before the Board-schools were opened, Liz herself neither knows nor comprehends. These schools have caused the disappearance of old characteristics once thought to be ingrained habits. Their civilizing influence during the last thirty years has been enormous. They have not only added millions to the numbers of those who read a great deal and perhaps—but this is doubtful—think a little, but they have abolished much of the old savagery. I declare that the life of this street as it was thirty or forty years ago simply could not be written down with any approach to truth in these pages.

Let me only quote the words of Professor Huxley, who began life by practising as a medical man in this quarter. 'I have seen the Polynesian savage,' I once heard him say in a speech, 'in his primitive condition, before the missionary or the blackbirder or the beach-comber got at him. With all his savagery, he was not half so savage, so unclean, so irreclaimable, as the tenant of a tenement in an East London slum.' These words open the door to unbounded flights of imagination. Leave that vanished world, leave the savage slum of Huxley's early manhood, to the region of poetry and fancy, to the unwritten, to the suggested, to the half-whispered. It exists no longer; it has been improved. . . .

Liz had got through her school-time; she must go to work.

Of course, she knew all along what awaited her. She must do as the others did, she must enter a factory. She contemplated the necessity without any misgiving. Why should she not go into a factory? It was all in the natural order of things, like getting hungry or waking up in the morning. Every girl had to be cuffed, every girl had to get out of the way when her father was drunk, every girl had to go to work as soon as she left school.

There is apparently a choice of work. There are many industries which employ girls. There is the match-making, there is the bottle-washing, there is the box-making, there is the paper-sorting, there is the jam-making, the fancy confectionery, the cracker industry, the making of ornaments for wedding-cakes, stockings for Christmas, and many others. There are many kinds of sewing. Virtually, how-ever, this child had no choice; her sisters were in the jam factory, her mother had been in the jam factory, she too went to the jam factory.

There are many branches of work more disagreeable than the jam factory. Liz found herself at half-past seven in the morning in a huge building, where she was one among a thousand working women and girls, men and boys, but chiefly girls. The place was heavily laden with an overpowering fragrance of fruit and sugar. In some rooms the fruit was boiling in great copper pots; in some girls were stirring the fruit, after it had been boiled, to get the steam out of it; in some machinery crushed and ground the sugar till it became as fine as flour. The place was like a mill. The flour of sugar hung about the room in a cloud of dust; it lay in such dust on the tables and the casks; it got into the girls' hair, so that they were fain to tie up their heads with white caps; it covered their clothes, and made them sticky; it made tables, benches, floor, all alike sticky. There were other developments of sugar; sometimes it lay on tables in huge, flat cakes of soft gray stuff like gelatine; they turned this mass, by their craft and subtlety, into innumerable threads of fine white silk; they drew it through machines, and brought it out in all the shapes that children love. Then there were rooms full of cocoanut. They treated casks full of dessicated cocoanut till that also became like flour. There were other rooms full of almonds, which they stripped and bleached and converted also into fine flour; or they turned boxes of gelatine into Turkish delight and jujubes. All day long and all the year round they made crackers; they made ornaments for wedding-cakes; they made favours; they made caramels; they made acidulated drops; they made things unnamed except by children. In all these rooms girls worked by hundreds, some sitting at long tables, some boiling the sugar, filling the pots with jam, stirring the boiling fruit, feeding machinery, filling moulds; all were as busy as bees and as mute as mice. Some of them wore white caps to cover their hair, some wore white aprons, some wore coarse sacking tied all round for a skirt to keep off stickiness. All day long the machinery whirred and pulsed an accompaniment to the activity and industry of the place.

'I like the smell,' said Liz. First impressions are the best; she continued to like the smell and the factory and the work. . . .

When she was seventeen Liz found a sweetheart.

He was a young fellow of twenty or thereabouts. He had come out of his native village, some place in the quiet country, a dull place, to enjoy the life of London. He was a highly skilled agricultural labourer: there was nothing on the farm that he could not do. He knew the fields and the woods, the wild creatures and the birds; he knew how to plough and to reap; he could keep an allotment full of vegetables all the year round; he understood a stable and a dairy, a paddock and sheepfold. Yet with all this knowledge he came to London, where it was of no earthly use to him. He threw over the best work that a country lad can have, and he became nothing but a pair of hands like this girl's father. He was a pair of hands; he was a strong back; his sturdy legs were fit to do the commonest, the heaviest, the most weary work in the world. One evening Liz was standing alone on the pavement, looking at something or other—a barrel-organ, a cheap Jack, one of the common sights and sounds—when this young fellow passed along, walking heavily, as one who has walked chiefly over ploughed fields. He looked at her. Something in her face,—it was an honest face,—something in her attitude of alertness and the sharp look of her eye struck his imagination. He hitched closer. In Brook Street it is permissible, it is laudable, to introduce yourself. He said huskily: 'I've seen you here before. What's your name? Mine is George.'

That was the beginning of it. Presently the other girls met Liz walking proudly along Brook Street with a big, well-set-up young fellow. They moved out of her way. Liz had got a chap. When would their turn come?

Next night they met again. On Sunday she walked with him along the Mile End Road without her apron and in her best hat. It was a parade and proclamation of an engagement. She told her mother, who was glad. 'A man,' she said, 'is a better friend than a woman. He sticks.' Liz did not tell the ladies of the club, but the other girls did, and the ladies looked grave and spoke seriously to her about responsibilities. . . .

Six months later Liz was married. It was on the August bank-holiday. The wedding took place at St James's Church, Ratcliffe. It was celebrated in a style which did honour to the quarter. The bride was dressed in heliotrope satin. She wore a large hat of purple plush. The bridesmaids were brilliantly attired in frocks of velveteen, green and crimson and blue. They too wore hats of plush. After the ceremony they adjourned to the residence of the bride, where a great feast was spread. The rejoicing lasted all day and all night. When the young couple began their wedded life it was with an empty purse and a week of borrowed food. I hope that George will not get drunk, will not knock his wife down, and will not take the strap to her. If he does, we must comfort ourselves with the thought that to Liz it will be no new thing, hitherto unknown in the land, not an unnatural thing when the drink is in a man, and, unless repeated in soberness, a trifle to be endured and forgotten and forgiven, even seventy times seven.

Here we must leave our girl. She is now a wife. For a little while she will go on at the factory; then she will stay at home. London Street will be enriched by half a dozen children all her own. Like their mother, these children will play in the dust and the mud; like her, they will go to school and be happy; like her, they will go to work in the factory. Liz will be repeated in her children. As long as she lives she will know and enjoy the same life, with the same pleasures, the same anxieties, the same luck. She will 'do' for her girls when they grow up. Now and then she will be taken on as a casual at the old factory. London Street will always be her whole world; she will have no interests outside, and when she dies it will be only the vanishing of one out of the multitudes which seem, as I said at the beginning, to be all alike, all living the same life, all enduring, hoping, loving, suffering, sinning, giving, helping, condoling, mourning, in the same kindly, cruel, beneficent, merciless, contradictory, womanly fashion that makes up the life of London Street.

Degeneration

CESARE LOMBROSO

From *The Criminal Man* (1876)

At the end of his career Cesare Lombroso (1835–1909) collaborated with his daughter, Gina Lombroso Ferrero (1872–1944), to prepare an English language summary of *The Criminal Man* (1876). Lombroso Ferrero, who did much of the writing, refers to Lombroso as 'my father.'

This is the difference between the Classical and the Modern School of Penal Jurisprudence. The Classical School based its doctrines on the assumption that all criminals, except in a few extreme cases, are endowed with intelligence and feelings like normal individuals, and that they commit misdeeds consciously, being prompted thereto by their unrestrained desire for evil. The offence alone was considered, and on it the whole existing penal system has been founded, the severity of the sentence meted out to the offender being regulated by the gravity of his misdeed.

The Modern, or Positive, School of Penal Jurisprudence, on the contrary, maintains that the anti-social tendencies of criminals are the result of their physical and psychic organisation, which differs essentially from that of normal individuals; and it aims at studying the morphology and various functional phenomena of the criminal with the object of curing, instead of punishing him. The Modern School is therefore founded on a new science, Criminal Anthropology, which may be defined as the Natural History of the Criminal, because it embraces his organic and psychic constitution and social life, just as anthropology does in the case of normal human beings and the different races.

If we examine a number of criminals, we shall find that they exhibit numerous anomalies in the face, skeleton, and various psychic and sensitive functions, so that they strongly resemble primitive races. It was these anomalies that first drew my father's attention to the close relationship between the criminal and the savage and made him suspect that criminal tendencies are of atavistic origin.

When a young doctor at the Asylum in Pavia, he was requested to make a post-mortem examination on a criminal named Vilella, an Italian Jack the Ripper,* who by atrocious crimes had spread terror in the Province of Lombardy. Scarcely had he laid open the skull, when he perceived at the base, on the spot where the internal occipital crest* or ridge is found in normal individuals, a small hollow, which he called *median occipital fossa.** This abnormal character was correlated to a still greater anomaly in the cerebellum, the hypertrophy of the vermis, *i.e.,* the spinal cord which separates the cerebellar lobes lying underneath the cerebral hemispheres.* This vermis was so enlarged in the case of Vilella, that it almost formed a small, intermediate cerebellum like that found in the lower types of apes, rodents, and birds. This anomaly is very rare among inferior races, with the exception of the South American Indian tribe of the Aymaras of Bolivia and Peru, in whom it is not infrequently found (40%). It is seldom met with in the insane or other degenerates, but later investigations have shown it to be prevalent in criminals.

This discovery was like a flash of light. 'At the sight of that skull,' says my father, 'I seemed to see all at once, standing out clearly illumined as in a vast plain under a flaming sky, the problem of the nature of the criminal, who reproduces in civilised times characteristics, not only of primitive savages, but of still lower types as far back as the carnivora.'

Thus was explained the origin of the enormous jaws, strong canines, prominent zygomae,* and strongly developed orbital arches* which he had so frequently remarked in criminals, for these peculiarities are common to carnivores and savages, who tear and devour raw flesh. Thus also it was easy to understand why the span of the arms in criminals so often exceeds the height, for this is a characteristic of apes, whose fore-limbs are used in walking and climbing. The other anomalies exhibited by criminals—the scanty beard as opposed to the general hairiness of the body, prehensile foot,* diminished number of lines in the palm of the hand, cheek-pouches, enormous development of the middle incisors and frequent absence of the lateral ones, flattened nose and angular or sugar-loaf form of the skull, common to criminals and apes; the excessive size of the orbits, which, combined with the hooked nose, so often imparts to criminals the aspect of birds of prey, the projection of the lower part of the face and jaws (prognathism) found in negroes and animals, and supernumerary teeth (amounting in some cases to a double row as in snakes) and cranial bones (epactal bone* as in the Peruvian Indians): all these characteristics pointed to one conclusion, the atavistic origin of the criminal, who reproduces physical, psychic, and functional qualities of remote ancestors.

Subsequent research on the part of my father and his disciples showed that other factors besides atavism come into play in determining the criminal type. These are: disease and environment. Later on, the study of innumerable offenders led them to the conclusion that all law-breakers cannot be classed in a single species, for their ranks include very diversified types, who differ not only in their bent towards a particular form of crime, but also in the degree of tenacity and intensity displayed by them in their perverse propensities, so that, in reality, they form a graduated scale leading from the born criminal to the normal individual.

Born criminals form about one third of the mass of offenders, but, though inferior in numbers, they constitute the most important part of the whole criminal army, partly because they are constantly appearing before the public and also because the crimes committed by them are of a peculiarly monstrous character; the other two thirds are composed of criminaloids (minor offenders), occasional and

habitual criminals, etc., who do not show such a marked degree of
diversity from normal persons.

GEORGE GISSING

From *The Nether World* (1889)

In this passage, John Snowdon is believed to be in possession of some
money obtained in Australia. Sixteen-year-old Clem Peckover and her
mother are scheming to take it away from him.

The bells of St James's, Clerkenwell, ring melodies in intervals of
the pealing for service-time. One morning of spring their music, like
the rain that fell intermittently, was flung westwards by the boisterous wind, away over Clerkenwell Close, until the notes failed one by
one, or were clashed out of existence by the clamour of a less civilised steeple. Had the wind been under mortal control it would
doubtless have blown thus violently and in this quarter in order that
the inhabitants of the House of Detention might derive no solace
from the melody. Yet I know not; just now the bells were playing
'There is a happy land, far, far away,' and that hymn makes too great
a demand upon the imagination to soothe amid instant miseries.

In Mrs Peckover's kitchen the music was audible in bursts. Clem
and her mother, however, it neither summoned to prepare for
church, nor lulled into a mood of restful reverie. The two were
sitting very close together before the fire, and holding intimate converse; their voices kept a low murmur, as if, though the door was
shut, they felt it necessary to use every precaution against being
overheard. Three years have come and gone since we saw these
persons. On the elder time has made little impression; but Clem has
developed noticeably. The girl is now in the very prime of her
ferocious beauty. She has grown taller and somewhat stouter; her
shoulders spread like those of a caryatid,* the arm with which she
props her head is as strong as a carter's and magnificently moulded.
The head itself looks immense with its pile of glossy hair. Reddened
by the rays of the fire, her features had a splendid savagery which
seemed strangely at discord with the paltry surroundings amid
which she sat; her eyes just now were gleaming with a crafty and

cruel speculation which would have become those of a barbarian in ambush. I wonder how it came about that her strain, after passing through the basest conditions of modern life, had thus reverted to a type of ancestral exuberance.

'If only he doesn't hear about the old man or the girl from somebody!' said Mrs Peckover. 'I've been afraid of it ever since he come into the 'ouse. There's so many people might tell him. You'll have to come round him sharp, Clem.'

The mother was dressed as her kind are wont to be on Sunday morning—that is to say, not dressed at all, but hung about with coarse garments, her hair in unbeautiful disarray. Clem, on the other hand, seemed to have devoted much attention to her morning toilet; she wore a dark dress trimmed with velveteen, and a metal ornament of primitive taste gleamed amid her hair.

'There ain't no mistake?' she asked, after a pause. 'You're jolly sure of that?'

'Mistake? What a blessed fool you must be! Didn't they advertise in the papers for him? Didn't the lawyers themselves say as it was something to his advantage? Don't you say yourself as Jane says her grandfather's often spoke about him and wished he could find him? How can it be a mistake? If it was only Bill's letter we had to go on, you might talk; but—there, don't be a ijiot!'

'If it turned out as he hadn't nothing,' remarked Clem resolutely, 'I'd leave him, if I was married fifty times.'

Her mother uttered a contemptuous sound. At the same time she moved her head as if listening; some one was, in fact, descending the stairs.

'Here he comes,' she whispered. 'Get the eggs ready, an' I'll make the corffee.'

A tap at the door, then entered a tallish man of perhaps forty, though he might be a year or two younger. His face was clean-shaven, harsh-featured, unwholesome of complexion; its chief peculiarity was the protuberance of the bone in front of each temple, which gave him a curiously animal aspect. His lower lip hung and jutted forward; when he smiled, as now in advancing to the fire, it slightly overlapped the one above. His hair was very sparse; he looked, indeed, like one who has received the tonsure.* The movement of his limbs betokened excessive indolence; he dragged his feet rather than walked. His attire was equally suggestive; not only had it fallen into the last degree of shabbiness (having originally been such as is worn by a man above the mechanic ranks), but it was patched with dirt of many kinds, and held together by a most inadequate supply of buttons. At present he wore no collar, and his waistcoat, half-open, exposed a red shirt.

'Why, you're all a-blowin' and a-growin' this morning, Miss Peckover,' was his first observation, as he dropped heavily into a wooden arm-chair. 'I shall begin to think that colour of yours ain't natural. Dare you let me rub it with a handkerchief?'

'Course I dare,' replied Clem, tossing her head. 'Don't be so forward, Mr Snowdon.'

'Forward? Not I. I'm behind time if anything. I hope I haven't kept you from church.'

He chuckled at his double joke. Mother and daughter laughed appreciatively.

OSCAR WILDE

From *The Picture of Dorian Gray* (1890)

'How sad it is!' murmured Dorian Gray, with his eyes still fixed upon his own portrait. 'How sad it is! I shall grow old, and horrible, and dreadful. But this picture will remain always young. It will never be older than this particular day of June. . . . If it were only the other way! If it were I who was to be always young, and the picture that was to grow old! For that—for that—I would give everything! Yes, there is nothing in the whole world I would not give! I would give my soul for that!'

'You would hardly care for such an arrangement, Basil,' cried Lord Henry, laughing. 'It would be rather hard lines on your work.'

'I should object very strongly, Harry,' said Hallward.

Dorian Gray turned and looked at him. 'I believe you would, Basil. You like your art better than your friends. I am no more to you than a green bronze figure. Hardly as much, I dare say.'

The painter stared in amazement. It was so unlike Dorian to speak like that. What had happened? He seemed quite angry. His face was flushed and his cheeks burning.

'Yes,' he continued, 'I am less to you than your ivory Hermes* or your silver Faun. You will like them always. How long will you like me? Till I have my first wrinkle, I suppose. I know, now, that when one loses one's good looks, whatever they may be, one loses everything. Your picture has taught me that. Lord Henry Wotton is perfectly right. Youth is the only thing worth having. When I find that I am growing old, I shall kill myself.'

Hallward turned pale, and caught his hand. 'Dorian! Dorian!' he cried, 'don't talk like that. I have never had such a friend as you, and I shall never have such another. You are not jealous of material things, are you?—you who are finer than any of them!'

'I am jealous of everything whose beauty does not die. I am jealous of the portrait you have painted of me. Why should it keep what I must lose? Every moment that passes takes something from me, and gives something to it. Oh, if it were only the other way! If the picture could change, and I could be always what I am now! Why did you paint it? It will mock me some day—mock me horribly!' The hot tears welled into his eyes; he tore his hand away, and, flinging himself on the divan, he buried his face in the cushions, as though he was praying. . . .

[*Years later the artist asks to see the portrait, which Dorian has hidden.*]

'So you think that it is only God who sees the soul, Basil? Draw that curtain back, and you will see mine.'

The voice that spoke was cold and cruel. 'You are mad, Dorian, or playing a part,' muttered Hallward, frowning.

'You won't? Then I must do it myself,' said the young man; and he tore the curtain from its rod, and flung it on the ground.

An exclamation of horror broke from the painter's lips as he saw in the dim light the hideous face on the canvas grinning at him. There was something in its expression that filled him with disgust and loathing. Good heavens! it was Dorian Gray's own face that he was looking at! The horror, whatever it was, had not yet entirely spoiled that marvellous beauty. There was still some gold in the thinning hair and some scarlet on the sensual mouth. The sodden eyes had kept something of the loveliness of their blue, the noble curves had not yet completely passed away from chiselled nostrils and from plastic throat. Yes, it was Dorian himself. But who had done it? He seemed to recognize his own brush-work, and the frame was his own design. The idea was monstrous, yet he felt afraid. He seized the lighted candle, and held it to the picture. In the left-hand corner was his own name, traced in long letters of bright vermilion.

It was some foul parody, some infamous, ignoble satire. He had never done that. Still, it was his own picture. He knew it, and he felt as if his blood had changed in a moment from fire to sluggish ice. His own picture! What did it mean? Why had it altered? He turned, and looked at Dorian Gray with the eyes of a sick man. His mouth twitched, and his parched tongue seemed unable to articulate. He passed his hand across his forehead. It was dank with clammy sweat.

The young man was leaning against the mantel-shelf, watching him with that strange expression that one sees on the faces of those who are absorbed in a play when some great artist is acting. There was neither real sorrow in it nor real joy. There was simply the passion of the spectator, with perhaps a flicker of triumph in his eyes. He had taken the flower out of his coat, and was smelling it, or pretending to do so.

'What does this mean?' cried Hallward, at last. His own voice sounded shrill and curious in his ears.

'Years ago, when I was a boy,' said Dorian Gray, crushing the flower in his hand, 'you met me, flattered me, and taught me to be vain of my good looks. One day you introduced me to a friend of yours, who explained to me the wonder of youth, and you finished a portrait of me that revealed to me the wonder of beauty. In a mad moment, that, even now, I don't know whether I regret or not, I made a wish, perhaps you would call it a prayer . . .'

'I remember it! Oh, how well I remember it! No! the thing is impossible. The room is damp. Mildew has got into the canvas. The paints I used had some wretched mineral poison in them. I tell you the thing is impossible.'

'Ah, what is impossible?' murmured the young man, going over to the window, and leaning his forehead against the cold, mist-stained glass.

'You told me you had destroyed it.'

'I was wrong. It has destroyed me.'

'I don't believe it is my picture.'

'Can't you see your ideal in it?' said Dorian, bitterly.

'My ideal, as you call it . . .'

'As you called it.'

'There was nothing evil in it, nothing shameful. You were to me such an ideal as I shall never meet again. This is the face of a satyr.'

'It is the face of my soul.'

'Christ! what a thing I must have worshipped! It has the eyes of a devil.'

'Each of us has Heaven and Hell in him, Basil,' cried Dorian, with a wild gesture of despair.

Hallward turned again to the portrait, and gazed at it. 'My God! if it is true,' he exclaimed, 'and this is what you have done with your life, why, you must be worse even than those who talk against you fancy you to be!' He held the light up again to the canvas, and examined it. The surface seemed to be quite undisturbed, and as he had left it. It was from within, apparently, that the foulness and horror had come. Through some strange quickening of inner life the leprosies of sin were slowly eating the thing away. The rotting of a corpse in a watery grave was not so fearful.

His hand shook, and the candle fell from its socket on the floor, and lay there sputtering. He placed his foot on it and put it out. Then he flung himself into the ricketty chair that was standing by the table and buried his face in his hands.

'Good God, Dorian, what a lesson! what an awful lesson!' There was no answer, but he could hear the young man sobbing at the window. 'Pray, Dorian, pray,' he murmured. 'What is it that one was taught to say in one's boyhood? "Lead us not into temptation. Forgive us our sins. Wash away our iniquities." Let us say that together. The prayer of your pride has been answered. The prayer of your repentance will be answered also. I worshipped you too much. I am punished for it. You worshipped yourself too much. We are both punished.'

Dorian Gray turned slowly around, and looked at him with tear-dimmed eyes. 'It is too late, Basil,' he faltered.

'It is never too late, Dorian. Let us kneel down and try if we cannot remember a prayer. Isn't there a verse somewhere, "Though your sins be as scarlet, yet I will make them as white as snow"?'*

'Those words mean nothing to me now.'

'Hush! don't say that. You have done enough evil in your life. My God! don't you see that accursed thing leering at us?'

Dorian Gray glanced at the picture, and suddenly an uncontrollable feeling of hatred for Basil Hallward came over him, as though it had been suggested to him by the image on the canvas, whispered into his ear by those grinning lips. The mad passions of a hunted animal stirred within him, and he loathed the man who was seated at the table, more than in his whole life he had ever loathed anything. He glanced wildly around. Something glimmered on the top of the painted chest that faced him. His eye fell on it. He knew what it was. It was a knife that he had brought up, some days before, to cut a piece of cord, and had forgotten to take away with him. He moved slowly towards it, passing Hallward as he did so. As soon as he got behind him, he seized it, and turned round. Hallward stirred in his chair as if he was going to rise. He rushed at him, and dug the knife into the great vein that is behind the ear, crushing the man's head down on the table, and stabbing again and again.

MAX NORDAU

From *Degeneration* (1892)

We have recognised the effect of diseases in these *fin-de-siècle* literary and artistic tendencies and fashions, as well as in the susceptibility of the public with regard to them, and we have succeeded in maintaining that these diseases are degeneracy and hysteria. We have now to inquire how these maladies of the day have originated, and why they appear with such extraordinary frequency at the present time.

Morel,* the great investigator of degeneracy, traces this chiefly to poisoning. A race which is regularly addicted, even without excess, to narcotics and stimulants in any form (such as fermented alcoholic drinks, tobacco, opium, hashish, arsenic), which partakes of tainted foods (bread made with bad corn), which absorbs organic poisons (marsh fever,* syphilis, tuberculosis, goitre), begets degenerate descendants who, if they remain exposed to the same influences, rapidly descend to the lowest degrees of degeneracy, to idiocy, to dwarfishness, etc. That the poisoning of civilized peoples continues and increases at a very rapid rate is widely attested by statistics. The consumption of tobacco has risen in France from 0.8 kilogramme per head in 1841 to 1.9 kilogrammes in 1890. The corresponding figures for England are 13 and 26 ounces; for Germany, 0.8 and 1.5 kilogrammes. The consumption of alcohol during the same period has risen in Germany (1844) from 5.45 quarts to (1867) 6.86 quarts; in England from 2.01 litres to 2.64 litres; in France from 1.33 to 4 litres. The increase in the consumption of opium and hashish is still greater, but we need not concern ourselves about that, since the chief sufferers from them are Eastern peoples, who play no part in the intellectual development of the white races. To these noxious influences, however, one more may be added, which Morel has not known, or has not taken into consideration—residence in large towns. The inhabitant of a large town, even the richest, who is surrounded by the greatest luxury, is continually exposed to unfavourable influences which diminish his vital powers far more than what is inevitable. He breathes an atmosphere charged with organic detritus; he eats stale, contaminated, adulterated food; he feels himself in a state of constant nervous excitement, and one can compare him without exaggeration to the inhabitant of a marshy district. The effect of a large town on the human organism offers the closest analogy to that of the Maremma,* and its population falls victim to the same fatality of degeneracy and destruction as the victims of malaria. The death-rate in a large town is more than a quarter greater than the average for the entire population; it is double that of the open country, though in reality it ought to be less, since in a large town the most vigorous ages predominate, during which the mortality is lower than in infancy and old age. And the children of large towns who are not carried off at an early age suffer from the peculiar arrested development which Morel has ascertained in the population of fever districts. They develop more or less normally until fourteen or fifteen years of age, are up to that time alert, sometimes brilliantly endowed, and give the highest promise; then suddenly there is a standstill, the mind loses its facility of comprehension, and the boy who, only yesterday, was a model scholar, becomes an obtuse, clumsy dunce, who can only be steered with the greatest difficulty through his examinations. With these mental changes bodily modifications go hand in hand. The growth of the long bones is extremely slow, or ceases entirely, the legs remain short, the pelvis retains a feminine form, certain other organs cease to develop, and the entire being presents a strange and repulsive mixture of incompleteness and decay.*

Now we know how, in the last generation, the number of the inhabitants of great towns increased to an extraordinary degree. At the present time an incomparably larger portion of the whole population is subjected to the destructive influences of large towns than was the case fifty years ago; hence the number of victims is proportionately more striking, and continually becomes more remarkable. Parallel with the growth of large towns is the increase in the number of the degenerate of all kinds—criminals, lunatics, and the 'higher degenerates' of Magnan;* and it is natural that these last should play an ever more prominent part in endeavouring to introduce an ever greater element of insanity into art and literature.

The enormous increase of hysteria* in our days is partly due to the same causes as degeneracy, besides which there is one cause much more general still than the growth of large towns—a cause which perhaps of itself would not be sufficient to bring about degeneracy, but which is unquestionably quite enough to produce hysteria and neurasthenia. This cause is the fatigue of the present generation. That hysteria is in reality a consequence of fatigue Féré* has conclusively demonstrated by convincing experiments. In a communication to the Biological Society of Paris, this distinguished investigator says: 'I have recently observed a certain number of facts which have made apparent the analogy existing between fatigue and the chronic condition of the hysterical. One knows that among the hysterical [involuntary!] symmetry of movements frequently shows itself in a very characteristic manner. I have proved that in normal subjects this same symmetry of movements is met with under the influence of fatigue. A phenomenon which shows itself in a very marked way in serious hysteria is that peculiar excitability which demonstrates that the energy of the voluntary movements, through peripheral stimulations or mental presentations, suffers rapid and transitory modifications co-existing with parallel modifications of sensibility, and of the functions of nutrition. This excitability can be equally manifested during fatigue. . . . Fatigue constitutes a true temporary experimental hysteria. It establishes a transition between the states which we call normal and the various states which we designate hysteria. One can change a normal into a hysterical individual by tiring him. . . . All these causes (which produce hysteria) can, as far as the pathogenic part they play is concerned, be traced to one simple physiological process—to fatigue, to depression of vitality.'

Now, to this cause—fatigue—which, according to Féré, changes healthy men into hysterical, the whole of civilized humanity has been exposed for half a century. All its conditions of life have, in this period of time, experienced a revolution unexampled in the history of the world. Humanity can point to no century in which the inventions which penetrate so deeply, so tyrannically, into the life of every individual are crowded so thick as in ours. The discovery of America, the Reformation, stirred men's minds powerfully, no doubt, and certainly also destroyed the equilibrium of thousands of brains which lacked staying power. But they did not change the material life of man. He got up and laid down, ate and drank, dressed, amused himself, passed his days and years as he had been always wont to do. In our times, on the contrary, steam and electricity have turned the customs of life of every member of the civilized nations upside down, even of the most obtuse and narrow-minded citizen, who is completely inaccessible to the impelling thoughts of the times. . . .

In 1840 there were in Europe 3,000 kilometres of railway; in 1891 there were 218,000 kilometres. The number of travellers in 1840, in Germany, France and England, amounted to 2½ millions; in 1891 it was 614 millions. In Germany every inhabitant received, in 1840, 85 letters; in 1888, 200 letters. In 1840 the post distributed in France 94 millions of letters; in England, 277 millions; in 1881, 595 and 1,299 millions respectively. The collective postal intercourse between all countries, without including the internal postage of each separate country, amounted, in 1840, to 92 millions; in 1889, to 2,759 millions. In Germany, in 1840, 305 newspapers were published; in 1891, 6,800; in France, 776 and 5,182; in England (1846), 551 and 2,255. The German book trade produced, in 1840, 1,100 new works; in 1891, 18,700. The exports and imports of the world had, in 1840, a value of 28, in 1889 of 74, milliards of marks. The ships which, in 1840, entered all the ports of Great Britain contained 9½, in 1890 74½, millions of tons. The whole British merchant navy measured, in 1840, 3,200,000; in 1890, 9,688,000 tons.

Let us now consider how these formidable figures arise. The 18,000 new publications, the 6,800 newspapers in Germany, desire to be read, although many of them desire in vain; the 2,759 millions of letters must be written; the larger commercial transactions, the numerous journeys, the increased marine intercourse, imply a correspondingly greater activity in individuals. The humblest village inhabitant has to-day a wider geographical horizon, more numerous and complex intellectual interests, than the prime minister of a petty, or even a second-rate state a century ago. If he do but read his paper, let it be the most innocent provincial rag, he takes part, certainly not by active interference and influence, but by a continuous and receptive curiosity, in the thousand events which take place in all parts of the globe, and he interests himself simultaneously in the issue of a revolution in Chili, in a bush-war in East Africa, a massacre in North China, a famine in Russia, a street-row in Spain, and an international exhibition in North America. A cook receives and sends more letters than a university professor did formerly, and a petty tradesman travels more and sees more countries and people than did the reigning prince of other times.

All these activities, however, even the simplest, involve an effort of the nervous system and a wearing of tissue. Every line we read or write, every human face we see, every conversation we carry on, every scene we perceive through the window of the flying express, sets in activity our sensory nerves and our brain centres. Even the little shocks of railway travelling, not perceived by consciousness, the perpetual noises, and the various sights in the streets of a large town, our suspense pending the sequel of progressing events, the constant expectation of the newspaper, of the postman, of visitors, cost our brains wear and tear. In the last fifty years the population of Europe has not doubled, whereas the sum of its labours has increased ten-fold, in part even fifty-fold. Every civilized man furnishes, at the present time, from five to twenty-five times as much work as was demanded of him half a century ago.

This enormous increase in organic expenditure has not, and cannot have, a corresponding increase of supply. Europeans now eat a little more and a little better than they did fifty years ago, but by no means in proportion to the increase of effort which to-day is required of them. And even if they had the choicest food in the greatest abundance, it would do nothing towards helping them, for they would be incapable of digesting it. Our stomachs cannot keep pace with the brain and nervous system. The latter demand very much more than the former are able to perform. And so there follows what always happens if great expenses are met by small incomes; first the savings are consumed, then comes bankruptcy.

SARAH GRAND

From *The Heavenly Twins* (1893)

The Heavenly Twins, one of the 'new woman' novels of the 1890s, follows the lives of three unhappily married women. Angelica, a tomboyish girl, impulsively marries a man twenty years her senior under the condition that he will let her do exactly as she likes. Evadne learns on her wedding day that her husband, Colonel Colquhoun, has been involved with other women, and she agrees to live with him only if they have no physical relations. Edith, whose married life is depicted here, catches syphilis from her husband, Mosely Menteith, and goes mad after giving birth to a syphilitic child and learning of her husband's past. Grand's novel was one of the first to depict the 'heredity of vice', the transmission of syphilis from one generation to the next. While syphilis was sometimes used as an illustration of how an 'acquired character' could be transmitted, syphilis is not 'hereditary' in the strict sense. A syphilitic father gives the disease to his child by infecting the mother, who passes it on to the child through her placenta. Grand's novel condemns social acceptance of men's youthful promiscuity, showing the grave consequences it can have for their families later in life.

Mrs Orton Beg's ankle was strong enough now for her to walk from her little house in the Close to the palace, but she had to use a stick. She was bleached by being so much indoors, and looked very fragile in the costly simplicity of her black draperies as she entered.

Mrs Beale and Edith received her affectionately, and Sir Mosley rose and transferred his scrutinizing gaze to her while they were so occupied. He inspected her dark glossy hair; eyes, nose, mouth, and figure, down to her feet; then looked into her eyes again, and bowed on being presented by Mrs Beale.

'Sir Mosley is in the Colquhoun Highlanders,' the latter explained to Mrs Orton Beg. 'He is just going out to Malta to join them.'

Mrs Orton Beg looked up at him with interest from the low chair into which she had subsided: 'Then you know my niece, I suppose,' she said—'Mrs Colquhoun?'

'I have not yet the pleasure,' he answered, smiling so that he showed his teeth. They were somewhat discoloured by tobacco, but the smile was a pleasant one, to which people instantly responded. He went to the tea-table when he had spoken, and stood there waiting to hand Mrs Orton Beg a cup of tea which Mrs Beale was pouring out for her. 'But I have seen Mrs Colquhoun,' he added. 'I was at the wedding—she looked remarkably well.' He fixed his eyes on vacancy here, and turned his attention inward in order to contemplate a vision of Evadne in her wedding dress. His first question about a strange woman was always; 'Is she good-looking?' and his first thought when one whom he knew happened to be mentioned was always as to whether she was attractive in appearance or not. He was one of several of Colonel Colquhoun's brother officers who had graced the wedding. There was not much variety amongst them. They were all excessively clean and neat in appearance, their manners in society were unexceptionable, the morals of most of them not worth describing because there was so little of them; and their comments to each other on the occasion neither original nor refined; generations of them had made the same remarks under similar circumstances.

The bishop came in during the little diversion caused by handing tea and cake to Mrs Orton Beg.

'Ah, how do you do?' he said, shaking hands with the latter. 'How is the foot? Better? That's right. Oh! is that you, Mosley? I beg your pardon, my dear boy'—here they shook hands—'I did not see you at first. Very glad you've come, I'm sure. How is your mother? Not with your regiment, eh?' He peered at Sir Mosley through a pair of very thick glasses he wore, and seemed to read an answer to each question as he put it, written on the latter's face.

'Will you have some tea, dear?' said Mrs Beale.

'Eh, what did you say, my dear? Tea? Yes, if you please. That is what I came for.'

He turned to the tea-table as he spoke, and stood over it rubbing his hands, and beaming about him blandly.

Sir Mosley Menteith had been a good deal at the palace as a youngster. He and Edith still called each other by their Christian names. The bishop had seen him grow up from a boy, and knew all about him—so he would have said—although he had not seen much of him and had heard absolutely nothing for several years.

'So you are not with your regiment?' he repeated interrogatively.

'I am just on my way to join it now,' the young man answered, looking up at the bishop from the chair near Edith on which he was again sitting, and giving the corners of his little light moustache a twirl on either side when he had spoken. All his features, except his eyes, preserved an imperturbable gravity; his lips moved, but without altering the expression of his face. His eyes, however, inspected the bishop intelligently; and always, when he spoke to him, they rested on some one point, his vest, his gaiters, his apron, the top of his bald head, the end of his nose.

'Dr Galbraith,' the footman announced; and the doctor entered in his easy, unaffected, but somewhat awkward way. He had his hat in his hand, and there was a shade of weariness or depression on his strong pale face; but his deep gray kindly eyes—the redeeming feature—were as sympathetically penetrating as usual.

He shook hands with them all, except Sir Mosley, at whom he just glanced sufficiently long to perceive that he was a stranger.

Mrs Beale named them to each other, and they both bowed slightly, looking at the ground, and then they exchanged glances.

'Not much like a medico if you are one,' thought Menteith.

'Not difficult to take your measure,' thought the doctor after which he turned at once to the tea-table, like one at home, and stood there waiting for a cup. . . .

Edith Beale had now been married for more than a year to Sir Mosley Menteith, and the whole of their life together had been to her a painful period of gradual disillusion—and all the more painful because she was totally unprepared even for the possibility of any troubles of the kind which had beset her. Parental opinion and prejudice, ignorance, education, and custom had combined to deceive her with regard to the transient nature of her own feeling for her lover; and it was also inevitable that she should lend herself enthusiastically to the deception; for who would not believe, if they could, that a state so ecstatic is enduring? Even people who do know better are apt to persuade themselves that an exception will be made in their favour, and this being so, it naturally follows that a girl like Edith, all faith and fondness, is foredoomed by every circumstance of her life and virtue of her nature, to make the fatal mistake. But, as Evadne told her, passion stands midway between love and hate, and is an introduction to either; and there is no doubt that, if Menteith had been the kind of repentant erring sinner she imagined him, her first wild desire would have cooled down into the lasting joy of tranquil love. Menteith, however, was not at all that kind of man, and, consequently, from the first the marriage had been a miserable example of the result of uniting the spiritual or better part of human nature with the essentially animal or most degraded side of it. In that position there was just one hope of happiness left for Edith, and that was in her children. If such a woman so situated can be happy anywhere it will be in her nursery. But Edith's child, which arrived pretty promptly, only proved to be another whip to scourge her. Although of an unmistakable type, he was apparently healthy when he was born, but had rapidly degenerated, and Edith herself was a wreck. . . .

Angelica had never been in the same house with a baby before, and she was all interest. Whatever defects of character the new women* may eventually acquire, lack of maternal affection will not be one of them.

'Have you seen the baby?' she asked Elizabeth, when the latter was brushing her hair for dinner. He had not been visible during the afternoon, but Angelica had thought of him incessantly.

'Yes, Miss,' Elizabeth answered.

'Is he a pretty baby?' Angelica wanted to know.

Elizabeth pursed up her lips with an air of reserve.

'You don't think so?' Angelica said—she had seen the maid's face in the mirror before her. 'What is he like?'

'He's exactly like the bishop, Miss.'

Angelica broke into a broad smile at herself in the glass. 'What! a little old man baby!' she exclaimed.

'Yes, Miss—with a cold in his head,' the maid said seriously.

When she was dressed, Angelica went to make his acquaintance. On the way she discovered her particular friend, the bishop, going furtively in the same direction, and slipped her hand through his arm.

'We'll go together,' she said confidentially, taking it for granted that his errand was the same as her own.

The nurse was undressing the child when they entered, and Edith sat watching her. She was already dressed for the evening, and looked worse in an elaborate toilet than she had done in her morning dress. A stranger would have found it hard to believe that only the year before she had been radiantly healthy and beautiful. The puzzled, pathetic expression was again in her eyes as she watched the child. She had no smile for him, and uttered no baby words to him—

nor had he a smile for her. He was old, old already, and exhausted with suffering, and as his gaze wandered from one to the other it was easy to believe that he was asking each dumbly why had he ever been born?

'Is *that* Edith's baby?' Angelica exclaimed in her astonishment and horror under her breath, slipping her hand from the bishop's arm.

She had seen enough in one momentary glance, and she fled from the room. The bishop followed her. Mrs Beale was there when they entered, standing behind her daughter's chair, but she did not look at her husband, nor he at her. For the first time in their married life, poor souls, they were afraid to meet each other's eyes.

The news that Edith had returned to the palace, bringing her little son for the first time, was soon known in the neighbourhood. The arrival of the boy was one of those events of life, originally destined to be a great joy, which soften the heart and make it tender. And very soon carriages came rolling up with ladies leaning forward in them all in a flutter of sympathy and interest, eager to offer their congratulations to the young mother, and to be introduced to the child. And meanwhile Mrs Beale sat beside her daughter's bed, patting her slender white hand from time to time as it lay upon the coverlet, with that little gesture which had struck Angelica as being so piteous. Edith had not spoken for hours; but suddenly she exclaimed: 'Evadne was right!'

Mrs Beale rocked herself to and fro, and the tears gathered in her eyes and slowly trickled down her cheeks. 'Edith, darling,' she said at last with a great effort, 'do you blame me?'

'Oh, no, mother! oh, no!' Edith cried, pressing her hand, and looking at her with a last flash of loving recognition. 'The same thing may happen now to any mother—to any daughter—and *will* happen so long as we refuse to know and resist.' A spasm of pain contracted her face. She pressed her mother's hand again gently, and closed her eyes.

Presently she laughed. 'I am quite, quite mad!' she said. 'Do you know what I have been doing? I've been murdering him! I've been creeping, creeping, with bare feet, to surprise him in his sleep; and I had a tiny knife—very sharp—and I felt for the artery'—she touched her neck—'and then stabbed quickly! and he awoke, and knew he must die—and cowered! and it was all a pleasure to me. Oh, yes! I am quite, quite mad!'

She did not notice the coming and going of people now, or anything that was done in her room that day. Only once when she heard a servant outside the door whisper: 'For her ladyship,' she asked what it was, and a silver salver was brought to her covered with visiting cards. She looked at one or two. 'Kind messages,' she said, 'great names! and I am a great lady too, I suppose! I made a splendid match. And now I have a lovely little boy—the one thing wanting to complete my happiness. What numbers of girls must envy me! Ah! they don't know! But tell them—tell them that I'm quite, quite mad!'

Mrs Beale was at last persuaded to go and rest, and Mrs Orton Beg replaced her.

'I am glad you have come,' said Edith. 'I want to show you my lovely little son. Naturally I want to show him to everyone!' and she laughed.

Late in the evening, when the room was lighted up, Edith noticed her father and mother and Dr Galbraith. Angelica was there too, but in the background.

'Oh-h!' Edith exclaimed with a sudden shriek, starting up in bed—'I want to kill—I want to kill *him*. I want to kill that monstrous child!'

Dr Galbraith was in time to prevent her springing out of bed.

'I know I am mad,' she moaned in a broken voice. 'I am quite, quite mad! I never hurt a creature in my life—never thought an evil thought of anyone; why must I suffer so? Father, my head.' Again she started up. 'Can't you—can't you save me?' she shrieked. 'Father, my head! my head!'

BRAM STOKER

From *Dracula* (1897)

This scene, narrated by the alienist John Seward, refers to the fourth blood transfusion administered to Lucy Westenra, who is being drained by Dracula. The donor is Quincey Morris, an American adventurer. Lucy's fiancé Arthur Holmwood, Seward, and the senior scientist Van Helsing have already given Lucy their blood. Like Holmwood, Seward and Morris once proposed marriage to Lucy, and she has expressed a secret wish that she could marry all three. Since the technique of blood typing was not discovered until 1900, it is highly unlikely that a patient would have survived four transfusions from random donors.

Once again we went through that ghastly operation. I have not the heart to go through with the details. Lucy had got a terrible shock, and it told on her more than before, for though plenty of blood went into her veins, her body did not respond to the treatment as well as on the other occasions. Her struggle back into life was something frightful to see and hear. However, the action of both heart and lungs improved, and Van Helsing made a subcutaneous injection of morphia, as before, and with good effect. Her faint became a profound slumber. The Professor watched whilst I went downstairs with Quincey Morris, and sent one of the maids to pay off one of the cabmen who were waiting. I left Quincey lying down after having a glass of wine, and told the cook to get ready a good breakfast. . . .

When I got back Quincey was waiting for me. I told him I would see him as soon as I knew about Lucy, and went up to her room. She was still sleeping, and the Professor seemingly had not moved from his seat at her side. From his putting his finger to his lips, I gathered that he expected her to wake before long and was afraid of forestalling nature. So I went down to Quincey and took him into the breakfast-room, where the blinds were not drawn down, and which was a little more cheerful, or rather less cheerless, than the other rooms. When we were alone, he said to me:—

'Jack Seward, I don't want to shove myself in anywhere where I've no right to be; but this is no ordinary case. You know I loved that girl and wanted to marry her; but, although that's all past and gone, I can't help feeling anxious about her all the same. What is it that's wrong with her? The Dutchman—and a fine old fellow he is; I can see that—said, that time you two came into the room, that you must have *another* transfusion of blood, and that both you and he were exhausted. Now I know well that you medical men speak *in camera*;* and that a man must not expect to know what they consult about in private. But this is no common matter, and, whatever it is, I have done my part. Is not that so?'

'That's so,' I said, and he went on:—

'I take it that both you and Van Helsing had done already what I did to-day. Is not that so?'

'That's so.'

'And I guess Art was in it too. When I saw him four days ago down at his own place he looked queer. I have not seen anything pulled down so quick since I was on the Pampas and had a mare that I was fond of go to grass all in a night. One of those big bats that they call vampires had got at her in the night, and, what with his gorge and the vein left open, there wasn't enough blood in her to let her stand up, and I had to put a bullet through her as she lay. Jack, if you may tell me without betraying confidence, Arthur was the first; is not that so?' As he spoke the poor fellow looked terribly anxious. He was in a torture of suspense regarding the woman he loved, and his utter ignorance of the terrible mystery which seemed to surround her intensified his pain. His very heart was bleeding, and it took all the manhood of him—and there was a royal lot of it, too—to keep him from breaking down. I paused before answering, for I felt that I must not betray anything which the Professor wished kept secret, but already he knew so much, and guessed so much, that there could be no reason for not answering, so I answered in the same phrase: 'That's so.'

'And how long has this been going on?'

'About ten days.'

'Ten days! Then I guess, Jack Seward, that that poor pretty creature that we all love has had put into her veins within that time the blood of four strong men. Man alive, her whole body wouldn't hold it.' Then, coming close to me, he spoke in a fierce half-whisper: 'What took it out?'

EPILOGUE: SCIENCE
AND LITERATURE

SIR JOHN HERSCHEL

Prose and Verse (1857)

I

To thee, fair Science, long and early loved,
    Hath been of old my open homage paid;
Nor false, nor recreant have I ever proved,
    Nor grudged the gift upon thy altar laid.
    And if from thy clear path my foot have strayed,
Truant awhile,—'twas but to turn, with warm
    And cheerful haste; while thou didst not upbraid,
Nor change thy guise, nor veil thy beauteous form,
But welcomedst back my heart with every wonted charm.

II

High truths, and prospect clear, and ample store
    Of lofty thoughts are thine! Yet love I well
That loftier far, but more mysterious lore,
    More dark of import, and yet not less real,
    Which Poetry reveals; what time with spell
High-wrought, the Muse, soft-plumed, and whisperingly
    Nightly descends, and beckoning leads to cell
Or haunted grove; where all inspiringly
She breathes her dirge of woe, or swells my heart with glee.

III

Oh! rosy fetters of sweet-linked Rhyme,
    Which charm while ye detain, and hold me drowned
In rich o'erpowering rapture! Space and Time
    Forgot, I linger in the mazy round
    Of loveliest combination. Thought and Sound,

And tender images, and forms of grace,
    Flit by, and on my brow the laurel bound
Sits lightly!—who would not worse chains embrace,
So he might meet that loved inspirer, face to face?

EXPLANATORY NOTES

EDGAR ALLAN POE

3 *Hamadryad*: wood-nymph.

Naiad: river-nymph.

JOHN TYNDALL

4 *its Helmholtz, its Huxley, and its Du Bois-Reymond*: the German physicist and physiologist Hermann von Helmholtz (1821–94) formulated the Law of Conservation of Energy in 1847. A superb writer, he was known for his popular essays on science (see also note to p. 62). The German physiologist Emil DuBois-Reymond (1818–96) worked with Helmholtz and wrote beautifully in both French and German. The British naturalist Thomas Henry Huxley got his start in science by explaining complex ideas in popular essays.

Anaxagoras: (*c*.500–428 BC), Greek pre-Socratic philosopher who discovered the cause of eclipses. He opposed earlier philosophers who believed in the unity of all things, arguing that the universe was composed of an infinite number of elements.

MATTHEW ARNOLD

6 *M. Renan*: the French philosopher and historian Ernest Renan (1823–92) wrote the controversial *Life of Jesus* (1863), which presented Christianity as a myth generated by stimulating the popular imagination.

7 *Wolf*: the German classicist Friedrich August Wolf (1759–1824) established the nineteenth-century field of philology. His *Prolegomena ad Homerum* (1795) challenged the idea that *The Iliad* and *The Odyssey* were written by a single author. Instead, Wolf saw them as part of a tradition of oral poetry.

ADA LOVELACE

18 *Jacquard*: between 1790 and 1806 Joseph-Marie Jacquard (1752–1834) developed an automatic loom directed by punch cards. Jacquard's loom altered the textile industry for ever and laid the groundwork for modern weaving techniques.

AUGUSTUS DE MORGAN

21 *Wollaston and Fraunhofer*: the British physician William Hyde Wollaston

(1766–1828) developed techniques for processing metals and discovered the elements palladium and rhodium. Best known for his achievements in metallurgy, Wollaston also performed experiments in chemistry, physics, and physiology. The German optician and glass-maker Joseph von Fraunhofer (1787–1826) devoted himself to producing the best optical instruments possible for the study of light. He greatly improved the diffraction gratings used in spectroscopy and mapped the spectral lines of visible light.

22 *Alexander and Bucephalus*: Alexander the Great (356–323 BC) created a massive empire centred on Macedonia and extending from India to North Africa. Bucephalus ('Ox-head') was Alexander's horse.

GEORGE BOOLE

24 *a distinguished writer*: the French mathematician Siméon-Denis Poisson (1781–1840); quotation from *Recherches sur la probabilité des jugemens* (1837).

25 *The key to the rude Ogham inscriptions*: Charles Graves, a mathematics professor at the University of Dublin, announced in 1848 that he had deciphered the Ogham inscriptions. Ogham writing was an Irish alphabet used from the fourth century AD in inscriptions on stone monuments.

Mr Layard: the British archaeologist Austen Henry Layard (1817–94) studied the civilizations of ancient Mesopotamia, now modern Iraq. In 1849 he discovered cuneiform tablets that had served as state records and offered vast amounts of information about the ancient culture. His successful book, *Discoveries in the Ruins of Nineveh and Babylon*, had appeared in 1853, one year before Boole's text. Layard was knighted in 1878.

LEWIS CARROLL

33 *the larger Diagram*: Carroll refers here to tables he has been describing throughout the first five chapters. On these tables, logical propositions like 'some x are y' can be represented with the digits 0 and 1.

GEORGE ELIOT

36 *Livonian*: from Livonia, a Baltic province of Russia, today Latvia and Estonia.

37 *napoleons*: gold coins worth twenty francs.

Rousseau: the French philosopher Jean Jacques Rousseau (1712–78) argued that education and social rituals corrupted people, destroying their natural potential for goodness.

39 *louis*: silver coins worth three or five francs, known in French as *écus*.

'*Faites votre jeu, mesdames et messieurs*': Place your bets, ladies and gentlemen.

'*Le jeu ne va plus*': The game is over.

H. G. WELLS

41 *Professor Simon Newcomb*: probably fictional.

SIR WILLIAM HERSCHEL

44 *the Georgian planet*: Uranus, discovered by Herschel in 1781.

Sirius, Arcturus: two very bright stars known since ancient times. Sirius, the Dog Star, was believed by the Egyptians to cause the annual flooding of the Nile. Arcturus, 'the bear guard', is part of the northern constellation Boötes, 'the herdsman', located near the tail of the Great Bear.

the doctrine of parallaxes: a technique used to measure the distance between an object and the earth by comparing its angle when observed from two different points. The parallax of an object directly overhead is zero; that of an object directly at the horizon is maximal.

magnitude: a system for classifying stars based on their perceived brightness, suggesting their distance from the earth. Used since the days of Ptolemy, this classificatory scheme suffered from subjective variations until the invention of the photometer in the late nineteenth century. Stars of first magnitude are the brightest; those of the sixth are barely visible to the naked eye; and those of seventh or higher can only be seen with telescopes.

$a^2 l / D^2$: Herschel has previously defined a as the aperture of the iris; l as the total quantity of light perceived by the eye; and D as the distance from the luminous object.

a Cygni, β Tauri: Alpha Cygni is the brightest star in the constellation Cygnus, the Swan, with visual magnitude 1.25; Beta Tauri is a star in the constellation Taurus, the Bull, with visual magnitude 1.65.

46 *γ Cygni, ε Bootis*: Gamma Cygni is another of the brightest stars in Cygnus, with visual magnitude 2.20; Epsilon Bootis is a star in the northern constellation Boötes, 'the herdsman', with visual magnitude 2.37.

47 *Perseus*: a prominent northern constellation named after the ancient Greek hero.

MR MESSIER: the French astronomer Charles Messier (1730–1817), the first scientist to attempt a systematic catalogue of nebulae and star clusters.

H Geminorum: a star in the constellation Gemini, the Twins.

DR HALLEY: the British astronomer Edmund Halley (1656–1742) collaborated with Isaac Newton to develop a theory about what forces held the planets in their orbits. Halley was the first astronomer to calculate the orbit of a comet. Theorizing that the bright comets sighted in 1531, 1607, and 1682 were all really the same comet, he predicted that it would return in 1758. When it did, astronomers named it after him. Eta and Zeta Herculis are faint stars in the constellation Hercules. The latter has a visual magnitude of 2.81.

47 *Andromeda . . . in 1612*: the spiral galaxy Andromeda is the nearest galaxy outside the Milky Way. In Herschel's time it was classified as a nebula, an indistinct light source in the night sky. Known to Arabic astronomers as early as 964, it was rediscovered in 1611 by German investigator Simon Marius (1573–1624), one of the first astronomers to use a telescope.

THOMAS CARLYLE

48 *Chartisms*: Chartism was a democratic, reformist movement 1837–48 advocating increased rights for workers.

Chactaw: the Choctaw, a native American tribe that originally lived in Mississippi and Alabama.

Stygian: referring to the River Styx (one of the rivers of the underworld) or to the underworld in general.

49 *Transcendental*: advocates of an idealist philosophy voiced by the American essayist Ralph Waldo Emerson (1803–82) and other New England writers in the period 1830–50.

Chronos . . . Socinian: Chronos, or Cronus, father of Zeus; Jove: Jupiter, chief of the Roman gods, equivalent to the Greek Zeus; Odin: chief of the Norse gods; St Olaf (995–1030), the first king of Norway, a strong political leader who helped to spread Christianity; Socinian: belonging to a sixteenth-century theological sect that denied the divinity of Christ.

in Puseyisms: Tractarianism, or the 'Oxford Movement,' initiated in 1833 by Edward Bouverie Pusey (1800–82), who wanted to revive some Catholic teachings in the Anglican Church.

50 *Ilion's or Latium's plains*: scenes of ancient, heroic wars, described in the epic poems of Homer and Virgil. Ilion: Troy; Latium: the region of ancient Italy in which Rome was built.

Phrygians: inhabitants of Western Turkey 1100–600 BC, whose civilization reached its peak after the fall of Troy; metaphorically, the Trojans.

Frost-jötuns, Marsh-giants: in Scandinavian mythology, jötuns (the old Swedish word for giant) were said to have inhabited the Northern countries before these lands were occupied by people. These mythological beings included frost-, marsh-, and mist-giants. I am grateful to Staffan Müller-Wille for this information.

WILLIAM THOMSON

61 *Mayer . . . Waterston*: the German physicist Julius Robert Mayer (1814–78) was one of the first scientists to propose the principle of the conservation of energy. Mayer studied the relation between heat and mechanical work and was especially interested in the ways living bodies converted the energy from food into work and heat. Scottish physicist John James Waterson (1811–83) studied solar radiation. In 1845 he proposed a kinetic theory of gases, which was overlooked until James Clerk Maxwell began his work in this field.

62 *Meteoric action . . . from independent evidence*: Thomson is quoting his article, 'On the Mechanical Energies of the Solar System', *Transactions of the Royal Society of Edinburgh*, 1854.

Helmholtz: see note to p. 4 above. Like Mayer, Hermann von Helmholtz was extremely interested in thermodynamics and studied the relationship between heat and mechanical work both in organic and inorganic systems.

Joule: the British physicist James Prescott Joule (1818–89), a gifted experimentalist, studied the relationship between electrical currents, mechanical work, and heat, and developed formulas for interconverting them.

63 *the sun . . . for 500,000,000 years*: according to current estimates, the sun has been emitting energy for over four billion years and will continue to do so for many billions of years longer.

JOHN TYNDALL

67 *this fine Nicol's prism*: described in a passage omitted here, this is a prism made of Iceland spar that can polarize light (screen out all rays of light except those moving in one given direction). When exposed to polarized light, a Nicol prism can either block or transmit the light depending on the prism's position.

69 *Anschauungsgabe and Einbildungskraft*: (German) the ability to work through ideas visually; the power of the imagination.

JAMES CLERK MAXWELL

74 *Tyndallic*: Maxwell refers to the physicist John Tyndall. See pp. 3–4, 63–70.

empyrean: from the highest level of the heavens, which in ancient mythology was said to consist of fire.

The double D, magnesian b, / And Thallium's living green: when substances are heated, they give off characteristic patterns of radiation. When analysed spectroscopically, chemical elements exhibit distinct patterns of coloured lines corresponding to the wavelengths of energy emitted as excited electrons move from one energy level to another. In 1868 British physicist Sir William Crookes (1832–1919) discovered thallium because of a bright green line that always appeared in the spectroscopic analysis of some mineral ores. 'Double D' and 'magnesian *b*' refer to specific spectral lines.

76 *ebonite*: vulcanite, a hard compound of india-rubber and sulphur fused together by intense heat.

triple messing: Maxwell is playing here with a line from Horace (*Odes* I. iii): 'Illi robur et aes triplex'. The ode is a propemptikon wishing Virgil a safe journey as he sails for Greece. The complete line reads: 'he had oak and triple layers of bronze around his chest who first entrusted fragile craft to cruel sea.' Maxwell is joking about the audacity of Rowland's experiment. I am indebted to George Greaney for this and other information about Horace's poetry.

77 *Rowland of Troy*: American physicist and engineer Henry Augustus Rowland (1848–1901) taught physics at the Rensselaer Polytechnic Institute in Troy, New York. He was a close friend of Maxwell, who admired his studies of the electrical permeability of metals. While working in Hermann von Helmholtz's laboratory, Rowland designed an experiment with a vulcanite disc to test whether the magnetic induction produced by electric currents was caused through an interaction with the conductor, or simply by the presence of a moving charge. Helmholtz praised the experiment as the first real evidence that moving charges caused magnetic effects. Rowland is best known for the concave diffraction grating he designed later in his career, which allowed physicists to map spectral lines much more accurately.

Archimage: a great wizard or chief magician. Maxwell is referring to Hermann von Helmholtz.

One Rowland to two Olivers: Continuing the epic allusions (Roland and Oliver in *La Chanson de Roland*); 'Oliver' is possibly a reference to Oliver Heaviside, a former telegrapher, who presented Maxwell's laws in terms of integrals, leading to their acceptance by the scientific community. See Jeff Mackowiak, 'Maxwell's "Quaint Verses"', unpublished essay, 4 June 1999. I am grateful to Mackowiak for his valuable work on Maxwell's poetry.

78 *marlinspike*: a pointed iron tool used by sailors to separate strands of rope, in order to splice them together.

homaloid: plane.

THOMAS HARDY

82 *Castor and Pollux*: alpha and beta Geminorum, the two brightest stars in the constellation Gemini, named after the twin sons of Leda in Greek mythology.

RICHARD A. PROCTOR

84 *Seemed to move . . . of the gods*: Wordsworth, *The Excursion*, iv. 701–3. I am grateful to Scott Harshbarger for identifying these lines from Wordsworth.

Their wandering course . . . standing still: Milton, *Paradise Lost*, viii. 126.

87 *Cerberus*: in Greek and Roman mythology, a watchdog guarding the entrance to the underworld.

polariscopy: the analysis of polarized light with an instrument using two plates or prisms.

Argus-eyed: as watchful as Argus, a creature in Greek mythology who had a hundred eyes.

WILHELM CONRAD ROENTGEN

88 *a Hittorf vacuum-tube, or through a Lenard tube, a Crookes tube*: the German physicist Johann Wilhelm Hittorf (1824–1914) studied the ways electrical currents affected the behaviour of ions. Phillipp Lenard (1862–1947) won the Nobel Prize for Physics in 1905 for his studies of cathode rays, streams of electrons emitted by the negative electrode in a tube containing a low-pressure gas. Lenard observed that cathode rays could pass through thin layers of metal and designed a special tube with an aluminium opening through which the rays could pass. Lenard also discovered some aspects of the photoelectric effect, noticing that cathode rays were produced when light collides with metals. Sir William Crookes (see pp. 545–6) showed that cathode rays could produce heat and phosphorescence under some conditions. He also discovered the theory behind the radiometer, which quantified light intensity by converting it into radial motion.

90 *photometer*: an instrument that indicates the intensity of electromagnetic radiation by converting it into a mechanical form such as the movement of a needle.

interference phenomena: patterns of nodes and anti-nodes created by the intersection of two series of waves.

91 *ether*: see Edgar Allan Poe, 'Mesmeric Revelation', pp. 568–9 below.

SAMUEL F. B. MORSE

92 *With regard to telegraphs constructed on the ordinary principles*: in the late eighteenth and early nineteenth centuries the term 'telegraph' referred to systems of visual signalling. Before the electro-magnetic telegraph came into use, 'telegraphs' consisted of series of signal towers on high ground whose observers used telescopes to read their neighbours' signals. As Morse points out, such systems could not be used at night or in bad weather.

92 *Franklin*: the American scientist and statesman Benjamin Franklin experimented extensively with electricity. Morse refers to an experiment in which Franklin transmitted electrical current over a wire strung across a Philadelphia river.

93 *if I have been rightly informed . . . more rapidly than light*: Morse has of course been misinformed. In 1834 the British physicist Charles Wheatstone (1802–75) had calculated the velocity of electricity along a wire to be over 250,000 miles per second (about 1.3 times the speed of light). Morse, an artist with no background in physics, may have heard this figure and confused the units. In 1856 the German physicists Wilhelm Weber (1804–91) and Rudolph Kohlrausch (1809–58) determined this velocity to be 3×10^8 metres per second, later discovered to be the speed of light.

the first cost: Morse has been discussing the cost of insulation.

THE TELEPHONE

97 *phonoautograph*: a device consisting of a membrane with an attached point (a 'style') capable of recording sound vibrations onto a revolving cylinder.

MARK TWAIN

99 *the Psychical Society of England*: in January 1882 William Barrett (1844–1925) and F. W. H. Myers (1843–1901) founded the Society for Psychical Research, whose aim was to investigate mesmerism, thought-reading, spiritualism, clairvoyance, and haunted houses in a rigorous, scientific way.

100 *A Tramp Abroad*: this book, published in 1880, describes Twain's 1878 tour of Germany, Italy, and Switzerland and contains his essay, 'The Awful German Language'.

Mr Metcalf was too wary for me: the highly respectable *North American Review* published essays on law, religion, philosophy, history, and the classics and was reputed to have made rather dull reading. While it is possible that Twain offered 'Mental Telegraphy' to its editor in 1878, Twain's introduction may simply be a fictional dig at this 'respectable' journal.

101 *Mr William H. Wright*: (1829–98, *nom de plume* Dan DeQuille), American journalist and humorist, editor of the Virginia City newspaper *The Territorial Enterprise* and a close friend of Twain's.

102 *. . . all invented it at the same time*: in 1832, while returning from Europe, the American artist Samuel F. B. Morse (1791–1872) thought of sending messages over a wire with electrical signals. Morse's idea was far from original. Scientists had proposed using electricity to 'transmit intelligence' since the 1750s and had constructed working electrical telegraphs

as early as 1795. Not until 1837, however, did they design efficient models that could work over significant distances. While struggling with his apparatus between 1832 and 1837, Morse was helped by the physicist Joseph Henry (1797–1878), who designed a booster system making it possible to transmit signals over any distance without loss of strength. In 1837 Morse, Charles Wheatstone, and the German physicist Karl August Steinheil (1801–70) presented the world with telegraphic systems almost simultaneously. While Twain's explanation of mental telegraphy seems apt, European and American scientists had been working on the telegraph for decades. It is not surprising that several finished simultaneously.

a literary friend of mine: the American critic and novelist William Dean Howells (1837–1920).

103 ... *a very striking and strong story*: Anne Moncure Crane Seemüller (1838–72) published *Emily Chester* in 1864; *Moods*, the first novel of Louisa May Alcott (1832–88), appeared in 1865.

Will Carleton's: American poet Will Carleton (1845–1912), author of *Farm Ballads* (1873) and *Farm Legends* (1875).

HENRY JAMES

106 *Picciola*: a popular novel by Joseph Xavier Boniface, *nom de plume* Saintine, published in 1836. In Italian, *picciola* means a small woman who may at first appear to be of little worth.

108 *port of Juno*: with the bearing and mannerisms of a queen. In Roman mythology, Juno was the wife of Jupiter and queen of heaven, corresponding to the Greek Hera. Juno was seen as a protector of women.

HERMANN VON HELMHOLTZ

122 *Newton ... Daniel Bernoulli ... Rumford ... Humphry Davy*: Helmholtz credits the physicists Sir Isaac Newton (1642–1727), Daniel Bernoulli (1700–82), Benjamin Thompson, Count Rumford (1753–1814), and Sir Humphry Davy (1778–1829) with having suggested the principle of conservation of energy. The versatile Bernoulli, a physician and mathematician as well as a gifted physicist, studied the mechanics of respiration and circulation and developed the science of hydrodynamics. Thompson studied ballistics and tried to disprove the caloric theory of heat. His greatest contribution as a scientist was to promote the study of science and technology; he founded the Royal Institution in 1799. Davy, a chemist, educated the public about the relevance of chemistry to everyday life. He was particularly interested in the physiological effects of various gases and the chemical action of electricity.

Mayer ... Joule: see notes to pp. 61–2 above.

LUIGI GALVANI

136　*Bartholinus*: Thomas Bartholin (1616–80), Danish anatomist who helped reveal the structure of the lymphatic system.

　　series of men: in the eighteenth century, it was common practice to transmit an electric shock along a 'human chain,' either as part of an experiment or as a parlour game. Particularly famous was Jean-Antoine Nollet's (1700–70) experiment of 1746 in which he transmitted an electric shock along a line of two hundred monks.

　　Leyden jar: invented by the Dutch physicist Petrus van Musschenbroek (1692–1761) in 1746, this glass jar coated with metal foil functioned as a capacitor, allowing eighteenth-century experimenters to store electric charge. Before the invention of the battery in 1800, scientists used it as an energy supply for their electrical experiments.

137　*nerve fluid*: from classical times until well into the eighteenth century, nerves were thought to be hollow tubes for conducting fluid from the brain to the muscles. In 1791 electricity was also thought to be a fluid, so it made sense to identify the nerve fluid with electricity.

　　described experiments: Galvani has been describing experiments in which he substituted an animal preparation for a Leyden jar; the animal tissue could be charged and discharged in much the same way.

　　torpedo: an electric fish known since classical times.

　　noble . . . imperfect metals: 'noble' metals were those highly resistant to oxidation, such as gold, silver, platinum, and mercury. 'Imperfect' metals were more reactive and more easily oxidized.

　　insulating plane: a flat surface of non-conducting material that supported an experimental set-up without electrically connecting the parts.

138　*armature*: a thin layer of metal wrapped around an object, as on a Leyden jar.

　　resinous and vitreous bodies: bodies charged with what were believed to be two different kinds of electricity: resinous (negative), created by rubbing amber, silk, or paper; and vitreous (positive), created by rubbing glass, animal fur, or precious stones

139　*animal spirits*: nerve fluid. Championed by René Descartes and debated by late-seventeenth-century scientists, the hypothesis of animal spirits dictated that fast-moving particles in the blood assembled in the brain and when necessary rushed to the muscles, allowing them to exert their force.

SIR HUMPHRY DAVY

140　*respiration*: the biochemical processes through which living organisms extract energy from food.

142　*sublime philosophy*: belonging to the highest forms of human thought.

MARY SHELLEY

144 *natural philosophy*: the study of all natural phenomena, encompassing what today are the natural and physical sciences.

145 *the Arabian who had been buried with the dead . . . light*: a reference to Sinbad's fourth voyage in *Tales of a Thousand and One Nights*. In this adventure, Sinbad describes a country where, if a person's spouse dies, he or she must be lowered into a burial pit along with the spouse's body. When Sinbad's own wife dies, he survives because he spots a 'tremulous speck of light' and escapes from the pit via a tunnel dug by animals.

XAVIER BICHAT

150 *azote*: nitrogen.

151 *nerves of animal life . . . of organic life*: the voluntary and autonomic nervous systems.

Muscles of organic life . . . of animal life: involuntary (smooth) muscle and voluntary (striated) muscle.

The serous: watery tissues.

The synovial: connective tissues that lubricate the joints.

Bordieu's time: probably Théophile de Bordeu (1722–76), a prominent anatomist who argued that each organ had its own life.

peritoneum: the double membrane lining the abdominal cavity.

152 *brouchia*: probably a misprint for bronchia.

GEORGE ELIOT

154 *Fielding*: the British novelist Henry Fielding (1707–54), author of *Joseph Andrews* (1742) and *Tom Jones* (1749).

each lady who saw medical truth in Wrench . . . medical perdition: Doctors Wrench and Toller are fictional characters whose names suggest the violent and 'taxing' nature of their treatments.

156 *makdom and her fairnesse*: from James I, 'A Treatise of the Airt of Scottis Poesie' (1585).

157 *Jenner*: Edward Jenner (1749–1823), the discoverer of vaccination.

158 *Herschel*: Sir William Herschel (1738–1822), an innovative astronomer who designed powerful, light-gathering telescopes and used them to explore the night skies in a systematic way. Born in Germany, Herschel fled to England in 1757 when the French occupied Hanover. Initially he supported himself by teaching music.

GEORGE HENRY LEWES

161 *ganglionic cells*: neurons, so called at this time because of the tendency of their cell bodies to cluster in visible, pulpy 'ganglia'.

162 *Ehrenberg ... the spinal ganglia*: Christian Gottfried Ehrenberg (1795–1876), one of the first anatomists to observe nerve cells in the cerebral cortex; and Robert Remak (1815–65), who demonstrated that the cell body and the axon (the extended outgrowth along which a neuron transmits signals over long distances) were both parts of the nerve cell.

motricity: the ability to provoke motion.

Schröder van der Kolk: the neuroanatomist Jacob Lodewik Koenraad Schroeder van der Kolk (1797–1862) studied how neurons in the spinal cord made reflex arcs possible.

163 *Wundt*: Wilhelm Wundt (1832–1920), one of the founders of experimental psychology, began his career as a neurophysiologist.

MARY SHELLEY

164 *typhus fever*: an infectious disease caused by Rickettsia, often transmitted by fleas or lice, and characterized by headache, fever, and a red rash. In the early nineteenth century, before it was known that typhus and typhoid were caused by two different micro-organisms, debates raged among physicians as to whether these two fevers were the same disease. Typhoid, which also involves a red rash, is caused by the bacterium *Salmonella typhi*.

Brobdignagians: gigantic beings depicted in the second part of Jonathan Swift's *Gulliver's Travels* (1726). They regard humans as vermin.

165 *Quito*: the capital of Ecuador, located at the foot of the volcano Pichincha.

Ryland: a fictional character. A man 'of obscure birth and of immense wealth', this republican politician opposes inherited privilege and tries to implement a more egalitarian social system. When the plague strikes, however, he proves to be a poor leader.

167 *New Holland*: Australia.

Van Diemen's Land: Tasmania.

SIR EDWIN CHADWICK

Mr Gilbert: Assistant Commissioner Thomas Gilbert, who studied lunacy and idiocy among paupers.

malaria: any fever believed to be caused by unwholesome air, such as that of marshy districts. Malaria was not associated with mosquitoes in 1842, nor did it denote a single, well-characterized disease.

168 *Dr Barham*: possibly Thomas Foster Barham, who received his MD from Queen's College, Cambridge, in 1820. Barham practised in Exeter and died in Devon in 1869.

170 *Dr Arnott*: a close friend of Jeremy Bentham, the British physician Neil Arnott (1788–1874) showed Chadwick the hospitals and sewers of

London and Edinburgh and convinced him that diseases were caused by noxious fumes from decaying matter. Arnott was especially interested in improving ventilation in the dwellings of the poor. *Wynds* are narrow alleys leading off of main streets.

Dr Alison: William Pulteney Alison (1790–1859), professor of medicine at the University of Edinburgh and Secretary of the Edinburgh Medico-Chirurgical Society. Alison was particularly interested in inflammation and was known for his textbook *Outlines of Physiology* (1831).

EDGAR ALLAN POE

171   *Avator*: avatar, the manifestation of a god in human form.

173   *litten*: lighted.

174   *'Hernani'*: Victor Hugo's (1802–85) innovative, controversial poetic drama that challenged theatrical conventions. Set in Spain, the play depicts the complex relations between the outlaw Hernani, the young woman he loves, the aristocratic protector determined to marry her, and the King courting her. At early performances of *Hernani* in 1830, romantic writers confronted theatrical traditionalists who objected to the play's format and style.

OLIVER WENDELL HOLMES

178   *hydrophobia*: rabies.

179   *Dr Gordon of Aberdeen*: the Scottish physician Alexander Gordon (1752–99) studied medicine in Aberdeen and Edinburgh and worked briefly as a ship's surgeon in the Royal Navy. After studying midwifery in London, he returned to Scotland where he spent most of his career directing the Aberdeen dispensary. Gordon specialized in obstetrics, and some scholars think that he, not Holmes or Semmelweis, should receive credit for demonstrating that puerperal fever was contagious.

180   *peritonitis*: inflammation of the tissue lining the abdominal cavity.

erysipelas: St Anthony's Fire, a bacteriologically caused skin disease involving inflammation and fever.

LOUIS PASTEUR

182   *albuminous*: having a composition similar to that of eggwhite, i.e. a suspension of proteins in water.

M. Cagniard de Latour: Charles Cagniard de Latour (1777–1859), had argued as early as 1835–6 that a living substance caused fermentation.

all true fermentations—viscous, lactic, butyric ... tartaric acid, malic acid, or urine: fermentation is the process by which living organisms extract energy from glucose in the absence of oxygen. The many types of fermentation are classified according to the end products into which the six-carbon glucose is broken down. In lactic fermentation, lactic acid, a three-carbon compound, is produced; butyric, tartaric, and malic acid fermentation lead to the production of four-carbon compounds. The type of fermentation a micro-organism will conduct depends upon the enzymes it possesses. By 1859 Pasteur could selectively bring about any known kind of fermentation, and he suspected that these different biochemical reactions were occurring because different micro-organisms were involved.

183 *guncotton*: cotton soaked in nitric and sulphuric acid, usually employed in blasting.

SIR JOSEPH LISTER

187 *It is now six years*: in 1861 Lister was placed in charge of the surgical wards at the Glasgow Royal Infirmary and began studying how wounds became infected.

granulating sore: a wound in the phase of normal healing characterized by small, round bumps caused by the outgrowth of capillaries.

THE LANCET: founded in 1823 by medical reformer Thomas Wakley, this British medical journal was the primary source of information for nineteenth-century English-speaking physicians and is still one of the world's most highly respected medical periodicals. In the 1860s its readers included not just doctors but educated lay people interested in medicine. George Eliot studied *The Lancet* to prepare for writing *Middlemarch*.

We know from the researches of Pasteur: until Lister learned of Pasteur's ideas in 1865, he had believed that dust caused sepsis, but he quickly became one of Pasteur's strongest supporters.

188 *vibrios*: a genus of mobile, 'vibrating', S-shaped or comma-shaped bacteria, some of which cause deadly diseases.

189 *pyogenic membrane*: a membrane holding back a large quantity of pus.

190 *sanious*: containing serum, pus, and some blood, like the thin fluid that emerges from a wound.

ANONYMOUS

193 *tubercle bacillus*: the bacterium that causes tuberculosis. Koch won world fame in March 1882, when he identified the bacillus that caused one of Europe's most widespread and deadly diseases.

anthrax: a bacteriological disease of cattle to which humans are also susceptible. Koch's study of the anthrax bacillus in 1876 provided the first evidence that a specific micro-organism caused a particular infectious disease. Louis Pasteur produced the first vaccine to a bacterially caused disease in 1881 with his famous experiment at Pouilly-le-Fort. He demonstrated that sheep inoculated with denatured anthrax bacillus survived, whereas uninoculated sheep died when both grazed in the same anthrax-infested field.

relapsing fever: an infectious disease caused by the spirochete *Borrelia* (a bacterium), spread by lice and ticks, that produces week-long attacks of fever at weekly intervals.

spirillum: a genus of large, spiral-shaped bacteria.

194 *Drs Kartulis and Schiess-Bey . . . Drs Strauss and Roux*: Greek microbiologist Alexander Kartulis (1852–1920), known for his studies of amoebic dysentery, and bacteriologists Isidore Straus (1845–1896), a Professor of Medicine at the University of Paris, and Émile Roux (1853–1933), an associate of Louis Pasteur. Schiess-Bey is not otherwise known.

196 *Hurdivar and Puri*: Haridwar, a city in Northern India, and Puri, a city in Eastern India on the Bay of Bengal, are important destinations for Hindu pilgrims.

H. G. WELLS

201 *Ravachol, Vaillant*: the French anarchist François Koenigstein (1859–92) used his mother's name, 'Ravachol'. A former grave-robber, Ravachol became famous for dynamiting public buildings. He was arrested, condemned to death, and guillotined in 1892. The French radical politician Édouard-Marie Vaillant (1840–1915), who had studied engineering and medicine, was exiled from France in 1871 for helping to organize the Paris Commune. Between 1871 and 1880 he lived in England, where he collaborated with Karl Marx. In 1880 he returned to France and from 1893 onward served in the National Assembly. Among the causes he supported were social security and an eight-hour workday.

CLAUDE BERNARD

204 *According to Galen . . . criminals condemned to death*: the Greek physician Galen of Pergamum (Claudios Galenos, AD 129–99) dissected monkeys to learn how the human body worked and proposed that people would remain healthy if they could maintain the balance between the four bodily humours. Attalus III (Philometor Euergetes, 170–133 BC, King of Pergamum 138–133 BC) was known as a tyrant but later became interested in learning. Pergamum, an important city in the Hellenistic Age, is located in modern Turkey.

Celsus . . . with the Ptolemies' consent: Aulus Cornelius Celsus, the 'Cicero of Physicians', was a Roman medical writer of the first century AD. His work *De Medicina* was widely read during the European renaissance. The Alexandrian physician Herophilus (335–280 BC) dissected human cadavers in public and performed important studies of brain anatomy. Erasistratus, another physician of Alexandria who was born several generations later, studied the nervous and circulatory systems and was able to distinguish sensory from motor nerves. The Ptolemies, a dynasty of Macedonian kings, ruled Egypt from 323 to 30 BC.

204 *Fallopius*: the Italian anatomist Gabriello Fallopio (1523–62) studied the female reproductive system and the inner ear.

nephrotomy: an incision into a kidney.

205 *Graaf . . . Magendie*: the Dutch physician Reinier de Graaf (1641–73) conducted anatomical studies of the human reproductive organs and discovered the ovarian follicles. The British physician William Harvey (1578–1657) explained how the blood circulated in his classic work, *Anatomical Exercises Concerning the Motion of the Heart and Blood in Animals* (1628). The Italian anatomist Gaspare Aselli (1581–1626) demonstrated how fluids moved through the lymphatic system. The anatomist Jean Pecquet (1622–74) performed numerous dissections of animals. The Swiss physiologist Albrecht von Haller (1708–77) explored the relationship between the muscles and the nerves. Bernard depicts his mentor, François Magendie (1783–1855) as heir to a great tradition of experimental physiology. One of the most important physiologists of the nineteenth century, Magendie demonstrated the distinct sensory and motor functions of the spinal nerves. All these scientists depended on experimental animals as sources of knowledge.

206 *helminthologist*: a specialist in the study of intestinal worms.

phthisis: tuberculosis of the lungs.

207 *Nero*: the fifth Roman emperor (AD 37–68), known for his cruelty.

Le Gallois: in the first decade of the nineteenth century, the physiologist Julien Jean César Le Gallois (1770–1814) had studied respiration in rabbits by decapitating them, then inflating their lungs with a syringe.

208 *Fontana and J. Müller*: the Italian physiologist Felice Fontana (1730–1805) advanced scientists' understanding of nerves and muscles by observing the way that different tissues reacted to chemical and electrical stimulation. The German physiologist Johannes Müller (1801–58) inspired a generation of experimental physiologists to analyse bodily functions in terms of physical and chemical laws.

SIR JAMES PAGET

213 *Before Hunter's time*: the surgeon John Hunter (1728–93) introduced English doctors to pathological anatomy and urged them to perform anatomical and physiological experiments.

FRANCES POWER COBBE

215 *Professor Hermann of Zurich*: Ludimar Hermann (1838–1914), author of *Die Vivisectionsfrage* (1877) and several influential physiology textbooks.

Nineteenth Century . . . Fortnightly Review: liberal journals for educated lay readers with no special knowledge of science. Founded in 1877 by J. T. Knowles, the *Nineteenth Century* offered readers debates on controversial issues. In 1890–1 it carried a heated exchange between William Gladstone and T. H. Huxley about the existence of miracles. The *Fortnightly Review*, founded in 1865, was first edited by George Henry Lewes. It carried no unsigned articles and was known for its high-quality serialized fiction.

216 *Dr Lauder Brunton*: Sir Thomas Lauder Brunton (1844–1916), an authority on pharmacology, circulation, and digestion.

'I believe that . . . the most humane persons': Cobbe is quoting Paget's 'Vivisection: Its Pains and Its Uses', a passage on the cruelty of sports omitted from the extracts above.

Claude Bernard's description: like other nineteenth-century writers, Cobbe read Bernard in the original French. She quotes Bernard's discussion of vivisection in *An Introduction to the Study of Experimental Medicine* (see pp. 203–8). Her wording differs from that of the selection above because she has translated the passage herself. The French reads: 'Le physiologiste n'est pas un homme du monde, c'est un savant, c'est un homme qui est saisi et absorbé par une idée scientifique qu'il poursuit: il n'entend plus les cris des animaux, il ne voit plus le sang qui coule, il ne voit que son idée et n'aperçoit que des organismes qui lui cachent des problèmes qu'il veut découvrir.'

Cyon's: Elie de Cyon (1843–1912), author of *Methodik der physiologischen Experimente und Vivisectionen* (1876), studied electrotherapy and the innervation of the heart.

217 *Paul Bert*: (1833–86), an expert on respiration and anaesthesiology, and a great admirer of Claude Bernard.

Schiff: the neurophysiologist J. Moritz Schiff (1823–96). Cobbe is citing Schiff's *Lezioni di fisiologia sperimentale sul sistema nervoso* (1873), an Italian translation of his *Untersuchung zur Physiologie des Nervensystems* (1855).

Flourens . . . Bell's: the neurophysiologist Marie-Jean-Pierre Flourens (1794–1867); the physiologist François Magendie (see note to p. 205 above); and neuroanatomist Sir Charles Bell (1774–1842). In 1811 Bell proposed that the anterior roots of spinal nerves were motor, and that the posterior were primarily sensory. When Magendie reproduced Bell's results eleven years later, he disputed Bell's priority for the discovery. Flourens supported Bell. Because the British anti-vivisection movement was stronger than the French, Bell had worked only with stunned animals and could never accurately have studied changes in their sensitivity.

Magendie worked with live, conscious animals. Although British anti-vivsectionists condemned him for his cruelty, he deserves credit for the discovery.

218 *Gull*: Sir William Withey Gull (1816–90), author of a treatise on anorexia nervosa.

Professor Yeo ... Professor Rutherford's victims: Gerald Francis Yeo (1845–1909), author of *A Manual of Physiology* (1884). William Rutherford, Professor of Medicine at the University of Edinburgh, studied digestion in the dog.

Fuegians: people of Tierra del Fuego, the southernmost tip of South America, described by Charles Darwin in his *Journal of Researches into the Geology and Natural History of the Various Countries Visited by H.M.S. Beagle* (1839).

curare: a poison that paralyses animals by preventing their nerves from transmitting impulses to their muscles.

Dr Burdon-Sanderson ... Dr Michael Foster: the physiologist John Scott Burdon-Sanderson (1828–1905), who wrote a guide an animal experimentation and was a common target of anti-vivisectionists; Sir George Murray Humphry (1820–96), who studied the human skeleton and the process of ageing; Ernest Abraham Hart (1835–98), who studied vaccination and the diseases of the eye; George John Romanes (1848–94), who at the time was studying the nervous systems of invertebrates; and Michael Foster (1836–1907), founder of the Cambridge School of Physiology and an expert on the neuro-muscular interactions that drive the heart.

219 *Professors Goltz, Flint ... Ferrier*: the neurophysiologist Friedrich Leopold Goltz (1834–1902); the physiologist Austin Flint (1836–1915), author of several successful physiology textbooks; the neurophysiologist Charles-Édouard Brown-Séquard (1817–94); the physiologist Jules Béclard (1817–87); the anatomist Auguste Chauveau (1827–1917), who experimented with the physiological effects of electricity; and the neurophysiologist David Ferrier (1843–1928), who attempted to associate bodily movements with specific locations in the brain.

Richet ... Mantegazza in Italy: the physiologist and psychologist Charles Robert Richet (1850–1935), who studied digestion, temperature regulation, anaphylaxis, and psychic phenomena; and the Italian physiologist Paolo Mantegazza (1831–1910), author of a series of popular books on the physiology of pain, pleasure, love, and the expression of feelings.

Gemonian stairs: a set of steps on the Aventine hill in ancient Rome down which the bodies of executed criminals were dragged in order to be thrown into the River Tiber.

220 *'SEINEN FREUNDEN ... VON DEM VERFASSER'*: 'Dedicated to his friends in England, from the author.'

Raleigh: the English explorer and poet Sir Walter Raleigh (1554–1618), a favourite of Elizabeth I, though later imprisoned and executed by James I.

H. G. WELLS

231 *L'Homme qui Rit*: (1869), a romance by Victor Hugo, set in late-seventeenth-century England, about a man disguised by having a smile carved into his face.

233 *houri*: in Islamic popular tradition, a beautiful nymph said to await the virtuous in paradise.

JEAN BAPTISTE DE LAMARCK

241 *In the preceding chapter*: in the previous chapter, Lamarck guided readers 'downward' through the animal kingdom, pointing out the 'continuous but irregular degradation in the organisation of animals'. In order to prepare readers for his main claim, the idea that living things evolve by responding to environmental pressures, he first needed to convince them that life can be seen as an accumulation of increasingly complex traits.

243 *solipeds*: animals with uncloven hoofs.

SIR CHARLES LYELL

247 *Champollion*: the French linguist and historian Jean-François Champollion (1790–1832) established Egyptology as a field. In 1821–2 he published a series of papers decoding the Egyptian hieroglyphics on the Rosetta stone. Champollion was the first European scholar to see that some hieroglyphic symbols were letters, some were syllables, and some represented entire concepts.

248 *Manetho*: an Egyptian priest who recorded the history of Egypt in Greek *c.*300 BC.

249 *Virgil's Elysium*: the Roman poet Publius Vergilius Maro (70–19 BC) is known for his epic, *The Aeneid* (30–19 BC), about the founding of Rome. In Book VI the souls awaiting rebirth are described in Elysium, part of the underworld.

Falloppio: see note to p. 204 above.

250 *Etna*: an active volcano in Eastern Sicily.

in reductâ . . . greges: 'in a secluded valley, he looks forth upon wandering herds of mooing cattle': Horace, *Epodes*, ii. 11–12.

251 *'cirque of Gavarnie'*: a natural amphitheatre in the French Pyrenees consisting of a relatively flat floor and three steep surrounding walls.

Trosachs: mountains in the central Scottish highlands. The quotation is from Walter Scott, *The Lady of the Lake* (1810), canto I, no. 14, lines 15–16.

251 *'yon dreary plain . . . pale and dreadful'*: Milton, *Paradise Lost*, i: 180–3.

252 *'As when heaven's fire . . . the blasted heath'*: Milton, *Paradise Lost*, i. 607–10. I am indebted to James Secord for the sources of Lyell's literary quotations.

WILLIAM WHEWELL

254 *Quádrupedánte . . . cámpum*: 'hooves pound the crumbling field with four-footed sound': Virgil, *Aeneid*, viii. 596. I thank George Greeney for locating these lines in the *Aeneid*.

ALFRED, LORD TENNYSON

256 *Ammonites*: fossilized molluscs with spiral, compartmentalized shells.

calumets: peace-pipes.

Claymore: broadsword from the Scottish highlands.

Malayan crease: (kris) a dagger, with a curved blade.

Agincourt . . . Ascalon: in the Battle of Agincourt (1415), a turning-point in the Hundred Years War, the British defeated the French because of their superior archers. Ascalon (Ashquelon) is a city in Israel. During the twelfth century it was a stronghold of European crusaders.

CHARLES DARWIN

259 *De Candolle*: the French botanist Augustin Pyramus de Candolle (1778–1841) argued that plant classification should be based on anatomy, not physiology. De Candolle's criteria establishing the relationships between plants supported Darwin's theories about how plants had evolved.

W. Herbert, Dean of Manchester: William Herbert (1778–1847) was a classicist and poet.

264 *Articulata*: one of Cuvier's four sub-kingdoms of animals (see note to p. 335), invertebrates such as insects and crustaceans that have a hard exoskeleton.

266 *Silurian*: a geological period 438 to 408 million years ago during which the first land plants and jawed fish appeared.

THOMAS HENRY HUXLEY

274 *'Warum treibt sich . . . er auch will'*: 'Why do the people rush around so and cry out? They want to feed themselves, have children, and feed them as best they can. No one can get beyond this, try as he may': Johann Wolfgang von Goethe (1749–1831), *Venetianische Epigramme*, Epigramm 8. I thank Christoph Hoffman and Jens Lachmund for helping to locate and translate these lines.

275 *'Debemur morti nos nostraque'*: 'We owe ourselves and what we have to death': Horace, *Ars Poetica*, 63.

the *'Peau de Chagrin'*: novel (1831) by the French realist Honoré de Balzac (1799–1850). Balzac was greatly interested in the relationship of animals (especially human beings) to their environment. The 1842 introduction to his great series of novels, *La Comédie humaine*, discusses this topic in terms of contemporary scientific debates.

GEORGE JOHN ROMANES

279 *'the proper study of mankind is man'*: Alexander Pope, 'An Essay on Man' (1733–4).

my previous works: *Animal Intelligence* (1882) and *Mental Evolution in Animals* (1883).

281 *ab initio*: from the outset.

282 *vis inertiae*: a retarding force.

the Negro: such sweeping generalizations about the mental inferiority of people of African descent were unfortunately common in nineteenth-century scientific writing. They stemmed from a distortion of evolutionary theory that presented non-Europeans as 'earlier' versions of what were regarded as socially more advanced peoples. See Stephen Jay Gould, *Ontogeny and Phylogeny* (Cambridge, Mass.: Belknap–Harvard University Press, 1977).

ALFRED, LORD TENNYSON

284 *fanes*: temples.

285 *Paul with beasts*: 1 Corinthians 15: 32: 'If after the manner of men I have fought with beasts at Epheseus, what advantageth it me, if the dead rise not? let us eat and drink, for tomorrow we die.'

HERBERT SPENCER

286 *multiaxial plant*: a plant that grows along many lines or axes.

Schleiden: Mathias Jacob Schleiden's (1804–81) microscopic studies of plants in the late 1830s led to the theory that all living organisms are composed of cells.

Protococcus: a genus of algae that grows on tree-trunks.

287 *Volvox globator*: a micro-organism that lives in round, hollow colonies one cell thick. Because *Volvox* has separate somatic and germ cells, it suggests how multicellular organisms may have evolved out of unicellular ones.

polype: one of the two bodily forms of Cnidarians (a phylum of marine invertebrates) in which one end is anchored and the other is hollow and surrounded by stinging tentacles that draw in prey.

287 *Hydrozoa*: a class of marine invertebrates, including the jelly-fish.

288 *Medusae*: the second body-form of Cnidarians, that of a jelly-fish.

Anacharis Alsinastrum: an American water-weed that 'invaded' England in 1842 and spread quickly throughout the country.

289 *gemmation*: budding.

Hectocotylus: a male generative organ of molluscs which in some species is detachable and remains with the female. In a famous zoological error, Georges Cuvier mistook the organ for a parasitic worm.

Echinus: sea-urchin.

THOMAS HARDY

290 *confervae*: green algae that grow in long filaments.

291 *Trilobites*: extinct crab-like animals with three-part bodies.

Zoophytes: organisms with properties of both animals and plants.

292 *megatherium . . . mylodon*: large, extinct and sloth-like animals.

iguanodon: large, extinct, plant-eating lizard.

ERNST HAECKEL

296 *Gastraea*: a putative ancestral sac-like animal from which Haeckel believed all animals were descended.

Ascidians: marine animals with pouch-like bodies believed to be a key link in the evolution of vertebrates. Once classified as molluscs, they are now considered chordates.

AUGUST WEISMANN

300 *tout ensemble*: entirety.

gemmules: tiny particles that Darwin believed were emitted by each cell in the body and travelled to the germ-cells to provide them with enough information to produce each individual cell. In chapter 27 of *The Variation of Plants and Animals under Domestication* (1868), Charles Darwin had proposed that such gemmules accounted for the germ-cells' ability to produce an entire organism, the hypothesis of Pangenesis. No scientist of the day was satisfied with this hypothesis, including Darwin himself.

301 *germ-cell*: a cell such as an egg or sperm capable of producing an entire organism when united with another germ-cell.

ontogeny: the development of an individual organism.

302 *acquired characters*: traits acquired during an organism's lifetime that are supposedly passed on to its offspring.

E. Roth: possibly Emanuel Roth (1850–?), known for his studies of hygiene and trade.

MAY KENDALL

303 *Monads*: hypothetical, ancestral unicellular organisms that the biologist Ernst Haeckel claimed gave rise to all existing multicellular ones.

304 *Monotremes*: simple, oviparous mammals native to Australia and New Guinea, including the spiny ant-eater and duck-billed platypus.

Kant. ... Hegel ... Mr Browning ... Mr Punch: the German philosophers Immanuel Kant (1724–1804) and Georg Wilhelm Friedrich Hegel (1770–1831); English poet Robert Browning (1812–89). The weekly comic magazine *Punch*, founded in 1841, was one of the most widely read Victorian journals; 'Lay of the Trilobite' appeared in *Punch* in 1885.

GERARD MANLEY HOPKINS

305 *chevy*: race.

Shivelights: narrow strips of light.

306 *potsherd*: piece of broken pottery.

HENRY RIDER HAGGARD

312 *oribé*: antelope.

Billali: an old man who is introducing the narrator, Holly, his attractive young ward, Leo Vincey, and their servant, Job, to the customs of the Amahagger, a people who live on the east coast of Africa.

CONSTANCE NADEN

317 *silex*: flint.

318 *Aves*: birds.

THOMAS DE QUINCEY

332 *φαρμακον νήπενθες*: a soothing drug.

l'Allegro ... Il Penseroso: 'The Cheerful Man' and 'The Pensive Man', poems by John Milton (1608–74).

ex cathedrâ: (Latin) literally, from the (teacher's) chair; with the full authority of office.

333 *meo periculo*: at my own risk; on my own authority.

334 *ponderibus librata suis*: balanced by its own weight.

MARSHALL HALL

335 *medulla oblongata ... spinalis*: the lowest portion of the brain, at which point it joins the spinal cord; and the spinal cord itself.

335 *Baron CUVIER*: the French zoologist Georges Cuvier (1769–1832), who worked at the Paris Natural History Museum, helped to establish the science of comparative anatomy. He argued that an animal's form was shaped through its interactions with its environment, an idea further developed by the novelist Honoré de Balzac. Cuvier opposed the eighteenth-century 'Great Chain of Being', which had classified animals in a continuous line from simplest to most complex. Instead, he devised a new, four-group system (Vertebrata, Mollusca, Articulata, and Radiata) to classify animal life. Cuvier's scheme was widely accepted by zoologists until evolutionary theory required the rethinking of relationships between animals in the 1860s.

NATHANIEL HAWTHORNE

343 *Powers*: Hiram Powers (1805–73), American sculptor.

HERMAN MELVILLE

347 *cannel coal ... anthracite*: cannel coal burns brightly, like a candle; anthracite is difficult to ignite but also difficult to extinguish.

THOMAS LAYCOCK

349 *teleorganic*: fulfilling the goals of organic life.
noetic: intellectual; relating to the mind or to the act of thinking and perceiving.
teleiotic: making perfect, tending toward perfection.

350 *Protozoa, Radiata, and lower Articulata and Mollusca*: protozoa are single-celled animals; radiata, one of Georges Cuvier's four classificatory divisions of the animal kingdom, include animals with radial symmetry like sea urchins and polyps; articulata: see note to p. 264 above; mollusca, Cuvier's classification for a sub-kingdom of animals, include shellfish, snails, and cuttlefish.

Hydrozoa and Polyzoa, the Polypes and Zoophytes: for hydrozoa and polypes see notes to p. 287 above; polyzoa: small, aquatic (colonial) invertebrates like the sea-mosses; for zoophytes, see note to p. 291 above.

351 *hymenoptera*: an order of insects with four wings, including ants, bees, and wasps.
recently investigated by Mr Huxley: Thomas Henry Huxley, *The Oceanic Hydrozoa*, Ray Society, 1859.
Remak: see note to p. 162.

S. WEIR MITCHELL

358 *the battle of Chickamauga*: fought on 19–20 September 1863, the battle of Chickamauga in north-west Georgia was the greatest Confederate

victory of the American Civil War. After major Union victories at Gettysburg and Vicksburg in early July 1863, Chickamauga gained strategic importance because of its proximity to the railway hub, Chattanooga, in Eastern Tennessee. Both sides sent large numbers of troops to the area, but the Confederate army, considerably smaller than the Union force, triumphed because of the Union generals' strategic blunders. Like the author, Mitchell, George Dedlow is a surgeon on the Union side. The battle produced 34,000 casualties.

360 *Stump Hospital . . . the United States Army Hospital for nervous diseases*: the 'Stump Hospital' and the US Army Hospital for Injuries and Diseases of the Nervous System are modelled on the Philadelphia hospitals where Mitchell worked as a contract surgeon during the American Civil War. In 1864 Surgeon General William Hammond founded the 400-bed Turner's Lane Hospital for soldiers with nerve injuries, where Mitchell worked as one of America's first neurologists. Mitchell's descriptions of Dedlow's sensations are based on his extensive interviews of his patients.

361 *les absents ont toujours tort*: the absent are always wrong.

HENRY MAUDSLEY

366 *prodromata*: warning symptoms that precede the onset of disease.

368 *primiparae*: first pregnancies.

asthenic: related to loss of physical strength.

WILLIAM B. CARPENTER

371 *hyperaemia*: excessive blood accumulation.

Ideation: the formation of mental images or ideas through recollected sensations.

372 *Dr Ferrier's recent experiments*: in an Appendix, Carpenter describes some controversial experiments which the neurophysiologist David Ferrier (1843–1928) conducted on dogs, cats, and monkeys in the mid-1870s. While trying to learn how epileptic seizures worked, Ferrier discovered that when he applied current to specific regions of the cerebral cortex, anaesthetized animals always responded with the same bodily movements. By systematically applying AC current to the motor cortex, Ferrier was able to 'map out' the region, identifying the areas that corresponded to each part of the body. Anti-vivisectionists objected to Ferrier's use of live dogs, and in 1882 he was tried for cruelty to animals.

Professor J. H. Bennett . . . Sir Robert Christison: John Hughes Bennett (1812–75) studied numerous physiological functions. His textbook, *Clinical Lectures on the Principles and Practice of Medicine* (1858), was widely read and went through many editions. Sir Robert Christison (1797–1882) studied the effects of poisons on the body.

WILLIAM JAMES

373 *spiritualistic*: relating to the belief that mental functions predominate over those of the body; not to be confused with spiritualism, the belief that the living can communicate with the souls of the dead.

374 *The 'associationist' schools of Herbart in Germany, and of Hume the Mills and Bain in Britain*: associationist philosophers and psychologists taught that all of consciousness could be developed through associations of its most basic elements, sensations and the ideas created by those sensations. To varying degrees, the Scottish philosopher David Hume (1711–76), the German philosopher and psychologist Johann Friedrich Herbart (1776–1841), the British philosophers James (1773–1836) and John Stuart Mill (1806–73), and the psychologist Alexander Bain (1818–1903) can all be tied to the associationist school.

376 *a parte ante . . . a parte post*: beforehand, after the fact.

GEORGE COMBE

377 *caeteris paribus*: all other things being equal.

380 *BELLINGHAM*: on 11 May 1812 John Bellingham, who was mentally ill, assassinated the Prime Minister Spencer Perceval in the House of Commons because of a personal grievance against the government.

GORDON: probably Lord George Gordon (1751–93). Of aristocratic birth, Gordon served in the navy and in parliament, where he assumed leadership of the anti-Catholic contingent. In 1780 he led a mob to the houses of parliament to protest the Catholic Relief Act and was tried for high treason for inciting a riot. After creating additional political and religious problems, Gordon ended his life in Newgate Prison.

381 *DENNIS . . . POPE*: in his 'Essay on Criticism' British poet Alexander Pope (1688–1744) poked fun at critic John Dennis's (1657–1734) unsuccessful tragedy, *Appius and Virginia* (1709), setting off a feud between the writers that lasted for years. Pope again mocked Dennis, who believed that emotion was the most important element in poetry, in his satire *The Dunciad* (1728), a protest against 'Dulness'.

BURNS, MOZART: the Scottish poet Robert Burns (1759–96), and the Austrian composer Wolfgang Amadeus Mozart (1756–91).

JOHANN GASPAR SPURZHEIM

382 *Lavater*: the Swiss Protestant Pastor Johann Kaspar Lavater (1741–1801) developed physiognomy as a science because he was looking for evidence of the divine in the human form. He was also very interested in animal magnetism. Lavater's *Essays on Physiognomy* (1789–98) quickly became well known throughout Europe.

383 *Esop and Socrates*: Aesop, a legendary author of Greek fables, was

probably not an actual person. On an Etuscan bowl held in the Vatican's collections and possibly known to Spurzheim, he is depicted as having a large nose and sloping forehead. The Greek philosopher Socrates (470–399 BC) was believed to have had a highly unattractive physical appearance.

Euripides, Plutarch, and Seneca: the Greek dramatist Euripides (484–406 BC); the Greek biographer and essayist Plutarch (AD 46–119); and the Roman philosopher and politician Lucius Annaeus Seneca (4 BC–AD 65).

Pericles: (495–429 BC), the Greek politician believed responsible for creating Athenian democracy.

La Porte, Lebrun: the literary critic Joseph de LaPorte (1713–79) and the artist Charles Lebrun (1619–90) both had a great interest in physiognomy.

384 *sincipital ... basilar*: relating to the front and base of the head, respectively.

GEORGE ELIOT

389 *Potter's 'Aeschylus' ... Francis's 'Horace'*: Robert Potter's *The Tragedies of Aeschylus* (1777) and Philip Francis's *Poetical Translation of the Works of Horace* (1747) were well-known English verse translations. I am indebted to Helen Small for this information.

CHAUNCEY HARE TOWNSEND

391 *WORDSWORTH*: from *The Excursion*, ix.: 'Discourse of the Wanderer, and an Evening Visit to the Lake'. I am grateful to Scott Harshbarger for locating this reference.

393 *Coleridge*: the English poet Samuel Taylor Coleridge (1772–1834) discusses the role of intuition in creating knowledge in his *Biographia Literaria* (1817), chapter XII.

394 *Newton*: the English physicist Sir Isaac Newton (1642–1727) changed his mind over the course of his career about whether there was an ether, a highly rarefied material between all discernible bodies. In the 1670s he argued for the existence of the ether, but in the first edition of *Principia* (1687) he questioned whether there could be such a substance, contending that it would disrupt the motions of the heavenly bodies. In 1693, however, he wrote to Bentley that it was absurd to suppose that any body could affect another over a distance 'without the mediation of anything else': Derek Gjertsen, *The Newton Handbook* (London: Routledge, 1986), 190–2. I thank Peter Dear for leading me to this source.

395 *Professor Playfair's beautifully expressed opinion of the queries*: probably the Scottish geologist and mathematician John Playfair (1748–1819), a professor of natural philosophy at the University of Edinburgh.

JOHN ELLIOTSON

396 *epigraphs*: the English writer Matthew Gregory Lewis (1775–1818) was known for his best-selling Gothic novel *The Monk* (1796). The French writer and scientist Bernard LeBovier Fontanelle (1657–1757) wrote opera librettos, philosophical dialogues, and scientific studies. His work *A Plurality of Worlds* (1688) helped to popularize Copernicus's view of the solar system.

W. Topham, Esq. . . . of Wellow Hall: William Topham, a barrister of the Middle Temple, served as mesmerist in the operation and was responsible for anaesthetizing the patient; Dr W. Squire Ward, a surgeon from the Ollerton Infirmary near Nottingham, performed the amputation. See Alison Winter, *Mesmerized: Powers of Mind in Victorian Britain* (Chicago: University of Chicago Press, 1998), 165–6.

398 *the Okeys*: the young maidservants Jane and Elizabeth O'Key, aged 15 and 16 respectively, were Elliotson's most celebrated patients. Both were believed to be suffering from hysteria and epilepsy, and Elliotson used mesmerism to treat them, demonstrating its effects to large audiences. Members of the medical community who distrusted mesmerism accused Elliotson of fraud and tried to prove that the O'Keys were feigning their trances. Although the 'trial' was inconclusive, the name 'O'Key' became associated with chicanery. See Winter, *Mesmerized*, 67–100.

399 *caeteris paribus*: see note to p. 377 above.

400 *sal volatile*: smelling salts.

EDGAR ALLAN POE

402 *phthisis*: see note to p. 206 above.

403 *Cousin*: Victor Cousin (1792–1867), the most influential French philosopher of Poe's day, tried to combine empiricism with traditional religious beliefs. Intellectually, Cousin did all he could to undermine materialism, which he thought was harmful to society. According to the modern eclectic school that he founded, the human soul consisted of three interdependent parts: sensation, reason, and heart.

The 'Charles Elwood' of Mr Brownson: in his novel, *Charles Elwood, or The Infidel Converted* (1840), Orestes Augustus Brownson (1803–76) relied on Victor Cousin's arguments to show how an atheist could be persuaded to change his views. Part autobiography and part fiction, Brownson's work is written in the first person, and by the author's own admission, Cousin's ideas figure prominently in its many philosophical discussions.

His end . . . Trinculo: 'the latter end of his commonwealth forgets the beginning': Shakespeare, *The Tempest*, II. i; 'his' refers to Gonzalo rather than Trinculo, however.

405 *luminiferous ether*: a rarefied substance that nineteenth-century scientists

believed occupied all space between the particles of matter and was responsible for transmitting waves of light and heat.

HARRIET MARTINEAU

406 *From the early summer of 1839, I was, till this autumn, a prisoner from illness*: in 1839, Martineau fell ill while travelling through Europe, and for the next five years she was almost incapacitated by physical pain. In addition to having a large uterine tumour, which placed pressure on her internal organs, she suffered from a prolapsed uterus and inflammation of the bladder. Her doctors prescribed opiates and advised bed rest and treatments with leeches, none of which alleviated her condition. Winter, *Mesmerized*, 218–30.

407 *Mr Spencer Hall*: (1812–85), a former stocking-maker and printer, first learned about mesmerism in 1841. After teaching himself how to mesmerize people, he travelled through Northern England giving lectures on mesmerism. Hall claimed to represent the common people, resisting professionally trained doctors' exclusive claims on healing techniques. Hall introduced Martineau to mesmerism, but she found him 'simple-minded' and preferred to be mesmerized by a female friend or her maid. See Winter, *Mesmerized*, 130–5.

Isis: an Egyptian goddess associated with fertility, agriculture, and healing.

409 *Mr Atkinson*: Henry G. Atkinson (1812–90), an independently wealthy man who dabbled in science, taking a particular interest in mesmerism and phrenology. He was one of Martineau's closest friends and helped introduce her to mesmerism. The two later collaborated to write a philosophical study, *Letters on the Laws of Man's Nature and Development* (1851), inspired in part by her mesmeric experiences. See Winter, *Mesmerized*, 223.

JAMES ESDAILE

413 *Moulavies*: Islamic doctors of law.

414 *teetotum*: a small spinning-top spun with the fingers.

ROBERT BROWNING

415 *water-butt*: rain barrel.

416 *calotypist's*: of a photographer.

FRANCES POWER COBBE

424 *like those of M. Doré*: by comparing dream images to the vivid illustrations of the French artist Gustave Doré (1832–83), Cobbe suggests the

creative power of the unconscious. One of the best known illustrators of the nineteenth century, Doré preferred working with religious and richly imaginative texts. Among the works he illustrated are the Bible, Dante's *Inferno*, Cervantes's *Don Quixote*, Milton's *Paradise Lost*, Coleridge's 'Rime of the Ancient Mariner', Poe's 'The Raven', and Tennyson's 'Idylls of the King'. Doré is also known for his medical drawings and his many sketches of the London poor.

425 *Undines*: water nymphs.

Lady Macbeth . . . 'little hand': William Shakespeare, *Macbeth*, v. i: 'All the perfumes of Arabia will not sweeten this little hand.'

Homo Noumenon, the Self of man: the German philosopher Immanuel Kant used the term *noumena* to represent things as they were in themselves, apart from any human sensory perception of them. The *homo noumenon* would be a purely rational being, independent of any elements of sense.

Plutarch . . . from vice: Greek biographer and essayist Plutarch (AD 46–119), and Greek philosopher Zeno of Citium (335–263 BC), the founder of Stoicism. Townsend is quoting Plutarch's *Moralia*, 'How a Man May Become Aware of his Progress in Virtue', 82.

Sir Thomas Browne: (1605–82), English physician who combined religious with medical studies and tried to eliminate popular superstitions.

426 *Coleridge's poem of Kubla Khan*: Samuel Taylor Coleridge wrote the poem 'Kubla Khan' (1797) immediately after awakening from an opium-induced dream.

Cabanis . . . Condillac: French philosopher Pierre-Jean-Georges Cabanis (1757–1808) studied the way that physical and moral forces interacted in individuals. French philosopher Étienne Bonnot Condillac (1715–80) was known for his writings on logic, epistemology, and the human senses.

Sir Edward Codrington: (1770–1851), British admiral.

AUGUST KEKULÉ

433 *Und wer nicht denkt . . . ohne Sorgen*: to the one who doesn't think, [truth] will be given; he'll have it with no trouble.

OLIVER WENDELL HOLMES

Jael . . . Sisera: when Sisera's army was holding the Israelites captive, Jael, the wife of Heber the Kenite, offered Sisera shelter, then stabbed and killed him by driving a tent stake into his temple; Judges 4.

434 *a Mother Cary's chicken*: sailors' name for the Stormy Petrel.

435 *the Burney girl who prophesied 'Evelina'*: Fanny Burney's epistolary novel *Evelina, or a Young Lady's Entrance into the World*, published

anonymously in 1778, tells the story of a girl who is first denied her birthright but then regains it.

S. WEIR MITCHELL

437 *Mrs Grandgrind*: the feeble-minded, invalid wife of overbearing Thomas Gradgrind in Charles Dickens's *Hard Times*.

J. R. M'CULLOCH

457 *Dr Colquhoun*: the early social scientist Patrick Colquhoun (1745–1820) studied education, commerce, industry, urban poverty, and law enforcement. His *Treatise on the Wealth, Power, and Resources of the British Empire* (1814) was a valuable source for M'Culloch.

AUGUSTE COMTE

464 *M. Fourier*: the French mathematician Jean-Baptiste-Joseph Fourier (1768–1830) developed the Fourier series starting in 1807 to analyse the diffusion of heat. The Fourier series is now used to describe complex wave functions as the sum of many simpler waves. Fourier formulated one equation to represent the diffusion of heat through an object and another to represent heat diffusing along its surface. He published his results in his *Analytical Theory of Heat* (1822).

465 *the labours of Aristotle and the school of Alexandria*: the Greek philosopher Aristotle (384–322 BC) tried to systematize knowledge by classifying all known objects and phenomena. Alexandria, a major centre for scientific study in the third century BC, was home to the mathematician Euclid.

Bacon ... Descartes ... Galileo: the English scientist Francis Bacon (1561–1626) taught that reliable knowledge could be obtained only through observation and experiment. The French philosopher René Descartes (1596–1650) sought knowledge through deductive reasoning. The Italian astronomer Galileo Galilei (1564–1642) redefined his field by associating astronomy with mathematics rather than philosophy.

CHARLES DICKENS

468 *galvanising apparatus*: equipment for applying therapeutic electric shocks to the body.

469 *Graminivorous*: grass-eating.

JOHN STUART MILL

470 *Epicurus*: the Greek philosopher Epicurus (341–270 BC) urged people to seek pleasure and peace of mind through rational thought. Occasionally

misunderstood as hedonists, his followers tried to eliminate their physical desires, not indulge them.

ROBERT KNOX

476 *Gibbon*: the historian Edward Gibbon (1737–94), author of *The Decline and Fall of the Roman Empire* (1776–88). In chapter 25, section iii of this work, Gibbon claims that Africans are mentally and socially inferior to people from northern civilizations.

Dr Tiedemann: the anatomist and physiologist Friedrich Tiedemann (1781–1861) compared the skulls of Europeans and non-Europeans.

Kaffirs: a derogatory name for the Bantu people of South Africa.

Sarmatian: referring to people of Iranian origin who migrated to Western Russia and Poland between 500 and 300 BC.

477 *Bosjeman and Hottentot*: Bosjeman is Dutch for Bushman; Hottentot is a pejorative term for the Khoikhoin. Both peoples live near the Cape of Good Hope in South Africa.

mesially: toward the midline of the body.

Von Tchudi: Johann Jakob von Tschudi (1818–89) wrote of his travels in Peru 1838–42.

interparietal bone: a plate between the left and right bones at the top of the skull.

Boschjiee women: women of the Bushman people.

transcendental anatomy: comparative anatomy.

478 *Copts*: Christian peoples of Egypt whose culture flourished AD 200–1200.

Van Diemen's Land: see note to p. 167.

SIR FRANCIS GALTON

479 *Sisyphus*: in Greek mythology, a king of Corinth condemned to an eternal torture in which he had to roll a heavy stone up to the top of a hill. In each trial, just as he reached the summit, the stone would roll back down again.

481 *Hereditary Genius*: in this work (1869), Galton argued that both mental and physical traits were inherited.

Dr Matthews Duncan: in *Fecundity, Fertility, Sterility* (Edinburgh: A. and C. Black, 1871).

FRIEDRICH ENGELS

488 *Mons Sacer*: sacred mountain; Kersall-moor is a hill near Manchester where workingmen held meetings. Engels links this to the *Mons Sacer* near Rome, scene of the secession of the plebeians in 494 and 449 BC.

491 *miasmatic gas*: in 1844 it was believed that foul-smelling, 'miasmatic' gases from decaying matter caused diseases.

'Poor-Law Bastille': in 1789 the French revolution began when a crowd of impoverished workers stormed the Bastille, a medieval fortress used in the eighteenth century to detain political prisoners. To the workers, the Bastille symbolized the abuses of state power. Engels implies that the Manchester workhouse plays an analogous role.

492 *the Leeds railway*: the Liverpool–Manchester Railway, which opened in 1830, was one of the first public railways built. Engineers planned to extend the line north-west to Leeds as early as 1831, but landowners resisted, and parliament did not approve the extension until 1836. Surveyed and built by George Stephenson, England's foremost railway engineer, the Manchester–Leeds line became operational in 1841.

helots: members of the serf class in ancient Sparta; figuratively, slaves.

HENRY MAYHEW

495 *Transportation*: the forced deportation of criminals to British colonies, especially to Australia.

ELIZABETH GASKELL

496 *Crampton*: a working-class neighbourhood in which the heroine, Margaret, is going to look for a new servant.

497 *Milton*: a fictional northern industrial city, patterned on Manchester, in which much of Gaskell's novel takes place.

498 *Helstone*: a fictional southern town in which Margaret was raised.

499 *Beulah*: Hebrew for 'married,' connoting happiness and bliss. See Isaiah 62: 4: 'Thou shalt no more be termed Forsaken; neither shall thy land any more be termed Desolate, but thou shalt be called Hephzibah, and thy land Beulah: for the Lord delighteth in thee, and thy land shall be married.' The Revised Standard Version translates 'Hephzibah' as 'My delight is in her'.

501 *'They shall hunger no more . . . nor any heat'*: Isaiah 49: 10.

methodee: Methodist. Organized in 1738 by John Wesley, Methodists tried to revitalize the Church of England by encouraging open-air and lay preaching in order to reach out to people alienated from the Church. Methodism was popular among impoverished workers and flourished in industrial areas.

MATTHEW ARNOLD

Bethnal Green . . . Spitalfields: densely populated working-class neighbourhoods in East London. Spitalfields, a ward of Stepney, contained East London's main market.

502 *Belgrave Square*: a fashionable district of London near Buckingham Palace.

GEORGE BERNARD SHAW

507 *Principal of Newnham*: head of Newnham College at Cambridge University. Founded in 1871, Newnham was the second college at Cambridge to admit women.

whitelead: a compound of lead carbonate and hydrated lead oxide that was used to make paints and seal joints.

WALTER BESANT

512 *Ratcliffe*: a working-class ward of Stepney located on the River Thames in East London.

Board-schools: schools established by the Education Act of 1870 and managed by local school boards.

CESARE LOMBROSO

517 *Jack the Ripper*: serial murderer of seven women in the Whitechapel district of East London between 7 August and 10 November 1888. The identity of Jack the Ripper was never determined.

internal occipital crest: a bony ridge along the rear, inside surface of the skull.

median occipital fossa: a hollow area along the back midline of the skull.

the cerebellum . . . underneath the cerebral hemispheres: the cerebellum is a region at the back of the brain that co-ordinates muscular movements. It consists of the vermis, a narrow strip along the middle, and one lobe on each side. The cerebrum, the upper, larger portion of the brain, is divided into left and right hemispheres.

518 *zygomae*: arches along the side of the head formed by the cheek bones and the bones of the skull.

orbital arches: the bone structures above the eye cavity.

prehensile foot: a foot that can grasp objects, as a monkey's can.

epactal bone: the ossa suturalia or wormian bone, a small, irregular bone between the sutures of the skull.

GEORGE GISSING

519 *caryatid*: in Greek architecture, a sculpture of a strong female body which acts as a supportive column.

520 *tonsure*: the shaving of one's head for the priesthood.

OSCAR WILDE

521 *your ivory Hermes*: a statue of the god Hermes; in Greek mythology, the messenger of the gods, associated with medicine, commerce, and communications of all kinds.

524 *"Though your sins be as scarlet, yet I will make them as white as snow"*: Isaiah 1: 18.

MAX NORDAU

525 *Morel*: Bénédict Auguste Morel (1809–73) was the first medical theorist to describe degeneration as a pathological, sociological phenomenon.

marsh fever: malaria.

526 *Maremma*: a marshy region of central Italy. By associating diseases with swampy areas rather than micro-organisms, Nordau recalls the miasma theory advocated by most physicians before the 1880s. Despite the discoveries of Pasteur, Koch, and Lister, many *fin de siècle* scientists and laymen continued to believe that places, not microbes, caused diseases.

With these mental changes . . . incompleteness and decay: Nordau cites Paul Brouardel (1837–1906), who conducted studies of drug use, poisoning, and infanticide.

527 *Magnan*: Valentin Magnan (1835–1916), known for his studies of alcoholism.

hysteria: a bodily disturbance such as paralysis, convulsions, or endless coughing that had no apparent organic cause and was thus believed to be caused by a psychological or nervous disorder.

Féré: Charles Féré (1852–1907) investigated human sensations, emotions, and sexuality.

SARAH GRAND

533 *new women*: an expression coined by Grand to describe young women of the 1890s who advocated suffrage, equal rights, and equal educational opportunities for women. Like Grand's characters Evadne and Angelica, the 'new women' attacked the sexual double standard.

BRAM STOKER

536 *in camera*: in private conference.

PUBLISHER'S ACKNOWLEDGEMENTS

We gratefully acknowledge permission to reprint the following copyright material:

Rudyard Kipling: 'The Deep-Sea Cables' first published in *The Seven Seas* (1896), reprinted from *The Writings in Prose and Verse of Rudyard Kipling: Verses 1889–1896* (Charles Scribner's Sons, New York, 1898), by permission of A. P. Watt Ltd. on behalf of The National Trust for Places of Historical Interest or Natural Beauty.

George Bernard Shaw: extract from *Mrs Warren's Profession: An Unpleasant Play* (Brentano's, New York, 1913) first published in *Plays: Pleasant and Unpleasant* (H. S. Stone, 1898), reprinted by permission of The Society of Authors on behalf of the Bernard Shaw Estate.

H. G. Wells: 'The Stolen Bacillus' reprinted from *The Stolen Bacillus* (Methuen, London, 1895); extract reprinted from *The Time Machine* (Heinemann, London, 1895), and extract reprinted from *The Island of Doctor Moreau* (Heinemann, London, 1896), by permission of A. P. Watt Ltd. on behalf of the Literary Executors of the Estate of H. G. Wells.

The Oxford World's Classics Website

www.worldsclassics.co.uk

- Browse the full range of Oxford World's Classics online

- Sign up for our monthly e-alert to receive information on new titles

- Read extracts from the Introductions

- Listen to our editors and translators talk about the world's greatest literature with our Oxford World's Classics audio guides

- Join the conversation, follow us on Twitter at OWC_Oxford

- Teachers and lecturers can order inspection copies quickly and simply via our website

www.worldsclassics.co.uk

American Literature

British and Irish Literature

Children's Literature

Classics and Ancient Literature

Colonial Literature

Eastern Literature

European Literature

Gothic Literature

History

Medieval Literature

Oxford English Drama

Poetry

Philosophy

Politics

Religion

The Oxford Shakespeare

A complete list of Oxford World's Classics, including Authors in Context, Oxford English Drama, and the Oxford Shakespeare, is available in the UK from the Marketing Services Department, Oxford University Press, Great Clarendon Street, Oxford OX2 6DP, or visit the website at www.oup.com/uk/worldsclassics.

In the USA, visit www.oup.com/us/owc for a complete title list.

Oxford World's Classics are available from all good bookshops. In case of difficulty, customers in the UK should contact Oxford University Press Bookshop, 116 High Street, Oxford OX1 4BR.

JANE AUSTEN	**Emma**
	Mansfield Park
	Persuasion
	Pride and Prejudice
	Sense and Sensibility
MRS BEETON	**Book of Household Management**
LADY ELIZABETH BRADDON	**Lady Audley's Secret**
ANNE BRONTË	**The Tenant of Wildfell Hall**
CHARLOTTE BRONTË	**Jane Eyre**
	Shirley
	Villette
EMILY BRONTË	**Wuthering Heights**
SAMUEL TAYLOR COLERIDGE	**The Major Works**
WILKIE COLLINS	**The Moonstone**
	No Name
	The Woman in White
CHARLES DARWIN	**The Origin of Species**
CHARLES DICKENS	**The Adventures of Oliver Twist**
	Bleak House
	David Copperfield
	Great Expectations
	Nicholas Nickleby
	The Old Curiosity Shop
	Our Mutual Friend
	The Pickwick Papers
	A Tale of Two Cities
GEORGE DU MAURIER	**Trilby**
MARIA EDGEWORTH	**Castle Rackrent**

GEORGE ELIOT	Daniel Deronda
	The Lifted Veil and Brother Jacob
	Middlemarch
	The Mill on the Floss
	Silas Marner
SUSAN FERRIER	Marriage
ELIZABETH GASKELL	Cranford
	The Life of Charlotte Brontë
	Mary Barton
	North and South
	Wives and Daughters
GEORGE GISSING	New Grub Street
	The Odd Woman
THOMAS HARDY	Far from the Madding Crowd
	Jude the Obscure
	The Mayor of Casterbridge
	The Return of the Native
	Tess of the d'Urbervilles
	The Woodlanders
WILLIAM HAZLITT	Selected Writings
JAMES HOGG	The Private Memoirs and Confessions of a
	Justified Sinner
JOHN KEATS	The Major Works
	Selected Letters
CHARLES MATURIN	Melmoth the Wanderer
WALTER SCOTT	The Antiquary
	Ivanhoe
	Rob Roy
MARY SHELLEY	Frankenstein
	The Last Man

TROLLOPE IN OXFORD WORLD'S CLASSICS

ANTHONY TROLLOPE

An Autobiography
The American Senator
Barchester Towers
Can You Forgive Her?
The Claverings
Cousin Henry
Doctor Thorne
The Duke's Children
The Eustace Diamonds
Framley Parsonage
He Knew He Was Right
Lady Anna
The Last Chronicle of Barset
Orley Farm
Phineas Finn
Phineas Redux
The Prime Minister
Rachel Ray
The Small House at Allington
The Warden
The Way We Live Now